# Philosophy of Education

Philosophy of education is a study both of the aims of education and the most appropriate means of achieving those aims. This volume contains substantial selections from those works widely regarded as central to the development of the field. These are the "essential texts" that lay the foundation for further study. The text is historically organized, moving from classical thought (Plato, Aristotle), through the medieval period (Augustine), to modern perspectives (Locke, Rousseau, Wollstonecraft), and twentieth-century thinkers (Whitehead, Dewey). Each selection is followed by an extended interpretative essay in which a noted authority of our time highlights essential points from the readings and places them in a wider context.

Exhibiting both breadth and depth, this text is ideal as a reader for courses in philosophy of education, foundations of education, and the history of ideas.

**Steven M. Cahn** is Professor of Philosophy at The City University of New York Graduate Center. Among the nine books he has authored are *The Eclipse of Excellence, Education and the Democratic Ideal, Saints and Scamps: Ethics in Academia,* revised edition, and *From Student to Scholar: A Candid Guide to Becoming a Professor.* He is also the editor of more than thirty volumes, including *Morality, Responsibility and the University: Studies in Academic Ethics, The Affirmative Action Debate* (Routledge), now in its second edition, and *Classics of Western Philosophy,* now in its seventh edition.

# Philosophy of Education

## The Essential Texts

Edited by Steven M. Cahn

 Routledge
Taylor & Francis Group

NEW YORK AND LONDON

First published 2009
by Routledge
270 Madison Ave, New York, NY 10016

Simultaneously published in the UK
by Routledge
2 Park Square, Milton Park, Abingdon, Oxon OX14 4RN

*Routledge is an imprint of the Taylor & Francis Group, an informa business*

© 2009 Taylor & Francis

Typeset in Minion by
Swales & Willis Ltd, Exeter, Devon
Printed and bound in the United States of America on acid-free paper by
Sheridan Books, Inc.

*Library of Congress Cataloging-in-Publication Data*
Philosophy of education: the essential texts / edited by Steven M. Cahn
    p. cm.
  1. Education—Philosophy—History.   I. Cahn, Steven M.
LB7.P55 2009
370.1—dc22
2008038504

ISBN10: 0–415–99755–0 (hbk)
ISBN10: 0–415–99440–3 (pbk)

ISBN13: 978–0–415–99755–3 (hbk)
ISBN13: 978–0–415–99440–8 (pbk)

To the memory of
**Charles Frankel**
(1917–1979)
Old Dominion Professor of Philosophy and Public Affairs, Columbia University

Assistant Secretary of State for Educational and Cultural Affairs

President and Director, National Humanities Center

# Contents

Preface                                                                    ix

1.  Plato                                                                    1
    *Meno* (complete)                                                        1
    *The Republic*                                                          30
    Afterword ROBERT S. BRUMBAUGH                                           94

2.  Aristotle                                                              109
    *Nicomachean Ethics*                                                   109
    *Politics*                                                             133
    Afterword RANDALL CURREN                                               148

3.  Augustine                                                              159
    *On the Teacher*                                                       159
    Afterword PHILIP L. QUINN                                              173

4.  John Locke                                                             179
    *Some Thoughts Concerning Education*                                   179
    Afterword PETER GAY                                                    200

5.  Jean-Jacques Rousseau                                                  205
    *Emile*                                                                205
    Afterword WILLIAM BOYD                                                 246

6.  Immanuel Kant                                                          253
    *Lectures on Pedagogy*                                                 253
    Afterword ROBERT B. LOUDEN                                             281

7.  Mary Wollstonecraft                                                    293
    *A Vindication of the Rights of Woman*                                 293
    Afterword JANE ROLAND MARTIN                                           308

 8. John Stuart Mill                                          321
    *Inaugural Address at St. Andrews* (complete)            321
    Afterword ELIZABETH ANDERSON                             355

 9. Alfred North Whitehead                                   361
    *The Aims of Education*                                  361
    Afterword NATHANIEL M. LAWRENCE                          373

10. John Dewey                                               379
    *Democracy and Education*                                379
    Afterword SIDNEY HOOK                                    490

    Permissions                                              499

# Preface

Philosophy of education is a study both of the aims of education and the most appropriate means of achieving those aims. Many of the leading figures in the history of philosophy made notable contributions to the philosophy of education, although in some cases their other philosophical writings are better known.

This volume contains substantial selections from those works widely regarded as central to the development of the field. Each author's writings are followed by an extended interpretative essay in which a noted authority of our time highlights essential points from the reading and places them in a wider context.

I am most grateful to Catherine Bernard, my editor at Routledge, for her encouragement and guidance. I also wish to express my appreciation to the staff at Routledge for its help throughout the stages of production.

My special thanks to Professor Randall Curren of the University of Rochester for his new essay on Aristotle and to Professor Robert B. Louden of the University of Southern Maine for his new essay on Kant.

# 1
## Plato

**Plato** (427–347 B.C.E.), born into a noble Athenian family, became a student of Socrates (469–399 B.C.E.), the famous teacher who himself wrote nothing, but in conversation was able to befuddle the most powerful minds of his day. Socrates was eventually found guilty of impiety and put to death by the Athenian democracy. Plato then traveled extensively in the Mediterranean region and eventually returned to Athens, where he founded his own school, the Academy. His dialogues form the foundation of all subsequent Western philosophy.

## *Meno*

### Introduction (70a–71d)

MEN: Can you tell me, Socrates, whether virtue is taught?[1] Or is it not taught but acquired by 70a practice? Or is it neither acquired by practice nor learnt, but present in men by nature or some other way?[2]

SOC: Meno, it used to be that Thessalians were famous among the Greeks for their wealth and skill with horses, but it seems now that they are admired for their wisdom, and not b least among them the Larisians, fellow citizens of your comrade Aristippus. Gorgias[3] is the reason. He came to Larisa and made the first men of the city eager for his wisdom—your friend Aristippus among them, and the foremost among the other Thessalians too. Specifically, he gave you your habit of answering any question fearlessly, in the c style of men who know; for he offers himself for questioning to any Greek who wishes,

71a on any subject he pleases, and there is no one he does not answer. But Meno, my friend, things are just the opposite here in Athens. There is, as it were, a drought of wisdom; very likely she has left our borders for yours. At any rate, if you mean to ask that kind of question of anyone here, he will laugh and say, "Stranger, you must think me fortunate indeed, if you suppose I know whether virtue is taught, or how it comes to be present. So far am I from knowing whether or not it is taught, I don't even know what it is at all."

b Now, I'm that way too, Meno. I share this poverty of my fellow citizens, and reproach myself for knowing nothing at all about virtue. And if I don't know what something is, how am I to know what pertains to it? Or do you think someone could determine, for instance, whether Meno is handsome or wealthy or wellborn, or the opposite of these things, without knowing at all who Meno is? Does that seem possible to you?

MEN: Not to me. But Socrates, is it really true that you don't know what virtue is? Is this the

c report I am to carry home about you?

SOC: Not only that, my friend, but also that I never met anyone else I thought did know.

MEN: Really? Didn't you meet Gorgias when he was here?

SOC: I did.

MEN: Well, didn't you think he knew?

SOC: I have a poor memory, Meno. I can't say at present what I thought then. Perhaps he did know, and you know what he used to say. Remind me of it. Or if you will, tell me

d yourself, for no doubt you are in agreement with him.

MEN: Yes, I am.

SOC: Then we may as well dismiss him, since he isn't here anyway.

## The Request for a Definition (71d–73c)

(*Socrates continues*) What do you say virtue is, Meno? Don't begrudge telling me, so that I may find, should it turn out that you and Gorgias know, that I was in most fortunate error when I said that I had never met anyone who knew.

e MEN: No difficulty, Socrates. First of all, if it is the virtue of a man you want, that is easy: the virtue of a man is to be capable of managing the affairs of his city, and in this management benefiting his friends and harming his enemies, taking care to suffer no such harm himself. And if it is the virtue of a woman you want, that is not difficult to explain either: she should manage her house well, preserving what is in it, and obey her

72a husband. There is another virtue for children, male and female; and for an old man, free or slave as you please. And there are a great many other virtues, so that there is no perplexity in saying what virtue is. For each of us, there is a virtue with respect to each particular activity and time of life, and in relation to each particular function. The same is also true of vice, Socrates.

SOC: This is quite a stroke of luck, Meno. I was looking for one virtue, and here I've found a whole swarm of them settled at your side. But still, Meno, please keep to this image of a

b swarm. Suppose I were to ask you what it is to be a bee, about its nature and reality, and you replied that there are many different kinds of bees. What would your answer be if I then asked you, "Do you mean that there are many different kinds, and that they differ from each other in respect to being bees? Do they differ in that way, or in some other way—in beauty or size, for example, or something else like that." Tell me, how would you answer such a question?

MEN: Why, that *as* bees, one is not different from another.

SOC: All right, suppose I went on and said, "Now that's the very thing I want you to tell me    c about, Meno: Just what do you say it is, in respect to which they do not differ but are the same?" You could surely tell me?

MEN: Of course.

SOC: So too then with virtues. Even if there are many different kinds, they surely all have a certain single characteristic which is the same, through which they are virtues; it is on this that he who would make clear what virtue is should fix his gaze. Do you under- stand what I mean?    d

MEN: I think I do. But I still don't quite grasp the point of your question.

SOC: Well Meno, do you think it is only true of virtue that it is one thing for a man, another for a woman, and so on? Or is this also true of health and size and strength? Do you think health is one thing for a man, and another for a woman? Or is health, if it is to be health, the same character everywhere, whether in man or anything else?    e

MEN: I would say that health is the same for both man and woman.

SOC: What about size and strength then? If a woman is strong, will she not be strong by reason of the same character, the same strength? By "the same" I mean this: strength does not differ, in respect of being strength, whether it be in a man or a woman. Or do you think there is some difference?

MEN: No.

SOC: Then will virtue differ, in respect of being virtue, whether it be in a woman or man, old    73a man or child?

MEN: Somehow, Socrates, I don't think this is like those others any more.

SOC: Really? Didn't you say that a man's virtue is to manage a city well, and a woman's a house?

MEN: Yes, I did.

SOC: Well, is it possible to manage city, house, or anything else well, without managing it temperately and justly?

MEN: Surely not.

SOC: Now, if people manage justly and temperately, they do so by reason of justice and    b temperance?

MEN: Necessarily.

SOC: So both men and women alike have need of the same things, namely justice and temperance, if they are to be good.

MEN: It appears they do.

SOC: What about a child or an old man. Could they be good if they were intemperate or unjust?

MEN: Surely not.

SOC: Only if temperate and just?

MEN: Yes.

c     SOC: Then all human beings are good in the same way: for they become good by obtaining the same things.

MEN: So it seems.

SOC: But surely they would not be good in the same way unless they possessed the same virtue.[4]

MEN: Of course not.

SOC: Since they all possess the same virtue, try to recollect and tell me what Gorgias, and you with him, say it is.

## Virtue as Ability to Rule (73c–74b)

MEN: Virtue is nothing else but ability to rule mankind, if you are after some one thing
d         common to all cases.

SOC: I am indeed. But does a child possess the same virtue, Meno, or a slave the ability to rule his master? Does it seem true to you that one who rules would still be a slave?

MEN: It surely doesn't, Socrates.

SOC: No, not likely, my friend. And there is a further point to consider: you say "ability to rule." Are we not to add to that "justly, not unjustly"?

MEN: Yes, I think so. For justice is virtue, Socrates.

e     SOC: Virtue, Meno? Or *a* virtue?

MEN: What do you mean by that?

SOC: Something which holds generally. For example, take roundness if you will. I'd say that it is *a* figure, but not figure without qualification. The reason I'd say so is that there are other figures too.

MEN: Yes, and you'd be right. I also say there are other virtues besides justice.

74a    SOC: What are they? As I'd cite other figures for you, if you asked, so please cite other virtues for me.

MEN: Well, I think courage is a virtue, and temperance, and wisdom, and dignity. And there are a great many others.

SOC: And now we're back where we started, Meno. Looking for one virtue, we've found many, though by a different way than a moment ago. But the one virtue which runs through them all we can't find.

b     MEN: No, for I can't yet do as you ask, Socrates, and grasp a single virtue common to all, as in the other cases.

## Requirements for Definition (74b–77b)

SOC: Naturally enough. But I'll try if I can to help us on. You understand, I suppose, that this holds generally: if someone asked you the question I put just now, "What is figure, Meno?" and you replied, "Roundness," and he then asked, as I did, "Is roundness figure or *a* figure?" you'd surely reply that it is *a* figure.

MEN: Of course.

c     SOC: And for this reason, that there are other figures too?

MEN: Yes.

SOC: And if he went on and asked you what they were, you'd tell him?

MEN: I would.

SOC: And again, if he asked in the same way what color is, and you said "white," and he went on to ask whether white is color or *a* color, you would say that it is *a* color, because there are other colors too.

MEN: I would.

SOC: And if he asked you to mention other colors, you'd mention others which are no less colors than white?                                                                                          d

MEN: Yes.

SOC: Suppose he pursued the argument as I did. Suppose he said, "We keep arriving at a plurality, and that's not what I want. Since you call that plurality by a single name and say that all of its members are figures even though they are opposite to each other, just what is this thing which encompasses the round no less than the straight and which you name figure, saying that the round is no more figure than the straight?" You do     e make that claim, don't you?

MEN: I do.

SOC: When you do, do you mean that the round is no more round than straight, the straight no more straight than round?

MEN: Of course not, Socrates.

SOC: Rather, you mean that the round is no more *figure* than the straight, and the straight no more than the round.

MEN: True.

SOC: Well then, what is this thing of which "figure" is the name? Try and say. Suppose when asked this question about figure or color you said, "I don't understand what you want,     75a Sir, nor do I know what you mean." Your questioner might well be surprised and say, "Don't you understand that I'm after what is the same over all these cases?" Would you have no reply, Meno, if someone asked, "What is it that is over the round and the straight and the rest, and which you call figure, as the same over all?" Try and answer, in order to get practice for your reply about virtue.

MEN: No, please, Socrates, you answer.                                                                                          b

SOC: You want me to gratify you?

MEN: Yes, indeed.

SOC: And then you'll tell me about virtue?

MEN: I will.

SOC: Then I must do my best, for it's worth it.

MEN: Yes, certainly.

SOC: Come then, let us try to say what figure is. See if this will do: let figure alone among things which are be that which ever follows color. Is that sufficient, or are you after something else? For my part, I'd be delighted to have you tell me about virtue even that way.                                                                                          c

MEN: Yes, but surely this is foolish, Socrates.

SOC: How do you mean?

MEN: According to your account, figure is what ever follows color. All right, suppose someone said he didn't know color, that he was as much at a loss there as he was about figure. What would you think of your answer then?

soc: That is the truth. And if my questioner were one of your contentious and eristical wise men, I'd tell him, "I've answered. If my answer is not good, it is your job to refute me." But with friends who wish to converse with each other, as in our case, a gentler answer is indicated, one more suited to dialectic. It is more dialectical not only to answer what is true, but to do so in terms which the questioner further agrees that he knows. So that's how I'll try to answer you. Tell me then, is there something you call an end? I mean something like a limit or a boundary—they are all about the same, though Prodicus[5] perhaps would disagree. But you surely call something limited and ended, and that is the kind of thing I mean—nothing fancy.

men: To be sure I do, and I think I understand what you mean.

soc: Well then, is there something you call a surface, and still another you call a solid, as in geometry?

men: Certainly.

soc: Then at this point you can understand what I say figure is. In respect of every figure, I say figure is that in which a solid terminates. More briefly, figure is the limit of a solid.

men: And what do you say color is, Socrates?

soc: You are outrageous, Meno. You put an old man to the trouble of answering, when you won't yourself recollect and say what Gorgias said virtue is.

men: You tell me this, Socrates, and I'll tell you that.

soc: A man could realize blindfolded, Meno, just from the way you converse, that you are handsome and still have admirers.

men: Why?

soc: Because you speak only to command, as spoiled favorites do, who play tyrant as long as the bloom of their beauty lasts. And at the same time you've probably noticed my weakness for the fair, so I'll gratify you and answer.

men: By all means do.

soc: Will you have me answer in the manner of Gorgias, which would be easiest for you to follow?

men: Why, of course.

soc: Well then, don't you and Gorgias talk about certain effluences among the things which are, in the same way as Empedocles?[6]

men: Yes, emphatically.

soc: And about pores or passages, into which and through which the effluences pass?

men: Certainly.

soc: And that some of the effluences fit certain of the pores, while some are too large or too small?

men: That is so.

soc: Again, there is something you call sight?

men: There is.

soc: Then "grasp what I tell you," as Pindar says.[7] Color is an effluence of figures, commensurable with sight, therefore perceptible.

men: Socrates, I think you've found an answer which is simply superb!

soc: No doubt because it is put in a way you're accustomed to. At the same time you realize,

I suppose, that in a similar way you could say what sound is, and smell, and many other things of the sort.                                                                                   e

MEN: Of course.

SOC: It is a stately style of answer, Meno, and so you like it better than my answer about figure.

MEN: Yes, I do.

SOC: And yet, son of Alexidemus, I myself am convinced the other answer was better, and I think you would come to agree too, if it weren't necessary for you, as you were saying yesterday, to leave before the mysteries are celebrated, and if you were able to stay to be initiated.[8]

MEN: Socrates, I would make it a point to stay if you gave me many such answers as that.      77a

SOC: Then I must spare no effort to do so, both for your sake and my own—though I'm afraid I may not be able to keep to a level like that for very long. But come, it's your turn to pay your promised debt and say what virtue as a whole is. And "stop making one into many," as the joke goes when somebody breaks something. Leave virtue whole and healthy and say what it is. Examples you have got from me.                         b

## Virtue as Desire for Good Things and Ability to Attain Them (77b–78c)

MEN: Well, I think, Socrates, that as the poet says, virtue is "to rejoice in things beautiful and be capable of them." And that, I claim, is virtue: desire for beautiful things and ability to attain them.

SOC: Do you say that to desire beautiful things is to desire good things?

MEN: Yes, of course.

SOC: Then do some men desire evils, and others goods? Does it not seem to you, my friend, that *all* men desire goods?                                                                           c

MEN: No, it doesn't.

SOC: Some desire evils?

MEN: Yes.

SOC: Supposing the evils to be goods, you mean, or recognizing that they are evils and still desiring them?

MEN: Both, I think.

SOC: You think, Meno, that anyone recognizes evils to be evils and still desires them?

MEN: Certainly.

SOC: What do you mean by "desire"? Desire to possess?

MEN: Why yes, of course.                                                                           d

SOC: Believing that evils benefit, or recognizing that evils harm, those who possess them?

MEN: Some believe evils benefit, others recognize that they harm.

SOC: Does it seem to you those who believe that evils benefit recognize evils to be evils?

MEN: No, I certainly don't think that.

SOC: Then it is clear that these people, who do not recognize evils for what they are, do not desire evils; rather, they desire things they suppose to be good, though in fact those things are evil. Hence, these people, not recognizing evils to be evils, and supposing    e
them to be goods, really desire goods. Not so?

MEN: Yes, very likely it is.

SOC: Now what about those who, as you claim, desire evils believing that evils harm their possessor. Surely they recognize they will be harmed by them?

MEN: They must.

78a SOC: Don't they suppose that people who are harmed are made wretched to the degree they are harmed?

MEN: Again, they must.

SOC: And aren't the wretched unhappy?

MEN: I should think so.

SOC: Now, does anyone wish to be wretched and unhappy?

MEN: I think not, Socrates.

SOC: Then nobody wishes for evils, Meno, unless he wishes to be in that condition. For what else is it to be wretched, than to desire evils and get them?

b MEN: You are very likely right, Socrates; nobody wishes for evils.

SOC: Now, you were just saying that virtue is to wish for good things and to be able to get them?

MEN: Yes, I did.

SOC: Well, of this claim, the wishing part applies to everybody, so in that respect, one person is no better than another.

MEN: So it appears.

SOC: But it is clear that if one person is better than another, it must be in respect to ability.

MEN: Certainly.

c SOC: So it seems that, according to your account, virtue is the ability to attain good things.

MEN: You have now expressed my opinion precisely.


## Virtue as Ability to Attain Good Things (78c–80d)

SOC: Then let us consider this and see if you are right, as you very likely are. You say that being able to attain goods is virtue?

MEN: I do.

SOC: And you call such things as health and wealth goods, do you not?

MEN: Yes, I count possession of gold and silver good, as well as civic honors and offices.

SOC: And you don't count other things good besides those sorts of things?

MEN: No, only things such as those.

d SOC: Very well. Then to attain gold and silver is virtue—so says Meno, ancestral guest-friend of the Great King of Persia. Do you add "justly and piously" to that attainment, Meno, or does it make no difference? If someone attains them unjustly, do you call it virtue all the same?

MEN: Surely not, Socrates.

SOC: Vice, rather?

MEN: Of course.

SOC: So it seems that justice or temperance or holiness, or some other part of virtue, must be

e present in the attainment. Otherwise, it will not be virtue even if it provides goods.

MEN: No, for how could it be virtue without them?

soc: And failure to provide gold and silver for oneself or for another when it would not be just to do so—that is virtue too, that very failure and perplexity of provision?

MEN: So it seems.

soc: So the provision of such goods is no more virtue than the failure to provide them. Rather, it seems what is accompanied by justice is virtue, and what is without anything of the sort will be vice. 79a

MEN: I think it must be as you say.

soc: Now we were saying a moment ago that justice and temperance and everything of the sort each are a part of virtue? b

MEN: Yes.

soc: Then, Meno, you're making fun of me.

MEN: But why, Socrates?

soc: Because I just now begged you not to break virtue up into bits and pieces, and gave you examples of how you should answer, and here you are paying no attention to that, but telling me that virtue is the ability to attain good things with justice. And justice, you say, is a part of virtue?

MEN: Yes.

soc: So it follows from your own admissions that virtue is doing whatever one may do with a part of virtue, since you say that justice and the rest are parts of virtue. What do I mean by that? Just this: I begged you to say what virtue is as a whole, but you, so far from saying what it is, claim that every action is virtue if it is done with a part of vir- tue—as though you already had said what virtue as a whole is, and I am at this point to c understand even if you break it into parts. So it seems to me that you must start from the beginning with the same question, my dear Meno: What is virtue? For that is what is being said when someone says that every action done with justice is virtue. Don't you think you need to go back to the original question? Or do you think someone knows what a part of virtue is, without knowing what virtue is?

MEN: I do not.

soc: No, for if you remember when I was answering you just now about figure, we discarded d the sort of answer which is given in terms of what is still under investigation and not yet agreed upon.

MEN: Yes, and we were right to do so, Socrates.

soc: Then my friend, as long as what virtue is as a whole is still under investigation, don't suppose that you will clarify virtue for anyone by answering in terms of its parts, or in any other terms which contain a similar obscurity. The original question needs to be e answered. You talk about virtue—but what is it? Do I seem to be talking nonsense?

MEN: Most certainly not.

soc: Then answer again from the beginning: what do you and your comrade Gorgias say virtue is?

MEN: Socrates, I kept hearing before I ever met you that you are yourself in perplexity, and cause perplexity in others. And now I think you've cast a spell on me; I am utterly 80a subdued by enchantment, so that I too have become full of perplexity. Am I allowed a small joke? You are both in appearance and other ways very like the stingray in the sea, which benumbs whatever it touches.[9] I think you've now done something of the sort to b  me. My tongue, my soul, are numb—truly—and I cannot answer you. And yet, I've said many things about virtue a thousand times, and to a host of people—and, as I thought, spoken well. But now I'm utterly at a loss to say even what it is. You do well, I think, not to journey abroad from here; for if you worked things like this as a stranger in another city, you might well be arrested as a sorcerer.

SOC: Meno, you are quite unscrupulous. You very nearly fooled me.

MEN: How could I, Socrates!

c  SOC: I see the motive in your comparison.

MEN: What do you think it is?

SOC: You want a comparison in return. This I know of all you handsome types—you delight in being compared, because you make a profit on it; your beauty leads to beautiful comparisons. But I won't give you a comparison. As for myself, if the stingray numbs itself as it numbs others, I am like it; otherwise not. For I don't cause perplexity in others while free of perplexities myself; the truth is rather that I cause perplexity in

d  others because I am myself perplexed. And so it is now with virtue. I don't know what it is, while you, who may have known before I touched you, are now in like way ignorant. Nevertheless, I wish to join with you in inquiring what it is.

## Inquiry and Recollection (80d–81e)

MEN: And how will you inquire into a thing, Socrates, when you are wholly ignorant of what it is? What sort of thing among those you don't know will you set up as the object of your inquiry? Even if you happen to bump right into it, how will you know that it is the thing you didn't know?

SOC: I understand what you want to say, Meno. Do you see what an eristical argument you're

e  spinning? It is thus impossible for a man to inquire either into what he knows, or into what he does not know. He cannot inquire into what he knows; for he knows it, and there is no need for inquiry into a thing like that. Nor would he inquire into what he does not know; for he does not know what it is he is to inquire into.

81a MEN: Well, don't you think that's a good argument, Socrates?

SOC: I do not.

MEN: Can you say why?

SOC: Yes. For I have heard from men and women who are wise in things divine—

MEN: What was it they told?

SOC: A noble truth, I think.

MEN: What was it? And who were they who told it?

SOC: Some were priests and priestesses who wanted to explain their observances. But Pindar

b  and as many other poets who are inspired have told it too. Here is their tale. See if you think it true. They say that the soul of man is immortal, sometimes reaching an end which men call dying, sometimes born again, but never perishing. Because this is so, one must live his whole life in utmost holiness; for from whomsoever

> Persephone shall accept requital for her ancient grief,
> Returning their souls in the ninth year to the upper light,

Their term of banishment to darkness done:

> From them illustrious kings shall spring, c
>
> Lords of rushing wisdom, and strength unsurpassed.

In all remaining time they shall be known

As heroes, and be sanctified by men.[10]

Seeing then that the soul is immortal, and has been born many times, and has beheld all things in this world and the world beyond, there is nothing it has not learnt: so it is not surprising that it can be reminded of virtue and other things which it knew before. For since the whole of nature is akin, and the soul has learned all things, there is   d nothing to prevent someone, upon being reminded of one single thing—which men call learning—from rediscovering all the rest, if he is courageous and faints not in the search. For learning and inquiry are then wholly recollection.[11] Therefore we need not be persuaded by the eristical argument, which would cause us to be idle; it is sweet only to the ear of the soft and weak, whereas this account induces industry and inquiry. I put my trust in its truth, and ask you to join me in inquiring what virtue is.   e

## A Proof of Recollection (81e–86c)

MEN: Yes, Socrates, but what do you mean by saying that we do not learn, that what we call learning is recollection? Can you teach me that this is so?

SOC: Why Meno, I just said you were unscrupulous, and now you are asking me to teach you, when I claim there is no teaching but recollection, just so I can straightway prove myself inconsistent.   82a

MEN: No, no, Socrates, that was surely not my aim. I just spoke from habit. If you can somehow prove it is as you say, please do so.

SOC: Well, it is not easy, but still, for you I will make the effort. You have many of your attendants here. Summon for me whichever one you please for the demonstration.   b

MEN: Certainly, (*Beckoning to a slave boy.*) You there, come here.

SOC: He's a Greek, I assume, and speaks Greek?

MEN: Oh yes, he was born and raised in our house.

SOC: Then pay close attention. See whether it appears to you that he recollects, or learns from me.

MEN: I certainly shall.

SOC: (*Turning to the boy.*) Tell me, my boy. Do you recognize that this sort of figure is a square? (*Socrates traces square ABCD in the sand at his feet.*)

BOY: I do.

SOC: Now, a square figure is one having all four of these sides equal? (*Indicating the sides.*)   c

BOY: Of course.

SOC: And so is one having these lines drawn through the middle equal too? (*Socrates draws in transversals bisecting each side.*)

BOY: Yes.

SOC: Now, a figure of this sort could be larger or smaller?

BOY: Of course.

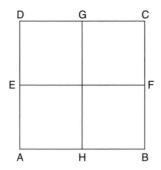

SOC: Now suppose that this side (AB) were two feet, and this one (AD) two feet. How many feet[12] would the whole be? Look at it this way: if it were two feet this way (AB) and only one foot that way (AE), wouldn't the figure be two feet taken once?

BOY: (*Inspecting ABFE*) Yes.

d   SOC: But since it is also two feet that way (AD), doesn't it become twice two?

BOY: It does.

SOC: Therefore it becomes twice two feet?

BOY: Yes.

SOC: Now, how many is twice two feet? Count and tell me. (*The boy looks at ABCD and counts the squares it contains.*)

BOY: Four, Socrates.

SOC: Now could there be another figure twice the size of this one, but similar to it—that is, having four sides equal to each other?

BOY: Yes.

SOC: How many feet will it be?

BOY: Eight.

SOC: Come then. Try and tell me how long each side of it will be. Each side of this one (ABCD) is two feet. What about the side of a figure double this?[13]

e   BOY: Clearly it will be double, Socrates.

SOC: Do you see, Meno, that I am teaching him nothing but am asking him all these things? And now he thinks he knows the length of the side from which the eight-foot figure will be generated. Do you agree?

MEN: I do.

SOC: Well, does he know?

MEN: Of course not.

SOC: He merely thinks it is generated from the doubled side?

MEN: Yes.

SOC: Now watch him recollect serially and in order, as is necessary for recollection. (*Turning to the boy*) Tell me: are you saying that the doubled figure is generated from the doubled

83a   side? The figure I mean is not to be long one way and short the other; it is to be equal on all sides, as this one (ABCD) is, but double it, eight feet. See if you still think it will result from double the side.

BOY: I do.

SOC: Now, this line (AB) becomes double (AX) if we add another of the same length here?

BOY: Of course.

SOC: So there will be an eight-foot figure from it, you say, if four such sides are generated?

BOY: Yes.

SOC: Then let us inscribe four equal sides from it. (*Socrates, beginning with base AX, inscribes AXYZ.*)  b

You say this would be eight feet?

BOY: Of course.

SOC: Now, there are four squares in it, each of which is equal to this four-foot figure (ABCD)? (*Socrates completes the transversals begun by DC and BC above.*)

BOY: Yes.

SOC: Then how big has it become? Four times as big?

BOY: Certainly.

SOC: Now, is four times the same as double?

BOY: Surely not.

SOC: How many?

BOY: Fourfold.

SOC: Then from double the line, my boy, not a double but a fourfold figure is generated.  c

BOY: True.

SOC: Since four times four is sixteen. Right?

BOY: Yes.

SOC: Well, then, an eight-foot figure will be generated from what line? That one (AX) gave us a four-fold figure, didn't it? (i.e., AXYZ)

BOY: Yes.

SOC: But half of it (AB) grave us four feet? (i.e., ABCD)

BOY: I agree.

SOC: Very well. But an eight-foot figure is double this (ABCD), and half that (AXYZ)?

BOY: Yes.

SOC: Then it will be from a side greater than this (AB) but smaller than that one there (AX), won't it?  d

BOY: Yes, I think so.

SOC: Excellent. Always answer what you think. Now tell me: wasn't this line (AB) two feet, and that one (AX) four?

BOY: Yes.

SOC: So the side of an eight-foot figure must be greater than this two-foot side here, but smaller than the four-foot side?

BOY: It must.

e SOC: Try and tell me how long you'd say it is.

BOY: Three feet.

SOC: Now, if it is to be three feet, we'll add (to AB) half of this (BX), and it will be three feet; for this (AB) is two, and that (BM) is one. And in the same way over here, this (AD) is two and that (DN) is one; and the figure you speak of is generated. (*Socrates as he speaks marks M and N on BX and DZ, and then completes the square.*)

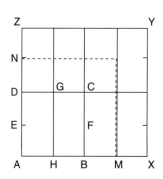

BOY: Yes.

SOC: Now if this (AM) is three and that (AN) is three, the whole figure generated is thrice three feet?

BOY: That follows.

SOC: And how many is thrice three?

BOY: Nine.

SOC: But the double (of the original square) had to be how many feet?

BOY: Eight.

SOC: So somehow the eight foot figure is not generated from the three-foot side either.

BOY: It certainly isn't.

SOC: But from what, then? Try and tell us exactly. If you don't want to count it out, just point
84a to it.

BOY: Socrates, I really don't know.

SOC: (*Turning to Meno.*) Here again, Meno, do you see the progress in recollection he's made so far? At first he didn't know the side required for an eight-foot figure—and he still doesn't. But earlier he supposed he knew and answered confidently, and did not believe
b he was in perplexity. But now he *does* believe it, and as he doesn't know, either does he suppose he knows.

MEN: You are right.

SOC: So he is now better off with respect to the thing which he did not know?

MEN: I agree.

SOC: Well, did we harm him any by numbing him like a stingray and making him aware of his perplexity?

MEN: I think not.

SOC: We have at any rate done something, it seems, to help him discover how things are, for in his present condition of ignorance, he will gladly inquire into the matter, whereas before he might easily have supposed he could speak well, and frequently, and before large audiences, about doubling the square and how the side must be double in length.    c

MEN: So it seems.

SOC: Well, do you think he would undertake to inquire into or learn what he thought he knew and did not, before he fell into perplexity and became convinced of his ignorance and longed to know?

MEN: I think not, Socrates.

SOC: So numbing benefited him?

MEN: Yes.

SOC: Then please observe what he will discover from this perplexity as he inquires with me—even though I will only ask questions and will not teach. Be on guard lest you find that I teach and explain to him, instead of questioning him about his own opinions.    d (*Socrates at this point rubs out the figures in the sand at his feet, leaving only rectangle ABCD, and turns to the boy.*) Now back to you. We've got this figure of four feet, don't we? Do you follow?

BOY: I do.

SOC: And we can add here another equal to it? (*Inscribes it*)

BOY: Yes.

SOC: And a third here, equal to each of those? (*Inscribes it*)

BOY: Yes.

SOC: Now, we can fill in the one here in the corner? (*Inscribes it*)

BOY: Of course.

SOC: So these four equal figures would be generated?

BOY: Yes.    e

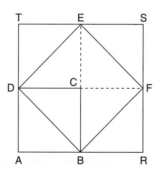

SOC: Now then. How many times larger than this (ABCD) does this whole (ARST) become?

BOY: Four times.

SOC: But we had to generate double. Do you recall?

BOY: Of course.

SOC: Now take this line from corner to corner. (*Socrates inscribes BFED.*) Does it cut each of these figures in two?    85a

BOY: Yes.

SOC: Now, have we generated four equal lines here (BD, DE, EF, FE), enclosing this figure (BFED)?

BOY: We have.

SOC: Then consider: how large is this figure?

BOY: I don't understand.

SOC: Hasn't each of these lines cut off the inner half of these four squares?

BOY: Yes.

SOC: Then how many (halves) of that size are in this (BFED)?

BOY: Four.

SOC: And how many in this one (ABCD)?

BOY: Two.

SOC: What is four to two?

BOY: Double.

b  SOC: So this becomes how many feet?

BOY: Eight feet.

SOC: From what line?

BOY: That one (BD).

SOC: That is, from the line stretching from corner to corner of the four-foot figure?

BOY: Yes.

SOC: Students of the subject call that the diagonal. So if that is the name for it, then you, Meno's slave, are stating as your view that the double figure would be generated from the diagonal.

BOY: Yes, certainly, Socrates.

SOC: (*Turning to Meno*) Well, Meno, what do you think? Did he reply with any opinion not his own?

c  MEN: No, they were his.

SOC: Yet he didn't *know*, as we were saying a little earlier.

MEN: True.

SOC: Yet these opinions were *in* him, weren't they?

MEN: Yes.

SOC: Therefore, while he is ignorant of these things he does not know, there are true opinions in him about these very things?

MEN: That follows.

SOC: For the moment, these opinions have been stirred up in him as in a dream; but if he were repeatedly asked these same questions in different ways, you may rest assured that

d  eventually he would know about these things as accurately as anyone.

MEN: It seems so.

SOC: Then he will know without being taught but only questioned, recovering knowledge out of himself?

MEN: Yes.

SOC: And his recovering knowledge which is in him is recollection?

MEN: Yes.

SOC: The knowledge he now has he either gained at some time or always had?

MEN: Yes.

SOC: Well, if he always had it, he always knew. And if he gained it at some time, he surely didn't do so in his present life. Or did someone teach him geometry? For he will do the very same thing all through geometry and every other study. Is there anyone who has   e taught him all this? You ought to know, especially since he was born in your house and raised there.

MEN: I do know: no one ever taught him.

SOC: But he has these opinions, does he not?

MEN: It appears he must, Socrates.

SOC: Well, if he did not get them in his present life, is it not at this point clear he got and   86a learned them at some other time?

MEN: It appears so.

SOC: A time when he was not in human form?

MEN: Yes.

SOC: So if we are to say that there are true opinions present in him both during the time when he is and is not a man, and that those opinions become knowledge when roused by questioning, then his soul will ever be in a state of having learned. For it is clear that through all time he either is or is not a man.

MEN: That follows.

SOC: Now, if the truth of things is always in our soul, the soul is immortal. So it is right to try boldly to inquire into and recollect what you do not happen to know at present—that   b is, what you do not remember.

MEN: I think you are right, Socrates—how, I don't know.

SOC: I think so too, Meno. There are other things about the argument I would not con-fidently affirm, but that we shall be better men, more courageous and less idle, if we think we ought to inquire into what we do not know, instead of thinking that because we cannot find what we do not know we ought not seek it—that I would do battle for,   c so far as possible, in word and deed.

MEN: Here again, I think you are right, Socrates.

SOC: Then since we are agreed that there must be inquiry about what one does not know, shall we together undertake to investigate what virtue is?

## The Method of Hypothesis (86c–87c)

MEN: By all means. But Socrates, what would please me most would be to take up the question I began with and hear you on it: whether virtue is something that is taught, or present by nature, or in what way it comes to be present in men.   d

SOC: If I not only ruled myself, Meno, but also ruled you, we'd not consider whether virtue is or is not taught before first considering what it is. But since you do not even attempt to rule yourself—being a free man, after all—and yet still try to rule me, and do, I must perforce go along. What else can I do? It seems then that we must inquire of what sort   e virtue is, when we don't yet know what it is. But please relax your rule over me a little, and consent to inquire by means of a hypothesis whether it is taught. I mean the sort of thing geometers often use in their inquiries. When someone asks them, say, about an area, whether it is possible for a given area to be stretched as a triangle into a given

87a circle, a geometer might say, "I don't know yet if it is possible, but I think there is, as it were, a hypothesis at hand to deal with the matter. It is this: if this area is such that, when applied along a line given for it, it falls short by an area of the same sort as the area which has already been applied. I think one thing follows: and a different thing follows in turn if it is impossible for the area to be so affected. So I wish to tell you what follows about the stretching out of it into the circle, whether it is possible or not, by

b using hypothesis."[14]

So too then for us about virtue. Since we know neither what it is nor what is true of it, let us use hypothesis in inquiring whether it is taught. As follows: among things of the soul, of what sort must virtue be if it is taught or if it is not taught? To begin with, if it is the same sort or a different sort than knowledge, is it or is it not taught?—or as we were just now saying, remembered? The name we use makes no difference here: is it

c taught? Or isn't it quite clear that a man is taught nothing but knowledge?

MEN: I think so.

SOC: So if virtue is a kind of knowledge, it clearly would be taught.

MEN: Certainly.

SOC: Then we have disposed of this point quickly: it is taught if it is of one sort, but not if of another.

MEN: Of course.

### That Virtue Is Knowledge (87c–89a)

SOC: The next step, it seems, is to inquire whether virtue is knowledge or of a sort other than knowledge.

d MEN: I agree: that must be examined next.

SOC: Well, then, do we say that virtue is good? Does that hypothesis stand fast for us, that it is good?

MEN: Certainly.

SOC: Now, if something is good, but other than and separate from knowledge, virtue perhaps would not be a kind of knowledge. But if there is nothing good which knowledge does not encompass, we may rightly suspect that virtue is a kind of knowledge.

MEN: True.

SOC: Again, it is by virtue that we are good?

MEN: Yes.

e SOC: And if good, beneficial. For all good things are beneficial, are they not?

MEN: Yes.

SOC: So virtue is beneficial, then?

MEN: Necessarily, from what has been agreed.

SOC: Then let us examine what sort of thing benefits us, taking particular examples. Health, we say, and strength, beauty, and no doubt wealth too—we hold that they and things like them are beneficial, do we not?

MEN: Yes.

88a SOC: But we say that those same things sometimes also do harm. Do you dispute that?

MEN: No, it is true.

SOC: Then let us consider what guides each of these things when they benefit us, and what guides them when they do harm. Don't they benefit us when there is right use, and harm us when there is not?

MEN: Certainly.

SOC: Next, consider things having to do with the soul. Is there something you call temperance, and justice and courage and quick wits, and memory and nobility of character and so on?

MEN: There is.   b

SOC: Then consider: do those among them which you think are not knowledge, but other than knowledge, sometimes benefit and sometimes harm? Take courage, for example. Suppose that courage is not wisdom but, as it were, a kind of boldness. When a man is bold without intelligence, he is harmed; with intelligence, he is benefited. Isn't that so?

MEN: Yes.

SOC: And so similarly with temperance and quick wits. Things learned or acquired by training are beneficial when accompanied by intelligence, but harmful without it.

MEN: Very true indeed.   c

SOC: To sum up then, everything that the soul undertakes or endures, when guided by wisdom, ends in happiness, and in the opposite when guided by folly?

MEN: It seems so.

SOC: Therefore, if virtue is something among things in the soul, and is necessarily beneficial, it must be wisdom, since everything which has to do with the soul is in itself neither beneficial nor harmful, but becomes one or the other by the addition of wisdom or folly.   d
According to this account, then, virtue, being beneficial, must be a kind of wisdom.

MEN: I agree.

SOC: Returning then to the other things we just mentioned as sometimes good and sometimes harmful—I mean wealth, and so on—isn't the same true there? Just as wisdom, guiding the rest of the soul, makes things of the soul beneficial, while folly makes them harmful, so too with these: the soul, guiding and using them rightly, makes them   e
beneficial; if not rightly, harmful.

MEN: Of course.

SOC: But it is the wise soul which guides rightly, and the foolish soul which guides with error?

MEN: True.

SOC: So this then is to be asserted generally: in man, all other things depend upon the soul; but things of the soul depend upon wisdom, if they are to be good. And by this account, the beneficial would be wisdom, while virtue, we say, is beneficial.   88a

MEN: Quite so.

SOC: Therefore, we say that virtue is wisdom, either all or some part?

MEN: I think these statements excellent, Socrates.

## That Virtue Is Not Taught (89a–e)

SOC: Now if this is true, good men are not good by nature.

MEN: No.

b   SOC: Otherwise, this would surely follow: if good men are good by nature, we would no doubt have among us people who could discern among our youth those whose natures are good; and we would take them, once revealed to us, and guard them in a lofty citadel, setting our seal upon them more surely than on our gold, so that no one might corrupt them. For when they reach maturity, they will be of service to their cities.

   MEN: Very likely, Socrates.

c   SOC: Then since good men are not good by nature, are they so by learning?

   MEN: At this point, it seems necessary. And, Socrates, it is clear from the hypothesis, if virtue is knowledge, it is taught.

   SOC: To be sure. But perhaps it was improper to agree to that.

   MEN: It surely seemed proper a moment ago.

   SOC: Yes, but if there is to be any soundness to it, shouldn't it seem proper not only "a moment ago," but now and in the future as well?

d   MEN: No doubt. But what do you see to make you uneasy? Why do you doubt that virtue is knowledge?

   SOC: I'll tell you, Meno. I'm not taking back as improper the claim that it is taught if it is knowledge. But consider whether you don't think it reasonable to doubt that it is knowledge. Just tell me this: if anything at all—not just virtue—is taught, must there not be teachers and students of it?

e   MEN: I think so.

   SOC: Then might we not reasonably conjecture that the opposite also holds—that should there be neither teachers nor students of it, it is not taught?

   MEN: Yes. But don't you think there are teachers of virtue?

   SOC: Well at any rate I've often inquired if there are, and try as I might, I couldn't find them. And yet I inquired among many people, especially those I thought most experienced in the matter.

### The Interview with Anytus (89e–96d)

   SOC: But look now, Meno. Here is Anytus sitting down beside us, and just at the right time.[15]

90a   Let us make him a partner in our inquiry. It is reasonable that we should, for in the first place, he is the son of a wise and wealthy father, Anthemion, who became rich not by gift or accident, like Ismenias the Theban[16] who has just recently come into the fortune of Polycrates,[17] but by his own diligence and skill. Then too, he seems to be a citizen who is not insolent, or pompous and offensive, but a man of good conduct and well-

b   ordered life. Finally, he raised and educated his son here well, as the majority of Athenians think; at any rate, they choose him for their highest offices. It is right, then, to inquire with such a man whether or not there are teachers of virtue, and who they are. So Anytus, please join us—your guest-friend Meno here, and me—and inquire into this matter of who the teachers of virtue may be. Consider this: if we wished Meno

c   here to become a good physician, to what teachers would we send him? To the physicians, I assume?

   ANY: Of course.

   SOC: What if we wished him to become a good cobbler. To the cobblers?

ANY: Yes.

SOC: And so in other cases?

ANY: Of course.

SOC: Then look again to the same examples and tell me this: We say we properly send him to the physicians if we wish him to become a physician. When we make that statement, do we mean that we'd be well advised to send him to people who lay claim to the art, rather than those who do not, and charge a fee precisely on that basis, declaring themselves teachers for anyone wishing to come and learn? Wouldn't this be our proper consideration in sending him?

ANY: Yes.

SOC: And isn't it just the same with flute playing and so on? It is the height of unreason, if we wish to make somebody a flute player, not to be willing to send him to people who promise to teach the art and charge for it, and instead to trouble others to teach him when they don't claim to be teachers and haven't got a single pupil in the subject. Don't you think that would be highly unreasonable?

ANY: I do, and stupid to boot.

SOC: Well said. Accordingly, you and I can now consult together about your guest-friend Meno here. He has been saying to me for some time, Anytus, that he desires the wisdom and virtue by which men properly order households and cities, and take care of their parents, and know how to welcome and take leave of fellow citizens and guest-friends in a manner worthy of a good man. To whom should we send him for this? Or is it clear from our account just now that we should send him to people who undertake to be teachers of virtue, declaring themselves available to any Greek who wishes to learn, and charging a set fee for it.

ANY: And just who do you mean, Socrates?

SOC: Why, you know as well as I do. The men people call sophists.

ANY: Good Lord, don't blaspheme, Socrates. Many none of my own, not family, not friends, no citizen, no guest, be seized with such madness as to go to these men and be ruined. For they clearly ruin and corrupt anyone who associates with them.

SOC: Why Anytus, what do you mean? Do they therefore differ so much from others who claim to know how to work some good, that they alone not only provide no benefit, as the rest do, to what is placed in their hands, but on the contrary corrupt it? They openly demand a fee for doing *that*? I can scarcely believe you. Why, I know one man, Protagoras,[18] who made more money from that wisdom of his than did Phidias,[19] who produced such conspicuously beautiful work, and any ten other sculptors you please. People who mend old shoes and patch cloaks, if they were to hand back articles in worse condition than they got them, would not escape detection for thirty days and would quickly starve to death if they tried. You surely utter a portent, then, if Protagoras for more than forty years corrupted those who associated with him, sent them back in worse condition than he got them, and escaped detection by the whole of Greece. He was nearly seventy when he died, I think; he had been forty years in his art; and in all that time, and to the present day, esteem for him has been unceasing. And not just for Protagoras, either. There have been a host of others, some born before him and some still alive now. Are we to say according to your account that they led astray and ruined the youth knowingly, or that they were not even aware of it themselves? Shall we then deem them mad, whom some say are the wisest men of all?

ANY: They are far from mad, Socrates. It is the youths who pay them money who are mad, still more the relatives who allow it, and most of all the cities which allow such men to enter and don't drive them out—whether they are foreigners or citizens.

SOC: But Anytus, why are you so hard on them? Has one of the sophists wronged you?

ANY: No indeed, I've never associated with any of them, nor permitted anyone of mine to do so.

SOC: So you have no experience of the fellows?

ANY: That's right. May it continue so.

SOC: Then, my friend, how do you know whether this affair has good or mischief in it, when you have no experience of it?

ANY: Easily. At any rate, I know who they are and what they are, whether I've had experience with them or not.

SOC: You must have second sight, Anytus! I can't see how else you'd know about them, from what you've said. Still, we weren't asking where Meno can go to be corrupted. Let it be to the sophists, if you wish. Tell us instead about the others. Benefit this friend of your father's house and inform him to whom he should go in this great city to become distinguished in respect to the virtue I just described.

ANY: Why don't you tell him yourself?

SOC: Why, I did mention whom I thought were teachers of it, though it happens I was talking nonsense. So you say, at least, and perhaps you are right. But now it's your turn. Tell him to whom he should go among the Athenians. Mention any name you please.

ANY: Why should he hear just one name? Any Athenian gentlemen he meets will make him better than would the sophists, provided he is willing to listen.

SOC: But did they become fine gentlemen spontaneously? Without having learned from anyone, can they nonetheless teach others what they themselves did not learn?

ANY: Why, I expect they learned from their elders, who were gentlemen too. Do you deny that there have been many good men in this city?

SOC: No, Anytus, I think there are good men in political life here, and that their predecessors were not inferior to them. But have they been good teachers of their own virtue? Our discussion is about that; not whether there are good men here now, or formerly, but whether virtue is taught. We've been asking for some time, and to ask that is to ask this: Do good men, whether of our time or earlier, actually know how to hand down to someone else the virtue in which their goodness consists, or is it impossible for a man to hand it on or receive it from another? That's what Meno and I have been after for some time. On the basis of your own account, consider: would you say Themistocles was a good man?

ANY: Of course. Eminently good.

SOC: So if anyone else could teach his own virtue, you'd say he'd be a good teacher?

ANY: I suppose so, at least if he wanted to.

SOC: But don't you suppose he'd have wished others to become good men, especially his own son? Do you think he'd treat a son with grudging jealousy, and purposefully not hand on the virtue in which his own goodness consisted? Surely you must have heard

how Themistocles[20] had his son Cleophantus taught to be a good horseman. Why, he      d
could ride a horse standing bolt upright, and aim a javelin doing it, and he could do
many other amazing things, because Themistocles educated him and made him skillful
in everything which can be got from good teachers. Surely you've heard all this from
your elders?

ANY: I have.

SOC: So no one could claim his son's nature was bad.

ANY: Perhaps not.      e

SOC: But what about this: Did you ever hear anybody, young or old, say that Cleophantus
son of Themistocles was good and wise, as his father was?

ANY: Certainly not.

SOC: Well, are we to suppose that he wished to educate his son in other things, but not to
make him any better than his neighbors in respect to the wisdom he himself possessed—that is, assuming virtue is taught?

ANY: Hardly.

SOC: So there's your teacher of virtue; yet even you agree he was one of the best men of past
generations. But let's examine someone else then, Aristides son of Lysimachus.[21] Or      94a
don't you agree he was good?

ANY: Of course I do.

SOC: Well, he too gave his son Lysimachus the best education in Athens, so far as it could be
got from teachers. Do you think it made him better than anybody at all? You've
associated with him; you see what he's like. Or if you will, take Pericles[22]—so splendidly
wise a man. You know he raised two sons, Paralus and Xanthippus?      b

ANY: Yes.

SOC: Then you also know he taught them to be horsemen inferior to none in Athens; he
educated them in music and gymnastics and everything that could be got by art, and
they excelled. Didn't he then wish to make them good men? I think he did, but perhaps
this is not taught. But lest you think this has been impossible only for a few Athenians
of a quite insignificant sort, think about Thucydides.[23] He also raised two sons, Mele-      c
sius and Stephanus, educated them well in other things, and made them the best
wrestlers in Athens. He had one of them trained by Xanthias and the other by Eudorus,
who were reputed to be the best wrestlers of their time. You recall?

MEN: Yes, I've heard that.

SOC: Well he clearly would never have gone to the expense needed to teach his children
wrestling, and yet fail to teach them at no cost to himself the thing needed to make      d
them good men—if it is taught. Was Thucydides perhaps insignificant, without a host
of friends in Athens and among the Allies? To the contrary: he was great in house and
great in power, in this city and in the rest of Greece. If the thing is taught, he'd certainly
have found out who it was, fellow countryman or foreigner, who would make his sons
good, if he himself lacked leisure due to cares of state. Anytus, my friend, it may well be      e
that virtue is not taught.

ANY: Socrates, it seems to me you slander men lightly. If you will be persuaded by me, I
would advise you to beware. It may be that in other cities too it is easier to do evil to
men than good. Certainly it is in this one. But then, I think you know that.      95a

SOC: Anytus seems angry, Meno. I'm not surprised. To begin with, he thinks I am disparaging these men; then too, he thinks he is one of them. If someday he should understand what slander really is, he will cease to be angry.[24] At present, he does not know.

But Meno, you tell me: there are gentlemen in your country too, are there not?

MEN: Of course.

b SOC: Well then, are they willing to offer themselves as teachers to the young? Would they agree they are teachers and that virtue is taught?

MEN: Emphatically not, Socrates; rather, sometimes you hear them say it is taught, and sometimes not.

SOC: Well, are we to say they are teachers of it, when they disagree on that very point?

MEN: I think not, Socrates.

c SOC: Then what about the sophists? They are the only ones who claim to be teachers of virtue. Do you think they are?

MEN: Socrates, that is why I especially admire Gorgias. You'd never hear him promise that: in fact, he laughs at those who do. He thinks it his business to make men clever speakers.

SOC: Then you don't think the sophists are teachers?

MEN: Socrates, I can't say. Actually, I'm just like everybody else: sometimes I think so, sometimes not.

SOC: But did you know that it's not just you and other people in public life who sometimes

d think it is taught and sometimes not? Even the poet Theognis said the same thing.[25]

MEN: Really? Where?

SOC: In his Elegaics, where he says,

> Sit with them, eat with them, drink with them;
> Be pleasing unto those whose power is great,
> For the good will teach you to be good.
e
> Mix with evil and your mind will be lost.

You see that in those lines he says virtue is taught?

MEN: Yes, apparently so.

SOC: But in others he shifts his ground a bit. I think it goes

> If thought were something to be made and put into a man,
> They would bear and carry many a fee and large.

Meaning by "they" the people who were able to do it. And again,

96a
> Never is a bad son born of a good father,
> For he is persuaded by precepts of wisdom.
> But never by teaching will you make the bad man good.

You notice how he contradicts himself?

MEN: Apparently.

SOC: Well, can you mention any other subject where those who claim to be teachers are not acknowledged as teachers, or even acknowledged to understand their own subject matter, but are thought to be bad at the very thing they claim to teach; whereas those acknowledged as accomplished in this subject matter sometimes claim it is taught and sometimes not. Can you in any proper sense say that people so confused are teachers?

MEN: Emphatically not.

SOC: Now, if neither sophists nor gentlemen are teachers of the thing, then clearly no one else is.

MEN: I agree.

SOC: And if no teachers, no students?

MEN: I think that's so.

SOC: And we agreed that if there are neither teachers nor students of a thing, then it is not taught.

MEN: We did.

SOC: Now, it turns out there are no teachers of virtue?

MEN: It does.

SOC: And if no teachers, no students?

MEN: That follows.

SOC: Therefore, virtue is not taught?

MEN: It seems not, provided that we've examined it correctly. But the result is that I really wonder, Socrates, whether there even are any good men, or how those who become good can do so.

## Knowledge and Right Opinion (96d–98b)

SOC: Very likely you and I are pretty poor types, Meno. Gorgias hasn't sufficiently educated you, nor Prodicus me. Beyond all else, we must pay close attention to ourselves and seek someone who will in some way make us better men. I say this with a view to the inquiry just concluded where we wittingly make ourselves ridiculous by neglecting the fact that it is not true that human affairs are carried on rightly and well only through the guidance of knowledge. That is perhaps why recognition of the way good men become good escapes us.

MEN: What do you mean, Socrates?

SOC: This: we have agreed—and rightly, since it could hardly be otherwise—that good men must be beneficial.

MEN: Yes.

SOC: And also that they will be beneficial if they guide matters rightly for us?

MEN: Yes.

SOC: But that there cannot be right guidance unless there is understanding—to that, it seems, we agreed wrongly.

MEN: Really? Why do you say that?

SOC: I'll tell you. Suppose someone who knew the road to Larissa,[26] or any place you please, were to walk there and guide others. He would guide them rightly and well, wouldn't he?

MEN: Of course.

SOC: But what if someone had right opinion as to the road, but had never taken it and did not know it. Wouldn't he guide rightly too?

MEN: Of course.

SOC: And presumably as long as he has right opinion about matters of which the other has knowledge, he will be no worse a guide than the man who understands it, even though he only believes truly without understanding.

MEN: Quite so.

SOC: Therefore true opinion, concerning rightness of action, is a guide not inferior to understanding; that is what we left out just now in our inquiry about what sort of thing virtue is. We said that understanding is the only guide to right action, whereas it seems there is also true opinion.

MEN: Yes, it seems so.

SOC: So right opinion is no less beneficial than knowledge.

MEN: Except in this way, Socrates, that a man with knowledge will always hit upon the right answer, whereas a man with right opinion sometimes will and sometimes won't.

SOC: How do you mean? Won't the man who always has right opinion always be right as long as his opinion is right?

MEN: It would appear he must. But Socrates, assuming this is true, I have to wonder that knowledge is much more highly valued than right opinion, and in what respect one is different from the other.

SOC: Do you know why you're surprised, or should I tell you?

MEN: Tell me, please.

SOC: It's because you haven't paid attention to the statues of Daedalus.[27] Maybe there aren't any in your country.

MEN: What are you getting at?

SOC: Those statues, if they aren't bound, actually get up and run away; but if bound, they stay.

MEN: Well, so?

SOC: It isn't worth a great deal to own one of his creations if it's loose; like a runaway slave, it will not stay. But it is worth quite a great deal when bound, for his works are very beautiful. What am I getting at? This bears on true opinions. For in fact, true opinions, as long as they stay, are beautiful possessions and accomplish all that is good, but they are unwilling to stay very long. They run away from the soul of a man, so that they are not worth much until someone binds them by reflection on the reason for them. And that, my friend Meno, is recollection, as we agreed before.[28] When bound, they in the first place become knowledge; and secondly, they abide. That is why knowledge is more to be valued than right opinion: Knowledge differs from right opinion by its bond.

MEN: Yes, Socrates, it certainly seems that way.

SOC: Still, I speak as one who conjectures, not as one who knows. But that right opinion is other than knowledge I think is surely not conjecture: if I were to say I knew anything—and I would say it of very little—this one thing I would surely place among things I know.

MEN: Yes, and correctly, Socrates.

**Conclusion (98b–100c)**

SOC: Well, then, isn't it correct that in each action the guidance of true opinion accomplishes results in no way inferior to those accomplished by knowledge?

MEN: There again, what you say seems true.

SOC: So right opinion is not worse or less beneficial than knowledge in respect to action; nor c is the man who has right opinion inferior to the man who knows.

MEN: True.

SOC: Moreover, we've agreed that good men are beneficial.

MEN: Yes.

SOC: Then since good men would benefit their cities, if they do, not only through knowledge but right opinion, and since neither of the two belongs to men by nature, but is acquired—or do you think either knowledge or right opinion is present by nature? d

MEN: No, I don't.

SOC: Then since they are not present by nature, good men are not good by nature.

MEN: Of course not.

SOC: Since good men are not good by nature, we next considered if virtue is taught.

MEN: Yes.

SOC: If virtue is wisdom, it seemed it would be taught.

MEN: Yes.

SOC: And if taught, it would be wisdom?

MEN: Of course.

SOC: And if there were teachers, it would be taught. If none, it would not be taught. e

MEN: Yes.

SOC: We have further agreed that there are no teachers of it?

MEN: That is so.

SOC: Therefore, we have agreed that it is neither taught nor wisdom?

MEN: Of course.

SOC: However, we surely agree that it is good.

MEN: Yes.

SOC: And that which guides rightly is useful and good?

MEN: Of course.

SOC: But only these two things, true opinion and knowledge, guide rightly, and a man guides 99a rightly only if he has them. Things which occur rightly by chance occur through no human guidance, but wherever a man guides rightly, one of these two, true opinion or knowledge, is found.

MEN: I agree.

SOC: Now, virtue no longer is knowledge, since it is not taught.

MEN: It appears not.

SOC: Therefore, of two good and beneficial things, one has been ruled out: knowledge would b not be a guide in political affairs.

MEN: I think not.

SOC: So it is not by a kind of wisdom or because they are wise that men such as Themistocles, and those like him whom Anytus here just mentioned, guide their cities. For they cannot make others like themselves, since they are not what they are because of knowledge.

MEN: That seems to be true, Socrates, as you say.

SOC: Then if not by knowledge, only true opinion is left. That is what men in political life use to direct their cities rightly, differing in no way from sooth-sayers and seers in respect to understanding. For the latter also say many things which are true, and understand nothing of what they are saying.

MEN: Very likely.

SOC: Now, Meno, isn't it proper to call men divine, when without possessing intelligence they bring a multitude of important things to successful issue in what they do and say?

MEN: Of course.

SOC: And therefore we rightly call those men divine whom we just mentioned—soothsayers and seers, and the whole race of poets. And surely we must say that our statesmen, by no means least among them, are divine and inspired. For when, by speaking, they bring a multitude of important things to successful issue without understanding what they are talking about, it is because they have been breathed upon and laid hold of by the god.

MEN: Of course.

SOC: And surely that is the tale the women tell: they call good men divine. And the Spartans, when they sing the praises of a good man, say, "He is a man divine."

MEN: Yes, Socrates, it appears you are right. But Anytus here may be angry at you for saying it.

SOC: That does not concern me. We shall doubtless talk with him another time, Meno. For the present, if this whole account of ours has been correctly examined and stated, virtue is neither present by nature nor taught: it comes to be present, in those to whom it comes, by divine apportionment, without intelligence—unless there is among statesmen a man who can make another man a statesman. If there is, that man might be said to be of the same sort among the living as Homer claimed Teiresias[29] was among the dead:

> Alone among those below he kept his wits.
> The rest are darting, fleeting shadows.

In the same way in this world with regard to virtue, such a man would be, as among shadows, a thing of reality and truth.

MEN: I think you put it most excellently, Socrates.

SOC: Then from this it appears, Meno, that virtue comes to be present by divine apportionment in those to whom it comes. But we shall only know that with clear certainty when, before inquiring how virtue comes to be present in men, we first undertake to inquire what virtue is.

The hour is come for me to go. Please persuade your host Anytus here of the things of which you yourself are now persuaded, so that his anger may be allayed. If you persuade him, you may also do some benefit to the Athenians.

## Notes

1. The word here translated "taught" may also mean "teachable." In what follows, it will be translated "taught." [translator's note]
2. Meno, a mercenary soldier, was a person of dubious character; hence, his questions carry a touch of irony.
3. Gorgias (c. 480–376) was one of the most famous of the Sophists, itinerant teachers of oratory who were paid for their services.
4. *Arete*, given its customary translation, "virtue," is "goodness." [translator's note]
5. Prodicus was a Sophist, best known for his precision in drawing verbal distinctions.
6. Empedocles (c. 493–c. 433 B.C.E.) was a pre-Socratic philosopher who thought that our perceptions are the result of effluences from physical objects entering our sense organs.
7. Pindar (518–438 B.C.E.) was a celebrated lyric poet.
8. The reference is to a religious ceremony.
9. The stingray, which paralyzed its victims, was a danger to Mediterranean swimmers.
10. The quotation is from Pindar.
11. Recollection is related to, but not identical with, memory. A distinction between the two may be that knowledge based on experience is remembered, whereas knowledge not based on experience is recollected.
12. It is customary here and in what follows to translate "feet" in appropriate contexts as "square feet," a concept for which Greek mathematics had no special term. I have kept to Greek usage. [translator's note]
13. Socrates asks the boy to find a line whose length is the square root of eight, an irrational number.
14. The passage is opaque. A cogent explanation of the mathematics that may be involved is provided by Judith I. Meyers in "Plato's Geometric Hypothesis: *Meno* 86E–87B," *Apeiron 21* (Fall 1988), pp. 173–180.
15. Anytus, who helped restore Athenian democracy, was one of the three accusers of Socrates at his trial.
16. Ismenias (d. 382 B.C.E.) was a noted statesman.
17. The money in question was probably a bribe. [translator's note]
18. Protagoras (*c.* 490–c. 420 B.C.E.) was one of the most prominent Sophists.
19. Phidias, active in the mid-fifth century B.C.E., was the most famous Athenian sculptor.
20. Themistocles (528–462 B.C.E.) was an Athenian statesman and general who helped defeat the Persians.
21. Aristides was an Athenian statesman and hero of the Persian War, renowned for his honesty.
22. Pericles (c. 495–429 B.C.E.), the most famous leader of democratic Athens, was celebrated for his incorruptible character.
23. Not the historian, but a political rival of Pericles. [translator's note]
24. The translation could also read. "If someday he should understand what speaking falsely is, he will cease to be angry."
25. Theognis was a sixth-century B.C.E. elegiac poet from Megara.
26. Larissa was the principal city of Thessaly, the region of Meno's birth.
27. Daedalus, a legendary artist, craftsman, and inventor, made lifelike figures that moved.
28. See 85c. [translator's note]
29. Tiresias was a legendary blind Theban, gifted with the power of prophecy.

# The Republic

## Book II

368  ... Glaucon, and all the rest with him, requested me by all means to give my assistance, and
not to let the conversation drop, but thoroughly to investigate what each of them is [justice
and injustice], and the truth with regard to their respective advantages. So I said what
seemed to me to be the case. The inquiry we are undertaking is no trivial one, but demands a

d  keen sight, as it appears to me. Therefore, since we are not all that clever, I think we had
better adopt a mode of inquiry which may be thus illustrated. Suppose we had been ordered
to read small writing at a distance, not having very good eyesight, and that one of us
discovered that the same writing was to be found somewhere else in larger letters, and upon a
larger space, we should have looked upon it as a piece of luck, I imagine, that we could read
the latter first, and then examine the smaller, and observe whether the two were the same.

Undoubtedly we should, said Adeimantus; but what parallel can you see to this, Socrates,

e  in our inquiry after justice?

I will tell you, I replied. We speak of justice as residing in an individual man, and also as
residing in an entire city, do we not?

Certainly we do, he said.

Well, a city is larger than one man.

It is.

Perhaps, then, justice may exist in larger proportions in the greater subject, and thus be

369  easier to discover; so, if you please, let us first investigate what justice is like in cities;
afterwards let us apply the same inquiry to the individual, looking for the counterpart of the
greater as it exists in the form of the less.

Indeed, he said, I think your plan is a good one.

If then we were to trace in speech the gradual formation of a city, should we also see the
growth of its justice or of its injustice?

Perhaps we should.

b  Then, if this were done, might we not hope to see more easily the object of our search?

Yes, much more easily.

Is it your advice, then, that we should attempt to carry out our plan? It is no trifling task, I
imagine; therefore consider it well.

We have considered it, said Adeimantus; yes, do so by all means.

Well then, I proceeded, the formation of a city is due, as I imagine, to this fact, that we are not individually self-sufficient, but have many wants. Or would you assign any other principle for the founding of cities?

No I agree with you, he replied.

Thus it is, then, that owing to our many wants, and because each seeks the aid of others to  c
supply his various requirements, we gather many associates and helpers into one dwelling-place, and give to this joint dwelling the name of city. Is it so?

Undoubtedly.

And everyone who gives or takes in exchange, whatever it be that he exchanges, does so from a belief that it is better for himself.

Certainly.

Now then, let us construe our city in speech from the beginning. It will owe its construction, it appears, to our needs.

Unquestionably.

Well, but the first and most pressing of all wants is that of sustenance to enable us to exist  d
as living creatures.

Most decidedly.

Our second want would be that of a house, and our third that of clothing and the like.

True.

Then let us know what will render our city adequate to the supply of so many things. Must we not begin with a farmer for one, and a house-builder, and besides these a weaver? Will these suffice, or shall we add to them a shoemaker, and perhaps some other person who ministers to our bodily wants?

By all means.

Then the smallest possible city will consist of four or five men.

So it seems.

To proceed then, ought each of these to place his own work at the disposal of the  e
community, so that the single farmer, for example, shall provide food for four, spending four
times the amount of time and labor upon the preparation of food, and sharing it with others;  370
or must he neglect them, and produce for his own consumption alone the fourth part of this quantity of food, in a fourth part of the time, spending the other three parts, one in making his house, another in procuring himself clothes, and the third in providing himself with shoes, saving himself the trouble of sharing with others, and doing his own business by himself, and for himself?

To this Adeimantus replied, Well, Socrates, perhaps the former plan is the easier of the two.

Really, I said, by Zeus, it is not improbable; for I recollect myself, after your answer, that, in the first place, no two persons are born exactly alike, but each differs in his nature, one being suited for one occupation, and another for another. Do you not think so?  b

I do.

Well, when is a man likely to succeed best? When he divides his exertions among many skills, or when he devotes himself exclusively to one?

When he devotes himself to one.

Again, it is also clear, I imagine, that if a person lets the right moment for any work go by, it never returns.

It is quite clear.

For the thing to be done does not choose, I imagine, to await the leisure of the doer, but
the doer must be at the call of the thing to be done, and not treat it as a secondary affair.

He must.

From these considerations it follows that all things will be produced in superior quantity
and quality, and with greater ease, when each man, being freed from other tasks, works at a
single occupation, in accordance with his nature and at the right moment.

Unquestionably.

More than four citizens, then, Adeimantus, are needed to provide the requisites which we
named. For the farmer, it appears, will not make his own plough, if it is to be a good one, nor
his hoe, nor any of the other tools employed in agriculture. No more will the builder make
the numerous tools which he also requires; and so of the weaver and the shoemaker.

True.

Then we shall have carpenters and smiths, and many other artisans of the kind, who will
become members of our little city, and create a population.

Certainly.

Still it will not yet be very large, supposing we add to them cowherds and shepherds, and
the rest of that class, in order that the farmers may have oxen for plowing, and the house-
builders, as well as the farmers, beasts of burden for hauling, and the weavers and shoe-
makers wool and leather.

It will not be a small city, either, if it contains all these.

Moreover, it is scarcely possible to plant the actual city in a place where it will have no
need of imports.

No, it is impossible.

Then it will further require a new class of persons to bring from other cities all that it
requires.

It will.

Well, but if the agent goes empty-handed, carrying with him none of the products in
demand among those people from whom our city is to procure what it requires, he will also
come empty-handed away, will he not?

I think so.

Then it must produce at home not only enough for itself, but also articles of the right kind
and quantity to accommodate those whose services it needs.

It must.

Then our city requires larger numbers both of farmers and other craftsmen.

Yes, it does.

And among the rest it will need more of those agents also, who are to export and import
the several products, and these are merchants, are they not?

Yes.

Then we shall require merchants also.

Certainly.

And if the commerce is carried on by sea, there will be a further demand for a considerable number of other persons, who are skilled in the practice of navigation.

A considerable number, undoubtedly.

But now tell me, In the city itself how are they to exchange their several productions? For it was to promote this exchange, you know, that we formed the community, and so founded our city.

Clearly, by buying and selling.

Then this will give rise to a market and a currency, for the sake of exchange.

Undoubtedly.

Suppose then that the farmer, or one of the other craftsmen, should come with some of his produce into the market, at a time when none of those who wish to make an exchange with him are there, is he to leave his occupation and sit idle in the market-place?    c

By no means, there are persons who, with an eye to this contingency, undertake the service required; and these in well-regulated cities are, generally speaking, persons of excessive physical weakness, who are of no use in other kinds of labor. Their business is to remain on    d the spot in the market, and give money for goods to those who want to sell, and goods for money to those who want to buy.

This demand, then, causes a class of tradesmen to spring up in our city. For do we not give the name of tradesmen to those who station themselves in the market, to minister to buying and selling, applying the term merchants to those who go about from city to city?

Exactly so.

In addition to these, I imagine, there is also another class of servants, consisting of those    e whose reasoning capacities do not recommend them as associates, but whose bodily strength is equal to hard labor. These, selling the use of their strength and calling the price of it wage, are thus named, I believe, wage-earners. Is it not so?

Precisely.

Then wage-earners also form, as it seems, a complementary portion of a city.

I think so.

Shall we say then, Adeimantus, that our city has at length grown to its full stature?

Perhaps so.

Where then shall we find justice and injustice in it? With which of these elements that we have contemplated, has it simultaneously made its entrance?

I have no notion, Socrates, unless perhaps it be discoverable somewhere in the mutual    372 relations of these same persons.

Well, perhaps you are right. We must investigate the matter, and not flinch from the task. Let us consider then, in the first place, what kind of life will be led by persons thus provided. I presume they will produce bread and wine, and clothes and shoes, and build themselves houses; and in summer, no doubt, they will generally work naked and without shoes, while in winter they will be suitably clothed and shod. And they will live, I suppose, on barley and    b wheat, baking cakes of the meal, and kneading loaves of the flour. And spreading these excellent cakes and loaves upon mats of straw or on clean leaves, and themselves reclining on rude beds of yew or myrtle-boughs, they will make merry, themselves and their children, drinking their wine, wearing garlands, and singing the praises of the gods, enjoying one another's society, and not begetting children beyond their means, through a prudent fear of poverty or war.    c

Glaucon here interrupted me, remarking, Apparently you describe your men as feasting without any seasonings.

True, I said, I had forgotten. Of course they will have something to season their food—salt, no doubt, and olives and cheese, together with the country fare of boiled onions and cabbage. We shall also set before them a dessert, I imagine, of figs and chickpeas and beans; and they may roast myrtle-berries and beech-nuts at the fire, taking wine with their fruit in

d moderation. And thus passing their days in peace and sound health, they will, in all probability, live to an advanced age, and dying, bequeath to their children a life in which their own will be reproduced.

Upon this Glaucon exclaimed, Why Socrates, if you were founding a community of swine, this is just the style in which you would fatten them up!

How then, said I, would you have them live, Glaucon?

In the customary manner, he replied. They ought to recline on couches, I should think, if

e they are not to have a hard life of it, and dine off tables, and have the usual dishes and dessert in the way we do now.

Very good. I understand. Apparently we are considering the growth not of a city merely, but of a luxurious city. I dare say it is not a bad plan, for by this extension of our inquiry we shall perhaps discover how it is that justice and injustice take root in cities. Now it appears to

373 me that the city which we have described is the true and, so to speak, healthy city. But if you wish us to contemplate a city that is suffering from inflammation, there is nothing to hinder us. Some people will not be satisfied, it seems, with the fare or the mode of life which we have described, but must have, in addition, couches and tables and every other article of furniture, as well as seasonings and fragrant oils, and perfumes, and courtesans, and confectionery; and all these in plentiful variety. Moreover, we must not limit ourselves now to essentials in those articles which we specified at first, I mean houses and clothes and shoes, but we must set painting and embroidery to work, and acquire gold and ivory, and all similar valuables, must we not?

b Yes.

Then we shall also have to enlarge our city, for our first or healthy city will not now be of sufficient size, but requires to be increased in bulk, and needs to be filled with a multitude of callings, which do not exist in cities to satisfy any natural want. For example, the whole class of hunters, and all who practice the art of imitation, including many who use forms and colors, and many who use music; and poets also—and their helpers, the rhapsodes, actors, dancers, contractors; and lastly, the craftsmen of all sorts of articles, and among others those who make parts of feminine adornments. We shall similarly require more personal servants, shall we not? That is to say, teachers, wet-nurses, dry-nurses, beauticians, barbers, and cooks moreover and butchers? Swineherds again are among the additions we shall require, a class of persons not to be found, because not needed, in our former city, but needed among the rest in this. We shall also need great quantities of all kinds of cattle, for those who may wish to eat them, shall we not?

Of course we shall.

d Then shall we not experience the need of medical men also, to a much greater extent under this than under the former life-style?

Yes, indeed.

The land too, I presume, which was formerly sufficient for the support of its then inhabitants will be now too small, and adequate no longer. Shall we say so?

Certainly.

Then must we not cut ourselves a slice of our neighbor's territory, if we are to have land enough both for pasture and tillage, while they will do the same to ours, if they, like us, permit themselves to overstep the limit of necessities, and plunge into the unbounded acquisition of wealth?

It must inevitably be so, Socrates.

Will our next step be to go to war, Glaucon, or how will it be?

As you say.

At this stage of our inquiry let us avoid asserting either that war does good or that it does harm, confining ourselves to this statement, that we have further traced the origin of war to causes which bring about whatever ills befall a city, either in its public capacity, or in its individual members.

Exactly so.

Once more then, my friend, our city must be larger and not just by a small extent, but by a whole army, which must go forth and do battle with all invaders in defense of its entire property, and of the things we were just now describing.

How so? he asked. Are not those persons sufficient of themselves?

They are not, if you and all the rest of us were right in the admissions which we made, when we were modeling our city. We admitted, I think, if you remember, that it was impossible for one man to work well at many crafts.

True.

Well then, is not the business of war looked upon as a craft in itself?

Undoubtedly.

And have we not as much reason to concern ourselves about the craft of war as the craft of shoemaking?

Quite as much.

But we cautioned the shoemaker, you know, against attempting to be a farmer or a weaver or a builder besides, with a view to our shoemaking work being well done; and to every other artisan we assigned in like manner one occupation, namely, that for which he was naturally fitted, and in which, if he let other things alone, and worked at it all his time without neglecting his opportunities, he was likely to prove a successful workman. Now is it not of the greatest moment that the work of war should be well done? Or is it so easy, that anyone can succeed in it and be at the same time a farmer or a shoemaker or a laborer at any other craft whatever, although there is no one in the world who could become a good checkers-player or dice-player by merely taking up the game at unoccupied moments, instead of pursuing it as his special study from his childhood? And will it be enough for a man merely to handle a shield or the other arms and implements of war? Will that make him competent to play his part well on that very day in an engagement of heavy troops or in any other military service—although the mere handling of any other instrument will never make anyone a true craftsman or athlete, nor will such instrument be even useful to one who has neither learnt its capabilities nor exercised himself sufficiently in its practical applications?

If it were so, these implements of war would be very valuable, he said.

In proportion, then, to the importance of the work which these guardians have to do,

it will require more leisure than most, as well as extraordinary skill and attention. I quite
e think so.

Will it not also require natural endowments suited to this particular occupation?

Undoubtedly.

Then, apparently, it will be up to us to choose, if we can, the kind of nature which qualifies its possessors for the guardianship of a city.

Certainly; it belongs to us.

Then, by Zeus, we have taken upon ourselves no trifling task; nevertheless, there must be no flinching, so long as our strength holds out.

No, there must not.

375 Do you think then, I asked, that there is any difference, in the qualities required for keeping guard, between a well-bred puppy and a gallant young man?

I do not quite understand you.

Why, I suppose, for instance, they both must be quick to see things and swift to overtake what they perceive, and strong also, in case they have to fight what they have caught.

Certainly, all these qualities are required.

Moreover, they must be brave if they are to fight well.

Undoubtedly.

But will either a horse, or a dog, or any other animal, be likely to be brave if it is not
b spirited? Or have you failed to observe what an irresistible and unconquerable thing is the spirit so that under its influence every creature will be fearless and unconquerable in the face of any danger?

I have observed it.

We know then what bodily qualities are required in our guardian.

We do.

And also what qualities of the soul, namely, that he must be spirited.

Yes.

How then, Glaucon, if such be their natural disposition, are they to be kept from behaving fiercely to one another, and to the rest of the citizens?

It will not be easy, by Zeus.

c Nevertheless, they certainly ought to be gentle to their friends, and dangerous only to their enemies—else they will not wait for others to destroy them, but will be the first to do it for themselves.

True.

What then shall we do? Where shall we find a character at once gentle and high-spirited? For I suppose a gentle nature is the opposite of a spirited one?

Apparently it is.

Nevertheless a man who is devoid of either gentleness or spirit cannot possibly make a good guardian. And as they seem to be incompatible, the result is, that a good guardian is an
d impossibility.

It looks like it, he said.

Here then I was perplexed, but having reconsidered our conversation, I said, We deserve, my friend, to be puzzled, for we have deserted the image which we set before us.

How so?

It never struck us, that after all there are natures, though we fancied there were none, which combine these opposite qualities.

And where is such a combination to be found?

You may see it in several animals, but particularly in the one which we ourselves compared to our guardian. For I suppose you know that it is the natural disposition of well-bred dogs to be perfectly gentle to their friends and acquaintance, but the reverse to strangers.

Certainly I do.

Therefore the thing is possible; and we are not contradicting nature in our endeavor to give such a character to our guardian.

So it would seem.

Then is it your opinion, that in one who is to make a good guardian it is further required that he be a philosopher as well as high-spirited?

How so? I do not understand you.

You will notice in dogs this other trait, which is really marvelous in the creature.

What is that?

Whenever they see someone they don't know they are irritated before they have been provoked by any ill treatment, but when they see someone they are acquainted with they welcome him, though they may never have experienced any kindness at his hands. Has this never excited your wonder?

I never paid attention to this before, but no doubt they do behave so.

Well, but this affection is a very clever thing in the dog, and truly philosophical.

How so?

Why, because the only mark by which he distinguishes between the appearance of a friend and that of an enemy is, that he knows the former and is ignorant of the latter. How, I ask, can the creature be other than fond of learning when it makes knowledge and ignorance the criteria of the familiar and the strange?

Beyond a question, it must be fond of learning.

Well, is not the love of learning the same thing as a philosophical disposition?

It is, he said.

Shall we not then assert with confidence in the case of a man also, that if he is to show a gentle disposition towards his relatives and acquaintances, he must have a turn for learning and philosophy?

Be it so, he said.

Then in our judgment the man who is a fine and good guardian of the city will be in his nature philosophical, high-spirited, swift-footed, and strong.

Undoubtedly he will.

This then will be the original character of our guardians. But in what way shall we rear and educate them? And will the investigation of this point help us on towards discovering that which is the object of all our speculations, namely, the manner in which justice and injustice grow up in a city? For I wish us neither to omit anything useful, nor to occupy ourselves with anything redundant, in our inquiry.

Hereupon Glaucon's brother observed, Well, for my part, I fully anticipate that this inquiry will be useful.

If so, by Zeus, I said, we must certainly not give it up, my dear Adeimantus, even though it should prove somewhat long.

Indeed we must not.

Come then, like leisurely story-tellers in a story, let us describe the education of our men.

e    Yes, let us do so.

What then is the education to be? Perhaps we could hardly find a better than that which the experience of the past has already discovered, which consists, I believe, in gymnastics for the body, and music for the soul.

It does.

Shall we not then begin our course of education with music rather than with gymnastics? Undoubtedly we shall.

Under the term music, do you include speeches or not?

I do.

And of speeches there are two kinds, the true and the false.

Yes.

377    And must we instruct our pupils in both but in the false first?

I do not understand what you mean.

Do you not understand that we begin with children by telling them stories? And these, I suppose, to speak generally, are false, though they contain some truths; and we employ such stories in the treatment of children at an earlier period than gymnastic exercises.

True.

That is what I meant when I said that music ought to be taken up before gymnastics.

You are right.

Then are you aware, that in every work the beginning is the most important part, espe-
b    cially in dealing with anything young and tender? That is the time when any impression one desires is most readily stamped upon it.

Precisely so.

Shall we then permit our children without scruple to hear any stories composed by any authors whatever, and so to receive into their souls opinions generally the reverse of those which *we* think they ought to entertain, when they are grown up to manhood?

No, we shall not permit it on any account.

Then apparently it will be our first duty to be in charge over the story-makers, selecting
c    their good productions, and rejecting the bad. And the selected stories we shall advise our nurses and mothers to repeat to their children, that they may thus shape their souls with stories even more than they shape their bodies with their hands. But we shall have to throw out the greater part of those which are now in vogue.

Which do you mean? he asked.

In the greater stories, I answered, we shall also be able to make out the lesser ones. For the
d    general character and tendency of both the greater and the lesser must doubtless be identical. Do you not think so?

I do; but I am equally uncertain which you mean by the greater.

I mean the stories which Hesiod, and Homer, and the other poets, tell us. For they, I imagine, have composed false stories which they told, and still tell, to men.

What kind of stories do you mean, and what is the fault that you find with them?

A fault, I replied, which deserves the earliest and gravest condemnation, especially if the lie has no beauty.

What is this fault?

It is whenever an author gives a poor representation of the characters of gods and heroes, like a painter whose picture bears no resemblance to the objects he wishes to paint.

Yes, it is quite right to condemn such faults; but explain further what we mean, and give some examples.

In the first place, the poet who conceived the greatest lie on the greatest subjects invented an ugly story when he told how Uranus acted as Hesiod declares he did, and also how Cronus had his revenge upon him. And again, even if the deeds of Cronus and his son's treatment of him were true, it would not have been right, I should have thought, to tell them so casually to young and thoughtless persons; on the contrary, it would be best to keep quiet; or, if for some reason they must be told, they should be imparted under the seal of secrecy to as few hearers as possible, and that after the sacrifice, not of a pig, but of some rare and costly victim, for the purpose of restricting their number as far as possible.

Certainly, these are offensive stories.

They are; and therefore, Adeimantus, they must not be repeated in our city. No; we must not tell a youthful listener that he will be doing nothing extraordinary if he commit the most extreme injustice, nor if he should chastise the unjust acts of a father in the most unscrupulous manner, but will simply be doing what the first and greatest of the gods have done before him.

I assure you, he said, I quite agree with you as to the impropriety of such stories.

Nor yet, I continued, is it proper to say in any case—what is indeed untrue—that gods wage war against gods, and intrigue and fight among themselves; that is, if the future guardians of our city are to deem it a most disgraceful thing to quarrel lightly with one another. Far less ought we to select as subjects for fiction and embroidery the battles of the giants and the various other feuds in which gods and heroes fight against their own family and kin. But if there is any possibility of persuading them that to quarrel with one's fellow is an impiety of which no member of a city was ever guilty, such ought rather to be the language told to our children from the first, by old men and old women, and when they grow older, our poets must be compelled to write in such a strain. But stories like the chaining of Hera by her son, and the flinging of Hephaestus out of heaven for trying to take his mother's part when his father was beating her, and all those battles of the gods which are to be found in Homer, must be refused admittance into our city, whether the meaning is hidden or not. For a child cannot discriminate between what is supposition and what is not; and whatever at that age is adopted as a matter of belief has a tendency to become fixed and indelible, and therefore, perhaps, we ought to esteem it of the greatest importance that the stories children first hear should be adapted in the most perfect manner to the promotion of virtue.

There is certainly reason in this. But if anyone were to proceed to ask us which these are, and which stories convey them, how should we answer him?

To which I replied, My dear Adeimantus, you and I are not poets, on the present occasion, but founders of a city. And founders ought certainly to know the molds in which their poets are to cast their stories, and from which they are not permitted to deviate; but they are not bound to compose stories themselves.

You are right; but to use your own words, what should these molds be in the case of theology?

I think they may be described as follows: It is right, I presume, always to represent god as he really is, whether the poet describe him in an epic or a lyrical or a dramatic poem.

Yes, it is right.

b  Then surely god is good in reality, and is to be so represented?

Unquestionably.

Well, but nothing that is good is harmful, is it?

I think not.

And does that which is not hurtful hurt?

By no means.

And does that which hurts not, do any harm?

I answer as before, no.

And that which does no harm cannot be the cause of any harm either?

How should it be?

Well, is that which is good beneficial?

Yes.

Then it is a cause of well-being?

Yes.

Then that which is good is not the cause of all things, but only of what is as it should be. It is not responsible for any bad things.

c  Exactly so.

If that be so, then god, inasmuch as he is good, cannot be the cause of all things, as the many say. On the contrary, he is the author of only a small part of human affairs; of the larger part he is not the author, for our harmful things far outnumber our good things; and the good things we must ascribe to no other than god, while we must seek elsewhere, and not in him, the causes of the harmful things.

That seems to me the very true.

Then we must express our disapproval, he said, if Homer, or any other poet, is guilty of
d  such a foolish blunder about the gods, as to tell us that . . .

e        Zeus is the dispenser unto men both of both weal and of woe.

And if anyone assert that the violation of oaths and treaties, of which Pandarus was the author, was brought about by Athena and Zeus, we shall not praise him. Nor can we allow it to be said that the strife and trial of strength between the gods was instigated by Themis and
380 Zeus, nor, again, must we let our young people hear that, in the words of Aeschylus,

When to destruction god will plague a house,
He plants the cause in mortals.

But if a poet writes about the sufferings of Niobe, as Aeschylus does in the play from which I have taken these lines, or the calamities of the house of Pelops, or the disasters at Troy, or any similar occurrences, either we must not allow him to call them the work of a god, or if they are to be so called, he must find out an account of them, such as that for which we are now
b  searching, and must say, that what the god did was just and good, and that the people

benefited from their being punished; but we cannot allow the poet to say that a god was the author of a punishment which made the objects of it miserable. Now, if he should say that because the wicked are miserable, these men needed punishment, and the infliction of it by the god was a benefit to them, we shall make no objection; but as to asserting that god, who is good, becomes the author of harm to any, we must do battle uncompromisingly against anyone saying these things; they shall neither be recited or heard in the city, by any member  c
of it, young or old, if it is to be a well-regulated city; because such language may not be used without irreverence, and is moreover both injurious to us and self-contradictory.

I vote with you, he said, for this law, and it pleases me.

Then one of those theological laws or molds, in accordance with which we shall require our speakers to speak, and our authors to write, will be to this effect, that god is not the author of all things, but only of such as are good.

You have proved it quite satisfactorily, he replied.

Well, here is a second for you to consider. Do you think that god is a wizard, and likely to appear for special purposes in different forms at different times, sometimes actually assum-  d
ing such forms, and altering his own person into a variety of shapes, and sometimes deceiving us and making us believe that such a transformation has taken place; or do you think that he is simple, and that it is the most unlikely thing that he should ever depart from his own proper form?

I cannot answer you all at once.

Then answer me this: If anything passes out of its proper forms must not the change be produced either by itself or some other thing?  e

It must.

And is it not the case that changes and motions, communicated by anything else, affect least the things that are best? For instance, the body is changed by food and drink and exertion, and every plant by sunshine and wind, and similar influences; but is not the change slightest in the plant or the body which is healthiest and strongest?

Undoubtedly it is.  381

So of the soul, is it not the bravest and the most prudent that will be the least disturbed and altered by any influence from without?

Yes.

Moreover, I suppose that the same argument applies to all manufactured things, such as furniture, houses, and clothes: those that are well made and in good condition, are least altered by time and other influences.

That is true.

So that everything which is good either by nature or by art, or by both, is least liable to be  b
changed by another thing.

So it would seem.

But surely god and the things of god are in every way most excellent.

Unquestionably.

Then god will be very unlikely to assume many shapes through external influence.

Very unlikely indeed.

But will he change and alter himself?

Clearly he must, if he alters at all.

Does he then, by changing himself, attain to something better and fairer, or to something worse and uglier than himself?

c  Something worse, necessarily, if he alters at all, for we shall not, I presume, affirm that there is any imperfection in the beauty or the goodness of god.

You are perfectly correct; and this being the case, do you think, Adeimantus, that any god or any man would willingly/voluntarily make himself worse than he is, in any respect?

It is impossible.

Then it is also impossible for a god to be willing to change himself, and therefore it would seem that every god, inasmuch as he is perfect to the utmost in beauty and goodness, abides ever simply and without variation in his own shape.

d  The inference is inevitable, I think. Then, my dear friend, let no poet tell us that

> Gods in the likeness of wandering strangers,
> Bodied in manifold forms, go roaming from city to city.

And let no one slander Proteus and Thetis, or introduce in tragedies or any other poems, Hera transformed, collecting in the guise of a priestess,

> Alms for the life-giving children of Inachus, river of Argos.

e  Not to mention many other similar falsehoods, which we must interdict. And once more, let not the mothers be persuaded by these poets into scaring their children by stories badly told, telling them how certain gods go about by night in the likeness of strangers from every land; so that they may not by one and the same acts defame the gods and foster timidity in their children.

No, let that be forbidden.

But perhaps, I continued, though the gods have no tendency to change in themselves, they induce us, by deception and magic, to believe that they appear in various forms.

Perhaps they do.

382  Would a god consent to lie, do you think, either in word, or by an act, such as that of putting a phantom before our eyes?

I don't know.

Don't you know that a true lie, if I may be allowed the expression, is hated by all gods and by all men?

I do not know what you mean.

I mean, that to lie with the highest part of himself, and concerning the highest subjects, is what no one voluntarily consents to do; on the contrary, everyone fears above all things to harbor a lie in that quarter.

I still do not understand you.

b  Because you think I have some mysterious meaning; whereas what I mean is simply this, for the soul to lie, to be deceived, and to be without knowledge concerning the things that are, and to have and hold instead a lie in that place—that is the last thing any man would consent to, for all men hold in special abhorrence a lie in a place like that.

Yes, in most especial abhorrence.

Well, but, as I was saying just now, this is what might most correctly be called a true lie, namely, ignorance residing in the soul of the deluded person. For the spoken lie is a kind of imitation of the affections of the soul, of which it is a secondary image, and not an altogether unadulterated lie; or am I wrong?

No, you are perfectly right.                                                                          c

Then a real lie is hated not only by gods, but likewise by men.

So I think. . . .

Then do you grant that we must devise a second principle regarding which all speaking    383
and writing about the gods must be molded, namely: That the gods neither metamorphose themselves like wizards, nor mislead us by lies expressed either in word or act?

I do grant it.

Then while we praise much in Homer, we shall refuse to praise the story of the dream sent by Zeus to Agamemnon, as well as that passage in Aeschylus where Thetis says that Apollo    b
singing at her marriage,

> Dwelt on her happy motherhood,
> The life from sickness free, and lengthened years.
> Then all-inclusively he blest my lot,
> Favored of heaven, in strains that cheer'd my soul.
> And I too fondly deem'd that Phoebus' lips divine
> Would be free of lies, fraught with prophetic skill;
> But he himself who sang, the marriage-guest
> Himself, who spake all this, 'twas even he
> That slew my son.

When a poet holds such language concerning the gods, we shall be angry with him, and    c
refuse him a chorus, neither shall we allow our teachers to use his writings for the instruction of the young, if we would have our guardians grow up to be as godlike and god-fearing as it is possible for a human to be.

I entirely acquiesce, said he, in the propriety of these principles, and would adopt them as laws.

## Book III

Concerning the gods, then, I continued, such, it would seem, are the things that should and    386
should not be heard, from childhood onwards, for those who are to honor the gods and their parents and to set no small value on mutual friendship.

Yes, he said; and I think our views are correct.

To proceed then. If we intend our citizens to be brave, must not such things be said to them as will make them least afraid of death? Or do you think a man can ever become brave    b
who is haunted by the fear of death?

No, by Zeus, I do not.

Well, do you imagine that a believer in Hades and its terrors will be free from all fear of death, and in the day of battle will prefer it to defeat and slavery?

Certainly not.

Then apparently we must assume some control over those who undertake to set forth these stories and others, requesting them not to revile the other world in that manner, but c rather to speak well of it, because what they say is neither true, nor beneficial to men who are meant to be war-like.

We certainly must.

Then we shall expunge the following passage, and with it all that are like it:

> I'd rather be a serf, and drudge on the lands of a master,
> Serving a man of no great estate and scanty means,
> Sooner than reign supreme in the realm of the dead that have perished.

387 These verses, and all that are like them, we shall entreat Homer and the other poets not to be
b angry if we erase, not because they are unpoetical, or disagreeable to the ears of most men; but because, in proportion as they are more poetical, so much the less ought they to be recited in the hearing of boys and men, whom we require to be free men, fearing slavery more than death.

By all means let us do so. . . .

389 But again, a high value must be set also upon truth. For if we were right in what we said
b just now, and falsehood is really useless to the gods, and only useful to men in the way of a medicine, it is plain that such an agent must be kept in the hands of physicians, and that private men must not meddle with it.

Evidently.

To the rulers of the city then, if to any, it is a proper right to use lies, to deceive either
c enemies or their own citizens, for the good of the city. And no one else may meddle with this privilege. In fact, for a private person to tell a lie to such rulers, we shall consider at least as great a mistake as for a patient to deceive his physician, or a pupil his training-master, concerning the state of his own body; or for a sailor to tell an untruth to a pilot concerning the ship and the crew, in describing his own condition or that of any of his fellow-sailors.

Most true.

If then he finds anyone else guilty of lying in the city,

d > Any of those that be craftsmen,
> Whether prophet or seer or healer of hurts, or worker in timber

he will punish him for introducing a practice as pernicious and subversive in a city as it is in a ship.

Yes, he said, if deeds be in accord with words. . . .

392 Let us then here close our discussion of the subject-matter of narratives: our next task, I
c imagine, is to investigate the question of their style; and this done, we shall have thoroughly considered both what ought to be said, and the mode of saying it. . . .

394 I divine, said he, that you are speculating whether we shall admit tragedy and comedy into
d our city, or not.

It may be so, I replied; and it may be that other claims will be questioned besides those of tragedy and comedy; in fact, I do not yet know myself; but we must go where the argument carries us, as a vessel runs before the wind.

You are quite right.

e Here then is a question for you to consider, Adeimantus: Should our guardians be apt imitators, or not? Or does it follow, from our previous admissions, that any individual may pursue with success one calling, but not many; or, if he attempts this, by his meddling with many he will fail in all, so far as to gain no distinction in any?

That would undoubtedly be the case.

Does not the same principle apply to imitation, or can the same person imitate many things as well as he can imitate one?

Certainly he cannot.

It is very improbable, then, that one who is engaged in any important calling will at the same time know how to imitate a variety of things, and be a successful imitator. Even two branches of imitation, which are thought to be closely allied, are more, I believe, than can be successfully pursued together by the same person—as, for instance, the writing of comedy and of tragedy, which you described just now as imitations, did you not? 395

I did; and you are right in saying that the same persons cannot succeed in both.

Nor yet can a man combine the professions of a rhapsode, a reciter of epic poetry, with that of an actor.

True.

In fact, the same actor cannot even play both tragedy and comedy. And all these are arts of imitation, are they not? b

They are.

And human nature appears to me, Adeimantus, to be split up into yet smaller parts than these, so that a man is unable to imitate many things well, or do the things themselves of which the imitations are likenesses.

Most true.

If, then, we are to maintain our first view, that our guardians ought to be released from every other craft, that they may very precisely be craftsmen of their city's freedom, and may c follow no other occupation but such as tends to this result, it will not be desirable for them either to practice or to imitate anything else; or if they do imitate, let them imitate right from childhood whatever is proper to their profession—brave, moderate, pious, free men, and the like—but slavishness and every other kind of baseness, let them neither practice nor be skilled to imitate, lest from the imitation they'd enjoy the reality. For have you not perceived d that imitations, whether of the body, sound, or thought, if they be persevered in from an early age, are apt to become habitual and natural?

Certainly I have.

Then we shall not permit those in whom we profess to take an interest, and who must themselves become good men, to imitate a woman, if they themselves are men, whether the woman be young or old, either railing at a husband, or striving and boasting against the e gods, in the belief of her own happiness, or taken up with misfortunes, and griefs, and complaints; much more shall we forbid them to imitate one that is ill, or in love, or in labor.

Exactly so.

Again, they must not be permitted to imitate slaves, whether male or female, engaged in the occupations of slaves.

No, they must not.

Nor yet bad men, it would seem, such as cowards, and generally those whose conduct is the reverse of what we described just now; men in the act of abusing and making fools of one another, and uttering obscenities, whether drunk or sober, or committing any of those 396 offences against others, or amongst themselves, of which such men both in word and in deed are guilty. I think also that we must not accustom them to liken themselves to madmen, in word or in act. For though it is right they should know mad and wicked men and women, they ought not to act like them, nor give imitations of them.

Most true.

Again, may they imitate smiths or any other craftsmen, working at their trade, or rowers b pulling at the oars in a galley, or those calling out the time, or anything else of the kind?

Impossible, he replied, since they are not to be permitted even to pay mind to any of these occupations. . . .

397 And is not this the reason why in a city like ours, and in no other, we shall find the e shoemaker a shoemaker, and not a pilot in addition, and the farmer a farmer, and not a juryman in addition, and the soldier a soldier, and not a tradesman in addition; and so on throughout?

True.

It is probable then, that if a man should arrive in our city, so wise as to be able to assume 398 any character and imitate all things, and should propose to make a public display of himself and his poems, we shall pay him reverence as a sacred, admirable, and charming person, but we shall tell him that in our city there is no one like him, and that our law excludes such characters. And we shall send him away to another city after pouring perfumed oil upon his b head, and crowning him with woolen ribbons; but for ourselves, we shall employ, for the sake of our benefit, that more austere and less fascinating poet and story-teller, who will imitate for us the style of the decent man, and will cast his narratives in those molds which we prescribed at the outset, when we were engaged with the education of our soldiers.

We shall certainly do so, if it be in our power.

Now then, my dear friend, it would seem that we have completely done with that part of music which relates to fables and other narratives; for we have described both what is to be said, and how it is to be said.

I think so too. . . .

401 This being the case, ought we to confine ourselves to supervising our poets, and compel-b ling them to impress on their products the likeness of a good character, or else not to compose such among us? Or ought we to extend our supervision to all craftsmen as well, and forbid them to impress those signs of a bad character, of dissoluteness, of meanness, and of ungracefulness, either on the likenesses of living creatures, or on buildings, or any other work c of their hands; altogether forbidding those who cannot do otherwise from working in our city, that our guardians may not be reared among images of vice, as upon unwholesome pastures, culling much every day little by little from many places, and feeding upon it, until they insensibly accumulate a large quantity of ill in their souls? Ought we not, on the contrary, to seek out those craftsmen who by the power of their good temperament can trace out the nature of the fair and the graceful, that our young men, dwelling as it were in a healthful region, may be benefited from everywhere, whence any emanation from noble d works may strike upon their eye or their ear, like a wind wafting health from beneficial lands, and win them imperceptibly from their earliest childhood into likeness, friendship, and harmony with beautiful speech?

Such a nurture, he replied, would be by far the best.

Is it then, Glaucon, on these accounts that we attach such supreme importance to a musical education, because rhythm and harmony sink most deeply into the recesses of the soul, and take most powerful hold of it, bringing gracefulness in their train, and making a man graceful if he be rightly nurtured, but if not, the reverse? And also because he that has been duly nurtured therein will have the keenest eye for defects, whether in the failures of art, or the mis-growths of nature; and feeling a most just disdain for them, will commend beautiful objects, and gladly receive them into his soul, and feed upon them, and grow to be noble and good; whereas he will rightly blame and hate all shameful objects, even in his childhood, before he is able to be reasoned with; and when reason comes, he will welcome her most cordially who can recognize her on account of its kinship, and because he has been so nurtured?

e

402

I have no doubt, he said, that such are the reasons for a musical education. . . .

Gymnastics will come after music in the education of our young men.

403

Certainly.

c

No doubt a careful training in gymnastics, as well as in music, ought to begin with their childhood, and go on through all their life. But the following is the true view of the case, in my opinion. See what you think of it. My belief is, not that a good body will by its own excellence, make the soul good; but on the contrary, that a good soul will by *its* excellence render the body the best it can be. What is your view?

d

The same as yours. . . .

Then, Glaucon, am I also right in saying that those who establish a system of education in music and gymnastics, are not moved by the purpose which some persons attribute to them, of applying the one to the improvement of the soul, the other to that of the body?

410

c

Why what can be their purpose, if it is not thus?

Probably they introduce both mainly for the sake of the soul.

How so?

Do you not observe the characteristics which distinguish the thought of those who have been familiar with gymnastics all their lives, without any acquaintance with music? And again, of those whose condition is the opposite of this?

To what do you refer?

To the wildness and hardness which mark the one, and the softness and tameness which mark the other.

d

Oh yes. Those who have devoted themselves to gymnastics exclusively, become wilder than they ought to be; while those who have devoted themselves to music are made softer than is good for them.

We know, however, that wildness is the natural product of the spirited element, which, if rightly nurtured, will be brave; but, if strained to an improper pitch, will in all probability become harsh and disagreeable.

I think so.

Well, and will not tameness be a property of the philosophic nature? And, if it is too much indulged, will it not produce an excess of softness; but, if rightly nurtured, it will render it gentle and orderly?

e

True. . . .

For those two parts of the soul, the spirited and the philosophic, it seems likely a god—or at least so I would maintain—has given two arts to humans, music and gymnastics, not specifically for soul and body, but only incidentally so. It is rather for the sake of harmonizing these two parts, by stretching and relaxing them as is fitting.

412

So it would appear.

Then whosoever can best blend gymnastics with music, and bring both to bear on the soul most judiciously, such a man we shall justly call perfect in music, and a master of true harmony, much rather than the artist who tunes the lyre string to string.

Yes, and with good reason, Socrates.

Then will not some such overseer be always needed in our city, Glaucon, if our constitution is to be saved?

b

Yes, indeed, such an officer will be quite indispensable.

Such then will be the models of our system of education and training. For why should one enter into details respecting the dances, the hunting and field-exercises, or the sports of the gymnasium and the race-course? It is tolerably clear that these must correspond with the foregoing models, and there will be no further difficulty in discovering them.

Perhaps not, he said.

Very good; then what will be the next point for us to settle? Is it not this, which of the persons so educated are to be the rulers, and which the ruled?

c

Unquestionably it is.

There can be no doubt that the rulers must be the elderly men, and the subjects would be the younger.

True.

And also that the rulers must be the best men among them.

True again.

Are not the best farmers those who are most skilled in farming?

Yes.

In the present case, as we require the best guardians, shall we not find them in those who are most capable of guarding a city?

Yes.

Then for this purpose must they not be prudent and powerful, and, moreover, care for the city?

d

They must.

And a man will care most for that which he loves?

Of course.

And assuredly he will love that most whose interests he regards as identical with his own, and in whose prosperity or adversity he believes his own fortunes to be involved.

Just so.

Then we must select from the whole body of guardians those men who appear to us, after due observation, to be remarkable above others for the zeal with which, through their whole

e

life, they have done what they have thought advantageous to the city, and inflexibly refused to do what they thought the reverse.

Yes, these are the suitable persons, he said.

Then I think we must watch them at every stage of their life, to see if they are tenacious guardians of this conviction, and never bewitched or forced into a forgetful banishment of the opinion that they ought to do what is best for the city. . . .

Yes.

413

We must also appoint them labors, and pains, and contests, in which we must watch for      d
the same symptoms of character.

Rightly so.

And, as a third kind of test, we must try them with witchcraft, and observe their behavior. And, just as young horses are taken into the presence of noise and tumult, to see whether they are timid, so must we bring our men, while still young, into the midst of objects of      e
terror, and soon transfer them to scenes of pleasure, testing them much more thoroughly than gold is tried in the fire, to find whether they show themselves under all circumstances inaccessible to witchcraft, and proper in their bearing, good guardians of themselves and of the music which they have been taught, proving themselves on every occasion true to the laws of rhythm and harmony, and acting in such a way as would render them most useful to  414
themselves and the city. And whoever, from time to time, after being put to the test as a child, as a youth, and as a man, comes forth uninjured from the trial, must be appointed a ruler and guardian of the city, and must receive honors in life and in death, and be admitted to the highest privileges, in the way of funeral rites and other tributes to his memory. And all who are the reverse of this character must be rejected. Such appears to me, Glaucon, to be the true method of selecting and appointing our rulers and guardians, described simply as a sketch, without accuracy in detail.

I am pretty much of your mind.

Is it not then entirely correct to give them the name of complete guardians, as being      b
qualified to take care that their friends at home shall not wish, and their enemies abroad not be able, to do any harm, and to call the young men, whom up to this time we called "guardians," "auxiliaries" and helpers with the decrees of the rulers?

I think so, he said.

This being the case, I continued, can we contrive any ingenious mode of bringing into play one of those lies of which we spoke just now, so that, propounding a single noble lie, we may persuade even the rulers themselves, if possible, or if not them, the rest of the city?      c

What kind of a lie?

Nothing new, but a Phoenician story, which has happened often before now, as the poets tell and mankind believe, but which in our time has not been, nor, so far as I know, is likely to happen, and which would require great powers of persuasion.

You seem very reluctant to tell it.

You will think my reluctance very natural when I have told it.

Speak out boldly and without fear.

Well I will; and yet I hardly know where I shall find the courage or where the words to      d
express myself. I shall try, I say, to persuade first the rulers themselves and the military class, and after them the rest of the city, that when we were training and instructing them, they only thought, as in dreams, that all this was happening to them and about them, while in truth they were in course of formation and training in the bowels of the earth, where they themselves, their armor, and the rest of their equipments were manufactured. As soon      e
as they were finished, the earth, their real mother, sent them up to its surface; and,

consequently, that they ought now to take thought for the land in which they dwell, as their mother and nurse, and repel all attacks upon it, and to feel towards their fellow-citizens as brothers born of the earth.

It was not without reason that you were so long ashamed to tell us your lie.

415    I dare say; nevertheless, hear the rest of the story. We shall tell our people, in mythical language: You are doubtless all brothers, as many as inhabit the city, but the god who created you mixed gold in the composition of such of you as are qualified to rule, which is why they are most honored, while in the auxiliaries he made silver an ingredient, assigning iron and bronze to the farmers and the other workmen. Therefore, inasmuch as you are all related to

b    one another, although your children will generally resemble their parents, yet sometimes a golden parent will produce a silver child, and a silver parent a golden child, and so on, each producing any. The rulers therefore have received this charge first and above all from the gods, to observe nothing more closely, as good guardians, than the children that are born, to see which of these metals is mixed in their souls. And if a child be born in their class with an alloy of bronze or iron, they are to have no manner of pity upon it, but giving it the value

c    that belongs to its nature, they are to thrust it among artisans or farmers; and if again among these latter a child be born with any admixture of gold or silver, they will honor it, and they are to raise it either to the class of guardians, or to that of auxiliaries, because there is an oracle which declares that the city shall then perish when it is guarded by iron or bronze. Can you suggest any device by which we can make them believe this story?

d    None at all by which we could persuade the men with whom we begin our new city; but I think there could be such a device for their sons, and the next generation, and all subsequent generations.

Well, I said, even this might have a good effect towards making them care more for the city and for one another; for I think I understand what you mean. However, we will leave this fiction to posterity; but for our part, when we have armed these children of the soil, let us lead them forward under the command of their officers, until they arrive at the city; then let them look around them to discover the most eligible position for their camp, from which

e    they may best coerce the inhabitants, if there be any disposition to refuse obedience to the laws, and repel foreigners, if an enemy should come down like a wolf on the flock. And when they have pitched their camp, and offered sacrifices to whom they ought, let them arrange their sleeping-places. Is all this right?

It is.

And these sleeping-places must be such as will keep out the weather both in winter and summer, must they not?

Certainly; you mean dwelling-houses, if I am not mistaken.

I do; but the dwelling-houses of soldiers, not of money-makers.

416    What is the difference which you imply?

I will endeavor to explain it to you, I replied. I presume it would be a most monstrous and scandalous proceeding in shepherds to keep as auxiliaries such a breed of dogs, to so treat them, that owing to unruly tempers, or hunger, or any bad habit whatever, the dogs themselves should begin to worry the sheep, and behave more like wolves than dogs.

It would be monstrous, undoubtedly.

b    Then must we not take every precaution that our auxiliary class, being stronger than the other citizens, may not act towards them in a similar fashion, and so resemble savage despots rather than friendly allies?

We must.

And will they not be furnished with the best of safeguards, if they are really well educated?

But they are *that* already, he exclaimed.

To which I replied, It is not worthwhile to be too sure about that point, my dear Glaucon. But it is most necessary to maintain what we said this minute, that they must have the right c education, whatever it may be, if they are to have what will be most effectual in rendering them tame to one another, and to those whom they guard.

True.

But besides this education a rational man would say that their dwellings and property generally should be arranged on such a scale as shall neither prevent them from being the best possible guardians, nor provoke them to do harm to the other citizens. d

He will say so with truth.

Consider then, I continued, whether the following plan is the right one for their lives and their dwellings, if they are to be of the character I have described. In the first place, no one should possess any private property, except as necessary; secondly, no one should have a dwelling or storehouse into which all who please may not enter; whatever necessaries are required by moderate and courageous men, who are trained to war, they should receive by regular appointment from their fellow-citizens, as wages for their services, and the amount e should be such as to leave neither a surplus on the year's consumption nor a deficit. They should attend common messes and live together as men do in a camp; as for gold and silver, we must tell them that they are in perpetual possession of a divine species of the precious metals placed in their souls by the gods themselves, and therefore have no need of the human sort; that in fact it would be profanation to pollute their spiritual riches by mixing them with 417 the mortal sort, because the world's coinage has been the cause of countless impieties, whereas theirs is undefiled. Therefore to them, as distinguished from the rest of the people, it is forbidden to handle or touch gold and silver, or enter under the same roof with them, or to wear them on their dresses, or to drink out of the precious metals. If they follow these rules, they will be safe themselves and the saviors of the city; but whenever they come to possess lands, and houses, and money of their own, they will be householders and farmers instead of b guardians, and will become hostile masters of their fellow-citizens rather than their allies. And so they will spend their whole lives, hating and hated, plotting and plotted against, standing in more frequent and intense alarm of their enemies at home than of their enemies abroad; by which time they and the rest of the city will be running on the very brink of ruin. On all these accounts, I asked, shall we say that the foregoing is the right arrangement of the houses and other concerns of our guardians, and shall we legislate accordingly; or not?

Yes, by all means, answered Glaucon.


**Book IV**

Here Adeimantus interposed, inquiring, Then what defense will you make, Socrates, if any- 419 one protests that you are not making these men particularly happy? And that it is their own fault, too, if they are not? For the city really belongs to them, and yet they derive nothing

good from it, as others do, who own lands and build fine large houses, and furnish them in corresponding style, and perform private sacrifices to the gods, and entertain their strangers, and, in fact, as you said just now, possess gold and silver, and everything that is usually necessary to be considered blessed. On the contrary, they appear to be posted in the city, as it
420 might be said, precisely like mercenary troops, wholly occupied keeping watch.

Yes, I said, and for this they are only fed, and do not receive pay in addition to their rations, like the rest, so that it will be out of their power to take any journeys on their own account, should they wish to do so, or to make presents to mistresses, or to lay out money in the gratification of any other desire, after the plan of those who are considered happy. These and many similar counts you leave out of the indictment.

Well, said he, let us suppose these to be included in the charge.
b    What defense then shall we make, you ask?

Yes.

By traveling the same road as before, we shall find, I think, what to say. We shall reply that, though it would not surprise us if, in the given circumstances, they too were very happy, yet that our object in the construction of our city is not to make any one class preeminently happy, but to make the whole city as happy as it can be made. For we thought that in such a city we should be most likely to discover justice, as, on the other hand, in the worst-regulated
c    city we should be most likely to discover injustice, and that after having observed them we might decide the question we have been so long investigating. At present, we believe we are forming the happy city, not by selecting a few of its members and making them happy, but by making the whole so. Soon we shall examine a city of the opposite kind. Now, if someone came up to us while we were painting statues, and blamed us for not putting the most beautiful colors on the most beautiful parts of the body, because the eyes, being the most beautiful part, were not painted purple, but black, we should think it a sufficient defense to
d    reply, Please, sir, do not suppose that we ought to make the eyes so beautiful as not to look like eyes, nor the other parts in like manner, but observe whether, by giving to every part what properly belongs to it, we make the whole beautiful. In the same way do not, in the present instance, compel us to attach to our guardians such a kind of happiness as shall make them anything but guardians. For we are well aware that we might, on the same principle,
e    clothe our farmers in long robes, and put gold on their heads, and tell them to till the land at their pleasure; and that we might stretch our potters at their ease on couches before the fire, to drink and make merry, placing the wheel by their side, with directions to ply their trade just so far as they should feel it agreeable; and that we might dispense this kind of bliss to all the rest, so that the entire city might thus be happy. But give not such advice to us, since, if we
421 comply with your recommendation, the farmer will be no farmer, the potter no potter; nor will any of those professions, which make up a city, maintain its proper character. For the other occupations it matters less—cobblers who become careless and corrupt and pretend to be what they are not, are not dangerous to a city; but when guardians of the laws and of the city are such in appearance only, and not in reality, you see that they utterly destroy the whole city, as, on the other hand, they alone can make them well-governed and happy. If then, while
b    *we* aim at making genuine guardians, who shall be as far as possible from doing harm to the city, the person speaking in opposition makes a class of farmers and, as it were, jovial feasters at a holiday gathering, rather than citizens of a city; he will be describing something which is

not a city. We should examine then whether our object in constituting our guardians should be to secure to them the greatest possible amount of happiness, or whether our duty, as regards happiness, is to see if our city as a whole enjoys it, persuading or compelling our auxiliaries and guardians to study only how to make themselves the best possible workmen at their own occupation, and treating all the rest in like manner, and thus, while the whole city grows and, being beautifully founded, we must let nature apportion happiness to each group. c

I think, he replied, that what you say is quite right. . . .

Really, my good Adeimantus, these injunctions of ours are not, as one might suppose, a number of arduous tasks, but they will all be inconsiderable, if the guardians diligently observe the one great point, as the saying is, though it should rather be called sufficient than great. 423 e

What is that?

Education, I said, and rearing. For if by a good education they be made reasonable men, they will readily see through all these questions, as well as others which we pass by for the present, such as the possession of women, marriage, and the procreation of children; in all 424 which things they will see that the proverb ought, as far as possible, to be followed, which says that "among friends all things are in common."

Yes, that would be the most correct plan.

And indeed, if a regime has once started well, it exhibits a kind of circular progress in its growth. Adherence to a sound system of nurture and education creates good natures, and sound natures, receiving the assistance of a good education, grow still better than chose before them, and better for procreation also, as is also seen in the lower animals.

Yes, naturally so. b

To speak briefly, therefore, the overseers of the city must hold fast to this principle, not allowing it to be impaired without their notice, out guarding it above everything; the principle, I mean, which for-bids any innovation, in either gymnastics or music, upon the established order, requiring it, on the contrary, to be most strictly maintained, from a fear lest, when it is said that men care most for the song

Which being newest is sung, and its music encircles the singers,

It might perhaps be imagined that the poet is speaking not of new songs, but of a new style of c music, and novelty should accordingly be commended. Whereas novelty ought not to be commended, nor ought the words to be so understood. For the introduction of a new kind of music must be shunned as endangering the whole city; since styles of music are never disturbed without affecting the most important political laws, at least so Damon affirms, and I believe him.

By all means include me too among the believers in this doctrine, said Adeimantus.

Then to all appearance, I continued, it is here in music that our guardians should erect d their guard-house.

At any rate, said he, it is here that lawlessness easily creeps in unawares.

Yes, in the guise of play, and professing to do no mischief.

No, and it does none, except that, gradually settling in, it quietly insinuates itself into character and customs; and from these it issues in greater force, and makes its way into mutual contracts with one another, and from contracts it goes on to attack laws and e     constitutions, displaying the utmost impudence, Socrates, until it ends by overturning everything, both in public and in private.

Well, said I: Is this so?

I think it is.

Then, as we said in the beginning, must not our children from the very first be restricted to more lawful play, because when play becomes lawless, and children take after them, it is

425    impossible for such children to grow into law-abiding and serious men.

Unquestionably.

Accordingly, when our children, engaging in well-ordered play from the beginning, play fairly and receive lawfulness from music, the result is the exact reverse of the former; for lawfulness accompanies them into everything and promotes their growth, and restores anything of the city which has previously been neglected.

Yes, that is true.

Consequently such persons make the discovery of those trivial regulations, as they are held to be, which had all been lost by those whom we described before.

What regulations do you mean?

b     Those, for example, which require the young to maintain an appropriate silence in the presence of their elders, stooping to them, and rising up at their entrance, and paying every attention to their parents; together with regulations as to the mode of wearing the hair, the style of dress and shoes, and bodily bearing in general, and everything else of the same kind. Is not this your opinion?

It is.

But to legislate on these matters would be foolish, I think. It is never done, I believe; nor could anything legislated in speech and in writing be permanent.

How could it be?

At any rate, it is probable, Adeimantus, that the bent given by education will determine all

c     that follows. For does not like always invite like?

Undoubtedly it does.

And so, I think, we should at last expect our system to end in some complete and grand result, whether this result be good or the reverse.

We certainly should.

On these grounds I should not attempt to extend our legislation to points like those.

With good reason. . . .

427    Then the organization of our city is now complete, son of Ariston; and the next thing for

d     you to do is to examine it, furnishing yourself with the necessary light from any quarter you can, and calling to your aid your brother and Polemarchus and the rest, in order to try, if we can, to see where justice may be found in it, and where injustice, and wherein they differ the one from the other, and which of the two the man who desires to be happy ought to possess, whether all gods and men know it or not.

That will not do! exclaimed Glaucon; it was you that engaged to make the inquiry, on the

e     ground that it would not be holy for you to refuse to give justice.

I recollect that it was as you say, I replied; and I must do so, but you also must assist me.

We will.

434    Now observe whether you hold the same opinion that I do. If a carpenter should under-

take to execute the work of a shoemaker, or a shoemaker that of a carpenter, either by interchanging their tools and honors, or by the same person undertaking both trades, with all the changes involved in it, do you think it would greatly damage the city?

Not very greatly.

But when one whom nature has made a craftsman, or a producer of any other kind, is so elated by wealth, or a large connection, or bodily strength, or any similar advantages, as to intrude himself into the class of the warriors; or when a warrior intrudes himself into the class of the counselors and guardians, of which he is unworthy, and when these interchange their tools and their distinctions, or when one and the same person attempts to discharge all these duties at once, then, I imagine, you will agree with me, that such change and meddling among these will be ruinous to the city.

Most assuredly they will.

Then any intermeddling in the three parts, or change from one to another, would inflict great damage on the city, and may properly be described, as doing the most extreme harm.

Quite so.

And will you not admit that the greatest harm towards one's own city is injustice?

Unquestionably.

This then is injustice. On the other hand, let us state that, conversely, adherence to their own business on the part of the money-makers, the military, and the guardians, each of these doing its own work in the city, is justice, and will render the city just.

I fully agree, he said.

Let us not state it yet quite positively; but if we find, on applying this form to the individual man, that there too it is recognized as constituting justice, we will then give our assent—for what more can we say? But if not, in that case we will begin a new inquiry. At present, however, let us complete the investigation which we undertook in the belief that, if we first endeavored to contemplate justice in some larger subject which contains it, we should find it easier to discern its nature in the individual man. Such a subject we recognized in a city, and accordingly we organized the best we could, being sure that justice must reside in a good city. The view, therefore, which presented itself to us there, let us now apply to the individual; and if it be admitted, we shall be satisfied; but if we should find something different in the case of the individual, we will again go back to our city, and put our theory to the test. And perhaps by considering the two cases side by side, and rubbing them together, we may cause justice to flash out from the contact, like fire from dry bits of wood, and when it has become visible to us, may settle it firmly in our own minds.

There is method in your proposal, he replied, and so let us do. . . .

Now, can we say that people sometimes are thirsty, and yet do not wish to drink?

Yes, certainly; it often happens to many people.

What then can one say of them, except that their soul contains one principle which commands, and another which forbids them to drink, the latter being distinct from and stronger than the former?

That is my opinion.

Whenever the authority which forbids such indulgences grows up in the soul, is it not engendered there by calculation; while the powers which lead and draw the soul towards them, owe their presence to passive and diseased states?

It would appear so.

Then we shall have reasonable grounds for assuming that these are two principles distinct one from the other, and for giving to that part of the soul with which it reasons the title of the rational principle, and to that part with which it loves and hungers and thirsts, and experiences the flutter of the other desires, the title of the irrational and appetitive principle, the ally of sundry indulgences and pleasures.

e   Yes, he replied; it will not be unreasonable to think so.

Let us consider it settled, then, that these two specific forms exist in the soul. But now, will spirit, or that by which we feel spirited, constitute a third distinct part? If not, which of the former two has the same nature?

Perhaps with the appetitive principle.

But I was once told a story, which I trust, to the effect, that Leontius, the son of Aglaion, as he was walking up from the Piraeus, and approaching the northern wall from the outside, observed some dead bodies on the ground, and the executioner standing by them. He immediately felt a desire to look at them, but at the same time loathing the thought he tried

440  to divert himself from it. For some time he struggled with himself, and covered his eyes, until at length, over-powered by the desire, he opened his eyes wide with his fingers, and running up to the bodies, exclaimed, "There, you wretches! Gaze your fill at the beautiful spectacle!"

I have heard this too.

This story, however, indicates that anger sometimes fights against the desires, which implies that they are two distinct principles.

True, it does indicate that.

And do we not often observe in other cases that when a man is overpowered by the desires

b   against the dictates of his reason, he reviles himself, and resents the violence thus exerted within him, and that, in this struggle of contending parties, the spirited sides with the rational? But that it should make common cause with the desires, when reason pronounces that they ought not to act against itself, is a thing which I suppose you will not profess to have experienced yourself, nor yet, I imagine, to have ever noticed in anyone else.

No, by Zeus, I have not.

c   Well, and when anyone thinks he is doing an injustice, is he not, in proportion to the nobleness of his character, so much the less able to be angry at being made to suffer hunger or cold or any similar pain at the hands of him who he thinks does so justly? Will not his spirit, as I describe it, refuse to be roused against the one punishing him?

True.

On the other hand, when anyone thinks he is suffering an injustice, does he not instantly boil and chafe, and enlist himself on the side of what he thinks to be justice; and whatever

d   extremities of hunger and cold and the like he may have to suffer, does he not endure until he conquers, never ceasing from his noble efforts, until he has either succeeded, or perished in the attempt, or been recalled and calmed by the voice of reason within, as a dog is called off by a shepherd?

Yes, he replied, the case answers very closely to your description; and in fact, in our city we made the auxiliaries, like sheep-dogs, subject to the rulers, who are as it were the shepherds of the city.

You rightly understand my meaning. But try whether you also apprehend my next observation.

What is it?

e

That our recent view of the spirited principle is exactly reversed. Then we thought it had something of the appetitive character, but now we say that, far from this being the case, it much more readily takes arms on the side of the rational principle in the conflict of the soul.

Decidedly it does.

Is it then distinct from this principle also; or is it only a modification of it, thus making two instead of three distinct principles in the soul, namely, the rational and the appetitive? Or ought we to say that, as the city was held together by three great classes, the money-making part, the auxiliary, and the deliberative, so also in the soul the spirited principle constitutes a third element, the natural ally of the rational principle, if it be not corrupted by bad training?

441

It must be a third, he replied.

Yes, I continued; if it shall appear to be distinct, from the rational principle, as we found it different from the appetitive.

That will easily appear. For even in little children anyone may see this, that from their very birth they have plenty of spirit, whereas reason is a principle to which most men only attain after many years, and some, in my opinion, never.

b

Well said, by Zeus. In beasts also one may see what you describe exemplified. And besides, that passage in Homer, which we quoted on a former occasion, will support our view:

> Smiting his breast, to his heart thus spake he in accents of chiding.

For in this line Homer has distinctly made a difference between the two principles, representing that which had calculated the good or the bad of the action as rebuking that which was irrationally spirited.

c

You are perfectly right.

Here then, I proceeded, after a hard swim, we have, though with difficulty, reached the land; and we are pretty well satisfied that there are corresponding divisions, equal in number, in a city, and in the soul of every individual.

True.

Then does it not necessarily follow that, as and whereby the city was wise, so and thereby the individual is wise?

Without doubt it does.

And that through which the individual is brave, thereby is the city brave. And everything conducing to virtue which is possessed by the one, finds its counterpart in the other?

d

It must be so.

Then we shall also assert, I imagine, Glaucon, that a man is just, in the same way in which we found the city to be just.

This too is necessary.

But surely we have not allowed ourselves to forget, that what makes the city just, is the fact of each of its three parts minding its own business.

No; I think we have not forgotten this.

We must bear in mind, then, that each of us also, if his inward parts mind their own
e   business, will, by virtue of that, be a just man, and mind his own business.

Certainly, it must be borne in mind.

Is it not then essentially the domain of the rational principle to command, inasmuch as it
is wise, and has to exercise forethought on behalf of the entire soul, and the domain of the
spirited principle to be its subject and ally?

Yes, certainly.

442   And will not the combination of music and gymnastics bring them, as we said, into uni-
son—elevating and fostering the one with lofty discourses and studies, and lowering the tone
of the other by soothing stories, until its wildness has been tamed by harmony and rhythm?

Yes, precisely so.

And so these two, having been thus trained, and having truly learned their parts and
having been educated, will exercise control over the appetitive principle, which in every man
forms the largest portion of the soul, and is by nature most insatiable. And they will watch it
narrowly, that it may not be filled with what are called the pleasures of the body, as to grow
b   large and strong, and forthwith refuse to mind its own business, and even aspire to subjugate
and dominate over that which it has no right to rule by virtue of its class, thus totally
upsetting the life of all.

Certainly they will.

And would not these two principles be the best qualified to guard the entire soul and body
against enemies from without—the one taking counsel, and the other fighting its battles, in
obedience to the ruling power, carrying out its order with courage?

True.

c   In like manner, I think, we call an individual courageous in virtue of the spirited element
of his nature, when this part of him holds fast, through pain and pleasure, the instructions of
the reason as to what is to be feared, and what is not.

Yes, and rightly.

And we call him wise, in virtue of that small part which reigns within him, and issues
these instructions, and which also in its turn contains within itself knowledge of what is
advantageous for the whole community composed of these three parts, and for each member
of it.

Exactly so.

Again, do we not call a man moderate, in virtue of the friendship and harmony of these
same principles, that is to say, when the two that are governed agree with that which governs
d   in regarding the rational principle as the part that ought to rule, and set up no opposition to
its authority?

Certainly, he replied; moderation is nothing else than this, whether in city or individual.

Lastly, a man will be just, in the way and by the means which we have repeatedly
described.

Unquestionably he will. . . .

443   And so there really was, Glaucon, an image of justice—and hence of its utility—in the
c   principle that it is right for a man whom nature intended for a shoemaker to confine himself
to shoemaking, and for a man who has a turn for carpentering to do carpenter's work, and
so on.

It appears so.

The truth being that justice is indeed, to all appearance, something of the kind, only that, instead of dealing with a man's outward performance of his own work, it has to do with that inward performance of it which truly concerns the man himself, and his own interests. So that the just man will not permit each part within him to do anything but mind its own business, nor allow the three classes in his soul to meddle with each other, but will really set his house in order; and having gained the mastery over himself, will so regulate his own character as to be on good terms with himself, and to set those three parts in tune together, as if they were truly three chords of a harmony, a highest and a lowest and a middle, and whatever may lie between these. And after he has bound all these together, and reduced the many elements of his nature to a real unity, as a moderate and harmonized man, he will then at length proceed to do whatever he may have to do, whether it involve a business transaction, or the care of his body, a political matter or a private contract. In all of these actions he will believe and profess that the just and fair course is that which preserves and assists in creating the aforesaid condition, and that the genuine knowledge which presides over such conduct is wisdom; while on the other hand, he will hold that an unjust action is one which tends to destroy this habit, and that the mere opinion which presides over unjust conduct, is folly.

What you say is thoroughly true, Socrates.

Very good; if we were to say we have discovered the just man and the just city, and what justice is as found in them, it would not be thought, I imagine, to be a complete lie.

No, by Zeus. It would not.

Shall we say so then?

We will.

Be it so, I continued. In the next place we have to investigate, I imagine, what injustice is.

Evidently we have.

Must it not then, as the reverse of justice, be a state of strife between the three parts, and the disposition to meddle and interfere, and the insurrection of a part of the soul against the whole, this part aspiring to the supreme power within the soul, to which it has no right, its proper place and destination being, on the contrary, to do service to any member of the rightfully ruling part? Such doings as these, I imagine, and the confusion and bewilderment of the aforesaid parts, will, in our opinion, constitute injustice, and licentiousness, and cowardice, and folly, and, in one word, all vice.

Yes, precisely so.

And is it not now quite clear to us what it is to act unjustly, and to be unjust, and, on the other hand, what it is to act justly, knowing as we do the nature of justice and injustice?

How so?

Because there happens to be no difference with regard to the health and disease of the body and the soul.

In what way?

The conditions of health, I presume, produce health, and those of disease engender disease.

Yes.

In the same way, does not the practice of justice beget the habit of justice, and the practice of injustice the habit of injustice?

Inevitably.

Now to produce health is so to constitute the bodily forces that they shall master and be mastered by one another in accordance with nature; and to produce disease is to make them govern and be governed by one another in a way which violates nature.

True.

Similarly, will it not be true that to beget justice is so to constitute the parts of the soul that they shall master and be mastered by one another in accordance with nature, and that to beget injustice is to make them rule and be ruled by one another in a way which violates nature?

Quite so.

Then virtue, it appears, will be a kind of health and beauty, and good habit of the soul;

e    and vice will be a disease, and deformity, and sickness of it.

True.

And may we not add, that all fair practices tend to the acquisition of virtue, and all foul practices to that of vice?

Undoubtedly they do.

What now remains for us, apparently, is to inquire whether it is also profitable to act justly,

445   and to pursue fair aims, and to be just, whether a man be known to be such or not, or to act unjustly, and to be unjust, if one suffer no punishment, and be not made a better man by paying the penalty.

But, Socrates, this appears to be ridiculous by now, seeing that each one has come to light as we described. If life does not seem livable, when the nature of body is ruined, though we

b    may have at our disposal all food and drink, and wealth and every sort of power, will it then be livable if the nature of that very thing by which we live is corrupted and ruined—even if a man does what he wishes except the one thing which will release him from bad and injustice and which will acquire him justice and virtue?

Yes, it is ludicrous, I replied. . . .


## Book V

449   . . . Polemarchus, who was seated a little further off than Adeimantus, put out his hand to

b    take hold of his cloak high up near the shoulder, drew him towards himself, and leaning forwards whispered a few words into his ear, of which we only caught the following: Shall we let him off then, or what shall we do?

Certainly not, said Adeimantus, beginning to speak aloud.

Whereupon I said, And what may that be which you are not going to let off?

You, he replied.

c    And how so? I further inquired.

We have an idea that you are lagging, and stealing a whole section, and that a very important one, from the argument, in order to avoid handling it. . . .

Must we not then first come to an agreement as to whether the regulations proposed are possible or not, and give to anyone, whether of a playful or serious turn, an opportunity of

453   raising the question, whether the nature of the human female is such as to enable her to share in all the deeds of the male, or whether she is wholly unequal to any, or equal to some and

not to others; and in particular how that is with respect to war? Will not this be the way to make the best beginning, and, in all probability, the best ending also?

Yes, quite so.

Would you like, then, that we should argue against ourselves in behalf of an objector, that the opposition may not be attacked without a defense?

There is no reason why we should not.

Then let us say on his behalf: "Socrates and Glaucon, there is no need for others to advance anything against you; for you yourselves, at the beginning of your scheme for constructing a city, admitted that every individual therein ought, in accordance with nature, to do the one work which belongs to him."

"We did admit this, I imagine; how could we do otherwise?"

"Can you deny that there is a very marked difference between the nature of woman and that of man?"

"Of course there is a difference."

"Then is it not fitting to assign to each sex a different work, appropriate to its peculiar nature?"

"Undoubtedly."

"Then if so, you must be in error now, and be contradicting yourselves when you go on to say, that men and women ought to engage in the same occupations, when their natures are so widely diverse?" Do you have any answer to that objection, my clever friend?

It is not so very easy to find one at a moment's notice; but I shall beg you, and I do so now, to state what the arguments on our side are, and to interpret them for us.

These objections, Glaucon, and many others like them, are what I anticipated all along; and that is why I was afraid and reluctant to meddle with the law that regulates the possession of the women and children, and the rearing of the latter.

By Zeus, it seems no easy task.

Why no; but the fact is, that whether you fall into a small swimming pool, or into the middle of the great ocean, you have to swim all the same.

Exactly so.

Then is it not best for us, in the present instance, to swim out and endeavor to emerge in safety from the discussion, in the hope that either a dolphin may take us on his back, or some other improbable rescue will present itself?

It would seem so.

Come then, I continued, let us see if we can find the way out. We admitted, you say, that different natures ought to have different occupations, and that the natures of men and women are different; but now we maintain that these different natures ought to engage in the same occupations. Is this your charge against us?

Precisely.

Truly, Glaucon, the power of the art of contradiction is very extraordinary.

How so?

Because it seems to me that many fall into it even against their will, and think they are discussing, when they are merely debating, because they cannot distinguish the various forms of what is said, but carry on their opposition to what is stated, by attacking the mere words, employing the art of eristical debate, and not that of dialectical discussion.

This is no doubt the case with many; does it apply to us at the present moment?

b    Most assuredly it does; at any rate there is every appearance of our having fallen unintentionally into a verbal contradiction.

How so?

Following only the name, we say, in the boldest style of eristical debate, that different natures ought not to engage in the same pursuits. But we did not in any way consider what form of sameness and difference of nature and what that referred to, and what we were distinguishing when we assigned different pursuits to different natures, and the same pursuits to the same natures.

It is true we have not considered that.

c    That being the case, it is open to us apparently to ask ourselves whether bald men and long-haired men are of the same or of opposite natures, and after admitting the latter to be the case, we may say that if bald men make shoes, long-haired men must not be allowed to make them, or if the long-haired men make them, the others must be forbidden to do so.

No, that would be ridiculous.

Is it ridiculous for any other reason than that we did not agree on "the same" and "different nature" in every respect, being engaged only with that form of likeness and difference which applied directly to the pursuits in question? For example, we said that a

d    male and female physician have the same nature and soul. Or do you not think so?

I do.

And that a man who would make a good physician had a different nature from one who would make a good carpenter.

Of course he has.

If, then, the class of men and women appear to differ in reference to any art, or other occupation, we shall say that such occupation must be assigned to the one or the other. But if

e    we find the difference to consist simply in the fact that the female bears and the male mounts, we shall assert that it has not yet been by any means demonstrated that the difference between man and woman touches our purpose; on the contrary, we shall still think it proper for our guardians and their wives to engage in the same pursuits.

And rightly.

455    Shall we not proceed to call upon our opponents to inform us what is that particular art or occupation connected with the organization of a city, in reference to which the nature of a man and a woman are not the same, but different?

We certainly are entitled to do so.

Well, perhaps it might be pleaded by others, as it was a little while ago by you, that it is not easy to give a satisfactory answer at a moment's notice; but that, with time for consideration, it would not be difficult to do so.

True, it might.

Would you, then, like us to beg the man who voices such objections to accompany us, to

b    see if we can show him that no occupation which belongs to the ordering of a city is peculiar to women?

By all means.

Well then, we will address him thus: "Tell us whether, when you say that one man is well-suited for a particular study, and that another is not, you mean that the former learns it easily, the latter with difficulty; and that the one with little instruction can find out much for himself in the subject he has studied, whereas the other after much teaching and practice cannot even retain what he has learned; and that the reasoning of the one is duly aided, that of the other thwarted, by the bodily powers? Are not these the only marks by which you define the possession and the want of natural talents for any pursuit?"   c

Everyone will say yes.

Well then, do you know of any branch of human industry in which the female sex is not inferior in these respects to the male? Or need we go the length of specifying the art of weaving, and the manufacture of pastry and preserves, in which women are thought to excel, and in which their defeat is most laughed at?   d

You are perfectly right, that in almost every employment the one class is vastly superior to the other. There are many women, no doubt, who are better in many things than many men; but, speaking generally, it is as you say.

I conclude then, my friend, that none of the occupations concerned with ordering a city belong to woman as woman, nor yet to man as man; but natural gifts are to be found here and there, in both animals alike; and, so far as her nature is concerned, the woman is   e admissible to all pursuits as well as the man; though in all of them the woman is weaker than the man.

Precisely so.

Shall we then appropriate all duties to men, and none to women?

How can we?

On the contrary, we shall hold, I imagine, that one woman may have talents for medicine, and another be without them; and that one may be musical, and another unmusical.

Undoubtedly.

And shall we not also say, that one woman may have qualifications for gymnastic exercises, and for war, and another be unwarlike, and without a taste for gymnastics?   456

I think we shall.

Again, may there not be a lover of wisdom in one, and a hatred of it in another? And may not one be spirited, and another without spirit?

True again.

If that be so, there are some women who are fit, and others who are unfit, for the office of guardians. For were not those the qualities that we selected, in the case of the men, as marking their fitness for that office?

Yes, they were.

Then as far as the guardianship of a city is concerned, there is no difference between the natures of the man and of the woman, but only various degrees of weakness and strength.

Apparently there is none.

Then we shall have to select duly qualified women also, to share in the life and guardian-   b ship with the duly qualified men; since we find that they are competent, and of kindred nature with the men.

Just so. . . .

Very well; if the question is how to render a woman fit for the office of guardian, we shall not have one education for men, and another for women, especially as the nature affected is the same in both cases.   d

No, the education will be the same. . . .

But I really think, Socrates, he continued, that if you be permitted to go on in this way, you will never recollect what you put aside some time ago before you entered on all these questions, namely, the task of showing that this regime is possible, and how it might be realized.

Well, then, I continued, in the first place we ought not to forget that we have been brought to this point by an inquiry into the nature of justice and injustice.

True; but what of that?

Why nothing. But, if we find out what justice is, shall we expect the character of a just man not to differ in any point from that of justice itself, but to be like justice in every way? Or shall we be content provided he comes as near it as is possible, and partakes more largely of it than the rest of the world?

We shall be content with the latter. . . .

Do you think any the worse of the merits of an artist, who has painted a paradigm of the most beautiful human being, and has left nothing lacking in the picture, because he cannot prove that such a man as he has painted might possibly exist?

No, indeed, I do not.

Well, were not we likewise professing to make in speech the paradigm of a good city?

Yes, certainly.

Then will our argument suffer at all, do you think, if we cannot prove that it is possible for a city to be organized in the way we have said?

Certainly not.

This then is the truth of it; but if for your gratification I must also exert myself and demonstrate in what way and under what conditions it is most possible, I must ask you to agree again to the same points for the sake of this demonstration.

Which do you mean?

Can anything be accomplished in the city as it is said? Or is it the case that practice by nature attains less to the truth than does speech? Never mind if some think otherwise; tell me whether you admit this fact or not.

I do admit it.

Then do not force me to exhibit the details in every way in deed as we went through them in speech; but if we find out how a city may be organized and gets very close to our description, you must admit that we have discovered the possibility of realizing the plan which you require me to consider. Shall you not be content if you gain this much? For my own part I shall be.

So shall I.

Then our next step apparently must be, to try to search out and demonstrate what there is now amiss in the working of our cities, preventing their being governed in the manner described, and what is the smallest change that would enable a city to assume this form of regime, confining ourselves, if possible, to a single change; if not, to two; or else, to such as are fewest in number and least important in their influence.

Let us by all means endeavor so to do.

Well, I proceeded, there is one change by which, as I think we might show, the required transformation would be secured; but it is certainly neither a small nor an easy change, though it is a possible one.

What is it? . . .

Unless it happen either that philosophers acquire the kingly power in cities, or that those who are now called kings and rulers be genuinely and adequately philosophical, that is to say, unless political power and philosophy be united in the same place, most of those who at present pursue one to the exclusion of the other being necessarily excluded from either, there will be no deliverance, my dear Glaucon, for cities, nor yet, I believe, for the human race; neither can the regime, which we have now sketched in speech, ever grow into a possibility until then, and see the light of the sun. But my awareness how entirely paradoxical this was made me all along so reluctant to give expression to it. It is difficult to see any other way by which happiness can be attained, by the city or by the individual. . . .

## Book VI

Here Adeimantus interposed and said: a person will tell you, that though at each question he cannot oppose you with words, yet in practice he sees that all the students of philosophy, who have devoted themselves to it for any length of time, instead of taking it up for educational purposes and dropping it while still young, in most cases become exceedingly eccentric, quite depraved in fact, while even those who appear the most respectable are nonetheless far worse off for the pursuit which you commend, they become useless to their cities.

When he had said this, I replied: Then do you think that what has been said is deceptive?

I am not sure, he answered; but I should be glad to hear what you think of it.

Let me tell you, that I think we were speaking the truth.

How then can it be right to assert that the miseries of our cities will find no relief, until those philosophers who, on our own admission, are useless to them, become their rulers?

You are asking a question, I replied, which I must answer by the help of an image.

And you, I suppose, have not been in the habit of using images.

Ah! Are you making fun of me, now that you have got me upon a subject in which demonstration is so difficult? However, listen to the illustration, that you may see still better how greedy I am for images. So cruel is the position in which those respectable men are placed, in reference to their cities, that there is no single thing whose position is analogous to theirs. Consequently I have to collect materials from several quarters for the image which I am to use in their defense, like painters when they paint goat-stags and similar monsters. Think of a fleet, or a single ship, in which the state of affairs on board is as follows. The owner, you are to suppose, is taller and stronger than any of the crew, but rather deaf, and rather near-sighted, and correspondingly deficient in nautical skill; and the sailors are quarreling together about piloting, each of them thinking he has a right to steer the vessel, although up to that moment he has never studied the art, and cannot name his instructor, or the time when he served his apprenticeship. More than this, they assert that it is a thing which positively cannot be taught, and are even ready to tear in pieces the person who affirms that it can. Meanwhile they crowd incessantly round the person of the ship-owner, begging and beseeching him with every importunity to entrust the helm to them; and occasionally, failing to persuade him, while others succeed better, these disappointed candidates kill their successful rivals, or fling them overboard, and, after binding the noble ship-owner hand and foot with drugs or strong drink, or disabling him by some other contrivance, they rule the ship, and apply its contents to their own purposes, and pass their time at sea in drinking and feasting, as you might expect with such a crew. And besides all

d     this, they compliment with the title of "able seaman," "pilot," "skillful navigator," any sailor that can second them cleverly in either persuading or forcing the ship-owner into installing them in command of the ship, while they condemn as useless everyone whose talents are of a different order, they don't know that the true pilot must devote his attention to the year and its seasons, to the sky, and the stars, and the winds, and all that concerns his art, if he intends

e     to be really fit to command a ship; and thinking it impossible to acquire and practice, along with the pilot's art, the art of maintaining the pilot's authority whether some of the crew like it or not. Such being the state of things on board, do you not think that the pilot who is really

489   master of his craft is sure to be called a useless, star-gazing babbler by those who form the crews of ships run like this?

Yes, that he will, replied Adeimantus.

Well, said I, I suppose you do not need to scrutinize my image, to remind you that it is a true picture of our cities insofar as their disposition towards philosophers is concerned; on the contrary, I think you understand my meaning.

Yes, quite.

That being the case, when a person expresses his astonishment that philosophers are not respected in our cities, begin by telling him our illustration and try to persuade him that it

b     would be far more astonishing if they were respected.

Well, I will.

And go on to tell him that he is right in saying that those most suitable for philosophy are considered most useless by the many; only recommend him to lay the blame for it not on these good people themselves, but upon those who decline their services. For it is not in the nature of things that a pilot should petition the sailors to submit to his authority, or that the wise should wait at the rich man's door. No, the author of that bit of cleverness was wrong.

c     For the real truth is, that, just as a sick man, whether he be rich or poor, must attend at the physician's door, so all who require to be ruled must attend at the gate of him who is able to rule, it being against nature that the ruler, supposing him to be really good for anything, should have to beg his subjects to submit to his rule. In fact, you will not be wrong, if you compare the statesmen of our time to the sailors whom we were just now describing, and the useless visionary talkers, as they are called by our politicians, you can compare to those who are truly pilots.

You are perfectly right.

Under these circumstances, and among men like these, it is not easy for that best of occupations to be in good repute with those to whose pursuits it is directly opposed. But far

d     the most grievous and most obstinate slander, under which philosophy labors, is due to her professed followers—who are doubtless the persons meant by the accuser of philosophy, when he declares, as you tell us, that most of those who approach her are utterly depraved, while even her best pupils are useless—to the truth of which remark I assented, did I not?

Yes, you did.

We have explained the reason why the good are useless, have we not?

Certainly we have. . . .

Well, then, this part of the subject having been laboriously completed, shall we proceed to  502
discuss the questions still remaining, in what way, and by the help of what studies and     d
practices, there will develop a group capable of saving the regime, and what must be the age
at which these studies are severally undertaken?

Let us do so by all means. . . .

Now consider what a small supply of these men you will, in all probability, find. For the
parts of that nature, which we described as essential to philosophers, will seldom grow
together in the same place. In most cases that nature grows disjointed.

What do you mean?                                                                           c

You are aware that persons endowed with a quick grasp, memory, sagacity, quickness, and
their attendant qualities, do not readily grow up to be at the same time so vigorous and
magnificent as to consent to live an orderly, calm, and steady life; on the contrary, such
persons are carried away by their quickness hither and thither, and all steadiness vanishes
from their life.

True.

On the other hand, those steady and invariable characters, whose trustiness makes one
readily depend on them, and who in war are slow to take alarm, behave in the same way     d
when pursuing their studies—that is to say, they are torpid and stupid, as if they were
benumbed, and are constantly dozing and yawning, whenever they have to toil at anything of
the kind.

That is true.

But we declare that, unless a person possesses a pretty fair amount of both qualifications,
he must not share in the strictest education, in honor, and in ruling.

We are right.

Then do you not anticipate a scanty supply of such characters?

Most assuredly I do.

Hence we must not be content with testing their behavior in the toils, dangers, and        e
pleasures, which we mentioned before; but we must go on to try them in ways which we then
omitted, exercising them in a variety of studies, and observing whether their character will be
able to support the greatest studies, or whether it will flinch from the trial, like those who
flinch under other circumstances.                                                          504

No doubt it is proper to examine them in this way. But which do you mean by the greatest
studies? . . .

Assuredly you have heard the answer many a time; but at this moment either you have
forgotten it, or else you intend to cause the trouble in turn. I incline to think this; for you  505
have often been told that the idea of the good is the highest study, and it is by relation to it
that just acts and other things become useful and advantageous. And at this moment you can
scarcely doubt that I am going to assert this, and to assert, besides, that we are not sufficiently
acquainted with this. And if so—if, I say, we know everything else perfectly, without knowing
this—you are aware that it will profit us nothing; just as it would be equally profitless to
possess everything without possessing what is good. Or do you imagine it would be an       b
advantage to possess all things that can be possessed, with the single exception of things
good; or to have an understanding of all things, without understanding what is good, while
understanding nothing with regard to the beautiful and the good?

Not I, by Zeus.

Moreover, you doubtless know besides, that the good is supposed by the multitude to be pleasure, and the enlightened think it is prudence?

Of course I know that.

And you are aware, my friend, that the advocates of this latter opinion are unable to explain what they mean by prudence, and are compelled at last to explain it as being about the good.

Yes, they are in a ludicrous difficulty.

c   They certainly are, since they reproach us with ignorance of that which is good, and then speak to us the next moment as if we knew what it was. For they tell us that the good is prudence about the good, assuming that we understand their meaning, as soon as they have uttered the term "good".

It is perfectly true.

Again, are not those, whose definition identifies pleasure with good, just as much infected with error as the preceding? For they are forced to admit the existence of bad pleasures, are they not?

Certainly they are.

From which it follows, I should suppose, that they must admit the same thing to be both good and bad. Does it not?

d   Certainly it does.

Then is it not evident that this is a subject often and severely disputed?

Doubtless it is.

Well then, is it not evident, that though many persons would be ready to do and seem to do, or to possess and seem to possess, what seems just and beautiful, without really being so; yet, when you come to things good, no one is content to acquire what only seems such; on the contrary, everybody seeks the reality, and semblances are here, if nowhere else, treated with universal contempt?

Yes, that is quite evident.

This good, then, is what every soul pursues, as the end of all its actions, divining its e   existence, but perplexed and unable to apprehend satisfactorily its nature, or to enjoy that steady confidence in relation to it, which it does enjoy in relation to other things. And because this is so, they fail to arrive at any advantage which it might have derived from those 506   same things. Are we to maintain that, on a subject of such overwhelming importance, the blindness we have described is a desirable feature in the character of those best members of the city in whose hands everything is to be placed?

Most certainly not.

At any rate, if it be not known in what way just things and beautiful things come to be also good, I imagine that such things will not possess a very valuable guardian in the person of him who is ignorant on this point. And I surmise that none will know the just and the beautiful satisfactorily until he knows the good.

You are right in your surmise.

Then will not the arrangement of our regime be perfect, provided it is overseen by a b   guardian who is a knower of these things?

Unquestionably. But tell us, Socrates, do *you* assert the good to be knowledge or pleasure or something different from both?

I saw long ago that you are the kind of man who would certainly not put up with the opinions of other people on these subjects.

Why, Socrates, it appears to me to be not just in one who has devoted so much time to these questions, to be able to state the opinions of others, without being able to state his own.  c

Well, I said, do you think it is just to speak as if one knows when one in fact does not know about these things?

Certainly not as if one knew, but I think it right to be willing to state one's opinion for what it is worth.

Well, but have you not noticed that opinions divorced from knowledge are all ugly? At the best they are blind. Or do you conceive that those who, unaided by intelligence, entertain a correct opinion, are at all superior to blind men, who manage to keep the straight path?

Not at all superior, he replied.

Then is it your desire to contemplate objects that are ugly, blind, and crooked, when it is in your power to learn from other people about bright and beautiful things?  d

I implore you in the name of Zeus, Socrates, cried Glaucon, not to hang back, as if you had come to the end. We shall be content even if you only discuss the subject of the good in the style in which you discussed justice, moderation, and the rest.

Yes, my friend, and I likewise should be thoroughly content. But I distrust my own powers, and I feel afraid that my awkward zeal will subject me to ridicule. No, I will have to put aside, for the present at any rate, all inquiry into the good itself. For, it seems to me, it is beyond the  e
measure of this effort to find the way to what is, after all, only my present opinion on the subject. But I am willing to talk to you about that which appears to be an off-shoot of the good, and bears the strongest resemblance to it, provided it is also agreeable to you; but if it is not, I will let it alone.

But please tell us about it, he replied. You shall remain in our debt for an account of the parent.

I wish that I could pay, and you receive, the parent sum, instead of having to content 507
ourselves with the interest springing from it. However, here I present you with the interest and the child of the good itself. Only take care that I do not involuntarily deceive you by handing in a spurious account of this offspring.

We will take all the care we can; only proceed.

I will do so as soon as we have come to a settlement together, and you have been reminded of certain statements made in a previous part of our conversation, and renewed before now again and again.

What statements exactly?  b

In the course of the discussion we have distinctly maintained the existence of a multiplicity of things that are beautiful, and good, and so on.

True, we have.

And also the existence of beauty itself, and good itself, and everything else which we previously regarded as many. We will now refer them to the single idea of each as if it were a single being, and address each as "that which is."

Just so. . . .

509
e

Suppose you take a line divided into two unequal parts—one to represent the visible class of objects, the other the intelligible—and divide each part again into two segments in the same proportion.

510

Then, if you make the lengths of the segments represent degrees of distinctness or indistinctness, one of the two segments of the part which stands for the visible world will represent all images—meaning by images, first of all, shadows; and, in the next place, reflections in water, and in close-grained, smooth, bright substances, and everything of the kind, if you understand me.

Yes, I do understand.

Let the other segment stand for that which corresponds to these images—namely, the animals about us, and everything that grows and the whole class of crafted things.

Let it be so.

Would you also consent to say that, with reference to this class, there is, in point of truth and the lack of it, the same distinction between the copy and the original, that there is between what is a matter of opinion and what is a matter of knowledge?

b

Certainly I should.

Then let us proceed to consider how we must divide that part of the whole line which represents the intelligible world.

How must we do it?

When the soul is compelled to investigate on the basis of hypotheses, it uses as images what were objects to be imitated in the previous argument, traveling not to a first principle but to a conclusion. The other segment will represent the soul, as it makes its way from a hypothesis to a first principle which is not hypothetical, unaided by those images which the former division employs, and shaping its journey by the sole help of the forms themselves.

I have not understood your description so well as I might wish.

c

Then we will try again. You will understand me more easily when I have made some additional observations. I think you know that the students of subjects like geometry and calculation, assume by way of materials, in each investigation, all odd and even numbers, figures, three kinds of angles, and other similar things. These things they assume as known, and having adopted them as hypotheses, they decline to give any account of them, either to themselves or to others, on the assumption that they are self-evident; and, making these their

d

starting point, they proceed to travel through the remainder of the subject, and arrive at last, with perfect unanimity, at that which they have proposed as the object of investigation.

I am perfectly aware of the fact, he replied.

Then you also know that they use visible forms, and discourse about them, though their thoughts are busy not with these forms, but with their originals, and though they discourse

e

not with a view to the particular square and diameter which they draw, but with a view to the square itself and the diameter itself, and so on. For while they employ by way of images those

511

figures and diagrams, which again have their shadows and images in water, they are really endeavoring to behold things themselves, which a person can only see with reasoning.

True.

This, then, was the form of things which I called intelligible; but I said that the soul is constrained to employ hypotheses while engaged in the investigation of them, not traveling to a first principle, because it is unable to step out of, and mount above, its hypotheses, but using as images the copies presented by things below, which copies, as compared with the originals, opined to be esteemed distinct and valued accordingly.

I understand you to be speaking of the subject matter of the various branches of geometry and the kindred arts.

Again, by the second segment of the intelligible world understand me to mean all that reason itself apprehends by the force of dialectic, when it considers hypotheses not as first principles, but in the truest sense, that is to say, as stepping-stones and impulses, whereby it may force its way up to something that it not hypothetical, and arrive at the first principle of everything, and seize it in its grasp. When it has grasped this, it turns round, and takes hold of that which takes hold of this first principle, until at last it comes down to a conclusion, calling in the aid of no sensible object whatever, but simply employing forms themselves, and going through forms to forms, it ends in forms.

I do not understand you so well as I could wish, for I believe you to be describing an arduous task; but at any rate I understand that you wish to differentiate between that which is (exists) and is intelligible, as contemplated by the knowledge of dialectics, is more clear than the field investigated by what are called the arts, in which hypotheses constitute first principles, which the students are compelled, it is true, to contemplate with the mind and not with the senses. But, at the same time, as they do not come back, in the course of inquiry, to a first principle, but push on from hypothetical premises, you think that they do not exercise mind on the questions that engage them, although taken in connection with a first principle these questions come within the domain of reason. And I believe you apply the term reasoning, not understanding, to the habit of such people as geometricians, regarding reasoning as something intermediate between opinion and understanding.

You have taken in my meaning most satisfactorily; and I beg you will accept these four dispositions in the soul, as corresponding to the four segments, namely understanding corresponding to the highest, reasoning to the second, trust to the third, and imagination to the last; and now arrange them in gradation, and believe them to partake of distinctness in a degree corresponding to the truth of their respective domains.

I understand you, said he. I quite agree with you, and will arrange them as you desire.

## Book VII

Now then, I proceeded to say, compare our natural condition, as far as education and the lack of education are concerned, to a state of things like the following. Imagine a number of human beings living in an underground cave-like chamber, with an entrance open to the light, extending along the entire length of the cave, in which they have been confined, from their childhood, with their legs and necks so shackled, that they are obliged to sit still and look straight forward, because their chains make it impossible for them to turn their heads round. And imagine a bright fire burning some way off, above and behind them, and a kind of roadway above which passes between the fire and the prisoners, with a low wall built along it, like the screens which puppeteers put up in front of their audience, and above which they exhibit their puppets.

I see, he replied.

Also picture to yourself a number of persons walking behind this wall, and carrying with

515 them statues of men, and images of other animals, fashioned in wood and stone and all kinds of materials, together with various other articles, which are above the wall. And, as you might expect, let some of the passers-by be talking, and others silent.

You are describing a strange scene, and strange prisoners.

They resemble us, I replied. For let me ask you, in the first place, whether persons so confined could have seen anything of themselves or of each other, beyond the shadows thrown by the fire upon the part of the cave facing them?

Certainly not, if you suppose them to have been compelled all their lifetime to keep their
b heads unmoved.

And what about the things carried past them? Is not the same true with regard to them?

Unquestionably it is.

And if they were able to converse with one another, do you not think that they would be in the habit of giving names to the things which they saw before them?

Doubtless they would.

Again, if their prison-house returned an echo from the part facing them, whenever one of the passers-by opened his lips, to what, let me ask you, could they refer the voice, if not to the shadow which was passing?

They would refer it to that, by Zeus.
c Then surely such persons would hold the shadows of those manufactured articles to be the only truth.

Without a doubt they would.

Now consider what would happen if the course of nature brought them a release from their fetters, and a remedy for their foolishness, in the following manner. Let us suppose that one of them has been released, and compelled suddenly to stand up, and turn his head around and walk with open eyes towards the light—and let us suppose that he goes through all these actions with pain, and that the dazzling splendor renders him incapable of perceiving those things of which he formerly used to see only the shadows. What answer should you
d expect him to give, if someone were to tell him that in those days he was watching foolery, but that now he is somewhat nearer to reality, and is turned towards things more real, and sees more correctly? Above all, what would you expect if he were to point out to him the several objects that are passing by, and question him, and compel him to answer what they are? Should you not expect him to be puzzled, and to regard his old visions as truer than the things now shown?

Yes, much truer.
e And if he were further compelled to gaze at the light itself, would not his eyes be distressed, do you think, and would he not shrink and turn away to the things which he could see distinctly, and consider them to be really clearer than the things pointed out to him?

Just so.

And if someone were to drag him violently up the rough and steep ascent from the cave,
516 and refuse to let him go until he had drawn him out into the light of the sun, do you not think that he would be vexed and indignant at such treatment, and on reaching the light, would he not find his eyes so dazzled by the glare as to be incapable of making out so much as one of the objects that are now called true?

Yes, he would find it so at first.

Hence, I suppose, it will be necessary for him to become accustomed before he is able to see the things above. At first he will be most successful in distinguishing shadows, then he will discern the images of men and other things in water, and afterwards the things themselves? And after this he will raise his eyes to encounter the light of the moon and stars, finding it less difficult to study the heavenly bodies and the heaven itself by night, than the    b
sun and the sun's light by day.

Doubtless.

Last of all, I imagine, he will be able to observe and contemplate the nature of the sun, not as it appears in water or on alien ground, but as it is in itself in its own region.

Of course.

His next step will be to draw the conclusion, that the sun is the provider of the seasons and the years, and the guardian of all things in the visible world, and in a manner the cause of all    c
those things which he and his companions used to see.

Obviously, this will be his next step.

What then? When he recalls to mind his first home, and the wisdom of the place, and his old fellow-prisoners, do you not think he will think himself happy on account of the change, and pity them?

Assuredly he will.

And if it was their practice in those days to receive honor and praise one from another, and to give prizes to him who had the keenest eye for the things passing by, and who remembered best all that used to precede and follow and accompany it, and from these    d
divined most ably what was going to come next, do you imagine that he will desire these prizes, and envy those who receive honor and exercise authority among them? Do you not rather imagine that he will feel what Homer describes, to "drudge on the lands of a master, serving a man of no great estate," and be ready to go through anything, rather than entertain those opinions, and live in that fashion?

For my own part, he replied, I am quite of that opinion. I believe he would consent to go    e
through anything rather than live in that way.

And now consider what would happen if such a man were to descend again and seat himself on his old seat? Coming so suddenly out of the sun, would he not find his eyes blinded with the darkness of the place?

Certainly, he would.

And if he were forced to form a judgment again, about those previously mentioned shadows, and to compete earnestly against those who had always been prisoners, while his sight continued dim, and his eyes unsteady, and if he needed quite some time to get    517
adjusted—would he not be made a laughingstock, and would it not be said of him, that he had gone up only to come back again with his eyesight destroyed, and that it was not worthwhile even to attempt the ascent? And if anyone endeavored to set them free and carry them to the light, would they not go so far as to put him to death, if they could only manage to get their hands on him?

Yes, that they would.

Now this imaginary case, my dear Glaucon, you must apply in all its parts to our former statements, by comparing the region which the eye reveals to the prison-house, and the light    b
of the fire to the power of the sun. And if, by the upward ascent and the contemplation of the

things above, you understand the journeying of the soul into the intelligible region, you will not disappoint my hopes, since you desire to be told what they are; though, indeed, god only knows whether they are true. But, be that as it may, the view which I take of the phenomena is the following: In the world of knowledge, the idea of the good is the limit of what can be

c seen, and it can barely be seen; but, when seen, we cannot help concluding that it is in every case the source of all that is right and beautiful, in the visible world giving birth to light and its master, and in the intelligible world, as master, providing truth and mind—and that whoever would act prudently, either in private or in public, must see it.

To the best of my power, said he, I quite agree with you.

That being the case, I continued, agree with me on another point, and do not be surprised, that those who have climbed so high are unwilling to mind the business of human beings,

d because their souls are eager to spend all their time in that upper region. For how could it be otherwise, if in turn it follows from the image we've discussed before?

True, it could scarcely be otherwise.

Well, do you think it amazing that a person who has turned from the contemplation of the divine to the study of human things, should betray awkwardness, and appear very ridiculous, when with his sight still dazed, and before he has become sufficiently accustomed to the surrounding darkness, he finds himself compelled to contend in courts of law, or elsewhere,

e about the shadows of justice, or images which cast the shadows, and to take up in what way these things are to be grasped by those who have never yet had a glimpse of justice itself?

No, it is anything but amazing.

518 But an intelligent person will remember that the eyes may be confused in two distinct ways and from two distinct causes, that is to say, by sudden transitions either from light to darkness, or from darkness to light. And, believing that these same things hold for the soul, whenever such a person sees a case in which the soul is perplexed and unable to distinguish objects, he will not laugh unintelligently, but will rather examine whether it has just come from a brighter life, and has been blinded by the novelty of darkness, or whether it has come

b from the depths of ignorance into a more brilliant life, and has been dazzled by the unusual splendor; and not until then will he consider the first soul happy in its life and condition, or have pity on the second. And if he chooses to laugh at the second soul, such laughter will be less ridiculous than that which is raised at the expense of the soul that has descended from the light of a higher region.

You are speaking in a sensible manner.

Hence, if this is true, we must consider the following about these matters, that education is not what certain men proclaim. They say, I think, that they can infuse the soul with know-

c ledge, when it was not in there, just as sight might be instilled in blinded eyes.

True, they do indeed assert that.

Whereas, our present argument shows us that there is a faculty residing in the soul of each person, and an instrument enabling each of us to learn; and that, just as we might suppose it to be impossible to turn the eye round from darkness to light without turning the whole body, so must this faculty, or this instrument, be wheeled round, in company with the entire soul, from the world of becoming, until it be enabled to endure the contemplation of the world of being and the brightest part thereof, which, according to us, is the idea of the good.

d Am I not right?

You are.

Hence, I continued, there should be an art of this turning around, involving the way that the change will most easily and most effectively be brought about. Its object will not be to produce in the person the power of seeing. On the contrary, it assumes that he possesses it, though he is turned in a wrong direction, and does not look towards the right quarter—and its aim is to remedy this defect.

So it would appear.

Hence, on the one hand, the other so-called virtues of the soul seem to resemble those of the body, inasmuch as they really do not pre-exist in the soul, but are formed in it in the course of time by habit and exercise; while the virtue of prudence, on the other hand, does, e above everything else, appear to be more divine, which never loses its energy, but depending on which way it is turned, becomes useful and serviceable, or else remains useless and harmful. For you must have noticed how keen-sighted are the puny souls of those who have 519 the reputation of being wise but vicious, and how sharply they distinguish the things to which they are directed, thus proving that their powers of vision are by no means feeble, though they have been compelled to become the servants of wickedness, so that the more sharply they see, the more numerous are the harms which they work.

Yes, indeed it is the case.

But, I proceeded, if from earliest childhood this part of their nature had been hammered out and its ties to becoming knocked off—those leaden, earth-born weights, which grow and b cling to the pleasures of eating and gluttonous enjoyments of a similar nature, and which keep the eye of the soul turned upon the things below—if, I repeat, they had been released from these snares, and turned round to look at true things, then these very same souls of these very same men would have had as keen an eye for such pursuits as they actually have for those in which they are now engaged.

Yes, probably it would be so.

Once more, is it not also probable, or rather does it not follow our previous remarks, that neither those who are uneducated and inexperienced in truth, nor those who spend their time continuously on their education all their life, can ever be adequate guardians of the city, c the former, because they have no single goal in life, to which they are to constitute the end and aim of all their conduct both in private and in public? And the latter, because they will not act without compulsion, believing that, while yet alive, they have emigrated to the islands of the blest?

That is true.

It is, therefore, our task as founders of the city, I continued, to constrain the best natures to arrive at that learning which we formerly pronounced the highest, and to set eyes upon the d good, and to mount that ascent we spoke of; and, when they have mounted and looked long enough, we must take care to refuse to permit them that which is at present allowed.

And what is that?

Staying where they are, and refusing to descend again to those prisoners, or partake of their toils and honors, be they humble or more serious.

Then are we to do them an injustice, and make them live a life that is worse than the one within their reach?

You have again forgotten, my friend, that law does not ask itself how some one part of a e

city is to live extraordinarily well. On the contrary, it tries to bring about this result in the
520  entire city—for which purpose it links the citizens together by persuasion and by constraint,
makes them share with one another the benefit which each individual can contribute to the
commonwealth, and does actually create men of this sort in the city, not with the intention
of letting them go each on his own way, but by using them to make a beginning towards
binding the city together.

True, he replied, I had forgotten.

Therefore reflect, Glaucon, that far from wronging the future philosophers of our city, we
shall only be treating them justly, if we put them under the additional obligation of guarding
b    and caring for the others. We shall say with good reason that when men of this type come to
be in other cities, it is likely that they will not partake in the labor of the city. For they take
root in a city spontaneously, against the will of the prevailing regime. And it is but just that a
self-sown plant, which is indebted to no one for support, should have no inclination to pay
to anybody wages for attendance. But in your case, it is we that have begotten you for the city
as well as for yourselves, to be like leaders and kings of a hive, better and more perfectly
c    educated than the rest, and more capable of playing a part in both lives. You must therefore
descend by turns, and associate with the rest of the community, and you must accustom
yourselves to the contemplation of these dark things. For, when accustomed, you will see ten
thousand times better than the residents, and you will recognize what each image is, and
what is its original, because you have seen the truth of beautiful and just and good things.
And in this way, for you and for us, the city is ruled in a waking state and not in a dream like
so many of our present cities, which are mostly composed of men who fight among themselves for shadows, and are feuding to gain rulership, which they regard as a great good.
d    Whereas I conceive that the truth is this. That city in which those who are going to rule are
least eager to rule will inevitably be ruled in the best and least factious manner, and a
contrary result will ensue if the rulers are of a contrary disposition.

You are perfectly right.

And do you imagine that our pupils, when addressed in this way, will disobey our commands, and refuse to toil with us in the city by turns, while they spend most of their time
together in that pure region?

e    Impossible, he replied, for certainly it is a just command and those who are to obey it are
just men. No, doubtless each of them will undertake ruling as a necessary thing—the opposite of what is pursued by the present rulers in each city.

True, my friend, the case stands thus. If you can find a life better than ruling for those who
521  are going to rule, you may possibly realize a well-governed city. For only in such a city will
the rulers be those who are really rich, not in gold, but in a good and prudent life, which is
the wealth necessary for a happy man. But if beggars, and persons who hunger after private
goods, take the reins of the city, supposing that they are privileged to snatch good from their
power, all goes wrong. For then ruling is made an object of strife, both civil war and family
feuds, and conflicts of this nature, ruin not only these men themselves, but also the rest of the
city.

That is most true.

b    And can you mention any life which despises political offices, except the life of true
philosophy?

No by Zeus, I cannot.

Well, but the task of ruling must be undertaken by persons who aren't lovers of it; otherwise, their rival lovers will fight.

Unquestionably it must.

Then what persons will you compel to become guardians of the city other than the ones who are most prudent about how best to rule the city and who have other honors and a life better than the political life?

None other, he said.

And now would you have us proceed to consider in what way such persons come about in the city, and how they are to be led up to the light, like those heroes who are said to have ascended up to the gods from Hades.

Certainly I would have you do so.

Apparently this is a question involving a soul, which is traversing a road leading from a kind of night-like day up to a true day—and this ascent to real being we shall truly declare to be true philosophy.

Exactly so.

Then must we not consider what branch of study possesses the power required?

Certainly we must.

Then, Glaucon, can you tell me of a study which tends to draw the soul from becoming to being? As I am talking, it just came to mind that we said, did we not, that our pupils must be trained in their youth for war?

Yes, we did say so.

Then the study which we are looking for must possess this feature as well as the former.

What feature?

That it can be turned to use by warlike men.

That is certainly advisable, if it be possible.

Now in the foregoing discussion we were training our pupils in music and gymnastics.

True.

Gymnastics, I believe, is engaged with becoming and perishing, for it presides over the growth and waste of the body.

That is evident.

Hence gymnastics cannot be the study we are looking for.

No, it cannot.

But what do you say to music, considered in the manner in which we previously discussed it?

But music, he replied, was only the counterpart of gymnastics, if you remember; for it trained our guardians through habit, and imparted to them, not knowledge but a kind of harmoniousness by means of harmony, and a kind of rhythm. And in the subjects which it treated, whether tales or speeches more true, it presented another series of kindred habits, but it contained no branch of study tending toward the sort of thing which you are now seeking.

Your memory is very exact, I answered; for it really did possess nothing of the kind. But, my excellent Glaucon, where are we to find the thing we want? All the arts, I believe, we thought merely mechanical.

Unquestionably we did; yet what other study is left, apart from music and gymnastics and the arts?

Come then, if we can find nothing beyond and independent of these, let us take one of those studies which applies to all.

Which one?

That common one, for example, of which all arts, reasonings, and knowledge make use, and which is also one of the first things that every one must learn.

Tell me the nature of it.

I refer to that simple process of distinguishing the numbers, one, two, and three. And, in short, I call that number and calculation. For may it not be said of these, that every art and science must partake of them?

Certainly it may.

And is that not true of the science of war also?

Beyond a doubt it is. . . .

Then can we help concluding, that to be able to calculate and count is necessary study for the warrior?

Yes, most indispensable, if he is to understand how to handle troops at all, or rather, if he is to be a human being.

And do you have the same thing in mind concerning this study?

What sort of thing do you mean?

What we are seeking seems to be by nature one of those studies leading to understanding, but no one appears to make the right use of it, as a thing which tends in every way to draw us towards being.

Explain your meaning.

I will try to make my own opinion clear to you. And you, on your side, must join me in looking at those things, which I distinguish in my own mind as leading or not leading to that which we said, and you must express your agreement or disagreement, in order that we may see more clearly, whether I am right in my surmises as to the sort of thing this is.

Please go on with your distinctions.

I will. If you observe, some of the things that we perceive do not call upon the understanding for examination, because they are thoroughly judged by perception; whereas others urge the intellect strenuously to examine them, because perception appears to produce nothing healthy.

It is plain you are talking of objects seen at a distance, and shadow-painting.

You have not quite grasped my meaning.

Then what sort of objects do you mean?

The sort of things that do not simultaneously go over into the opposite perception I call things that do not call upon the intellect. On the other hand, all things which do go over I consider evocative, calling upon the intellect—meaning whenever perception, being hit upon either from near or from a distance, indicates one thing no more than its opposite. You will understand my meaning more clearly in this way: Here you have three fingers, you say, the little finger, the second, and the middle.

Very good.

Well, suppose me to be speaking of them as they appear on a close inspection. Now here is the point which I wish you to examine with reference to them.

What is it?

It is evident that they are all equally fingers; and, so far, it makes no difference whether the one we are looking at be in the middle or out-side, whether it be white or black, thick or thin, and so on. For, so long as we confine ourselves to these points, the soul of the many seldom feels compelled to ask the understanding what a finger is, because in no instance has the sight informed the soul at the same moment, that the finger is the opposite of a finger.   d

No, certainly not.

Then, naturally, such impressions cannot be stimulating or awaken the understanding.   e

True.

But how is it with the bigness and littleness of the fingers? Does the sight distinguish them satisfactorily, and does it make no difference to it, whether the position of one of them be in the middle, or at the outside? And in like manner, does the touch estimate thickness and thinness, softness and hardness, satisfactorily? And is there no defect in the similar declaration of the other senses? Or, do they not all rather proceed in this way? To begin with the perception that is set over hard things, is it not necessarily also set over soft things, and does   524 it not announce to the soul that it feels the same thing to be both hard and soft?

It does.

In such cases, then, must not the soul be at a loss to know what this perception means by hard, since it declares the same thing to be also soft—and what the perception of weight means by light and heavy, when it means that the heavy is light, and the light heavy?

Why yes, he answered, such interpretations will be strange to the soul, and will require   b examination.

Hence it is natural for the soul in such circumstances to call in the aid of calculation and understanding, and to attempt to determine whether the things reported are one or two.

Undoubtedly.

And if it appears to be two, will not each be distinct and one?

That is evident.

If then each is one, and both together make two, the soul will conclude that the two are separable. For if they were inseparable, it could only conclude that they are one, not two.   c

True.

Well, sight, we say, saw the great and the small, not as separate, but as mixed together. Am I not right?

You are.

But, in order to clear this up, the understanding, reversing the process of the sight, was compelled to look at great and small as things distinct, not mixed together.

True.

Then is it not some contradiction of this kind that first prompts us to ask, "What then, after all, is greatness, and what smallness?"

No doubt it is.

And thus we are led to distinguish between the intelligible and the visible.

Most rightly so.   d

This, then, was the meaning which I was just now attempting to convey, when I said that some things are evocative to reasoning and others are not, defining as "evocative" those that hit upon perception simultaneously with their opposite, while those that do not arouse the understanding are not.

Now I understand, he replied, and I agree with you.

Well, to which of the two classes do you think that number and one belong?

I cannot make up my mind.

Let our previous remarks help you figure it out. If one, in and by itself, is adequately grasped by sight or any other sense, like the finger we spoke of, it cannot draw the soul e toward being. But if the opposite is always seen at the same time, so that it does not appear much more one than its opposite, then the need would arise for something to judge, and in this case the soul would be at a loss and inquire, moving its understanding and asking: 525 "What, after all, is the one in itself?" And thus the study of the one will be among those things which turn and lead us to the contemplation of what is.

You are right, said he; sight of the one has that property to a remarkable degree. For we see the same thing as one and as an unlimited plurality.

Then, if this is the case with one, is it not also the case with all numbers without exception?

Doubtless it is.

Well, but calculation and arithmetic treat of number exclusively.

Certainly they do.

b And, apparently, they lead us to truth.

Yes, in a manner quite extraordinary.

Hence it would appear that they must be among the studies we are seeking. For the warrior finds a knowledge of it indispensable in drawing up his troops, and the philosopher must study it because he is bound to rise above becoming and cling to being, or never becoming skilled in calculation.

True.

But our guardian, as it happens, is both warrior and philosopher.

Undoubtedly he is.

Therefore, Glaucon, it will be proper to enforce the study by legislative enactment, and to c persuade those who are going to take part in the greatest affairs of the city to study calculation and devote themselves to it, not like private men, but perseveringly, until, by the aid of the understanding, they have attained to the contemplation of the nature of numbers, not cultivating it with a view to buying and selling, as merchants or shopkeepers, but for purposes of war, and to facilitate the turn-around of the soul itself from becoming to truth and being.

What you say is admirable.

Indeed, I continued, talking of this study which treats of calculation, it has only just d occurred to me how elegant it is, and how valuable it may be to us in many ways in carrying out our wishes, provided it be pursued for the sake of knowledge, and not for purposes of trade.

How so? he asked.

Because, as we were saying just now, it mightily draws the soul upwards, and compels it to reason about numbers themselves, steadily declining the discussion when any numbers are

proposed which have bodies that can be seen and touched. For I presume you are aware that those who are clever in these things ridicule and disallow any attempt to cut the one itself in the course of argument—and if you divide it into pieces, like small change, they multiply it      e
back again, and take every precaution to prevent the unit from ever losing its unity, and presenting an appearance of multiplicity.

That is quite true.

Now suppose, Glaucon, that someone were to ask them the following question: "My   526
excellent friends, what kind of numbers are you discussing? Where are the numbers in which the one realizes your description of it, which is, that every one is equal, each to each, without the smallest difference, and contains within itself no parts?" What answer should you expect them to make?

If you ask me, I should expect them to say, that the numbers about which they talk, are only capable of being conceived in thought, and cannot be dealt with in any other way.

Then, my friend, do you see that this study is, in all likelihood, absolutely necessary to us,   b
since it evidently obliges the soul to employ the understanding in pursuit of truth itself?

It certainly possesses this quality in an eminent degree.

Again, have you ever noticed that those who have a natural bent for calculation are, with scarcely any exceptions, naturally quick at all studies; and that men who are slow, if they are trained and exercised in this study, even supposing they derive no other benefit from it, at any rate progress so far as to become invariably quicker than they were before?

That is true.

And I am pretty sure, also, that you will not easily find many studies that give the learner   c
and student so much trouble and toil as this.

No, certainly you will not.

Then on all these accounts, so far from rejecting this study, we must employ it in the education of the best natures.

I agree with you, said he.

Then let us consider this one point settled. In the second place, let us inquire whether the study which borders on this is suitable.

What is that? Do you mean geometry?

The very one, I replied.

It is obvious, he continued, that all that part of it which bears upon strategy does concern   d
us. For in encamping, in occupying positions, in closing up and deploying troops, and in executing all the other maneuvers of an army in the field of battle or on the march, it will make every difference to a military man, whether or not he is a good geometrician.

Nevertheless, I replied, a trifling portion of geometry and calculation will suffice for these purposes. The question is, whether the larger and more advanced part of the study tends at all to facilitate our contemplation of the idea of the good. Now, according to us, this is the   e
tendency of everything that compels the soul to turn towards that region in which is the happiest of being, which it is above all necessary for it to see.

You are right.

Consequently if geometry compels the soul to contemplate being, it does concern us; but if becoming, it does not concern us.

Yes, so we affirm.

527   Well then, on one point at any rate we shall encounter no opposition from those who have even a little experience with geometry, when we assert that this science holds a position which flatly contradicts the language employed by those who practice it.

How so?

They talk, I believe, in a very ridiculous and constrained style. For they speak invariably of squaring, and producing, and adding, and so on, as if they were engaged in some business,

b   and as if all their propositions had a practical end in view; whereas in reality I conceive that the study is pursued wholly for the sake of knowledge.

Assuredly it is.

There is still a point about which we must be agreed, is there not?

What is it?

That it is for the sake of the knowledge of that which is always, and not of what comes into existence at a particular time, and then perishes.

We shall soon be agreed about that. Geometry, no doubt, is a knowledge of what is always.

If that be so, my noble friend, geometry must tend to draw the soul towards truth, and to produce philosophical reasoning, contributing to raise up what, at present, we so wrongly keep down.

Yes, it will do so most forcibly.

c   Then you must, in the most forcible manner, direct the citizens of your beautiful city on no account to fail to apply themselves to geometry. For even its secondary advantages are not trifling.

And what are they?

The things you mentioned as bearing upon the conduct of war, and I would insist particularly upon the fact, of which we are assured, that, when it comes to a finer understanding of any study, it will make all the difference whether the pupil has applied himself to geometry or not.

Yes, by Zeus, it will.

Shall we, then, impose this, as a secondary study, upon our young men?

Yes, let us do so, he replied.

d   Again, shall we make astronomy a third study? Or do you disapprove?

I quite approve of it, said he. For to have an intimate acquaintance with seasons, and months, and years, is an advantage not only to the farmer and the navigator, but also, in an equal degree, to the general.

You amuse me by your evident alarm lest the multitude should think that you insist upon useless studies. Yet indeed it is no easy matter, but on the contrary a very hard one, to trust that in the midst of these studies an instrument of our souls is purified and rekindled when it has been blinded and destroyed by other pursuits—an instrument whose preservation is of

e   more importance than ten thousand eyes; because only by it can truth be seen. Consequently, those who think with us will think you speak very well; while those who have no inkling at all of this, will think them valueless, because they see no considerable advantage to be gained

528  from them. Therefore consider at once with which of the two parties you are conversing; or else, if you are carrying on the discussion chiefly on your own account, without any reference to either party, you surely will not grudge another man any advantage which he may derive from the conversation.

I prefer the latter course; I mean to speak, put my questions, and give my answers, chiefly on my own account.

Then take a step backwards, I continued. We were wrong a moment ago in what we took to follow.

What did we take?

Why, after considering plane surfaces, we proceeded to take solids in motion, before considering solids in themselves. Whereas the correct way is, to proceed from two dimensions to three—which brings us, I believe, to cubical dimensions, and figures into which depth enters.

True, Socrates; but these subjects, I think, have not yet been explored.

They have not, I replied, and for two reasons. In the first place, they are difficult problems, and but feebly investigated, because no city holds them in honor, and, in the second place, those who do investigate them need a supervisor without whom they will make no discoveries. Now, to find such a person is a hard task to begin with; and then, supposing one were found, as matters stand now, the pride of those who are inquisitive about the subject would prevent their listening to his suggestions. But if the entire city were to pay honor to the study, and constitute itself supervisor thereof, these students would obey, and the real nature of the subject, thus continuously and vigorously investigated, would be brought to light. For even now, slighted and curtailed as it is not only by the many, but also by professed inquirers, who can give no account of the extent of its usefulness, it nevertheless makes progress, in spite of all these obstacles, by its inherent elegance; and I should not be at all surprised if it came to light.

There certainly is a peculiar fascination about it. But explain more clearly what you were saying just now. I think you defined geometry as the investigation of plane surfaces.

I did.

You then proceeded to place astronomy next to geometry—though afterwards you drew back.

Yes, I said, the more I hasten to travel over this ground, the slower I move. The investigation of space of three dimensions is the next thing in order; but because of its ridiculous state, I passed it over, and spoke of astronomy, which implies motion of solid bodies, as the next step after geometry.

You are right.

Then let us assign the fourth place in our studies to astronomy, regarding the existence of the study now omitted as only waiting for the time when the city will take it up.

It is likely, Socrates. And to return to the rebuke which you gave me a little while ago for my vulgar praise of astronomy, I can now praise the plan on which you pursue it. For I suppose it is clear to everyone, that astronomy at all events compels the soul to look upwards, and draws it from the things of this world to the other.

It is not clear to me, I replied, though perhaps it may be to everyone else, for it does not seem to me to be thus.

Then what is your opinion?

It seems to me that astronomy, as now handled by those who embark on philosophy, positively makes the soul look downwards.

How so?

I think you are very generous in your conception of the study of things above. For probably, if a person were to throw his head back, and learn something from the contempla-
b tion of a carved ceiling, you would suppose him to be contemplating it, not with his eyes, but with his understanding. Now, perhaps your notion is right, and mine foolish. For my own part, I cannot conceive that any study makes the soul look upwards, unless it has to do with the things that are and are invisible. It makes no difference whether a person stares stupidly at the sky, or looks with half-shut eyes upon the ground—so long as he is trying to study the
c perceptible, I deny that he can ever be said to have learned anything, because it is impossible to have knowledge of these sorts of things, and I maintain that his soul is looking down-wards, not upwards, though he may be lying on his back, like a swimmer, to study, either in the sea, or on dry land.

I am paying a just penalty, he said, for I deserved your rebuke. But what did you mean by saying that astronomy ought to be studied in a way contrary to the present one, if it is to be studied profitably for the purposes that we have in view?

I will tell you. Since this ornamented sky is still a part of the visible world, we are bound to
d regard it, though the most beautiful and precise of visible things, as far inferior nevertheless to those true movements, which are really swift, and are really slow, existing in true number, and in all true figures, and are moved with respect to each other, carrying with them all that they contain. They are grasped by argument and reasoning, not by sight. Or do you think differently?

No, indeed, he replied.

Therefore we must employ that decorated sky as a paradigm to forward the study of these
e other things, just as one might employ diagrams, which fell in his way, carefully drawn and elaborated by Daedalus or some other artist or painter. For, I imagine, a person acquainted with geometry, on seeing such diagrams, would think them most beautifully finished, but
530 would hold it ridiculous to study them seriously in the hope of detecting thereby the truths of equals, doubles, or any other proportion.

No doubt it would be ridiculous.

And do you not think that the genuine astronomer will be similarly persuaded when viewing the motions of the stars? That is to say, will he not regard the heaven itself, and the bodies which it contains, as framed by the craftsman of heaven with the utmost beauty of which such works are susceptible? But as to the proportion which the day bears to the night, both to the month, the month to the year, and the other stars to the sun and moon, and to
b one another, will he not, do you think, look down upon the man who believes such corporeal and visible objects to be changeless and exempt from all deviation? And will he not think it strange to apprehend their truth in every way?

Yes, I think so, now that I hear you suggest it.

Hence, we shall pursue astronomy with the help of problems, just as we pursue geometry; but we shall let the heavenly bodies alone, if it is our design to become really acquainted with astronomy, and by that means to convert the natural prudence of the soul from a useless into
c a useful possession.

The plan which you prescribe, said he, is, I am confident, many times more laborious than the present mode of studying astronomy.

Yes, I replied, and I imagine we shall prescribe everything else on the same scale, if we are to be of any use as legislators. But to proceed, what other study can you suggest?

I cannot suggest any, on such short notice.

Well, motion, if I am not mistaken, admits of certainly more than one variety: A perfect enumeration of these varieties may perhaps be supplied by some wise man. Those which are    d
clear to people like us are two in number.

And what are they?

We have already described astronomy. The other is its counterpart.

What is that?

It would seem, I replied, that our ears were intended to detect harmonious movements, just as our eyes were intended to detect the motions of the heavenly bodies; and that these constitute in a manner two sister sciences, as the Pythagoreans assert, and as we, Glaucon, are ready to grant. If not, what other course do we take?

We take the course you mentioned first; we grant the fact.

Then, as the business promises to be a long one, we will consult the Pythagoreans upon    e
this question, and perhaps upon some other questions too, guarding our interest throughout.

What principle do you mean?

Never to let our pupils attempt to study any imperfect branch of these sciences, or anything that ever fails to arrive ultimately at that point which all things ought to reach, as we said just now in treating of astronomy. For you can scarcely be ignorant that harmony 531
also is treated just like astronomy in this, that its professors, like the astronomers, are content to measure the notes and sounds distinguished by the ear, one against another, and therefore toil without result.

Yes, by the gods, and they make themselves quite ridiculous. They talk about repetitions, and apply their ears closely, as if they were bent on extracting a note from their neighbors; and then one party asserts that an intermediate sound can still be detected, which is the smallest interval, and ought to be the unit of measure; while the other party contends that now the sounds are identical—both put ears before the mind.    b

I see you are alluding to those good men who tease and torture the chords, and rack them upon the pegs. But not to make the image too elaborate by enlarging upon the blows given by the plectrum, and the accusations and denials and boasting of the strings, I here abandon this, and tell you that I do not mean these persons, but those whom we resolved just now to consult on the subject of harmony. For they act just like the astronomers—that is, they    c
investigate the numerical relations subsisting between these audible concords, but they refuse to apply themselves to problems, with the object of examining what numbers are, and what numbers are not, consonant, and what is the reason of the difference.

The work you describe would require divine faculties.

Call it, rather, a work useful in the search after the beautiful and the good, though useless if pursued with other ends.

Yes, that is not unlikely.

In addition to this, I continued, if the inquiry into all these things we have enumerated, arrives at some mutual association and relationship, and draws conclusions about their    d
kinship, I believe that the diligent treatment of them will contribute to what we have in view, and that the labor, which otherwise would be fruitless, will be well spent.

I surmise it the same way, Socrates. But the work you speak of is a very great one.

Do you allude to the prelude? I replied. Or to what? Surely we do not require to be reminded that all this is but the prelude to the actual song, which we have to learn? For I presume you do not look at those who are clever at this as dialecticians.

No, by Zeus, I do not, with the exception of a few that have come my way.

But of course you do not suppose that persons unable to give or receive an account, can be said to know anything of what we affirm they ought to know.

No, that again is not my opinion.

Then, Glaucon, have we not here the actual song which dialectics sings? This hymn, falling as it does within the domain of the intelligible, is imitated by the faculty of sight, which, as we said, strives to look steadily, first at animals themselves, then at the stars themselves, and last of all at the very sun itself. In the same way, whenever a person strives, by the help of dialectic, to start in pursuit of what each thing is by itself by using argument, independent of all sensations, never flinching, until by an act of the understanding he has grasped the good itself, he arrives at the very end of the intelligible world, just as the last-mentioned person arrived at the end of the visible world.

Unquestionably.

And this journey you name dialectic, do you not?

Certainly I do.

On the other hand, the release of the prisoners from their chains, and their transition from the shadows to the images themselves and to the light, and their ascent from the cave into the sunshine; and, when there, the fact of their being able to look, not at the animals and vegetables and the sun's light, but still only at their appearances in water, which are indeed divine and shadows of things that are, instead of being shadows of images thrown by a light which may itself be called an image, when compared with the sun—these points, I say, find their counterpart in all this pursuit of the above-mentioned arts, which possesses this power of elevating the best part of the soul, and advancing it towards the contemplation of that which is best in the things that are, just as in the other case the clearest thing of the body was furthered to the contemplation of that which is brightest in the corporeal and visible region.

For myself, he replied, I accept this statement. And yet I must confess that I find it hard to accept; though at the same time, looking at it in another way, I find it hard to deny. However, as the discussion of it need not be confined to the present occasion, but may be repeated on many future occasions, let us assume that what you have said is so, and so proceed to the song itself, and discuss it, as we have discussed the prelude. Tell us, therefore, what is the general character of the power of dialectic, and into what specific parts it is divided, and lastly what paths it follows. For these will, in all likelihood, be the roads that lead to the very spot where we are to close our march, and end our journey.

My dear Glaucon, I replied, you would not be able to follow me further, though I am willing to lead you. You would no longer be looking at the image of that whereof we speak, but at the truth itself, how it appears to me. Whether I am right or not, I dare not go so far as to decide positively; but we must maintain that there is something to see. Must we not?

Undoubtedly we must.

And may I not also affirm, that the power of dialectic can alone reveal the truth to one who is experienced in the things which we have just enumerated—and that in no other way is it possible?

Yes, on that point also you also have a right to insist.

At any rate, I continued, no one will contradict us when we assert that there is no other b way of inquiry which attempts methodically and in all cases to grasp what each thing individually is. On the contrary, all the arts, with few exceptions, are wholly addressed to the opinions and wants of men, or else concern themselves about the production and composition of bodies, or the treatment of things which grow and are put together. And as for the few exceptions, such as geometry and its accompanying sciences, which, according to us, to some extent apprehend what is—we find that, though they may dream about what is, they cannot behold it in a waking state, so long as they use hypotheses which they leave c unexamined, and of which they can give no account. For when a person assumes a first principle which he does not know, and the end and things in between are woven together out of things not known—what mechanism is there to turn such an arrangement into knowledge?

It is indeed impossible.

Hence the dialectical way of inquiry, and that alone, adopts the following course. It carries back its hypotheses to the very first principle of all, in order to establish them firmly; and finding the eye of the soul absolutely buried in a swamp of barbarous ignorance, it gently d draws and raises it upwards, employing as handmaids in this work of turning around the arts which we have discussed. These we have often called sciences, because it is customary to do so, but they require another name, which indicates that they are clearer than opinion, but darker than science. Reasoning, I think, was the term we used previously. But it appears to me to be no part of our business to dispute about a name, when we have proposed to ourselves the consideration of such important subjects. e

You are quite right, said he.

Indeed I am content, I proceeded, to call as before the first division knowledge, the second reasoning, the third trust, and the fourth imagination—the two latter jointly constituting 534 opinion, and the two former understanding. Opinion deals with becoming, understanding with being; and as being as to becoming, so is understanding to opinion; and as understanding is to opinion, so is science to trust, and reasoning to imagination. But we had better omit the proportion between the things over which these are set and the twofold division of the domains of opinion and of understanding, Glaucon, to prevent burdening ourselves with discussions far outnumbering all the former.

Well, I certainly agree with you upon those other points, so far as I can follow you. b

Do you also give the title of dialectician to the person who gives an account of the being of each thing? And will you admit that, so far as a person has no such account to give to himself and to others, so far he fails to exercise his intellect upon the subject?

Yes, I cannot doubt it, he replied.

Then shall you not also hold the same concerning the good? Unless a person can strictly define by a process of thought the idea of the good, differentiated from everything else; and unless he can fight his way as it were through all objections, eager to cross-examine them, not c according to opinion, but according to being; and unless in all these conflicts he travels to his conclusion without making one false step in his train of thought, unless he does all this, shall you not assert that he knows neither the good itself, nor any other good; and that any image of it, which he may chance to apprehend, is the fruit of opinion and not of knowledge; and d that he dreams and sleeps away his present life, and never wakes on this side, but goes to Hades, where he is doomed to sleep forever?

Yes, by Zeus, he said. I shall most decidedly assert all this.

Then what of your children, whom you are rearing and educating in speech? If you were to do so in deed, I cannot suppose that you would allow them to be rulers in the city, with authority to decide the weightiest matters, while they are as unreasonable as irrational lines.

No, indeed I should not.

You will pass a law, no doubt, ordering them to apply themselves especially to
e that education which will enable them to question and answer in the most knowledgeable way.

I shall legislate along with you.

Then does it not seem to you that dialectic lies, like a capstone, at the top of these studies,
535 and that it would be wrong to place any other study above it, because the series is now complete?

Yes, I believe you are right, he replied.

Hence, I continued, it only remains for you to fix upon the persons to whom we are to assign these studies, and the principle of their distribution.

That is evidently the case.

Do you remember what kind of persons we selected, when we were choosing the rulers some time ago?

Of course I do.

Well, with regard to requirements, then, these are the natures that must be chosen. That is to say, we are bound to prefer the most steady, the most courageous, and, as far as we can, the
b most handsome. But in addition, besides requiring in them a noble and fierce disposition, they must also possess such qualifications as are favorable to this system of education.

And which do you determine these to be?

They must bring with them a piercing eye for their studies, my excellent friend, and they must learn with ease. For assuredly souls are much more likely to give up when it comes to hard studies than in gymnastics, because the labor is closer to home in the former case, as it is limited to the soul, instead of being shared by the body.

True.

c Then we must include in the objects of our search a memory, a firm demeanor, and a thorough love of work. How else can you expect to induce a man to go through with his bodily labors, and learn and practice so much besides?

No, we can hold out no inducement to a man who does not possess an entirely good nature.

At any rate, I continued, it is certain that the false view of philosophy which at present prevails, and the dishonor into which she has fallen, may be traced, as I said before, to the fact, that people apply themselves to philosophy who are untrustworthy; whereas the study of her is the privilege of her genuine sons, to the exclusion of bastards.

What do you mean by genuine?

d In the first place, he that would study her must not be lame in his love of work. He must not be half-laborious, and half-indolent, which is the case when a man loves exercise, and the hunt, and all bodily toil, but dislikes study, and feels an aversion for listening and inquiring, and in fact hates all intellectual labor. On the other hand, those people are equally lame whose love of work has taken the opposite form.

What you say is perfectly true.

In the same way, may we not affirm that a soul is crippled with reference to truth, if, while it hates voluntary falsehood, and cannot endure it in itself, and is exceedingly indignant    e when other people are guilty of an untruth, it nevertheless calmly accepts involuntary false-hood, and instead of being distressed when it's caught being ignorant, is fain to wallow in ignorance with the complacency of a swinish beast?

No doubt you are right.    536

Above all, I proceeded, we must watch the genuine and the bastard with regard to moder-ation, courage, magnificence, and all the separate virtues. For whenever cities or private persons have no eye for qualities like these, they unwittingly employ, as rulers or as friends, men who are lame and illegitimate in one or other respects.

Unquestionably it is so.

Hence we, on our side, must take every precaution in all matters of this description. For, if we can procure persons sound in limb, and sound in mind, and train them up under the    b influence of these important studies and exercises, justice herself will find no fault with us, and we shall preserve our city and regime; whereas, if we select pupils of a different stamp, our success will be turned into failure, and we shall draw down upon philosophy a still heavier storm of ridicule.

That would be indeed a disgrace.

It certainly would. But very likely I made myself ridiculous just this minute.

How so? he asked.

I forgot, I replied, that we were being playful, and spoke too intensely. For, as I spoke, I    c looked towards philosophy, and seeing her besmirched with mud, I was so indignant, and so angry with those who are responsible for it, that I believe I expressed myself too seriously.

No, by Zeus, you did not—at least, in listening, I did not think so.

Well, in speaking, it struck me that I did. But, to proceed, let us not forget, that it will be impossible in this instance to select persons advanced in years, as we did in the former. For    d we must not be persuaded by Solon into thinking that a man, as he grows old, can learn many things. On the contrary, an old man can sooner run than learn; and the wide range of severe labors must fall wholly on the young.

Unquestionably so.

Calculation, therefore, and geometry, and all the branches of that preliminary education which is to pave the way for dialectic, must be taught our pupils in their childhood—care being taken to convey instruction in such a way as not to make it look like compulsory learning.

Why so?

Because, I replied, no trace of slavery ought to mix with the studies of the freeborn man.    e For the constrained performance of bodily labors does, it is true, exert no harmful influence upon the body; but in the case of the soul, no study, pursued under compulsion, remains rooted in the soul.

That is true.

Hence, my excellent friend, you must train the children in their studies in a playful

537 manner, and without force, with the further object of discerning more readily the natural bent of their respective characters.

Your advice is reasonable.

Do you remember our saying that the children must also be taken on horseback within sight of actual war; and that, on any safe occasion, they must be brought into the field, and made to taste blood, like the puppies?

I do remember it, he replied.

Accordingly we must make a select list, including everyone who has shown himself best prepared and ready to go in the midst of all these labors, studies, and fears.

b      At what age must that be done?

As soon as they are released from the required gymnastic exercises, during which, whether they last two or three years, nothing else can be done. For weariness and sleep are enemies to study. And, besides, the behavior of each in his exercises is itself an important test.

Doubtless it is.

After this period, I continued, those selected from the ranks of the young men of twenty, must receive higher honors than the rest; and the studies in which they were educated as c      children, without any particular order, must now be brought within the compass of a single survey, to show the kinship which exists between them, and that which is.

Certainly this is the only kind of instruction which will be found abiding in those who receive it.

Yes, and it is also the greatest test of the nature which is dialectical. For depending on whether someone can or cannot see the whole together, he either is or is not a dialectician.

I agree with you.

Hence it will be your duty to have an eye to those who show the greatest ability in these d      questions, and the greatest firmness, not only in study, but also in war and in the other things established by law. And when they are thirty years old and upwards, you must select them out of the ranks of your picked men, and raise them to greater honors, and try them by the test of dialectic ability, in order to see who is able to release himself from his eyes and his other senses, going toward that which itself is, accompanied by truth. And here it is, my friend, that great caution is required.

For what special reason? he inquired.

e      Do you not perceive, I said, what great harm comes at present from the practice of dialectic?

What is it?

Lawlessness, I replied, with which I believe dialecticians to be tainted.

Indeed you are right.

Are you at all surprised at the fact, and do you make no allowance for the persons in question?

Do explain yourself.

By way of parallel case, imagine to yourself a child that has been secretly substituted, brought up in the midst of great wealth, and extensive connections of high family, and 538 surrounded by flatterers; and suppose him, on arriving at manhood, to learn that his alleged parents are not his real parents, though he cannot discover the latter. Can you guess what his behavior would be towards his flatterers and towards his spurious parents, first while he was ignorant of the fact of his substitution, and secondly after he became aware of it? Or would you like to listen to my own conjectures?

I should, he replied.

Well, I suspect that, so long as he is ignorant of the truth, he will honor his father and his mother and his other apparent relations, more than his flatterers; and be less likely to   b
overlook the needs of the former than the latter; and that he will be less likely to be unlawful in word or deed and of disobedience in important things towards his flatterers, than towards his supposed parents.

Probably he will.

On the other hand, I suspect that, after he has learned the truth, his esteem and regard for his parents will be diminished, while his respect for his flatterers will be heightened, to whom he will now listen very much more than before, and proceed to live as they would have him   c
live, associating with them undisguisedly, and wholly abandoning all concern for that father, and the rest of pretended relations, unless he is by nature kind.

Your description is just as it would happen. But how does this image bear upon those who apply themselves to arguments?

I will tell you. We have, I believe, from childhood, opinions about things just and beautiful; and we have been brought up to obey and honor these opinions, just as we have grown up in submission to our parents.

True.

Now these opinions are combated by certain pleasurable pursuits, which flatter our soul   d
and try to draw it over to their side; though they fail to persuade us, if we are at all sensible— in which case, we honor those ancestral opinions, and continue loyal to them.

True.

Well, but when such a person is met by the question, "What is beauty?" And, having given the answer, which he used to hear from the legislator, he is refuted by the argument; and when frequent and various defeats have forced him to believe that there is as much ugliness   e
as beauty in what he calls beauty, and that justice, goodness, and all the things, which he used to honor most, are similar—how do you think he will behave thenceforth toward what he heard from legislators, so far as honor and obedience are concerned?

Of course he will not pay them the same honor or the same obedience as before.

And so long as he neither honors nor acknowledges his former belief, as he used to do, while at the same time he fails to discover true ones, is not that flattering life the only one to   539
which he will be likely to attach himself?

It is.

In other words, he will appear, I suppose, to have abandoned his loyalty, and to have become lawless.

There cannot be a doubt of it.

Well now, is not this a condition of the student who takes up arguments, and, as I said just now, does he not deserve to be treated with much sympathy?

Yes, and with pity too, he replied.

Then in order that you may not have to feel this pity for those men of thirty, must you not use every precaution when you turn them to arguments?

Certainly.

b And will it not be one great precaution to forbid their meddling with it while young? For I suppose you have noticed, that whenever boys taste arguments for the first time, they pervert it into an amusement, and always employ it for purposes of contradiction, and imitate in their own persons the refutations of those who refuted them, delighting, like puppies, in pulling and tearing to pieces with argument anyone who comes near them.

They do, to an extravagant extent.

Hence, when they have experienced many triumphs and many defeats, they fall, quickly c and vehemently, into an utter disbelief of their former beliefs; and thereby both they and the whole of philosophy have been slanderous in the eyes of the world.

That is perfectly true.

The man of more advanced years, on the contrary, will not let himself be led away by such madness; but will imitate those who are resolved to discuss and examine truth, rather than d those who play at contradiction for amusement; and, as a consequence of his being more sensible, will increase instead of diminishing, the general respect for the pursuit.

You are right.

Again, were we not admonishing precaution throughout, when we said some time back, that those natures whom we have partake of arguments, must be stable and orderly, in opposition to the present system, which allows anybody, however unfit, to enter the field?

Certainly we were.

Would it suffice, then, for the acquisition of argument, that a man should continue constantly and strenuously devoted to the study, resigning every other pursuit for it, just as, in its turn, he resigned everything for gymnastics, during a period twice as long as that which he spent on bodily gymnastics?

e Do you mean six years, or four?

It does not matter much, I replied, say five. After this you will have to send them down again into the cave we described, and compel them to take commands in war, and to hold such offices as befit young men, that they will not be inferior to others in experience. And here again you must put them to the test, to see whether they will continue steadfast notwith-
540 standing every seduction, or whether possibly they may be a little shaken.

And how long a time do you assign for this?

Fifteen years, I replied. Then, as soon as they are fifty years old, those who have passed safely through all temptations, and who have won every distinction in every branch whether of action or of knowledge, must be forthwith introduced to their final task, and must be compelled to lift up the eye of the soul, and fix it upon that which gives light to all things; and having seen the good itself, they must take it as a paradigm, to be copied in that work of
b ordering their city and their fellow-citizens that is to occupy each in turn during the rest of life; and though they are to spend most of their time in philosophy, yet each, when his turn comes, is to devote himself to the hard duties of public life, and rule for their city's sake, not as a desirable, but as an unavoidable occupation. And thus having educated others like themselves to fill their place as guardians of the city, they will depart and take up their abode in the islands of the blessed. And the city will put up monuments to their memory at public
c expense, and offer sacrifices to them, as demigods, if the Pythian oracle will authorize it, or at least as highly-favored and godlike men.

Like a sculptor, Socrates, you have fashioned ruling men who are beautiful in every way.

Say ruling women too, Glaucon. For do not suppose that my remarks were intended to apply at all more to men than to women, so long as we can find women with adequate natures.

You are right, he said, if they are to share with the men everything in common equally, according to our account.

Well then, do you agree that what we have said about the city and the regime is not a mere prayer, but, though full of difficulties, possible in one way, and only one, which, as we have said, requires that one, if not more, of the true philosophers come to power in a city, and despise the honors of the present day, in the belief that they are mean and worthless; and that, deeply impressed with the supreme importance of right and of the honors to be derived from it, and regarding justice as the highest and most binding of all obligations, he shall, as the special servant and admirer of justice, provide for his own city.

How is that to be done?

All who are above ten years old in the city must be dispatched into the country, and their children must be taken and brought up removed from that disposition which they now have in common with their parents, and instead must be raised in their own manners and laws, the nature of which we have described above; and, tell me, will not this be the quickest and easiest way to enable a city and a constitution, such as we have represented, to establish itself and prosper, and at the same time to make happy the nation in which it has taken root?

Yes, quite so, he replied, and I believe, Socrates, you have stated correctly the means that would be employed, if such a regime were ever realized.

And have we not by this time discussed this city enough, and the individual that resembles it? For I presume it is also clear what sort of person we shall expect him to be.

It is clear, he replied; and the present inquiry is, I believe, concluded.

# Afterword

## Robert S. Brumbaugh*

### I. Platonic Origins of Educational Thought

Plato's dialogues, because of their extraordinary quality of raising the right questions and identifying the important ideas relevant to their answers, have had more impact and influence on Western philosophy and Western educational theory than any other writings in these fields. Plato's works offer, therefore, a natural beginning for our discussion of the questions great philosophers have asked and the answers they proposed when they turned their attention to education. But it would certainly be a mistake to think of Plato solely in historical terms, for the Platonic dialogues are more widely read than any other philosophic works. From high school to graduate school or adult discussions of great books, most Americans make their first acquaintance with philosophy by way of Plato.

Plato's ideas on the subject of education not only are found in his text as historical facts, but are, many of them, living doctrines in constant use. In some cases they have become so much a part of our educational thinking and planning that we do not even see sensible alternatives to them. The use of discussion method as part of instruction; the idea of a university as the highest point of a public system of educational institutions, primarily directed toward teaching and research; the division of levels of schools and curricula into elementary, secondary, and advanced; coeducation; the combination of physical with mental "education" on the pre-research level—all of these ideas, as well as many more, originated as Platonic concepts.

We are thus reminded not only that Plato was an unsurpassed philosopher and a brilliant author but that his practical vocation in life was that of an educator. Plato's stature as a philosopher and his genius for practical embodiment of ideas in educational programs and institutions place him in the first rank in the history of education; he knows from experience what he is talking about, he cares about it, and he proposes to do something original with education....

---

* Robert S. Brumbaugh was Professor of Philosophy at Yale University.

## II. Plato's Philosophy

Plato's philosophy brings together three important themes. The first is his view of philosophy as shared inquiry, as a search for self-knowledge and self-realization. He had been convinced by his teacher and hero, Socrates, that the human self is a far more mysterious thing than anyone up to that time had suspected. Plato's early philosophical writings are all dialogues, in which Socrates talks with leading politicians, educators, and citizens of his day about problems of human nature and human society. The second leading theme in Plato's philosophy is the discovery of form. The mathematicians of ancient Greece had developed an appreciation of the ability to reason "formally": to abstract and generalize, to talk about numbers and shapes "in general." Applying mathematics revealed many quantitative laws and patterns in nature and art and seemed to promise a whole new world of scientific discovery and precision. The third major theme in Plato's thought, mainly his own discovery, is that of the relation of form to value. We can see what this means when we look at a Platonic dialogue as an attempt to present some insight that is true, important, and beautiful. There has seldom been, in Western literature, a more meticulous attention to "literary form," in the interest of creating value. Socrates was concerned with ethical and psychological questions in his later life, and no doubt it was he who caused Plato to look for the relation of value to form. But it was Plato's contribution to recognize that ideals, goals, and criteria are ends to which form, in the sense of definite structure, is a means, and that ideals actually operate as causes in nature and human life. Plato saw that neither evaluating something nor describing it can be carried very far without the other. As a result he refused to separate questions of "fact" from those of "value."

*Inquiry*

Plato learned two main ideas from Socrates. One concerned the difficulty and complexity of self-knowledge. Socrates was condemned to death in 399 B.C. for refusing to stop his public inquiry into moral, social, and political matters. He embarrassed his persecutors by refusing to escape when he had a chance, drank the prescribed fatal cup of hemlock, and died. He was martyr to a frightened and stupid "people's government" that had little use for individual conscience. Plato, on the verge of a career as a young politician, was disillusioned by the unthinking conservatism that led to Socrates' death. He turned to education as a means of instilling the passion for self-knowledge in the young citizens of Athens.

*Form*

A second idea, less personally vivid but equally exciting, was the discovery we have mentioned, that one could study the formal features of things, apart from the things themselves. A hundred years before Plato, Pythagoras had begun to develop the science of "pure" mathematics, as opposed to accounting and computation. We can deal with the number two itself without limiting this concept to a pair of fish or of countesses. Again, when we talk about "triangles," we recognize triangularity as a common form even though different *instances* of triangularity may be equilateral, isosceles, and scalene and may be made of chalk lines, stylus marks on wax, or bronze strips. . . .

Plato's forms are the characteristics that give things their identities. Two chairs, for example, share the property or form of chairness; this is why we call them by the same name, differentiating them from, say, bookcases. Just as we recognize that two mathematical triangles have the same "form," which is common to both, a Platonist thinks of two persons or chairs as having a common "form" that makes them alike. These forms are not things in the sense of material objects in space and time; they are rather sets of general characteristics, which do not change. We cannot see or touch them, but we can recognize them by using our minds to compare and classify and generalize the concrete things about us that we *can* touch and see. Plato intends to say that the forms are actually present in things and therefore are not simply arbitrary ideas in human minds. I think and say that two chairs are alike because there is something essential and common in the chairs themselves which makes them alike. . . .

Their mathematical ancestry suggests to us that Platonic forms may be thought of as structures; however, they are more than structures. The forms are also, in his view, ideals and criteria of value. Some chairs are better, as chairs, than others. Thus we might say, "That's a real chair," or "That's not really a chair," to indicate that although a common structure is recognizable, there are degrees of realizing the form of "chairness," and these degrees are degrees of worth. One of the most important things to notice about the Platonic forms is that they are related to each other in a definite system. Some forms include others: the form of "furniture," for example, includes the form of "chair." This means that if anything has the form of chair, it also has the form of furniture. Some forms exclude others: odd and even, for example. Everything that has any form must also have all the other forms that include the one it has, and cannot have any of the other forms that are excluded by its own. Reasoning and logic consist in tracing these systematic connections among forms themselves; they apply to actual experience because each form, as it is realized, brings with it all of its systematic relations to the others. The forms are ordered in a rational system, which does not change, and we can "reason" by tracing their relations. For example, if the form of "furniture" includes the form of "chair," we recognize that all chairs are furniture. In the same way, if "number" is divided into "odd" and "even," and "odd" excludes "two," then "two" must be an even number.

### Value

Like the mathematicians, Socrates had directed his inquiries toward finding some common nature present in the objects of human knowledge, but Socrates chose as his objects the study of the things that men live by: instances of courage, temperance, or friendship. Plato, carrying on Socrates' concern with the human self, turned his attention to the underlying forms which are the causes of value.

Value seems always to require a form which is the basis of coherent order: Beauty requires organic pattern, virtue requires a harmonious relation of man's powers and faculties, truth requires a systematic coherence of steps in a proof or inquiry. These forms—virtue, truth, and beauty—therefore themselves are instances of a still higher form. The highest form in his system Plato calls the "good," the essence of all that is right, proper, and orderly. This form must be, in some measure, present in all things, giving them that value which lures us into wanting to possess them or to know about them. . . .

We always want to know *why* things have the shapes they do. In the case of the chair, and other artificial things, their "good" lies in how well they perform a certain useful function, and so we can relate them to the user and to their maker's intention. In inanimate nature—the world of crystals, stones, and stars—we wonder why the same patterns repeat so often: The reason a modern scientist gives is that patterns in nature tend toward those with minimum free energy; that is, they tend always to have a maximum symmetry, stability, and balance (crystals are a particularly good example). A Pythagorean scientist would regard this selection of stable shapes as involving a kind of goal or desire, an innate natural tendency in things. A modern philosopher might be willing to agree that we can *describe* it as a search by each thing for an arrangement and identity that will be stable. Similarly, with animals there is a certain nonreflective desire for immortality manifested in the instinct for preservation of the species. There is, even on a low level of life, an innate drive toward self-realization. In man, there emerges a vision of ideals, a drive toward self-transcendence.

On every level, knowledge of the goals of the things we encounter helps us to explain and understand their structures. Structures are the fixities and finalities of things, whether they be the arch that the bridge is, or the oak that the acorn will become. They stay just what they are, and they bring a system of limits and relations to the particulars they characterize. But if we were to restrict our idea of "forms" to structures detached from value or purpose, they would become unimportant and unintelligible. The conclusion drawn by Plato was that values are objective and knowable forms and that the realm of the ideal is in fact causally related to the realm of the actual, so that we cannot really separate "description" and "evaluation." in greater or less degree, in all actual "organization men." All valuation requires a standard, and most standards are ideals.

Plato's philosophy is also a formalism, for the ideals are themselves forms. They are not mere targets toward which things tend or aim. They are present in actual things, giving them the definite structure that the things have. Every actual thing incarnates many forms. Some of the forms, however, are not *essential* to the thing, that is, they do not give it its most important identity. A chair, for example, may embody rectangularity and brownness, but neither of these gives it its identity as a chair; that is given by the form of chairness. The same thing holds true of human nature; we should be able, if Plato is right, to recognize an essential form of man, which represents the true goals of life. According to Platonic doctrine, then, the problem of education, in whatever field, is that of bringing a latent awareness of ideal forms—a latent awareness which every man has—to as clear and high a level of realization as one's talents will permit. The happiness both of society and of the individual will, ultimately, depend on our success in getting and communicating a clear vision of essential form.

## III. The Divided Line: Knowledge and the Curriculum

From this summary of leading themes in Plato's overall philosophy, it will be clear that the attempt to isolate a "philosophy of education" from his dialogues is a difficult enterprise. Plato would agree completely with Dewey's comment that philosophy of education is the same thing as philosophy itself, broadly interpreted.

Accordingly, we are lucky that Plato, in his *Republic*, gives us . . . a treatment of the theory of education in considerable depth. It exemplifies a method of teaching, develops a theory of knowledge, outlines an educational curriculum, locates education in its social role, and gives an analysis of human nature. We will follow the method of the *Republic* in our own presentation, supplementing it by the special treatment of motivation, inquiry, and discussion offered in Plato's earlier dialogues, particularly the *Meno*.

In the *Republic* Socrates leads a discussion of "justice." What is a "just" man? What is a "just" society? Why are they both called "just"? In Book vi he explains that in a good society policy must be made by legislators who really know what their aims are, rather than by the practical "political technicians" of the day. As part of this explanation, Socrates asks Glaucon, Plato's brother, to visualize a vertical line divided into four parts, each representing a different degree of "clearness of knowledge." . . . We will discuss them from bottom to top, in order.

### *Eikasia*—Hearsay and Fiction

The bottom segment of Plato's line is "knowledge" that rests primarily on images and imagination. It is a world of story, myth, hearsay, and conjecture. The term suggests a kind of picture thinking, and evidently Plato has some notion that to "know" in this way is nothing more than "having a picture in my mind." *Eikasia* has a personal subjective quality, a vividness, and a romance to its imagery. For example, really to "see" what an abstract argument or proposition means to me as a unique individual, a "myth" is essential. But obviously this kind of thinking, for all its authenticity and color, is wholly unreliable when we compare it to the common-sense world of objects and techniques in space and time; a carpenter, not a poet, knows how to make a table. *Eikasia* has the lowest position on the divided line because we are arranging kinds of knowing in an order of clarity, objectivity, and genuine explanatory power. All the same, images and myths, imagination and fancy, are not to be scorned. Plato himself ends the *Republic* with a myth presenting his beliefs concerning human immortality, thus showing the need for imagery even at a very high level of understanding.

### *Pistis*—Grounded Belief and "Know-How"

The second level of knowing is called *pistis*, testable belief as opposed to individual imagination. This is the stage of technique, of familiarity with how things behave. *Pistis* refers to a "public" world. Plato illustrates the difference between these two levels in the analogy of "The Cave." Here he pictures the bulk of mankind underground, fixed in their seats, watching the play of shadows at the end of a cave. For some the only reality lies in these images. Others are able to turn and see the actual puppets whose firelit images are thrown on the cave wall. The puppets stand for the actual world, the shadows stand for the partial representation of that world which most men confine themselves to. Even this actual world is an incomplete vision of reality, however, which is only revealed to the philosopher who leaves the cave and stands at last confronting the sun, the source and sustainer of all that is. The sun, in this tale, represents the form of all forms, the good. We will see in a moment where "the good" stands in the ladder of knowledge.

*Pistis* is essentially know-how. It is what the mechanic has that Jones does not. . . . Most practical knowledge is of this sort: "If I do so and so, then such and such happens." Plato calls this practical knack *empeirea*. We get our word "empirical" from this Greek term, and we use it to refer to knowledge gained from experience. It is at the level of *pistis* that we first encounter the idea that if something is true, it is true for all. "True for me" can only make sense at the level of individual imagination, *eikasia*.

### *Dianoia*—Generalization and Knowing Why

There is a third kind of knowledge, clearer than knowing *that* and knowing *how*. This Plato calls *dianoia*, which is a kind of knowing *why*. *Dianoia* is the kind of knowledge a scientist has of my television set, as opposed to that of the competent repairman. The repairman has a circuit diagram and tests each element and connection to see how it is working; why it works that way is clear only when we see the behavior of each part as a special case of general physical theory. Mathematics is an ideal example of dianoetic explanation: Experiments, from now until eternity, might well make us *believe* that there is only one even prime number, and give us a technique for determining whether any given number was even and prime, but it takes a different kind of explanation to show that this must be true in every case, and why. The *why* here is given by deducing the solution to our question from the very general definitions and operations of the number system, which are found by "generalization" or "recognition of a form." *Dianoia* recognizes the unchanging types and laws that limit and control the behavior of actual objects and processes in the commonsense world of public space and time. The forms, as we have said, are the causes both of definiteness and order and also of value. *Dianoia* concentrates on the forms in the first of these roles. It finds general laws and descriptions but cannot, with its formal method, resolve questions of evaluation. For this a still more adequate recognition of "form" must be required.

### *Noesis*—Tested Theory and Evaluation

The fourth segment of Plato's line is called *noesis*; this is the knowledge that has true certainty. This fourth kind of knowledge includes the certainty that we know, that our combination of theory and data has produced an answer that is a good one. Since *dianoia* is, as we have just seen, a method of explanation by deduction from general hypotheses, there can be more than one hypothesis that will "explain" a particular situation. If it is hard to imagine this in arithmetic, it is certainly easy in social science: Different presupposed definitions of human nature could all have some explanatory power. One task of knowledge on this highest level is to examine these explanatory presuppositions. We want the best hypotheses. We want to know whether or not the hypothesis explains all the relevant facts it is supposed to explain. At this level we pursue ideals of clarity, universality, and simplicity, which are higher aims than that of just letting appearance speak for itself, or letting experience speak for itself, or even putting up a plausible theory. The whole explanatory enterprise is dominated by a desire to get the best possible understanding from a personal point of view, from a practical public point of view, from a theoretical point of view. It thus ends with an evaluation, and Plato puts the form of "the good," the criterion we have been using without clear awareness of it, at the very top of the line in his diagram.

### *To Agathon*—the Form of the Good

The highest object of *noesis* in Plato's system is the form of the good, standing at the summit of the divided line. This is the form which is responsible for the value and attraction of the other forms, and which therefore holds together all of reality in systematic interconnection. . . .

The account of the divided line brings out, in its discussion of degrees and dimensions of knowledge, the complexity of the human self and of the world we inhabit. The human self is at once a partially separate, changing, unique individual in space and time and a timeless being able to know laws that are universal, values that do not change. Our existence is a complex interplay of transitory adventure and awareness of eternal ideals, which we can partially realize.

There is an immediate implication for educational practice and educational theory. It would be a serious mistake to omit any dimension of human existence from either. Education, to be realistic, must combine the values of adventure, social activity, intellectual discipline, and vision of a moral ideal. For all of these are aspects of the human self, and all are parts of our cosmic environment, causally related to each other. . . .

## IV. Motivation and the Method of Inquiry

. . . What is an educational experience like, from the learner's point of view? Is there a need for engagement in a quest for self-improvement, a genuine and absorbed desire to know, if education is to make the student better? Must learning be by grasping truths for oneself? Or should we settle for a student who pays attention, retains information, practices exercises, and knows where to find references and authorities that give information? The way we measure what degree of educational effectiveness we have attained, the way we grade students, select materials, and conduct classes, depends, finally, on the way we picture "learning" as it goes on in the mind of the student. The professional teachers of Plato's time, the Sophists, held learning to be mainly a retention of information and the mastery of rhetoric in using information. The benefit for the student was instrumental, as a way to wealth or power. The student's state of mind was that of attentive memory, patient drill, for the sake of an external goal in the future. Socrates disagreed. Aren't there aspirations and ideals of the student's inner self? Isn't self-realization intrinsically rewarding, without external prizes for motivation?

Socrates had been confused in the minds of some Athenians with the Sophists; Plato disabuses them in a brilliant dialogue which centers on the opposition of the two ideas of education. The *Meno*, which we analyze in some detail, is named for its respondent, a talented young man who has had the benefit of upper-class education at the hands of the Sophist, Gorgias. Visiting Athens, Meno encounters Socrates, and it becomes obvious that his Sophistication has not made him a really educated person. Plato describes Meno's changes in feeling as he tries to "learn" for himself, instead of merely remembering, thereby establishing motivation as coming either from within or not at all.

It is obvious at the outset of Plato's dialogue that Meno has not been taught to be a good human being. He cannot generalize. He expects Socrates to tell him the answer to his question "Can virtue be taught?" He becomes discouraged and abusive when Socrates offers to help him inquire into the question. Yet he is clever, wealthy, unusually attractive: he is not unpromising material. "How can we possibly inquire into something neither of us knows?" asks Meno, when Socrates will not give a simple answer to his question. "Even if we found it, we wouldn't know we had the answer!" And, indeed, if "knowledge" were only items of information in reference works, this would be true. Socrates responds with a myth, an experiment, and a general statement of the method of inquiry. There is a myth, he tells Meno, that all knowledge is recollection; the soul, "before it was a man," knew the natures and truths of all things, and has within it latent memories. When we inquire, we are trying to become clear about something which we already know. But it takes an effort to "remember," and unless some problem makes us want to recover this inner insight, we do not make the effort to inquire. There is, then, no way to impart knowledge mechanically, by filling a mind with facts as though it were a storage bin. The student must provide the motivation, and take an active part in order to "recall" any knowledge with an inner conviction that it is true. Socrates himself will not argue that all the details of this myth are true, but he is ready to defend the conclusion that we will be wiser and better if we do inquire than if we do not.

Plato's use of this myth in the *Meno* is a popular presentation of a point that is essential to his educational theory. The latent power of the soul to remember truths it has already seen corresponds to the mind's power to discern unchanging forms in the changing world it confronts. The comparison to trying to remember brings out well the feeling that a learning situation always has. For the forms are realized in things in different degrees of exactness and adequacy, and are "seen" by the human observer with more or less clarity, depending on ability and training. "Knowing" is not, in Plato's view, a simple either-or relation, with the only alternatives "knowing" something or "not knowing" it. On the contrary, all of us "know" the forms in a dim and confused way—it is because we have some notion at the outset that there is a form of "virtue," for example, that we are motivated to inquire about it, and that we have a definite direction in our inquiry. Whether and how far Plato believed this doctrine of recollection literally is an interesting scholarly problem but irrelevant to the apparently novel and certainly correct conclusion that he drew: namely, that learning must begin with the student's desire to know; that it requires active attention for the student to have the feeling of "insight" or "recognition" that comes with "seeing" an answer; and that the basic capacities for educational progress must be present in the learner.

Meno "somehow likes what Socrates is saying." To convince him further, Socrates performs an experiment which has become a classical example of teaching method. A slave boy, who knows no geometry but thinks that doubling its sides will double the area of a square, is brought by leading questions to recognize that this is not the answer, then to "remember" that the square on the diagonal will be double the original square. The surprising thing about this performance, particularly for a modern teacher or student who has not appreciated Plato's intended Socrates-Gorgias contrast, is Meno's bewildered assurance that he has watched closely and seen that Socrates *has not "taught" the boy anything*. We feel that Meno was tricked, for Socrates certainly has used "leading questions" repeatedly, and diagrams as well. But the fact is that in Meno's limited sense of "teaching" as authoritative, external *instruction*, Socrates has not taught the boy the answer. The method Meno has in mind obviously won't account for the result; he may still distrust the myth of recollection, but he will have to admit that a student challenged to think can learn by directed inquiry.

Socrates then suggests that he and Meno return to their question of what virtue is, but Meno insists that instead they return to *his* question, and ask if it can be taught. The method Socrates uses is "the method of hypothesis": given a problem, we see what general assumptions would lead to a solution; then we deduce and check the consequences of such generalizations. For example, if virtue were knowledge, it could be taught, and since virtue is good, any person who knew it would also embody it and therefore certainly would be willing to teach it. We thus find that, if virtue is knowledge, there should be teachers of it. Suppose that teaching is either by precept or by example. Gorgias and his student Meno are evident proof that the leading Sophists do not succeed by the method of precept: Gorgias, indeed, as Meno recalls, thinks none of them teaches virtue at all.

Here Plato has Anytus, the democratic leader who inspired the execution of Socrates, enter the discussion, for Anytus believes virtue is taught by example. Just as a child learns to speak Greek from the community, without a special tutor, so young Athenians learn to be good by following the example of gentlemen, and of the great men of Athens. Socrates doubts this. For example, Pericles was not able to make either his sons or the Athenian public good through his example. If he had been, and was a good man himself, clearly the Athenian public would not have rejected his leadership after his many years in office! Anytus withdraws angrily, and Socrates and Meno are left with an inconclusive end to their discussion.

It is not hard to see that Plato intended to demonstrate for us that virtue can be taught neither by precept nor by example, but by the method used by Socrates. For during their conversation Meno does indeed seem to become (if only temporarily) wiser, more energetic, less vain, and "better."

Plato himself never forgot the educational significance of this Socratic discovery of freedom of the self, with its implication that true learning is founded on motivation. Throughout his work he indicates that the use of compulsion, pain, and fear as external motivation in education is immeral and worse than ineffectual, because it makes students dislike learning. For young students, education should begin as directed play. The suggestions for introducing youngsters to arithmetic, written into the educational statutes of the *Laws*, sound almost like a contemporary first-grade or kindergarten program. But the aim of secondary and higher education is excellence in the appreciation of form, i.e., the permanent laws and structures that govern individual persons and things.

Socrates' discovery that teaching must begin in the accepted challenge to inquire is one of his lasting contributions to modern educational thought. The Platonic myths give a vivid picture of the love of inquiry as arising from a sense of incompleteness and desire. Plato envisions the soul in the context of a world that stretches far beyond our immediate environing space and time, a self which recognizes its freedom and responsibility for choice. . . .

## V. Education and Society

In the present section we are concerned with a "public" or "social" self, and with "education" as a community affair, aimed at citizenship, technique, and social adaptation. Can we take such an objective view without denying the importance and right of each individual to a private self, and his own quest for excellence? Does the shaping of "the organization man" necessarily crush the soul beneath a weight of social pressure? For Plato this issue was not merely an abstract question but a vital personal one. As a young man he had seen his own relatives set up an interim dictatorship and become so power-mad that he indignantly refused their invitation to join them. He had seen the Athenian state under a shaky democratic government try and execute Socrates for insisting on the need to ask questions, even if the answers were not always the conventional patriotic ones the government wanted to hear. Did the Athenian city-state have either to fall into absolute obedience to the whim of the majority or else to become the scene of a struggle between powerful minorities?

Plato's effort to solve this problem is not simple and it does not always match our own ideas. The problem can be stated in a simple way, however. We strive, as a society, for the best possible state. As individuals, we strive for personal excellence. Must there be a conflict? Clearly there was, in the case of Socrates. What the state thought it most wanted of its citizens, unquestioning acceptance of its rule, was exactly counter to the life of inquiry necessary to an individual's self-development. So the state executed its finest citizen.

The Greek citizen or politician was even more committed than we are today to the notion that the function of society is to transmit tradition, to teach useful skills, and to shape character, so that younger students may fit in with the economic needs and political "common sense" of the community. Education as training in the interest of society, as a social institution less concerned with the demands of the ideal of human life than with the need for social stability, was part of the common sense of the day. In fact, "the state" made a powerful claim on the individual, since effective life in a community was understood to be a necessary part of civilized living. Moreover, loyalty to the state was one way in which, by identifying himself with something larger and more enduring, the individual could reach beyond his own finite life toward immortality. Yet "the state," as administered by a dictatorship of influential Athenian conservatives, Athenian democratic politicians, the military in Sparta, the dictator in Syracuse, or the Chamber of Commerce in Corinth, would certainly neither produce nor tolerate a truly excellent human individual. Was it a necessary consequence of society's nature that state and individual could not realize excellence together?

Only a clear analysis of the forms of state and individual could decide. In the *Republic* Plato gives his answer to this problem: The excesses of existing governments and the demand for mediocrity as the touchstone of "good social adjustment" in the local societies were not inevitable, but the result of unclear vision and errors in judgment as to the nature of the public good. The situation was correctable, Plato argued. By a close attention to education, the society could further the virtue of its citizens, and they in turn could modify its traditions and institutions for the better.

Education is meant to serve both the state and the person. To the person it owes the opportunity for the best realization of one's abilities. To the state it has the responsibility of developing citizens trained and happy in the roles whereby they carry on community life. A just state is one in which these roles are carried out by properly trained and motivated individuals. A just person is one in whom the various parts of the soul, the inner life, operate in the same harmonious way. Justice (the closest translation we can get for the Greek *dikē*) in both the individual and the state is the aim of education. Justice is "*each part performing its proper share*"; it is the ideal "form" for both the constitution of the state and the constitution of the individual. But, as we have seen, a "form" is capable of different degrees and, indeed, of different kinds, of approximation. We share a common "human nature," but there are individual differences—Plato thinks they may well be hereditary—which mean that our interests and aptitudes will differ. Could there be such a relation between state and individual that the social function of each person was exactly the one found most rewarding and freely chosen?

This depends, of course, on the relation of the ranges of individual differences and of specialized social functions. Plato analyzes the human self into three distinct "parts" (drives, dispositions, or interests). They are distinct, though *not separate*, for they can come into opposition with one another in the same situation. One of these "parts of the soul" is appetite; a second is "spirit," which we can think of as "ambition" plus a desire for competition and overt action; "reason" is the third. It is within every one's power to lead an intelligent life, not allowing desire for fame or fortune to run beyond all limits, creating inevitable unhappiness. But, given their physiques and innate tendencies of character, some will find their satisfaction in competitions and contests, others will rather prefer craftmanship or farming, while a third group will choose a life of intellectual inquiry and research. If we think of social "classes" in terms of function rather than accidental characteristics, such as property or family background, it turns out that there are also three such functional "classes" in a good state. There must be producers, protectors, and directors. Plato can now offer a solution to his problem, though it is one that runs radically counter to Greek thought and practice of the time: When each individual has a place in the social class which one's interests and talents match, then justice is possible at the same time for the person as self and for the society as organic whole. The details involved in applying this theory were too complex and novel for Plato to develop thoroughly, but the *Republic* had done what it was meant to, and proved that, while the state is a super-organism with its own goal and individuality, there was no necessary conflict between the society and the individual. In a state which knew how to use talent for the general good, a truly good person would not be executed but would be a useful and respected citizen.

To meet the needs of the three classes, a system of public education would have to be devised. The aims and content of this educational scheme occupy the central part of the *Republic*.

The *Republic* is thus the result of a critique of the idea of education as social adaptation (the conventional view) or as life adjustment (the Sophists' position). In a series of earlier dialogues between Plato's Socrates and the various leading Sophists and statesmen of the day, Plato had argued that adaptation should be realistic—and, in Plato's philosophy, the forms are a part of reality. Neither uncritical preservation of convention nor powerful control of tools for manipulating public opinion takes account of the true ends of state and individual. The "finishing school" approach of the Sophists, teaching graces and skills to an economic elite, seemed to Plato very unrealistic in its notion of adaptation.

Education and applied intelligence can modify and serve society but such service can be exacted only where the social gains lead to the individual's self-betterment as well. Life gains in vividness and authenticity from being lived in a *polis*. We share experience with our friends, argue in the assembly, applaud in the theater, march in the processions, and have conversations over a bowl of wine. This can enhance, not destroy, our individuality, in Plato's view. He would not understand an idea of education that posited an antagonism between self-realization and social effectiveness: the two are compatible in principle, and in practice can become so if we attend to improving education as a way of improving society.

What conclusions follow from this philosophic analysis? First, since education plays such a central part in society and since it is through education alone that individual ability and social function can be made to coincide, society should establish free public schools. This unprecedented notion, along with his insistence on the equality of women, alone would mark Plato as the great educational revolutionist of his time. Second, the Director of Education must be one of the most carefully chosen and respected officers of the state. In the *Republic*, the two tasks of the most talented and educated guardian class are legislation and education; the teacher and the legislator are the twin guardians of society. Third, socialization need not be destructive of individuality. Practice in social action will teach certain habits of cooperation and conformity, and perhaps in any actual state that Plato knew, those habits were fatal to self-realization. This, he says in one of the letters he wrote late in his life, is why he has not been an active politician, but an educator. But there is no necessity that forever keeps the good person and the good citizen from being the same, and perhaps this goal will be realized—if not in Athens, soon, then perhaps in some remoter time, in some more distant, foreign country.

We may disagree with Plato's view that a culture or a community is a kind of living reality. We may think that the conditions of modern civilization make socialization more opposed to individuality than an ancient Greek would have imagined. But we can hardly deny that some form of social effectiveness is a legitimate aim of education.

## VI. The Concrete Curriculum

. . . In the present section we will consider the subject matter of an ideal curriculum. This consideration emphasizes the *structure*—definite method, content, and order—of education, looking at the form of education from the standpoint of *dianoia*, the third level of the divided line. Here we expect to find Plato treating the problems, and perhaps sharing the insights, of liberal arts humanism.

The schools in the *Republic* are of three kinds. The elementary school provides a basic general education for everyone. A secondary school offers a more rigorous physical and intellectual training for students with special aptitude for and interest in military, civil service, research, and legislative work. And a center of higher education continues the training of a more highly selected group of students, who will become research scientists, educators, and legislators.

Elementary education has as its content *musikē*, a study of literature, music, and civics, and *gymnastikē*, athletics and the dance. Its aim is to elicit love of grace and beauty, to develop the temperance of the student. "Temperance" is the virtue of moderation and self-control: the recognition that excess in pursuit of pleasure or of wealth is not only bad taste but self-defeating. If we cannot convince our producers and consumers that living graciously is different from luxury and conspicuous waste, creation of new wants and a constant desire to "have more" will make everyone in the community dissatisfied with an individual share of comfort and commodities. The result will be to upset the economic sanity of the state.

The aim of the elementary level of schooling is to teach aesthetic and ethical value. This is to be taught by practice of graceful action and by study of great works of literature which combine excellence of style and form with plots and characters that excite the student's admiration and respect. Our students learn in part by imitation and inspiration: putting themselves in the place of tragic heroes, of their parents, of great athletes. And the tendency of actions to produce habits means that these students will grow to resemble the things they are imitating. This, Plato believes, imposes a need for the strictest selection and censorship. Far from being the humanist who believes that universality of appeal selects and preserves the best that has come from the past, Plato devotes two books of the *Republic* to criticizing Homer, whose epics were taught in elementary schools at that time as the supreme example of literature, and also as a civics text; Homer's *Iliad* played a role comparable to that of our Bible. The trouble with Homer is that he is able to persuade us, by the beauty of his poetry, that Achilles is a hero worthy of imitation. But Achilles, looked at through the more objective eyes of a Platonic ruler, is often hysterical, vindictive, greedy, undisciplined, and unreliable! The "idea of a gentleman" of the Homeric age was, Plato saw, unsuitable and ridiculous as a model for society of Plato's day.

Although he is willing to take issue with the most universally accepted humanistic value-judgment of the day when he finds Homer unsuitable reading for students, Plato's awareness of the influence of environment on character and his appreciation of form do lead him into an extreme conservatism. He does not want his students to have any occasion for first-hand imitation of intemperance and illiberality, and he supposes that the directors of education can select an environment in which there will be no such temptation or opportunity. From the discoveries in music and poetry, in dancing and craftsmanship, of the past, he proposes to choose only the very best, and by rigid censorship to exclude whatever fails to embody the very highest excellence. By "best" he means *both* most satisfying aesthetically and most noble in ethical effect. Censorship, whether we call it by this name or simply talk about selecting educational materials, is a controversial topic, even now. There are few people who do not believe in some censorship. Shall we have fifth-graders read Henry Miller? The question of censorship is never one of "whether"; it is one of "how much." Like all modern psychologists, Plato believes that the early formative influences are the critical ones. Taking the whole picture into account, however, we feel it necessary to say that Plato here plays the role of classical humanist so vigorously that he is led into philosophic inconsistency. Modern humanism holds that we must not only respect the discoveries of form that are a high point of the past but also see that new forms are needed as culture goes on.

The secondary school in the *Republic* is designed to test and train the intelligence of its students by "ten years of pure mathematics as a mental discipline." (In its context, since Plato seems to have been making several points by exaggeration, one is inclined to take both the ten-year period and the absolute purity of this prescription with several grains of salt, though there is no doubt that the recommendation of mathematics as training in reasoning is quite seriously meant.) They are to learn to look for the permanent patterns and forms by progressive study of arithmetic, plane geometry, solid geometry, theoretical astronomy, and harmonics (ratio theory). This training is intended to develop appreciation of truth as a value: precision, rigor, and consistency in the art of thinking.

From the brief description of the next level of education, it is clear that a primary reason for this discipline is for training in a general method of thinking, which must become automatic and ingrained before the student can go on to a higher education. No discipline should be spared in the training of those on whom the greatest responsibilities will rest. Executives and legislators must use intelligence; they cannot trust to mere guesswork or short-term "savvy" in their political actions. . . . For the students who do not go on to higher education, and who are to be the army, civil service, public engineers, and police force, the training is not useless, for their problems are precisely those of applying legislative rules, given to them as axioms, to particular situations, without contradictions or inconsistencies in the deduced application. This notion of teaching a method of thought is an attractive idea, and one that has enlisted many defenders in later educational theory. But it supposes that study of empty pattern will be interesting, applicable to life, and automatically transferable; and experience has tended to cast doubt on each of these claims. . . .

The higher education, for future legislators, will consist of "dialectic." Dialectic is a term with a varied history of meanings, and Plato himself uses it sometimes in the informal sense of directed conversation, sometimes as naming a practical method of inquiry, sometimes for logical precision in defining and classifying. Glaucon asks Socrates to tell him what "dialectic" is, but the answer is rather sketchy. However, if all students are to pursue this as their single course, it is clear that Plato's idea of "subject matter" on this level is not at all our own notion of departmentalization within the college and division into professional schools within the university. We do get several pieces of information about the intended course, and by putting them together we can see why Plato left the details so incomplete in his discussion of curriculum.

It seems evident that Plato here thinks of dialectic as an application of the clear, logical methods of mathematics to the tangled phenomena of human nature and conduct. The result would be, if this program were carried out, an inquiry into such concepts as "justice," on the pattern of the "divided line." . . .

Beyond skill in dialectic lies the vision of the good, the end of all philosophic understanding. The idea of the good permeates all the levels of understanding, providing them with that worth which lures us to self-realization by our knowledge of them. Plato says of this form of all forms that it is like the sun. The sun is the ultimate source of light by which actual things are seen—that is, are known and apprehended. It also sustains them in their very existence. So also the good is what illuminates what we *understand*, and the very reality of these things is dependent upon it.

"The good" is one of Plato's most difficult ideas, and volumes have been written about it. For our purposes it stands as the apex of value, upon which all other value depends. The educational development of people depends on how far their talents and motivation carry them toward this highest vision. Plato's highest judgment seems to have been that this vision cannot be translated into a doctrine and presented in textbook or lecture form, though the route of inquiry may be marked out.

Notice that Plato's idea of higher education is one of synthesis, not of specialization. . . . [T]he higher learning is to be practiced in appreciating and ordering general and expert findings into unified theories. If there is to be research into details of medicine, mathematics, law, or zoology, it should come later, so that the scholar has constantly in mind the ideal of knowledge and can use it as a criterion of importance in work on detail.

Platonic education is thus a training in what he would call "philosophy" and "philosophic vision." In American higher education today we are still concerned with this question. Should college, all of it, or at least the first two years, be devoted to giving the student a "general education"? If so, can this best be done by wide sampling of detailed courses in different "areas," or by specially designed "survey" or "general" courses that cross traditional departmental boundaries? Is the "major" for undergraduate upperclassmen to be considered specialized preprofessional training or a continuation of less specialized liberal education? Is there any necessity for "major" fields to coincide with the existing departments, or should there be flexibility in providing for "divisional" or "interdepartmental" study here? These are vital, immediate questions, and, by implication, they are also important for secondary education. If high school education is to be terminal for some students, does this mean that there should also be some attention to synthesis and synoptic vision on this level? Or is the best we can attain merely competence in socialization and in those instrumental techniques that a citizen needs in order to be "adapted" and "effective"?

There are similar questions posed by the high school and elementary school curricula Plato proposed. . . . [W]e can summarize Plato's curricular plan by noticing that it is intended to develop each individual's intellectual powers to choose formal studies which will best make one aware of the beautiful, the good, and the true.

# 2
## Aristotle

**Aristotle** (384–322 B.C.E.), born in northern Greece, spent two decades as a student in Plato's Academy. After teaching outside Athens for a dozen years, possibly including three as tutor to the young prince who later became known as Alexander the Great, Aristotle returned to Athens and founded his own school, the Lyceum. His intellectual achievements were vast. He founded the study of logic, wrote monumental philosophical treatises, and produced groundbreaking results in biology, psychology, zoology, meteorology, and astronomy. His later influence was so profound that during the Middle Ages he was often referred to simply as "the philosopher."

## *Nicomachean Ethics*

### Book I

#### 1. The Good as the Aim of Action

Every art or applied science and every systematic investigation, and similarly every action and choice, seem to aim at some good; the good, therefore, has been well defined as that at which all things aim. . . .

Since there are many activities, arts, and sciences, the number of ends is correspondingly large: of medicine the end is health, of shipbuilding, a vessel, of strategy, victory, and of household management, wealth. In many instances several such pursuits are grouped together under a single capacity: the art of bridle-making, for example, and everything else pertaining to the equipment of a horse are grouped together under horsemanship; horsemanship in turn, along with every other military action, is grouped together under strategy; and other pursuits are grouped together under other capacities. In all these cases the ends of the master sciences are preferable to the ends of the subordinate sciences, since the latter are pursued for the sake of the former. . . .

## 2. Politics as the Master Science of the Good

Now, if there exists an end in the realm of action which we desire for its own sake, an end which determines all our other desires; if, in other words, we do not make all our choices for the sake of something else—for in this way the process will go on infinitely so that our desire would be futile and pointless—then obviously this end will be the good, that is, the highest good. Will not the knowledge of this good, consequently, be very important to our lives? Would it not better equip us, like archers who have a target to aim at, to hit the proper mark? If so, we must try to comprehend in outline at least what this good is. . . .

## 3. The Limitations of Ethics and Politics

Our discussion will be adequate if it achieves clarity within the limits of the subject matter. For precision cannot be expected in the treatment of all subjects alike, any more than it can be expected in all manufactured articles. Problems of what is noble and just, which politics examines, present so much variety and irregularity that some people believe that they exist only by convention and not by nature. The problem of the good, too, presents a similar kind of irregularity, because in many cases good things bring harmful results. There are instances of men ruined by wealth, and others by courage. Therefore, in a discussion of such subjects, which has to start from a basis of this kind, we must be satisfied to indicate the truth with a rough and general sketch: when the subject and the basis of a discussion consist of matters that hold good only as a general rule, but not always, the conclusions reached must be of the same order. The various points that are made must be received in the same spirit. For a well-schooled man is one who searches for that degree of precision in each kind of study which the nature of the subject at hand admits: it is obviously just as foolish to accept arguments of probability from a mathematician as to demand strict demonstrations from an orator.

Each man can judge competently the things he knows, and of these he is a good judge. Accordingly, a good judge in each particular field is one who has been trained in it, and a good judge in general, a man who has received an all-round schooling. For that reason, a young man is not equipped to be a student of politics; for he has no experience in the actions which life demands of him, and these actions form the basis and subject matter of the discussion. Moreover, since he follows his emotions, his study will be pointless and unprofitable, for the end of this kind of study is not knowledge but action. Whether he is young in years or immature in character makes no difference; for his deficiency is not a matter of time but of living and of pursuing all his interests under the influence of his emotions. Knowledge brings no benefit to this kind of person, just as it brings none to the morally weak. But those who regulate their desires and actions by a rational principle will greatly benefit from a knowledge of this subject. So much by way of a preface about the student, the limitations which have to be accepted, and the objective before us. . . .

## 7. The Good is Final and Self-sufficient; Happiness is Defined

. . . Since there are evidently several ends, and since we choose some of these—e.g., wealth, flutes, and instruments generally—as a means to something else, it is obvious that not all ends are final. The highest good, on the other hand, must be something final. Thus, if there is only one final end, this will be the good we are seeking; if there are several, it will be the most final and perfect of them. We call that which is pursued as an end in itself more final than an end which is pursued for the sake of something else; and what is never chosen as a means to something else we call more final than that which is chosen both as an end in itself and as a means to something else. What is always chosen as an end in itself and never as a means to something else is called final in an unqualified sense. This description seems to apply to happiness above all else: for we always choose happiness as an end in itself and never for the sake of something else. Honor, pleasure, intelligence, and all virtue we choose partly for themselves—for we would choose each of them even if no further advantage would accrue from them—but we also choose them partly for the sake of happiness, because we assume that it is through them that we will be happy. On the other hand, no one chooses happiness for the sake of honor, pleasure, and the like, nor as a means to anything at all. . . .

We see then that happiness is something final and self-sufficient and the end of our actions.

To call happiness the highest good is perhaps a little trite, and a clearer account of what it is, is still required. Perhaps this is best done by first ascertaining the proper function of man. For just as the goodness and performance of a flute player, a sculptor, or any kind of expert, and generally of anyone who fulfills some function or performs some action, are thought to reside in his proper function, so the goodness and performance of man would seem to reside in whatever is his proper function. Is it then possible that while a carpenter and a shoemaker have their own proper functions and spheres of action, man as man has none, but was left by nature a good-for-nothing without a function? Should we not assume that just as the eye, the hand, the foot, and in general each part of the body clearly has its own proper function, so man too has some function over and above the functions of his parts? What can this function possibly be? Simply living? He shares that even with plants, but we are now looking for something peculiar to man. Accordingly, the life of nutrition and growth must be excluded. Next in line there is a life of sense perception. But this, too, man has in common with the horse, the ox, and every animal. There remains then an active life of the rational element. The rational element has two parts: one is rational in that it obeys the rule of reason, the other in that it possesses and conceives rational rules. Since the expression "life of the rational element" also can be used in two senses, we must make it clear that we mean a life determined by the activity, as opposed to the mere possession, of the rational element. For the activity, it seems, has a greater claim to be the function of man.

The proper function of man, then, consists in an activity of the soul in conformity with a rational principle or, at least, not without it. In speaking of the proper function of a given individual we mean that it is the same in kind as the function of an individual who sets high standards for himself: the proper function of a harpist, for example, is the same as the function of a harpist who has set high standards for himself. The same applies to any and every group of individuals: the full attainment of excellence must be added to the mere function. In other words, the function of the harpist is to play the harp; the function of the harpist who has high standards is to play it well. On these assumptions, if we take the proper function of man to be a certain kind of life, and if this kind of life is an activity of the soul and consists in actions performed in conjunction with the rational element, and if a man of high standards is he who performs these actions well and properly, and if a function is well performed when it is performed in accordance with the excellence appropriate to it; we reach the conclusion that the good of man is an activity of the soul in conformity with excellence or virtue, and if there are several virtues, in conformity with the best and most complete.

But we must add "in a complete life." For one swallow does not make a spring, nor does one sunny day; similarly, one day or a short time does not make a man blessed and happy. . . .

### 13. The Psychological Foundations of the Virtues

Since happiness is a certain activity of the soul in conformity with perfect virtue, we must now examine what virtue or excellence is. For such an inquiry will perhaps better enable us to discover the nature of happiness. Moreover, the man who is truly concerned about politics seems to devote special attention to excellence, since it is his aim to make the citizens good and law-abiding. We have an example of this in the lawgivers of Crete and Sparta and in other great legislators. If an examination of virtue is part of politics, this question clearly fits into the pattern of our original plan.

There can be no doubt that the virtue which we have to study is human virtue. For the good which we have been seeking is a human good and the happiness a human happiness. By human virtue we do not mean the excellence of the body, but that of the soul, and we define happiness as an activity of the soul. If this is true, the student of politics must obviously have some knowledge of the workings of the soul, just as the man who is to heal eyes must know something about the whole body. In fact, knowledge is all the more important for the former, inasmuch as politics is better and more valuable than medicine, and cultivated physicians devote much time and trouble to gain knowledge about the body. Thus, the student of politics must study the soul, but he must do so with his own aim in view, and only to the extent that the objects of his inquiry demand: to go into it in greater detail would perhaps be more laborious than his purposes require.

Some things that are said about the soul in our less technical discussions are adequate enough to be used here, for instance, that the soul consists of two elements, one irrational and one rational. . . .

In addition to this, there seems to be another integral element of the soul which, though irrational, still does partake of reason in some way. In morally strong and morally weak men we praise the reason that guides them and the rational element of the soul, because it exhorts them to follow the right path and to do what is best. Yet we see in them also another natural strain different from the rational, which fights and resists the guidance of reason. The soul behaves in precisely the same manner as do the paralyzed limbs of the body. When we intend to move the limbs to the right, they turn to the left, and similarly, the impulses of morally weak persons turn in the direction opposite to that in which reason leads them. However, while the aberration of the body is visible, that of the soul is not. But perhaps we must accept it as a fact, nevertheless, that there is something in the soul besides the rational element, which opposes and reacts against it. In what way the two are distinct need not concern us here. But, as we have stated, it too seems to partake of reason; at any rate, in a morally strong man it accepts the leadership of reason, and is perhaps more obedient still in a self-controlled and courageous man, since in him everything is in harmony with the voice of reason.

Thus we see that the irrational element of the soul has two parts: the one is vegetative and has no share in reason at all, the other is the seat of the appetites and of desire in general and partakes of reason insofar as it complies with reason and accepts its leadership; it possesses reason in the sense that we say it is "reasonable" to accept the advice of a father and of friends, not in the sense that we have a "rational" understanding of mathematical propositions. That the irrational element can be persuaded by the rational is shown by the fact that admonition and all manner of rebuke and exhortation are possible. If it is correct to say that the appetitive part, too, has reason, it follows that the rational element of the soul has two subdivisions: the one possesses reason in the strict sense, contained within itself, and the other possesses reason in the sense that it listens to reason as one would listen to a father.

Virtue, too, is differentiated in line with this division of the soul. We call some virtues "intellectual" and others "moral": theoretical wisdom, understanding, and practical wisdom are intellectual virtues, generosity and self-control moral virtues. In speaking of a man's character, we do not describe him as wise or understanding, but as gentle or self-controlled; but we praise the wise man, too, for his characteristic, and praiseworthy characteristics are what we call virtues.

## Book II

### 1. Moral Virtue as the Result of Habits

Virtue, as we have seen, consists of two kinds, intellectual virtue and moral virtue. Intellectual virtue or excellence owes its origin and development chiefly to teaching, and for that reason requires experience and time. Moral virtue, on the other hand, is formed by habit, *ethos*, and its name, *ēthikē*, is therefore derived, by a slight variation, from *ethos*. This shows, too, that none of the moral virtues is implanted in us by nature, for nothing which exists by nature can be changed by habit. For example, it is impossible for a stone, which has a natural downward movement, to become habituated to moving upward, even if one should try ten thousand times to inculcate the habit by throwing it in the air; nor can fire be made to move downward, nor can the direction of any nature-given tendency be changed by habituation. Thus, the virtues are implanted in us neither by nature nor contrary to nature: we are by nature equipped with the ability to receive them, and habit brings this ability to completion and fulfillment.[1]

Furthermore, of all the qualities with which we are endowed by nature, we are provided with the capacity first, and display the activity afterward. That this is true is shown by the senses: it is not by frequent seeing or frequent hearing that we acquired our senses, but on the contrary we first possess and then use them; we do not acquire them by use. The virtues, on the other hand, we acquire by first having put them into action, and the same is also true of the arts. For the things which we have to learn before we can do them we learn by doing: men become builders by building houses, and harpists by playing the harp. Similarly, we become just by the practice of just actions, self-controlled by exercising self-control, and courageous by performing acts of courage.

This is corroborated by what happens in states. Lawgivers make the citizens good by inculcating (good) habits in them, and this is the aim of every lawgiver; if he does not succeed in doing that, his legislation is a failure. It is in this that a good constitution differs from a bad one.

Moreover, the same causes and the same means that produce any excellence or virtue can also destroy it, and this is also true of every art. It is by playing the harp that men become both good and bad harpists, and correspondingly with builders and all the other craftsmen: a man who builds well will be a good builder, one who builds badly a bad one. For if this were not so, there would be no need for an instructor, but everybody would be born as a good or a bad craftsman. The same holds true of the virtues: in our transactions with other men it is by action that some become just and others unjust, and it is by acting in the face of danger and by developing the habit of feeling fear or confidence that some become brave men and others cowards. The same applies to the appetites and feelings of anger: by reacting in one way or in another to given circumstances some people become self-controlled and gentle, and others self-indulgent and short-tempered. In a word, characteristics develop from corresponding activities. For that reason, we must see to it that our activities are of a certain kind, since any variations in them will be reflected in our characteristics. Hence it is no small matter whether one habit or another is inculcated in us from early childhood; on the contrary, it makes a considerable difference, or, rather, all the difference.

## 2. Method in the Practical Sciences

The purpose of the present study is not, as it is in other inquiries, the attainment of theoretical knowledge: we are not conducting this inquiry in order to know what virtue is, but in order to become good, else there would be no advantage in studying it. For that reason, it becomes necessary to examine the problem of actions, and to ask how they are to be performed. For, as we have said, the actions determine what kind of characteristics are developed.

That we must act according to right reason is generally conceded and may be assumed as the basis of our discussion. . . . But let us first agree that any discussion on matters of action cannot be more than an outline and is bound to lack precision; for as we stated at the outset, one can demand of a discussion only what the subject matter permits, and there are no fixed data in matters concerning action and questions of what is beneficial, any more than there are in matters of health. And if this is true of our general discussion, our treatment of particular problems will be even less precise, since these do not come under the head of any art which can be transmitted by precept, but the agent must consider on each different occasion what the situation demands, just as in medicine and in navigation. But although such is the kind of discussion in which we are engaged, we must do our best.

First of all, it must be observed that the nature of moral qualities is such that they are destroyed by defect and by excess. We see the same thing happen in the case of strength and of health, to illustrate, as we must, the invisible by means of visible examples: excess as well as deficiency of physical exercise destroys our strength, and similarly, too much and too little food and drink destroys our health; the proportionate amount, however, produces, increases, and preserves it. The same applies to self-control, courage, and the other virtues: the man who shuns and fears everything and never stands his ground becomes a coward, whereas a man who knows no fear at all and goes to meet every danger becomes reckless. Similarly, a man who revels in every pleasure and abstains from none becomes self-indulgent, while he who avoids every pleasure like a boor becomes what might be called insensitive. Thus we see that self-control and courage are destroyed by excess and by deficiency and are preserved by the mean.

Not only are the same actions which are responsible for and instrumental in the origin and development of the virtues also the causes and means of their destruction, but they will also be manifested in the active exercise of the virtues. We can see the truth of this in the case of other more visible qualities, e.g., strength. Strength is produced by consuming plenty of food and by enduring much hard work, and it is the strong man who is best able to do these things. The same is also true of the virtues: by abstaining from pleasures we become self-controlled, and once we are self-controlled we are best able to abstain from pleasures. So also with courage: by becoming habituated to despise and to endure terrors we become courageous, and once we have become courageous we will best be able to endure terror.

## 4. Virtuous Action and Virtue

However, the question may be raised what we mean by saying that men become just by performing just actions and self-controlled by practicing self-control. For if they perform just actions and exercise self-control, they are already just and self-controlled, in the same way as they are literate and musical if they write correctly and practice music.

But is this objection really valid, even as regards the arts? No, for it is possible for a man to write a piece correctly by chance or at the prompting of another: but he will be literate only if he produces a piece of writing in a literate way, and that means doing it in accordance with the skill of literate composition which he has in himself.

Moreover, the factors involved in the arts and in the virtues are not the same. In the arts, excellence lies in the result itself, so that it is sufficient if it is of a certain kind. But in the case of the virtues an act is not performed justly or with self-control if the act itself is of a certain kind, but only if in addition the agent has certain characteristics as he performs it: first of all, he must know what he is doing; secondly, he must choose to act the way he does, and he must choose it for its own sake; and in the third place, the act must spring from a firm and unchangeable character. With the exception of knowing what one is about, these considerations do not enter into the mastery of the arts; for the mastery of the virtues, however, knowledge is of little or no importance, whereas the other two conditions count not for a little but are all-decisive, since repeated acts of justice and self-control result in the possession of these virtues. In other words, acts are called just and self-controlled when they are the kind of acts which a just or self-controlled man would perform; but the just and self-controlled man is not he who performs these acts, but he who also performs them in the way just and self-controlled men do.

Thus our assertion that a man becomes just by performing just acts and self-controlled by performing acts of self-control is correct; without performing them, nobody could even be on the way to becoming good. Yet most men do not perform such acts, but by taking refuge in argument they think that they are engaged in philosophy and that they will become good in this way. In so doing, they act like sick men who listen attentively to what the doctor says, but fail to do any of the things he prescribes. That kind of philosophical activity will not bring health to the soul any more than this sort of treatment will produce a healthy body.

### 6. Virtue Defined: The Differentia

. . . [V]irtue or excellence is a characteristic involving choice, and that it consists in observing the mean relative to us, a mean which is defined by a rational principle, such as a man of practical wisdom would use to determine it. It is the mean by reference to two vices: the one of excess and the other of deficiency. It is, moreover, a mean because some vices exceed and others fall short of what is required in emotion and in action, whereas virtue finds and chooses the median. Hence, in respect of its essence and the definition of its essential nature virtue is a mean, but in regard to goodness and excellence it is an extreme.

Not every action nor every emotion admits of a mean. There are some actions and emotions whose very names connote baseness, e.g., spite, shamelessness, envy; and among actions, adultery, theft, and murder. These and similar emotions and actions imply by their very names that they are bad; it is not their excess nor their deficiency which is called bad. It is, therefore, impossible ever to do right in performing them: to perform them is always to do wrong. In cases of this sort, let us say adultery, rightness and wrongness do not depend on committing it with the right woman at the right time and in the right manner, but the mere fact of committing such action at all is to do wrong. It would be just as absurd to suppose that there is a mean, an excess, and a deficiency in an unjust or a cowardly or a self-indulgent act. For if there were, we would have a mean of excess and a mean of deficiency, and an excess of excess and a deficiency of deficiency. Just as there cannot be an excess and a deficiency of self-control and courage—because the intermediate is, in a sense, an extreme—so there cannot be a mean, excess, and deficiency in their respective opposites: their opposites are wrong regardless of how they are performed; for, in general, there is no such thing as the mean of an excess or a deficiency, or the excess and deficiency of a mean.

### 9. How to Attain the Mean

Our discussion has sufficiently established (1) that moral virtue is a mean and in what sense it is a mean; (2) that it is a mean between two vices, one of which is marked by excess and the other by deficiency; and (3) that it is a mean in the sense that it aims at the median in the emotions and in actions. That is why it is a hard task to be good; in every case it is a task to find the median: for instance, not everyone can find the middle of a circle, but only a man who has the proper knowledge. Similarly, anyone can get angry—that is easy—or can give away money or spend it; but to do all this to the right person, to the right extent, at the right time, for the right reason, and in the right way is no longer something easy that anyone can do. It is for this reason that good conduct is rare, praiseworthy, and noble.

The first concern of a man who aims at the median should, therefore, be to avoid the extreme which is more opposed to it, as Calypso advises: "Keep clear your ship of yonder spray and surf."[2] For one of the two extremes is more in error than the other, and since it is extremely difficult to hit the mean, we must, as the saying has it, sail in the second best way and take the lesser evil; and we can best do that in the manner we have described.

Moreover, we must watch the errors which have the greatest attraction for us personally. For the natural inclination of one man differs from that of another, and we each come to recognize our own by observing the pleasure and pain produced in us [by the different extremes]. We must then draw ourselves away in the opposite direction, for by pulling away from error we shall reach the middle, as men do when they straighten warped timber. In every case we must be especially on our guard against pleasure and what is pleasant, for when it comes to pleasure we cannot act as unbiased judges. Our attitude toward pleasure should be the same as that of the Trojan elders was toward Helen, and we should repeat on every occasion the words they addressed to her.[3] For if we dismiss pleasure as they dismissed her, we shall make fewer mistakes.

In summary, then, it is by acting in this way that we shall best be able to hit the median. But this is no doubt difficult, especially when particular cases are concerned. For it is not easy to determine in what manner, with what person, on what occasion, and for how long a time one ought to be angry. There are times when we praise those who are deficient in anger and call them gentle, and other times when we praise violently angry persons and call them manly. However, we do not blame a man for slightly deviating from the course of goodness, whether he strays toward excess or toward deficiency, but we do blame him if his deviation is great and cannot pass unnoticed. It is not easy to determine by a formula at what point and for how great a divergence a man deserves blame; but this difficulty is, after all, true of all objects of sense perception: determinations of this kind depend upon particular circumstances, and the decision rests with our (moral) sense.

This much, at any rate, is clear: that the median characteristic is in all fields the one that deserves praise, and that it is sometimes necessary to incline toward the excess and sometimes toward the deficiency. For it is in this way that we will most easily hit upon the median, which is the point of excellence.


## Book VI


### 1. Moral and Intellectual Excellence. The Psychological Foundations of Intellectual Excellence

We stated earlier that we must choose the median, and not excess or deficiency, and that the median is what right reason dictates. Let us now analyze this second point.

In all the characteristics we have discussed, as in all others, there is some target on which a rational man keeps his eye as he bends and relaxes his efforts to attain it. There is also a standard that determines the several means which, as we claim, lie between excess and deficiency, and which are fixed by right reason. But this statement, true though it is, lacks clarity. In all other fields of endeavor in which scientific knowledge is possible, it is indeed true to say that we must exert ourselves or relax neither too much nor too little, but to an intermediate extent and as right reason demands. But if this is the only thing a person knows, he will be none the wiser: he will, for example, not know what kind of medicines to apply to his body, if he is merely told to apply whatever medical science prescribes and in a manner in which a medical expert applies them. Accordingly, in discussing the characteristics of the soul, too, it is not enough that the statement we have made be true. We must also have a definition of what right reason is and what standard determines it.

In analyzing the virtues of the soul we said that some are virtues of character and others excellence of thought or understanding. We have now discussed the moral virtues, [i.e., the virtues of character]. In what follows, we will deal with the others, [i.e., the intellectual virtues,] beginning with some prefatory remarks about the soul. We said in our earlier discussion that the soul consists of two parts, one rational and one irrational. We must now make a similar distinction in regard to the rational part. Let it be assumed that there are two rational elements: with one of these we apprehend the realities whose fundamental principles do not admit of being other than they are, and with the other we apprehend things which do admit of being other. For if we grant that knowledge presupposes a certain likeness and kinship of subject and object, there will be a generically different part of the soul naturally corresponding to each of two different kinds of object. Let us call one the scientific and the other the calculative element. Deliberating and calculating are the same thing, and no one deliberates about objects that cannot be other than they are. This means that the calculative constitutes one element of the rational part of the soul. Accordingly, we must now take up the question which is the best characteristic of each element, since that constitutes the excellence or virtue of each. But the virtue of a thing is relative to its proper function.

## 2. The Two Kinds of Intellectual Excellence and their Objects

Now, there are three elements in the soul which control action and truth: sense perception, intelligence, and desire. Of these sense perception does not initiate any action. We can see this from the fact that animals have sense perception but have no share in action. What affirmation and negation are in the realm of thought, pursuit and avoidance are in the realm of desire. Therefore, since moral virtue is a characteristic involving choice, and since choice is a deliberate desire, it follows that, if the choice is to be good, the reasoning must be true and the desire correct; that is, reasoning must affirm what desire pursues. This then is the kind of thought and the kind of truth that is practical and concerned with action. On the other hand, in the kind of thought involved in theoretical knowledge and not in action or production, the good and the bad state are, respectively, truth and falsehood; in fact, the attainment of truth is the function of the intellectual faculty as a whole. But in intellectual activity concerned with action, the good state is truth in harmony with correct desire. . . .

Choice is the starting point of action. . . . The starting point of choice, however, is desire and reasoning directed toward some end. That is why there cannot be choice either without intelligence and thought or without some moral characteristic; for good and bad action in human conduct are not possible without thought and character. Now thought alone moves nothing; only thought which is directed to some end and concerned with action can do so.

## 5. Practical Wisdom

We may approach the subject of practical wisdom by studying the persons to whom we attribute it. Now, the capacity of deliberating well about what is good and advantageous for oneself is regarded as typical of a man of practical wisdom—not deliberating well about what is good and advantageous in a partial sense, for example, what contributes to health or strength, but what sort of thing contributes to the good life in general. This is shown by the fact that we speak of men as having practical wisdom in a particular respect (i.e., not in an unqualified sense), when they calculate well with respect to some worthwhile end, one that cannot be attained by an applied science or art. It follows that, in general, a man of practical wisdom is he who has the ability to deliberate.

Now no one deliberates about things that cannot be other than they are or about actions that he cannot possibly perform. Since, as we saw, pure science involves demonstration, while things whose starting points or first causes can be other than they are do not admit of demonstration—for such things too (and not merely their first causes) can all be other than they are—and since it is impossible to deliberate about what exists by necessity, we may conclude that practical wisdom is neither a pure science nor an art. It is not a pure science, because matters of action admit of being other than they are, and it is not an applied science or art, because action and production are generically different.

What remains, then, is that it is a truthful characteristic of acting rationally in matters good and bad for man. For production has an end other than itself, but action does not: good action is itself an end. That is why we think that Pericles and men like him have practical wisdom. They have the capacity of seeing what is good for themselves and for mankind, and these are, we believe, the qualities of men capable of managing households and states. . . .

## 7. Theoretical Wisdom

We attribute "wisdom" in the arts to the most precise and perfect masters of their skills: we attribute it to Phidias as a sculptor in marble and to Polycletus as a sculptor in bronze. In this sense we signify by "wisdom" nothing but excellence of art or craftsmanship. However, we regard some men as being wise in general, not in any partial sense or in some other particular respect, as Homer says in the *Margites:*

> The gods let him not be a digger or a ploughman nor wise at anything.[5]

It is, therefore, clear, that wisdom must be the most precise and perfect form of knowledge. Consequently, a wise man must not only know what follows from fundamental principles, but he must also have true knowledge of the fundamental principles themselves. . . .

For it would be strange to regard politics or practical wisdom as the highest kind of knowledge, when in fact man is not the best thing in the universe. Surely, if "healthy" and "good" mean one thing for men and another for fishes, whereas "white" and "straight" always mean the same, "wise" must mean the same for everyone, but "practically wise" will be different. For each particular being ascribes practical wisdom in matters relating to itself to that thing which observes its interests well, and it will entrust itself to that thing. . . .

That is why it is said that men like Anaxagoras and Thales have theoretical but not practical wisdom: when we see that they do not know what is advantageous to them, we admit that they know extraordinary, wonderful, difficult, and superhuman things, but call their knowledge useless because the good they are seeking is not human.

Practical wisdom, on the other hand, is concerned with human affairs and with matters about which deliberation is possible. As we have said, the most characteristic function of a man of practical wisdom is to deliberate well: no one deliberates about things that cannot be other than they are, nor about things that are not directed to some end, an end that is a good attainable by action. In an unqualified sense, that man is good at deliberating who, by reasoning, can aim at and hit the best thing attainable to man by action.

Nor does practical wisdom deal only with universals. It must also be familiar with particulars, since it is concerned with action and action has to do with particulars. This explains why some men who have no scientific knowledge are more adept in practical matters, especially if they have experience, than those who do have scientific knowledge. For if a person were to know that light meat is easily digested, and hence wholesome, but did not know what sort of meat is light, he will not produce health, whereas someone who knows that poultry is light and wholesome is more likely to produce health. . . .

## 8. Practical Wisdom and Politics

. . . [P]ractical wisdom is primarily concerned with one's own person, i.e., with the individual, and it is this kind that bears the name "practical wisdom," which properly belongs to others as well. The other kinds are called household management, legislation, and politics. . . .

Now, knowing what is good for oneself is, to be sure, one kind of knowledge; but it is very different from the other kinds. A man who knows and concerns himself with his own interests is regarded as a man of practical wisdom, while men whose concern is politics are looked upon as busybodies. . . .

For people seek their own good and think that this is what they should do. This opinion has given rise to the view that it is such men who have practical wisdom. And yet, surely one's own good cannot exist without household management nor without a political system. . . .

An indication that what we have said is correct is the following common observation. While young men do indeed become good geometricians and mathematicians and attain theoretical wisdom in such matters, they apparently do not attain practical wisdom. The reason is that practical wisdom is concerned with particulars as well [as with universals], and knowledge of particulars comes from experience. But a young man has no experience, for experience is the product of a long time. In fact, one might also raise the question why it is that a boy may become a mathematician but not a philosopher or a natural scientist. The answer may be that the objects of mathematics are the result of abstraction, whereas the fundamental principles of philosophy and natural science come from experience. Young men can assert philosophical and scientific principles but can have no genuine convictions about them, whereas there is no obscurity about the essential definitions in mathematics. . . .

## 12. The Use of Theoretical and Practical Wisdom

. . . [A] man fulfills his proper function only by way of practical wisdom and moral excellence or virtue: virtue makes us aim at the right target, and practical wisdom makes us use the right means. . . .

Finally, the argument has to be met that our ability to perform noble and just acts is in no way enhanced by practical wisdom. We have to begin a little further back and take the following as our starting point. It is our contention that people may perform just acts without actually being just men, as in the case of people who do what has been laid down by the laws but do so either involuntarily or through ignorance or for an ulterior motive, and not for the sake of performing just acts. [Such persons are not just men] despite the fact that they act the way they should, and perform all the actions which a morally good man ought to perform. On the other hand, it seems that it is possible for a man to be of such a character that he performs each particular act in such a way as to make him a good man—I mean that his acts are due to choice and are performed for the sake of the acts themselves. Now, it is virtue which makes our choice right. It is not virtue, however, but a different capacity, which determines the steps which, in the nature of the case, must be taken to implement this choice.

We must stop for a moment to make this point clearer. There exists a capacity called "cleverness," which is the power to perform those steps which are conducive to a goal we have set for ourselves and to attain that goal. If the goal is noble, cleverness deserves praise; if the goal is base, cleverness is knavery. That is why men of practical wisdom are often described as "clever" and "knavish." But in fact this capacity [alone] is not practical wisdom, although practical wisdom does not exist without it. Without virtue or excellence, this eye of the soul, [intelligence,] does not acquire the characteristic [of practical wisdom]: that is what we have just stated and it is obvious. For the syllogisms which express the principles initiating action run: "Since the end, or the highest good, is such-and-such . . ."—whatever it may be; what it really is does not matter for our present argument. But whatever the true end may be, only a good man can judge it correctly. For wickedness distorts and causes us to be completely mistaken about the fundamental principles of action. Hence it is clear that a man cannot have practical wisdom unless he is good.

## Book VII

## 2. Problems in the Current Beliefs about Moral Strength and Moral Weakness

. . . [H]ow can a man be morally weak in his actions, when his basic assumption is correct [as to what he should do]? Some people claim that it is impossible for him to be morally weak if he has knowledge [of what he ought to do]. Socrates, for example, believed that it would be strange if, when a man possesses knowledge, something else should overpower it and drag it about like a slave. In fact, Socrates was completely opposed to the view [that a man may know what is right but do what is wrong], and did not believe that moral weakness exists. He claimed that no one acts contrary to what is best in the conviction [that what he is doing is bad], but through ignorance [of the fact that it is bad].

Now this theory is plainly at variance with the observed facts, and one ought to investigate the emotion [involved in the acts of a morally weak man]: if it comes about through ignorance, what manner of ignorance is it? For evidently a man who is morally weak in his actions does not think [that he ought to act the way he does] before he is in the grip of emotion.

There are some people who accept only certain points [of Socrates' theory], but reject others. They agree that nothing is better or more powerful than *knowledge*, but they do not agree that no one acts contrary to what he *thought* was the better thing to do. Therefore, they say, a morally weak person does not have knowledge but opinion when he is overpowered by pleasures.

However, if it really is opinion and not knowledge, if, in other words, the basic conviction which resists [the emotion] is not strong but weak, as it is when people are in doubt, we can forgive a man for not sticking to his opinions in the face of strong appetites. But we do not forgive wickedness or anything else that deserves blame [as moral weakness does. Hence it must be something stronger than opinion which is overpowered]. But does that mean that it is practical wisdom which resists [the appetite]? This, after all, is the strongest [kind of conviction]. But that would be absurd: for it would mean that the same man will have practical wisdom and be morally weak at the same time, and there is no one who would assert that it is the mark of a man of practical wisdom to perform voluntarily the basest actions. . . .

### 3. Some Problems Solved: Moral Weakness and Knowledge

. . . The contention that it is true opinion rather than knowledge which a morally weak man violates in his actions has no bearing on our argument. For some people have no doubts when they hold an opinion, and think they have exact knowledge. Accordingly, if we are going to say that the weakness of their belief is the reason why those who hold opinion will be more liable to act against their conviction than those who have knowledge, we shall find that there is no difference between knowledge and opinion. For some people are no less firmly convinced of what they believe than others are of what they know: Heraclitus is a case in point. (a) But the verb "to know" has two meanings: a man is said to "know" both when he does not use the knowledge he has and when he does use it. Accordingly, when a man does wrong it will make a difference whether he is not exercising the knowledge he has, [viz., that it is wrong to do what he is doing], or whether he is exercising it. In the latter case, we would be baffled, but not if he acted without exercising his knowledge.

Moreover, (b) since there are two kinds of premise, sleep, madness, and drink; and beginning students can reel off the words they have heard, but they do not yet know the subject. The subject must grow to be part of them, and that takes time. We must, therefore, assume that a man who displays moral weakness repeats the formulae [of moral knowledge] in the same way as an actor speaks his lines.

Further, (d) we may also look at the cause [of moral weakness] from the viewpoint of the science of human nature, in the following way. [In the practical syllogism,] one of the premises, the universal, is a current belief, while the other involves particular facts which fall within the domain of sense perception. When two premises are combined into one, [i.e., when the universal rule is realized in a particular case,] the soul is thereupon bound to affirm the conclusion, and if the premises involve action, the soul is bound to perform this act at once. For example, if [the premises are]: "Everything sweet ought to be tasted" and "This thing before me is sweet" ("this thing" perceived as an individual particular object), a man who is able [to taste] and is not prevented is bound to act accordingly at once.

Now, suppose that there is within us one universal opinion forbidding us to taste [things of this kind], and another [universal] opinion which tells us that everything sweet is pleasant, and also [a concrete perception], determining our activity, that the particular thing before us is sweet; and suppose further that the appetite [for pleasure] happens to be present. [The result is that] one opinion tells us to avoid that thing, while appetite, capable as it is of setting in motion each part of our body, drives us to it. [This is the case we have been looking for, the defeat of reason in moral weakness.] Thus it turns out that a morally weak man acts under the influence of some kind of reasoning and opinion, an opinion which is not intrinsically but only incidentally opposed to right reason; for it is not opinion but appetite that is opposed to right reason. And this explains why animals cannot be morally weak: they do not have conceptions of universals, but have only the power to form mental images and memory of particulars.

How is the [temporary] ignorance of a morally weak person dispelled and how does he regain his [active] knowledge [of what is good]? The explanation is the same as it is for drunkenness and sleep, and it is not peculiar to the affect of moral weakness. To get it we have to go to the students of natural science.

The final premise, consisting as it does in an opinion about an object perceived by the senses, determines our action. When in the grip of emotion, a morally weak man either does not have this premise, or he has it not in the sense of knowing it, but in the sense of uttering it as a drunken man may utter verses of Empedocles. [Because he is not in active possession of this premise,] and because the final [concrete] term of his reasoning is not a universal and does not seem to be an object of scientific knowledge in the same way that a universal is, [for both these reasons] we seem to be led to the conclusion which Socrates sought to establish. Moral weakness does not occur in the presence of knowledge in the strict sense, and it is sensory knowledge, not science, which is dragged about by emotion.

This completes our discussion of the question whether a morally weak person acts with knowledge or without knowledge, and in what sense it is possible for him to act knowingly.

## Book X

### 6. Happiness and Activity

Now that we have completed our discussion of the virtues, . . . it remains to sketch an outline of happiness, since, as we assert, it is the end or goal of human [aspirations]. Our account will be more concise if we recapitulate what we have said so far.

We stated, then, that happiness is not a characteristic; [if it were,] a person who passes his whole life in sleep, vegetating like a plant, or someone who experiences the greatest misfortunes could possess it. If, then, such a conclusion is unacceptable, we must, in accordance with our earlier discussion, classify happiness as some sort of activity. Now, some activities are necessary and desirable only for the sake of something else, while others are desirable in themselves. Obviously, happiness must be classed as an activity desirable in itself and not for the sake of something else. For happiness lacks nothing and is self-sufficient. Activities desirable in themselves are those from which we seek to derive nothing beyond the actual exercise of the activity. Actions in conformity with virtue evidently constitute such activities; for to perform noble and good deeds is something desirable for its own sake.

Pleasant amusements, too, [are desirable for their own sake]. We do not choose them for the sake of something else, since they lead to harm rather than good when we become neglectful of our bodies and our property. But most of those who are considered happy find an escape in pastimes of this sort, and this is why people who are well versed in such pastimes find favor at the courts of tyrants; they make themselves pleasant by providing what the tyrants are after, and what they want is amusement. Accordingly, such amusements are regarded as being conducive to happiness, because men who are in positions of power devote their leisure to them. But perhaps such persons cannot be [regarded as] evidence. For virtue and intelligence, which are the sources of morally good activities, do not consist in wielding power. Also, if these men, who have never tasted pure and generous pleasure, find an escape in the pleasures of the body, this is no sufficient reason for thinking that such pleasures are in fact more desirable. For children, too, think that what they value is actually the best. It is, therefore, not surprising that as children apparently do not attach value to the same things as do adults, so bad men do not attach value to the same things as do good men. Accordingly, as we have stated repeatedly, what is valuable and pleasant to a morally good man actually is valuable and pleasant. Each individual considers that activity most desirable which corresponds to his own proper characteristic condition, and a morally good man, of course, so considers activity in conformity with virtue.

Consequently, happiness does not consist in amusement. In fact, it would be strange if our end were amusement, and if we were to labor and suffer hardships all our life long merely to amuse ourselves. For, one might say, we choose everything for the sake of something else—except happiness; for happiness is an end. Obviously, it is foolish and all too childish to exert serious efforts and toil for purposes of amusement. Anacharsis[6] seems to be right when he advises to play in order to be serious; for amusement is a form of rest, and since we cannot work continuously we need rest. Thus rest is not an end, for we take it for the sake of [further] activity. The happy life is regarded as a life in conformity with virtue. It is a life which involves effort and is not spent in amusement.

Moreover, we say that what is morally good is better than what is ridiculous and brings amusement, and the better the organ or man—whichever may be involved in a particular case—the greater the moral value of the activity. But the activity of the better organ or the better man is in itself superior and more conducive to happiness.

Furthermore, any person at all, even a slave, can enjoy bodily pleasures no less than the best of men. But no one would grant that a slave has a share in happiness any more than that he lives a life of his own. For happiness does not consist in pastimes of this sort, but in activities that conform with virtue, as we have stated earlier.

## 7. Happiness, Intelligence, and the Contemplative Life

Now, if happiness is activity in conformity with virtue, it is to be expected that it should conform with the highest virtue, and that is the virtue of the best part of us. Whether this is intelligence or something else which, it is thought, by its very nature rules and guides us and which gives us our notions of what is noble and divine; whether it is itself divine or the most divine thing in us; it is the activity of this part [when operating] in conformity with the excellence or virtue proper to it that will be complete happiness. That it is an activity concerned with theoretical knowledge or contemplation has already been stated.

This would seem to be consistent with our earlier statements as well as the truth. For this activity is not only the highest—for intelligence is the highest possession we have in us, and the objects which are the concern of intelligence are the highest objects of knowledge—but also the most continuous: we are able to study continuously more easily than to perform any kind of action. Furthermore, we think of pleasure as a necessary ingredient in happiness. Now everyone agrees that of all the activities that conform with virtue activity in conformity with theoretical wisdom is the most pleasant. At any rate, it seems that [the pursuit of wisdom or] philosophy holds pleasures marvellous in purity and certainty, and it is not surprising that time spent in knowledge is more pleasant than time spent in research. Moreover, what is usually called "self-sufficiency" will be found in the highest degree in the activity which is concerned with theoretical knowledge. Like a just man and any other virtuous man, a wise man requires the necessities of life; once these have been adequately provided, a just man still needs people toward whom and in company with whom to act justly, and the same is true of a self-controlled man, a courageous man, and all the rest. But a wise man is able to study even by himself, and the wiser he is the more is he able to do it. Perhaps he could do it better if he had colleagues to work with him, but he still is the most self-sufficient of all. Again, study seems to be the only activity which is loved for its own sake. For while we derive a greater or a smaller advantage from practical pursuits beyond the action itself, from study we derive nothing beyond the activity of studying. Also, we regard happiness as depending on leisure; for our purpose in being busy is to have leisure, and we wage war in order to have peace. Now, the practical virtues are activated in political and military pursuits, but the actions involved in these pursuits seem to be unleisurely. This is completely true of military pursuits, since no one chooses to wage war or foments war for the sake of war; he would have to be utterly bloodthirsty if he were to make enemies of his friends simply in order to have battle and slaughter. But the activity of the statesman, too, has no leisure. It attempts to gain advantages beyond political action, advantages such as political power, prestige, or at least happiness for the statesman himself and his fellow citizens, and that is something other than political activity: after all, the very fact that we investigate politics shows that it is not the same [as happiness]. Therefore, if we take as established (1) that political and military actions surpass all other actions that conform with virtue in nobility and grandeur; (2) that they are unleisurely, aim at an end, and are not chosen for their own sake; (3) that the activity of our intelligence, inasmuch as it is an activity concerned with theoretical knowledge, is thought to be of greater value than the others, aims at no end beyond itself, and has a pleasure proper to itself—and pleasure increases activity; and (4) that the qualities of this activity evidently are self-sufficiency, leisure, as much freedom from fatigue as a human being can have, and whatever else falls to the lot of a supremely happy man; it follows that the activity of our intelligence constitutes the complete happiness of man, provided that it encompasses a complete span of life; for nothing connected with happiness must be incomplete.

However, such a life would be more than human. A man who would live it would do so not insofar as he is human, but because there is a divine element within him. This divine element is as far above our composite nature, as its activity is above the active exercise of the other, [i.e., practical,] kind of virtue. So if it is true that intelligence is divine in comparison with man, then a life guided by intelligence is divine in comparison with human life. We must not follow those who advise us to have human thoughts, since we are [only] men, and mortal thoughts, as mortals should; on the contrary, we should try to become immortal as far as that is possible and do our utmost to live in accordance with what is highest in us. For though this is a small portion [of our nature], it far surpasses everything else in power and value. One might even regard it as each man's true self, since it is the controlling and better part. It would, therefore, be strange if a man chose not to live his own life but someone else's.

Moreover, what we stated before will apply here, too: what is by nature proper to each thing will be at once the best and the most pleasant for it. In other words, a life guided by intelligence is the best and most pleasant for man, inasmuch as intelligence, above all else, is man. Consequently, this kind of life is the happiest.

## 8. The Advantages of the Contemplative Life

A life guided by the other kind of virtue, [the practical,] is happy in a secondary sense, since its active exercise is confined to man. It is in our dealings with one another that we perform just, courageous, and other virtuous acts, when we observe the proper kind of behaviour toward each man in private transactions, in meeting his needs, in all manner of actions, and in our emotions, and all of these are, as we see, peculiarly human. Moreover, some moral acts seem to be determined by our bodily condition, and virtue or excellence of character seems in many ways closely related to the emotions. There is also a close mutual connection between practical wisdom and excellence of character, since the fundamental principles of practical wisdom are determined by the virtues of character, while practical wisdom determines the right standard for the moral virtues. The fact that these virtues are also bound up with the emotions indicates that they belong to our composite nature, and the virtues of our composite nature are human virtues; consequently, a life guided by these virtues and the happiness [that goes with it are likewise human]. The happiness of the intelligence, however, is quite separate [from that kind of happiness]. That is all we shall say about it here, for a more detailed treatment lies beyond the scope of our present task.

It also seems that such happiness has little need of external trimmings, or less need than moral virtue has. Even if we grant that both stand in equal need of the necessities of life, and even if the labors of a statesman are more concerned with the needs of our body and things of that sort—in that respect the difference between them may be small—yet, in what they need for the exercise of their activities, their difference will be great. A generous man will need money to perform generous acts, and a just man will need it to meet his obligations. For the mere wish to perform such acts is inscrutable, and even an unjust man can pretend that he wishes to act justly. And a courageous man will need strength if he is to accomplish an act that conforms with his virtue, and a man of self-control the possibility of indulgence. How else can he or any other virtuous man make manifest his excellence? Also, it is debatable whether the moral purpose or the action is the more decisive element in virtue, since virtue depends on both. It is clear of course that completeness depends on both. But many things are needed for the performance of actions, and the greater and nobler the actions the more is needed. But a man engaged in study has no need of any of these things, at least not for the active exercise of studying; in fact one might even go so far as to say that they are a hindrance to study. But insofar as he is human and lives in the society of his fellow men, he chooses to act as virtue demands, and accordingly, he will need externals for living as a human being.

A further indication that complete happiness consists in some kind of contemplative activity is this. We assume that the gods are in the highest degree blessed and happy. But what kind of actions are we to attribute to them? Acts of justice? Will they not look ridiculous making contracts with one another, returning deposits, and so forth? Perhaps acts of courage—withstanding terror and taking risks, because it is noble to do so? Or generous actions? But to whom will they give? It would be strange to think that they actually have currency or something of the sort. Acts of self-control? What would they be? Surely, it would be in poor taste to praise them for not having bad appetites. If we went through the whole list we would see that a concern with actions is petty and unworthy of the gods. Nevertheless, we all assume that the gods exist and, consequently, that they are active; for surely we do not assume them to be always asleep like Endymion.[7] Now, if we take away action from a living being, to say nothing of production, what is left except contemplation? Therefore, the activity of the divinity which surpasses all others in bliss must be a contemplative activity, and the human activity which is most closely akin to it is, therefore, most conducive to happiness.

This is further shown by the fact that no other living being has a share in happiness, since they all are completely denied this kind of activity. The gods enjoy a life blessed in its entirety; men enjoy it to the extent that they attain something resembling the divine activity; but none of the other living beings can be happy, because they have no share at all in contemplation or study. So happiness is coextensive with study, and the greater the opportunity for studying, the greater the happiness, not as an incidental effect but as inherent in study; for study is in itself worthy of honor. Consequently, happiness is some kind of study or contemplation.

But we shall also need external well-being, since we are only human. Our nature is not self-sufficient for engaging in study: our body must be healthy and we must have food and generally be cared for. Nevertheless, if it is not possible for a man to be supremely happy without external goods, we must not think that his needs will be great and many in order to be happy; for self-sufficiency and moral action do not consist in an excess [of possessions]. It is possible to perform noble actions even without being ruler of land and sea; a man's actions can be guided by virtue also if his means are moderate. That this is so can be clearly seen in the fact that private individuals evidently do not act less honorably but even more honorably than powerful rulers. It is enough to have moderate means at one's disposal, for the life of a man whose activity is guided by virtue will be happy.

Solon certainly gave a good description of a happy man, when he said that he is a man moderately supplied with external goods, who had performed what he, Solon, thought were the noblest actions, and who had lived with self-control. For it is possible to do what one should even with moderate possessions. Also Anaxagoras, it seems, did not assume that a happy man had to be rich and powerful. He said that he would not be surprised if a happy man would strike the common run of people as strange, since they judge by externals and perceive nothing but externals. So it seems that our account is in harmony with the opinion of the wise.

Now, though such considerations carry some conviction, in the field of moral action truth is judged by the actual facts of life, for it is in them that the decisive element lies. So we must examine the conclusions we have reached so far by applying them to the actual facts of life: if they are in harmony with the facts we must accept them, and if they clash we must assume that they are mere words.

A man whose activity is guided by intelligence, who cultivates his intelligence and keeps it in the best condition, seems to be most beloved by the gods. For if the gods have any concern for human affairs—and they seem to have—it is to be expected that they rejoice in what is best and most akin to them, and that is our intelligence; it is also to be expected that they requite with good those who most love and honor intelligence, as being men who care for what is dear to the gods and who act rightly and nobly. That a wise man, more than any other, has all these qualities is perfectly clear. Consequently, he is the most beloved by the gods, and as such he is, presumably, also the happiest. Therefore, we have here a further indication that a wise man attains a higher degree of happiness than anyone.

## 9. Ethics and Politics

Now that we have given an adequate outline of these matters, of the virtues, and also of friendship and pleasure, can we regard our project as having reached its completion? Must we not rather abide by the maxim that in matters of action the end is not to study and attain knowledge of the particular things to be done, but rather to do them? Surely, knowing about excellence or virtue is not enough: we must try to possess it and use it, or find some other way in which we may become good.

Now, if words alone would suffice to make us good, they would rightly "harvest many rewards and great," as Theognis says, and we would have to provide them. But as it is, while words evidently do have the power to encourage and stimulate young men of generous mind, and while they can cause a character well-born and truly enamored of what is noble to be possessed by virtue, they do not have the capacity to turn the common run of people to goodness and nobility. For the natural tendency of most people is to be swayed not by a sense of shame but by fear, and to refrain from acting basely not because it is disgraceful, but because of the punishment it brings. Living under the sway of emotion, they pursue their own proper pleasures and the means by which they can obtain them, and they avoid the pains that are opposed to them. But they do not even have a notion of what is noble and truly pleasant, since they have never tasted it. What argument indeed can transform people like that? To change by argument what has long been ingrained in a character is impossible or, at least, not easy. Perhaps we must be satisfied if we have whatever we think it takes to become good and attain a modicum of excellence.

Some people believe that it is nature that makes men good, others that it is habit, and others again that it is teaching. Now, whatever goodness comes from nature is obviously not in our power, but is present in truly fortunate men as the result of some divine cause. Argument and teaching, I am afraid, are not effective in all cases: the soul of the listener must first have been conditioned by habits to the right kind of likes and dislikes, just as land [must be cultivated before it is able] to foster the seed. For a man whose life is guided by emotion will not listen to an argument that dissuades him, nor will he understand it. How can we possibly persuade a man like that to change his ways? And in general it seems that emotion does not yield to argument but only to force. Therefore, there must first be a character that somehow has an affinity for excellence or virtue, a character that loves what is noble and feels disgust at what is base.

To obtain the right training for virtue from youth up is difficult, unless one has been brought up under the right laws. To live a life of self-control and tenacity is not pleasant for most people, especially for the young. Therefore, their upbringing and pursuits must be regulated by laws; for once they have become familiar, they will no longer be painful. But it is perhaps not enough that they receive the right upbringing and attention only in their youth. Since they must carry on these pursuits and cultivate them by habit when they have grown up, we probably need laws for this, too, and for the whole of life in general. For most people are swayed rather by compulsion than argument, and by punishments rather than by [a sense of] what is noble. This is why some believe that lawgivers ought to exhort and try to influence people toward [a life of] virtue because of its inherent nobility, in the hope that those who have made good progress through their habits will listen to them. Chastisement and penalties, they think, should be imposed upon those who do not obey and are of an inferior nature, while the incorrigible ought to be banished abroad. A good man, they think, who orients his life by what is noble will accept the guidance of reason, while a bad man, whose desire is for pleasure, is corrected by pain like a beast of burden. For the same reason, they say that the pains inflicted must be those that are most directly opposed to the pleasures he loves.

Accordingly, if, as we have said, a man must receive a good upbringing and discipline in order to be good, and must subsequently lead the same kind of life, pursuing what is good and never involuntarily or voluntarily doing anything base, this can be effected by living under the guidance of a kind of intelligence and right order which can be enforced. Now, a father's command does not have the power to enforce or to compel, nor does, in general, the command of a single man, unless he is a king or someone in a similar position. But law does have the power or capacity to compel, being the rule of reason derived from some sort of practical wisdom and intelligence. While people hate any men who oppose, however rightly, their impulses, the law is not invidious when it enjoins what is right.

But, with a few exceptions, Sparta is the only state in which the lawgiver seems to have paid attention to upbringing and pursuits. In most states such matters are utterly neglected, and each man lives as he pleases, "dealing out law to his children and his wife" as the Cyclopes do.[8] Now, the best thing would be to make the correct care of these matters a common concern. But if the community neglects them, it would seem to be incumbent upon every man to help his children and friends attain virtue. This he will be capable of doing, or at least intend to do.

It follows from our discussion that he will be better capable of doing it if he knows something about legislation. For clearly matters of common concern are regulated by laws, and good concerns by laws which set high moral standards. Whether the laws are written or unwritten would seem to make no difference, nor whether they give education to one person or many, just as it makes no difference in the case of mental or physical training or any other pursuit. For just as legal traditions and [national] character prevail in states, so paternal words and [ancestral] habits prevail in households—and the latter have an even greater authority because of the tie of kinship and of benefits rendered, [for members of a household] have the requisite natural affection and obedience [toward the father] to start with. Furthermore, individual treatment is superior to group treatment in education as it is in medicine. As a general rule, rest and abstaining from food are good for a man with a fever, but perhaps they are not good in a particular case. And an expert boxer perhaps does not make all his pupils adopt the same style of fighting. It seems that each particular is worked out with greater precision if private attention is given, since each person has more of an opportunity to get what he needs.

But a physician, a physical trainer, or any other such person can take the best care in a particular case when he knows the general rules, that is, when he knows what is good for everyone or what is good for a particular kind of person; for the sciences are said to be, and actually are, concerned with what is common to particular cases. Of course, there is probably nothing to prevent even a person with no scientific knowledge from taking good care of a particular case, if he has accurately observed by experience what happens in a particular case, just as there are some who seem to be their own best physicians, even though they are incapable of giving aid to another. Nevertheless, if a man wants to master a skill or art or some theoretical knowledge, he ought, one would think, probably to go on to a universal principle, and to gain knowledge of it as best as possible. For, as we have stated, it is with this that the sciences are concerned.

Moreover, a man who wants to make others better by devoting his care to them—regardless of whether they are many or few—should try to learn something about legislation, if indeed laws can make us good. To inculcate a good disposition in any person, that is, any person who presents himself, is not a job for just anyone; if anyone can do it, it is the man who knows, just as it is in medicine and in all other matters that involve some sort of care and practical wisdom.

Is it not, then, our next task to examine from whom and how we can learn to become legislators? Is it not, as always, from the experts, in this case the masters of politics? For, as we saw, legislation is a part of politics. Or does politics not appear to be like the rest of the sciences and capacities?[9] In the other sciences and faculties we find that the people who transmit the capacity are at the same time actively engaged in practicing what they know, as, for example, physicians and painters. The Sophists, on the other hand, profess to teach social and political matters, but none of them practices them. That is done by the politicians, whose practice, it would seem, owes more to some sort of native capacity and to experience than to thought. We find that they neither discuss nor write about these matters—though that would certainly be nobler than making speeches for the law courts and the assemblies—nor again that they have succeeded in making masters of politics of their own sons or any of their friends. But one would expect that they would have done so, had they been able; for they could not have left a better bequest to their cities, nor is there anything they would rather choose to have for themselves, and thus also for those dearest to them, than a capacity of this kind. Nonetheless, experience does seem to make no mean contribution; for they would not have become masters of politics simply through their familiarity with political matters. This is why those who aim at a knowledge of politics also seem to need experience.

But, as we can see, those Sophists who profess to teach politics are very far from teaching it. By and large, they do not even know what sort of thing it is or with what kind of subjects it deals. For [if they did,] they would not have classified it as identical with or even inferior to rhetoric; nor would they have believed that it is easy to legislate by collecting the most highly regarded laws. They think that it is possible to select the best laws, as if the very selection were not an act of understanding and as if correct judgement were not the most important thing here, as it is in matters of music. In every field, it is those who are experienced that judge its products correctly, and are privy to the means and the manner in which they were accomplished and understand what combinations are harmonious. The inexperienced, on the other hand, must be satisfied if they do not fail to recognize whether the work has been produced well or badly. That is the case, for example, in painting. Laws are, as it were, the products of politics. Accordingly, how can a man learn from them to become a legislator or to judge which are the best? We do not even find men becoming medical experts by reading textbooks. Yet medical writers try at least not only to describe the treatments, but also how particular patients, whom they distinguish by their various characteristics, can be cured and how the treatments are to be applied. Though their books seem useful for experienced people, they are useless for those who do not have the requisite knowledge. So also collections of laws and constitutions may perhaps be of good use to those who have the capacity to study them and judge what enactments are good and which are not, and what kind of measures are appropriate to what circumstances. But those who go through such collections without the trained ability [to do so] do not have the requisite good judgment, unless they have it spontaneously, though they may perhaps gain a deeper understanding of these matters.

Accordingly, since previous writers have left the subject of legislation unexamined, it is perhaps best if we ourselves investigate it and the general problem of the constitution of a state, in order to complete as best we can our philosophy of human affairs.[10] First of all, then, let us try to review any discussion of merit contributed by our predecessors on some particular aspect; and then, on the basis of our collection of constitutions, let us study what sort of thing preserves and what destroys states, what preserves and destroys each particular kind of constitution, and what the causes are that make some states well administered and others not. Once we have studied this, we shall perhaps also gain a more comprehensive view of the best form of constitution, of the way in which each is organized, and what laws and customs are current in each. So let us begin our discussion.

## Notes

1. What we get in this paragraph is Aristotle's answer to the problem raised at the opening of Plato's *Meno* (70a) whether excellence is acquired by teaching, by practice, or by nature.
2. Homer, *Odyssey* XII, 219–220.
3. The reference is to Homer, *Iliad* III, 156–160.

4. The name of Pericles (ca. 495–429 B.C.E.) is almost synonymous with the Athenian democracy.

5. The *Margites* was a mock-heroic poem, ascribed by the ancients to Homer.

6. Anacharsis, who is said to have lived early in the sixth century, B.C.E., was a Scythian whose travels all over the Greek world brought him a reputation for wisdom.

7. Supposedly the most beautiful of men, Endymion was loved by the Moon, who cast him into a perpetual sleep that she might descend and embrace him each night.

8. Homer, *Odyssey* IX, 114–115. The Cyclopes, according to Homer, were savage one-eyed giants.

9. The same point is made by Plato, *Meno*, 91a–100c.

10. This final paragraph of the *Nicomachean Ethics* leads us back to the point made at the opening of the work in I, 2: the study of ethics is a part of politics. At the same time, this paragraph serves as a general introduction to the *Politics*.

# *Politics*

## Book VII

### Chapter 4

... [W]e may now embark on the rest of our theme by asking "What are the necessary presuppositions for the construction of a city which will be just as one would desire?" The best constitution cannot, of course, come into being unless it is equipped with the appropriate resources. We must therefore assume everything as we would wish it to be, though nothing we assume must be impossible. These conditions include, among others, a citizen body and a territory. All producers—weavers, for instance, or shipwrights—must have the materials proper to their particular work; and the better prepared these materials are, the better will be the products of their skill. In the same way, the statesman and the lawmaker must have their proper materials, and they must have them in a condition which is suited to their needs. The primary factor necessary, in the equipment of a city, is the human material; and this involves us in considering the ... quantity of the population naturally required.

Experience shows that it is difficult, if not indeed impossible, for a very populous city to enjoy good government. Observation tells us that none of the cities which have a reputation for being well governed are without some limit of population. But the point can also be established on the evidence of the words themselves. Law [*nomos*] is a system of order; and good government [*eunom-ia*] must therefore involve a general system of orderliness.

But an unlimited number cannot partake in order. That is a task for the divine power which holds together the whole [of this universe], for fineness of form generally depends on number and magnitude. We may therefore conclude that the finest city will be one which combines magnitude with the principle just mentioned. But we may also note that cities, like all other things (animals, plants, and inanimate instruments), have a definite measure of size. Any object will lose its power of performing its proper function if it is either excessively small or of an excessive size. Sometimes it will wholly forfeit its nature; sometimes, short of that, it will merely be defective. We may take the example of a ship. A ship which is only 6 inches in length, or is as much as 1,200 feet long, will not be a ship at all; and even a ship of more moderate size may still cause difficulties of navigation, either because it is not large enough or because it is excessively large. The same is true of cities. A city composed of too few members is a city without self-sufficiency (and the city, by its definition, is self-sufficient). One composed of too many will indeed be self-sufficient in the matter of material necessities (as a nation may be) but it will not be a city, since it can hardly have a constitution. Who can be the general of a mass so excessively large? And who can be its herald, unless he has Stentor's voice?[1]

The initial stage of the city may therefore be said to require such an initial amount of population as will be self-sufficient for the purpose of achieving a good way of life in the shape and form of a political association. A city which exceeds this initial amount may be a still greater city; but such increase of size, as has already been noticed, cannot continue indefinitely. What the limit of increase should be is a question easily answered if we look at the actual facts. The activities of a city are partly the activities of its governors, and partly those of the governed. The function of governors is to issue commands and give decisions. Both in order to give decisions in matters of disputed rights, and to distribute the offices of government according to the merit of candidates, the citizens of a city must know one another's characters. Where this is not the case, the distribution of offices and the giving of decisions will suffer. Both are matters in which it is wrong to operate by guesswork; but that is what obviously happens where the population is over-large. Another thing also happens under these conditions. Foreigners and resident aliens readily assume a share in the constitution: it is easy for them to go undetected among the crowd.[2]

These considerations indicate clearly the optimum standard of population. It is, in a word, "the greatest surveyable number required for achieving a life of self-sufficiency". Here we may end our discussion of the proper size of the population. . . .

## Chapter 8

We must inquire how many elements are necessary for the existence of the city. . . . The first thing to be provided is food. The next is crafts; for life requires many tools. The third is arms: the members of a city must bear arms in person, partly in order to maintain their rule over those who disobey, and partly in order to meet any threat of external aggression. The fourth thing which has to be provided is a certain supply of property, alike for domestic use and for military purposes. The fifth (but really first) is an establishment for the service of the gods, or, as it is called, public worship. The sixth thing, and the most vitally necessary, is a method of deciding what is demanded by the public interest and what is just in men's private dealings. These are the services which every city may be said to need. A city is not a mere casual group. It is a group which, as we have said, must be self-sufficient for the purposes of life; and if any of these services is missing it cannot be totally self-sufficient. A city should accordingly be so constituted as to be competent for all these services. It must therefore contain a body of farmers to produce the necessary food; craftsmen; a military force; a propertied class; priests; and those who decide necessary issues and determine what is the public interest.

## Chapter 9

Now that these points have been determined, it remains to consider whether everyone should share in the performance of all these services? (That is a possibility: the same people may all be engaged simultaneously in farm work, the practice of arts and crafts, and the work of deliberation and jurisdiction.) Or should we assume different people for each of the different services? Or, again, should some of the services be assigned to different sets of people, and others be shared by all? The system is not the same in every constitution, for, as we have noted, it is possible for all to share in all functions, and also for all not to share in all but for [only] some people to share in some of them. These alternatives lead to the different constitutions: in democracies everyone shares in all functions, while the opposite practice is followed in oligarchies. Here we are concerned only with the best constitution. Now the best constitution is that under which the city can attain the greatest happiness; and that, as we have already stated, cannot exist without goodness. Upon these principles it clearly follows that in a city with the best possible constitution—a city which has for its members people who are absolutely just, rather than ones who are merely just in relation to some particular standard—the citizens must not live the life of mechanics or shopkeepers, which is ignoble and inimical to goodness. Nor can those who are to be citizens engage in farming: leisure is a necessity, both for growth in goodness and for the pursuit of political activities.

On the other hand, a military force and a body to deliberate on matters of public interest and to give decisions in matters of justice are both essential, and are evidently "parts" of the city in a special sense. Should they be kept separate? or should both functions be given to one and the same set of people? The obvious answer is that from one point of view they should be given to the same people, but from another point of view they ought to be given to different ones. Either function requires a different prime of life: one needs wisdom while the other needs strength; from this point of view they ought to go to different people. But those who are strong enough to use force (or to prevent it from being used) cannot possibly be expected to remain in subjection; and from this point of view the two functions should go to the same people. After all those who have military power also have the power to determine whether or not the constitution will survive. The only course thus left to us is to vest these constitutional powers in one set of the people—that is, in both age-groups—but not at the same time. The order of nature gives strength to youth and wisdom to years; and it is prudent to follow that order in distributing powers among both age-groups. It is just, as well as prudent; for distribution on such a basis is in proportion to desert.

Property must also belong to these people, for the citizens must have a supply of property and these are citizens. The class of mechanics has no share in the city; nor has any other class which is not a "producer" of goodness. This conclusion clearly follows from the principle [of the best city]. That principle requires that happiness should go hand in hand with goodness, and in calling a city happy we should have regard, not just to a part of it, but to all the citizens.[3] A further argument is provided for the view that property ought to belong to citizens, if we consider that the farm-workers ought to be slaves or barbarian serfs.

Of the elements which we enumerated, only the priesthood is left. The plan on which it ought to be based is clear. Nobody belonging to the farming or the mechanic class should be made a priest. The cult of the gods should be undertaken by citizens. Now the citizen body has been divided into two sections, the military and the deliberative. Moreover, it is appropriate for the service of the gods and the relaxation which it brings to be assigned to those who have given up [these tasks] through age. It is to these people, therefore, that the priestly offices should be assigned.

This completes our survey of the factors without which a city cannot exist, and those which constitute "parts" of the city. Farm-workers, craftsmen, and the general body of day-labourers, must necessarily be present in cities, while the military force and the deliberative body are parts of the city. . . .

## Chapter 14

As all political associations are composed of rulers and ruled, we have to consider whether different people should be rulers and the ruled or whether the same people [should occupy these roles] throughout their lives. The system of education will necessarily vary according to the answer we give. We may imagine one set of circumstances in which it would be obviously better that the one group should once and for all be rulers and one group should be ruled. This would be if there were one class in the city surpassing all others as much as gods and heroes are supposed to surpass mankind—a class so outstanding, physically as well as mentally, that the superiority of the rulers was indisputably clear to those over whom they ruled. But that is a difficult assumption to make; and we have nothing in actual life like the gulf between kings and subjects which the writer Scylax describes as existing in India. We may therefore draw the conclusion, which can be defended on many grounds, that all should share alike in a system of government under which they rule and are ruled by turns. In a society of peers equality means that all should have the same [privileges]: and a constitution can hardly survive if it is founded on injustice. Along with those who are ruled there will be all those [serfs] from the countryside who want a revolution; those who belong to the citizen body cannot possibly be sufficient in number to overcome all these.[4] On the other hand, it cannot be denied that there should be a difference between governors and governed. How they can differ, and yet share alike, is a dilemma which legislators have to solve. . . .

Nature, we have suggested, has provided us with the distinction we need. She has divided a body identical in species into two different age-groups, a younger and an older, one of them meant to be ruled and the other to rule. No one in his youth resents being ruled, or thinks himself better [than his rulers]; especially if he knows that he will redeem his contribution on reaching the proper age. In one sense, therefore, it has to be said that rulers and ruled are the same; in another, that they are different. The same will be true of their education: from one point of view it must be the same; from another it has to be different, and, as the saying goes, one who would learn to rule well, must first learn to be ruled. Ruling, as has already been said in our first part, takes two forms, one for the benefit of the rulers, the other for the benefit of the ruled. The former is what we call "despotic"; the latter involves ruling over freemen.

Some of the duties imposed [on the free] differ [from those of slaves] not in the work they involve, but in the object for which they are to be done. This means that a good deal of the work which is generally accounted menial may none the less be the sort of work which young freemen can honourably do. It is not the inherent nature of actions, but the end or object for which they are done, which makes one action differ from another in the way of honour or dishonour.

We have said that the excellence of the citizen who is a ruler is the same as that of the good man and that the same person who begins by being ruled must later be a ruler. It follows on this that the legislator must labour to ensure that his citizens become good men. He must therefore know what institutions will produce this result, and what is the end or aim to which a good life is directed.

There are two different parts of the soul. One of these parts has reason intrinsically and in its own nature. The other has not; but it has the capacity for obeying such a principle. When we speak of a man as being "good", we mean that he has the goodnesses of these two parts of the soul. But in which of the parts is the end of man's life more particularly to be found? The answer is one which admits of no doubt to those who accept the division just made. In the world of nature as well as of art that which is worse always exists for the sake of that which is better. The part which has reason is the better part. But this part is in turn divided, on the scheme which we generally follow, into two parts of its own. Reason, according to that scheme, is partly practical, partly speculative. It is obvious, therefore, that the part of the soul which has this principle must fall into two corresponding parts. We may add that the same goes for the activities [of those parts]. It follows that those who can attain all the activities possible, or two of those activities, will be bound to prefer the activity of the part which is in its nature better. All of us always prefer the highest we can attain.

Life as a whole is also divided into action and leisure, war and peace; and actions are divided into those which are [merely] necessary, or useful, and those which have value [in themselves]. The same [pattern of] choice applies to these as applies to the parts of the soul and their different activities—war for the sake of peace; work for the sake of leisure; and acts which are merely necessary or useful for the sake of those which are valuable in themselves. The legislation of the true statesman must be framed with a view to all of these factors: it must cover the different parts of the soul and their different activities and should be directed more to the higher than the lower, and rather to ends than means. The same goes for the different parts or ways of life and for the choice of different activities. It is true that one must be able to engage in work and in war; but one must be even more able to lead a life of leisure and peace. It is true, again, that one must be able to do necessary or useful acts; but one must be even more able to do deeds of value. These are the general aims which ought to be followed in the education of childhood and of the stages of the life which still require education. . . .

## Chapter 15

The final end of human beings is the same whether they are acting individually or acting collectively; and the standard followed by the best man is thus the same as the standard followed by the best constitution. It is therefore evident that the qualities required for the use of leisure must belong [to the city as well as the individual]; for, as we have repeatedly argued, peace is the final end of war, and leisure the final end of work. The good qualities required for the use of leisure and the cultivation of the mind are twofold. Some of them are operative during leisure itself: some are operative while we are at work. A number of necessary conditions must be present, before leisure is possible. This is why a city must possess the quality of temperance, and why, again, it must possess the quality of courage and endurance. "There's no leisure for slaves", as the proverb goes, and those who cannot face danger courageously become the slaves of those who attack them. The quality of courage and endurance is required for work: wisdom is required for leisure: temperance and justice are qualities required for both times—though they are particularly required by those who enjoy peace and leisure. War automatically enforces temperance and justice: the enjoyment of prosperity, and leisure accompanied by peace, is more apt to make people overbearing. A great deal of justice and a great deal of temperance is therefore required in those who appear to be faring exceptionally well and enjoying all that is generally accounted to be happiness, like those, if there are any, who dwell in "the happy isles" of which poets sing; and the greater the leisure which these people enjoy, when they are set among an abundance of blessings, the greater too will be their need of wisdom, as well as of temperance and justice.

We can now understand why a city which seeks to achieve happiness, and to be good, must share in these virtues. If some shame must always attach to anyone who cannot use properly the goods of life, a special measure of shame must attach to those who cannot use them properly in times of leisure—to those who show themselves good in work and war, but sink to the level of slaves in times of peace and leisure. . . .

## Chapter 17

When children are born, the sort of nourishment which they are given can be expected to make a great difference to their physical powers. . . . It is good to habituate children to the endurance of cold from their earliest infancy; and this is a practice which greatly conduces to their general health, as well as hardening them in advance for military service. Wherever it is possible to implant a habit in children, it is best to begin the process of habituation in their earliest years, and then to increase it gradually. . . .

The earliest years will best be handled in the ways we have just described, and in other similar ways. The next stage of the child's life, which lasts to the age of 5, is one which cannot be set any lessons, or put to any compulsory tasks, for fear of hindering its growth. But it is a stage which needs some practice in movement, to prevent the body from becoming limp; and this should be provided by games, as well as in other ways. The games should be neither laborious nor undisciplined, but such as become a freeman. Care should also be taken by the officers in charge (who are generally termed the superintendents of education) to determine the sort of tales and stories which children of this age ought to be told. All these things should prepare the way for the occupations of later years; and even the games of children should be for the most part mimicries of what will later be earnest. . . .

The superintendents of education must exercise a general control over the way in which children pass their time. In particular, they must be careful that very little of their time is passed in the company of slaves. The stage of life through which children pass down to the age of 7 is bound to be one of home training; and, young as they are, they will be likely to contract slave-like habits from what they hear or see. It should therefore be a primary duty of the legislator to exorcize the use of bad language everywhere in our city. The use of bad language leads to similar kinds of behaviour. The young, especially, should be kept free from hearing, or using, any such language. Those who are found talking or acting in any of the prohibited ways must be punished accordingly. The younger freemen who are not yet allowed to recline at the common tables,[5] must be subjected to corporal punishment and other indignities; and men of an older age should pay the penalty for behaving like slaves by undergoing indignities of a slave-like character.

If talk of this kind is proscribed, it is obvious that we must also prevent the young from seeing indecent pictures and [hearing] indecent speeches. It should therefore be the duty of those in office to prohibit all statuary and painting which portrays any sort of indecent action. An exception may, however, be made for the festivals of deities where even the use of scurrility is licensed by the law. (But here, we may note, the law also allows men who have reached a proper maturity to worship the gods on behalf of their wives and children as well as for themselves.) Legislation should forbid the young from attending iambics or comedies, until they have reached the age when they are allowed to share in the practice of reclining and taking wine [at the common tables]. By that time their education will have made them all immune from the evil effects of such performances. . . .

Perhaps there is point in the remark of Theodorus, the tragic actor, that he had never yet allowed any other actor, however poor he might be, to make his entrance before he did, because (as he put it) "spectators get fond of those they hear first". This is a fate which is apt to befall us not only when we are dealing with people, but also when we are dealing with things: we always prefer what we come across first. The young must therefore be kept from an early familiarity with anything that is low, and especially anything that may suggest depravity or malice.

When the first five years are safely over, children should then spend the next two years, down to the age of 7, in watching others at work on the lessons which they will afterwards have to learn themselves.

There should be two different periods of education—the first from the age of 7 to that of puberty; the second from puberty to the age of 21. Those who divide man's life into seven-year periods are on the whole right. But the divisions which we ought to follow are those made by nature herself. The purpose of education, like that of every kind of art, is to make good nature's deficiencies. Three subjects here suggest themselves for our consideration. The first is whether there ought to be some code of regulations concerning children. The second is whether the care of children should be a matter for the city, or should be conducted on a private basis, as it still is, even today, in the great majority of cases. The third question which we have to consider is what this code of regulations should be.

## Book VIII

### Chapter 1

All would agree that the legislator should make the education of the young his chief and foremost concern. After all, the constitution of a city will suffer if this does not happen. The form of education must be related to each form of constitution. The type of character appropriate to a constitution tends to sustain that constitution as well as to bring it into being. The democratic type of character creates and sustains democracy; the oligarchical type creates and sustains oligarchy; and in every case the best type of character will always tend to produce a better form of constitution. What is more, every capacity, and every form of art, requires as a condition of its exercise some measure of previous training and some amount of preliminary habituation, so the same must clearly go for acts embodying goodness of character.

The city as a whole has a single end. Evidently, therefore, the system of education must also be one and the same for all, and the provision of this system must be a matter of public action. It cannot be left, as it is at present, to private enterprise, with each parent making provision privately for his own children, and having them privately instructed as he himself thinks fit. Training for an end which is common should also itself be common. We must not regard a citizen as belonging just to himself: we must rather regard every citizen as belonging to the city, since each is a part of the city; and the provision made for each part will naturally be adjusted to the provision made for the whole. Here the Spartans are to be praised. They pay the greatest attention to the training of the young; and they pay attention collectively, and not in their private capacity.

## Chapter 2

It is now evident both that there ought to be laws to regulate education and that education ought to be conducted by the city. But we have to consider what education should be given, and the methods by which it should be given. At present opinion is divided about the subjects of education. All do not share the same opinion about what should be learned by the young, with a view to goodness or to the best life; nor is opinion clear whether education should be directed mainly to the understanding, or mainly to moral character. If we look at actual practice, the result is confusing; it throws no light on the problem whether there should be training in those pursuits which are useful in life, or those which make for goodness, or those which go beyond the ordinary run [of knowledge]. Each sort of study receives some votes in its favour. There is, for example, a total absence of agreement about the studies which make for goodness. To begin with, those who honour goodness do not all have the same conception of goodness; so it is hardly surprising that they should also differ about the right methods of practising it.

There can be no doubt that such useful subjects as are really necessary ought to be part of the instruction of children. But this does not mean the inclusion of every useful subject. Occupations are divided into those which are fit for freemen and those which are unfit for them; and clearly children should take part in useful occupations only to the extent that they do not turn those taking part in them into "mechanical" types. The term "mechanical" [*banausos*] should properly be applied to any occupation, art, or instruction which is calculated to make the body, or soul, or mind of a freeman unfit for the pursuit and practice of goodness. We may accordingly apply the word "mechanical" to any art or craft which adversely affects men's physical fitness, and to any employment which is pursued for the sake of gain; these preoccupy and debase the mind. Much the same may also be said of those branches of knowledge which are fit for a freeman. It is not out of keeping with freeman's character to study these up to a certain point; but too much concentration upon them, with a view to attaining perfection, is liable to cause the same evil effects that have just been mentioned. A good deal depends on the purpose for which acts are done or subjects are studied. Doing these to satisfy a personal need, or to help a friend, or to attain goodness, is not unfitting for a freeman; but the very same act, when done repeatedly at the instance of other people, may be counted menial and servile.

# Chapter 3

The studies now generally established as parts of the curriculum may be regarded, as has already been said, from two different points of view. There are some four subjects which are usually included in education. They are reading and writing, physical training, and music; and some would also add drawing. Reading and writing together with drawing are generally regarded as useful for the practical purposes of life in a number of different ways. Physical training is commonly thought to foster courage. But there is a doubt about music. At present, indeed, it is mainly studied as if its object were pleasure; but the real reason which originally led to its being made a subject of education is that our very nature (as we have often remarked) seeks the power, not only to work in the right way but also to use leisure well; indeed leisure, as we would once more repeat, is the basis of everything. It is true that work and leisure are both necessary; but it is also true that leisure is preferable, and is more of an end. We must consider, therefore, what we should do to occupy our leisure. It cannot be playing, since play would then be the end for the sake of which we live. That is an impossibility. Play is a thing to be chiefly used in connection with work. Those who labour need relaxation; and play exists for the purpose of relaxation. Work involves labour and exertion. We may therefore conclude that play should be admitted into our city at the proper times, and should be applied as a kind of medicine. The effect which play produces in the mind is one of relief from exertion; and the pleasure it gives provides relaxation. Leisure of itself, so it seems, involves pleasure, happiness, and well-being. This is the condition, not of those who are at work, but of those who are at leisure. Those who work do so with a view to some end which they regard as still unattained. But happiness is an end; and all men think of it as accompanied by pleasure and not by pain. It is true that all do not conceive this pleasure in the same way. Different people conceive it differently, according to their own personality and disposition. But the highest pleasure, derived from the noblest sources, will be that of the man of greatest goodness.

It is clear, therefore, that there are some branches of learning and education which ought to be studied with a view to living a life of leisure. It is clear, too, that these forms of education and of learning are valued for their own sake, while those studied with a view to work should be regarded merely as matters of necessity and valued as means to other things. This will explain why our forefathers made music a part of education. They did not do so because it was necessary: it is nothing of the sort. Nor did they do so because it is useful, as reading and writing are useful for money-making, for household management, for the acquisition of knowledge, and for many political activities. Drawing may be held to be useful in helping us to judge more correctly the works of different craftsmen. Nor is music, like physical training, useful in improving health and strength: it has no visible effect upon either. We are thus left with its value for living a life of leisure. This is evidently the reason for its being introduced into education: it ranks as one of the ways in which a freeman should pass his time. This is the meaning of the lines in Homer, beginning,

> Such are they who alone should be called to the bountiful banquet

and continuing (after a mention of various guests) with the words:

> With them call they a minstrel, to pleasure all men with his music.

Again, in another passage, Odysseus is made to say that music is the best of pastimes when men are all merry, and

> They who feast in the hall lend their ears to the minstrel in silence, Sitting in order due.[6]

We may take it as evident, from what has been said, that there is a kind of education in which parents should have their sons trained not because it is necessary, or because it is useful, but simply because it befits a freeman and is good in itself. Whether this kind of education is confined to a single subject, or includes a number of subjects; what the subjects are, and how they should be studied—all this must be left for further discussion. But we have already reached a point at which we are entitled to say that the evidence of tradition supports our general view. This is shown by the old-established subjects of study; and the example of music is sufficient to make it clear. We are also entitled to say that some of the useful subjects—for example, reading and writing—ought to be taught to children, not only because they are useful, but also because, by their means, many other kinds of learning become possible. Similarly the object of instruction in drawing is not so much to save people from making mistakes in their private purchases, or from being deceived in the buying and selling of articles; it is rather to give them an observant eye for beauty of form and figure. To aim at utility everywhere is utterly unbecoming to the high-minded and to those who have the character of freemen.

In educating children we must clearly make use of habit before reason, and we must deal with the body before we deal with the mind. We must therefore begin by putting them into the hands of physical instructors and games masters. The former is concerned with the proper condition of the body: the latter with what it can do.

## Chapter 4

Among the cities which are generally regarded as paying the greatest attention to the training of youth, there are some which create an athletic habit of body at the cost of impairing both the appearance of the body and its growth. The Spartans have not made this particular error; but they give the young a savage character by imposing rigorous exercises, on the assumption that this is the best way of fostering courage. It is, however, a mistake, as we have repeatedly said, to direct the training of youth exclusively, or mainly, to this one end; and even if courage were the main object, the Spartans are wrong in their way of encouraging it. Both in the animal world, and among tribal peoples, courage is always found, as observation will show us, not in association with the greatest ferocity, but in connection with a gentler and more lion-like temperament. Even the Spartans themselves, as we know from experience, were superior to others only so long as they were the only people who assiduously practised the rigours of discipline; and nowadays they are beaten both in athletic contests and in actual war. Their previous superiority was not due to the particular training which they gave to their youth: it was simply and solely due to their having some sort of discipline when their antagonists had none at all. Nobility of character, rather than ferocity of temper, should take pride of place. It is not wolves, or other savage animals, that will fight a good fight in the presence of a noble danger, but the good man. To let youth run wild in savage pursuits, and to leave them untrained in the disciplines they really need, is really to degrade them into vulgarity. It is to make them serve the statesman's purposes in one respect, and one only; and even there, as our argument shows, it is to make them of less service than those who have been differently trained. We must not judge the Spartans on the grounds of their former achievement, but on the grounds of their present position. The Spartan training has now to face rivals. Formerly it had none.

There is general agreement about the necessity of physical training, and about the way in which it ought to be given. Till the age of puberty the exercises used should be light, and there should be no rigorous dieting or violent exertion, such as may hinder the proper growth of the body. The effects of these practices are strikingly evident. In the lists of Olympic victors there are only two or three cases of the same person having won in the men's events who had previously won in the boys'; and the reason is that early training, and the compulsory exercises which it involved, had resulted in loss of strength. After that age is reached, the next three years may be spent in other studies; and then the next period of development may properly be given to hard exercise and strict diet. It is not right to do work with the mind and the body at the same time. The two different sorts of work tend naturally to produce different, and indeed opposite, effects. Physical work clogs the mind; and mental work hampers the body.

## Chapter 5

Some questions concerning music have already been raised at an earlier stage of our argument; but it will be well to pick up the thread again here, and to pursue the matter further.[7] We may thus provide something in the nature of a preface to the considerations which would naturally be advanced in any full view of the subject. It is difficult to define the exact effects of music; and it is equally difficult to define the purpose for which it ought to be studied. Some would hold that the purpose of music, like that of sleeping or drinking, is simply amusement and relaxation. Sleep and drink are not in themselves good things; but they are at any rate pleasurable things, and, as Euripides says,[8] they "give us rest from care". It is on this ground that music is sometimes ranked with them both, and that sleep and drink and music (to which dancing may also be added) are all treated in just the same way. Another possible view is that music should be regarded as something of an influence making for goodness, inasmuch as it has the power of giving a tone to our character (just as physical training can give a tone to our bodies) by habituating us to feel pleasure in the right sort of way. There is still a third possible view—that music has some contribution to make to a cultivated way of living and to the growth of wisdom.

It is clear that amusement is not the object with a view to which the young should be educated. Learning is not a matter of amusement. It is attended by effort and pain. On the other hand, it is also true that a cultivated way of living is not a thing which is proper for children or the young of a tender age. Those who are themselves still short of their own end cannot yet cope with the ultimate end. Perhaps the serious studies of children are means to the amusement which they will be able to enjoy when they reach their full growth as adults, But if that view be taken, why (we may ask) should children be taught to play music themselves? Why should they not follow the example of the Persian and Median kings, and get their pleasure and instruction through listening to others making music? Those who make it an occupation and a profession are bound to attain a better result than those who only practise it long enough just to learn. We may add that if children are to be made to work away at musical performances, they ought equally to be made to work at the business of cooking—which is absurd.

The same problem arises if we look at music as a power which can improve character. Here, too, we may ask, "Why should children learn to perform themselves, and why should not listening to the music of others be enough to give them the power of enjoying and appreciating music in the right sort of way?" The Spartans act on that principle: they do not learn to play; but, so it is said, they are able to appreciate properly the difference between good and bad tunes. The same is true if we take the third view about music, and hold that it ought to be used to promote a way of living that is both pleasant and worthy of a freeman. Why, for this purpose, should we learn ourselves, instead of drawing on the services of others? Here we shall do well to remember the conception we hold of the gods. The Zeus of our poets does not sing, or play on the harp. We are apt to regard as vulgar those who do otherwise, and we think of them as behaving in a way in which a man would not behave unless he were drunk or jesting.

This, however, is perhaps a matter for later consideration. We must first inquire "Should music be included in education, or should it not?" and "Which of the three effects previously distinguished does it have?" "Does it contribute to education, or to amusement, or to a cultivated way of living?" There are reasons for connecting it with all three; for it evidently embraces elements common to all. For example, amusement is intended to produce relaxation; and relaxation, which is in its nature a remedy for the pain produced by exertion, must necessarily be pleasant. Similarly, again, it is generally agreed that a cultivated way of living must include pleasure, as well as nobility, since these are both part of the happy life. Now we all agree that music, whether instrumental or accompanied by the voice, is one of the greatest of pleasures. At any rate we can cite the testimony of the poet Musaeus:[9]

> Song is to mortals the sweetest;

and here we may see the reason why people very naturally enlist the aid of music for their social parties and pastimes—it has the power of gladdening their hearts. We may therefore conclude that this is one of the reasons why children ought to be educated in music. All innocent pleasures have a double use: they not only help us to achieve our end, but they also serve us as a means of relaxation. It is seldom that people attain their end. But they can often relax, and indulge themselves in amusements (not so much with a view to something beyond, but just for pleasure); and it may therefore be well that they should rest and relax for a while in the pleasures which come from music.

People fall, it is true, into a way of making amusements the end of their life. The reason for their doing so is that the end of life would seem to involve a kind of pleasure. This kind of pleasure is not the ordinary, but in their search for it people are apt to mistake ordinary pleasure for it; and they do so because pleasure generally has some sort of likeness to the ultimate end of their activity. This end is desirable just for itself, and not for the sake of any future result; and the pleasures of amusement are similar—they are not desired for the sake of some result in the future, but rather because of something which has happened in the past, that is to say, the exertion and pain [which have already been undergone]. This, it may reasonably be held, is the cause which induces people to seek happiness from pleasures of this sort.

Pleasure is not the only reason for having recourse to music. Another reason is its utility in furnishing relaxation. This is how the case for it seems to stand. But we have to inquire whether it does not possess a natural character which is of higher value than the uses hitherto mentioned. Perhaps there is more in question than our sharing in the common pleasure which everyone senses in music—a pleasure, indeed, which is natural, and which explains why the use of music appeals to all ages and all types of character—and perhaps we ought to consider whether music has not also some sort of bearing on our characters and our souls. It will clearly have such a bearing if our characters are actually affected by music. That they are so affected is evident from the influence exercised by a number of different tunes, but especially by those of Olympus.[10] His tunes, by general consent, have an inspiring effect on the soul; and a feeling of inspiration is an affection of the soul's character. We may add that, in listening to imitative [music], everyone is moved to feelings of sympathy, quite apart from the effects of rhythm and melody.

Since music belongs to the category of pleasures, and since goodness consists in feeling delight where one should, and loving and hating aright, we may clearly draw some conclusions. First, there is no lesson which we are so much concerned to learn, and no habit which we are so much concerned to acquire, as that of forming right judgements on, and feeling delight in, fine characters and good actions. Next, rhythm and melodies provide us with images of states of character, which come closer to their actual nature than anything else can do—images of anger and of calm, of courage and of temperance, and of their opposites, images, in fact, of every state of character. This is a fact which is clear from experience; to listen to these images is to undergo a real change of the soul. Now to acquire a habit of feeling pain or taking delight in an image is something closely allied to feeling pain or taking delight in the actual reality. For example, if someone finds delight in looking at the image of some object purely on the ground of its form, he will also be bound to find pleasure in looking at the actual object whose image he now sees. It is true that the objects of some of the senses, such as touch and taste, cannot furnish any resemblance to states of character. Objects of sight may do so, but only to a slight extent. There are indeed shapes and figures which bear a resemblance to states of character, but the resemblance is not great; and [we have to remember that] everyone shares this sense. Moreover, the shapes and colours [presented by visual art] are not representations of states of character: they are merely indications. And they are indications which can only be given by depicting the body when under the influence of some emotion. But in so far as there is any difference between the effects of looking at different works of art, the young should be discouraged from looking at the works of Pauso, and encouraged to study the works of Polygnotus and any other painter or sculptor who depicts moral character.[11]

With musical compositions, however, the case is different. They involve representations of states of character themselves. This is an evident fact. In the first place, the nature of the modes varies; and listeners will be differently affected according as they listen to different modes.[12] The effect of some will be to produce a sadder and graver temperament; this is the case, for example, with the mode called the Mixolydian. The effect of others (such as the soft modes) is to relax the tone of the mind. Another mode is specially calculated to produce a moderate and collected temperament; this is held to be the peculiar power of the Dorian mode, while the Phrygian mode is held to give inspiration and fire. Those who have studied this kind of education do well to make these points, for the evidence by which they support their theories is derived from actual facts. The same goes for the various rhythms: some have a more steady character while others have a lively quality; and these last may again be divided, according as they move with a more vulgar rhythm or move in a manner more suited to freemen.

What we have said makes it clear that music possesses the power of producing an effect on the character of the soul. If it can produce this effect, it must clearly be made a subject of study and taught to the young. We may add that the teaching of music is congenial to the natural character of youth. Owing to their tender years, the young will not willingly tolerate any unsweetened fare; and music, by its nature, has a quality of sweetness. Nor is that all. The modes and rhythms of music have an affinity [with the soul], as well as a natural sweetness. This explains why many thinkers connect the soul with harmony—some saying that it is a harmony, and others that it possesses the attribute of harmony.

## Chapter 6

It remains to answer the question, which has already been raised, whether children ought to learn music by actually singing and playing. It is clear that it makes a great difference to the acquisition of an aptitude if one has taken part in performances. It is difficult, if not impossible, for those who have never taken part in performances to become good judges of others. Children, too, should always have something to keep them occupied; and the rattle of Archytas[13] (which parents give to children in order to divert their attention and stop them from breaking things in the house) must be counted an admirable invention. Young things can never keep quiet: so a rattle suits children in infancy, while education serves as a rattle for older children.

These considerations make it plain that a musical education should include some share in its actual performance. There is no difficulty in determining what is suitable or unsuitable for the different ages of growth or in answering the objection that this is a vulgar "mechanical" kind of occupation. We must begin by noting that the purpose for which the young should join in the actual performance of music is only that they should be able to judge [musical performances]. This means that they ought to practise execution in their earlier years; but it also means that they ought to be released from it at a later age, when the education they have received in their youth should have made them able to judge what is good and to appreciate music properly. The censure which is sometimes passed on music—that it produces a professional or mechanical turn of mind—may be easily answered. . . .

We may take it for granted that the study [of music] should neither impede the activities of later years, nor produce a vulgar mechanical kind of body which is ineffective for the purposes of the period of military and civic training—ineffective, initially, in bodily exercise, and afterwards in the acquisition of knowledge. The study of music might follow these lines if two conditions were observed—first, that pupils were not set to work on the sort of performances which belong to professional competitions; secondly, that they were not made to attempt the extraordinary and extravagant feats of execution which have recently been introduced into competitions, and have thence passed on into education. Even so, performances should be carried only to the point at which students begin to be able to appreciate good melodies and rhythms, and are not content merely to enjoy that common element in music which is felt by some of the animals and by nearly all slaves and children.

## Notes

1. According to Homer (*Iliad* v. 785), Stentor had a voice as loud as fifty men.
2. This chapter indicates very strikingly some of the major differences between the Greek *polis*, which depended on face-to-face contact and personal knowledge, and modern states. It is notable that Aristotle expects citizens to draw on their personal knowledge of those involved in electing officials and settling legal disputes. Without this kind of personal knowledge constitutional rule as Aristotle understands it is impossible.
3. This passage is, no doubt, intended as a criticism of Plato's *Republic*, where the guardians are forbidden to have property.
4. I.e. if the constitution allows one group to rule permanently over another even though they are really of the same quality, the group in the inferior position will join forces with the serfs to overthrow the constitution.
5. The Greeks normally reclined on couches while dining but the younger men would be expected to sit on chairs.
6. The first of these lines is not in Homer's poetry as we have it; the second corresponds roughly to *Odyssey* xvii, 385; the third quotation is *Odyssey* ix, 7–8.
7. Very little Greek music has survived and our knowledge of it, as compared with other Greek art forms, is very limited. In this chapter Aristotle, like Plato in the *Republic*, takes it for granted that music has great emotional power. Not only can it represent or depict the emotions much more effectively than any other medium but it also tends to create those feelings in the listener. In this way it has the power to shape the characters, particularly of the young.
8. *Bacchae* 381.
9. A legendary pre-Homeric poet. Collections of verses attributed to him were evidently highly prized.
10. A semi-legendary composer.
11. Polygnotus was a celebrated painter active in the fifth century, B.C.E. His major works were largely mural paintings on public buildings in Athens and elsewhere. He was particularly noted for his ability to portray character. Pauso was evidently a painter of lesser state.
12. Greek music was based on a system of modes—different ways of arranging the notes on the scale. Different modes were held to be expressive of different emotions.
13. Archytas of Tarentum, famous both as a statesman and as a mathematician, was a contemporary of Plato. It is not clear why a child's rattle should bear his name.

# Afterword

Randall Curren*

To understand Aristotle's educational ideas, one must understand the overall plan of his *Nicomachean Ethics* (*NE*) and *Politics* (*Pol.*). These works are records of a distinct series of lectures presented by Aristotle (384–322 B.C.E.) at his school, the Lyceum, in Athens. One concerns ethics and the other "legislative science," but they are closely related to each other as parts of the larger field of "political science." Aristotle regarded political science as a form of inquiry into the nature of happiness (*eudaimonia*) and how to arrange human affairs in such a way as to achieve it. As such, political science sought to determine the truth about these matters and to guide human conduct on the basis of its findings. The audience Aristotle sought to guide included both statesmen and citizens in their private lives. He sought to guide both the affairs of societies, encouraging political reforms that would enable people to lead better, more satisfying lives, and also the affairs of individuals in managing their own lives and households. Ethics provides an understanding of happiness or the highest good for human beings, the nature and acquisition of virtue, the importance of virtue for a happy life, and various related matters such as the nature of friendship and its role in a good life and a good society. Politics, or legislative science, is concerned with putting this understanding into practice through two interrelated tools of governance: law and education. It addresses the nature and proper aim of a political community, the different kinds of constitutions (including the best that is feasible for most societies, and the best that can be hoped for in the best possible circumstances), the measures that may be taken to stabilize and improve societies, education, and various related matters such as the significance of wealth for citizenship and personal well-being.

At the end of the *Nicomachean Ethics*, Aristotle offers a preview of the *Politics* and makes his case for why everyone would benefit from not only a course in ethics, but also a course in legislation. It may seem odd that he would think that everyone who manages a household should have knowledge of legislative science. He argues it is "through laws" that people can become good, and becoming good is essential to living a happy life, so whether one is responsible for the care of many people (as a statesman is) or the care of just a few people (as the head of a household is), one must know how to legislate. This argument incorporates

---

* Randall Curren is Professor of Philosophy at the University of Rochester.

three propositions foundational to Aristotle's educational thought: (1) Good law is educative; it communicates truths about living well as a human being and a member of a society. (2) Virtue is a prerequisite for happiness. (3) Societies, heads of households, and educational institutions should all enable people to achieve happiness or the highest good for human beings, and should do so by enabling them to acquire and exercise virtue, goodness, or excellence (*arête*). The fact that Aristotle relies on these propositions in explaining the relationship between his *Nicomachean Ethics* and *Politics* illustrates how important education is to his whole philosophy of human affairs. To understand his educational ideas, it won't suffice to concentrate on the one part of his writings where education is addressed at some length: Book VIII of his *Politics*.

The purpose of what follows is to survey those aspects of the *Nicomachean Ethics* and *Politics* that are most important to an appreciation of Aristotle's educational ideas, and to offer some closing reflections on the enduring value of these ideas. We must consider the moral and intellectual virtues, how they are acquired and how they are related to one another; the happiest kind of life and the role of virtue in achieving it; the nature of a political community; Aristotle's theory of constitutions; the "best possible" society described in Book VII of the *Politics*; the context these provide for the account of education in Book VIII of the *Politics*; and what is of most enduring value in Aristotle's philosophy of education.

## 1. The Moral and Intellectual Virtues, How they are Acquired and How they are Related to One Another

In the final book of the *Nicomachean Ethics* (X.9), Aristotle observes that reasoned arguments alone are not enough to make people good. Many people are not moved by arguments based on what is admirable or appropriate (*kalon*), because they lack even a conception of what is *kalon*, having never been exposed to it. This echoes the opening lines of Plato's *Republic*, in which Socrates expresses a preference for using persuasion instead of force, and is met with the reply that people may not be willing to listen and be persuaded. Some central themes of the *Republic* are thereby introduced: Socrates is committed to an ethic of respect for persons as rational beings, which requires dealing with them as much as possible through truthful and reasoned instruction and persuasion, and as little as possible through force and violence. Plato is committed to the same ethic, but sees that people are not always ready to listen to reason. Thrasymachus, who appears later in Book I, is portrayed as unable to understand how Socrates could be moved by anything more admirable than a desire to prevail in verbal contests, having never developed beyond a love of victory and honor himself. How a person could care about truth and be moved by respect for sound reasoning and evidence is beyond him. Plato offers Thrasymachus as one illustration of the fact that reasonableness is a trait that comes in degrees and must be nurtured or *cultivated* in people. A society that is serious about respecting people as rational beings—beings who are potentially reasonable, and are better off to the extent they are reasonable and reasoned with instead of coerced or deceived—must be systematic in its efforts to nurture reasonableness. This requires government involvement to ensure that everyone receives an appropriate education. These same ideas animate Aristotle's *Politics* and *Nicomachean Ethics*.

The passage in *NE* X.9 goes on to say that "nature" (i.e., traits with which one is born), habituation (training in doing the right things), and teaching must *all* be favorable in order for a person to become good, so there is little chance of becoming good if one does not grow up under good laws. We learn in Books VII and VIII of the *Politics* that those laws should, among other things, provide schooling that is public and "the same for all." Plainly, Aristotle's view is that although our own actions play a crucial role in forming our character, the factors that shape our character are largely beyond our control. If he didn't think this, he would have little reason to open Book VIII of the *Politics* with the suggestion that legislators should obviously be concerned above all with educating the young. This is a remarkable statement, especially considering the fact that *public* education was all but unknown in his world. It reflects a conviction that adults have a fundamental, collective duty—a duty falling on governments—to enable young people to develop into good and flourishing adults. The laws should regulate birth and early training in order to ensure the healthy development of the body and "irrational" psyche, all with an eye to the development of "reason and mind." Aristotle says this sequence of development is "natural," but this does not imply that favorable development will occur spontaneously. The fulfillment of a person's highest potential is something rare and difficult to achieve, in fact.

Aristotle distinguishes between the moral virtues and the intellectual virtues, and he associates this distinction with a division of the psyche or soul, which he identifies as the source and cause of growth and movement. Moral virtues, such as generosity and courage, are identified as states of the desiring aspect of the soul (a part of the irrational element). Intellectual virtues, such as contemplative wisdom (*sophia*) and practical wisdom (*phronêsis*), are identified as states of the rational element of the soul. Moral virtues are defined as dispositions to feel and be moved by our desires or emotions neither too weakly nor too strongly, but in a way that moves us to act as reason would dictate, and to take pleasure in doing so. Intellectual virtues are defined as capacities or powers of understanding, judgment, and reasoning that enable the rational soul to attain truth.

Having distinguished the moral and intellectual virtues in this way, Aristotle says the former mainly arise as a result of habit and the latter mainly arise as a result of teaching. The understanding of Aristotle's conception of moral development often comes to an abrupt halt with the associated idea that we become brave by repeatedly doing the right thing in the face of danger and become cowardly by repeatedly fleeing or turning to jelly in the face of danger. Yet, there are two very important further aspects to Aristotle's conception of moral virtue and its development. The first is that "habit" cannot mean thoughtless, unguided repetition. The conduct in question must be shaped in all its details toward what is desirable. This requires supervision to ensure that the learner does the right thing, instead of never moving beyond an initial paralysis (the "jelly in the face of danger" stage) or resistance (the "I don't *like* to share, so I'm not going to" stage), and coaching which leads her through progressive mastery of various nuances of what she is doing, calling her attention to aspects of it she will not have *perceived* or had any language to describe. Supervision and coaching enable learners to *progress* in their practice and habits.

The second further crucial aspect of Aristotle's conception of moral development is that the moral virtues are a necessary step toward, and only completed by, the acquisition of the intellectual virtue of practical wisdom or good judgment. Aristotle asserts a *unity of virtue* thesis, which holds there are interdependencies between the possession of good judgment and the possession of moral virtue. No moral virtue is a *true* virtue unless it is guided by good judgment, and no one can develop good judgment without first possessing natural or habituated forms of the moral virtues. Moral virtues are dispositions of desire, emotion, and perception that lead us to choose and do what it is reasonable for us to choose and do, all the while *perceiving* our choices and actions to be reasonable. Moral virtues thereby establish the ends we aim at, while good judgment enables us to achieve those ends. Moral virtues that are not guided by good judgment may serve us in familiar circumstances, but will not *reliably* guide us to the right or best act, and are thus not true virtues at all, or virtues without qualification. Were the 9/11 hijackers *courageous*? Were they *loyal* team players? Such questions make us squirm. The hijackers were courageous and loyal in one sense, but not without qualification. A true virtue is supposed to be good without qualification, but in that case it must be guided by good judgment which prevents the possessor of that virtue from doing something wrong. In the absence of good judgment, a merely habitual virtue may be described as "blind," as in "He was led astray by blind loyalty to an unscrupulous superior." The moral virtues are *completed* by good judgment.

The unity of virtue thesis also holds that in order to have good judgment one must possess all the moral virtues. The possession of good judgment is only possible if one perceives the world accurately in all its moral particularity, and according to Aristotle our perceptions are largely shaped by what we have experienced as normal, including what we have experienced as normal in our own conduct. The ways we have habitually acted and the ends we have habitually pursued will seem to us acceptable and good. An aspect of the formation of (habitual) moral virtues or vices is thus the habituation of corresponding perceptions, accurate or inaccurate. Since good judgment requires accurate perceptions, it also requires the possession of the moral virtues. As Aristotle conceives those virtues, they pertain to different spheres and aspects of conduct, such as the sharing or not of wealth, fidelity to significant others, self-restraint in the face of temptation, and courage in the face of danger or threats. A person who lacks any one virtue will be deficient in the perception of associated moral particulars and conception of what is acceptable, and to that extent would suffer impaired judgment.

By Aristotle's lights, good practical judgment subsumes particular cases, well perceived, under universal principles acquired through teaching. Perceiving the particulars well requires virtue, as we have seen, but also experience and discussion that enables one to benefit from the perceptions of others. Learning the universal principles begins with the acquisition of true ethical beliefs in the course of a sound moral upbringing. On that basis, one must then study political science as Aristotle understands it. In the course of that study, the true beliefs one begins from can be refined and formed into a systematic, interconnected whole—a "scientific" understanding of human affairs.

## 2. The Happiest Kind of Life and the Role of Virtue in Achieving It

The *Nicomachean Ethics* opens with the idea that if there is something people pursue for its own sake, and not for the sake of anything else, that would be the highest good they aim at. He argues that there is such a highest good for human beings in general, and that it is the proper aim of politics and political science. People all conceive of this highest good as happiness, but have different ideas about what qualifies as a happy life. Is it a life which focuses on sensual pleasures as its highest aim? Is it a life focused on honor, conquest, or social status as its highest aim? To identify a specific kind of pleasure as the highest aim of a life is not, of course, to imply it is not a life without other forms of satisfaction. It is to identify an aim which will determine, in one's circumstances, the extent to which, and ways in which, one will experience other forms of satisfaction.

Aristotle employs a whole battery of arguments in Books I and X of the *Nicomachean Ethics* and Book VII of the *Politics* to show that the highest good and happiest life for human beings is a life devoted to intellectual inquiry or "contemplation" as its highest aim. The most intuitive of his reasons is that what is most satisfying is putting our greatest gifts, our intellectual capacities, to good use. As he says in *NE* I.7, the highest good for human beings is activity that exhibits virtue of the "best and most complete" kind, or in other words *sophia*, the wisdom that pertains to intellectual inquiry or "contemplation." Another argument compares the two strongest candidates for being the highest good: the life that takes contemplation as its highest end and the life that takes statesmanship or political leadership as its highest end. The contemplative life qualifies as the highest good for human beings, because it is not only desirable for itself (being intrinsically satisfying), but aims at nothing beyond itself. The political life cannot qualify as a highest good, because the activity of statesmanship aims at something beyond itself—power perhaps, or honor, or the happiness of some or all of the statesman's society. In aiming at something beyond itself it is not "complete" in itself, and the virtue it exhibits is not "complete." The political life may be a happy life for some, if it genuinely exhibits the virtue of practical wisdom—the second best and most complete human virtue—but it cannot constitute the best kind of life or highest good for a human being. Other arguments invoke the gods as a standard of perfection by which human beings and the quality of their lives are properly judged. The life of contemplation is said to be the most divine, in the sense of being the most like the life Aristotle imagines the gods to lead, as well as the most self-sufficient, and the one that most perfectly exercises the rational soul or intellect, the most "divine" element in our nature.

Once one recognizes that Aristotle identifies only two kinds of lives as genuinely happy, the contemplative life being the happiest and the political life being happy "in a secondary degree," it is easy to understand his deepest argument for believing that only someone who possesses moral virtue can be happy. It is intrinsic to both of these kinds of lives that they involve the exercise of intellectual virtues which, according to the *unity of virtue* thesis, cannot be possessed by someone who lacks the moral virtues. The accurate perceptions associated with the moral virtues are required for both *phronêsis* and *sophia*, since both are concerned with truth, including truths about human affairs. Understanding this sheds light on Aristotle's idea in *Politics* VII that the training of the irrational psyche should aim at "reason and mind." It should prepare the way for the acquisition of the intellectual virtues, whose exercise is central to a happy life, by ensuring that a person's perceptions of what is good and appropriate are not corrupted by growing accustomed to doing bad or inappropriate things.

This argument for the dependence of happiness on virtue is "deep" in the sense that it hinges on claims about the human psyche. Aristotle's account of friendship seems to provide an independent argument, relying on the idea that friendship is the most important of the "external goods" for a happy life, external goods beings ones which are not qualities of the person herself. Aristotle holds that the best kind of friendship is only possible for people who are virtuous, and it is only in such friendships that a person can reveal her true self. If intimate friendships are essential to a happy life, then one must be a good person in order to have a happy life.

## 3. The Nature of a Political Community

Aristotle's *Politics* begins with an account of the origin and growth of cities, and his famous claim that human beings are "political animals" (*politikon zôon*). What this means is not that people naturally engage in political activities, or are happier if they do, but that it is natural for them—for us—to *live in cities*. Greek *polises*, or city-states as they are often called, were politically autonomous urban centers surrounded by farmland. Aristotle describes the growth of social units from families, to villages, to polises, as consensual and mutually beneficial. The natural and proper aim of these social units is to enable everyone in them to live the best kind of life, so far as they are able, but only the polis is big enough to be self-sufficient for this purpose. One sense in which it is natural for people to live in a polis or city is thus that they *need* to in order to live the best kind of life of which they are capable. It is also natural in the sense that people are drawn together by mutual attraction or the pleasantness of living together instead of living alone, and the further sense that the capacity for language equips people to live as a *community* consciously organized in pursuit of the best kind of life. As Aristotle conceives it, a political society should be a mutually beneficial partnership to which everyone freely consents. Membership must be voluntary and citizens must all have a right to share in the society's collective governance. As a *partnership* in pursuit of the best kind of life, a political community must be socially unified, of one mind in its conception of the best kind of life, and egalitarian. A true political community is unified by friendship, and friendship requires at least a semblance of equality.

How might such a community be created? Certainly there were no such communities in Aristotle's world. Conflict, especially between the rich and the desperately poor, was common, and governments usually did not last long. Existing societies are not unified, Aristotle says. His concern, like Plato's, was how societies might become more peaceful, stable, and secure against factional conflict. In the *Republic*, Plato imagined a scheme for common rearing of children in which parents would not even know whose child was whose. He imagined that, in this way, rivalries between families might end and a stronger sense of civic community might emerge. In Book II of the *Politics*, Aristotle rejects this scheme. He agrees that a society needs to be unified by friendship in a way that provides security against factional conflict, but he thinks a more promising way to accomplish this is through civic institutions that nurture friendships bridging all social groups. The most important of these civic institutions is *common schools*—public day schools—in which a city's diverse children "grow up together" at least a few hours a day. It is through education that societies can be unified and made into a community, Aristotle advises.

## 4. The Theory of Constitutions

Aristotle goes on to elaborate an account of constitutions and the proper forms of political rule, distinguishing the true, just, or legitimate forms of constitution from those that are corrupt, unjust, or illegitimate. As one would expect, the former aim at the common good and operate on the basis of consent, while the latter aim only at the good of the rulers and rely on force. The former promote partnership in living well, hence mutual trust and goodwill, while the latter may seek to divide and enfeeble the populace in order to prevent unified and effective resistance to its rule. The laws of just regimes are worthy of respect; they respect rights and help everyone to live in accordance with the best element in themselves. Just regimes are indeed based upon a *rule of law*, which no one is at liberty to flaunt. Unjust regimes are by contrast "lawless" or "unconstitutional," and the unjust requirements they announce as laws have no claim to being obeyed.

Within each of these categories, constitutions might involve rule by one person, by a few people, or by many people. Thus, there are six basic forms of constitution. The just ones are: kingship, aristocracy or rule by a few who are genuinely the best (the *aristoi*), and polity or constitutional rule. The unjust ones are: tyranny, oligarchy or rule by a wealthy few, and democracy or rule by the poor. It may surprise a modern audience that Aristotle counts democracy as corrupt, but in the ancient Greek world, rule by the *demos* or poor and rule by the oligarchs or rich were both forms of unconstitutional rule, or systems in which one class imposed rule on the other in the interest of the rulers and without constitutional limits on the power of the rulers to harm the ruled.

Of the just forms of constitution, polity is the best that can be attained by most societies, and it is for that reason the goal toward which the reform of actual societies should aim. It is on the one hand a "mixed" constitution, and on the other hand a "middle" constitution. To say that it is the former is to say that its institutions of government provide forms of direct participation for citizens of all social classes. Aristotle regarded this as just, inasmuch as all citizens have a right to participate. More precisely, he thought that citizens have rights of participation proportional to how virtuous or practically wise they are, and he held that polities should operate on that basis, allowing people of ordinary virtue to deliberate with others on juries and in legislative assemblies, and selecting citizens of more outstanding good judgment for offices or roles in which the judgment of one person carried more weight. A "mixed" constitution also contributes to constitutional stability by making it possible for members of all social classes to protect their interests by working within the system. To say a polity is a "middle" constitution is to say that it is socially and politically dominated by a large middle class. This is beneficial because moderation of wealth is conducive to living well, avoiding both the hazards of poverty and the seductions of great wealth, and a large middle class serves as a bulwark against destructive political polarization and loss of belief in equal citizenship, impartial justice, and a common good. Political reforms to move existing constitutions closer to polity should protect rights, ensure political accountability and widespread political participation, restrain inequalities of wealth, and institute public education. Contemporary democracies are polities or constitutional systems, but rather oligarchic ones by Aristotle's standards. He considered voting an oligarchic political institution, because wealthy people can exercise undue influence on the outcomes of elections.

Kingship is Aristotle's theoretically ideal system, but he dismisses it as "unattainable." Because he praises the superior collective wisdom of the many, and asserts a universal right of citizens to participate in governance to the extent they have a share of practical wisdom, he could only approve of a monarch whose wisdom so far eclipses that of ordinary human beings that their collected wisdom could add *nothing* to his. Such a king would be a *god* among men. If we could ever be confident we were in such good hands, we could all spend more time enjoying the pleasures of intellectual contemplation. What could be better? Since there are no gods (or goddesses) among men, the best constitution that is actually *possible* is something else, namely the ideal form of aristocracy described in Book VII.

## 5. Politics VII: The Best Possible City

An ordinary aristocracy is a legitimate form of constitution, but it involves rule by only the few best people. In Book VII of the *Politics*, Aristotle imagines a constitution in which *all* of the citizens rule *and they all possess the true virtue required to live the best kind of life.* This would be an ideal aristocracy, and Aristotle presents it as the best form of political society that human beings could actually create. It would be a classless society in which all of the citizens are voluntary partners in living the best kind of life. It would satisfy Aristotle's conception of a true political community.

Book VII describes how, in very favorable circumstances, such a society might be created. It will be a classless society of equals, so far as the citizens are concerned, and their number shall be large enough for self-sufficiency, but not so large as to interfere with assigning offices according to merit. They should be both intelligent and courageous, and thus fit for self-rule. Since the citizens will be partners in living the best kind of life, they must have leisure from productive activities so they can acquire the highest virtue and make activity in accordance with it the dominating concern of their lives. Those who engage in productive activity, namely artisans, traders, and farmers, are necessary to the political society but not part of it. They may be resident aliens at best, but not citizens, though dealings with them must still be based on mutual benefit. (Aristotle would presumably want the proportion of citizens in the polis to be as large as possible, and the proportion of resident aliens and slaves to be as small as possible. How any amount of slavery could be acceptable is a question to which he has no good answer.) Citizens will share in ruling and being ruled, serving in their youth as soldiers and in their old age as priests. Land holdings will be divided among the citizens, assuring the moderation of wealth conducive to equal citizenship and a life of virtue, while reserving some for public needs. Three institutions are mentioned as conducive to virtue and the social unity necessary to a true community: common meals or dining clubs, common religious observances, and common schools. In the closing chapters of Book VII, we come to matters of childbirth, childcare and the training of habits, and schooling, where (as we have seen) everything should aim at the proper development of the rational element of the psyche—the "best part" in human nature, the flourishing of which is intrinsic to living the best kind of life. Since this "ideal aristocracy" is to be a society of virtuous equals living in partnership in pursuit of the best kind of life, the education must arguably be public and the same for all. Every citizen must receive an education in virtue, and should receive it in the context of common schools in which all citizen children are educated together.

## 6. Education

Two ideas dominate the opening of Book VIII of the *Politics*. One is that education is a prerequisite for the practice of virtue, and is thus a matter of public concern. The foregoing makes this easy enough to understand: The proper aim of politics is to enable citizens to live the best kind of life. In order to live such a life, a person must be virtuous. The development of virtue depends on a variety of things beyond a person's control. To educate someone is to train and teach him so that he acquires the moral and intellectual virtues, develops the good judgment needed for prudent self-governance and participation in political rule, and learns to take pleasure in the excellent activities with which a good life will be occupied. It makes perfect sense that Aristotle says in VIII.5 that the main concern of education is to cultivate good judgment and delight in good dispositions and admirable actions. He says elsewhere that to be educated is to be able to form a sound judgment of an investigation or exposition, a person of "universal education" being one who is able to do this in all or nearly all domains of knowledge.

Note well that education is a preparation for leisure "spent in intellectual activity," according to Aristotle. It is not a preparation for work, as is so often now assumed. Greek education in *gymnastikē* (athletics) and *musikē* (music, poetry, and narratives—the "Arts of the Muses") was from the beginning a preparation for leisure. The knightly warriors of Athens who originally received it spent their daytime leisure in athletic contests and their nighttime leisure at drinking parties where they entertained each other with music and recitations. The subsequent democratization of Athens and invention of group lessons altered this "old education," in part by introducing the commercially useful arts of reading, writing, and arithmetic. Leisure was, in any case, not equated with mere *amusement*. It was contrasted with *productive labor* in such a way that public service—even military service—was generally considered a use of leisure, or time not spent in satisfying material needs. For Aristotle, leisure provided the opportunity to flourish as a human being or to pursue what is intrinsically, not just instrumentally, good.

Education should include "necessary" practical arts, according to Aristotle, but it should focus on what is "liberal" or conducive to spending one's leisure in activities that express the best in human nature or best and most complete virtue. Aristotle's lengthy discussion of music emphasizes its capacity to shape character and judgment. Yet, he notes that even music becomes illiberal or "mechanical," if it is pursued in order to entertain others (making it an activity that is not complete in itself) and is pursued in such a way that it interferes with the development and exercise of virtue. He is not specific about what counts as "necessary" practical arts, but he probably has in mind what is necessary to meeting one's material needs and exercising virtues that involve the use of external goods. His model is probably a landowner of moderate means who needs to read, write, draw, and use arithmetic to prudently manage his farm.

The second dominating idea at the opening of *Politics* VIII, is that citizens should be molded "to suit the form of government" or constitution. The character of citizens matters to *preserving* constitutions and also to their *quality*. The better the character of the citizens, the better the constitution, Aristotle says. This is somewhat puzzling. Everything surveyed in this Afterword appears to suggest that constitutions should be made to suit the needs of the citizen, not the other way around. Moreover, in *Politics* III.4, Aristotle says that it is only in the best constitution that the virtues expected of a citizen fully coincide with the virtues of a human being as such. Only the best kind of society fully enables the development of independent good judgment and encourages the universal expression of that judgment in public and private life. Since the proper aim of *any* political society is to enable citizens to develop and exercise the best and most complete human virtue, it is not clear how it could be legitimate for any government to educate citizens to have any virtues that deviate from these. What are we to make of all this?

First it is important to realize that Aristotle says a great deal in the middle books of the *Politics* about the measures that actual regimes should take to preserve themselves. He identifies injustice as the most important general cause of political instability, and his advice to governments has the effect of encouraging reforms that will make them both more just and longer lasting. To the extent that defective regimes adopt his proposed reforms, they will become more like a polity, which is the best form of constitution most societies could ever enact. Public education is introduced in this context as the most valuable of the reforms that can be adopted. Like other reforms, it will not leave a deficient system as it is, but will instead both stabilize and improve it. Indeed, Aristotle says quite explicitly in *Politics* V.9 that the education that "suits" a constitution is not the kind of education preferred by the rulers of an unjust system. It is education that will create a more balanced and moderate ("mixed" and "middle") system that better serves the interests of all citizens. A critic might object at this point that education should not support anything less than an ideal system. Aristotle's implicit answer is that the best course in human affairs is to proceed through incremental reform transacted through public consultation and shared governance. Education that prepares everyone to employ independent good judgment in shared governance is progress.

Second, it must be recognized that in order for constitutions to "suit the needs of the citizen," citizens must have certain desirable qualities. This is inescapable. A constitution is not simply a blueprint for a form of government, but a functioning political system whose actual patterns are heavily determined by the characteristics of the people involved. Molding the constitution in such a way as to enable citizens to live the best kind of life requires measures to ensure that citizens are prepared to treat each other with mutual respect and friendly regard for each other's well-being. It requires that citizens have fellow citizens who will in a variety of ways allow them the satisfaction of fulfilling their human potential.

## 7. The Enduring Relevance of Aristotle's Philosophy of Education

Understood within the larger context of his philosophy of human affairs, Aristotle's philosophy of education offers valuable starting points for addressing several topics of enduring interest. One must surely count among these his conception of what is good for human beings, his account of the virtues and their development, his ideas about the relationships between virtue, law, and education, and his defense of public education.

If we set aside Aristotle's idea that there is one best life for human beings, there is still much to be said for his idea that what is most satisfying in life is experiencing the development and self-directed employment of our abilities. This is evident in the contemporary debate between psychologists about the relative merits of eudaimonistic and hedonistic theories of happiness. The eudaimonists identify the satisfaction of psychological needs to experience *competence, self-determination,* and *good relationships* with others as basic to happiness. Some contemporary philosophers of education are similarly influenced by Aristotle in arguing that education should aim to enable people to live flourishing and self-determining lives, in part by enabling them to engage in a variety of satisfying forms of human endeavor. Others could be considered Aristotelian to the extent that they emphasize the educational development of reasoned judgment through initiation into diverse forms of human inquiry.

Aristotle's account of the virtues has been fundamental to a major movement in moral theory and related scholarship on moral development in recent decades. Suffice it to say that his ideas about the development of reason and their importance for how we understand the relationships between goodness, law, and education are important, but relatively neglected. If reasonableness is a human quality that needs assistance to develop, and an ethic of respect for people as rational beings requires dealing with people as much as possible through truthful and reasoned instruction and persuasion and as little as possible through force and violence, then the foundations of law and government rest more crucially on adequate education for everyone than we generally realize. The legitimacy of a government and a rule of law will rest on prior, conscientious education which prepares everyone to voluntarily accept the reasonable expectations of law on the basis of their independent good judgment. This is not an easy educational mission to accomplish, but justice seems to require it.

These ideas about the foundations of a rule of law lurk in the background of Aristotle's defense of education that is public and the same for all. In the foreground are concerns about equity in enabling all the members of a society to live well, the need for civic education to promote intelligent cooperation in the enterprise of shared governance, and the value of schooling different kinds of children together so they may learn to know and respect each other as equals. These are still important concerns, and wealth and poverty matter to all of them today, just as they did in Aristotle's world. His was not a multicultural world in the way ours is, but the patterns of conflict to be resolved are not so different. Before we go any farther in allowing children to be educated apart from each other in their separate worlds, we would do well to take Aristotle's defense of public education seriously.

# 3
# Augustine

St. Augustine (354–430), born in North Africa, studied rhetoric in Carthage, taught that subject in Rome and Milan, then converted to Christianity. He was ordained as a priest and eventually became Bishop of Hippo in Africa. His literary output was enormous, and he came to be widely regarded as the most influential of the Church Fathers.

## *On the Teacher*

### The Purpose of Language

AUGUSTINE: When we speak, what does it seem to you we want to accomplish?

ADEODATUS: So far as it now strikes me, either to teach or to learn.

AUGUSTINE: I see one of these points and I agree with it, for it's clear that by speaking we want to teach. But to learn? How?

ADEODATUS: How do you suppose we learn, after all, if not when we ask questions?

AUGUSTINE: Even then I think that we want only to teach. I ask you: do you question someone for any reason other than to teach him what you want [to hear]?

ADEODATUS: You're right.

AUGUSTINE: So now you see that we seek nothing by speaking except to teach.

ADEODATUS: I don't see it clearly. If speaking is nothing but uttering words, I see that we do this when we're singing. Given that we often sing while we're alone, without anyone present who might learn, I don't think we want to teach anything.

AUGUSTINE: Well, for my part I think there is a certain kind of teaching through reminding— a very important kind, as our discussion will itself bring out. Yet if you don't hold that we learn when we remember or that the person who reminds us is teaching, I won't oppose you. I now stipulate two reasons for speaking: to teach or to remind either others or ourselves. We do this even when we're singing. Doesn't it seem so to you?

ADEODATUS: Not exactly. I would seldom sing to remind myself; I do it only to please myself.

AUGUSTINE: I see what you mean. But aren't you aware that what pleases you in a song is its melody? Since this melody can be either added to or taken away from the words, speaking is one thing and singing is another. There are [musical] songs on flutes or on the guitar, and birds sing, and we occasionally make some musical sound without words. This sound can be called "singing" but can't be called "speaking." Is there anything here you would object to?

ADEODATUS: Nothing at all.

AUGUSTINE: Then doesn't it seem to you that speaking is undertaken only for the sake of teaching or reminding?

ADEODATUS: It would seem so were I not troubled by the fact that we certainly speak while we're praying, and yet it isn't right to believe that we teach God or remind Him of anything.

AUGUSTINE: I dare say you don't know that we are instructed to pray "in closed chambers"[1]—a phrase that signifies the inner recesses of the mind—precisely because God does not seek to be taught or reminded by our speaking in order to provide us what we want. Anyone who speaks gives an external sign of his will by means of an articulated sound. Yet God is to be sought and entreated in the hidden parts of the rational soul, which is called the "inner man"; for He wanted those parts to be His temples. . . .

There is accordingly no need for speaking when we pray. That is, there is no need for spoken words—except perhaps to speak as priests do, for the sake of signifying what is in their minds: not that God might hear, but that men might do so and by remembering might, with one accord, be raised to God. Do you hold otherwise?

ADEODATUS: I agree completely.

AUGUSTINE: . . . Someone might object that, although we don't produce any sound, nonetheless we do "speak" internally in the mind, since we think these very words. Yet I believe you're also aware that in "speaking" in this way we do nothing but remind ourselves, since by repeating the words our memory, in which the words inhere, makes the very things of which the words are signs come to mind.

ADEODATUS: I understand, and I go along with this.

## The Nature of Signs

AUGUSTINE: Then we are in agreement: words are signs.

ADEODATUS: Yes.

AUGUSTINE: Well, can a sign be a sign if it doesn't signify anything?

ADEODATUS: It can't.

AUGUSTINE: Consider this line of verse:[2]

If nothing from so great a city it pleases the gods be left . . .
How many words are there?

ADEODATUS: Thirteen.

AUGUSTINE: Then there are thirteen signs?

ADEODATUS: Yes.

AUGUSTINE: I believe you understand this line of verse.

ADEODATUS: Quite well, I think.

AUGUSTINE: Tell me what each word signifies.

ADEODATUS: Well, I do see what "if" signifies, but I don't know any other word by which it can be explained.

AUGUSTINE: At least you know where anything signified by this word would be.

ADEODATUS: It seems to me that "if" signifies doubt. Now where is doubt but in the mind?

AUGUSTINE: I accept that for now. Continue with the other words.

ADEODATUS: What else does "nothing" signify except that which doesn't exist?

AUGUSTINE: Perhaps you're right, but I'm hesitant to agree with you, because you granted above that there is no sign unless it signifies something. Yet what does not exist can't in any way be something. Accordingly, the second word in this line of verse isn't a sign, because it doesn't signify anything. So we were wrong to agree either that all words are signs or that every sign signifies something.

ADEODATUS: You're really pushing too hard. It's stupid to utter a word when we don't have anything to signify. Yet in speaking with me now I believe you yourself aren't making a sound pointlessly. Instead, you're giving a sign to me with everything that comes out of your mouth, so that I may understand something. Thus you shouldn't enunciate those two syllables ["*nothing*"] when you speak if you don't signify anything with them! If you see that they are necessary for producing an enunciation, and that we are taught or reminded when they strike the ears, then surely you also see what I want to say but can't explain.

AUGUSTINE: What then are we to do? Given that one doesn't see a thing and furthermore finds (or thinks oneself to have found) that it doesn't exist, shall we not say that this word ["nothing"] signifies a certain state of mind rather than the very thing that is nothing?

ADEODATUS: Perhaps this is the very point I was trying to explain.

AUGUSTINE: Then be the matter as it may, let us move on from here so that the most absurd thing of all doesn't happen to us.

ADEODATUS: Which is?

AUGUSTINE: If *nothing* holds us back, and we suffer delays!

ADEODATUS: This is ridiculous, and yet somehow I see that it can happen—or rather, I clearly see that it has happened.

AUGUSTINE: We shall understand this kind of difficulty more clearly in due order, God willing. Now return to that line of verse and try to explain, as best you can, what the other words in it signify.

ADEODATUS: The third word is the preposition "from," for which I think we can say "out of."

AUGUSTINE: I'm not looking for this, that in place of one familiar word you say another equally familiar word that signifies the same thing—if really it does signify the same thing; but for now let us grant that this is so. Surely if the poet had said "out of so great a city" instead of "from so great a city" and I were to ask you what "out of" signifies, you would say "from," since these words ["from" and "out of"]—that is, these signs—do signify some one thing, as you think. I'm asking for that one thing itself, whatever it is, that is signified by these two signs.

ADEODATUS: It seems to me that they signify some kind of separation with regard to a thing in which something had been. This ["something"] is said to be "from" that thing, whether that thing (*a*) does not continue to exist, as for example in this line of verse some Trojans were able to be "from" the city when it no longer existed; or it (*b*) continues to exist, as we say that there are traders in Africa "from" the city of Rome.

AUGUSTINE: Even supposing that I grant you these claims and do not enumerate how many exceptions to your rule may perhaps be discovered, surely it's easy for you to notice that you have explained words by means of words. That is to say, you have explained signs by means of signs and familiar things by the same familiar things. I would like you to show me the very things of which these words are the signs, if you can.

ADEODATUS: I'm surprised that you don't know, or that you're pretending not to know, that what you want can't be done in my answer while we're engaged in discussion, where we can only answer with words. Furthermore, you're asking about things that, whatever they may be, surely aren't words—and yet you're also asking me about them with words! First raise the question without words, so that I may then answer under that stipulation of yours.

AUGUSTINE: You're within your rights, I admit. But if when one says "*wall*" I were to ask what this one-syllable word signifies, couldn't you show me with your finger? Then when you pointed it out I would straightway see the very thing of which this one-syllable word is a sign, although you used no words.

ADEODATUS: I grant that this can happen only in the case of names that signify bodies, so long as the bodies themselves are present.

AUGUSTINE: Do we call color a body? Don't we instead call it a quality of a body?

ADEODATUS: That's true.

AUGUSTINE: Then why can this too be pointed out with a finger? Are you also adding the qualities of bodies to bodies [in your proposal], so that those qualities too, when they are present, may nonetheless be taught without words?

ADEODATUS: Well, although I said "bodies," I wanted all corporeal things—that is, all the things sensed in bodies—to be understood [in my proposal].

AUGUSTINE: Consider whether you should make some exceptions even to this claim.

ADEODATUS: Your warning is a good one! I should have said "all *visible* things" rather than "all *corporeal* things." I admit that sound, smell, flavor, weight, heat, and other things that pertain to the rest of the senses, despite the fact that they can't be sensed without bodies and consequently are corporeal, nevertheless can't be exhibited through [pointing] a finger.

AUGUSTINE: Haven't you ever seen that men "converse" with deaf people by gesturing? That deaf people themselves, no less by gesturing, raise and answer questions, teach, and indicate all the things they want, or at least most of them? When this happens, they show us without words not only visible things, but also sounds and flavors and other things of this sort. Even actors in the theaters unfold and set forth entire stories without words—for the most part, by pantomime.

ADEODATUS: I have nothing to say against this, except that neither I nor even that pantomiming actor could show you without words what "from" signifies.

AUGUSTINE: Perhaps you're right, but let's imagine that he can. You do not doubt, I suppose, that any bodily movement he uses to try to point out to me the thing signified by the word ["from"] isn't going to be the thing itself but a sign [of the thing]. Accordingly, he too won't indicate a word with a word. He'll nonetheless still indicate a sign with a sign. The result is that this syllable "*from*" and his gesture signify some one thing, which I should like to be exhibited for me without signifying.

ADEODATUS: Who can do what you're asking, pray tell?

AUGUSTINE: In the way in which the wall could [be exhibited].

ADEODATUS: Not even [the wall] can be shown without a sign, as our developing argument has taught us. Aiming a finger is certainly not the wall. Instead, through aiming a finger a sign is given by means of which the wall may be seen. I see nothing, therefore, that can be shown without signs.

AUGUSTINE: What if I should ask you what walking is, and you were then to get up and do it? Wouldn't you be using the thing itself to teach me, rather than using words or any other signs?

ADEODATUS: I admit that this is the case. I'm embarrassed not to have seen a point so obvious. On this basis, too, thousands of things now occur to me that can be exhibited through themselves rather than through signs: for example, eating, drinking, sitting, standing, shouting, and countless others.

AUGUSTINE: Now do this: tell me—if I were completely ignorant of the meaning of the word ["walking"] and were to ask you what walking is while you were walking, how would you teach me?

ADEODATUS: I would do it a little bit more quickly, so that after your question you would be prompted by something novel [in my behavior], and yet nothing would take place other than what was to be shown.

AUGUSTINE: Don't you know that *walking* is one thing and *hurrying* another? A person who is walking doesn't necessarily hurry, and a person who is hurrying doesn't necessarily walk. We speak of "hurrying" in writing and in reading and in countless other matters. Hence given that after my question you kept on doing what you were doing, [only] faster, I might have thought walking was precisely hurrying—for you added that as something new—and for that reason I would have been misled.

ADEODATUS: I admit that we can't exhibit a thing without a sign if we should be questioned while we are doing it. If we add nothing [to our behavior], the person who raises the question will think that we don't want to show him and that we are persisting in what we were doing while paying no heed to him. Yet if he should ask about things we can do, but when we aren't doing them, after his question we can point out what he's asking about by doing the action itself rather than by a sign. (That is, unless he should happen to ask me what speaking is while I'm speaking, namely because no matter what I say I must be speaking to teach him.) In this way I'll confidently teach him, until I make clear to him what he wants, neither getting away from the thing itself that he wanted to be pointed out nor casting about beyond the thing itself for signs with which I might show it.

AUGUSTINE: Very acute. See then whether we're now in agreement that the following things can be pointed out without signs: (*a*) things we aren't doing when we are asked [about them] and yet can do on the spot; (*b*) the very signs we happen to be "doing" [when asked about them], just as when we speak we are making signs (and [the word] "signifying" is derived from this [activity]).

ADEODATUS: Agreed.

## Fundamental Division of Signs

AUGUSTINE: Thus [1] when a question is raised about certain signs, these signs can be exhibited by means of signs. Yet [2] when a question is raised about things that aren't signs, [these things can be exhibited] either [(*a*)] by doing them after the query [has been made], if they can be done, or [(*b*)] by giving signs with which they may be brought to one's attention.

ADEODATUS: That's right.

## Discussion of Division [2(a)]

. . . [L]et's now analyze more completely the class of things we said can be exhibited through themselves, without signs, such as speaking, walking, sitting, lying down, and the like.

ADEODATUS: I now recall what you're describing.

AUGUSTINE: Does it seem to you that all the things we can do once we've been asked about them can be exhibited without a sign? Is there any exception?

ADEODATUS: Considering this whole class over and over again, I still don't find *anything* that can be taught without a sign—except perhaps speaking, and possibly if someone should happen to ask the very question "What is it to teach?"—for I see that no matter what I do after his question so that he may learn, he doesn't learn from the very thing he wants exhibited to him.

For example, if anyone should ask me what it is to walk while I was resting or doing something else, as was said, and I should attempt to teach him what he asked about without a sign, by immediately walking, how shall I guard against his thinking that it's just the amount of walking I have done? He'll be mistaken if he thinks this. He'll think that anyone who walks farther than I have, or not as far, hasn't walked at all. Yet what I have said about this one word ["walking"] applies to all the things I had agreed can be exhibited without a sign, apart from the two exceptions we made.

AUGUSTINE: I agree with this point. Yet doesn't it seem to you that speaking is one thing and teaching another?

ADEODATUS: It does. If they were the same, nobody would teach except by speaking; but seeing that we also teach many things with other signs besides words, who would have any doubt that there is a difference?

AUGUSTINE: Well, is there any difference between teaching and signifying, or not?

ADEODATUS: I think they're the same.

AUGUSTINE: Anyone who says that we signify in order to teach is right, isn't he?

ADEODATUS: Completely right.

AUGUSTINE: Well, if someone else were to say that we teach in order to signify, wouldn't he easily be refuted by the view given above?

ADEODATUS: That is so.

AUGUSTINE: Then if we signify in order to teach, and we don't teach in order to signify, teaching is one thing and signifying another.

ADEODATUS: You're right. I was wrong in answering that they are the same.

AUGUSTINE: Now answer this: does the person teaching what it is to teach do so by signifying, or in another way?

ADEODATUS: I don't see how he can do it in another way.

AUGUSTINE: Then you stated a falsehood a little while ago, namely that a thing can be taught without signs when the question is raised what teaching itself is. Now we see that not even this can be done without signification, since you granted that signifying is one thing and teaching another: if they're different things, as they appear to be, and the latter is shown only through the former, then it isn't shown through itself, as you thought. So we haven't yet uncovered anything that can be exhibited through itself—except speaking, which also signifies itself, among other things. Since speaking itself is also a sign, though, it isn't yet entirely apparent whether anything seems able to be taught without signs.

ADEODATUS: I have no reason for not agreeing.

AUGUSTINE: Then it has been established that nothing is taught without signs, and that knowledge itself should be more valuable to us than the signs by means of which we know, although not all things signified can be superior to their signs.

ADEODATUS: So it seems. . . .

AUGUSTINE: . . . Well then, let's straightaway reconsider now whether you were correct. Consider this example. Suppose that someone unfamiliar with how to trick birds (which is done with reeds and birdlime) should run into a birdcatcher outfitted with his tools, not birdcatching but on his way to do so. On seeing this birdcatcher, he follows closely in his footsteps, and, as it happens, he reflects and asks himself in his astonishment what exactly the man's equipment means. Now the birdcatcher, wanting to show off after seeing the attention focused on him, prepares his reeds and with his birdcall and his hawk intercepts, subdues, and captures some little bird he has noticed nearby. I ask you: wouldn't he then teach the man watching him what he wanted to know by the thing itself rather than by anything that signifies?

ADEODATUS: I'm afraid that everything here is like what I said about the man who asks what it is to walk. Here, too, I don't see that the whole of birdcatching has been exhibited.

AUGUSTINE: It's easy to get rid of your worry. I add that he's so intelligent that he recognizes the kind of craft as a whole on the basis of what he has seen. It's surely enough for the matter at hand that some men can be taught about some things, even if not all, without a sign.

ADEODATUS: I also can add this to the other case! If he is sufficiently intelligent, he'll know the whole of what it is to walk, once walking has been illustrated by a few steps.

AUGUSTINE: You may do so as far as I'm concerned; not only do I not offer any objection, I even support you! You see, each of us has established that some people can be taught some things without signs, and what seemed apparent to us a little earlier—that there is absolutely nothing that can be shown without signs—is false. These examples already suggest not one or another but thousands of things that are exhibited through themselves, without any sign being given.

Why, I ask you, should we doubt this? For example (passing over the performances of men in all the theaters who display things themselves without a sign), doesn't God or Nature show and display to those paying attention, by themselves, this sun and the light pervading and clothing all things present, the moon and the other stars, the lands and the seas, and the countless things begotten in them?

## Discussion of Division [2(b)]

Well, if we should consider this more carefully, perhaps you'll discover that nothing is learned through its signs. When a sign is given to me, it can teach me nothing if it finds me ignorant of the thing of which it is the sign; but if I'm not ignorant, what do I learn through the sign?

For example, when I read:[3]

> . . . and their *sarabarae* were unchanged.

the word doesn't show me the thing it signifies. If certain headcoverings are denominated by this name ["*sarabarae*"], have I learned upon hearing it what the head is or what coverings are? I knew these things before; my conception of them wasn't fashioned because they were named by others, but because I saw them. The first time the syllable "*head*" struck my ears I was just as ignorant of what it signified as when I first heard or read "*sarabarae*". Yet since "*head*" was often pronounced, nothing and observing when it was pronounced, I discovered that it was the term for a thing already familiar to me by sight. Before I made this discovery, the word was a mere sound to me; but I learned that it was a sign when I found out of what thing it is the sign—and, as I said, I learned this not by anything that signifies but by its appearance. Therefore, a sign is learned when the thing is known, rather than the thing being learned when the sign is given.

So that you may understand this more clearly, suppose that we hear "*head*" now for the first time. Not knowing whether that utterance is a mere noise or also signifies something, we ask what "head" is. (Remember we want to have a conception not of the thing signified but of the sign itself, which we surely don't have as long as we don't know what it's the sign of.) If, then, the thing is pointed out with the finger after we raise the question, once it has been seen we learn the sign, which we had only heard and didn't know at that point.

Now there are two elements in the sign: the sound and the signification. We don't perceive the sound by the sign, but when it strikes the ear. We perceive the signification, however, by seeing the thing signified. Aiming with the finger can only signify what the finger is aimed at, and it's aimed not at the sign but at the bodily part called the head. Consequently, by aiming the finger I can't know either the thing (which I knew already) or the sign (at which the finger isn't aimed).

I don't much care about aiming with the finger, because it seems to me to be a sign of the pointing-out itself rather than of any things that are pointed out. It's like the exclamation "look!"—we typically also aim the finger along with this exclamation, in case one sign of the pointing-out isn't enough.

Most of all I'm trying to persuade you, if I'll be able to, that we don't learn anything by these signs called words. As I have stated, we learn the meaning of a word—that is, the signification hidden in the sound—once the thing signified is itself known, rather than our perceiving it by means of such signification.

What I've said about "head" I also might have said about "coverings" (and about countless other things!). Although I already knew them, I still don't yet know them to be *sarabarae*. If anyone should signify them to me with a gesture, or represent them, or show me something similar to them, I won't say that he didn't teach me—a claim I might easily maintain should I care to speak a little longer—but I do state something close to it: he didn't teach me with words. Even if he happens to see them when I'm around and should call them to my attention by saying "Look: *sarabarae*!" I wouldn't learn the thing I was ignorant of by the words that he has spoken, but by looking at it. This is the way it came to pass that I know and grasp what meaning the name has. When I learned the thing itself, I trusted my eyes, not the words of another—though perhaps I trusted the words to direct my attention, that is, to find out what I would see by looking.

To give them as much credit as possible, words have force only to the extent that they remind us to look for things; they don't display them for us to know. Yet someone who presents what I want to know to my eyes, or to any of my bodily senses, or even to my mind itself, does teach me something.

From words, then, we learn only words—rather, the sound and noise of the words. If things that aren't signs can't be words, then although I have already heard a word, I don't know that it is a word until I know what it signifies. Therefore, knowledge of words is made complete once the things are known. On the other hand, when words are [only] heard, not even the words are learned. We don't learn words we know. Also, we have to admit that we learn words we didn't know only after their signification has been perceived, and this happens not by hearing the mere sounds uttered but by knowing the things signified. This is a truthful and solid argument: when words are spoken we either know what they signify or we don't; if we know, then it's reminding rather than learning; but if we don't know, it isn't even reminding, though perhaps we recollect that we should inquire.

You may object: granted that (*a*) it's only by sight that we can know those head-coverings, whose name ["*sarabarae*"] we only take as a sound; and (*b*) we know the name itself more fully only when the things are themselves known. Yet we do accept the story of those boys—how they overcame King Nebuchadnezzar and his flames by their faith and religion, what praises they sang to God, and what honors they merited even from their enemy himself.[4] Have we learned these things otherwise than by words?

I reply to this objection that everything signified by those words was already known to us. I'm already familiar with what three boys are, what a furnace is, what fire is, what a king is, and finally what being unharmed by fire is, and all the other things that those words signify.

Yet Ananias, Azarias, and Misahel are just as unknown to me as the *sarabarae*, and these names didn't help me at all to know them, nor could they help me.

I do admit that I *believe* rather than *know* that everything we read in the story happened then just as it is written. Those whom we believe are themselves not unaware of the difference, for the Prophet says:[5]

Unless you believe, you shall not understand.

He surely would not have said this if he had thought there was no difference. Therefore, what I understand I also believe, but not everything I believe I also understand. Again, everything I understand I know; not everything I believe I know. Hence I'm not unaware how useful it is to believe even many things I do not know, and I also include in this usefulness the story of the three boys. According, although the majority of things can't possibly be known by me, I still know how useful it is to believe them.

Regarding each of the things we understand, however, we don't consult a speaker who makes sounds outside us, but the Truth that presides within over the mind itself, though perhaps words prompt us to consult Him. What is more, He Who is consulted, He Who is said to *dwell in the inner man,*[6] does teach: Christ—that is, *the unchangeable power and everlasting wisdom of God,*[7] which every rational soul does consult, but is disclosed to anyone, to the extent that he can apprehend it, according to his good or evil will. If at times one is mistaken, this doesn't happen by means of a defect in the Truth consulted, just as it isn't a defect in light outside that the eyes of the body are often mistaken—and we admit that we consult this light regarding visible things, that it may show them to us to the extent that we have the ability to make them out.

Now, on the one hand, regarding colors we consult light, and regarding other things we sense through the body we consult the elements of this world, the selfsame bodies we sense, and the senses themselves that the mind employs as interpreters to know such things. On the other hand, regarding things that are understood we consult the inner Truth by means of reason. What then can be said to show that we learn something by words aside from the mere sound that strikes the ears?

Everything we perceive, we perceive either by one of the bodily senses or by the mind. We name the former sensible, the latter intelligible—or, to speak in the fashion of our authorities, carnal and spiritual. When we are asked about the former, we answer, so long as the things we sense are present at hand. For example, while looking at the new moon we're asked what sort of thing it is or where it is. In this case if the person raising the question doesn't see the object, he merely believes our words (and often he doesn't believe them!). He doesn't learn at all unless he himself sees what is described, where he then learns not from words but from the things themselves and his senses. Words make the same sounds for the one who sees the object as for the one who doesn't see it.

When a question is raised not about things we sense at present but about things we sensed in the past, then we speak of not the things themselves but of the images impressed by them and committed to memory. I don't know how we state truths even though we look upon these false [images], unless it's because we report not that we are seeing or sensing [the things themselves], but that we have seen or sensed them. We carry these images in the recesses of our memory in this way as certain attestations of things sensed previously. Contemplating them in the mind, we have the good conscience that we aren't lying when we speak. Yet they are proofs for us [alone]. If anyone hearing me was then present and sensed these things, he doesn't learn from my words but knows them again from the images stored away within himself. If he hasn't sensed them, isn't it obvious that he merely believes my words rather than learns from them?

When we deal with things that we perceive by the mind, namely by the intellect and reason, we're speaking of things that we look upon immediately in the inner light of Truth, in virtue of which the so-called inner man is illuminated and rejoices. Under these conditions our listener, if he likewise sees these things with his inward and undivided eye, knows what I'm saying from his own contemplation, not from my words. Therefore, when I'm stating truths, I don't even teach the person who is looking upon these truths. He's taught not by my words but by the things themselves made manifest within when God discloses them. Hence if he were questioned, he could give answers even about these matters. What is more absurd than thinking that he's taught by my speaking, when even before I spoke he could explain these very matters were he questioned?

Now it often happens that someone denies something when questioned about it, and is brought around by further questions to admit it. This happens because of the weakness of his discernment. He can't consult that light regarding the whole matter. Yet he is prompted to do it part-by-part when he's questioned about the very parts that make up the whole, which he didn't have the ability to discern. If he's guided in this case by the words of his questioner, the words nevertheless do not teach him, but they raise questions in such a way that he who is questioned learns within, corresponding to his ability to do so.

For example, if I were to ask you about the very matter at issue, namely whether it's true that nothing can be taught by words, at first it would seem absurd to you, since you aren't able to examine it as a whole. It would therefore be necessary to ask you questions suited to your abilities to hear the Teacher within you. Thus I might say: "The things I'm saying that you admit to be truths, and that you're certain of, and that you affirm yourself to know— where did you learn them?" Maybe you would reply that I had taught them to you. Then I would rejoin: "What if I should say that I had seen a flying man? Do my words then make you as certain as if you were to hear that wise men are better than fools?" Surely you would deny it and reply that you do not believe the former statement, or even if you did believe it that you do not know it; whereas you know the latter statement with utter certainty. As a result, you would then understand that you hadn't learned anything from my words, neither in the former case (where you did not know although I was asserting it) nor in the latter case (where you knew quite well), seeing that when questioned about each case you would swear the former was unknown and the latter known to you. Yet at that point you would be admitting the whole that you had [initially] denied. You came to know that the [parts] in which it consists are clear and certain—namely, that whatever we may say, the hearer either (a) doesn't know whether it is true; (b) knows that it is false; or (c) knows that it is true. In (a) he either believes it or has an opinion about it or doubts it; in (b) he opposes and rejects it; in (c) he bears witness to the truth. Hence in none of these three cases does he learn. We have established that the one who doesn't know the thing, the one who knows that he has heard falsehoods, and the one who could when questioned have answered precisely what was said, have each clearly learned nothing from my words.

Consequently, even in the case of matters discerned by the mind, anyone who can't discern them hears in vain the discourse of one who does, save that it's useful to believe such things so long as they aren't known. Yet anyone who can discern them is inwardly a student of Truth and outwardly a judge of the speaker, or rather of what he says. Often he knows what is said even when the speaker doesn't know it. For example, if anyone believing the Epicureans and thinking that the soul is mortal should set forth the arguments for its immortality (discussed by more prudent thinkers) in the hearing of someone able to look upon spiritual things, then he judges that the speaker is stating truths. The speaker is unaware that he's stating truths. Instead, he holds them to be completely false. Should it then be thought that he teaches what he doesn't know? Yet he uses the very same words that someone who does know also could use.

Accordingly, words don't have even the minimal function of indicating the speaker's mind, since it's uncertain whether he knows the truth of what he says. Moreover, in the case of liars and deceivers it's easy to understand that their minds are not only not revealed but are even concealed by their words. I don't by any means doubt, of course, that the words of those who tell the truth attempt to make the speaker's mind evident and somehow declare it. They would accomplish this, everyone agrees, if liars were not permitted to speak.

We have often had the experience in ourselves and in others, however, of words being uttered that don't correspond to the things thought about. I see that this can happen in two ways: (*a*) when a speech that has been committed to memory and often run through pours out of the mouth of someone thinking about other things, as frequently happens to us while we're singing a hymn; (*b*) when by a slip of the tongue some words rush out in place of others against our will, and here too signs are heard that aren't about the things we have in mind. (Liars also think of the things they say, so that although we don't know whether they're speaking the truth, we know that they have in mind what they're saying should neither (*a*) nor (*b*) occur.) If anyone contends that (*a*) and (*b*) occur only occasionally and that it's apparent when they occur, I make no objection, though they are often unnoticed and they have often deceived me upon hearing them.

There is another class in addition to these, one that is widespread and the source of countless disagreements and quarrels: when the speaker does signify the selfsame things he's thinking about, but for the most part only to himself and to certain others, whereas he doesn't signify the same thing to the person to whom he's speaking and again to several other persons.

For example, let someone say in our hearing that man is surpassed in virtue by some brute animals. We immediately can't bear this, and with great vehemence we refute it as false and harmful. Yet perhaps he's calling physical strength "virtue" and enunciating what he was thinking about with this name. He would be neither lying nor in error about things. Nor is he reeling off words committed to memory while turning something else over in his mind. Nor does he utter by a slip of the tongue something other than he wanted. Instead, he's merely calling the thing he's thinking about by another name than we do; we should at once agree with him about it if we could look into his thinking, which he wasn't yet able to disclose to us by the words he had already uttered in expressing his view.

They say that definitions can remedy this kind of error, so that in this case if the speaker were to define what "virtue" is, he would make it plain, they say, that the dispute is over the word and not the thing. Now I might grant this to be so. Yet how many people can be found who are good at definitions? In any event, there are many arguments against the system of definitions, but it isn't opportune to discuss them here; nor do I altogether approve them.

I pass over the fact that there are many things we don't hear clearly, and we argue forcefully at great length about them as if they were things we heard. For example, you were saying recently, Adeodatus, that although I had asserted that *mercy* is signified by a certain Punic word, you had heard from those more familiar with this language that it signifies *piety*. Well, I objected to this, insisting that you completely forgot what you were told, because it seemed to me that you had said *faith* rather than *piety*—though you were sitting right next to me, and these two names don't at all trick the ear by any similarity in sound. Yet for a long time I thought you didn't know what was said to you, whereas it was I who didn't know what you had said. If I had heard you clearly, it would never have seemed absurd to me that piety and mercy are named by a single Punic word.

These things often happen. Let's pass over them, as I said, so that I not seem to be stirring up quibbles against words because of the carelessness of hearing, or even of men's deafness. The cases we listed above are more bothersome, where we can't know the thoughts of the speakers, though we speak the same language and the words are Latin and are clearly heard.

See here: I now give in and concede that when words are heard by someone who knows them, he can know that the speaker had been thinking about the things they signify. Yet does he for this reason also learn whether the speaker has stated truths, which is the question at hand?

Do teachers hold that it is their thoughts that are perceived and grasped rather than the very disciplines they take themselves to pass on by speaking? After all, who is so foolishly curious as to send his son to school to learn what the teacher thinks? When the teachers have explained by means of words all the disciplines they profess to teach, even the disciplines of virtue and of wisdom, then those who are called "students" consider within themselves whether truths have been stated. They do so by looking upon the inner Truth, according to their abilities. That is therefore the point at which they learn. When they inwardly discover that truths have been stated, they offer their praises—not knowing that they are praising them not as teachers but as persons who have been taught, if their teachers also know what they are saying. Men are mistaken in calling persons "teachers" who are not, which they do because generally there is no delay between the time of speaking and the time of knowing; and since they are quick to learn internally after the prompting of the lecturer, they suppose that they have learned externally from the one who prompted them.

At another time we shall, God willing, look into the whole problem of the usefulness of words—which, if considered properly, is not negligible! For the present, I have prompted you that we should not attribute more to words than is suitable. As a result, we should by now not only believe but also begin to understand how truly it has been written on divine authority that we should not call anyone on earth our teacher, since *there is one in heaven Who is the Teacher of all.* Furthermore, He Himself will teach us what "in heaven" is—He Who prompts us externally through men by means of signs, so that we are instructed to be inwardly turned toward Him. To know and love Him is the happy life which all proclaim they seek, although there are few who may rejoice in having really found it.

Now I would like you to tell me what you think of this whole disquisition of mine. On the one hand, if you know that what has been said is true, then if you were questioned about each of the points you would have said that you knew them. Therefore, you see from Whom you have learned these points. It isn't from me. You would have given all the answers to me were I to have questioned you. On the other hand, if you don't know that what has been said is true, neither I nor He has taught you—not I, since I can never teach; not He, since you still are not able to learn.

ADEODATUS: For my part, I have learned from the prompting of your words that words do nothing but prompt man to learn, and that the extent to which the speaker's thought is apparent in his speaking amounts to very little. Moreover, I have learned that it is He alone who teaches us whether what is said is true—and, when He spoke externally, He reminded us that He was dwelling within. With His help, I shall love Him the more ardently the more I advance in learning.

However, I'm especially grateful for this disquisition of yours, which you delivered without interruption, for this reason: it has anticipated and resolved everything that I had been prepared to say against it, and you didn't overlook anything at all that had produced a doubt in me; that private Oracle answered me about everything exactly as you stated in your words.

## Notes

1. Matthew 6: 6.
2. Vergil, *Aeneid* 2: 659.
3. Daniel 3: 94.
4. Anaias, Azarias, and Misahel were cast into a fiery furnace by King Nebuchadnezzar; because of their piety, God made the flames powerless to harm them, whereupon they were hauled out, pardoned, and richly rewarded by the king. This story is recounted in Daniel 3.
5. Isaiah 7: 9.
6. Ephesians 3: 16–17.
7. I Corinthians 1: 24.

# Afterword

## Philip L. Quinn[*]

How can people learn to understand the truth? Augustine of Hippo tries to answer this question about the education of the mind in *The Teacher* (*De magistro*). There he refutes the knowledge-transfer model of education, according to which a teacher transfers knowledge to a learner by means of speech or writing. The teacher transfers knowledge by encoding it into language and uttering the appropriate sounds; the learner, hearing the utterances and knowing the language, decodes language back into thoughts. Augustine formulates the transfer model as follows: "Nor is there any other reason for signifying, or for giving signs, except for bringing forth and transferring to another mind the action of the mind in the person who makes the sign" (*On Christian Doctrine* 2.2.2). Augustine's alternative view is that much, if not all, of what we know we learn from the teacher within, who is Christ.

*The Teacher* is a dialogue in which Augustine's interlocutor is his son, Adeodatus. It deals with problems in the philosophy of language: for instance, how does language connect with the world? Augustine and Adeodatus try to understand how we learn what is signified by signs that signify non-signs. They examine the hypothesis that ostensive teaching can exhibit the thing signified to the senses. They recognize that learning by ostension presents a problem. Suppose you ask me what the word "red" signifies, and I show you a red color patch. How do you learn that the patch's color rather than its shape is signified by the word and that the particular shade of the patch's color is not what is signified by the word? Augustine and Adeodatus agree that intelligent people somehow manage to learn ostensively despite such ambiguities. And so Augustine begins the monologue that takes up the last quarter of the work by concluding that "some people can be taught some things without signs" (*The Teacher* 10.32.103). This conclusion is consistent with the further claim that some people can also be taught some things through signs, through the medium of language.

But Augustine argues, for the stronger thesis that "nothing is learned through its signs" (*The Teacher* 10.33.115), and this thesis is inconsistent with the knowledge-transfer model of education. He initially presents the argument as a version of the learner's paradox. Signs can draw our attention to or prompt us to search for the sensible things they signify. But we do not know what they signify until we have sensed those things, and only then do we know that

[*] Philip L. Quinn was Professor of Philosophy at the University of Notre Dame.

they are signs. Once we do know that they are signs, however, presenting them to us can only serve to remind us of something we already know. Augustine thus endorses the following argument for words signifying sensible things: "we either know what they signify or we don't; if we know, then it's reminding rather than learning; but if we don't know, it isn't even reminding, though perhaps we recollect that we should inquire" (*The Teacher* 11.36. 15–18).

Augustine divides the things we perceive into the sensible and the intelligible. He says: "Everything we perceive, we perceive either by one of the bodily senses or by the mind" (*The Teacher* 12.39.9). He also maintains that "someone who presents what I want to know to my eyes, or to any of my bodily senses, or even to my mind itself, does teach me something" (*The Teacher* 11.36.3–4). In other words, teaching consists in one person bringing it about that something is shown or presented to another person who desires to know. I can teach what the color red is because, by means of a color patch, I can show or present the color red to another's sense of vision. Though nature is not a person and hence, strictly speaking, not a teacher, we can learn from nature because it shows or presents things to our bodily senses. As Augustine notes, nature can and does "show and display to those paying attention, by themselves, this sun and the light pervading and clothing all things present, the moon and the other stars, the lands and the seas, and the countless things begotten in them" (*The Teacher* 10.32.110–14).

But neither nature nor I can show or present to anyone intelligible things that can only be perceived by the mind. I can, of course, utter the English word "two" or inscribe the arabic numeral "2," and this word and that numeral signify the number two. They do not, however, show or present the number two to the bodily senses; nor do they show or present it directly to the mind. So I cannot teach anyone what the number two is. Nature cannot do so either. Augustine thinks God can. He tells us:

> When we deal with things that we perceive by the mind, namely by the intellect and reason, we're speaking of things that we look upon immediately in the inner light of Truth, in virtue of which the so-called inner man is illuminated and rejoices. Under these conditions our listener, if he likewise sees these things with his inward and undivided eye, knows what I'm saying from his own contemplating, not from my words. Therefore, when I'm stating truths, I don't even teach the person who is looking upon these truths. He's taught not by my words but by the things themselves made manifest within when God discloses them.
>
> (*The Teacher* 12.40.29–37)

In short, God teaches us about intelligible things by showing or presenting them directly to our minds.

The suggestion that our understanding of formal logic and mathematics depends upon some sort of inner vision or illumination has considerable plausibility. Many of us have had the experience of going over the steps of a mathematical proof without understanding how the proof works; only after a flash of insight do we come to understand the proof. There is a cognitive difference between our situation before and after the flash of insight. Like Augustine, we often describe this difference with visual metaphors.

There is some reason to believe that Augustine intends this account of divine illumination to cover more than our knowledge of such subjects as logic and mathematics. In a famous passage, he boldly claims:

> Regarding each of the things we understand, however, we don't consult a speaker who makes sounds outside us, but the Truth that presides within over the mind itself, though perhaps words prompt us to consult Him. What is more, He Who is consulted, He Who is said to *dwell in the inner man*, does teach: Christ—that is, *the unchangeable power and everlasting wisdom of God*, which every rational soul does consult, but is disclosed to anyone, to the extent that he can apprehend it, according to his good or evil will.
>
> (*The Teacher* 11.38.44–51)

So apparently Augustine thinks that Christ, God the Son and the teacher within, explains how we understand any of the things we really do understand.

Some explanation is needed for Augustine's choice of Christ to play the role of the teacher within. Augustine believes that God is a trinity of persons. Hence he asks whether the teacher within is one of these persons acting alone, two of them acting together in the absence of the third, or all three acting in concert. Introspection yields no answer to this question. Augustine thinks scripture, which he takes to be revealed truth, points to the answer he favors. The scriptural texts from which he derives his answer are alluded to by the phrases emphasized in the passage quoted above. The first is Ephesians 3: 16–17: "I pray that, according to the riches of his glory, he may grant that you may be strengthened in your inner being with power through his Spirit, and that Christ may dwell in your hearts through faith, as you are being rooted and grounded in love." This suggests that the teacher within is the Holy Spirit, Christ or both. The second text is 1 Corinthians 22–4: "For Jews demand signs and Greeks desire wisdom, but we proclaim Christ crucified, a stumbling block to Jews and foolishness to Gentiles, but to those who are the called, both Jews and Greeks, Christ the power of God and the wisdom of God." It seems fitting that the wisdom of God personified should impart understanding to us, and so Christ's claim on the role of the teacher within has, as Augustine sees it, the support of scriptural authority.

How does Christ play the role of the teacher within? I think it would be a mistake to suppose that he does so by means of some inner analogue of human speech. Such divine speech would give the learner nothing more than signs for intelligible things that are only perceived by the mind. It could not guarantee that the learner understood what is signified by such signs. Such a supposition would merely replicate at the level of the divine teacher the problem Augustine believes human teachers confront. According to Augustine, humans teach by showing or presenting to the learner sensible things signified by signs for them. It seems to me best to think of the divine teacher as operating in an analogous fashion. Christ teaches by showing or presenting directly to the learner's mind, not signs for intelligible things, but the intelligible things signified by such signs. This is what seems to me to be suggested by the claim quoted above that we are taught about intelligible things by the things themselves made manifest within when God discloses them. In short, like human teaching, divine teaching is showing rather than telling. The difference is that the divine teacher can show the learner's mind intelligible things and human teachers cannot.

I am inclined to think that Christians can reasonably endorse Augustine's claim that

Christ is the teacher within. It is not refuted by the fact that non-Christians often succeed in understanding things at least as well as Christians do, for Christ might operate within the minds of non-Christians unbeknownst to them. The doctrine of the teacher within is supposed to explain certain cognitive achievements. Like other explanatory theories, it is entitled to postulate unobservable occurrences in order to explain observable phenomena. Christ could be at work in any human person's mind without the person being introspectively aware of it.

There are, of course, rivals to Augustine's identification of the teacher within with Christ. According to Descartes, the role of the teacher within is played by the stock of innate ideas and the natural light of reason with which God endows people when he creates them. According to modern naturalists, the role of the teacher within could be played by hard-wired cognitive dispositions that form part of our evolutionary legacy. So it is only to be expected that there will be disagreement about who or what the teacher within is even among those who agree that something must be postulated to play the role of the teacher within.

Is it plausible to suppose that we need to postulate an inner teacher of some sort in order to explain some of our cognitive achievements? I think that, by means of examples, it can be made at least somewhat plausible in cases where we understand non-sensible truths. Augustine provides an example in his *Confessions*, when he describes his struggles to interpret Genesis 1: 2: "The earth was invisible and without form [*Terra erat invisibilis et incomposita*]."

> I used to use the word formless not for that which lacked form but for that which had a form such that, if it had appeared, my mind would have experienced revulsion from its extraordinary and bizarre shape, and my human weakness would have been plunged into confusion. But the picture I had in mind was not the privation of all form, but that which is relatively formless by comparison with more beautiful shapes. True reasoning convinced me that I should wholly subtract all remnants of every kind of form if I wished to conceive the absolutely formless. I could not achieve this. I found it easier to suppose something deprived of all form to be non-existent than to think that something could stand between form and nothingness, neither endowed with form nor nothing, but formless and so almost nothing.
>
> (*Confessions* 12.6.6)

Unless he can interpret the sentence "The earth was invisible and without form" in a satisfactory fashion, Augustine thinks he cannot find within himself the truth it expresses. Although he can believe that the sentence "The earth was invisible and without form" is true, he cannot grasp its truth. He can get out of his predicament if he can figure out for himself, consulting the teacher within, what the sentence means or what proposition it expresses. Faithful to his own understanding of who the teacher within is, Augustine praises God for "all that you disentangled for me in examining this question" (*Confessions* 12.6.6).

Augustine concludes his assault on the knowledge-transfer model of education by pointing out cases in which speech does not convey to the hearer the thoughts of the speaker. They include lies and other deceptions, recitations of a memorized speech when the speaker's mind is on something else, slips of the tongue, misunderstandings and mishearings. But even if such cases are set aside and it is granted that the hearer grasps the thoughts of the speaker, Augustine argues, the hearer does not thereby learn whether what the speaker has said is true. Instead, he claims, "when the teachers have explained by means of words all the disciplines they profess, even the disciplines of virtue and of wisdom, then those who are called 'students' consider within themselves whether truths have been stated" (*The Teacher* 14.45.5–8). They do this by consulting the teacher within, and that is the point at which they learn. The illusion that students learn from their human teachers arises, Augustine suggests, because there is usually no delay between the time of speaking and the time of learning. "Since they are quick to learn internally after the prompting of the lecturer," he says, "they suppose that they have learned externally from the one who prompted them" (*The Teacher* 14.45.15–16).

Teachers of many subjects could learn a becoming modesty from Augustine's refutation of the knowledge-transfer model of education. For example, a mathematician who walks into a classroom and writes on the blackboard a proof of some theorem she knows should be aware that she is not thereby transferring her knowledge into the minds of the students who copy the proof into their notebooks. Even if the bright students understand the proof right away, others will have to pore over their notebooks after class before they see for themselves how the proof goes. All the students in the class will have to acquire for themselves an understanding of the proof. To be sure, our mathematician will typically provide some commentary intended to facilitate understanding along with her presentation of the proof. But she should also be aware that, though such commentary may prompt understanding, it is not by itself guaranteed to produce it. Understanding of the proof requires the cooperation of something within the learner, whether it be literally an inner teacher who is a divine person, as Augustine thought, or the activation of some cognitive disposition that is not itself a person, as others suppose. Of course good mathematics teachers are at least tacitly aware of these things. But perhaps some helpful conversations about how teachers can prompt and facilitate the learning of their students would ensue if this awareness were made more explicit in discussions of mathematical pedagogy.

I think the point I have tried to make in terms of the imaginary mathematician of my example can be applied to the teachers of quite a few other subjects. At any rate, I would apply it to teachers of any science that has a good deal of theoretical content and to teachers of any of the humanities that involve interpreting difficult texts. Much of what such teachers do is not imparting understanding; it is instead prompting students to acquire it for themselves.

# 4

## John Locke

**John Locke** (1632–1704) attended the University of Oxford, where he spent much of his life as a lecturer in Greek, rhetoric, and philosophy. Educated also in medicine and chemistry, he later became secretary, physician, and advisor to the prominent English statesman Anthony Ashley Cooper, who became the 1st Earl of Shaftesbury. Through Locke's writings he earned a prominent place in both the history of philosophy as well as the history of political theory.

## *Some Thoughts Concerning Education*

1. A sound mind in a sound body, is a short but full description of a happy state in this world: he that has these two, has little more to wish for; and he that wants either of them, will be but little the better for anything else. Men's happiness or misery is [for the] most part of their own making. He whose mind directs not wisely, will never take the right way; and he whose body is crazy and feeble, will never be able to advance in it. I confess, there are some men's constitutions of body and mind so vigorous, and well framed by nature, that they need not much assistance from others; but, by the strength of their natural genius, they are, from their cradles, carried towards what is excellent; and, by the privilege of their happy constitutions, are able to do wonders. But examples of this kind are but few; and I think I may say, that, of all the men we meet with, nine parts of ten are what they are, good or evil, useful or not, by their education. It is that which makes the great difference in mankind. The little, or almost insensible, impressions on our tender infancies, have very important and lasting consequences: and there it is, as in the fountains of some rivers, where a gentle application of the hand turns the flexible waters into channels, that make them take quite contrary courses;

and by this little direction, given them at first, in the source, they receive different tendencies, and arrive at last at very remote and distant places.

32. If what I have said in the beginning of this discourse be true, as I do not doubt but it is, viz. that the difference to be found in the manners and abilities of men is owing more to their education than to anything else; we have reason to conclude, that great care is to be had of the forming children's minds, and giving them that seasoning early, which shall influence their lives always after. For when they do well or ill, the praise or blame will be laid there: and when anything is done awkwardly, the common saying will pass upon them, that it is suitable to their breeding.

33. As the strength of the body lies chiefly in being able to endure hardships, so also does that of the mind. And the great principle and foundation of all virtue and worth is placed in this, that a man is able to deny himself his own desires, cross his own inclinations, and purely follow what reason directs as best, though the appetite lean the other way.

34. The great mistake I have observed in people's breeding their children has been, that this has not been taken care enough of in its due season; that the mind has not been made obedient to discipline, and pliant to reason, when at first it was most tender, most easy to be bowed. Parents being wisely ordained by nature to love their children, are very apt, if reason watch not that natural affection very warily; are apt, I say, to let it run into fondness. They love their little ones, and it is their duty: but they often with them cherish their faults too. They must not be crossed, forsooth; they must be permitted to have their wills in all things; and they being in their infancies not capable of great vices, their parents think they may safely enough indulge their little irregularities, and make them-selves sport with that pretty perverseness, which they think well enough becomes that innocent age. But to a fond parent, that would not have his child corrected for a perverse trick, but excused it, saying it was a small matter; Solon very well replied, "Ay, but custom is a great one."

38. It seems plain to me, that the principle of all virtue and excellency lies in a power of denying ourselves the satisfaction of our own desires, where reason does not authorize them. This power is to be got and improved by custom, made easy and familiar by an early practice. If therefore I might be heard, I would advise, that, contrary to the ordinary way, children should be used to submit their desires, and go without their longings, even from their very cradles. The very first thing they should learn to know, should be, that they were not to have anything, because it pleased them, but because it was thought fit for them. If things suitable to their wants were supplied to them, so that they were never suffered to have what they once cried for, they would learn to be content without it; would never with bawling and peevish-ness contend for mastery; nor be half so uneasy to themselves and others as they are, because from the first beginning they are not thus handled. If they were never suffered to obtain their desire by the impatience they expressed for it, they would no more cry for other things than they do for the moon.

39. I say not this as if children were not to be indulged in anything, or that I expected they should, in hanging-sleeves, have the reason and conduct of counsellors. I consider them as children, who must be tenderly used, who must play, and have play things. That which I mean is, that whenever they craved what was not fit for them to have, or do, they should not be permitted it, because they were little and desired it: nay, whatever they were importunate

for, they should be sure, for that very reason, to be denied. I have seen children at a table, who, whatever was there, never asked for anything, but contentedly took what was given them: and at another place I have seen others cry for every thing they saw, must be served out of every dish, and that first too. What made this vast difference but this, that one was accustomed to have what they called or cried for, the other to go without it? The younger they are, the less, I think, are their unruly and disorderly appetites to be complied with; and the less reason they have of their own, the more are they to be under the absolute power and restraint of those, in whose hands they are. From which I confess, it will follow, that none but discreet people should be about them. If the world commonly does otherwise, I cannot help that. I am saying what I think should be; which, if it were already in fashion, I should not need to trouble the world with a discourse on this subject. But yet I doubt not but, when it is considered, there will be others of opinion with me, that the sooner this way is begun with children, the easier it will be for them, and their governors too: and that this ought to be observed as an inviolable maxim, that whatever once is denied them, they are certainly not to obtain by crying or importunity; unless one has a mind to teach them to be impatient and troublesome, by rewarding them for it, when they are so.

40. Those therefore that intend ever to govern their children, should begin it whilst they are very little; and look that they perfectly comply with the will of their parents. Would you have your son obedient to you, when past a child? Be sure then to establish the authority of a father, as soon as he is capable of submission, and can understand in whose power he is. If you would have him stand in awe of you, imprint it in his infancy; and, as he approaches more to a man, admit him nearer to your familiarity: so shall you have him your obedient subject (as is fit) whilst he is a child, and your affectionate friend when he is a man. For methinks they mightily misplace the treatment due to their children, who are indulgent and familiar when they are little, but severe to them, and keep them at a distance, when they are grown up. For liberty and indulgence can do no good to children: their want of judgment makes them stand in need of restraint and discipline. And, on the contrary, imperiousness and severity is but an ill way of treating men, who have reason of their own to guide them, unless you have a mind to make your children, when grown up, weary of you; and secretly to say within themselves, "When will you die, father?"

41. I imagine everyone will judge it reasonable, that their children, when little, should look upon their parents as their lords, their absolute governors; and, as such, stand in awe of them: and that, when they come to riper years, they should look on them as their best, as their only sure friends: and, as such, love and reverence them. The way I have mentioned, if I mistake not, is the only one to obtain this. We must look upon our children, when grown up, to be like ourselves; with the same passions, the same desires. We would be thought rational creatures, and have our freedom; we love not to be uneasy under constant rebukes and brow-beatings; nor can we bear severe humours, and great distance, in those we converse with. Whoever has such treatment when he is a man, will look out other company, other friends, other conversation, with whom he can be at ease. If therefore a strict hand be kept over children from the beginning, they will in that age be tractable, and quietly submit to it, as never having known any other: and if, as they grow up to the use of reason, the rigour of government be, as they deserve it, gently relaxed, the father's brow more smoothed to them, and the distance by degrees abated: his former restraints will increase their love, when they

find it was only a kindness for them, and a care to make them capable to deserve the favour of their parents, and the esteem of everybody else.

42. Thus much for the settling your authority over children in general. Fear and awe ought to give you the first power over their minds, and love and friendship in riper years to hold it: for the time must come, when they will be past the rod and correction; and then, if the love of you make them not obedient and dutiful; if the love of virtue and reputation keep them not in laudable courses; I ask, what hold will you have upon them, to turn them to it? Indeed, fear of having a scanty portion, if they displease you, may make them slaves to your estate; but they will be nevertheless ill and wicked in private, and that restraint will not last always. Every man must some time or other be trusted to himself, and his own conduct; and he that is a good, a virtuous, and able man, must be made so within. And therefore, what he is to receive from education, what is to sway and influence his life, must be something put into him betimes: habits woven into the very principles of his nature; and not a counterfeit carriage, and dissembled outside, put on by fear, only to avoid the present anger of a father, who perhaps may disinherit him.

43. This being laid down in general, as the course ought to be taken, it is fit we come now to consider the parts of the discipline to be used, a little more particularly. I have spoken so much of carrying a strict hand over children, that perhaps I shall be suspected of not considering enough what is due to their tender age and constitutions. But that opinion will vanish, when you have heard me a little farther. For I am very apt to think, that great severity of punishment does but very little good; nay, great harm in education: and I believe it will be found, that, *caeteris paribus*, those children who have been most chastised, seldom make the best men. All that I have hitherto contended for, is, that whatsoever rigour is necessary, it is more to be used, the younger children are; and, having by a due application wrought its effect, it is to be relaxed, and changed into a milder sort of government.

44. A compliance, and suppleness of their wills, being by a steady hand introduced by parents, before children have memories to retain the beginnings of it, will seem natural to them, and work afterwards in them, as if it were so; preventing all occasions of struggling, or repining. The only care is, that it be begun early, and inflexibly kept to, till awe and respect be grown familiar, and there appears not the least reluctancy in the submission and ready obedience of their minds. When this reverence is once thus established (which it must be early, or else it will cost pains and blows to recover it, and the more, the longer it is deferred) it is by it, mixed still with as much indulgence as they made not an ill use of, and not by beating, chiding, or other servile punishments, they are for the future to be governed, as they grow up to more understanding.

45. That this is so, will be easily allowed, when it is but considered what is to be aimed at, in an ingenuous education; and upon what it turns.

(1.) He that has not a mastery over his inclinations, he that knows not how to resist the importunity of present pleasure or pain, for the sake of what reason tells him is fit to be done, wants the true principle of virtue and industry; and is in danger of never being good for anything. This temper, therefore, so contrary to unguided nature, is to be got betimes; and this habit, as the true foundation of future ability and happiness, is to be wrought into the mind, as early as may be, even from the first dawnings of any knowledge or apprehension in children; and so to be confirmed in them, by all the care and ways imaginable, by those who have the oversight of their education.

46. (2.) On the other side, if the mind be curbed, and humbled too much in children; if their spirits be abased and broken much, by too strict a hand over them; they lose all their vigour and industry, and are in a worse state than the former. For extravagant young fellows, that have liveliness and spirit, come sometimes to be set right, and so make able and great men: but dejected minds, timorous and tame, and low spirits, are hardly ever to be raised, and very seldom attain to anything. To avoid the danger that is on either hand is the great art: and he that has found a way how to keep up a child's spirit, easy, active, and free; and yet, at the same time, to restrain him from many things he has a mind to, and to draw him to things that are uneasy to him; he, I say, that knows how to reconcile these seeming contradictions, has, in my opinion, got the true secret of education.

47. The usual lazy and short way by chastisement, and the rod, which is the only instrument of government that tutors generally know, or ever think of, is the most unfit of any to be used in education; because it tends to both those mischiefs; which as we have shown, are the Scylla and Charybdis, which, on the one hand or the other, ruin all that miscarry.

48. (1.) This kind of punishment contributes not at all to the mastery of our natural propensity to indulge corporal and present pleasure and to avoid pain at any rate; but rather encourages it; and thereby strengthens that in us, which is the root, from whence spring all vicious actions and the irregularities of life. From what other motive, but of sensual pleasure, and pain, does a child act, who drudges at his book against his inclination, or abstains from eating unwholesome fruit, that he takes pleasure in, only out of fear of whipping? He in this only prefers the greater corporal pleasure, or avoids the greater corporal pain. And what is it to govern his actions, and direct his conduct, by such motives as these? what is it, I say, but to cherish that principle in him, which it is our business to root out and destroy? And therefore I cannot think any correction useful to a child, where the shame of suffering for having done amiss does not work more upon him than the pain.

49. (2.) This sort of correction naturally breeds an aversion to that which it is the tutor's business to create a liking to. How obvious is it to observe, that children come to hate things which were at first acceptable to them, when they find themselves whipped, and chided, and teased about them? And it is not to be wondered at in them; when grown men would not be able to be reconciled to anything by such ways. Who is there that would not be disgusted with any innocent recreation, in itself indifferent to him, if he should with blows, or ill language, be hauled to it, when he had no mind? or be constantly so treated, for some circumstances in his application to it? This is natural to be so. Offensive circumstances ordinarily infect innocent things, which they are joined with: and the very sight of a cup, wherein anyone uses to take nauseous physic, turns his stomach; so that nothing will relish well out of it, though the cup be ever so clean, and well-shaped, and of the richest materials.

50. (3.) Such a sort of slavish discipline makes a slavish temper. The child submits, and dissembles obedience, whilst the fear of the rod hangs over him; but when that is removed, and, by being out of sight, he can promise himself impunity, he gives the greater scope to his natural inclination; which by this way is not at all altered, but on the contrary heightened and increased in him; and after such restraint, breaks out usually with the more violence. Or,

51. (4.) If severity carried to the highest pitch does prevail, and works a cure upon the

present unruly distemper, it is often bringing in the room of it worse and more dangerous disease, by breaking the mind; and then, in the place of a disorderly young fellow, you have a low-spirited moped creature: who, however with his unnatural sobriety he may please silly people, who commend tame inactive children, because they make no noise, nor give them any trouble; yet, at last, will probably prove as uncomfortable a thing to his friends, as he will be, all his life, an useless thing to himself and others.

52. Beating then, and all other sorts of slavish and corporal punishments, are not the discipline fit to be used in the education of those who would have wise, good, and ingenuous men; and therefore very rarely to be applied, and that only on great occasions, and cases of extremity. On the other side, to flatter children by rewards of things that are pleasant to them, is as carefully to be avoided. He that will give to his son apples, or sugar-plums, or what else of this kind he is most delighted with, to make him learn his book, does but authorise his love of pleasure, and cocker up that dangerous propensity, which he ought by all means to subdue and stifle in him. You can never hope to teach him to master it, whilst you compound for the check you give his inclination in one place, by the satisfaction you propose to it in another. To make a good, a wise, and a virtuous man, it is fit he should learn to cross his appetite, and deny his inclination to riches, finery, or pleasing his palate, &c. whenever his reason advises the contrary, and his duty requires it. But when you draw him to do anything that is fit, by the offer of money; or reward the pains of learning his book, by the pleasure of a luscious morsel; when you promise him a lace-cravat, or a fine new suit, upon performance of some of his little tasks; what do you, by proposing these as rewards, but allow them to be the good things he should aim at, and thereby encourage his longing for them, and accustom him to place his happiness in them? Thus people, to prevail with children to be industrious about their grammar, dancing, or some other such matter, of no great moment to the happiness or usefulness of their lives, by misapplied rewards and punishments, sacrifice their virtue, invert the order of their education, and teach them luxury, pride, or covetousness, &c. For in this way, flattering those wrong inclinations, which they should restrain and suppress, they lay the foundations of those future vices, which cannot be avoided, but by curbing our desires and accustoming them early to submit to reason.

53. I say not this that I would have children kept from the conveniences or pleasures of life that are not injurious to their health or virtue. On the contrary, I would have their lives made as pleasant and as agreeable to them as may be in a plentiful enjoyment of whatsoever might innocently delight them: provided it be with this caution, that they have those enjoyments only as the consequences of the state of esteem and acceptation they are in with their parents and governors; but they should never be offered or bestowed on them as the rewards of this or that particular performance that they show an aversion to or to which they would not have applied themselves without that temptation.

54. But if you take away the rod, on one hand, and these little encouragements, which they are taken with, on the other, how then (will you say) shall children be governed? Remove hope and fear, and there is an end of all discipline. I grant that good and evil, reward and punishment, are the only motives to a rational creature; these are the spur and reins whereby all mankind are set on work and guided, and therefore they are to be made use of to children too. For I advise their parents and governors always to carry this in their minds, that children are to be treated as rational creatures.

55. Rewards, I grant, and punishments must be proposed to children, if we intend to work upon them. The mistake, I imagine, is that those that are generally made use of are ill chosen. The pains and pleasures of the body are, I think, of ill consequence when made the rewards and punishments whereby men would prevail on their children: for, as I said before, they serve but to increase and strengthen those inclinations which it is our business to subdue and master. What principle of virtue do you lay in a child if you will redeem his desires of one pleasure by the proposal of another? This is but to enlarge his appetite and instruct it to wander. If a child cries for an unwholesome and dangerous fruit, you purchase his quiet by giving him a less hurtful sweetmeat. This perhaps may preserve his health, but spoils his mind and sets that farther out of order. For here you only change the object, but flatter still his appetite and allow that must be satisfied wherein, as I have showed, lies the root of the mischief; and till you bring him to be able to bear a denial of that satisfaction, the child may at present be quiet and orderly, but the disease is not cured. By this way of proceeding you foment and cherish in him that which is the spring from whence all the evil flows, which will be sure on the next occasion to break out again with more violence, give him stronger longings, and you more trouble.

56. The rewards and punishments then, whereby we should keep children in order, are quite of another kind and of that force, that when we can get them once to work, the business, I think, is done and the difficulty is over. Esteem and disgrace are, of all others, the most powerful incentives to the mind, when once it is brought to relish them. If you can once get into children a love of credit and an apprehension of shame and disgrace, you have put into them the true principle, which will constantly work and incline them to the right. But it will be asked, how shall this be done?

I confess it does not at first appearance want some difficulty; but yet I think it worth our while to seek the ways (and practice them when found) to attain this, which I look on as the great secret of education.

57. First, children (earlier perhaps than we think) are very sensible of praise and commendation. They find a pleasure in being esteemed and valued, especially by their parents, and those whom they depend on. If therefore the father caress and commend them, when they do well; show a cold and neglectful countenance to them upon doing ill; and this accompanied by a like carriage of the mother, and all others that are about them; it will in a little time make them sensible of the difference: and this, if constantly observed, I doubt not but will of itself work more than threats or blows, which lose their force, when once grown common, and are of no use when shame does not attend them; and therefore are to be forborn, and never to be used, but in the case hereafter mentioned, when it is brought to extremity.

58. But, secondly, to make the sense of esteem or disgrace sink the deeper, and be of the more weight, other agreeable or disagreeable things should constantly accompany these different states; not as particular rewards and punishments of this or that particular action, but as necessarily belonging to, and constantly attending one, who by his carriage has brought himself into a state of disgrace or commendation. By which way of treating them, children may as much as possible be brought to conceive, that those that are commended and in esteem for doing well, will necessarily be beloved and cherished by everybody, and have all other good things as a consequence of it; and, on the other side, when anyone by

miscarriage falls into dis-esteem, and cares not to preserve his credit, he will unavoidably fall under neglect and contempt: and, in that state, the want of whatever might satisfy or delight him, will follow. In this way the objects of their desires are made assisting to virtue; when a settled experience from the beginning teaches children, that the things they delight in, belong to, and are to be enjoyed by those only, who are in a state of reputation. If by these means you can come once to shame them out of their faults (for besides that, I would willingly have no punishment) and make them in love with the pleasure of being well thought on, you may turn them as you please, and they will be in love with all the ways of virtue.

63. But if a right course be taken with children, there will not be so much need of the application of the common reward and punishments, as we imagined, and as the general practice has established. For all their innocent folly, playing, and childish actions, are to be left perfectly free and unrestrained, as far as they can consist with the respect due to those that are present; and that with the greatest allowance. If these faults of their age, rather than of the children themselves, were, as they should be, left only to time, and imitation, and riper years to cure, children would escape a great deal of misapplied and useless correction; which either fails to overpower the natural disposition of their childhood, and so, by an ineffectual familiarity, makes correction in other necessary cases of less use; or else if it be of force to restrain the natural gaiety of that age, it serves only to spoil the temper both of body and mind. If the noise and bustle of their play prove at any time inconvenient, or unsuitable to the place or company they are in (which can only be where their parents are), a look or a word from the father or mother, if they have established the authority they should, will be enough either to remove, or quiet them for that time. But this gamesome humour, which is wisely adapted by nature to their age and temper, should rather be encouraged, to keep up their spirits, and improve their strength and health, than curbed or restrained: and the chief art is to make all that they have to do, sport and play too.

64. And here give me leave to take notice of one thing I think a fault in the ordinary method of education; and that is, the charging of children's memories, upon all occasions, with rules and precepts, which they often do not understand, and are constantly as soon forgot as given. If it be some action you would have done, or done otherwise; whenever they forget, or do it awkwardly, make them do it over and over again, till they are perfect: whereby you will get these two advantages: first, to see whether it be an action they can do, or is fit to be expected of them. For sometimes children are bid to do things, which, upon trial, they are found not able to do; and had need be taught and exercised in, before they are required to do them. But it is much easier for a tutor to command, than to teach. Secondly, another thing got by it will be this, that by repeating the same action, till it be grown habitual in them, the performance will not depend on memory, or reflection, the concomitant of prudence and age, and not of childhood; but will be natural in them. Thus, bowing to a gentleman when he salutes him, and looking in his face when he speaks to him, is by constant use as natural to a well-bred man, as breathing; it requires no thought, no reflection. Having this way cured in your child any fault, it is cured for ever: and thus, one by one, you may weed them out all, and plant what habits you please.

65. I have seen parents so heap rules on their children, that it was impossible for the poor little ones to remember a tenth part of them, much less to observe them. However, they were either by words or blows corrected for the breach of those multiplied and often very

impertinent precepts. Whence it naturally followed, that the children minded not what was said to them; when it was evident to them, that no attention they were capable of, was sufficient to preserve them from transgression, and the rebukes which followed it.

Let therefore your rules to your son be as few as is possible, and rather fewer than more than seem absolutely necessary. For if you burden him with many rules, one of these two things must necessarily follow, that either he must be very often punished, which will be of ill consequence, by making punishment too frequent and familiar; or else you must let the transgressions of some of your rules go unpunished, whereby they will of course grow contemptible, and your authority become cheap to him. Make but few laws but see they be well observed, when once made. Few years require but few laws; and as his age increases, when one rule is by practice well established, you may add another.

66. But pray remember, children are not to be taught by rules, which will be always slipping out of their memories. What you think necessary for them to do, settle in them by an indispensable practice, as often as the occasion returns; and, if it be possible, make occasions. This will beget habits in them, which, being once established, operate of them-selves easily and naturally, without the assistance of the memory. But here let me give two cautions: 1. The one is, that you keep them to the practice of what you would have grow into a habit in them, by kind words and gentle admonitions, rather as minding them of what they forget, than by harsh rebukes and chiding, as if they were wilfully guilty. Secondly, another thing you are to take care of, is, not to endeavour to settle too many habits at once, lest by a variety you confound them, and so perfect none. When constant custom has made any one thing easy and natural to them, and they practise it without reflection, you may then go on to another.

This method of teaching children by a repeated practice, and the same action done over and over again, under the eye and direction of the tutor, till they have got the habit of doing it well, and not by relying on rules trusted to their memories; has so many advantages, which way soever we consider it, that I cannot but wonder (if ill customs could be wondered at in any thing) how it could possibly be so much neglected. I shall name one more that comes now in my way. By this method we shall see, whether what is required of him be adapted to his capacity, and any way suited to the child's natural genius and constitution: for that too must be considered in a right education. We must not hope wholly to change their original tempers, nor make the gay pensive and grave, nor the melancholy sportive, without spoiling them. God has stamped certain characters upon men's minds, which, like their shapes, may perhaps be a little mended; but can hardly be totally altered and transformed into the contrary.

He therefore, that is about children, should well study their natures and aptitudes, and see, by often trials, what turn they easily take, and what becomes them; observe what their native stock is, how it may be improved, and what it is fit for: he should consider what they want, whether they be capable of having it wrought into them by industry, and incorporated there by practice; and whether it be worth while to endeavour it. For, in many cases, all that we can do, or should aim at, is, to make the best of what nature has given, to prevent the vices and faults to which such a constitution is most inclined, and give it all the advantages it is capable of. Every one's natural genius should be carried as far as it could; but to attempt the putting another upon him, will be but labour in vain;

and what is so plaistered on will at best sit but untowardly, and have always hanging to it the ungracefulness of constraint and affectation.

Affectation is not, I confess, an early fault of childhood, or the product of untaught nature: it is of that sort of weeds, which grow not in the wild uncultivated waste, but in garden-plots, under the negligent hand, or unskilful care of a gardener. Management and instruction, and some sense of the necessity of breeding, are requisite to make any one capable of affectation, which endeavours to correct natural defects, and has always the laudable aim of pleasing, though it always misses it; and the more it labours to put on gracefulness, the farther it is from it. For this reason it is the more carefully to be watched, because it is the proper fault of education; a perverted education indeed, but such as young people often fall into, either by their own mistake, or the ill conduct of those about them.

He that will examine wherein that gracefulness lies, which always pleases, will find it arises from that natural coherence, which appears between the thing done, and such a temper of mind, as cannot but be approved of as suitable to the occasion. We cannot but be pleased with an humane, friendly, civil temper, wherever we meet with it. A mind free, and master of itself and all its actions, not low and narrow, not haughty and insolent, not blemished with any great defect; is what every one is taken with. The actions, which naturally flow from such a well-formed mind, please us also, as the genuine marks of it; and being, as it were, natural emanations from the spirit and disposition within, cannot but be easy and unconstrained. This seems to me to be that beauty, which shines through some men's actions, sets off all that they do, and takes with all they come near; when by a constant practice they have fashioned their carriage, and made all those little expressions of civility and respect, which nature or custom has established in conversation, so easy to themselves, that they seem not artificial or studied, but naturally to follow from a sweetness of mind and a well-turned disposition.

On the other side, affection is an awkward and forced imitation of what should be genuine and easy, wanting the beauty that accompanies what is natural; because there is always a disagreement between the outward action, and the mind within, one of these two ways:

1. Either when a man would outwardly put on a disposition of mind, which then he really has not, but endeavours by a forced carriage to make show of; yet so, that the constraint he is under discovers itself: and thus men affect sometimes to appear sad, merry, or kind, when, in truth, they are not so.
2. The other is, when they do not endeavour to make show of dispositions of mind which they have not, but to express those they have by a carriage not suited to them: and such in conversation are all constrained motions, actions, words, or looks, which, though designed to show either their respect or civility to the company, or their satisfaction and easiness in it, are not yet natural nor genuine marks of the one or the other; but rather of some defect or mistake within. Imitation of others, without discerning what is graceful in them, or what is peculiar to their characters, often makes a great part of this. But affectation of all kinds, whencesoever it proceeds, is always offensive: because we naturally hate whatever is counterfeit; and condemn those who have nothing better to recommend themselves by.

Plain and rough nature, left to itself, is much better than an artificial ungracefulness, and such studied ways of being ill-fashioned. The want of an accomplishment, or some defect in our behaviour, coming short of the utmost gracefulness, often escapes observation and censure. But affectation in any part of our carriage is lighting up a candle to our defects; and never fails to make us be taken notice of, either as wanting sense, or wanting sincerity. This governors ought the more diligently to look after, because, as I above observed, it is an acquired ugliness, owing to mistaken education; few being guilty of it, but those who pretend to breeding, and would not be thought ignorant of what is fashionable and becoming in conversation: and, if I mistake not, it has often its rise from the lazy admonitions of those who give rules, and propose examples, without joining practice with their instructions, and making their pupils repeat the action in their sight, that they may correct what is indecent or constrained in it, till it be perfected into an habitual and becoming easiness.

67. Manners, as they call it, about which children are so often perplexed, and have so many goodly exhortations made them, by their wise maids and governesses, I think, are rather to be learned by example than rules; and then children, if kept out of ill company, will take a pride to behave themselves prettily, after the fashion of others, perceiving themselves esteemed and commended for it. But if, by a little negligence in this part, the boy should not put off his hat, nor make legs very gracefully, a dancing-master will cure that defect, and wipe off all that plainness of nature, which the à-la-mode people call clownishness. And since nothing appears to me to give children so much becoming confidence and behaviour, and so to raise them to the conversation of those above their age, as dancing; I think they should be taught to dance, as soon as they are capable of learning it. For, though this consist only in outward gracefulness of motion, yet, I know not how, it gives children manly thoughts and carriage, more than any thing. But otherwise I would not have little children much tormented about punctilios, or niceties of breeding.

Never trouble yourself about those faults in them which you know age will cure.

71. . . . I must here take the liberty to mind parents of this one thing, viz. that he that will have his son have a respect for him and his orders, must himself have a great reverence for his son. "*Maxima debetur pueris reverentia.*" You must do nothing before him, which you would not have him imitate. If anything escape you, which you would have pass for a fault in him, he will be sure to shelter himself under your example, and shelter himself so, as that it will not be easy to come at him to correct it in him the right way. If you punish him for what he sees you practise yourself, he will not think that severity to proceed from kindness in you, or carefulness to amend a fault in him; but will be apt to interpret it the peevishness and arbitrary imperiousness of a father, who, without any ground for it, would deny his son the liberty and pleasures he takes himself. Or if you assume to yourself the liberty you have taken, as a privilege belonging to riper years, to which a child must not aspire, you do but add new force to your example, and recommend the action the more powerfully to him. For you must always remember, that children affect to be men earlier than is thought: and they love breeches, not for their cut, or ease, but because the having them is a mark or a step towards manhood. What I say of the father's carriage before his children, must extend itself to all those who have any authority over them, or for whom he would have them have any respect.

73. (1.) None of the things they are to learn should ever be made a burden to them, or

imposed on them as a task. Whatever is so proposed presently becomes irksome: the mind takes an aversion to it, though before it were a thing of delight or indifferency. Let a child be but ordered to whip his top at a certain time every day, whether he has or has not a mind to it; let this be but required of him as a duty, wherein he must spend so many hours morning and afternoon, and see whether he will not soon be weary of any play at this rate. Is it not so with grown men? What they do cheerfully of themselves, do they not presently grow sick of, and can no more endure, as soon as they find it is expected of them as a duty? Children have as much a mind to show that they are free that their own good actions come from themselves, that they are absolute and independent, as any of the proudest of you grown men, think of them as you please.

74. (2.) As a consequence of this, they should seldom be put about doing even those things you have got an inclination in them to, but when they have a mind and disposition to it. He that loves reading, writing, music, &c. finds yet in himself certain seasons wherein those things have no relish to him: and, if at that time he forces himself to it, he only pothers and wearies himself to no purpose. So it is with children. This change of temper should be carefully observed in them, and the favourable seasons of aptitude and inclination be heedfully laid hold of: and if they are not often enough forward to themselves, a good disposition should be talked into them, before they be set upon anything. . . .

81. It will perhaps be wondered, that I mention reasoning with children: and yet I cannot but think that the true way of dealing with them. They understand it as early as they do language; and, if I misobserve not, they love to be treated as rational creatures sooner than is imagined. It is a pride should be cherished in them, and, as much as can be, made the greatest instrument to turn them by.

But when I talk of reasoning, I do not intend any other but such as is suited to the child's capacity and apprehension. Nobody can think a boy of three or seven years old should be argued with as a grown man. Long discourses, and philosophical reasonings, at best amaze and confound, but do not instruct, children. When I say, therefore, that they must be treated as rational creatures, I mean, that you should make them sensible, by the mildness of your carriage, and the composure, even in your correction of them, that what you do is reasonable in you, and useful and necessary for them; and that it is not out of caprice, passion, or fancy, that you command or forbid them anything. This they are capable of understanding; and there is no virtue they should be excited to, nor fault they should be kept from, which I do not think they may be convinced of: but it must be by such reasons as their age and understanding are capable of, and those proposed always in very few and plain words. The foundations on which several duties are built, and the fountains of right and wrong, from which they spring, are not, perhaps, easily to be let into the minds of grown men, not used to abstract their thoughts from common received opinions. Much less are children capable of reasonings from remote principles. They cannot conceive the force of long deductions: the reasons that move them must be obvious, and level to their thoughts, and such as may (if I may so say) be felt and touched. But yet, if their age, temper, and inclinations, be considered, they will never want such motives as may be sufficient to convince them. If there be no other more particular, yet these will always be intelligible, and of force, to deter them from any fault fit to be taken notice of in them, viz. that it will be a discredit and disgrace to them, and displease you.

95. . . . [A] father will do well, as his son grows up, and is capable of it, to talk familiarly with him; nay, ask his advice, and consult with him, about those things wherein he has any knowledge or understanding. By this the father will gain two things, both of great moment. The one is, that it will put serious considerations into his son's thoughts, better than any rules or advices he can give him. The sooner you treat him as a man, the sooner he will begin to be one: and if you admit him into serious discourses sometimes with you, you will insensibly raise his mind above the usual amusements of youth, and those trifling occupations which it is commonly wasted in. For it is easy to observe, that many young men continue longer in the thought and conversation of schoolboys, than otherwise they would, because their parents keep them at that distance, and in that low rank, by all their carriage to them.

118. Curiosity in children . . . is but an appetite after knowledge, and therefore ought to be encouraged in them, not only as a good sign, but as the great instrument nature has provided, to remove that ignorance they were born with, and which without this busy inquisitiveness will make them dull and useless creatures. The ways to encourage it, and keep it active and busy, are, I suppose, these following:

(1.) Not to check or discountenance any inquiries he shall make, nor suffer them to be laughed at; but to answer all his questions, and explain the matters he desires to know, so as to make them as much intelligible to him, as suits the capacity of his age and knowledge. But confound not his understanding with explications or notions that are above it, or with the variety or number of things that are not to his present purpose. Mark what it is his mind aims at in the question, and not what words he expresses it in: and, when you have informed and satisfied him in that, you shall see how his thoughts will enlarge themselves, and how by fit answers he may be led on farther than perhaps you could imagine. For knowledge is grateful to the understanding, as light to the eyes: children are pleased and delighted with it exceedingly, especially if they see that their inquiries are regarded, and that their desire of knowing is encouraged and commended. And I doubt not but one great reason, why many children abandon themselves wholly to silly sports, and trifle away all their time insipidly, is, because they have found their curiosity baulked, and their inquiries neglected. But had they been treated with more kindness and respect, and their questions answered, as they should, to their satisfaction, I doubt not but they would have taken more pleasure in learning, and improving their knowledge, wherein there would be still newness and variety, which is what they are delighted with, than in returning over and over to the same play and play things.

119. (2.) To this serious answering their questions, and informing their understandings in what they desire, as if it were a matter that needed it, should be added some peculiar ways of commendation. Let others, whom they esteem, be told before their faces of the knowledge they have in such and such things; and since we are all, even from our cradles, vain and proud creatures, let their vanity be flattered with things that will do them good; and let their pride set them on work on something which may turn to their advantage. Upon this ground you shall find, that there cannot be a greater spur to the attaining what you would have the elder learn and know himself, than to set him upon teaching it to his younger brothers and sisters.

120. (3.) As children's inquiries are not to be slighted, so also great care is to be taken, that they never receive deceitful and illuding answers. They easily perceive when they are slighted

or deceived, and quickly learn the trick of neglect, dissimulation, and falsehood, which they observe others to make use of. We are not to intrench upon truth in any conversation, but least of all with children; since, if we play false with them, we not only deceive their expectation, and hinder their knowledge, but corrupt their innocence, and teach them the worst of vices. They are travellers newly arrived in a strange country, of which they know nothing: we should therefore make conscience not to mislead them. And though their questions seem sometimes not very material, yet they should be seriously answered; for however they may appear to us (to whom they are long since known) inquiries not worth the making, they are of moment to those who are wholly ignorant. Children are strangers to all we are acquainted with; and all the things they meet with, are at first unknown to them, as they once were to us: and happy are they who meet with civil people, that will comply with their ignorance, and help them to get out of it. . . .

133. This is what I have thought concerning the general method of educating a young gentleman; which, though I am apt to suppose may have some influence on the whole course of his education, yet I am far from imagining it contains all those particulars which his growing years, or peculiar temper, may require. But this being premised in general, we shall, in the next place, descend to a more particular consideration of the several parts of his education.

134. That which every gentleman (that takes any care of his education) desires for his son, besides the estate he leaves him, is contained (I suppose) in these four things, virtue, wisdom, breeding, and learning. . . .

135. I place virtue as the first and most necessary of those endowments that belong to a man or a gentleman, as absolutely requisite to make him valued and beloved by others, acceptable or tolerable to himself. Without that, I think, he will be happy neither in this, nor the other world.

140. Wisdom I take, in the popular acceptation, for a man's managing his business ably, and with foresight, in this world. . . . To accustom a child to have true notions of things, and not to be satisfied till he has them; to raise his mind to great and worthy thoughts; and to keep him at a distance from falsehood, and cunning, which has always a broad mixture of falsehood in it; is the fittest preparation of a child for wisdom. The rest, which is to be learned from time, experience, and observation, and an acquaintance with men, their tempers and designs, is not to be expected in the ignorance and inadvertency of childhood, or the inconsiderate heat and unwariness of youth: all that can be done towards it, during this unripe age, is, as I have said, to accustom them to truth and sincerity; to a submission to reason; and, as much as may be, to reflection on their own actions.

141. The next good quality belonging to a gentleman, is good-breeding. There are two sorts of ill-breeding; the one, a sheepish bashfulness; and the other, a misbecoming negligence and disrespect in our carriage; both which are avoided, by duly observing this one rule, Not to think meanly of ourselves, and not to think meanly of others.

147. You will wonder, perhaps, that I put learning last, especially if I tell you I think it the least part. This may seem strange in the mouth of a bookish man: and this making usually the chief, if not only bustle and stir about children, this being almost that alone which is thought on, when people talk of education, makes it the greater paradox. When I consider what ado is made about a little Latin and Greek, how many years are spent in it, and what a

noise and business it makes to no purpose, I can hardly forbear thinking, that the parents of children still live in fear of the schoolmaster's rod, which they look on as the only instrument of education; as if a language or two were its whole business. How else is it possible, that a child should be chained to the oar seven, eight, or ten of the best years of his life, to get a language or two, which I think might be had at a great deal cheaper rate of pains and time, and be learned almost in playing?

Forgive me, therefore, if I say, I cannot with patience think, that a young gentleman should be put into the herd, and be driven with a whip and scourge, as if he were to run the gauntlet through the several classes. . . . "What then, say you, would you not have him write and read? Shall he be more ignorant than the clerk of our parish, who takes Hopkins and Sternhold for the best poets in the world, whom yet he makes worse than they are, by his ill reading?" Not so, not so fast, I beseech you. Reading, and writing, and learning, I allow to be necessary, but yet not the chief business. I imagine you would think him a very foolish fellow, that should not value a virtuous, or a wise man, infinitely before a great scholar. Not but that I think learning a great help to both, in well disposed minds; but yet it must be confessed also, that in others not so disposed, it helps them only to be the more foolish, or worse men. . . .

148. When he can talk, it is time he should begin to learn to read. But as to this, give me leave here to inculcate again what is very apt to be forgotten, viz. that a great care is to be taken, that it be never made as a business to him, nor he look on it as a task. We naturally, as I said, even from our cradles, love liberty, and have therefore an aversion to many things, for no other reason, but because they are enjoined us. I have always had a fancy, that learning might be made a play and recreation to children; and that they might be brought to desire to be taught, if it were proposed to them as a thing of honour, credit, desire and recreation, or as a reward for doing something else, and if they were never chided or corrected for the neglect of it. That which confirms me in this opinion is, that amongst the Portuguese, it is so much a fashion and emulation amongst their children to learn to read and write, that they cannot hinder them from it: they will learn it one from another, and are as intent on it as if it were forbid them. I remember, that being at a friend's house, whose younger son, a child in coats, was not easily brought to his book (being taught to read at home by his mother); I advised to try another way than requiring it of him as his duty. We therefore, in a discourse on purpose amongst ourselves, in his hearing, but without taking any notice of him, declared, that it was the privilege and advantage of heirs and elder brothers, to be scholars; that this made them fine gentlemen, and beloved by everybody: and that for younger brothers, it was a favour to admit them to breeding; to be taught to read and write was more than came to their share; they might be ignorant bumpkins and clowns, if they pleased. This so wrought upon the child, that afterwards he desired to be taught; would come himself to his mother to learn; and would not let his maid be quiet, till she heard him his lesson. I doubt not but some way like this might be taken with other children; and, when their tempers are found, some thoughts be instilled into them, that might set them upon desiring of learning themselves, and make them seek it, as another sort of play or recreation. But then, as I said before, it must never be imposed as a task, nor made a trouble to them. . . .

167. . . . There is yet a farther reason, why masters and teachers should raise no difficulties to their scholars; but, on the contrary, should smooth their way, and readily help them forwards, where they find them stop. Children's minds are narrow and weak, and usually

susceptible but of one thought at once. Whatever is in a child's head, fills it for the time, especially if set on with any passion. It should therefore be the skill and art of the teacher, to clear their heads of all other thoughts, whilst they are learning of anything, the better to make room for what he would instil into them, that it may be received with attention and application, without which it leaves no impression. The natural temper of children disposes their minds to wander. Novelty alone takes them; whatever that presents, they are presently eager to have a taste of, and are as soon satiated with it. They quickly grow weary of the same thing, and so have almost their whole delight in change and variety. It is a contradiction to the natural state of childhood, for them to fix their fleeting thoughts. Whether this be owing to the temper of their brains, or the quickness or instability of their animal spirits, over which the mind has not yet got a full command; this is visible, that it is a pain to children to keep their thoughts steady to anything. A lasting continued attention is one of the hardest tasks can be imposed on them: and therefore, he that requires their application, should endeavour to make what he proposes as grateful and agreeable as possible; at least, he ought to take care not to join any displeasing or frightful idea with it. If they come not to their books with some kind of liking and relish, it is no wonder their thoughts should be perpetually shifting from what disgusts them, and seek better entertainment in more pleasing objects. . . .

It is, I know, the usual method of tutors, to endeavour to procure attention in their scholars, and to fix their minds to the business in hand, by rebukes and corrections, if they find them ever so little wandering. But such treatment is sure to produce the quite contrary effect. Passionate words or blows from the tutor fill the child's mind with terror and affrightment, which immediately takes it wholly up, and leaves no room for other impressions. I believe there is nobody, that reads this, but may recollect, what disorder hasty or imperious words from his parents or teachers have caused in his thoughts; how for the time it has turned his brains, so what he scarce knew what was said by, or to him: he presently lost the sight of what he was upon; his mind was filled with disorder and confusion, and in that state was no longer capable of attention to anything else.

It is true, parents and governors ought to settle and establish their authority, by an awe over the minds of those under their tuition; and to rule them by that: but when they have got an ascendant over them, they should use it with great moderation, and not make themselves such scarecrows, that their scholars should always tremble in their sight. Such an austerity may make their government easy to themselves but of very little use to their pupils. It is impossible children should learn anything, whilst their thoughts are possessed and disturbed with any passion, especially fear, which makes the strongest impression on their yet tender and weak spirits. Keep the mind in an easy calm temper, when you would have it receive your instructions, or any increase of knowledge. It is as impossible to draw fair and regular characters on a trembling mind, as on a shaking paper.

The great skill of a teacher is to get and keep the attention of his scholar: whilst he has that, he is sure to advance as fast as the learner's abilities will carry him; and without that, all his bustle and pother will be to little or no purpose. To attain this, he should make the child comprehend (as much as may be) the usefulness of what he teaches him; and let him see, by what he has learned, that he can do something which he could not do before; something which gives him some power and real advantage above others, who are ignorant of it. To this he should add sweetness in all his instructions; and by a certain tenderness in his whole carriage, make the child sensible that he loves him, and designs nothing but his good; the only way to beget love in the child, which will make him hearken to his lessons, and relish what he teaches him.

Nothing but obstinacy should meet with any imperiousness or rough usage. All other faults should be corrected with a gentle hand; and kind encouraging words will work better and more effectually upon a willing mind, and even prevent a good deal of that perverseness, which rough and imperious usage often produces in well-disposed and generous minds. It is true, obstinacy and wilful neglects must be mastered, even though it costs blows to do it: but I am apt to think perverseness in the pupils is often the effect of forwardness in the tutor; and that most children would seldom have deserved blows, if needless and misapplied roughness had not taught them ill-nature, and given them an aversion to their teacher, and all that comes from him.

Inadvertency, forgetfulness, unsteadiness, and wandering of thought, are the natural faults of childhood: and therefore, when they are not observed to be wilful, are to be mentioned softly, and gained upon by time. If every slip of this kind produces anger and rating, the occasions of rebuke and corrections will return so often, that the tutor will be a constant terror and uneasiness to his pupils; which one thing is enough to hinder their profiting by his lessons, and to defeat all his methods of instruction.

Let the awe he has got upon their minds be so tempered with the constant marks of tenderness and good will, that affection may spur them to their duty, and make them find a pleasure in complying with his dictates. This will bring them with satisfaction to their tutor; make them hearken to him, as to one who is their friend, that cherishes them, and takes pains for their good; this will keep their thoughts easy and free, whilst they are with him, the only temper wherein the mind is capable of receiving new information, and of admitting into itself those impressions, which if not taken and retained, all that they and their teacher do together is lost labour; there is much uneasiness, and little learning.

177. But under whose care soever a child is put to be taught, during the tender and flexible years of his life, this is certain, it should be one who thinks Latin and language the least part of education; one, who knowing how much virtue, and a well-tempered soul, is to be perferred to any sort of learning or language, makes it his chief business to form the mind of his scholars, and give that a right disposition: which, if once got, though all the rest should be neglected, would, in due time, produce all the rest; and which if it be not got, and settled, so as to keep out ill and vicious habits, languages and sciences, and all the other accomplishments of education, will be to no purpose, but to make the worse or more dangerous man. . . .

178. At the same time that he is learning French and Latin, a child, as has been said, may also be entered in arithmetic, geography, chronology, history, and geometry too. For if these be taught him in French or Latin, when he begins once to understand either of these tongues, he will get a knowledge in these sciences, and the language to boot.

Geography, I think, should be begun with; for the learning of the figure of the globe, the situation and boundaries of the four parts of the world, and that of particular kingdoms and countries, being only an exercise of the eyes and memory, a child with pleasure will learn and retain them. . . .

179. When he has the natural parts of the globe well fixed in his memory, it may then be time to begin arithmetic. By the natural parts of the globe, I mean several positions of the parts of the earth and sea, under different names and distinctions of countries; not coming yet to those artificial and imaginary lines, which have been invented, and are only supposed, for the better improvement of that science.

180. Arithmetic is the easiest, and, consequently, the first sort of abstract reasoning, which the mind commonly bears, or accustoms itself to: and is of so general use in all parts of life and business, that scarce any thing is to be done without it. This is certain, a man cannot have too much of it, nor too perfectly; he should therefore begin to be exercised in counting, as soon, and as far, as he is capable of it; and do something in it every day, till he is master of the art of numbers. When he understands addition and subtraction, he may then be advanced farther in geography, and after he is acquainted with the poles, zones, parallel circles, and meridians, be taught longitude and latitude, and by them be made to understand the use of maps, and by the numbers placed on their sides, to know the respective situation of countries, and how to find them out on the terrestrial globe. Which when he can readily do, he may then be entered in the celestial; and there going over all the circles again, with a more particular observation of the ecliptic or zodiac, to fix them all very clearly and distinctly in his mind, he may be taught the figure and position of the several constellations, which may be showed him first upon the globe, and then in the heavens.

When that is done, and he knows pretty well the constellations of this our hemisphere, it may be time to give him some notions of this our planetary world, and to that purpose it may not be amiss to make him a draught of the Copernican system; and therein explain to him the situation of the planets, their respective distances from the sun, the centre of their revolutions. This will prepare him to understand the motion and theory of the planets, the most easy and natural way. For, since astronomers no longer doubt of the motion of the planets about the sun, it is fit he should proceed upon that hypothesis, which is not only the simplest and least perplexed for a learner, but also the likeliest to be true in itself. But in this, as in all other parts of instruction, great care must be taken with children, to begin with that which is plain and simple, and to teach them as little as can be at once, and settle that well in their heads, before you proceed to the next, or any thing new in that science. Give them first one simple idea, and see that they take it right, and perfectly comprehend it, before you go any farther; and then add some other simple idea, which lies next in your way to what you aim at; and so proceeding by gentle and insensible steps, children, without confusion and amazement, will have their understandings opened, and their thoughts extended, farther than could have been expected. And when any one has learned any thing himself, there is no such way to fix it in his memory, and to encourage him to go on, as to set him to teach it others.

181. When he has once got such an acquaintance with the globes, as is above-mentioned, he may be fit to be tried a little in geometry; wherein I think the six first books of Euclid enough for him to be taught. For I am in some doubt, whether more to a man of business be necessary or useful; at least if he have a genius and inclination to it, being entered so far by his tutor, he will be able to go on of himself without a teacher.

The globes, therefore, must be studied, and that diligently, and, I think, may be begun betimes, if the tutor will but be careful to distinguish what the child is capable of knowing, and what not; for which this may be a rule, that perhaps will go a pretty way, (viz.) that children may be taught any thing that falls under their senses, especially their sight, as far as their memories only are exercised: and thus a child very young may learn, which is the equator, which the meridian, &c. which Europe, and which England, upon the globes, as soon almost as he knows the rooms of the house he lives in; if care be taken not to teach him too much at once, nor to set him upon a new part, till that, which he is upon, be perfectly learned and fixed in his memory.

182. With geography, chronology ought to go hand in hand; I mean the general part of it, so that he may have in his mind a view of the whole current of time, and the several considerable epochs that are made use of in history. Without these two, history, which is the great mistress of prudence and civil knowledge; and ought to be the proper study of a gentleman, or man of business in the world; without geography and chronology, I say, history will be very ill retained, and very little useful; but be only a jumble of matters of fact, confusedly heaped together without order or instruction. It is by these two that the actions of mankind are ranked into their proper places of times and countries; under which circumstances, they are not only much easier kept in the memory, but, in that natural order, are only capable to afford those observations, which make a man the better and the abler for reading them.

187. It would be strange to suppose an English gentleman should be ignorant of the law of his country. This, whatever station he is in, is so requisite, that, from a justice of the peace to a minister of state, I know no place he can well fill without it. I do not mean the chicane or wrangling and captious part of the law; a gentleman whose business is to seek the true measures of right and wrong, and not the arts how to avoid doing the one, and secure himself in doing the other, ought to be as far from such a study of the law, as he is concerned diligently to apply himself to that wherein he may be serviceable to his country. And to that purpose I think the right way for a gentleman to study our law, which he does not design for his calling, is to take a view of our English constitution and government, in the ancient books of the common law, and some more modern writers, who out of them have given an account of this government. And having got a true idea of that, then to read our history, and with it join in every king's reign the laws then made. This will give an insight into the reason of our statutes, and show the true ground upon which they came to be made, and what weight they ought to have.

188. Rhetoric and logic being the arts that in the ordinary method usually follow immediately after grammar, it may perhaps be wondered, that I have said so little of them. The reason is, because of the little advantage young people receive by them; for I have seldom or never observed any one to get the skill of reasoning well, or speaking handsomely, by studying those rules which pretend to teach it: and therefore I would have a young gentleman take a view of them in the shortest systems could be found, without dwelling long on the contemplation and study of those formalities. Right reasoning is founded on something else than the predicaments and predicables, and does not consist in talking in mode and figure itself. But it is besides my present business to enlarge upon this speculation. . . .

189. If the use and end of right reasoning be to have right notions, and a right judgment of things; to distinguish between truth and falsehood, right and wrong, and to act

accordingly; be sure not to let your son be bred up in the art and formality of disputing, either practising it himself, or admiring it in others; unless, instead of an able man, you desire to have him an insignificant wrangler, opiniated in discourse, and priding himself in contradicting others; or, which is worse, questioning every thing, and thinking there is no such thing as truth to be sought, but only victory, in disputing. There cannot be any thing so disingenuous, so misbecoming a gentleman, or any one who pretends to be a rational creature, as not to yield to plain reason, and the conviction of clear arguments. For this, in short, is the way and perfection of logical disputes, that the opponent never takes any answer, nor the respondent ever yields to any argument. This neither of them must do, whatever becomes of truth or knowledge, unless he will pass for a poor baffled wretch, and lie under the disgrace of not being able to maintain whatever he has once affirmed, which is the great aim and glory in disputing. Truth is to be found and supported by a mature and due consideration of things themselves, and not by artificial terms and ways of arguing: these lead not men so much into the discovery of truth, as into a captious and fallacious use of doubtful words, which is the most useless and most offensive way of talking, and such as least suits a gentleman or a lover of truth of any thing in the world.

There can scarce be a greater defect in a gentleman, than not to express himself well, either in writing or speaking. But yet, I think, I may ask my reader, Whether he doth not know a great many, who live upon their estates, and so, with the name, should have the qualities of gentlemen, who cannot so much as tell a story as they should, much less speak clearly and persuasively in any business? This I think not to be so much their fault, as the fault of their education; for I must, without partiality, do my countrymen this right, that where they apply themselves, I see none of their neighbours outgo them. They have been taught rhetoric, but yet never taught how to express themselves handsomely with their tongues, or pens, in the language they are always to use; as if the names of the figures, that embellished the discourses of those who understood the art of speaking, were the very art and skill of speaking well. This, as all other things of practice, is to be learned not by a few or a great many rules given, but by exercise and application, according to good rules, or rather patterns, till habits are got, and a facility of doing it well.

Agreeable hereunto, perhaps it might not be amiss to make children, as soon as they are capable of it, often to tell a story of anything they know; and to correct at first the most remarkable fault they are guilty of, in their way of putting it together. When that fault is cured, then to show them the next, and so on, till, one after another, all, at least the gross ones, are mended. When they can tell tales pretty well, then it may be time to make them write them. . . .

When they understand how to write English with due connexion, propriety, and order, and are pretty well masters of a tolerable narrative style, they may be advanced to writing of letters; wherein they should not be put upon any strains of wit or compliment, but taught to express their own plain easy sense, without any incoherence, confusion, or roughness. . . . The writing of letters has so much to do in all the occurrences of human life, that no gentleman can avoid showing himself in this kind of writing: occasions will daily force him to make this use of his pen, which, besides the consequences, that, in his affairs, his well or ill managing of it often draws after it, always lays him open to a severer examination of his breeding, sense, and abilities, than oral discourses; whose transient faults, dying for the most part with the sound that gives them life, and so not subject to a strict review, more easily escape observation and censure. . . .

194. Though the systems of physics that I have met with afford little encouragement to look for certainty, or science, in any treatise, which shall pretend to give us a body of natural philosophy from the first principles of bodies in general; yet the incomparable Mr. Newton has shown, how far mathematics, applied to some parts of nature, may, upon principles that matter of fact justify, carry us in the knowledge of some, as I may so call them, particular provinces of the incomprehensible universe. And if others could give us so good and clear an account of other parts of nature, as he has of this our planetary world, and the most considerable phænomena observable in it, in his admirable book "Philosophiæ naturalis Principia mathematica," we might in time hope to be furnished with more true and certain knowledge in several parts of this stupendous machine, than hitherto we could have expected. And though there are very few that have mathematics enough to understand his demonstrations; yet the most accurate mathematicians, who have examined them, allowing them to be such, his book will deserve to be read, and give no small light and pleasure to those, who, willing to understand the motions, properties, and operations of the great masses of matter in this our solar system, will but carefully mind his conclusions, which may be depended on as propositions well proved.

195. . . . To conclude this part, which concerns a young gentleman's studies; his tutor should remember, that his business is not so much to teach him all that is knowable, as to raise in him a love and esteem of knowledge; and to put him in the right way of knowing and improving himself, when he has a mind to it.

216. Though I am now come to a conclusion of what obvious remarks have suggested to me concerning education, I would not have it thought, that I look on it as a just treatise on this subject. There are a thousand other things that may need consideration; especially if one should take in the various tempers, different inclinations, and particular defaults, that are to be found in children; and prescribe proper remedies. The variety is so great, that it would require a volume; nor would that reach it. Each man's mind has some peculiarity, as well as his face, that distinguishes him from all others; and there are possibly scarce two children, who can be conducted by exactly the same method. Besides that, I think a prince, a noble-man, and an ordinary gentleman's son, should have different ways of breeding. But having had here only some general views, in reference to the main end and aims in education, and those designed for a gentleman's son, whom, being then very little, I considered only as white paper, or wax, to be moulded and fashioned as one pleases; I have touched little more than those heads, which I judged necessary for the breeding of a young gentleman of his condition in general; and have now published these my occasional thoughts, with this hope, that, though this be far from being a complete treatise on this subject, or such as that every one may find what will just fit his child in it; yet it may give some small light to those, whose concern for their dear little ones makes them so irregularly bold, that they dare venture to consult their own reason, in the education of their children, rather than wholly to rely upon old custom.

# Afterword

## Peter Gay*

I

Like many another revolutionary, John Locke was also a conservative, at once transmitting and transforming traditional ideas. His treatise on education stands at the beginning of the long cycle of modernity, but it stands, too, at the end, and as the climax, of a long evolution—the discovery of the child. During the Middle Ages, and during the Renaissance, adults treated children as toys, strange animals, or small grownups. Children mixed readily in adult company, played infantile adaptations of adult games, dressed in cut-down versions of adult clothing, overheard the grossest sexual allusions, and participated in overt sexual play. The precise age of the child was unknown and, if known, irrelevant: the educational process knew nothing of our automatic allocation of children to classes or grades. Most children, of course, remained illiterate; but even among the educated, some began their schooling early, others late; some were confided to tutors at home, while others went away to school; some completed their education in three years, others in ten. Educators had little if any conception of the gradual evolution of rationality and self-discipline in the growing child or of the orderly development of subject matter. . . .

    Locke was both an expression and a cause of this shift in sensibility. The sixteenth and seventeenth centuries saw the growing rationalization of the world. There was a new calendar; there were mechanical clocks, improved administrative techniques (if only for the purpose of collecting taxes and suppressing dissent), and energetic inquiries into the sources and nature of knowledge. There were, above all, the magnificent, cumulative discoveries of "new philosophy." These changes were expressed in new kinds of schools, in which students were carefully differentiated by grades and guided by thoughtfully worked-out programs of study. But bold as they were, these academies and *collèges* had grave flaws; as everyone knows, it is rare that the moral and psychological possibilities suggested by new discoveries are fully

* Peter Gay is Professor Emeritus of History at Yale University.

embodied in social institutions. When Locke wrote *Some Thoughts Concerning Education*, most children remained beyond the pale of literacy, the schools then in existence taught by rote and disciplined with brutality, and the very understanding of childhood as a reputable phase in the life cycle remained the property of a few. It took books like Locke's and a half-century of insistent propaganda to diffuse the notion that children are human, with their own rights, their own rhythm of development, and their own pedagogical needs. . . .

## II

The main reason for the immediate, and lasting, popularity of Locke's pedagogic writings was their intimate and obvious connection with his philosophy, a philosophy that came to dominate the eighteenth century. Like every true philosopher of education, Locke developed his pedagogical program, not in isolation, but as part of a total view of the world. It was as a philosopher that Locke the educator appealed to experience, expressed confidence in the flexibility of human nature, regarded human beings as organisms of interacting psychological and physical characteristics, and advocated humane treatment and utilitarian training. . . .

Locke's *Thoughts Concerning Education* . . . is by nature didactic, but its many rules are based on experience. They suggest that Locke had watched the children he knew with open and benign eyes. Moreover, Locke's educational program was not a divine pattern or a moral improbability, but a sensible, attainable reality: it aimed to produce the civic-minded, well-mannered, and soundly informed English gentleman.

Nor is this all. Locke did not go as far as Rousseau was to go in recommending an education that concentrated first on experience and only later on reading, but his concern with exposing the child to life as well as to books is remarkable for his time. Children understand reasoning early and take pride in "being treated as rational creatures"; yet, Locke warns, "when I talk of reasoning, I do not intend any other, but such as is suited to the child's capacity and apprehension. Nobody can think a boy of three or seven years old, should be argued with, as a grown man. Long discourses, and philosophical reasonings, at best, amaze and confound, but do not instruct children." This piece of advice sounds much like Rousseau's *Emile*. So does Locke's admonition to show young children pictures and objects to accompany their reading.

Beyond this, Locke recognizes that education is not confined to formal exercises, but goes on in all transactions between adults and children, and among children themselves. That is why the *Thoughts Concerning Education* deals with the child's total environment. It warns against intimate commerce with servants, encourages children to study—and profit from—the art of conversation, and urges the inculcation of good habits through practice: "Pray remember, children are not to be taught by rules, which will be always slipping out of their memories. What you think necessary for them to do, settle in them by an indispensable practice, as often as the occasion returns; and, if it be possible, make occasions." Since children learn by imitation, they must be given experiences worth imitating.

This sort of pragmatic empiricism is closely tied to Locke's doctrine that man's nature is receptive and malleable, especially in early youth. Locke does not deny the existence of intuition. Nor does he deny the presence of innate capacities. He does deny that men have authoritative knowledge of such important matters as God, apart from experience and reflection on that experience; he affirms, conversely, that the environment exercises a pervasive power over men's minds.

The relevance of this view to education is obvious. To be sure, Locke, always moderate, concedes that "God has stamped certain characters upon men's minds, which, like their shapes, may perhaps be a little mended; but can hardly be totally altered and transformed into the contrary." The good teacher does not try to force grave children to become gay and gay children to become grave, for "what is so plaistered on will at best sit but untowardly." Yet if, as Locke says in the *Essay*, the child's mind at birth is like "white paper, void of all characters," skillful educators may develop their pupil's "natural genius" to its limit. . . .

One reason for Locke's moderation was that he saw the child's mind embedded in his total organism. As a physician, Locke begins his *Thoughts Concerning Education* with a quotation from Juvenal—"a sound mind in a sound body"—and continues with thirty paragraphs on the child's health, his food, his clothing. . . .

This was a bold step for Locke to take; even if some of his advice would make today's physicians, or parents, wince, his recognition that mental development is related to physical condition is thoroughly modern. It was this recognition, too, that permitted him to understand the relation between motivation and learning. A listless and dreamy child must not be forced to learn, for he will only forget what he has learned, and quickly, too. On the contrary, the teacher must awaken the child's natural appetite for experience by appealing to his ruling passions. "Where there is no desire," Locke writes, reasonably enough, "there will be no industry." On this point Locke insisted over and over again. Compulsion, the prevailing method of training the young, is absurd. Children naturally enjoy "variety and freedom," and they naturally "hate to be idle." It follows that they will enjoy learning as soon as it is made enjoyable: "None of the things they are to learn should ever be made a burden to them, or imposed on them as a task."

These words show Locke not merely as a physician; they also reveal a personal quality on which I have already touched: Locke was a humane man. Humanitarianism was a personal quality, but, like his empiricism, it was also part of his general philosophy, and his legacy to the dawning Enlightenment. The idea that individuals are precious pervades Locke's thought. His political liberalism teaches that the state is the agent rather than the master of the individual; his theory of toleration teaches that opinion, even erroneous opinion, has its value and should be heard. In politics, as in education, it is repression, not liberty, that breeds the cancer of sullen rebellion. Just as the individual exists, not for the state, but for himself, so the child is neither the slave nor the plaything of adults, but a human being with his own worth.

This does not mean that Locke advocated the relaxation of all discipline; he was not *that* modern. Rather, he insisted that children owe respect and obedience to their elders. He insisted, too, that all the wishes of children ought not to be granted, and that habits of self-denial should be inculcated early: "He that has not a mastery over his inclinations, he that knows not how to resist the importunity of present pleasure or pain, for the sake of what reason tells him is fit to be done, wants the true principle of virtue and industry, and is in danger never to be good for anything." At the same time, Locke had nothing but contempt for the accepted form of punishment—beating—which he called the "usual lazy and short way." Beating a child has no educational function of any sort: it does not get at the roots of misbehavior; it fosters disgust with learning rather than pleasure in it; it encourages either blind rebellion or slavish obedience, both undesirable traits in children as in adults. By breaking the mind, Locke warns, one creates a "low-spirited, moped creature," fit only to please foolish grownups by his unnatural silence or servile obedience. The child is father to the man: the boy whose spirit has been broken will grow up "an useless thing to himself and others."

Kindliness, then, is desirable for its own sake; it is appropriate to the human dignity of the child as much as to the dignity of the adult. But Locke offers another justification for it: it works. Locke, in fact, is persistently concerned with the consequences of his recommendations in daily life, with the utility of his program. Indeed, a utilitarian streak colors his educational proposals in general. Here we encounter a strain in Locke's thinking typical of much liberal theorizing down to the nineteenth century: Locke is radical, but he is also embedded in his time. He wants reform, but not for all. . . . On the one hand, Locke was impatient with the educational practices of his day which produced, he thought, idle and empty-headed wastrels. Listing the qualities he wishes to see cultivated in children, he begins with virtue (by which he means a gentle but courageous religiosity free from both "superstition" and "enthusiasm") and continues with respect for truth; to these he adds wisdom and good breeding. Learning comes last, a placement to which he refers, a little self-consciously, as "strange in the mouth of a bookish man." But Locke knew what he was about: "Learning must be had, but in the second place, as subservient only to greater qualities." Let the pupil learn English well and read his Bible; let him be taught French. Latin, "absolutely necessary to a gentleman," comes later, contrary to accepted practice, which makes a fetish of this dead language: "Can there be anything more ridiculous than that a father should waste his own money, and his son's time, in setting him to learn the Roman language, when, at the same time, he designs him for a trade, wherein he, having no use of Latin, fails not to forget that little which he brought from school, and which it is ten to one he abhors for the ill usage it procured him?" Latin is necessary for some, but not for all; time-honored subjects like logic or Greek might well be omitted; history, geography, and anatomy might well be substituted for useless learning—in a word, the educational system should adjust itself to the needs of life. Are not these notions (just a little philistine even in Locke's pure diction) all too familiar in our own time?

But the very real affinity of Locke's radical notions with our age of democratic education should not blind us to their equally real distance from it. Locke was, after all, addressing his little book on education to a gentleman, on the subject of the education of that gentleman's son and in the hope that other gentlemen would read it. It never occurred to him that every child should be educated or that all those to be educated should be educated alike. Locke believed that until the school system was reformed, a gentleman ought to have his son trained at home by a tutor, and he devoted some lengthy paragraphs of his *Thoughts Concerning Education* to the proper qualifications of such a tutor. As for the poor, they do not appear in Locke's little book at all. . . .

## III

. . . it is easy to forget just how different the seventeenth century was from our own. The lot of man was scarcity, not abundance; social hierarchies remained steep and class divisions sharp. Egalitarian democracy in education would have seemed the wildest of Utopian dreams to men in Locke's time. Indeed, in his own day, Locke was denounced as a radical, in education as in religion, and it is significant that Rousseau's *Emile*, probably the most influential revolutionary tract on education that we have, shows Locke's influence on page after page. Therefore, if we seek the roots of what is valuable in modern educational philosophy, we must turn to Locke's *Thoughts Concerning Education*, even if many of its specific recommendations are now out of date or wholly irrelevant. And more: if we want to remind ourselves why we really wish to educate children, if we seek a philosophy that insists on the relevance of subject matter to experience without neglecting the pleasure of cultivation for its own sake, that emphasizes recognition of the child's needs without ignoring the uses of discipline, that urges the relation of morale to learning without denying the virtue of hard study, that seeks to form men and women fit for modern life without forgetting that this fitness requires cultivation of the higher sensibilities and a profound knowledge of the great literature of the past—if we seek such an educational theory we would do well to read, and reread, Locke with care.

# 5
## Jean-Jacques Rousseau

**Jean-Jacques Rousseau** (1712–1778) was born in Geneva, the son of a watchmaker. His first interest was music, and he composed operas. Throughout most of his life he traveled throughout Europe, writing and engaging in controversy. Although troubled in his personal relationships, he became one of the most influential of all political philosophers.

# *Emile*

### The Author's Preface

This collection of reflections and comments, loosely strung together, was begun to please a good intelligent mother who was concerned about the education of her son. My first intention was to write a memoir of a few pages. But the subject ran away with me, and before I quite realised it the memoir had grown into a kind of book which was rather big for all that is in it but too small for its subject. After trying vainly to improve it I have decided that I ought to publish it as it stands in the hope of directing public attention to the matter. Even if my own ideas should prove bad, my labour will not have been in vain if I manage to stimulate good ones in other people.

I shall not say much about the importance of a good education or stop to demonstrate that the ordinary education is bad. A great many people have said that before me, and there is no need for me to fill a book with things that everybody knows. I will only remark that from time immemorial there has been constant complaint about the established practice but never a plan for anything better. In spite of all the writings that have the public utility for their aim, the first of all the utilities, which is the forming of man, continues to be overlooked.

Nothing is known about childhood. With our false ideas of it the more we do, the more we blunder. The wisest people are so much concerned with what grown ups should know that they never consider what children are capable of learning. They keep looking for the man in the child, not thinking of what he is before he becomes a man. It is to this study I have given special thought, in the hope that even if my method should prove chimerical and false there will always be profit in my observations. I may have gone off wrong in my view of what is needed, but I believe I am right in my view of the person on whom we have to work. Begin then by studying your pupils better; for assuredly you do not know them. If you read the book with this in view I am sure you will find it quite useful.

It is with regard to what may be called the systematic part of the book, which simply follows the natural development of the child, that there is most chance of misunderstanding on the part of the reader. He will think he is reading the dreams of a visionary rather than a treatise on education. What can I do about it? It is not other people's ideas of education I am presenting but my own. It is a long standing reproach that I see things differently from other people. If sometimes I take a dogmatic tone it is not to force my views on the reader but just to talk to him as the thoughts come to me.

I am always being told to suggest something feasible. What in effect is being said to me is that I should propound the ordinary methods or at least combine something good with the existing evil. A plan like this is really more fantastic than mine, for in this combination the good gets spoiled and the bad is not cured. I would rather follow the established methods in their entirety and avoid the contradiction that would be produced in man by making for two discordant ends.

In every kind of project two things have to be considered. The first is the goodness of the project in itself; the second is the ease of execution. In the present case, the first question is whether the education I propose is suitable for mankind, and congenial to the human heart. And is it practicable? That depends on the conditions under which it is tried. These conditions may vary indefinitely. The kind of education good for France will not suit Switzerland; that suitable for the middle classes will not suit the nobility. The greater or less ease of execution depends on a thousand circumstances which it is impossible to define except in a particular application of the method to this country or that, to this condition or that; and these particular applications are no part of my plan. All I am concerned with is that my plan should be capable of application wherever men are born. More I cannot promise.

## Book I

Everything is good as it comes from the hands of the Maker of the world but degenerates once it gets into the hands of man. Man makes one land yield the products of another, disregards differences of climates, elements and seasons, mutilates his dogs and horses, perverts and disfigures everything. Not content to leave anything as nature has made it, he must needs shape man himself to his notions, as he does the trees in his garden.

But under present conditions, human beings would be even worse than they are without this fashioning. A man left entirely to himself from birth would be the most misshapen of creatures. Prejudices, authority, necessity, example, the social institutions in which we are immersed, would crush out nature in him without putting anything in its place. He would fare like a shrub that has grown up by chance in the middle of a road, and got trampled underfoot by the passers-by.

Plants are fashioned by cultivation, men by education. We are born feeble and need strength; possessing nothing, we need assistance; beginning without intelligence, we need judgment. All that we lack at birth and need when grown up is given us by education. This education comes to us from nature, from men, or from things. The internal development of our faculties and organs is the education of nature. The use we learn to make of this development is the education of men. What comes to us from our experience of the things that affect us is the education of things. Each of us therefore is fashioned by three kinds of teachers. When their lessons are at variance the pupil is badly educated, and is never at peace with himself. When they coincide and lead to a common goal he goes straight to his mark and lives single-minded. Now, of these three educations the one due to nature is independent of us, and the one from things only depends on us to a limited extent. The education that comes from men is the only one within our control, and even that is doubtful. Who can hope to have the entire direction of the words and deeds of all the people around a child?

It is only by good luck that the goal can be reached. What is this goal? It is nature's own goal. Since the three educations must work together for a perfect result, the one that cannot be modified determines the course of the other two. But perhaps "nature" is too vague a word. We must try to fix its meaning. Nature, it has been said, is only habit. Is that really so? Are there not habits which are formed under pressure, leaving the original nature unchanged? One example is the habit of plants which have been forced away from the upright direction. When set free, the plant retains the bent forced upon it; but the sap has not changed its first direction and any new growth the plant makes returns to the vertical. It is the same with human inclinations. So long as there is no change in conditions the inclinations due to habits, however unnatural, remain unchanged, but immediately the restraint is removed the habit vanishes and nature reasserts itself.

We are born capable of sensation and from birth are affected in diverse ways by the objects around us. As soon as we become conscious of our sensations we are inclined to seek or to avoid the objects which produce them: at first, because they are agreeable or disagreeable to us, later because we discover that they suit or do not suit us, and ultimately because of the judgments we pass on them by reference to the idea of happiness or perfection we get from reason. These inclinations extend and strengthen with the growth of sensibility and intelligence, but under the pressure of habit they are changed to some extent with our opinions. The inclinations before this change are what I call our nature. In my view everything ought to be in conformity with these original inclinations.

There would be no difficulty if our three educations were merely different. But what is to be done when they are at cross purposes? Consistency is plainly impossible when we seek to educate a man for others, instead of for himself. If we have to combat either nature or society, we must choose between making a man or making a citizen. We cannot make both. There is an inevitable conflict of aims, from which come two opposing forms of education: the one communal and public, the other individual and domestic.

To get a good idea of communal education, read Plato's *Republic*. It is not a political treatise, as those who merely judge books by their titles think. It is the finest treatise on education ever written. Communal education in this sense, however, does not and can not now exist. There are no longer any real fatherlands and therefore no real citizens. The words "fatherland" and "citizen" should be expunged from modern languages.

I do not regard the instruction given in those ridiculous establishments called colleges as "public," any more than the ordinary kind of education. This education makes for two opposite goals and reaches neither. The men it turns out are double-minded, seemingly concerned for others, but really only concerned for themselves. From this contradiction comes the conflict we never cease to experience in ourselves. We are drawn in different directions by nature and by man, and take a midway path that leads us nowhere. In this state of confusion we go through life and end up with our contradictions unsolved, never having been any good to ourselves or to other people.

There remains then domestic education, the education of nature. But how will a man who has been educated entirely for himself get on with other people? If there were any way of combining in a single person the twofold aim, and removing the contradictions of life, a great obstacle to happiness would be removed. But before passing judgment on this kind of man it would be necessary to follow his development and see him fully formed. It would be necessary, in word, to make the acquaintance of the natural man. This is the subject of our quest in this book.

What can be done to produce this very exceptional person? In point of fact all we have to do is to prevent anything being done. When it is only a matter of sailing against the wind it is enough to tack, but when the sea runs high and you want to stay where you are, you must throw out the anchor.

In the social order where all stations in life are fixed, every one needs to be brought up for his own station. The individual who leaves the place for which he has been trained is useless in any other. In Egypt, where the son was obliged to follow in his father's footsteps, education had at least an assured aim: in our country where social ranks are fixed, but the men in them are constantly changing, nobody knows whether he is doing his son a good or a bad turn when he educates him for his own rank.

In the natural order where all men are equal, manhood is the common vocation. One who is well educated for that will not do badly in the duties that pertain to it. The fact that my pupil is intended for the army, the church or the bar, does not greatly concern me. Before the vocation determined by his parents comes the call of nature to the life of human kind. Life is the business I would have him learn. When he leaves my hands, I admit he will not be a magistrate, or a soldier, or a priest. First and foremost, he will be a man. All that a man must be he will be when the need arises, as well as anyone else. Whatever the changes of fortune he will always be able to find a place for himself. . . .

A man of high rank once suggested that I should be his son's tutor. But having had experience already I knew myself unfit and I refused. Instead of the difficult task of educating a child, I now undertake the easier task of writing about it. To provide details and examples in illustration of my views and to avoid wandering off into airy speculations, I propose to set forth the education of Emile, an imaginary pupil, from birth to manhood. I take for granted that I am the right man for the duties in respect of age, health, knowledge and talents.

A tutor is not bound to his charge by the ties of nature as the father is, and so is entitled to choose his pupil, especially when as in this case he is providing a model for the education of other children. I assume that Emile is no genius, but a boy of ordinary ability: that he is the inhabitant of some temperate climate, since it is only in temperate climates that human beings develop completely; that he is rich, since it is only the rich who have need of the natural education that would fit them to live under all conditions; that he is to all intents and purposes an orphan, whose tutor having undertaken the parents' duties will also have their right to control all the circumstances of his upbringing; and, finally, that he is a vigorous, healthy, well-built child. . . .

We are born with a capacity for learning, but know nothing and distinguish nothing. The mind is cramped by imperfect half-formed organs and has not even the consciousness of its own existence. The movements, and cries of the new born child are purely mechanical, quite devoid of understanding and will.

Children's first sensations are wholly in the realm of feeling. They are only aware of pleasure and pain. With walking and grasp undeveloped, it takes a long time for them to construct the representative sensations which acquaint them with external objects; but even before these objects reach up to and depart from their eyes, if one may put it so, the recurrence of the sensations begins to subject them to the bondage of habit. You see their eyes always turning to the light and unconsciously taking the direction from which the light comes, so that you have to be careful to keep them facing the light in order to prevent them acquiring a squint or becoming cross-eyed. Similarly, they have to be accustomed quite early to darkness, or soon they will wail and cry if they find themselves in the dark. Food and sleep, if too precisely organised, come to be necessary at definite intervals, and soon the desire for them is due not to need but to habit. Or rather, habit adds a new need to that of nature. That is something to be avoided.

The only habit the child should be allowed to acquire is to contract none. He should not be carried on one arm more than the other or allowed to make use of one hand more than the other, or to want to eat, sleep or do things at definite hours; and he should be able to remain alone by night or day. Prepare in good time for the reign of freedom and the exercise of his powers, by allowing his body its natural habits and accustoming him always to be his own master and follow the dictates of his will as soon as he has a will of his own. . . .

**Book II**

. . . The more children can do for themselves the less help they need from other people. Added strength brings with it the sense needed for its direction. With the coming of self-consciousness at this second stage individual life really begins. Memory extends the sense of identity over all the moments of the child's existence. He becomes one and the same person, capable of happiness or sorrow. From this point on it is essential to regard him as a moral being. . . .

Your first duty is to be humane. Love childhood. Look with friendly eyes on its games, its pleasures, its amiable dispositions. Which of you does not sometimes look back regretfully on the age when laughter was ever on the lips and the heart free of care? Why steal from the little innocents the enjoyment of a time that passes all too quickly?

Already I hear the clamour of the false wisdom that regards the present as of no account and is for ever chasing a future which flees as we advance. This is the time to correct the evil inclinations of mankind, you reply. Suffering should be increased in childhood when it is least felt, to reduce it at the age of reason. But how do you know that all the fine lessons with which you oppress the feeble mind of the child will not do more harm than good? Can you prove that these bad tendencies you profess to be correcting are not due to your own misguided efforts rather than to nature?

If we are to keep in touch with reality we must never forget what befits our condition. Humanity has its place in the scheme of things. Childhood has its place in the scheme of human life. We must view the man as a man, and the child as a child. The best way to ensure human well-being is to give each person his place in life and keep him there, regulating the passions in accordance with the individual constitution. The rest depends on external factors without our control.

We can never know absolute good or evil. Everything in this life is mixed. We never experience a pure sentiment, or remain in the same state for two successive moments. Weal and woe are common to us all, but in differing measure. The happiest man is the one who suffers least: the most miserable the one who has least pleasure. Always the sufferings outweigh the enjoyments. The felicity of man here below is therefore a negative state, to be measured by the fewness of his ills. Every feeling of pain is inseparable from the desire to escape from it: every idea of pleasure inseparable from the desire for its enjoyment. Privation is implicit in desire, and all privations are painful. Consequently unhappiness consists in the excess of desire over power. A conscious being whose powers equalled his desires would be absolutely happy.

In what then does the human wisdom that leads to true happiness consist? Not simply in the diminution of desires, for if they fell below our power to achieve, part of our faculties would be unemployed and our entire being would not be satisfied. Neither does it consist in the extension of our faculties, for a disproportionate increase in our desires would only make us more miserable. True happiness comes with equality of power and will. The only man who gets his own way is the one who does not need another's help to get it: from which it follows that the supreme good is not authority, but freedom. The true freeman wants only what he can get, and does only what pleases him. This is my fundamental maxim. Apply it to childhood and all the rules of education follow.

There are two kinds of dependence: dependence on things, which is natural, and dependence on men, which is social. Dependence on things being nonmoral is not prejudicial to freedom and engenders no vices: dependence on men being capricious engenders them all. The only cure for this evil in society would be to put the law in place of the individual, and to arm the general will with a real power that made it superior to every individual will.

Keep the child in sole dependence on things and you will follow the natural order in the course of his education. Put only physical obstacles in the way of indiscreet wishes and let his punishments spring from his own actions. Without forbidding wrong-doing, be content to prevent it. Experience or impotence apart from anything else should take the place of law for him. Satisfy his desires, not because of his demands but because of his needs. He should have no consciousness of obedience when he acts, nor of mastery when someone acts for him. Let him experience liberty equally in his actions and in yours.

Be specially careful not to give the child empty formulae of politeness, to serve as magic words for subjecting his surroundings to his will and getting him what he wants at once. For my part I am less afraid of rudeness than of arrogance in Emile, and would rather have him say "Do this" as a request, than "Please" as a command. I am not concerned with the words he uses, but with what they imply.

Excessive severity and excessive indulgence are equally to be avoided. If you let children suffer you endanger health and life. If you are over-careful in shielding them from trouble of every kind you are laying up much unhappiness for the future: you are withdrawing them from the common lot of man, to which they must one day become subject in spite of you.

You will tell me that I am making the same mistake as those bad fathers whom I blamed for sacrificing their children's happiness for the sake of a distant time that may never come. That is not so, for the liberty I allow my pupil amply compensates for the slight hardships I let him experience. I see little scamps playing in the snow, blue and stiff with cold and scarcely able to move a finger. There is nothing to hinder them warming themselves, but they don't. If they were forced to come indoors they would feel the rigours of constraint a hundred times more than the cold. What then is there to complain about? Am I making the child unhappy by exposing him to hardships which he is quite willing to endure? I am doing him good at the present moment by leaving him free. I am doing him good in the future by arming him against inevitable evils. If he had to choose between being my pupil or yours, do you think he would hesitate for an instant?

The surest way to make your child unhappy is to accustom him to get everything he wants. With desire constantly increasing through easy satisfaction, lack of power will sooner or later force you to a refusal in spite of yourself, and the unwonted refusal will cause him deeper annoyance than the mere lack of what he desires. First he will want the stick in your hand, then the bird that flies past, then the star that shines above him. Everything he sees he will want: and unless you were God you could never hope to satisfy him. How could such a child possibly be happy? Happy! He is a despot, at once the meanest of slaves and the most wretched of creatures. Let us get back to the primitive way. Nature made children to be loved and helped, not to be obeyed and feared. Is there in the world a being more feeble and unhappy, more at the mercy of his environment, more in need of pity and protection than a child? Surely then there is nothing more offensive or more unseemly than the sight of a dictatorial headstrong child, issuing orders to those around him and assuming the tone of a master to people without whom he would perish.

On the other hand, it should be obvious that with the many restrictions imposed on children by their own weakness it is barbarous for us to add subjection to our caprices to the natural subjection, and take from them such limited liberty as they possess. Social servitude will come with the age of reason. Why anticipate it by a domestic servitude? Let one moment of life be free from this yoke which nature has not imposed, and leave the child to the enjoyment of his natural liberty.

I come back to practice. I have already said that what your child gets he should get because he needs it, not because he asks for it, and that he should never act from obedience but only from necessity. For this reason, the words "obey" and "command" must be banished from his vocabulary, still more the words "duty" and "obligation"; but "force," "necessity," "weakness" and "constraint" should be emphasised. It is impossible to form any idea of moral facts or social relations before the age of reason. Consequently the use of terms which express such ideas should as far as possible be avoided, for fear the child comes to attach to these words false ideas which cannot or will not be eradicated at a later time.

"Reason with children" was Locke's chief maxim. It is the one most popular today, but it does not seem to me justified by success. For my part I do not see any children more stupid than those who have been much reasoned with. Of all the human faculties, reason which may be said to be compounded of all the rest develops most slowly and with greatest difficulty. Yet it is reason that people want to use in the development of the first faculties. A reasonable man is the masterwork of a good education: and we actually pretend to be educating children by means of reason! That is beginning at the end. If children appreciated reason they would not need to be educated.

Instead of appealing to reason, say to the child: "You must not do that!" "Why not?" "Because it is wrong." "Why is it wrong?" "Because it is forbidden." "Why is it forbidden?" "Because it is wrong." That is the inevitable circle. To distinguish right from wrong and appreciate the reason for the duties of man is beyond a child's powers.

Nature wants children to be children before they are men. If we deliberately depart from this order we shall get premature fruits which are neither ripe nor well flavoured and which soon decay. We shall have youthful sages and grown up children. Childhood has ways of seeing, thinking and feeling peculiar to itself: nothing can be more foolish than to seek to substitute our ways for them. I should as soon expect a child of ten to be five feet in height as to be possessed of judgment.

Treat your pupil according to his age. Begin by putting him in his place and keep him in it so firmly that he will not think of leaving it. Then he will practice the most important lesson of wisdom before he knows what wisdom is. Give him absolutely no orders of any kind. Do not even let him imagine that you claim any authority over him. Let him only know that he is weak and you are strong, and that therefore he is at your mercy. Quite early let him feel the heavy yoke which nature imposes on man, the yoke of the necessity in things as opposed to human caprice. If there is anything he should not do, do not forbid him, but prevent him without explanation or reasoning. Whatever you give, give at the first word without prayers or entreaty, and above all without conditions. Give with pleasure, refuse with regret, but let your refusals be irrevocable. Your "No" once uttered must be a wall of brass which the child will stop trying to batter down once he has exhausted his strength on it five or six times.

It is strange that all the time people have been bringing up children nobody has thought of any instruments for their direction but emulation, jealousy, envy, vanity, greed or base fear; most dangerous passions all of them, sure to corrupt the soul. Foolish teachers think they are working wonders when they are simply making the children wicked in the attempt to teach them about goodness. Then they announce gravely: such is man. Yes, such is the man you have made. All the instruments have been tried but one, and that as it happens is the only one that can succeed: well regulated liberty.

Avoid verbal lessons with your pupil. The only kind of lesson he should get is that of experience. Never inflict any punishment, for he does not know what it is to be at fault. Being devoid of all morality in his actions he can do nothing morally wrong, nothing that deserves either punishment or reprimand.

Let us lay it down as an incontestable principle that the first impulses of nature are always right. There is no original perversity in the human heart. Of every vice we can say how it entered and whence it came. The only passion natural to man is self-love, or self-esteem in a broad sense. This self-esteem has no necessary reference to other people. In so far as it relates to ourselves it is good and useful. It only becomes good or bad in the social application we make of it. Until reason, which is the guide of self-esteem, makes its appearance, the child should not do anything because he is seen or heard by other people, but only do what nature demands of him. Then he will do nothing but what is right.

I do not mean to say that he will never do any mischief: that he will never hurt himself, for example, or break a valuable bit of furniture. He might do a great deal that was bad without being bad, because the wrong action depends on harmful intention and that he will never have. When children are left free to blunder it is better to remove everything that would make blundering costly, and not leave anything fragile and precious within reach. Their room should be furnished with plain solid furniture, without mirrors, china, or ornaments. My Emile whom I am bringing up in the country will have nothing in his room to distinguish it from that of a peasant. If in spite of your precautions the child manages to upset things and break some useful articles, do not punish or scold him for your own negligence. Do not even let him guess that he has annoyed you. Behave as if the furniture had got broken of itself. Consider you have done very well if you can avoid saying anything.

May I set forth at this point the most important and the most useful rule in all education? It is not to save time but to waste it. The most dangerous period in human life is that between birth and the age of twelve. This is the age when errors and vices sprout, before there is any instrument for their destruction. When the instrument is available the roots have gone too deep to be extracted. The mind should remain inactive till it has all its faculties.

It follows from this that the first education should be purely negative. It consists not in teaching virtue and truth, but in preserving the heart from vice and the mind from error. If you could do nothing and let nothing be done, so that your pupil came to the age of twelve strong and healthy but unable to distinguish his right hand from his left, the eyes of his understanding would be open to reason from your very first lessons. In the absence of both prejudices and habits there would be nothing in him to oppose the effects of your teaching and care.

Do the opposite of what is usually done and you will almost always be right. Fathers and teachers, anxious to make a learned doctor instead of a child, correct, reprove, flatter, threaten, instruct, reason. There is a better way. Be reasonable and do not reason with your pupil. It is a mistake to try to get him to approve of things he dislikes. To bring reason into what is disagreeable at this stage will only discredit it. Exercise body, senses, powers, but keep the mind inactive as long as possible. Let childhood ripen in children.

The practical value of this method is confirmed by consideration of the distinctive genius of the child. Each mind has a form of its own in conformity with which it must be directed. If you are a wise man you will observe your pupil carefully before saying a word to him. In the first instance leave his essential character full liberty to manifest itself, in order to get a better view of his whole personality.

But where are we to place this child of ours when we are bringing him up like an automaton unaffected by anything outside himself? Must we keep him up in the moon or in some desert island? Are we to separate him from all human beings? Will he not see other children of his own age? Will he not see his relatives, his neighbours, his nurse, his lackey, even his tutor, who will assuredly be no angel? This is a very substantial objection. I have never pretended that it was easy to make education natural. Perhaps the difficulties are insurmountable. I do not say that anyone will reach the goal I have set, but I do say that the one who comes nearest will succeed best.

Remember that before you dare undertake the making of a man you must be a man yourself. While the child is as yet without knowledge of the world there is still time to make sure that everything around him is proper for him to see. To ensure this you must make yourself worthy of the respect and love of everybody, so that all will seek to please you. You will not be the child's master unless you are master of everything that surrounds him. This is another reason for bringing Emile up in the country, far from the filthy morals of the towns. The glitter of town life is seductive and corrupting while the gross vices of country people are more likely to repel than to seduce. In a village the tutor will be in much better control of the objects he wants the child to see. If he is helpful to the people, they will all be eager to oblige him and appear to his pupil as if they were in reality what the master would like them to be. If they do not correct their vices, they will at any rate refrain from scandalous behaviour, and that is all that is wanted for our purpose.

Be simple and hold yourself in check, you zealous teachers. Never be in a hurry to act. So far as you can, refrain from a good instruction for fear of giving a bad one. Since you cannot prevent the child learning from the examples set by others, confine your care to impressing these examples on his mind in the form which suits him best. The impetuous passions have a great effect on the child who witnesses them. Anger is so noisy in its expression that it cannot but be noticed by any one near. Here is obviously a chance for a pedagogue to concoct a fine discourse. But no fine discourses for you: not a word. Leave the child to come to you. Astounded by the sight of an angry man he will be sure to ask questions. Your answer is simple. It is suggested by the very things that have struck the senses. He sees an inflamed countenance, flashing eyes, threatening gestures; he hears cries: all signs that something is wrong with the body. Tell him quietly: "The poor man is ill, he has an attack of fever." Such an idea if given at the proper time will have as salutary effects as the most long-winded discourse, and it will have useful applications later on. On this way of thinking you are entitled, if the necessity arises, to treat a rebellious child as an invalid. You can confine him to his room, perhaps send him to bed, put him on a diet, and so make him afraid of his budding vices without him ever regarding the severity you are perhaps forced to use for their cure as a punishment. And should it happen that in a moment of heat you lose your own composure and moderation do not try to hide your faults. Just say to him frankly with a tender reproach: "You have made me ill."

My plan is not to go into details, but only to set forth general principles and give examples in difficult cases. I do not think it is possible to bring up a child to the age of twelve in society without giving him some idea of the relations of man to man and the moral aspects of human conduct. The best one can do is to postpone these necessary notions as long as possible, and when they can be no longer postponed to limit them to the immediate requirement.

Our first duties are to ourselves. Self is the centre of the primitive sentiments. The natural impulses all relate in the first instance to our preservation and well-being. Hence the first sentiment of justice does not come to us from what we owe others, but from what others owe us. It is another of the blunders of the ordinary education to talk to children about their duties, and say nothing about their rights. This takes them beyond their comprehension and their interest.

The first idea a child should have given him is not that of liberty but of property. To get that he must possess something of his own. To tell him that he owns his clothes, his furniture, his toys, means nothing to him. Though he uses them he does not know why or how they are his. He must be taken back to the origin of property.

The easiest way for him to learn about property is through the work he does in the garden in imitation of the gardener. He plants beans and when they come up they "belong" to him. To explain what that term means I make him feel that he has put his time, his work, his effort, himself into them. Then one day he finds his beans dug up by Robert the gardener. The ground "belongs" to the gardener and he must come to an arrangement with the man before he can raise beans again. The destructive child has to learn his lesson in another way. He breaks the windows of his room, Let the wind blow on him night and day and do not worry about him catching cold. It is better for him to catch cold than to be a fool. If he goes on breaking windows shut him up in a dark room without windows. The time will come when he has learned what property means and he is willing to respect other people's belongings.

We are now in the moral world and the door is open to vice. With conventions and duties come deceit and lying. As soon as we can do what we ought not to do, we seek to hide our misdeeds. With the failure to prevent evildoing the question of punishment arises. On fact there is never any need to inflict punishment as such on children. It should always come to them as the natural consequence of their bad conduct. In the case of lying, for example, you need not punish them because they have lied, but so arrange that if they lie they will not be believed even when they speak the truth, and will be accused of bad things they have not done.

Actually children's lies are all the work of their teachers. They try to teach them to tell the truth and in doing so teach them to lie. As for those of us who only give our pupils lessons of a practical kind and prefer them to be good rather than clever, we never demand the truth from them for fear they should hide it, and we never exact any promise lest they be tempted to break it. If something wrong has been done in my absence and I do not know the culprit, I take care not to accuse Emile or to ask: "Was it you?" Nothing could be more indiscreet than such a question, especially if the child is guilty. If he thinks you know he has done wrong you will seem to be trying to trap him and the idea will turn him against you. If he thinks you do not know he will ask: "Why should I reveal my fault?" and the imprudent question will be a temptation to lying.

What has been said about lying applies in many respects to all the other duties prescribed for children. To make them pious you take them to church where they are bored. You make them gabble prayers till they look forward to the happy time when they will no longer pray to God. You make them give alms to inspire charity, as if almsgiving were a matter for children only. Drop these pretences, teachers. Be virtuous and good yourselves, and the examples you set will impress themselves on your pupils' memories, and in due season will enter their hearts.

The apparent ease with which children learn is their misfortune. It is not seen that this very facility proves that they are learning nothing. Their smooth polished brain is like a mirror which throws back the objects presented to it. Nothing gets in, nothing remains behind. They remember words but ideas are reflected off. Those who listen to them understand what the words mean but they themselves do not.

Though memory and reasoning are essentially different faculties they depend on each other in their development. Before the age of reason the child receives images but not ideas. The difference between them is that images are simply the exact pictures of sense-given objects, whereas ideas are notions of the objects determined by their relations. An image may exist by itself in the imagining mind, but every idea presupposes other ideas. Imagination is just seeing, but conception implies comparison. Our sensations are purely passive, different from our perceptions or ideas which are the outcome of an active principle of judgment.

That is why I say that children being incapable of judgment have no true memory. They retain sounds, shapes, sensations, but rarely ideas, and still more rarely their relations. It may be objected that they learn some of the elements of geometry, but really that only shows that so far from being able to reason for themselves they cannot even recollect the reasoning of others. For if you follow these little geometricians in their lesson you will find that all they have recollected is the exact picture of the figure and the words of the demonstration. The least new question upsets them and so does any change of figure. Their knowledge is all in sensation; nothing has got through to the understanding. Their memory itself is scarcely any more perfect than the other faculties since they nearly always have to re-learn the things whose names they learned in childhood when they grow up. Nevertheless I am far from thinking that children have no kind of reasoning. On the contrary, I notice that they think very well on everything which bears on their present and obvious interest. Where people go wrong is in regard to the things they actually know. They credit them with knowledge they do not possess, and make them reason about things beyond their comprehension.

The professional pedagogues speak differently, but it is evident from their own performance that they think exactly as I do. For what in fact do they teach? Nothing but words. Among the various sciences they boast of teaching their pupils, they take good care not to include those which are really useful, because these would be the sciences dealing with facts, in which the children's failure would be evident. They choose subjects like heraldry, geography, chronology and the languages in which acquaintance with terms gives the appearance of knowledge: studies so remote from men and especially from children that it would be surprising if ever they came to be of use even once in a lifetime.

*Languages.* It may seem strange that I reckon the study of languages among the futilities of education, but it must be remembered that I am only speaking now about the studies of the early years; and whatever may be said I do not believe that, apart from prodigies, any child under twelve or fifteen has ever really learned two languages. I agree that if the study of language was merely one of words it would be quite proper for children, but with the change in symbols the ideas represented are also modified. It is only the thought that is common: the spirit in each language has its own distinctive form. Of these different forms the child has only the one he uses, and he is limited to it till the age of reason. To have two languages he would have to be able to compare ideas, and how can he compare ideas he can barely conceive? He can then learn only a single language. But, you will tell me, some pupils learn several languages. I deny that. I have seen little prodigies who were supposed to speak five or six languages. I have heard them speak German, then use Latin, French and Italian in succession. Actually they made use of five or six different vocabularies, but in every case it was German they were speaking. The words were changed, but not the language.

To conceal their own incapacity teachers prefer the dead languages in which there are no longer any judges to call them in question. The familiar use of these languages has been lost a long time ago and we have to be content to imitate the language found in books. That is what is called "speaking the language". If the teachers' Latin and Greek are like that, judge what the children's are like.

*Geography.* In any study whatever, the representing symbols mean nothing apart from the idea of the things represented. But children are always limited to symbols. The teacher thinks he is giving them a description of the earth in geography, but actually he is only giving them a knowledge of maps. He tells them the names of towns, countries, rivers, but the children have no notion that they exist anywhere but on the paper shown to them. I remember seeing somewhere a geography which began: "What is the world? It is a cardboard globe." There you have the child's geography. I maintain in fact that after two years of the sphere and cosmography, there is not a ten-year-old child who could find his way from Paris to St. Denis by the rules he has been taught. These are the learned doctors who know just where Pekin, Ispahan, Mexico and all the countries of the world are.

*History.* It is still more ridiculous to set children to study history. History is supposed to be a collection of facts within their comprehension. But what is meant by "facts"? Is it credible that the relations determining historical facts should be so easy to grasp that the ideas of them should readily take shape in children's minds? Or that there can be a real knowledge of events without a knowledge of their causes and their effects? If history is no more than an account of human actions in purely physical terms there is absolutely nothing to be learned from it. Try to make children appreciate these actions in terms of moral relations and you will see then whether they are old enough to learn history.

It is easy to put into their mouths words like "king," "empire," "war," "conquest," "revolution," "law," but when it comes to a question of attaching precise ideas to such words, the explanations will be very different from those Emile got in his dealings with Robert the gardener.

Even if there is no book study the kind of memory the child has does not remain idle. All that he sees and hears makes its impression on him and he remembers it. He keeps a record in himself of the deeds and words of people. The world around him is the book in which without knowing it he is continually adding to the stores of memory, against the time when his judgment can profit by them. It is in the choice of these objects and in the constant care taken to put before him the things he can know and hide from him the things he ought not to know that the art of memory training consists. This is what must be done to form a storehouse of the knowledge which is to serve for his education in youth and for his conduct all through life.

*Fables.* Emile will never learn anything by heart, not even fables like those of La Fontaine, simple and charming though they be; for the words of fables are no more fables than the words of history are history. How can people be so blind as to call fables the ethics of childhood and not realise that the moral which amuses also misleads? Fables may instruct men, but it is necessary to speak the naked truth to children. My contention is that the child does not understand the fables he is taught, for whatever you do to make them simple the instruction you want to draw from them implies ideas beyond his grasp.

In all La Fontaine's book of fables there are only five or six of childlike simplicity. The first and best of these is "The Crow and the Fox". Analyse it line by line and it will be evident how very unsuitable it is for children. "*Mr. Crow, on a tree perched.*" Have the children seen a crow? Do they know what a crow is? Why "Mr."? The usual order of words would be: "perched on a tree." Why the inversion? "*Held in his beak a cheese.*" What kind of a cheese? Could a crow hold a cheese in its beak? There are difficulties in every line, not merely of understanding, but of morals. The fox flatters and lies to get the crow to drop the cheese. What conclusion will the child draw? Watch children learning their fables and you will see that the morals they draw are just the opposite of what they were intended to draw. They laugh at the crow but are fond of the fox.

*Reading.* When I get rid of all the usual tasks of children in this way I also get rid of the books which are the chief cause of unhappiness to them. Reading is the greatest plague of childhood. Emile at the age of twelve will scarcely know what a book is. But at least, I will be told, he must be able to read. I agree. He must be able to read when he needs to read. Before that it will only be a bother to him.

If nothing is to be exacted from children by way of obedience it follows that they will only learn what they feel to be of actual and present advantage, either because they like it, or because it is of use to them. Otherwise, what motive would they have for learning? The art of speaking to absent people and hearing from them, of communicating personally our sentiments and our wishes, is an art whose usefulness can be made obvious to people of all ages; but by some strange perversity it has become a torment for childhood. Why should this be? Because the children have been compelled to learn it against their will, and made to put it to purposes which mean nothing for them.

Great stress is laid on finding better methods of teaching children to read. Reading cases and cards have been invented, and the child's room has been turned into a printer's shop. Locke suggested the use of dice. Fancy all this elaborate contrivance! A surer way that nobody thinks of is to create the desire to read. Give the child this desire and have done with gadgets and any method will be good.

Present interest: that is the great motive impulse, the only one that leads sure and far. Emile sometimes receives from his father or his friends letters inviting him to a dinner, a walk, a boating party, or some public entertainment. These notes are short, clear, precise and well written. He must find some one to read them for him. This person is either not to be found at the right moment or is no more disposed to be helpful to the boy than the boy was to him the night before. In this way the chance is lost. By the time the note is read the time is past. If only he could read himself! He receives more letters and does his best to read them; and finally deciphers half a letter, something about going out tomorrow to eat cream. But where? And with whom? How hard he tries to read the rest! I do not think Emile will have any need of reading devices. Shall I go on now to speak about writing? Oh no. I am ashamed to amuse myself with such trifles in an educational treatise. . . .

I have now brought my pupils through the land of the sensations right up to the bounds of childish reason. The first step beyond this should take him towards manhood. But before entering on this new stage let us cast our eyes backward for a moment on the one we have traversed. Each age and state of life has its own proper perfection, its own distinctive maturity. People sometimes speak about a complete man. Let us think rather of a complete child. This vision will be new for us and perhaps not less agreeable.

When I picture to myself a boy of ten or twelve, healthy, strong and well built for his age, only pleasant thoughts arise in me, whether for his present or for his future. I see him bright, eager, vigorous, care-free, completely absorbed in the present, rejoicing in abounding vitality. I see him in the years ahead using senses, mind and power as they develop from day to day. I view him as a child and he pleases me. I think of him as a man and he pleases me still more. His warm blood seems to heat my own. I feel as if I were living in his life and am rejuvenated by his vivacity.

The clock strikes and all is changed. In an instant his eye grows dull and his merriment disappears. No more mirth, no more games! A severe, hardfaced man takes him by the hand, says gravely, "Come away, sir," and leads him off. In the room they enter I get a glimpse of books. Books! What a cheerless equipment for his age. As he is dragged away in silence, he casts a regretful look around him. His eyes are swollen with tears he dare not shed, his heart heavy with sighs he dare not utter.

Come, my happy pupil, and console us for the departure of the wretched boy. Here comes Emile, and at his approach I have a thrill of joy in which I see he shares. It is his friend and comrade, the companion of his games to whom he comes. His person, his bearing, his countenance reveal assurance and contentment. Health glows in his face. His firm step gives him an air of vigour. His complexion is refined without being effeminate; sun and wind have put on it the honourable imprint of his sex. His eyes are still unlighted by the fires of sentiment and have all their native serenity. His manner is open and free without the least insolence or vanity.

His ideas are limited but precise. If he knows nothing by heart, he knows a great deal by experience. If he is not as good a reader in books as other children, he reads better in the book of nature. His mind is not in his tongue but in his head. He has less memory but more judgment. He only knows one language, but he understands what he says; and if he does not talk as well as other children he can do things better than they can.

Habit, routine and custom mean nothing to him. What he did yesterday has no effect on what he does today. He never follows a fixed rule and never accepts authority or example. He only does or says what seems good to himself. For this reason you must not expect stock speeches or studied manners from him but just the faithful expression of his ideas and the conduct that comes from his inclinations.

You will find in him a few moral notions relating to his own situation, but not being an active member of society he has none relating to manhood. Talk to him about liberty, property and even convention, and he may understand you thus far. But speak to him about duty and obedience, and he will not know what you mean. Command him to do something, and he will pay no heed. But say to him: "If you will do me this favour, I will do the same for you another time"; and immediately he will hasten to oblige. For his part, if he needs any help he will ask the first person he meets as a matter of course. If you grant his request he will not thank you, but will feel that he has contracted a debt. If you refuse, he will neither complain nor insist. He will only say: "It could not be done." He does not rebel against necessity once he recognises it.

Work and play are all the same to him. His games are his occupations: he is not aware of any difference. He goes into everything he does with a pleasing interest and freedom. It is indeed a charming spectacle to see a nice boy of this age with open smiling countenance, doing the most serious things in his play or profoundly occupied with the most frivolous amusements.

Emile has lived a child's life and has arrived at the maturity of childhood, without any sacrifice of happiness in the achievement of his own perfection. He has acquired all the reason possible for his age, and in doing so has been as free and as happy as his nature allowed him to be. If by chance the fatal scythe were to cut down the flower of our hopes we would not have to bewail at the same time his life and his death, nor add to our griefs the memory of those we caused him. We would say that at any rate he had enjoyed his childhood and that nothing we had done had deprived him of what nature gave.

## Book III

The whole course of life up to adolescence is a time of weakness, but there is one point during this first age of man at which strength exceeds the demands made on it by needs, and the growing creature though still absolutely weak becomes relatively strong. With needs incompletely developed, his powers more than suffice. As a man he would be very feeble: as a child he is very strong. This is the third stage of early life which for lack of a better word I continue to call childhood. It is not yet the age of puberty, but adolescence draws near.

At twelve or thirteen the child's powers develop much more rapidly than his needs. The sex passions, the most violent and terrible of all, have not yet awakened. He is indifferent to the rigours of weather and seasons, and braves them light-heartedly. His growing body heat takes the place of clothing. Appetite is his sauce, and everything nourishing tastes good. When he is tired he stretches himself out on the ground and goes to sleep. He is not troubled by imaginary wants. What people think does not trouble him. Not only is he self-sufficient but his strength goes beyond his requirements. . . .

Nevertheless, it will probably be necessary to give him a little guidance. But let it be very little, and avoid the appearance of it. If he goes wrong, do not correct his errors. Say nothing till he sees them and corrects them himself; or at most, arrange some practical situation which will make him realise things personally. If he never made mistakes he would never learn properly. In any case, the important thing is not that he should know the topography of the country, but that he should be able to get his information for himself. It does not matter greatly whether he has maps in his head, provided he knows what they represent and has a clear idea of the art of their construction.

The essential principle in my method is not to teach the child a great many things but to allow him to form only clear, exact ideas. It would not matter greatly if he knew nothing so long as he did not go wrong in his thinking. I only put truths into his head to save him from the errors he might learn instead. Reason and judgment are slow to come, but prejudices crowd in; and it is necessary to protect him from them.

During the first period of life time was plentiful. We only sought to have it occupied in any way at all to prevent it being put to a bad use. Now it is just the opposite, and we have not enough time to get all done that is useful. Bear in mind that the passions are near at hand, and that as soon as they knock at the door your pupil will no longer attend to anything else. The quiet period of intellect passes so rapidly and has so many other necessary occupations that it is folly to try to make the child a scholar within its span. It is not a question of teaching him the sciences, but of giving him a taste for them, and methods of acquiring them when this taste is better developed. This is most certainly a fundamental principle in all good education. . . .

With the child's advance in intelligence other considerations compel greater care in the choice of his occupations. As soon as he comes to know himself well enough to understand what constitutes happiness for him and can judge what is fitting and what is not, he is in a position to appreciate the difference between work and play, and to regard play as relaxation from work. Thereafter matters of real utility may enter into his studies and lead him to apply himself more diligently than he did to mere amusements. The law of necessity, always operative, soon teaches man to do what he does not like, in order to avoid evils he would like still less. Such is the practice of foresight; and from foresight, well or ill directed, comes all the wisdom or all the unhappiness of mankind.

When children foresee their needs their intelligence has made real progress. They begin to know the value of time. For this reason, it is important to accustom them to employ their time on objects of an obvious utility that are within their understanding. All that pertains to the moral order and to social usage should not be put before them yet, because it does not mean anything for them. Why do you want to set a child to the studies of an age he may never reach, to the detriment of studies suited for the present? But you will ask: "Will there be time for him to learn what he ought to know when the occasion for its use arises?" That I do not know. What I do know is that it is impossible for him to learn it sooner. Our real teachers are experience and feeling, and no one ever appreciates what is proper to manhood till he enters into its situations. A child knows that he is destined to become a man. Such of the ideas of adult life as are within his comprehension are occasions of instruction for him, but he ought to be kept in absolute ignorance of all the rest. This whole book is one long demonstration of this educational principle.

As soon as we have managed to give our pupil some idea of what the word "utility" means, we have another strong hold on him. This word makes a deep impression on him, provided it has meaning for him on his own age level and he can see its bearing on his present well being. "What is the good of that?" Henceforth this is the sacred question, the decisive question between him and me, in all the situations of our life. This is my infallible response to all his questions, and it serves to check the multitude of foolish queries with which children constantly bother people. Note what a powerful instrument I am putting into your hands for dealing with your pupil. Since he does not know the reason of anything, you can reduce him to silence at will while you with your knowledge and experience can show him the use of all you put before him. But make no mistake about it: when you ask him this question you are teaching him to put it to you in his turn. You can be sure that in future he will never fail to ask about anything you tell him: "What is the good of it?"

I do not like explanatory speeches. Young people pay little attention to them and rarely remember them. Give them facts. I cannot say often enough, that we allow too great power to words. With our babbling education we only make babblers.

Suppose, when I am studying with my pupil the course of the sun and how to find our direction, he suddenly stops me to ask what good purpose all this serves. What a fine discourse I could give him—especially if people were listening in to our conversation—about the use of travel, the advantages of commerce, the special products of different regions, the customs of different peoples, the use of the calendar, the reckoning of the seasons for agriculture, the art of navigation. Politics, natural history, astronomy, even ethics and the law of nations, might enter into my explanation so as to give my pupil a great idea of all these subjects and a great desire to learn them. But not a single idea of all this would the boy understand. Unless he feared that he would be bothering me, he would ask what was the use of taking one's bearings. Actually our Emile, brought up in the country and accustomed to get ideas the hard way, would not listen to a single word of all this. At the first sentence he did not understand he would run off and leave me to perorate by myself. We must look for a more ordinary solution. My display of science is of no use to him.

When Emile wants to learn what use it is to know the position of the forest north of Montemorency, I put him off and next morning take him for a walk before breakfast. We get lost and the more we wander the more tired and hungry we become. We sit down to consider how we can get out. Crying is no use. "Let us see your watch. What time is it?" "It is noon," says Emile, "and I am so hungry." At twelve o'clock the day before, he is reminded, we were observing the position of the forest from Montmorency. "Did we not say that the forest was . . .?" "North of Montmorency," says Emile, "So Montmorency lies. . . ." "South of the forest." But we know how to find the north at midday. "Yes," says Emile, "by the direction of the shadows," and comes to the conclusion that if we go the opposite way from the shadows we will find the town. And this we do. It is evident that astronomy is of some use after all.

I hate books. They only teach us to talk about what we do not know. It is said that Hermes engraved the elements of science on pillars for fear his discoveries might perish in a deluge. If he had impressed them firmly on the human brain, they would have been kept safe there by tradition.

Is there no way of bringing together all the lessons scattered through a multitude of books and grouping them together round some common object which, even at this age, might be easy to see, interesting to follow and thought-provoking? If it were possible to invent a situation in which all the natural needs of mankind were made obvious to the mind of a child, and the ways of providing for these needs made equally clear, the simple lifelike picture of this condition of things would give the child's imagination its first training.

Eager philosopher, I see your own imagination lighting up. Do not trouble yourself. This situation has been found, and with all respect to you has been described better than you could do it, at any rate with greater truth and simplicity. Since it is essential that there should be books, there happens to be one book which in my opinion furnishes the most satisfactory treatise on natural education. This is the first book my Emile will read. For a long time it will constitute his entire library, and will always occupy an honoured place in it. It will be the text on which all our talks on the natural sciences will form a commentary. It will serve as a touchstone for our judgment as we progress, and so long as our taste remains unspoiled, it will continue to give us pleasure. What is this marvellous book? Is it Aristotle? Or Pliny? Or Buffon? Oh no, it is *Robinson Crusoe*.

Robinson Crusoe alone on his island, without the help of his fellows and the tools of the various arts, yet managing to procure food and safety, and even a measure of well-being: here is something of interest for every age, capable of being made attractive to children in a thousand ways. This condition, I admit, is not that of social man, and probably it is not to be that of Emile, but he should use it in the evaluation of all other conditions. The surest way for him to rise above prejudices and to bring his own judgments into line with the true relations of things is to put himself at the point of view of a solitary man, and to judge everything as this man would with reference to its real utility.

Rid of all its lumber, this novel, beginning with the shipwreck of Robinson near his island and concluding with the arrival of the ship that is to take him away, will furnish Emile with both amusement and instruction during the period of life under consideration. I want his head to be turned by it, and to have him busy himself unceasingly with his castle, his goats and his plantations. I want him to learn, not from books but from experience, all the things he would need to know in such a situation. I want him to think he is Robinson and imagine himself clothed in skins, with a large hat, a large sabre and all the grotesque equipment of the character, even to the umbrella he will not need. I want him to be concerned about the measures he would take if any one thing happened to be lacking, scrutinising his hero's conduct to see whether anything has been omitted or could be done better. You may be sure that he will plan a house for himself like Crusoe's. This is the veritable castle in Spain of this blessed age, when all that is required for happiness is freedom and the necessaries of life.

What an opportunity there is in this phantasy for a skilful grown-up who knows how to awaken it and use it to advantage. The child, eager to build a storehouse for his island will be more zealous to learn than the master to teach. He will concentrate on everything that is of use for the purpose. You will no longer have to direct him, only to hold him back. For the rest, let us hasten to establish him on this island while he is able to find complete happiness on it, for the day draws near when he will no longer want to live alone, and when Friday's company will not content him.

The practice of the natural arts for which a single man is sufficient leads to the pursuit of the industrial arts which call for the co-operation of many hands. The former can be practised by solitaries and savages, but the latter can only come into being in the society which they make necessary. So long as there is only physical need each man is self-sufficient. It is the introduction of luxuries that makes the sharing and differentiation of labour essential. . . .

Your main endeavour should be to keep away from your pupil all the notions of social relations which are beyond his comprehension; but when the interrelation of knowledge forces you to show him the mutual dependence of men, avoid the moral aspects and direct his attention to industry and the mechanical arts which make them useful to each other. As you take him from one workshop to another, never let him see any kind of work without putting his hand to it, and never let him leave till he knows perfectly the reason for all that he has observed. With that in view, set him an example by working yourself in the different occupations. To make him a master become an apprentice. You can be sure that he will learn more from an hour's work than he would remember after a day's explanations. . . .

Reader, do not give too much thought to the bodily activity and the skill of hand of our pupil. Consider rather the direction we are giving to his childish curiosities. Consider his senses, his inventive mind, his foresight. Consider the good head he will have. He will want to know all about everything he sees and does, and will take nothing for granted. He will refuse to learn anything until he acquires the knowledge that is implied in it. When he sees a spring made he will want to know how the steel was got from the mine. If he sees the pieces of a box put together, he will want to know how the tree was cut. When he is using a tool himself he will not fail to say of the tool he uses: "If I did not have this tool, how would I make one like it, or manage without it?"

At the beginning of this period of life we have taken advantage of the fact that our strength greatly exceeds our needs, to get away beyond ourselves. We have soared into the heavens and have surveyed the earth. We have studied the laws of nature. In a word, we have traversed the whole of our island. Now we come back gradually to our own dwelling. What is there for us to do when we have completed the study of our surroundings? We must convert them as much as we can to our own purposes. Up to this point, we have provided ourselves with all kinds of instruments without knowing which of them we will need. It may be that those which are of no use to us may be of service to other people and that we in turn may need theirs. In this way we will all find ourselves gaining by these exchanges. For this we must know the mutual needs of men; what each of us has to give and to get. Suppose there are ten men, each with ten kinds of needs, each applying himself to ten different kinds of work to provide for the necessities of life. The ten, because of differences of gift and talent, are likely to be less apt at some tasks than others, and all will be badly served when each does everything. But make a society of these ten, and let each man apply himself for his own benefit and that of the other nine to the kind of work that suits him best. Each one will profit by the talents of the others as if he personally had them all, and at the same time grow more perfect in his own line of work by constant practice. So it will come that the whole ten are perfectly provided for and will still have something left for others. This is the obvious basis of all our social institutions.

In this way the ideas of social relations take shape in the child's mind little by little, even before he becomes an active member of society himself. Emile sees that in order to have things for his own use he must have some he can exchange with other people. It is easy to lead him to feel the need for such exchanges and put himself in a position to profit by them.

As soon as he knows what life is, my first concern will be to teach him to preserve it. Up to this point I have ignored differences of station, rank or fortune, and I shall say little more about them in what follows, because man is the same in all stations. The rich man's stomach is no bigger than the poor man's, and his digestion no better. The master's arms are no longer and no stronger than the slave's. A "great" man is no greater than a man of the people. Natural needs being everywhere alike, the means of satisfying them should likewise be equal. Fit man's education to what man really is. Do you not see that if you try to fit him exclusively for one way of life you make him useless for every other? You put your trust in the existing social order and do not take into account the fact that that order is subject to inevitable revolutions, and that you can neither foresee nor prevent the revolution that may affect your children. . . .

Here is our child, ready to cease being a child and to enter on an individual life. More than ever he feels the necessity which binds him to things. After training his body and his senses, we have trained his mind and his judgment. In short, we have combined the use of his limbs with that of his faculties. We have made him an efficient thinking being and nothing further remains for us in the production of a complete man but to make him a loving, sensitive being: in fact, to perfect reason through sentiment. But before entering on this new order of things let us look back over the one we are leaving, and see where we have reached.

To begin with, our pupil had only sensations, now he has ideas: he had only feelings, now he judges; for from the comparison of several sensations, whether successive or simultaneous, and the judgment passed on them, there comes a sort of mixed or complex sensation which I call an idea. It is the particular way of forming ideas that gives its character to the human mind. A solid mind forms its ideas on real relations: a superficial one is content with appearances. Greater or less aptitude in the comparison of ideas and the discovery of relations is what makes the difference in the mental capacity of different people.

In sensation, judgment is purely passive—we feel what we feel: in perception or idea, it is active—it connects, compares, determines relations. It is never the sensation that is wrong but the judgment passed on it. The child says about the ice cream that it burns. That is a right sensation but a wrong judgment. So with the experiences of those who see a mirror for the first time, or enter a cellar at different times of the year, or dip a warm or cold hand into lukewarm water, or see the clouds passing over the moon as if they were stationary, or think the stick immersed in water is broken. All our mistakes in these cases come from judgment. Unfortunately social man is dependent on a great many things about which he has to judge. He must therefore be taught to reason correctly.

I will be told that in training the child to judge, I am departing from nature. I do not think so. Nature chooses her instruments, and makes use of them not according to opinion but according to necessity. There is a great difference between natural man living in nature and natural man living in the social state. Emile is not a savage to be banished to the deserts: he is a savage made to live in a town. He must know how to get a living in towns, and how to get on with their inhabitants, and to live with them, if not to live like them.

The best way of learning to judge correctly is to simplify our sense experiences as much as possible. To do this we must learn to check the reports of each sense by itself, over and above the check from the other senses. Then each sensation will become an idea, and this idea will always conform to the truth. This is the kind of acquirement I have tried to secure in this third stage of childhood.

Emile, who has been compelled to learn for himself and use his reason, has a limited knowledge, but the knowledge he has is his own, none of it half-known. Among the small number of things he really knows the most important is that there is much he does not know which he may one day come to know, much more that other people know that he will never know, and an infinity of things that nobody will ever know. He has a universal mind, not because of what he knows but from his faculty for acquiring knowledge: a mind open, intelligent, responsive, and (as Montaigne says) if not instructed, capable of being instructed. I am content if he knows the "wherefore" of all he does, and the "why" of all he believes.

The only knowledge Emile has at this stage is in the sphere of natural and physical facts. He does not even know the name of history, nor what meta-physics and ethics are. He knows the essential relations between man and things, but none of the moral relations between man and man. He has little ability to form general ideas or abstractions. He sees the qualities common to certain bodies without reasoning about the qualities in themselves. He knows abstract space by means of geometrical figures, and abstract quantity by means of algebraic symbols. These figures and signs are the basis of the abstractions, on which his senses rest. He does not seek to know things in themselves, but through the relations which interest him. He only judges external facts by their relation to himself, but this judgment of his is sound. Nothing fantastic or conventional enters into it. He sets most store on what is useful for him, and as he never departs from this method of evaluation, he is not swayed by accepted opinion.

Emile is hard working, temperate, patient, stable and courageous. His imagination, still unstimulated, does not exaggerate dangers. Few evils affect him and he can endure suffering calmly because he has learned not to fight against fate. As for death, he does not yet know what it is, but being accustomed to submit unresistingly to the laws of nature, he will die if he must without a struggle. To live a free man and hold human affairs lightly is the best way to prepare for death. In a word, Emile has every personal virtue. To add the social virtues he only needs to know the relations which call them into being. That knowledge his mind is now quite ready to receive.

He still thinks of himself without regard to others and is quite satisfied that others should give no thought to him. He asks nothing from other people and does not believe that he owes anything to them. Thus far he stands alone in human society. He is self-dependent and is better entitled to be so than any other person, since he is all that a child could be at his age. He has no mistaken ideas and no vices, other than those that nobody can avoid. He has a healthy body, agile limbs, a true mind free from prejudice, a free heart devoid of passion. Self-esteem, the first and most natural of all the passions, has still to awaken in him. Without disturbing anybody's peace he has lived happy, contented and free within the bounds of nature. Do you think that a child who has reached his fifteenth year like this has wasted his childhood?

**Book IV**

We are born twice over; the first time for existence, the second for life; once as human beings and later as men or as women. Up to puberty, children of the two sexes have nothing obvious to distinguish them. They are similar in features, in figure, in complexion, in voice. Girls are children, boys are children. The same name suffices for beings so much alike.

But man is not meant to remain a child for ever. At the time prescribed by nature he passes out of his childhood. As the fretting of the sea precedes the distant storm, this disturbing change is announced by the murmur of nascent passions. A change of mood, frequent tantrums, a constant unease of mind make the child hard to manage. He no longer listens to his master's voice. He is a lion in a fever. He mistrusts his guide and is averse to control.

With the moral signs of changing mood go patent physical changes. His countenance develops and takes on the imprint of a definite character. The soft slight down on his cheeks grows darker and firmer. His voice breaks, or rather, gets lost. He is neither child nor man, and he speaks like neither. His eyes, organs of the soul, which have hitherto said nothing, find language and expression as they light up with a new fire. He is becoming conscious that they can tell too much and he is learning to lower them and blush. He is disturbed for no reason whatever.

This is the second birth of which I spoke. Now is the time that man really enters into life and finds nothing alien to him. So far his guardian's responsibility has been child's play: it is only now that his task comes to have real importance. This stage at which ordinary educations end is just that when ours should begin.

The passions are the chief instruments for our preservation. The child's first sentiment is self-love, the only passion that is born with man. The second, which is derived from it, is the love he has for the people he sees ready to help him, and from this develops a kindly feeling for mankind. But with fresh needs and growing dependence on others comes the consciousness of social relations and with it the sense of duties and preferences. It is at this point that the child may become domineering, jealous, deceitful, vindictive. Self-love being concerned only with ourselves is content when our real needs are satisfied, but self-esteem which involves comparisons with other people never is and never can be content because it makes the impossible demand that others should prefer us to themselves. That is how it comes that the gentle kindly passions issue from self-love, while hate and anger spring from self-esteem. Great care and skill are required to prevent the human heart being depraved by the new needs of social life.

The proper study of man is that of his relationships. So long as he is aware of himself only as a physical being he should study himself in his relations with things. That is the task of childhood. When he comes to consciousness of himself as a moral being he should study himself in his relations with his fellows. This is the occupation of his whole life, beginning at the point we have now reached. . . .

At last we are entering the moral sphere. We have reached the second stage of manhood. If this were the place for it, I would try to show how the first impulses of the heart give rise to the first utterances of conscience, and how from the sentiments of love and hate come the first ideas of good and evil. I would demonstrate that justice and goodness are not merely abstract terms, moral entities created by the understanding, but real affections of the soul enlightened by reason which have developed from our primitive affections. I would show too that it is impossible to establish any natural law by reason alone, independent of conscience, and that natural rights are an empty dream unless they are based on the natural needs of the human heart. But I do not think I am called on to write treatises on metaphysics and ethics or detail any courses of study whatever.

Up to the present, my Emile has thought only about himself. The first thought he gives to his fellows leads him to compare himself with them; and the first sentiment excited in him by this comparison is a desire for priority. It is at this point that self-love changes into self-esteem and that all the passions pertaining to the latter begin to be active. But to determine whether the passions which will dominate his character are to be humane and kindly, or cruel and malevolent, we must know what he regards as his proper place among men and what kind of obstacles he thinks he will have to overcome to reach it. We have already let him see the chances of life which are common to all mankind. We must now for his guidance in this quest show him the differences among men and give him a picture of the whole social order.

Here it is important to take the opposite course from the one we have been following so far, and let the young man learn from other people's experience rather than his own. I would have you choose a young man's associates so that he may think well of those who live with him, and at the same time I would have you teach him to know the world so well that he may think ill of all that goes on in it. You want him to know and feel that man is naturally good, and to judge his neighbour by himself: equally, you want him to see how society corrupts men and to find in their prejudices the source of all their vices. This method, I have to admit, has its drawbacks and it is not easy to put into practice. If a young man is set to observe men too early and too close up, he will take a hateful pleasure in interpreting everything as badness and fail to see anything good in what is really good. Soon the general perversity will serve him as an excuse rather than as a warning, and he will say that if this is what man is, he himself has no wish to be different.

To get over this obstacle and bring him to an understanding of the human heart without risk of spoiling himself I would show him men in other times and places, in such a way that he can look on the scene as an outsider. This is the time for history. By means of it he will read the hearts of men without the lessons of philosophy, and look on them as a mere spectator without prejudice and without passion: judging them, but neither their accomplice nor their accuser.

Unfortunately this study has dangers and drawbacks of various kinds. It is difficult to put one's self at a point of view from which to judge one's fellows fairly. One of the great vices of history is the portrayal of men by what is bad in them rather than by what is good. It is from revolutions and catastrophes that it derives its interest. So long as a nation grows and prospers in the calm of peaceful government, history has nothing to say about it. It only begins to tell about nations when they are no longer self-sufficient and have got mixed up in their neighbours' affairs. It only records their story when they enter on their decline. Our historians all begin where they ought to finish. Only bad men achieve fame: the good are either forgotten or held up to ridicule. Like philosophy, history always slanders mankind.

Moreover, the facts described in history never give an exact picture of what actually happened. They change form in the historian's head. They get moulded by his interests and take on the hue of his prejudices. Who can put the reader at the precise point where an event can be seen just as it took place? Ignorance or partisanship distorts everything. Without even altering a single feature a quite different face can be put on events by a broader or a narrower view of the relevant circumstances. How often a tree more or less, a rock to the right or the left, a cloud of dust blown up by the wind, have decided the outcome of a battle without anybody being aware of it! But that does not prevent the historian telling you the causes of defeat or victory with as much assurance as if he had been everywhere himself. In any case, what do the facts matter when the reason for them is unknown? And what lessons can I draw from an event when I am ignorant of the real cause of it? The historian gives me an explanation, but it is his own invention. And is not criticism itself, of which there is so much talk, only an art of guessing, the art of choosing among various lies the one most like the truth?

I will be told that historical precision is of less consequence than the truth about men and manners. So long as the human heart is well depicted, it will be said, it does not greatly matter whether events are accurately narrated or not. That is right, if the pictures are drawn close enough to nature. If, however, most of them are coloured by the historian's imagination, we are back again to the difficulty we set out to avoid, and are allowing writers an authority which has been denied the teacher. If my pupil is only to see pictures of fancy, I prefer to have them traced by my own hand. They will at least be those best suited for him.

The worst historians for a young man are those who pass judgment. Give him the facts and let him judge for himself. That is how he will learn to know men. If he is always guided by some author's judgment, he only sees through another's eyes: when he lacks these eyes he cannot see. . . .

To all these considerations must be added the fact that history is more concerned with actions than with men. It takes men at certain chosen moments when they are in full dress. It only depicts the public man when he is prepared to be seen, and does not follow him into the intimacies of friendship and private life. It is the coat rather than the person that is portrayed.

I would much rather have the study of human nature begin with the reading of the life story of individual men. In these stories the historian gets on the track of the man, and there is no escape from his scrutiny. . . .

It is true that the genius of nations, or of men in association, is very different from the character of man as an individual; and the knowledge of human nature got without examination of the form it assumes in the multitude, would be very imperfect. But it is no less true that it is necessary to begin with the study of man in order to form a judgment about men, and that one who had a complete knowledge of the dispositions of the constituent individuals might be able to foresee their joint effects in the body politic. . . .

One step more and we reach the goal. Self-esteem is a useful instrument but it has its dangers. Often it wounds the hand that employs it and rarely does good without also doing evil. Emile, comparing himself with other human beings and finding himself very fortunately situated, will be tempted to give credit to his own reason for the work of his guardian, and to attribute to his own merit the effects of his good fortune. He will say: "I am wise, and men are foolish." This is the error most to be feared, because it is the one hardest to eradicate. If choice had to be made I do not know whether I would not prefer the illusion of prejudice to the illusion of pride.

There is no remedy for vanity but experience. It is doubtful indeed if it can be cured at all; but at any rate its growth may be checked when it appears. Do not waste your time on fine arguments and try to convince an adolescent that he is a man like other men and subject to the same weaknesses. Make him feel it for himself, or he will never learn it. Once again, I have to make an exception to my own rules, by deliberately exposing my pupil to the mischances which may prove to him that he is no wiser than the rest of us. I will let flatterers get the better of him. If fools were to entice him into some extravagance or other I would let him run the risk. I will allow him to be duped by card sharpers, and leave him to be swindled by them. The only snares from which I would guard him with special care would be those of prostitutes. Actually Emile would not be readily tempted in these ways. It should be kept in mind that my constant plan is to take things at their worst. I try in the first place to prevent the vice, and then I assume its existence in order to show how it can be remedied.

The time for faults is the time for fables. Censure of an offender under cover of a fiction gives instruction without offence. The young man learns in this way that the moral of the tale is not a lie, from the truth that finds application in his own case. The child who has never been deceived by flattery sees no point in the fable of *The Fox and the Crow*, but the silly person who has been gulled by a flatterer understands perfectly what a fool the crow was. From a fact he draws a moral, and the experience which would speedily have been forgotten is engraved in his mind by the fable. There is no moral knowledge which cannot be acquired either through the experience of other people or of ourselves. Where the experience is too dangerous for the young man to get it at first hand, the lesson can be drawn from history. When the test has no serious consequences it is good for him to be exposed to it and to have the particular cases known to him summed up as maxims. I do not mean, however, that these maxims should be expounded or even stated. The moral at the end of most fables is badly conceived. Before I put the inimitable fables of La Fontaine into the hands of a young man I would cut out all the conclusions in which he takes the trouble to explain what he had just said so clearly and agreeably. If your pupil does not understand the fable without the explanation, you can be sure that he will not understand it in any case. Only men can learn from fables and now is the time for Emile to begin.

When I see young people confined to the speculative studies at the most active time of life and then cast suddenly into the world of affairs without the least experience, I find it as contrary to reason as to nature and am not at all surprised that so few people manage their lives well. By some strange perversity we are taught all sorts of useless things, but nothing is done about the art of conduct. We are supposed to be getting trained for society but are taught as if each one of us were going to live a life of contemplation in a solitary cell. You think you are preparing children for life when you teach them certain bodily contortions and meaningless strings of words. I also have been a teacher of the art of conduct. I have taught my Emile to live his own life, and more than that to earn his own bread. But that is not enough. To live in the world one must get on with people and know how to get a hold on them. It is necessary also to be able to estimate the action and reaction of individual interests in civil society and so forecast events as to be rarely at fault in one's enterprises.

It is by doing good that we become good. I know of no surer way. Keep your pupil occupied with all the good deeds within his power. Let him help poor people with money and with service, and get justice for the oppressed. Active benevolence will lead him to reconcile the quarrels of his comrades and to be concerned about the sufferings of the afflicted. By putting his kindly feelings into action in this way and drawing his own conclusions from the outcome of his efforts, he will get a great deal of useful knowledge. In addition to college lore he will acquire the still more important ability of applying his knowledge to the purposes of life.

My readers, I foresee, will be surprised to see me take my pupil through the whole of the early years without mentioning religion. At fifteen he was not aware that he had a soul, and perhaps at eighteen it is not yet time for him to learn. For if he learns sooner than is necessary he runs the risk of never knowing.

My picture of hopeless stupidity is a pedant teaching the catechism to children. If I wanted to make a child dull I would compel him to explain what he says when he repeats his catechism. It may be objected that since most of the Christian doctrines are mysteries it would be necessary for the proper understanding of them to wait, not merely till the child becomes a man but till the man is no more. To that I reply, in the first place, that there are mysteries man can neither conceive nor believe and that I see no purpose in teaching them to children unless it be to teach them to lie. I say, further, that to admit there are mysteries one must understand that they are incomprehensible, and that this is an idea which is quite beyond children. For an age when all is mystery, there can be no mysteries, properly so-called.

Let us be on guard against presenting the truth to those unable to comprehend it. The effect of that is to substitute error for truth. It would be better to have no idea of the Divine Being than to have ideas that are mean, fantastic and unworthy. "I would rather people believed there was no Plutarch in the world," says the good Plutarch, "than that it should be said that he was unjust, envious, jealous, and such a tyrant that he exacts more than can be performed."

The worst thing about the distorted images of the Deity imprinted on children's minds, is that they endure all their lives, so that even when they grow up their God is still the God of their childhood. Every child who believes in God is an idolater, or rather he thinks of God in human shape. Once the imagination has seen God, it is very seldom that the understanding conceives Him. I once met in Switzerland a good pious mother who was so convinced of this that she would not teach her son religion in his early years, for fear he might be content with this crude instruction and neglect a better when he came to the age of reason. This child never heard God spoken about save with devotion and reverence, and he was silenced when he tried to speak of Him, on the ground that the subject was too great and too sublime for him. This reserve roused his curiosity, and his pride made him look forward to the time when he would know the mystery so carefully hidden from him. The less that was said about God the more he thought of Him. The child saw God everywhere. My own fear is that this air of mystery might excite a young man's imagination overmuch and turn his head so that he would become a fanatic rather than a believer.

But there is no fear of anything like that happening with my Emile. He always refuses to pay any attention to everything beyond his grasp and hears with indifference things he does not understand. When he does begin to be troubled by these great questions, it will not be because they have been put before him, but because the natural progress of his intelligence is taking his inquiries in that direction.

At this point I see a difficulty ahead: a difficulty all the greater because it is due less to the facts of the situation than to the cowardice of those who are afraid to face up to it. Let us at least be bold enough to state the problem. A child has to be brought up in his father's religion, and always gets ample proof that this religion, whatever it is, is the only true one, and all the others are absurd and ridiculous. In matters of religion more than in any other opinion triumphs. What then are we, who profess to cast off the yoke of opinion and seek to be independent of authority, to do about this? We do not wish to teach our Emile anything which he could not learn for himself in any country. In what religion are we to bring him up? With which sect is the man of nature to be connected? The answer it seems to me is very simple. We will not make him join this sect or that, but put him in the position to choose the one to which he himself is led by the best use of his reason. . . .

So long as we take no account of the authority of man or the prejudices of the country of our birth and educate according to nature, the light of reason by itself can lead us no further than to natural religion: and to that I confine myself with Emile. If he is to have another religion I have no longer the right to be his guide. The choice is his alone.

We are working in concert with nature. While she is forming the physical man we are seeking to form the moral man; but the two do not progress at the same rate. The body is already strong and sturdy while the soul remains dull and feeble, and in spite of all that human skill can do the temperament is always ahead of the reason. So far as we have gone our main endeavour has been to hold back the one side and bring on the other so that as far as possible the man we are training may be at one with himself. In developing his nature we have controlled his sensibility by cultivating the reason. By taking him to the essence of things we have saved him from the domination of the senses. It has been easy to lead him from the study of nature to the search for its Author.

In doing this we have gained a fresh hold on our pupil. It is only now that he has come to have a real interest in being good and doing good, whether anyone sees him or not and without the compulsion of law; and is concerned to be on right terms with God and do his duty whatever the cost. He has learned to cherish virtue not merely for the love of social order (which for all of us is subordinate to the love of self) but for the love of the Author of his being which enters into his self-love, so that in the end he may enjoy the lasting happiness which peace of conscience and the contemplation of God promise him in another life after he has made good use of the present life. . . .

Emile is not destined to remain a solitary forever. He is a member of society and must fulfil its obligations. Destined to live with men, he has to know them. He knows man in general already; the next thing is for him to know individual men. He knows what goes on in the world: the next thing is for him to know how people live in it. The time has come to take him to the front of that great stage, of which he already knows the hidden workings. He will not look on it now with the foolish wonder of a young dolt, but with the discrimination of a sober, straightforward, thinking man.

As there is a fitting time for the study of the sciences, so is there a time for getting a good understanding of the ways of the world. Anyone who learns these ways too young follows them without proper discrimination or reflection his whole life long. But one who learns them with an appreciation of the reasons for them, follows them with greater discernment and in consequence more exactly and more finely. Give me a child of twelve who knows nothing at all, and at fifteen I will give him back to you as wise as the one you have instructed from the beginning. The difference will be that your child will have his knowledge in his memory, while mine will have it in his judgment. Similarly a young man of twenty introduced into the world under proper guidance will become more agreeable and more refined in a year's time than one who has been brought up in it from the beginning.

You need a mate, I say to the young man. Let us go in search of one to suit you. We may not find her easily, since real merit is always rare. But we will not hurry, and we will not be discouraged. Without doubt there is such a person and in the end we will find her, or some one very like her. With this attractive project I introduce him into society. What need to say more?

You can see that in portraying the destined mistress I will be able to make dear and pleasing to him the qualities he ought to love, and set his mind against the things he should avoid. I would have to be very stupid if I did not rouse his passions in anticipation of the unknown woman. The fact that the picture I paint is an imaginary one is of no consequence. People are more in love with the image they make for themselves than with its object. To see what we love exactly as it is, would make an end of love on the earth. . . .

Let us now look at Emile as he enters into society, not to become a leader but to become acquainted with it and to find his mate. Whatever the rank into which he may be born, whatever the society he enters, his first appearance will be simple and unpretentious. He neither has nor desires the qualities that make an immediate impression. He sets too little store by the opinions of men to be concerned about their prejudices, and is not concerned to have people esteem him till they know him. His way of presenting himself is neither modest nor conceited, but just natural and sincere. He knows neither constraint nor concealment. He is the same in company as when he is alone. He speaks little, because he has no desire to attract notice. For the same reason he only speaks about things that are of practical value, being too well informed ever to be a babbler. Far from despising the ways of other people, he conforms quite readily to them: not for the sake of appearing versed in the conventions or affecting fashionable airs, but simply to avoid notice. He is never more at his ease than when nobody is paying him any attention.

When he studies the ways of men in society as he formerly studied their passions in history, he will often have occasion to reflect on the things that gratify or offend the human heart. This will lead him to philosophise on the principles of taste, and this is the study that is most fitting for this period of life.

There is no need to go far for a definition of taste. Taste is simply the faculty of judging what pleases or displeases the greatest number of people. This does not mean that there are more people of taste than others. For though the majority judge sanely about any particular thing, there are few who possess this sanity about everything. Taste is like beauty. Though the most general tastes put together make good taste, there are not many people of taste, just as beauty is constituted by an assemblage of the most common traits and yet there are few beautiful persons.

We are not concerned here with the things we like because they are useful, or dislike because they are harmful. Taste has nothing to do with the necessities of life: it applies to things which are indifferent to us or at most have the interest that goes with our amusements. This is what makes decisions of taste so difficult and seemingly so arbitrary. I should add that taste has local rules which make it dependent in very many ways on region, custom, government and institutions, as well as other rules relating to age, sex and character. That is why there can be no disputing about tastes.

Taste is natural to all men, but all do not possess it in equal measure. The degree of taste we may have depends on native sensibility: the form it takes under cultivation depends on the social groups in which we have lived. In the first place, it is necessary to live in numerous social groups and make many comparisons. In the second place, these must be groups for amusement and leisure, for in those that have to do with practical affairs it is interest and not pleasure that has to be considered. In the third place, there must not be too great inequality in the group and the tyranny of opinion must not be excessive: otherwise fashion stifles taste and people no longer desire what pleases but what gives distinction.

This matter of taste is one to which Emile cannot be indifferent in his present enquiries. The knowledge of what may be agreeable or disagreeable to men is essential to one who has need of them, and no less to one who wants to be useful to them. It is important to please people if you want to serve them. . . .

To keep his taste pure and healthy I will . . . arrange to have useful conversations with him, and by directing the talk to topics that please him I will make these conversations both amusing and instructive. Now is the time to read agreeable books, and to teach him to analyse speech and appreciate all the beauties of eloquence and diction. Contrary to the general belief, there is little to be gained from the study of languages for themselves; but the study of languages leads to the study of the general principles of grammar. It is necessary to know Latin to get a proper knowledge of French. To learn the rules of the art of speech we must study and compare the two languages.

There is moreover a certain simplicity of taste that goes to the heart, which is to be found only in the writings of the ancients. In oratory, in poetry, in every kind of literature, the pupil will find them, as in history, abundant in matter and sober in judgment. In contrast with this our authors talk much and say little. To be always accepting their judgment as right is not the way to acquire a judgment of our own. . . .

Generally speaking Emile will have more liking for the writings of the ancients than our own, for the good reason that coming first they are nearer nature and their genius is more distinctive. Whatever may be said to the contrary the human reason shows no advance. What is gained in one direction is lost in another. All minds start from the same point, and the time spent in learning what others think is so much time lost for learning to think for ourselves. As time goes on there is more acquired knowledge and less vigour of mind.

It is not for the study of morals but of taste that I take Emile to the theatre, for it is there above all that taste reveals itself to thinking people. "Give no thought to moral precepts," I will say to him: "it is not here that you will learn them." The theatre is not intended to give truth but to humour and amuse. Nowhere can the art of pleasing men and touching the human heart be so well learned. The study of drama leads to the study of poetry: their object is the same. If Emile has even a glimmering of taste for poetry he will cultivate Greek, Latin and Italian—the languages of the poets—with great pleasure. The study of them will give him unlimited entertainment, and will profit him all the more on that account. They will bring him delight at an age and in circumstances when the heart finds charm in every kind of beauty. Imagine on the one hand my Emile, and, on the other, some young college scamp, reading the Fourth Book of the *Aeneid*, or Tibullus, or Plato's *Banquet*. What a difference there is: the heart of the one stirred to its depth by something that does not impress the other at all. Stop the reading, young man: you are too greatly moved. I want you to find pleasure in the language of love, but not to be carried away by it. Be a man of feeling, but also a wise man. Actually, it is of no consequence whether Emile succeeds in the dead languages, in literature, in poetry or not. It would not matter greatly if he were ignorant of them all. His education is not really concerned with such diversions.

My main object in teaching him to feel and love beauty in every form is to fix his affections and his tastes on it and prevent his natural appetites from deteriorating so that he comes to look for the means of happiness in his wealth instead of finding it within himself. As I have said elsewhere, taste is simply the art of appreciating the little things, but since the pleasure of life depends on a multitude of little things such concern is not unimportant. It is by means of them that we come to enrich our lives with the good things at our disposal. . . .

## Book V

We have reached the last act in the drama of youth but the denouement has still to come.

It is not good for man to be alone. Emile is now a man. We must give him the mate we have promised him. The mate is Sophie. Once we know what kind of a person she is, we will know better where to find her and we will be able to complete our task.

Sophie should be as typically woman as Emile is man. She must possess all the characteristics of humanity and of womanhood which she needs for playing her part in the physical and the moral order. Let us begin by considering in what respects her sex and ours agree and differ.

In everything that does not relate to sex the woman is as the man: they are alike in organs, needs and capacities. In whatever way we look at them the difference is only one of less or more. In everything that relates to sex there are correspondences and differences. The difficulty is to determine what in their constitution is due to sex and what is not. All we know with certainty is that the common features are due to the species and the differences to sex. From this twofold point of view we find so many likenesses and so many contrasts that we cannot but marvel that nature has been able to create two beings so much alike with constitutions so different.

The sameness and the difference cannot but have an effect on mentality. This is borne out by experience and shows the futility of discussions about sex superiorities and inequalities. A perfect man and a perfect woman should no more resemble each other in mind than in countenance: and perfection does not admit of degrees.

In the mating of the sexes each contributes in equal measure to the common end but not in the same way. From this diversity comes the *first* difference which has to be noted in their personal relations. It is the part of the one to be active and strong, and of the other to be passive and weak. Accept this principle and it follows in the *second* place that woman is intended to please man. If the man requires to please the woman in turn the necessity is less direct. Masterfulness is his special attribute. He pleases by the very fact that he is strong. This is not the law of love, I admit. But it is the law of nature, which is more ancient than love.

If woman is made to please and to be dominated, she ought to make herself agreeable to man and avoid provocation. Her strength is in her charms and through them she should constrain him to discover his powers and make use of them. The surest way of bringing these powers into active operation is to make it necessary by her resistance. In this way self-esteem is added to desire and the man triumphs in the victory which the woman has compelled him to achieve. Out of this relation comes attack and defence, boldness on the one side and timidity on the other, and in the end the modesty and sense of shame with which nature has armed the weak for the subjugation of the strong.

Hence as a *third* consequence of the different constitution of the sexes, the stronger may appear to be master, and yet actually be dependent on the weaker: not because of a superficial practice of gallantry or the prideful generosity of the protective sex, but by reason of an enduring law of nature. By giving woman the capacity to stimulate desires greater than can be satisfied, nature has made man dependent on woman's good will and constrained him to seek to please her as a condition of her submission. Always there remains for man in his conquest the pleasing doubt whether strength has mastered weakness, or there has been a willing subjection; and the woman has usually the guile to leave the doubt unresolved.

Men and women are unequally affected by sex. The male is only a male at times; the female is a female all her life and can never forget her sex.

Plato in his *Republic* gives women the same physical training as men. That is what might be expected. Having made an end of private families in his state and not knowing what to do with the women, he found himself compelled to make men of them. That wonderful genius provided for everything in his plans, and went out of his way to meet an objection that nobody was likely to make, while missing the real objection. I am not speaking about the so-called community of wives, so often charged against him by people who have not read him. What I refer to is the social promiscuity which ignored the differences of sex by giving men and women the same occupations, and sacrificed the sweetest sentiments of nature to the artificial sentiment of loyalty which could not exist without them. He did not realise that the bonds of convention always develop from some natural attachment: that the love one has for his neighbours is the basis of his devotion to the state; that the heart is linked with the great fatherland through the little fatherland of the home; that it is the good son, the good husband, the good father, that makes the good citizen.

Once it has been shown that men and women are essentially different in character and temperament, it follows that they ought not to have the same education. In accordance with the direction of nature they ought to co-operate in action, but not to do the same things. To complete the attempt we have been making to form the man of nature, we must now go on to consider how the fitting mate for him is to be formed.

If you want right guidance, always follow the leadings of nature. Everything that characterises sex should be respected as established by nature. Men's pride leads them astray when, comparing women with themselves, they say, as they are continually doing, that women have this or that defect, which is absent in men. What would be defects in men are good qualities in women, which are necessary to make things go on well. Women on their side never stop complaining that we men make coquettes of them and keep amusing them with trifles in order to maintain our ascendency. What a foolish idea! When have men ever had to do with the education of girls? Who prevents the mothers bringing up their daughters as they please? Are we men to blame if girls please us by their beauty and attract us by the art they have learned from their mothers? Well, try to educate them like men. They will be quite willing. But the more they resemble men the less will be their power over men, and the greater their own subjection.

The faculties common to the sexes are not equally shared between them; but take them all in all, they are well balanced. The more womanly a woman is, the better. Whenever she exercises her own proper powers she gains by it: when she tries to usurp ours she becomes our inferior. Believe me, wise mother, it is a mistake to bring up your daughter to be like a good man. Make her a good woman, and you can be sure that she will be worth more for herself and for us. This does not mean that she should be brought up in utter ignorance and confined to domestic tasks. A man does not want to make his companion a servant and deprive himself of the peculiar charms of her company. That is quite against the teaching of nature, which has endowed women with quick pleasing minds. Nature means them to think, to judge, to love, to know and to cultivate the mind as well as the countenance. This is the equipment nature has given them to compensate for their lack of strength and enable them to direct the strength of men.

As I see it, the special functions of women, their inclinations and their duties, combine to suggest the kind of education they require. Men and women are made for each other but they differ in the measure of their dependence on each other. We could get on better without women than women could get on without us. To play their part in life they must have our willing help, and for that they must earn our esteem. By the very law of nature women are at the mercy of men's judgments both for themselves and or their children. It is not enough that they should be estimable: they must be esteemed. It is not enough that they should be beautiful: they must be pleasing. It is not enough that they should be wise: their wisdom must be recognised. Their honour does not rest on their conduct but on their reputation. Hence the kind of education they get should be the very opposite of men's in this respect. Public opinion is the tomb of a man's virtue but the throne of a woman's.

On the good constitution of the mothers depends that of the children and the early education of men is in their hands. On women too depend the morals, the passions, the tastes, the pleasures, aye and the happiness of men. For this reason their education must be wholly directed to their relations with men. To give them pleasure, to be useful to them, to win their love and esteem, to train them in their childhood, to care for them when they grow up, to give them counsel and consolation, to make life sweet and agreeable for them: these are the tasks of women in all times for which they should be trained from childhood. . . .

Children of the two sexes have many amusements in common, and that is right since it will be the same when they grow up. But they have also distinctive tastes. Boys like movement and noise: their toys are drums, tops and go-carts. Girls would rather have things that look well and serve for adornment: mirrors, jewels, dress materials and most of all dolls. The doll is the special plaything of the sex. Here the girl's liking is plainly directed towards her lifework. For her the art of pleasing finds its physical expression in dress. That is all a child can acquire of this art.

Look at the little girl, busy with her doll all day long, changing its trappings, dressing and undressing it hundreds of times, always on the outlook for new ways of decoration whether good or bad. Her fingers are clumsy and her taste unformed, but already her bent is evident. "But," you may say, "she is dressing her doll, not herself." No doubt! The fact is that she sees her doll and not herself. For the time being she herself does not matter. She is absorbed in the doll and her coquetry is expressed through it. But the time will come when she will be her own doll.

Here then right at the beginning is a well-marked taste. You have only to follow it up and give it direction. What the little one wishes most of all is to decorate her doll, to make bows, tippets, sashes, lacework for it. In all this she has to depend on the good will of others for help and it would be more convenient in every way if she could do it herself. Here is a motive for the first lessons given to her. They are not tasks prescribed for her but favours conferred. As a matter of fact nearly all little girls greatly dislike learning to read and write but they are always willing to learn to use the needle. They imagine themselves grown up and think happily of the time when they will be using their talents in adorning themselves.

This first open road is easy to follow. Tapestry which is the amusement of women is not much to the liking of girls, and furnishings, having nothing to do with the person, are remote from their interests. But needlework, embroidery and lacemaking come readily to them. The same willing progress leads on easily to drawing, for this art is not unrelated to that of dressing one's self with good taste. I would not have girls taught to draw landscape or to do figure painting. It will be enough if they draw leaves, flowers, fruit, draperies, anything that can add to the elegance of dress and enable them to make their own embroidery patterns. If it is important for men to confine their studies in the main to everyday knowledge, it is even more important for women whose way of life, though less laborious, does not permit them to devote themselves to the talent of their choice at the expense of their duties.

Whatever the humorists may say, good sense is common to the two sexes. Girls are generally more docile than boys and in any case have more need to be brought under authority. But this does not mean that they should be required to do things without seeing the use of them. The maternal art is to make evident the purpose of everything that is prescribed to them; and this is all the easier to do since the girl's intelligence is more precocious than the boy's. This principle excludes for both boys and girls not only studies which serve no obvious purpose but even those which only become useful at a later stage. If it is wrong to urge a boy to learn to read it is even worse to compel little girls to do so before making them realise the value of reading. After all what need have girls to read and write at an early age? They are not going to have a household to manage for a long time to come. All of them have curiosity enough to make sure that they will learn without compulsion when leisure and the occasion come. Possibly they should learn to count first of all. Counting has an obvious utility at all stages and much practice is required to avoid errors in calculation. I guarantee that if a little girl does not get cherries at tea-time till she has performed some arithmetical exercise she will very soon learn to count.

Always justify the tasks you impose on young girls but impose them all the same. Idleness and indocility are their most dangerous faults and are most difficult to cure once they are contracted. Not only should girls be careful and industrious but they should be kept under control from an early age. This hardship, if it be a hardship, is inseparable from their sex. All their lives they will be under the hard, unceasing constraints of the proprieties. They must be disciplined to endure them till they come to take them as a matter of course and learn to overcome caprice and bow to authority. If they are inclined to be always busy they should sometimes be compelled to do nothing whatever. To save them from dissipation, caprice and fickleness they must learn above all to master themselves.

Do not let girls get bored with their occupations and turn too keen on their amusements, as happens in the ordinary education where, as Fénelon says, all the boredom is on the one side and all the pleasure on the other. A girl will only be bored with her tasks if she gets on badly with the people around her. A little one who loves her mother or some darling friend will work in their company day in day out and never become tired. The constraint put on the child, so far from weakening the affection she has for her mother, will make it stronger; for dependence is a state natural to women, and girls realise that they are made for obedience.

And just because they have, or ought to have, little freedom, they carry the freedom they have to excess. Extreme in all things, they devote themselves to their play with greater zeal than boys. This is the second defect. This zeal must be kept within bounds. It is the cause of several vices peculiar to women, among others the capricious changing of their tastes from day to day. Do not deprive them of mirth, laughter, noise and romping games, but prevent them tiring of one game and turning to another. They must get used to being stopped in the middle of their play and put to other tasks without protest on their part. This daily constraint will produce the docility that women need all their lives. The first and most important quality of a woman is sweetness. Being destined to obey a being so imperfect as man (often with many vices and always with many shortcomings), she must learn to submit uncomplainingly to unjust treatment and marital wrongs. Not for his sake but for her own she must preserve her sweetness.

Girls should always be submissive, but mothers should not always be inexorable. To make a young person docile there is no call to make her unhappy. Indeed I should not be sorry if sometimes she were allowed to exercise a little cunning, not to elude punishment but to escape having to obey. Guile is a natural gift of her sex; and being convinced that all natural dispositions are good and right in themselves I think that this one should be cultivated like the rest. The characteristic cunning with which women are endowed is an equitable compensation for their lesser strength. Without it women would not be the comrade of man but his slave. This talent gives her the superiority that keeps her his equal and enables her to rule him even while she obeys. . . .

It is well to keep in mind that up to the age when reason becomes active and the growth of sentiment makes conscience speak, good or bad for young women is only what those around them so regard. What they are told to do is good: what they are forbidden is bad. That is all they have to know. From this it is evident how important is the choice of those who are to be with them and exercise authority over them, even more than in the case of boys. But in due course the moment will come when they begin to form their own judgment and then the plan of their education must be changed. We cannot leave them with social prejudices as the only law of their lives. For all human beings there is a rule of conduct which comes before public opinion. All other rules are subject to the inflexible direction of this rule. Even prejudices must be judged by it, and it is only in so far as the values of men are in accord with it that they are entitled to have authority over us. This rule is conscience, the inner conviction (*sentiment*). Unless the two rules are in concord in women's education, it is bound to be defective. Personal conviction without regard for public opinion will fail to give them that fineness of soul which puts the hallmark of worldly honour on good conduct; and public opinion lacking personal conviction will only make false, dishonest women with a sham virtue. For the co-ordination of the two guides to right living, women need to cultivate a faculty to arbitrate between them, to prevent conscience going astray on the one hand and correct the errors of prejudice on the other. This faculty is reason. But at the mention of reason all sorts of questions arise. Are women capable of sound reasoning? Is it necessary for them to cultivate it? If they do cultivate it, will it be of any use to them in the functions imposed on them? Is it compatible with a becoming simplicity?

The reason that brings a man to a knowledge of his duties is not very complex. The reason that brings a woman to hers is simpler still. The obedience and loyalty she owes to her husband and the tender care she owes her children are such obvious and natural consequences of her position that she cannot without bad faith refuse to listen to the inner sentiment which is her guide, nor fail to recognise her duty in her natural inclination. Since she depends on her own conscience and on the opinion of other people she must learn to compare and harmomise the two rules. This can best be done by cultivating her understanding and her reason.

Let us now look at the picture of Sophie which has been put before Emile, the image he has of the woman who can make him happy.

Sophie is well born and has a good natural disposition. She has a feeling heart which sometimes makes her imagination difficult to control. Her mind is acute rather than precise: her temper easy but variable; her person ordinary but pleasing. Her countenance gives indication of a soul—with truth. Some girls have good qualities she lacks and others have the qualities she possesses in fuller measure; but none has these qualities better combined in a happy character. Without being very striking, she interests and charms, and it is difficult to say why. . . .

Let us give Emile his Sophie. Let us bring this sweet girl to life . . . A pupil of nature like Emile, she is better suited for him than any other woman. She is indeed his woman, his equal in birth and merit, his inferior in fortune. Her special charm only reveals itself gradually, as one comes to know her, and her husband will appreciate it more than anyone. Her education is in no way exceptional. She has taste without study, talents without art, judgment without knowledge. Her mind is still vacant but has been trained to learn: it is well-tilled land only waiting for the grain. What a pleasing ignorance! Happy is the man destined to instruct her. She will be her husband's disciple, not his teacher. Far from wanting to impose her tastes on him, she will share his. It is time they met. . . .

If I go into the simple, unsophisticated story of their innocent love I will be considered frivolous, but that is a mistake. Not sufficient consideration is given to the influence of the first relations of man and woman on the whole course of the future lives of both. People do not realise the lasting effect of an experience so vivid as the first love, throughout the years, on to death. We are given in educational treatises long wordy discourses on the imaginery duties of children, but not a word is spoken about the most important and most difficult part of their education, the crisis which marks the transition from child to adult. If I have been specially helpful in this book it will be because I have dealt at length with this essential matter which others omit, and have not allowed myself to be diverted from this enterprise by false delicacy or the difficulty of finding fitting language.

Once he is Sophie's accepted lover and has become really anxious to please her, Emile begins to realise the value of the agreeable talents which he has acquired. Sophie is fond of singing. He sings with her: more than that, he teaches her music. She is lively and nimble and is fond of skipping. He dances with her and changes her steps into perfect dance movements. These lessons are charming and are inspired by a light-hearted gaiety. It is right for a lover to be the master of his mistress.

There is an old harpsichord which is in very bad condition. Emile mends it and puts it in tune. It has always been his rule to learn to do everything he can for himself, where possible: he is an instrument maker and mender as well as a carpenter. The house is in a picturesque situation. He makes various drawings of it with some help from Sophie, for her father's room. When she sees Emile drawing she imitates him and improves her own drawing. She cultivates all her talents, and her charm embellishes them.

It is both touching and funny to see. Emile bent on teaching Sophie everything he knows, regardless of whether she wants to learn or whether it is suitable for her. He talks to her about everything, and explains things with boyish eagerness. He assumes that he has only to talk and immediately she will listen. He looks forward to discussing things with her and regards everything he has learned which cannot be told to her as of no account. He almost blushes at the thought of knowing something she does not know.

Here then is Emile teaching her philosophy, physics, mathematics, history, everything in fact. She lends herself with pleasure to his zeal, and tries to profit by it. The art of thinking is not alien to women, but they only need a nodding acquaintance with logic and metaphysics. Sophie forms some idea of everything, but most of what she learns is soon forgotten. She makes best progress in matters of conduct and taste. In the case of physics she has only a limited idea of the general laws and system of the universe. Sometimes when the pair contemplate the wonders of nature in the course of their walks their pure and innocent hearts seek to rise to its Author and they fearlessly pour out their hearts before Him together. . . .

One morning when they had not seen each other for two days I went into Emile's room with a letter in my hand. Looking at him fixedly, I said: "What would you do if someone were to inform you that Sophie is dead?" He gave a loud cry, sprang up and struck his hands, and without a word looked at me with haggard eyes. "Reassure yourself," I said; "she is alive and well, and we are expected tonight. Let us go for a short stroll and we can talk things over. We must be happy, dear Emile," I said. "Happiness is the end of every sentient being. It is the first desire impressed on us by nature and the only one that never leaves us. But where is happiness to be found? Nobody knows. Everybody seeks it: nobody finds it. All through life we pursue it, but die without attaining it. If you want to live happily fix your heart on the beauty that never perishes. Let your desires be limited by your condition in life and put your duties before your inclinations. Extend the law of necessity into the sphere of morals and learn to lose whatever can be taken from you, and to rise above the chances of life. Then you will be happy in spite of fortune and wise in spite of passion. In the good things that are most fragile you will find a pleasure that nothing can disturb. They will not possess you but you will possess them; and you will discover that in this passing world man only enjoys what he is ready to give up. You will not have the illusion of imaginary pleasures, it is true, but neither will you suffer the sorrows that attend them. When you no longer attach an undue importance to life you will pass your own life untroubled and come to the end of it without fear. Others, terror-stricken, may believe that when death comes they will cease to be. You, being aware of the nothingness of this life, will know that the real life is just beginning."

Emile listened with anxious attention. He foresaw the hard discipline to which I had it in mind to subject him. "What must I do?" he asked, with eyes downcast. "You must leave Sophie. Sophie is not yet eighteen and you are barely twenty-two. This is the age for love but not for marriage. You are too young to be the father and mother of a family. Do you not know how premature motherhood can weaken the constitution, ruin the health and shorten the life of young women? When mother and child are both growing and the substance needed for the growth of each of them has to be shared between the two, neither get what nature meant them to get. As for yourself, have you given proper thought to the duties you undertake when you become a husband and a father? When you become the head of a family you become a member of the state. Do you know what that involves? You have studied the duties of a man but do you know what the duties of a citizen are? Do you know what is meant by 'government,' 'laws,' 'country'? Do you know the price that has to be paid for life and the causes for which you must be ready to die? Before entering the civil order seek to realise and understand what is your proper place in it."

Emile stood silent for a moment, then looked at me steadily: "When do we start?" he said. "In a week's time," I replied. Sophie I consoled and reassured. Let her keep faith with him as he would with her, and I swear that they will be married in two years' time.

The question is much discussed whether it is good for young people to travel. A better way of putting it would be to ask whether it is enough for an educated man to know only his own countrymen. For my part I am firmly convinced that anyone who only knows the people among whom he lives does not know mankind. But even admitting the utility of travel, does it follow that it is good for everybody? Far from it. It is only good for the few people who are strong enough in themselves to listen to the voice of error and not let themselves be seduced, and see examples of vice and not be led astray. Travel develops the natural bent and makes a man either good or bad. More come back bad than good because more start off with an inclination to badness. But those who are well born and have a good nature which has been well trained, those who travel with a definite purpose of learning, all come back better than they went away. That applies to my Emile.

Everything done rationally should have its rules. This holds good for travel, considered as a part of education. To travel merely for the sake of travelling is to wander about like a vagabond. Even to travel for instruction is too vague a matter. A journey without some definite aim is of no use. I would give a young man an obvious interest in learning, and this interest (if well chosen) would in turn fix the nature of the instruction. After he has considered his physical relations with the world and his moral relations with other men, it remains for him to consider his civic relations with his compatriots. For this he must study the nature of government in general, then the different forms of government, and finally the particular government under which he has been born, in order to know whether it is the one suited for him. By a right which nothing can annul, every man when he reaches his majority and becomes his own master is entitled to renounce the contract by which he is bound to the community and leave the country of his birth. It is only by staying on in that country after coming to the age of reason that he is judged to confirm tacitly the engagement made by his ancestors. Yet the place of his birth being a gift of nature, he gives up something of his own if he renounces it.

Here is what I would say to Emile. "Up to this time you have not been your own master but have lived under my direction. You are coming to the age when the law allows you the control of your property and makes you master of your person. You have in mind establishing a household of your own, and that is as it should be: it is one of the duties of a man. But before you marry you must know what kind of man you want to be, how you mean to spend your life, what measures you are going to take to ensure a living for yourself and your family. Are you willing to depend on men you despise? Are you willing to have your fortune and your social position determined by civil relations which will subject you for all time to the discretion of other people?" Next, I would describe to him all the different ways of turning his possessions to account in commerce, in public office, in finance, and show him that in every case his position would be precarious and dependent. There is another way of employing his time and himself, I would tell him. You can join the army and hire yourself out at a very high rate to go and kill people who never did you any harm. But far from making you independent of other resources, this job only makes them more necessary for you.

It may be surmised that none of these occupations will be greatly to Emile's taste. "Do you think I have forgotten the games of my childhood," he will say to me. "Have I lost my arms? Has my strength failed? Can I no longer work? All the property I want is a little farm in some corner of the world. My only ambition will be to work it and live free from worry. With Sophie and my land I will be rich." "You speak of your own land, dear Emile. But where are you going to find it? In what corner of the earth can you say: 'I am my own master and master of the ground I occupy?' There are places where a man can become rich: none where he can spend his life without riches. Nowhere is it possible to live a free and independent life, doing ill to no one, fearing ill from no one. Your plan, Emile, is a fine one and an honourable one, and it would certainly bring you happiness. Let us do our best to realise it. I have a proposal to make. Let us devote the two years till you are due to return to Sophie to looking for a place of refuge somewhere in Europe where you can live happily with your family, secure from danger. If we succeed you will have found the happiness which is sought in vain by so many others. If we do not succeed, you will be cured of an illusion. You will console yourself for an unavoidable evil, and submit to the law of necessity."

The time has come to draw to an end. We must bring Emile back to Sophie. We have spent almost two years going through some of the great states of Europe and many of the small ones. We have learned two or three of the chief languages. We have seen the unusual things in natural history, government, arts and men. Emile, consumed with impatience, calls my attention to the fact that the time is nearly up. Then I say to him: "Well, my friend, you remember the main object of our travels. What conclusions have you reached after all your observations?" Unless I have been wrong in my method he will answer something like this: "What conclusion? To remain the kind of person you have trained me to be, and not to add by my own will any bonds to those which nature and the laws have put on me. The more I examine the work of men in their institutions, the more I see that in seeking independence they make themselves slaves. To avoid being carried away by the torrent of things they form a thousand attachments: then when they try to take a step forward they are surprised to find themselves being held back. It seems to me that the way to become free is just to do nothing, and give up trying to be free. You yourself, master, have made me free by teaching me to yield to necessity. What matters the fortune left me by my parents? I will begin by not depending on it. If I am allowed I will keep it: if it is taken from me I will not let myself be carried away with it. Rich or poor I will be free. What does my earthly condition matter? Wherever there are men I am among brothers: where there are none I have still my own home. If my belongings enslave me I will give them up without hesitation. I can work for my living. Whatever time death comes I will defy it. Having accepted things as they are I will never need to struggle against destiny. There is one and only one chain I shall always wear, and in that I will glory. Give me Sophie, and I am free."

"My dear Emile," I reply, "I am very pleased to hear you speak like a man. Before you set out on your travels I knew what the outcome would be. I knew that when you made acquaintance with our institutions you would not be tempted to put greater confidence in them than they deserve. Men vainly aspire to freedom under safeguard of the laws. Liberty is not to be found in any form of government. It is in the heart of the free man. He takes it with him everywhere. If I were to speak to you about the duties of citizenship you would perhaps ask me 'Where is my country?' and think you had confounded me. You would be wrong, however. You must not say: 'What does it matter to me where I live?' It does matter than you should be where you can fulfil all your duties as a man, and one of these duties is to be loyal to the place of your birth. Your fellow-countrymen protected you in childhood. They are entitled to your love when you become a man. You should live among them, or wherever you can be most useful to them. For that, I am not urging you to go and reside in a big town. On the contrary, one of the examples good men can give to others is that of a patriarchal life in the country. That was the first life of man, and still the finest and most natural to those with unspoiled hearts." I like to think how Emile and Sophie in their simple retreat may spread benefits around them, putting fresh life into the country and reviving the worn-out spirits of unfortunate villagers.

At last I see approaching the most delightful day in Emile's life and the happiest in mine. I see the crown set on my labours. The goodly couple are united in an indissoluble bond. Their lips utter and their hearts confirm enduring vows. They are wedded.

"My children," I say to them as I take them both by the hand, "it is three years since I saw the beginnings of the ardent love that makes you happy today. It has gone on growing steadily, and I see from your eyes that now it has reached its greatest intensity. After this it can only decline." My readers can imagine the indignant vows of Emile, and the scornful air with which Sophie withdraws her hand from mine, and the protesting glances of mutual adoration they exchange. I let them have their way, and then I proceed. "I have often thought that if it were possible to prolong the happiness of love in marriage we would have a heaven on earth. Would you like me to tell you what in my belief is the only way to secure that?" They look at each other with a mocking smile. "It is simple and easy," I continue. "It is to go on being lovers after you are married." "That will not be hard for us," says Emile, laughing at my secret. "Perhaps harder than you think," I reply. "Knots which are too tightly drawn break. That is what happens to the marriage tie when too great a strain is put on it. The faithfulness required of a married couple is the most sacred of all obligations but the power it gives one partner over the other is too great. Constraint and love go ill together, and the pleasures of marriage are not to be had on demand. It is impossible to make a duty of tender affection and to treat the sweetest pledges of love as a right. What right there is comes from mutual desire: nature knows no other. Neither belongs to the other except by his or her own good will. Both must remain master of their persons and their caresses.

"When Emile became your husband, Sophie, he became your head and by the will of nature you owe him obedience. But when the wife is like you it is good for the husband to be guided by her: that is also the law of nature and it gives you as much authority over his heart as his sex gives him over your person. Make yourself dear to him by your favours and respected by your refusals. On these terms you will get his confidence; he will listen to your advice and settle nothing without consulting you. After love has lasted a considerable time a sweet habit takes its place, and the attraction of confidence succeeds the transports of passion. When you cease to be Emile's mistress you will be his wife and sweetheart and the mother of his children, and you will enjoy the closest intimacy. Remember that if your husband lives happily with you, you will be a happy woman."

"Dear Emile," I say to the young husband, "all through life a man has need of a counsellor and guide. Up to the present I have tried to fulfil that duty to you. At this point my lengthy task comes to an end and another takes it over. Today I abdicate the authority you have allowed me. From this time on, Sophie is your tutor."

Gradually the first rapture calms down and leaves them to experience in peace the delights of their new state. Happy lovers, worthy spouses! How often I am enraptured as I contemplate my work in them, and my heart beats quicker. How often I take their hands in mine, blessing Providence and uttering heartfelt sighs; and they in their turn are affected and share my transports. If happiness is to be found anywhere in earth, it is to be found in the retreat where we live.

Some months later Emile comes into my room and embraces me. "Master," he says, "congratulate your boy. He hopes soon to have the honour to be a father. There will be new cares for us and for you. I do not mean to let you bring up the son as you have brought up the father. God forbid that a task so sweet and holy should fall to any one but me. But remain the teacher of the young teachers. Advise and direct us, and we will be ready to learn. I will have need of you as long as I live. I need you more than ever now that the tasks of my manhood are beginning. You have completed your own tasks. Lead me to imitate you, and enjoy your well-earned rest."

# Afterword

## William Boyd*

Having followed Emile in his educational career from birth to marriage, we have now to look back and ask what there was in this romantic tale to impress so many of Rousseau's contemporaries and give a new direction to education up to our own time. The question is easier to answer for the eighteenth century than for the twentieth. At the time of its composition, Rousseau was living insecurely among people of wealth and rank, whose families were all being educated tutorially at home. The book in its present form was intended for the edification and entertainment of some of his patronesses, for whom he turned what was originally meant to be a treatise into a kind of a story that would serve to enlighten them about the education of their families. The general scheme was certainly different from the ordinary practice in some respects, but not nearly so different as it is from ours. The story form of the exposition, it is true, presented some difficulty. Did Rousseau mean the story to be taken literally? Did he think that boys and girls should be, or could be, educated like Emile and Sophie? When asked, Rousseau sometimes said "Yes" and sometimes said "No." Actually there was no reason for not saying "Yes." The tutor acting *in loco parentis* and demanding complete authority made an obvious difficulty. But as Rousseau himself made clear at the beginning and again at the end of the book, the tutor was incidental to the story and not essential to it. The real educators in a "natural" education, he was careful to insist, were the father and mother. In the good family, there is just such a control of conditions and just such individual guidance to the child as the symbolical tutor provides in the *Emile.* . . .

What . . . is the enduring lesson of the *Emile*? . . .

The tutor and the tutorial education under country conditions had their place in the aristocratic way of life in the eighteenth century, but they are merely incidents in Rousseau's discussion of education. The big truth in his view, the truth that gives it application to the education of the children of all times and all conditions, is that the educator should take full account of human nature, and especially the nature of the child. Begin by studying the child, he said; and by not merely saying it, but by trying to do it himself in this book about Emile, he impressed the idea on all subsequent education.

The task he set himself and us was not an easy one. There is a seeming simplicity about the

* William Boyd was Reader in Education at the University of Glasgow.

idea of making education conform to nature. It can be translated into everyday language as a call to use common sense and see the foolishness of social usages which have lost their meaning and possibly have even become harmful. The insistence by Rousseau on sensible methods of feeding and clothing babies, and again on the learning of some trade in the teens as an insurance against an uncertain future, illustrates its value. But get deeper down into the maxim, and philosophical and scientific problems, not to mention problems of practice, make their appearance. Leaving aside the question of what "nature" is, we may ask what is "human nature?" What again is implied in speaking of the "nature" of the child? Rousseau has his own answers to these questions, and he gives them in a way that challenges us to agreement or disagreement.

In the forefront of his theory of life is his conviction that man in himself, man as a natural being, is good. Here he breaks with the Calvinism of Geneva: according to him if man in society is bad, it is not because he is bad by nature but because he has been made bad by society. Actually the goodness with which he credits man is of a rather neutral kind. It is not that child or man can be allowed to do what he likes and that he will inevitably take the right course, but rather that if he is not led into vice or error by others he will come to make the right adaptation to the necessities of the natural and the social worlds, and so reach truth and virtue. The way of the good life is a hard way: happiness can only be achieved by keeping desire within the limits imposed by the nature of things. The educational implication of this doctrine for Rosseau are interesting. The postulate of the scheme is that in man there is an active principle at work. The child does not become good or intelligent by having the habits or the opinions of society imposed on him. What he does or knows should be the outcome of a personal reaction on life situations. The truth for me is what I have convinced myself is true: the good I appreciate by the inner light. The difficulty is that such response as a child can make to life is limited to sense-given facts. The ordinary instruction supplies him with ready-made habits and views ahead of the time when he can understand things and form his own judgments. That in Rousseau's opinion is what makes it bad. What is learned at second-hand in this way prevents him learning things for himself when he attains the necessary maturity. Better therefore no education than one that prejudices the future development like this. There is plenty of time for morals and science when the mind is able to do its proper work. Indoctrination is always wrong.

The realisation of the difference between child and man is fundamental in the new education Rousseau advocated. To take proper account of the child's nature at its different stages, it is necessary to make such a study of childhood as no one had even attempted before his time. What are the essential differences between a child of 2 and a child of 10? Between a child of 10, and one of 16 or 18 or 20? These are hard questions to answer, and it cannot be said that Rousseau or any of his successors has been altogether successful in answering them. But in trying to define the mental changes which take place as the child grows by successive changes into manhood he made some important advances towards a dynamic psychology. He still talked as if the mind were made up of a number of separate faculties, which appear one after another: sensations in infancy, sense judgments in childhood, practical thinking in the early teens, reasoning and abstraction in adolescence. But in contrast with the materialistic philosophers with whom he shared this faculty psychology, he recognised the existence of a co-ordinating self that is active at all stages of life. While he emphasised the fact that it was the child's right to live a full life as a child and professed himself indifferent to his future occupation, he knew quite well that the child needs the right kind of training for manhood. Thinking in terms of mental self-activity, he anticipated later psychology by connecting physical and mental energy. It is the powers set free by the growth of the body in the early teens that extend the child's intellectual horizon. Even more important, it is the physical changes of puberty that bring about the manifold transformations of adolescence. Rousseau's discussion of adolescence from this point of view was a revolutionary event in educational thought.

It is easy to criticise much of what Rousseau wrote about the education of the child at the different periods of immature life. It is evident to us now that in stressing the differences between one period and another he did less than justice to the continuity of growth; that in fact he met the one-sidedness of common practice which ignores these differences with a one-sidedness of his own. Children are adults in the making: children have their rights as children and their own way of life. There is truth in both views. But as happens with adults, always more concerned about their own side of the relation with children, the half-truth most needing attention is the one with which Rousseau challenged his own age and still challenges ours. The new education he initiated attempts to secure a proper balance by trying to take into account the distinctive nature of the child in the education that fits him for society. Its aim is to make both man and citizen, but it gives special thought to the making of the man.

The problem of effecting a reconciliation of the interests of society and the individual with which Rousseau wrestles in the *Emile* is still with us. It is in fact the problem of democracy, and of the schooling which prepares boys and girls for the democratic way of life; and we all of us are democratic enough to take it for granted that home and school and the adult communities to which we belong should bring personal satisfaction through our membership of them. The problem has been largely solved in the good home, and we are trying to solve it in the good school. What help has Rousseau to give us here? Does his discussion of curriculum and methods in the *Emile*, when taken out of its story setting, have any useful applications in the work of the modern school?

Let us begin with his scheme for education in boyhood in Book Two. The emphasis here is largely on what he calls "negative education"—on the habits and ideas the boy is not to acquire. There are really two different lines of thought in this, and it is important to distinguish them. The one is that it only does harm to children to teach them things that are beyond personal comprehension and appreciation. If history or literature or morals or religion need a mature mind to have significance—as Rousseau firmly believes—they can only be taught verbally in childhood, and the verbal learning will prejudice the deeper experiences of later life. The other line is that even if it is possible to teach children to read or write or count, it is a mistake to do so before they are conscious of the need for them. The only satisfactory motive for learning is the interest on the level of childhood that comes from realised need. With the latter, intelligent teachers are in the main agreed: the practical difficulty experienced in putting the idea into practice is met (up to a point) by some form of the project method, in which the learner is set to a task of his own choosing which makes it necessary for him to read, write or count. The former raises more serious issues, because it runs counter to the universal practice of indoctrinating children with the great social ideals and faiths. Children, we say, must learn to be good. They must have impressed on them the best things in our social heritage; science, art, literature, music. They must be brought up in the religious faith of their fathers. But what if the children are not really learning the lessons we think we are teaching them? Take history, for example: what can immature persons of limited knowledge, and possibly of limited intelligence, make of the complex sequences and interrelations of events that constitute any great social movement, or of the personalities of those taking part in them? Or again think of religion with its combination of dogma and worship; what personal meaning can it have for children before the awakening of mind and spirit at adolescence? In the whole cultural domain, there is good cause for paying heed to Rousseau's warning against premature instruction. With his usual vehemence of conviction he has over-stated his case. Every adult capacity has its origins in childhood. Some sense of beauty, some realisation of the past, some religious awe, some of the wonder out of which science comes are present from the earliest years. The spiritual faculties must all be nurtured by the appropriate culture from the beginning of life. But so long as adults think of children as but smaller editions of themselves, and fail to realise their mental and moral limitations, Rousseau's emphasis on what children cannot learn, and should not learn, will serve to remind parents and teachers that children must be allowed to act and think as persons in their own right, if they are ever to achieve full personality. In school practice there is no need for the clean sweep of adult interests which Rousseau seems to advocate in the case of Emile. He himself shows the way to a sane child-centred education in the case of mathematics. In effect, his method was to make the pupil want to learn, and thereafter teach him by an appeal to concrete experiences in his everyday life. The same course can be taken within the limits of childish capacity in every sphere. Partly by looking on at grown-up ways, partly by enjoying the simpler unintellectualised experiences in the aesthetic, moral and religious spheres, the child gets prepared for his future life without knowing it. In the light of all the educational experiments made since Rousseau's time in his spirit, it is possible to conceive of a school in which children sharing in community life may get a real initiation into the varied richness of humanity, without losing the satisfactions of a happy childhood.

The educational scheme for the teen-ages before and after puberty, set forth in Books Three and Four, presents fewer difficulties to the modern reader of Rousseau than the scheme for boyhood. Allowing for the differences between the eighteenth and the twentieth centuries, he will find himself in considerable agreement with much that is said about the teaching of science and of the humanities. Even if critical of the view that social understanding does not come till after puberty, and that consequently the social studies cannot be included between 12 and 15, he will accept Rousseau's admission of geography and physical science at this stage as in accord with present experience and practice, and will appreciate the value assigned to craftsmanship both for the immediate interest and as a preparation for the future. The organisation of adolescent education round the developing sex interest, again, gives a view of what is happening as the young man or woman moves onward through personal friendships and the broad human relations to life as a member of society, which was quite new when first propounded, and which has not lost its freshness even yet. Just as the primary school is inclined to stress instrumental arts like reading, writing and counting, with more concern about their later use than their present interest, so the secondary school stresses the more complex instruments of languages, mathematics, sciences and arts for their utility in the occupations and pursuits that lie ahead. Rousseau's lively account of the personal training in history, language, economics, religion and literature in response to the needs of youth serves as a reminder that the making of the worthy man is quite as important as the making of the good citizen; and that in order to achieve this the adolescent studies must not only prepare for the future but yield their own proper satisfactions in their season.

Finally come, in Book Five, the education of Sophie and the last stages of Emile's education. The education of men and women, he maintains, must be fundamentally different. By reason of their sex they differ in character and temperament: man strong and active, woman weak and passive; man dominating woman, woman holding her own by the charms that make her pleasing to man. Their natures being different they must be educated differently: the boy to be independent of public opinion and recognising no authority but what approves itself to him, the girl to be socially docile, accepting the authority of parents in childhood and later of husband and society. Here plainly "Nature" speaks the language of eighteenth century prejudice. . . .

In any case, the value of Rousseau's discussion of the age and sex differences in education depends not on his practical suggestions but on the basic principles which have found expression in his educational writings. He himself says as much in the preface to the *Emile*, and his followers, through whom his teaching has passed into the stream of European thought, have confirmed it by developing methods of their own very different from his. The question for us is not whether we should educate children in Rousseau's way but whether there is essential truth in the idea of a "natural" education as propounded by him. The assumption that underlies the view of education presented in the *Emile* is that children are living, growing beings who at every stage of their upgrowing are persons in their own right, capable of being properly prepared for later maturity only through the active interests of their own age and condition. It is in effect the democratic conception of humanity applied to childhood and youth, and is accepted in some fashion by all modern educators as an integral element in the educational ideal. Even if in their practice they find it an ideal hard to realise and are sometimes faithless to its spirit, the schools of today (we hope) are moving slowly but surely towards an education that will make their pupils both citizens and men: a national and a natural education.

The revolutionary idea in education, expressed with strange compelling power in the *Emile*, is at once simple and profound. It is, in a word, that education to be effective in the making of good human beings and through them of a good society, must be child-centred. Educators before him had stressed the need to take proper account of the child's point of view, but always they had thought of children as limited creatures requiring to be fashioned after the adult pattern. Jesus indeed had set the child in the midst and told the older people that they must become as children if they were to enter the kingdom of heaven, but till Rousseau nobody had ever tried to give practical effect to this precept. It was because poor frustrated Rousseau had so much of the child in himself that he was able to look at life through the eyes of a child, and appreciate the child's point of view. And thus he was led to realise, as no one had done before, that it was only by living his own kind of life in all its fullness that the child could develop into adult man. From that conception of the child as a being with rights and duties on his own level of experience everything else followed: the idea of natural education (that is, of education in accordance with the nature of the child); the need for definite knowledge of children, both boys and girls, at the successive stages of their growth, and the need also for a knowledge of their individual characteristics; the training for life through life in a country environment from which all influences that might lead to vice or error are excluded by a wise direction; the limitation of learning to matters of personal concern and interest till maturity brings fitness for adult studies; the impersonal discipline of consequences to check waywardness and misconduct. These principles, presented concretely in the romantic tale of Emile and Sophie, and interwoven in more abstract form with the biographical detail, laid hold on the imagination of a great number of Rousseau's contemporaries. Fathers and mothers paid him the compliment of believing that their children should be educated like the original pair. Educators in various lands—outstanding men like Kant . . .—were led to re-think their opinions about education and to devise ways and means of creating a better education suited to their own conditions. The French Revolution and its aftermath brought a reaction, and Rousseau and his works sank for a time in common esteem, but the magic of the *Emile* never wholly lost its power and its essential ideas gradually found their way into the educational ideals, and to some extent into the educational practice, of Europe. These ideas were in the main the inspiring faith of the New Schools which came into being in England, America, Germany and other countries at the end of the nineteenth and the beginning of the twentieth century, and they have since spread over the world. . . .

# 6
## Immanuel Kant

**Immanuel Kant** (1724–1804) is a preeminent figure in the history of philosophy. Born and raised in the Prussian town of Königsberg (now Kaliningrad), he attended its university and was eventually appointed to its chair of logic and metaphysics. Although he never traveled beyond the environs of his home city, his intellectual scope was far-ranging. Beginning in his early years with studies in physics and astronomy, he eventually made numerous ground-breaking contributions to all the major fields of philosophy.

## *Lectures on Pedagogy*

### Introduction

The human being is the only creature that must be educated. By education we mean specific-ally care (maintenance, support), discipline (training) and instruction, together with formation. Accordingly, the human being is first infant, then pupil, and then apprentice.

Animals use their powers as soon as they have any in a regular manner; that is to say, in such a way that they do not harm themselves. It is indeed wonderful to note, for instance, that young swallows, when scarcely hatched out of their eggs and still blind, nevertheless know how to make their own excrement fall out of their nests. This is why animals need no care, but at most food, warmth, and guidance or a certain protection. Most animals indeed need nourishment, but not care. For by care is meant the precaution of the parents that children not make any harmful use of their powers. For example, were an animal to cry immediately when it comes into the world, as children do, it would inevitably become the prey of wolves and other wild animals, who would be attracted by its crying.

Discipline or training changes animal nature into human nature. An animal is already all that it can be because of its instinct; a foreign intelligence has already taken care of everything for it. But the human being needs his own intelligence. He has no instinct and must work out the plan of his conduct for himself. However, since the human being is not immediately in a position to do this, because he is in a raw state when he comes into the world, others must do it for him.

The human species is supposed to bring out, little by little, humanity's entire natural predisposition by means of its own effort. One generation educates the next. One can see the first beginnings of education in either a crude or in a perfect, developed state. If the latter is assumed to have preceded and come first, then the human being must, however, afterwards have once more grown savage and fallen into a raw state.

Discipline prevents the human being from deviating by means of his animal impulses from his destiny: humanity. Discipline, for example, must restrain him so that he does not wildly and thoughtlessly put himself in danger. Training is therefore merely negative, that is to say, it is the action by means of which man's tendency to savagery is taken away. Instruction, on the other hand, is the positive part of education.

Savagery is independence from laws. Through discipline the human being is submitted to the laws of humanity and is first made to feel their constraint. But this must happen early. Thus, for example, children are sent to school initially not already with the intention that they should learn something there, but rather that they may grow accustomed to sitting still and observing punctually what they are told, so that in the future they may not put into practice actually and instantly each notion that strikes them.

Now by nature the human being has such a powerful propensity towards freedom that when he has grown accustomed to it for a while, he will sacrifice everything for it. And it is precisely for this reason that discipline must, as already said, be applied very early; for if this does not happen, it is difficult to change the human being later on. He then follows every whim. It is also observable in savage nations that, though they may be in the service of Europeans for a long time, they can never grow accustomed to the European way of life. But with them this is not a noble propensity towards freedom, as Rousseau and others believe; rather it is a certain raw state in that the animal in this case has so to speak not yet developed the humanity inside itself. Therefore the human being must be accustomed early to subject himself to the precepts of reason. If he is allowed to have his own way and is in no way opposed in his youth, then he will retain a certain savagery throughout his life. And it is also of no help to those who in their youth have been spared by all too much motherly affection, for later on they will be opposed all the more from all sides, and receive blows everywhere, as soon as they get involved in the business of the world.

It is a common error made in the education of princes that, because they are destined to become rulers, no one really opposes them in their youth. Because of the human being's propensity towards freedom, a polishing of his crudity is necessary; whereas with the animal, on account of its instincts, this is not necessary. . . .

The human being can only become human through education. He is nothing except what education makes out of him. It must be noted that the human being is educated only by human beings, human beings who likewise have been educated. That is also why the lack of discipline and instruction in some people makes them in turn bad educators of their pupils. If some day a being of a higher kind were to look after our education, then one would see what the human being could become. But since education partly teaches the human being something and partly merely develops something within him, one can never know how far his natural predispositions reach. If at least an experiment were conducted here through support of the rulers and through the united powers of many people, then we might even by this means gain disclosure as to how far the human being might rise. But it is as important for the speculative mind as it is sad for the philanthropist to observe how the rulers for the most part care only for themselves and take no part in the important experiments of education in such a manner that nature may take a step closer to perfection.

There is no one who, having been neglected in his youth, would not recognize in mature age in what regard he had been neglected, whether as regards discipline or as regards culture (the latter being another term for instruction). He who is uncultured is raw; he who is undisciplined is savage. Omission of discipline is a greater evil than omission of culture, for the latter can be made up for later in life; but savagery cannot be taken away, and negligence in discipline can never be made good. Perhaps education will get better and better and each generation will move one step closer to the perfection of humanity; for behind education lies the great secret of the perfection of human nature. Henceforth this may happen. Because now for the first time we are beginning to judge rightly and understand clearly what actually belongs to a good education. It is delightful to imagine that human nature will be developed better and better by means of education, and that the latter can be brought into a form appropriate for humanity. This opens to us the prospect of a future happier human species.

An outline of a theory of education is a noble ideal, and it does no harm if we are not immediately in a position to realize it. One must be careful not to consider the idea to be chimerical and disparage it as a beautiful dream, simply because in its execution hindrances occur.

An idea is nothing other than the concept of a perfection which is not yet to be found in experience—as is the case of a perfect republic governed by rules of justice. Is the latter therefore impossible? If our idea is only correct, then it is by no means impossible, despite all of the obstacles which stand in the way of its execution. If, for example, everyone were to lie, would truth-telling therefore become a mere whim? Now the idea of education which develops all the human being's natural predispositions is indeed truthful.

With the present education the human being does not fully reach the purpose of his existence. For how differently do people live! There can only be uniformity among them if they act according to the same principles, and these principles would have to become their second nature. What we can do is work out the plan of an education more suited to the human being's purpose and hand down instructions to that effect to posterity, which can realize the plan little by little. It is observable, for instance, that the auricula only bears flowers of one and the same color when cultivated from a root. On the other hand, if it is grown from seed one gets flowers of totally different and most varied colors. Thus nature has after all placed the germs in these plants, and it is merely a matter of proper sowing and planting that these germs develop in the plants. The same holds true with human beings.

Many germs lie within humanity, and now it is our business to develop the natural dispositions proportionally and to unfold humanity from its germs and to make it happen that the human being reaches his vocation. Animals fulfill their vocation automatically and unknowingly. The human being must first seek to reach his, but this cannot happen if he does not even have a concept of his vocation. It is also completely impossible for the individual to reach the vocation. Let us assume a fully formed first human couple, and let us see how they educate their pupils. The first parents already give the children an example which the latter imitate, and that way some natural predispositions are developed. But not all predispositions can be developed in this manner, for the children only see these examples in occasional circumstances. Formerly, human beings did not even have a conception of the perfection which human nature can reach. We ourselves are not even yet clear about this concept. But this much is certain, that individual human beings, no matter what degree of formation they are able to bring to their pupils, cannot make it happen that they reach their vocation. Not individual human beings, but rather the human species, shall get there.

Education is an art, the practice of which must be perfected over the course of many generations. Each generation, provided with the knowledge of the preceding ones, is ever more able to bring about an education which develops all of the human being's natural predispositions proportionally and purposively, thus leading the whole human species towards its vocation. Providence has willed that the human being shall bring forth by himself that which is good, and he speaks, as it were, to him: "Go forth into the world," so might the creator address humanity, "I have equipped you with all predispositions toward the good. It is up to you to develop them, and thus your own happiness and unhappiness depend on you yourself."

It is the human being himself who is supposed to first develop his predispositions toward the good. Providence has not placed them already finished in him; they are mere predispositions and without the distinction of morality. The human being shall make himself better, cultivate himself, and, if he is evil, bring forth morality in himself. If one thinks this over carefully, one finds that it is very difficult. That is why education is the greatest and most difficult problem that can be given to the human being. For insight depends on education and education in turn depends on insight. For that reason education can only move forward slowly and step by step, and a correct concept of the manner of education can only arise if each generation transmits its experience and knowledge to the next, each in turn adding something before handing it over to the next. . . .

Since the development of the natural predispositions in the human being does not take place by itself, all education is an art. Nature has placed no instinct in him for this. The origin as well as the continuation of this art is either *mechanical*, without plan and ordered by given circumstances, or *judicious*. The art of education arises mechanically only on those chance occasions when we learn by experience whether something is harmful or useful to people. All educational art which arises merely mechanically must carry with it many mistakes and defects, because it has no plan for its foundation. The art of education or pedagogy must therefore become judicious if it is to develop human nature so that the latter can reach its vocation. Parents who are already educated are examples for imitation by means of which children form themselves. But if children are to become better, pedagogy must become a course of study. Otherwise, there is nothing to hope from it. Otherwise one whose education is corrupted will educate the other one. The mechanism in the art of education must be transformed into science, otherwise it will never become a coherent endeavor, and one generation might tear down what another has already built up.

One principle of the art of education, which particularly those men who are educational planners should have before their eyes, is this: children should be educated not only with regard to the present but rather for a better condition of the human species that might be possible in the future; that is, in a manner appropriate to the idea of humanity and its complete vocation. This principle is of great importance. Parents usually educate their children merely so that they fit in with the present world, however corrupt it may be. However, they ought to educate them better, so that a future, better condition may thereby be brought forth. But here we encounter two obstacles:

1) Parents usually care only that their children get on well in the world, and 2) princes regard their subjects merely as instruments for their own designs.

Parents care for the home, princes for the state. Neither have as their final end the best for the world and the perfection to which humanity is destined, and for which it also has the predisposition. However, the design for a plan of education must be made in a cosmopolitan manner. And is, then, the best for the world an idea which can be harmful to us in our best private condition? Never! For even though it appears that something must be sacrificed for it, through it one nevertheless always promotes the best of one's present condition. And then, what glorious consequences accompany it! Good education is exactly that from which all the good in the world arises. The germs which lie in the human being must only be developed further and further. For one does not find grounds of evil in the natural predispositions of the human being. The only cause of evil is this, that nature is not brought under rules. In the human being lie only germs for the good.

But from where is the better condition of the world supposed to come? From the princes, or from the subjects? Should the latter first better themselves on their own and meet a good government halfway? If it is to be brought about by the princes, then the education of the princes must first become better—an education which for some time has always had the large defect, that in their youth no one resisted them. But a tree which stands alone in the field grows crooked and spreads its branches wide. By contrast, a tree which stands in the middle of the forest grows straight towards the sun and air above it, because the trees next to it offer opposition. It is the same with the princes. Still, it is better yet that they be educated by someone from among their subjects rather than by one from their own rank. We can therefore expect the good to come from above only if the education there is the superior one. That is why this matter depends mainly on private efforts and not so much on the assistance of the princes. . . . For experience teaches that the princes first of all have not so much the best for the world in mind but rather the well-being of their state, so that they may reach their own goals. If, however, they provide the money, then the design of the plan must after all be left to their discretion. This is the case in everything which concerns the education of the human spirit, the enlargement of human knowledge. Power and money do not accomplish it, but at most facilitate it. . . .

Accordingly, the set-up of the schools should depend entirely on the judgment of the most enlightened experts. All culture begins with private individuals and extends outward from there. It is only through the efforts of people of more extended inclinations, who take an interest in the best world and who are capable of conceiving the idea of a future improved condition, that the gradual approach of human nature to its purpose is possible. Every now and then many a ruler still looks upon his people as, so to speak, merely a part of the realm of nature, and directs his attention merely to their propagation. At most the ruler then further demands skillfulness, but merely in order to be able to better use his subjects for his purposes. Admittedly, at first private individuals must also have nature's purpose before their eyes, but they must furthermore reflect especially on the development of humanity, and see to it that humanity becomes not merely skillful but also moral and, what is most difficult of all, they must try to bring posterity further than they themselves have gone.

In his education the human being must therefore 1) be *disciplined*. To discipline means to seek to prevent animality from doing damage to humanity, both in the individual and in society. Discipline is therefore merely the taming of savagery.

2) The human being must be *cultivated*. Culture includes instruction and teaching. It is the procurement of skillfulness. The latter is the possession of a faculty which is sufficient for the carrying out of whatever purpose. Thus skillfulness determines no ends at all, but leaves this to the later circumstances.

Some kinds of skillfulness are good in all cases, for example reading and writing; others only for some purposes, for example music, which makes us popular with others. Because of the multitude of purposes, skillfulness becomes, as it were, infinite.

3) It must be seen that the human being becomes *prudent* also, well suited for human society, popular, and influential. This requires a certain form of culture, which is called *civilizing*. Its prerequisites are manners, good behavior and a certain prudence in virtue of which one is able to use all human beings for one's own final purposes. This form of culture conforms to the changeable taste of each age. Thus just a few decades ago ceremonies were still loved in social intercourse.

4) One must also pay attention to *moralization*. The human being should not merely be skilled for all sorts of ends, but should also acquire the disposition to choose nothing but good ends. Good ends are those which are necessarily approved by everyone and which can be the simultaneous ends of everyone.

The human being can either be merely trained, conditioned, mechanically taught, or actually enlightened. One trains dogs and horses, and one can also train human beings. . . .

But to have trained one's children is not enough, rather, what really matters is that they learn *to think*. This aims at principles from which all actions arise. Thus we see that in a true education there is a great deal to be done. In private education, however, it usually still happens that the fourth, most important point is little observed. For children are mainly educated in such a manner that their moralization is left up to the preacher. But how immensely important it is that children are taught from youth to detest vice, not merely on the ground that God has forbidden it, but rather because it is detestable in itself! Otherwise they easily get the idea that they could always practice vice and that it would after all be quite permitted if only God had not forbidden it, and that God can easily make an exception for once. God is the holiest being and wills only that which is good, and demands that we should practice virtue because of its own inner worth and not because He demands it.

We live in a time of disciplinary training, culture, and civilization, but not by any means in a time of moralization. Under the present conditions of human beings one can say that the happiness of states grows simultaneously with the misery of human beings. And there is still the question whether we would not be happier in a raw state, without all this culture, than we are in our present condition. For how can one make human beings happy, if one does not make them moral and wise? Otherwise, the quantity of evil is not diminished.

Experimental schools must be established before normal schools can be established. Education and instruction must not be merely mechanical but must be based on principles. But neither must education be merely through rational argument, rather it must still be mechanical in a certain way. . . .

It is even commonly imagined that experiments in education are not necessary, and that one can already judge according to reason whether something will be good or bad. But this is very mistaken, and experience teaches that our experiments often show quite different effects from the ones expected. One sees therefore that since experiments matter, no one generation can present a complete plan of education. . . . Education includes *care* and *formation*. Formation is 1) *negative*, viz., the discipline which merely prevents errors; 2) *positive*, viz., instruction and guidance, and insofar forms a part of culture. *Guidance* is direction in the exercise of that which one has learned. Thus arises the difference between the *instructor*, who is merely a teacher, and the *tutor*, who is a guide. The former educates merely for the school, the latter for life.

The first stage in the pupil's development is that in which he must show obsequiousness and passive obedience; in the other he is allowed to make use of reflection and of his freedom, though under laws. In the first there is a mechanical, in the other a moral coercion. . . .

Education is either *private* or *public*. The latter concerns only instruction, and this can always remain public. The practice of the precepts is left to the former. A complete public education is one which unites both instruction and moral formation. . . .

But to what extent might private education have an advantage over public education or vice versa? In general, it appears that public education is more advantageous than domestic, not only as regards skillfulness but also with respect to the character of a citizen. Quite often, domestic education not only frequently brings forth family mistakes but also reproduces them. . . .

The obsequiousness of the pupil is either *positive*, when he must do what is prescribed to him, because he cannot himself judge, and the mere capacity of imitation still continues in him; or *negative*, when he must do what others want if he wants others to do some favor for him in return. With the first, he may come in for punishment; with the second, others may not do what he wants. In the latter case, although he can already think for himself, he is nevertheless dependent for his pleasure.

One of the biggest problems of education is how one can unite submission under lawful constraint with the capacity to use one's freedom. For constraint is necessary. How do I cultivate freedom under constraint? I shall accustom my pupil to tolerate a constraint of his freedom, and I shall at the same time lead him to make good use of his freedom. Without this everything is a mere mechanism, and the pupil who is released from education does not know how to use his freedom. He must feel early the inevitable resistance of society, in order to get to know the difficulty of supporting himself, of being deprived and of acquiring—in a word: of being independent.

Here the following must be observed: 1) From earliest childhood the child must be allowed to be free in all matters (except in those where it might injure himself, as, for example, when it grabs an open knife), although not in such a manner that it is in the way of others' freedom; as, for example, if it screams or is merry in too loud a way, it already burdens others. 2) The child must be shown that it can only reach its goals by letting others also reach theirs, for example, that it will not be pleased if it does not do what one wants it to do, that it should learn, etc. 3) One must prove to it that restraint is put on it in order that it be led to the use of its own freedom, that it is cultivated so that it may one day be free, that is, so that it need not depend on the care of others. This third point is the last to be grasped by the child. For with children the consideration only comes late, that, for example, later in life they will have to support themselves. They think that it will always be as it is in the parents' house, that they will receive food and drink without having to be responsible for it. Without such treatment children (especially children of rich parents and sons of princes) remain children throughout their entire lives. . . . Here public education has its obvious advantages, because by means of it one learns both to measure one's powers, one learns restrictions through the rights of others. Here no one enjoys any advantages, because one feels resistance everywhere, and because one can only make oneself noticed by distinguishing oneself through merit. Public education provides the best model of the future citizen. . . .

## Treatise

Pedagogy or the doctrine of education is either *physical* or *practical*. *Physical* education is the education part which the human being has in common with animals, or maintenance. *Practical* or *moral* education is the education by which the human being is to be formed so that he can live as a freely acting being. (We call *practical* everything which has a relation to freedom.) Practical education is education towards personality, the education of a freely acting being who can support itself and be a member of society, but who can have an inner value for itself.

Accordingly, practical education consists of: 1) *scholastic-mechanical* formation with regard to skillfulness, which is therefore *didactic* (the job of the instructor), 2) *pragmatic* formation with regard to prudence (the task of the tutor), 3) *moral* formation with regard to ethics.

The human being needs *scholastic* formation or instruction in order to become skillful for the attainment of all of his ends. It gives him value in relation to himself as an individual. But by means of formation towards prudence he is formed into a citizen, thus receiving public value. There he learns not only how to direct civil society for his purposes, but also how to fit in with civil society. Finally, through *moral* formation he receives value in view of the entire human race.

Scholastic formation is the earliest and the first. For all prudence presupposes skillfulness. Prudence is the faculty of using one's skillfulness effectively. Moral formation, in so far as it is based on principles which the human being should comprehend himself, comes last; but in so far as it is based on common human understanding, it must be observed right from the start and already with physical education. For otherwise, mistakes easily take root against which all educational art afterwards labors in vain. In view of skillfulness and prudence everything must correspond to the age of the student. Being childishly skillful, childishly prudent and good-natured, rather than cunning in a manly way, suits the child as little as for a grown-up to have a childish mind. . . .

Even though he who undertakes an education as tutor does not receive the children under his supervision early enough that he can also attend to their physical education, nevertheless it is useful to know all that is necessary to observe in education from beginning to end. Even though as tutor one may only be dealing with older children, it may well happen that new children are born in the house. And if one conducts oneself well one is always entitled to be a confidant of the parents and to be consulted about the physical education of their children as well. Besides, one is often the only scholar in the house. Therefore an acquaintance with this subject is also necessary for a tutor. . . .

In general it should be observed that the first stage of education must be merely negative, i.e., one should not add some new provision to that of nature, but merely leave nature undisturbed. The only art permitted in the educational process is that of hardening. . . .

To come immediately to the child's assistance when it cries, to sing something to it, etc. . . . is very harmful. This is usually the first undoing of the child, for if it sees that everyone rallies at its cries, then it repeats its cries more often.

It can no doubt be said with truth that the children of the common people are being spoiled much more than the children of high-ranking families. For the common people play with their children, like monkeys do. They sing to them, hug and kiss them, and dance with them. They think they are doing something good to the child if they run over and play with it, etc., as soon as it cries. But this only makes them cry more often. If, on the other hand, one does not care about their cries, they finally stop. For no creature enjoys a futile task. If children are accustomed to having all of their whims fulfilled, then afterwards the breaking of the will comes too late. If one lets them cry, then they will grow weary of it by themselves. But if all of their whims are fulfilled in early youth, their heart and their morals are thereby spoiled.

To be sure the child does not yet have any concept of morals, but its natural disposition is thereby spoiled in such a way that afterwards very strict punishment must be applied in order to repair that which has been spoiled. Later, when one tries to cure them of having someone always hasten to them on demand, these children when crying express such great a rage as only grown-ups are capable of, except that they lack the power to act upon it. For so long they needed only to call, and everything came to them; they ruled entirely despotically. When this rule now stops, they are quite naturally irritated. For even grown-up human beings who have been in possession of power for some time find it very difficult to wean themselves suddenly from it. . . .

As concerns the formation of the mind, which in a certain sense can actually also be called physical, it should mainly be noted that the discipline not be slavish. Rather, the child must always feel its freedom; in such a way, however, that it not hinder the freedom of others. Therefore it must find resistance. Some parents refuse their children everything in order to exercise the patience of their children, thereby demanding more patience of the children than they themselves have. But this is cruel. Give the child as much as is useful to it, and then say to it: You have enough! But then it is also absolutely necessary that this be irrevocable. Pay no attention to the cries of the children and do not comply with them when they want to get something by screaming. But give them that which they ask for in a friendly manner, provided it is useful to them. In this way the child will also become accustomed to being frank, and since it does not annoy anybody by its crying, everyone in turn will also be friendly to it. Providence seems indeed to have given children friendly expressions so that they can win people over. In breaking their self-will nothing is more harmful than a vexatious, slavish discipline.

It is customary to say to children: "Shame on you! That is not proper!" etc. But this sort of thing should not occur in the first stage of education at all. The child does not yet have concepts of shame and propriety. It has nothing to be ashamed of and should not feel ashamed, and only becomes shy as a result. It becomes embarrassed when others look at it and seeks to hide from other people. As a result reserve and a disadvantageous concealment develop. No longer does the child dare to ask for anything, and yet it should be able to ask for everything; it conceals its disposition and always appears different from what it is, instead of being allowed to say everything frankly. Instead of always being with the parents, it avoids them and throws itself into the arms of the more compliant household servants.

Trifling and continually caressing are no better than such a vexatious education. This reinforces the child in its own will and makes it deceitful, and by betraying to it a weakness in the parents, robs from them necessary respect in the eyes of the child. But if it is educated in such a way that it cannot get anything by crying, then it will be free without being insolent, and modest without being shy. . . . A bold human being is not liked. Some men have such bold faces that one must always fear some coarseness from them, just as one can look at other faces and see instantly that they are unable to say a coarse word to anyone. One can always appear frank, provided that this is united with a certain goodness. . . .

We come now to the culture of the soul, which in a way can also be called physical. One must, however, distinguish between nature and freedom. Giving laws to freedom is something entirely different from forming nature. The nature of the body and that of the soul agree in this, that in the formation of each of them one seeks to prevent some corruption—and that art furthermore adds something to both of them. One can therefore call the formation of the soul in a way just as physical as the formation of the body.

However, this physical formation of the mind is distinguished from the moral formation of the mind in that the latter aims solely at freedom; the former solely at nature. A human being can be highly cultivated in physical terms, he can have a well-formed mind, but can still be poorly cultivated in moral terms, and thus be an evil creature. . . .

Various educational plans have been drawn up for the commendable goal of ascertaining which method in education is the best. Among other things, one has hit upon the idea to let children learn everything as if in play. . . . This is entirely counterproductive. The child should play, it should have its hours of recreation, but it must also learn to work. To be sure, the culture of its skill is as valuable as the culture of its mind, but the two kinds of culture must be practised at different times. Besides, it is already a particular misfortune for the human being that he is so much inclined to inactivity. The more a human being has been lazy, the harder it is for him to resolve to work.

In work the activity is not pleasant in itself, rather one undertakes it on account of another aim. By contrast, in play the activity is pleasant in itself without intending any further purpose. When one goes for a walk, going for a walk is itself the aim, and therefore the longer the walk is, the more pleasant it is for us. But if we go somewhere in particular, then the company which is to be found in that place or something else is the aim of our walk, and we gladly choose the shortest way. It is the same with card games. It is really remarkable to see how reasonable men often are able to sit for hours and shuffle cards. This shows that human beings do not easily cease being children. For how is that game better than the children's playing ball? It is true that adults do not exactly ride on a stick, but they ride on other hobby horses all the same.

It is of the greatest importance that children learn to work. The human being is the only animal which must work. He must first undertake many preparations before he can enjoy something for his living. The question whether heaven would not have cared for us more kindly if it had let us find everything already prepared so that we should not need to work at all, is certainly to be answered in the negative. For the human being requires occupations, including those that involve a certain constraint. Just as false is the idea that if Adam and Eve had only remained in paradise they would have done nothing there but sit together, sing arcadian songs, and observe the beauty of nature. Certainly boredom would have tortured them just as much as it does other people in a similar situation.

The human being must be so occupied that he is filled with the purpose which he has before his eyes, in such a way that he is not conscious of himself at all, and the best rest for him is that which comes after work. The child must therefore be accustomed to working. And where else than at school should the inclination to work be cultivated? School is compulsory culture. It is extremely harmful if one accustoms the child to view everything as play. The child must have time to relax, but there must also be a time for it to work. Even if the child does not see immediately how this compulsion is useful, nevertheless in the future it will become aware of its great usefulness. Actually it would only seriously pamper children's nosiness if one were always to answer their question "What is this good for and what is that good for?" Education must be compulsory, but this does not mean that it must be slavish.

As concerns the free culture of the powers of mind, it must be noted that it is always in progress. It really concerns the higher powers. The lower powers are always cultivated in the process, but only in relation to the higher ones; wit, for example, is cultivated in relation to the understanding. The main rule here is that no power of mind is to be cultivated separately but each in relation to the other; for example, the power of imagination is to be cultivated only for the advantage of the understanding.

The lower powers have no value in themselves; take the example of a human being who has a great memory, but no power of judgment. Someone like that is then a living lexicon. Such pack mules of Parnassus are also necessary, for even if they themselves cannot accomplish anything sensible, they still can drag along materials out of which others can bring about something good.—Wit results in pure silliness if not joined by the power of judgment. Understanding is the knowledge of the universal. The power of judgment is the application of the universal to the particular. Reason is the faculty to see the connection of the universal with the particular. This free culture runs its course from childhood on until the time that the youth is released from all education. If a youth, for example, cites a universal rule, then one can have him cite cases from history and fables in which this rule is disguised, and passages from poets where it is already expressed, and thus give him reason to exercise his wit, his memory, and so forth.

The saying, *tantum scimus, quantum memoria tenemus*[1] is certainly correct, and that is why the culture of the memory is quite necessary. All things are such that the understanding only follows upon the sensuous impressions, and the memory must retain these impressions. So it is, for example, with languages. One can either learn them by formal memorization or by social intercourse, and with living languages the latter is the best method. Learning the vocabulary is indeed necessary, but it is certainly best to have those words learned which occur in the author that one is reading just then with the youth. The youth must have its certain and fixed workload. Thus one also learns geography best by means of a certain mechanism. The memory in particular loves this mechanism, and in a lot of cases it is also very useful. Up to now no really suitable mechanism for learning history has been found; it is true that tables have been tried, but it also seems that they, too, do not work right. But history is an excellent means for exercising the understanding in judgment. Memorization is very much needed, but as a mere exercise it is useless; for example, having them memorize speeches. At most it only helps to promote boldness, and besides, declaiming is only a thing for adult men. Here belong also all those things that one learns merely for a future examination or with respect to *futuram oblivionem.*[2] One must occupy the memory only with those things which for us are important to remember and which have a relation to real life. The worst thing is when children read novels, namely because they will use them for nothing but the entertainment they provide in the very moment of being read. Reading novels weakens the memory. For it would be ridiculous to want to remember novels and recount them to others. That is why all novels should be taken out of the hands of children. While they read them they form within the novel a new novel by developing the circumstances differently for themselves, going into raptures and sitting there thoughtlessly.

Distractions must never be tolerated, least of all at school, for they eventually produce a certain tendency in that direction, a certain habit. Even the most beautiful talents perish in one who is subject to distractions. Although children become distracted through their entertainments, nevertheless they soon compose themselves again. However, one sees them most distracted when they have bad pranks in mind, for then they ponder how they can conceal them or make good for them. Then they only hear half of everything, answer wrongly, do not know what they are reading, and so forth.

One must cultivate the memory early on, but must also cultivate the understanding in the process.

The memory is cultivated 1) by remembering the names in stories; 2) by reading and writing; but the former must be exercised with understanding and not by means of spelling the letters; 3) by means of languages, which children must be taught first by hearing, before they even read anything. Then a suitably constructed so-called *Orbis pictus*[3] serves well, and one can make a beginning with botanizing, with mineralogy, and the description of nature. Sketching these objects provides the occasion for drawing and modeling, for which mathematics is needed. It is most advantageous to have the first scientific instruction be concerned with geography, mathematical as much as physical. Travel accounts, illustrated by means of engravings and maps, then lead to political geography. From the present condition of the earth's surface one then goes back to its previous condition, moving on to ancient geography, ancient history, and so forth.

In the instruction of children one must seek gradually to combine knowledge and ability. Of all the sciences mathematics appears to be the one that satisfies this final purpose best. Furthermore, knowledge and speech must be combined (eloquence, fluency, ease in talking). But the child must also learn to distinguish very well knowledge from mere opinion and belief. Thus one prepares the way for a correct understanding and a *correct* taste rather than a *fine* or *delicate* taste. This taste must first be that of the senses, particularly that of the eyes, but eventually that of ideas.

Rules must be found in everything that is to cultivate the understanding. It is very useful also to abstract the rules so that the understanding may proceed not merely mechanically but rather with the consciousness of a rule.

It is also very good to arrange the rules in a certain formula and thus to entrust them to the memory. If we have the rule in our memory but have forgotten its application, we still shall soon find our way again. Here the question is: should the rules precede merely *in abstracto*, and should rules first be learned afterwards, when one has completed the application, or should rule and application go hand in hand? The latter alone is advisable. In the other case the application is very uncertain until one reaches the rules. But rules must also occasionally be arranged into classes, for one does not retain them if they do not stand in connection with one another. Thus in language instruction grammar must always precede ever so slightly.

But now we must also give a systematic concept of the entire purpose of education and the means by which it can be attained.

1) *The general culture of the powers of the mind,* as distinguished from the particular culture. It aims at skillfulness and perfection. The point is not to inform the pupil in any particular area but to strengthen his powers of mind. The general culture of the powers of the mind is

a) either *physical.* Here everything is based on exercise and discipline and the children must not know any maxims. It is *passive* for the apprentice, he must be obedient to the direction of someone else. Others think for him.

b) or *moral.* In this case it is based not on discipline but on maxims. Everything is spoiled if one tries to ground this culture on examples, threats, punishments, and so forth. Then it would be merely discipline. One must see to it that the pupil acts from his own maxims, not from habit, that he not only does the good, but that he does it because it is good. For the entire moral value of actions consists in the maxims concerning the good. Physical education differs from moral education in that the former is passive for the pupil while the latter is active. He must at all times comprehend the ground of the action and its derivation from the concepts of duty.

2) *The particular culture of the powers of the mind.* This includes the culture of the cognitive faculty, of the senses, of the imagination, of the memory, of the strength of attention and wit, in short what concerns the *lower powers* of the understanding. Of the culture of the senses, for example that of the sense of proportion, we have spoken above. As concerns the culture of the imagination, the following is to be noted. Children have an exceedingly

strong imagination, which does not need to be strained further and expanded by fairy tales at all. Rather it needs to be reined in and brought under rules, but all the same one must not leave the imagination entirely unoccupied.

Maps have something in them which appeals to all children, even the smallest ones. When they are weary of everything else, they still learn something when maps are used. And this is a good entertainment for children, in which their imagination cannot wander but must stick to a certain figure, as it were. One could actually begin with geography in teaching children. Figures of animals, plants, and so forth can be combined with that simultaneously; they must enliven geography. But history should rather come in at a later point.

As concerns the strengthening of attention, it should be noted that this must be strengthened in general. A rigid attachment of our thoughts to an object is not so much a talent as a weakness of our inner sense, which in such a case is inflexible and does not allow itself to be applied as one likes. Distraction is the enemy of all education. Memory, however, is based on attention.

But as concerns the *higher powers of understanding*, they include the culture of the understanding, of the power of judgment, and of reason. In the beginning, the understanding, too, can be formed passively, as it were, by referring to examples for the rule, or, conversely, by discerning the rule for the individual cases. The power of judgement indicates what use is to be made of the understanding. It is required in order to understand what one learns or says, and in order not to repeat things without understanding them. How many read and hear something without understanding it, even though they believe they do! This holds for images and things.

By means of reason one grasps grounds. But one must keep in mind that here one is talking about a reason that is still being guided. It must therefore not always want to argue, but one must also not present it with arguments which transcend its concepts. We are not speaking here of speculative reason, but of the reflection on that which happens, regarding its causes and effects. It is a reason which is practical in its management and arrangement.

The best way of cultivating the powers of the mind is to do everything that one wants to accomplish by oneself; for example, immediately to apply the grammatical rule that one has learned. One understands a map best when one can draw it oneself. The biggest aid to understanding something is to produce it. One learns most thoroughly and retains best that which one learns as it were from oneself. Only a few human beings, however, are able to do this. They are called autodidacts.

In the formation of reason one must proceed Socratically. For *Socrates*, who called himself the midwife of his listeners' knowledge, gives in his dialogues, which Plato has preserved for us faithfully, examples of how even in the case of old people, one can bring forth a good deal from their own reason. On many matters children do not need to exercise reason. They must not reason about everything. They do not need to know the reasons for everything which is meant to make them well-educated. But as soon as duty is concerned, then the reasons in question must be made known to them. However, in general one must see to it that one does not carry rational knowledge into them but rather extracts it from them. The Socratic method should be the rule for the catechetical method. That method is admittedly somewhat slow, and it is difficult to arrange things such that when one extracts knowledge from one child the others also learn something in the process. The mechanical-catechetical method is also good for some sciences; for example, in instruction in revealed religion. However, in the case of universal religion one must use the Socratic method. For the mechanical-catechetical method particularly recommends itself for what must be learned historically.

The formation of the feeling of pleasure or displeasure also belongs here. It must be negative and the feeling itself must not be coddled. A tendency towards ease is worse for the human being than all evils of life. It is therefore extremely important that children learn to work from early on. If children have not already been coddled, they really love amusements which are connected with exertion, occupations for which forces are required. One must not make children dainty nor let them have a choice when it comes to what they enjoy. Generally mothers spoil their children in this respect and coddle them altogether. And yet one notices that the children, especially the sons, love their fathers more than their mothers. This is probably because the mothers do not let them jump around, run around and so forth at all, for fear that they might be injured. However, the father, who scolds and perhaps beats them when they have been naughty, now and then also takes them out into the field and there lets them run around very boyishly, play, and be happy.

It is thought that children can be taught patience by letting them wait a long time for something. This, however, hardly seems necessary. But they do need patience during illnesses and so forth. Patience is twofold. It consists either in giving up all hope or in seizing new courage. The first is not necessary, provided that one always demands only what is possible, and one always needs the latter, provided that one desires only what is right. During illnesses hopelessness aggravates the situation just as much as courage can ameliorate it. And he who is still capable of summoning up courage with regard to his physical or moral condition also does not give up hope.

Children must also not be made shy. This happens especially when one shouts at them with words of scolding, and makes them feel ashamed repeatedly. Here belongs particularly the exclamation of many parents: "Shame on you!" It is not at all clear what children should actually be ashamed about when they, for example, stick their fingers in their mouths and so forth. One can say to them that this is not customary or not good manners, but one must never shout "Shame on you!" to them, except in case they are lying. Nature has given the sense of shame to the human being so that he betrays himself as soon as he lies. Hence if parents never talk to their children of shame except when they lie, the children will then keep this blush of shame with respect to lying for their entire lifetime. But when they are constantly put to shame, then this establishes a shyness which continues to stick to them irrevocably.

As already said above, the will of children must not be broken but merely directed in such a way that it yields to natural hindrances. In the beginning of course the child must obey blindly. It is unnatural that the child should command by its crying, and that the strong should obey a weak one. One must therefore never comply with the crying of children, even in their first years, and allow them to extort something by this means. The parents commonly err in this and afterwards try to compensate for it by refusing the children in later years everything they ask for. But it is very wrong to refuse them something without cause which they expect from the kindness of their parents, merely in order to resist them and to make them, the weaker ones, feel the superior strength of the elders.

Children are spoiled if one complies with their wills, and quite wrongly educated if one acts directly contrary to their wills and desires. The former generally happens as long as they are a plaything of the parents, especially at the time when they begin to talk. But from spoiling the child very great harm arises for its entire life. It is true that by acting contrary to the wills of the children one hinders them at the same time from showing their indignation, which admittedly must happen, but their inner rage is all the stronger. They have not yet learned how they should conduct themselves. The rule which must be observed with children from their earliest years is this: When they cry and one believes that they are being harmed, one should come to their aid, but when they cry merely from indignation, one should let them lie. And a similar procedure must also be observed unrelentingly later on. The resistance which the child finds in this case is quite natural and in fact only negative, consisting simply in not acceding to it. By contrast, many children get everything they demand from their parents merely by resorting to entreaties. If children are allowed to get everything by crying, they become malicious; but if they obtain everything by asking, they become soft. If there is thus no important reason to the contrary, one must fulfill the child's request. But if one finds a reason not to fulfill it, one must not allow oneself to be moved even by constant entreaties. Every refusal must be irrevocable. This soon has the effect that one will not need to make frequent refusals.

Suppose—and this is something that can be assumed only extremely rarely—that the child has a natural predisposition to stubbornness. Then it is best to deal with it such that if it does nothing to please us, we also do nothing to please it. Breaking the child's will brings about a slavish way of thinking; but natural resistance produces docility.

Moral culture must be based on maxims, not on discipline. The latter prevents bad habits, the former forms the way of thinking. One must see to it that the child accustoms itself to act according to maxims and not according to certain incentives. Discipline leaves us only with a habit, which, after all, fades away over the years. The child should learn to act according to maxims whose fairness it itself understands. It is easy to see that this is hard to bring about in children, and that moral formation therefore also demands the most insight from the side of the parents and the teachers.

If the child, for example, lies, it must not be punished but rather met with contempt, and it must be told that in the future one will not believe it, and the like. But if a child is punished when it does something bad and rewarded when it does something good, then it does something good in order to be well off. Later when the child enters the world where things are different, where it can do something good without being rewarded and something bad without being punished, it will become a human being who cares only how it can get on well in the world and is good or bad depending on what it finds most conducive to that end.

Maxims must originate from the human being himself. One should try to convey concepts concerning good and evil to children already early on in moral culture. If one wants to ground morality, one must not punish. Morality is something so holy and sublime that one must not degrade it and place it on the same level with discipline. The first effort in moral education is the grounding of character. Character consists in the aptitude of acting according to maxims. In the beginning these are school maxims and later maxims of humanity. In the beginning the child obeys laws. Maxims too are laws, but subjective ones; they originate from the human being's own understanding. No violation of the school law may go unpunished, although the punishment must always be commensurate with the violation.

If one wishes to form a character in children, it is very important to draw their attention to a certain plan in all things, certain laws, known to them, which they must follow exactly. Thus, for example, one sets for them a time for sleep, for work, for amusement, and these one must then not extend or shorten. In indifferent things one can allow children the choice of time, but what they have made their law they must afterwards always follow.—In children, however, one must form not the character of a citizen but rather that of a child.

Human beings who have not given themselves certain rules are unreliable. One often cannot figure them out, and one can never really know what they are up to. It is true that people who always act according to rules are frequently reprimanded; for example, the man who has fixed a certain time for each action according to the clock. But often such reprimanding is unjustified, and this exactness, though it looks like punctiliousness, is a disposition for [the formation of] a character.

To the character of a child, especially of a pupil, there belongs above all things obedience. This is twofold: first, obedience to the *absolute will* of a leader, but also, second, obedience to the will of a leader who is recognized to be *reasonable and good*. Obedience can be derived from constraint, and then it is *absolute*; or it can be derived from confidence, and then it is of the other sort. This *voluntary* obedience is very important; but the former is also extremely necessary, for it prepares the child for the fulfillment of such laws as it will in the future have to fulfill as a citizen, even though it may not like them.

Children must therefore stand under a certain law of necessity. This law, however, must be a universal one, a point that one has to observe especially in schools. The teacher must not show any predilection or preference for one child over others. For then the law ceases to be universal. As soon as the child sees that not all the others must submit to the same law, it becomes rebellious.

One talks a lot about having to present things to children in such a way that they might do it from inclination. In some cases this is certainly good, but there is also a great deal which one must prescribe to them as duty. Later this is of great benefit to them for their entire lives. For when it comes to public taxes, the labors of office and in many other cases only duty, not inclination, can guide us. Even if the child is unable to understand the duty, it is nevertheless better this way. And that something is its duty as a child, it may well understand, but it will be harder for it to understand that something is its duty as a human being. If it could also understand the latter kind of duty (which, however, is only possible with advancing age), then its obedience would be still more perfect.

Every transgression of a command by a child is a lack of obedience, and this brings on punishment. Even in the case of a careless transgression of the command, punishment is not superfluous. This punishment is either *physical* or *moral*.

One punishes *morally* by harming the inclinations to be honored and loved, which are aids to morality; for example, when one makes the child feel ashamed and treats it frostily and coldly. The inclinations to be honored and loved are to be preserved as far as possible. Therefore this kind of punishment is the best, since it comes to the aid of morality; for example, if a child lies, a look of contempt is punishment enough and is the most appropriate punishment.

*Physical* punishment consists either in refusing what is desired, or in the infliction of punishments. The first kind is related to moral punishment and is negative. The other punishments must be used with caution, so that no *indoles servilis*[4] arises. It is not good to give children rewards; as a result they become selfish and an *indoles mercennaria*[5] arises.

Furthermore obedience is either that of the *child* or of the *adolescent*. The transgression of obedience is followed by punishment. This is either a really *natural* punishment, which the human being brings upon himself by his behavior—for example, that the child becomes sick when it eats too much. And these punishments are the best, for the human being experiences them throughout his entire life and not only as a child. Or, on the other hand, the punishment is *artificial*. The inclination to be respected and loved is a sure means for arranging the chastisements in such a way that they are lasting. Physical punishments must be merely supplements to the insufficiency of the moral punishments. If moral punishments do not help any more at all and one proceeds to physical punishment, this will no longer form a good character. However, at the beginning physical constraint must take the place of reflection, which is lacking in children.

Punishments which are carried out with signs of rage have the wrong effects. Children then regard them merely as consequences of someone else's affect, and they regard themselves as the objects of such an affect. In general punishments must be inflicted on children with caution, so that they may see that their final purpose is the improvement of the children. To make children express thanks when they have been punished and to make them kiss their parents' hands and so forth is foolish and makes the children slavish. If physical punishments are repeated often, children become stubborn, and if parents punish their children because of obstinacy, then this only makes them all the more obstinate.—Besides, stubborn people are by no means the worst, rather they often yield easily to kind remonstrances.

The obedience of the adolescent is different from the obedience of the child. It consists in submission to the rules of duty. To do something from duty means to obey reason. To talk to children about duty is futile labor. In the end they regard duty as something the transgression of which is followed by the rod. The child could be led by means of mere instincts, but as soon as it grows up the concept of duty must step in. Neither must shame be used with children, rather it should first be used in the years of adolescence. For shame can only occur when the concept of honor has already taken root.

A second principal feature in the grounding of character in children is truthfulness. It is the fundamental trait and what is essential in a character. A human being who lies has no character at all, and if he has anything good in him, this is merely due to his temperament. Some children have a propensity towards lying, which quite often is to be derived from a lively imagination. It is the father's business to see to it that the children break this habit. For the mothers usually regard it as a matter of no or merely slight significance; indeed, they often find in it proof of the excellent talents and abilities of their children, with which they flatter themselves. Now this is the place to make use of the feeling of shame, for in this case the child understands it well. The blush of shame betrays us when we lie, but is not always proof of it. For we often blush over the shamelessness with which someone else accuses us of wrongdoing. Under no circumstances must one try to force the truth from children by means of punishments, except when their lie results in some immediate damage; and then they are to be punished on account of this damage. The withdrawal of respect is the only appropriate punishment for lying.

Punishments may also be divided into *negative* and *positive* punishments, the first of which may take place with laziness or immorality; for example, with lies, noncompliance, and quarrelsomeness. The positive punishments, however, are for indignation. But above all things one must beware never to bear grudges against children.

A third feature in the character of a child must be *sociability*. The child must maintain friendships with others and not remain by itself all the time. Some teachers, it is true, are opposed to these friendships in schools; but this is very wrong. Children should prepare themselves for the sweetest enjoyment of life. However, teachers must not prefer one child over another because of its talents but only because of its character, for otherwise resentment develops, which is contrary to friendship.

Children must be openhearted too, and as bright as the sun in their expressions. The cheerful heart alone is capable of rejoicing in the good. A religion which makes the human being gloomy is false; for he must serve God with a cheerful heart and not out of constraint. The cheerful heart must not always be held strictly under the constraints of the school, for in that case it will soon be suppressed. When it has freedom, it recovers again. This purpose is well served by certain games, in which the child has freedom and where it tries always to outdo others. Then the soul brightens up again.

Many people think that the years of their youth were the best and most pleasant of their lives. But this is hardly so. They are the most arduous years, because one is under strict discipline, can seldom have a real friend, and even more seldom can have freedom.

Children must be taught only those things that are suitable to their age. Some parents are pleased when their children can talk in a precocious manner at an early age. But usually nothing comes such children. A child must only be intelligent in the manner of a child. It must not blindly ape everything. But a child that has precocious moral sayings is totally beyond what its years call for, and it apes others. It should have only the understanding of a child and should not appear in public too early. Such a child will never become a man of insights and of brightened understanding. It is just as insufferable when a child already wants to keep up with all the latest fashions; for example, to have its hair dressed, wear ruffled cuffs, or even to carry a snuffbox. It acquires an affected nature, which does not suit a child. Civilized society is a burden to it, and in the end it lacks entirely the uprightness of a man. And for this very reason one must counteract its vanity early on, or, better put, not give it occasion to become vain. But children become vain when one chatters to them quite early about how beautiful they are, how well this or that finery becomes them, or when such finery is promised to them and given to them as a reward. Finery is not suitable for children. They must receive their neat and simple clothing only as a bare necessity. But the parents also must attach no value to these things, not look at themselves in the mirror, for here as everywhere example is all-powerful and reinforces or destroys good teaching.

**Of Practical Education**

Practical education includes 1) skill, 2) worldly prudence and 3) morality. As concerns *skill,* one must see that it is thorough and not superficial. One must not assume the appearance of knowing things that later one cannot bring about. In skill there must be thoroughness, which must gradually become a habit in the way of thinking. It is the essential thing for the character of a man. Skill is necessary for talent.

As concerns *worldly prudence*, it consists in the art of using our skillfulness effectively, that is, of how to use human beings for one's purposes. For this various things are needed. Strictly speaking, it is the last thing attained by the human being, but in terms of its worth it occupies the second rank.

If the child is to be given over to worldly prudence, then it must be able to conceal itself and make itself impenetrable, but at the same time be able to scrutinize the other person. It must conceal itself particularly in regard to its character. The art of external appearance is propriety. And one must possess this art. To scrutinize others is difficult, but it is necessary to know this art well while making oneself impenetrable. This includes dissimulation, that is, holding back one's faults, and the previously mentioned external appearance. Dissimulation is not always hypocrisy, and can sometimes be allowed, but it borders very closely on dishonesty. Dissimulation is a desperate means. It is part of worldly prudence not to suddenly fly into a rage; but one must also not be too indolent. Thus one must not be vehement, but yet upright. Being upright is quite different from being vehement. An *upright man* is one who takes pleasure in willing. This is a part of the moderation of affect. Worldly prudence is a matter of temperament.

*Morality* is a matter of character. *Sustine et abstine*[6] is the preparatior for a wise moderation. If one wants to form a good character, one must first clear away the passions. In regard to his inclinations the human being must learn not to let his inclinations become passions. Rather, he must learn to do without something when it is refused to him. *Sustine* means endure and accustom yourself to enduring.

Courage and inclination are required if one wants to learn to do without something. One must become accustomed to refusals, opposition and so forth.

Temperament includes sympathy. Children must be prevented from any yearning, languishing sympathizing. Sympathizing is actually sensitivity; it agrees only with a character that is sensitive. It is still different from compassion and is an evil which consists merely in bemoaning a thing. One should give children some pocket money with which they could help the needy, and then one would see whether they are compassionate or not. But if they are always only generous with their parents' money, compassion drops out.

The saying *festina lente*[7] indicates a perpetual activity, where one must hurry in order to learn a great deal—that is, *festina*. But one must also learn thoroughly, and thus take time with everything—that is, *lente*. The question now arises, whether it is preferable to have a great range of knowledge, or only a smaller one, but one which is thorough. It is better to know little, but to know this little thoroughly, than to know a lot and know it superficially, for in the latter case the shallowness of this knowledge eventually shows. But the child of course does not know in which circumstances it will need this or that knowledge, and therefore it is best that it knows thoroughly something of everything. Otherwise it will deceive and dazzle others with its superficially learned knowledge.

Finally there is the grounding of character. This consists in the firm resolution of willing to do something, and then also in the actual performance of it. . . . For example, if I have promised something to someone, then I must indeed keep it, even if it were to bring me harm. For a man who resolves to do something but who does not do it cannot trust himself any longer. For example, if someone resolves always to get up early in order to study, or to do this or that, or in order to take a walk, and then during the spring excuses himself, stating that it is still too cold in the morning, and it could do him harm; while in the summer he states that one can sleep so well and that sleep is pleasant to him, and thus always from one day to the next puts off his resolution—then in the end he does not trust himself any more.

That which is contrary to morals forms an exception to such resolutions. In the case of an evil human being the character is very bad, and is already called stubbornness. Yet we like it when he carries out his resolutions and is steadfast, although it would be better if he showed the same persistence in good things.

Not much can be thought of someone who always puts off the execution of his resolutions. The so-called future conversion is of this sort. For the human being who has always led a depraved life and wants to be converted in an instant cannot possibly get there, for it would be nothing short of a miracle for him to become in an instant the same as someone who has conducted himself well during his entire life and always thought upright thoughts. For the same reason there is nothing to be expected from pilgrimages, castigations, and fasting; for it is not possible to conceive how pilgrimages and other customs can help make an honest man out of a depraved one on the spot.

How can there be uprightness and improvement, if one fasts by day and enjoys so much more at night, or imposes a penance to one's body, which can contribute nothing to the transformation of the soul?

In order to ground a moral character in children, we must note the following:

One must teach them the duties that they have to fulfill as much as possible by examples and orders. The duties which a child has to perform are after all only ordinary duties to itself and to others. These duties must therefore be drawn from the nature of things. Therefore we have to consider more closely:

a) duties to oneself. These do not consist in buying fine clothes for oneself, having splendid meals and so forth, although everything must be clean. Nor do they consist in trying to satisfy one's desires and inclinations, for on the contrary one must be very moderate and temperate. Rather they consist in the human being having a certain dignity within himself which ennobles him before all creatures, and it his duty not to deny this dignity of humanity in his own person.

But we deny the dignity of humanity when we, for example, take to drinking, commit unnatural sins, practice all kinds of immoderation, and so forth, all of which degrade the human being far below the animals. Further, when a human being grovels before others, always making compliments, in order—as he believes—to ingratiate himself by such undignified behavior, then this is also contrary to the dignity of humanity.

The dignity of the human being could also be made perceptible already to the child with regard to itself; for example, in cases of uncleanliness, which after all is unbecoming for humanity. But the child can indeed also degrade itself below the dignity of humanity through lying, since the child is already able to think and to communicate its thoughts to others. Lying makes the human being an object of universal contempt and is a means of robbing him of the respect and credibility for himself which everyone should have.

b) duties to others. Reverence and respect for the rights of human beings must be instilled into the child at a very early age, and one must carefully see to it that the child puts these into practice. For example, if a child meets another, poorer child and haughtily pushes it out of the way or away from itself, gives it a blow and so forth, then one must not say: "Don't do that, it hurts the other one. You should have pity! It is a poor child," and so forth. Rather one must treat it just as haughtily and noticeably, because its behavior was contrary to the rights of humanity. But children do not yet really have any generosity. One can, for example, infer this from the following fact: when parents tell their child to hand over half of its piece of bread and butter to another child, but without receiving that much more from the parents later, then either it does not obey at all, or very seldom and unwillingly. Besides, one cannot say much about generosity to a child anyway, since it has nothing yet in its power.

Many writers . . . have entirely overlooked or incorrectly explained the chapter of morals which contains the doctrine of duties to oneself. But the duty to oneself consists, as already said, in preserving the dignity of humanity in one's own person. The human being reprimands himself when he has the idea of humanity before his eyes. He has an original in his idea with which he compares himself. When he grows older, when the inclination towards the other sex begins to stir him, then is the critical point in time in which only the dignity of the human being is able to restrain the youth. But one must give the youth pointers early on as to how he must guard himself against this or that.

In our schools something is almost universally lacking, something which would nevertheless greatly promote the formation of uprightness in children, namely a catechism of right. It would have to contain cases which would be popular, which occur in ordinary life, and which would always naturally raise the question whether something is right or not. For example, if someone who should pay his creditor today is touched through the sight of someone in need and gives him the sum which he owes and should now pay—is this right or not? No! It is not right, for I must be free if I want to perform charitable acts. And when I give money to the poor man, I perform a meritorious deed; but when I pay my debt, I perform an obligatory deed. Further, whether a white lie should be permitted? No! There is not one conceivable case in which it would be excusable, and least of all before children, who would then look upon each tiny thing as such an emergency situation and often allow themselves to tell lies. If there were such a book already, then one could set aside an hour daily with much benefit, teaching children to know and to take to heart the rights of humanity, this apple of God's eye on earth.

As concerns the obligation of beneficence, it is only an imperfect obligation. One must not so much soften the hearts of children in order for them to be affected by the fate of others, but rather make them upright. The child should not be full of feeling but rather full of the idea of duty. Many people, indeed, become hard-hearted because, having formerly been compassionate, they often found themselves deceived. It is useless to try to make the meritorious nature of actions understandable to a child. Clergymen often make the mistake of representing acts of beneficence as something meritorious. Putting aside the fact that with respect to God we can do no more than our obligation, it is also only our duty to do good to the poor. For the inequality of the wealth of human beings comes only from accidental circumstances. Thus if I possess wealth, I owe it only to the seizing of these circumstances, which has turned out well either for me or my predecessor, but the regard for the whole still remains the same.

Envy is aroused when one points out to a child to value itself according to the value of others. Instead the child should value itself according to the concepts of its own reason. That is why humility is actually nothing else than a comparison of one's worth with moral perfection. Thus the Christian religion, for instance, does not so much preach humility as make the human being humble because he must compare himself to the highest model of perfection. It is quite wrong to let humility consist in valuing oneself less than others.—"See how such and such child behaves!" and so forth. An exclamation of this kind produces a quite ignoble way of thinking. When the human being values his worth according to others, he seeks either to raise himself above others or to diminish the value of the other one. The latter, however, is envy. One then always tries only to impute a wrong to the other one. For if he were not there, then one also could not be compared with him, and so one would be the best. The inappropriate spirit of emulation merely stirs up envy. The case in which emulation could be of some use would be to convince someone of the feasibility of a thing; for example, if I demand of a child that a certain lesson be learned and show the child that others can do it.

One must in no way allow one child to shame another. One must seek to avoid all pride which is grounded on the advantages of good fortune. But at the same time one must seek to establish frankness in children. Frankness is a modest confidence in oneself. By means of it the human being is placed in a position to display all of his talents in a proper way. It is to be distinguished completely from impertinence, which consists in indifference toward the judgment of others.

All desires of the human being are either formal (freedom and capacity) or material (related to an object)—the latter being desires of delusion or of pleasure; or, finally, they relate to the mere continuation of both as elements of happiness.

Desires of the first kind are ambition, lust for power, and greed; desires of the second kind are the pleasures of sex (lust), of things (luxurious living), or of society (taste in entertainment). Desires of the third kind, finally, are love of life, of health, and of ease (freedom from care concerning the future).

But the vices are those of malice, or of baseness, or of narrow-mindedness. To the first kind belong envy, thanklessness, and joy in someone else's misfortune; to those of the second kind belong injustice, unfaithfulness (deceitfulness), dissoluteness in the squandering of goods as well as of health (intemperance) and honor. Vices of the third kind are unkindness, stinginess, and indolence (effeminacy).

The virtues are either virtues of *merit* or merely of *obligation* or *innocence*. To the first kind belong magnanimity (in self-conquest regarding revenge as well as ease and greed), beneficence, and self-mastery; to the second kind belong uprightness, decency, and peaceableness; to the third kind, finally, belong honesty, modesty, and frugality.

Now we come to the question whether the human being is by nature morally good or evil. He is neither of the two because by nature he is not a moral being at all; he only becomes one when his reason raises itself to the concepts of duty and of law. However, one can say that originally he has impulses to all vices in himself, for he has inclinations and instincts which incite him, although reason drives him in the opposite direction. Therefore he can only become good by means of virtue, that is, by self-constraint; although without impulses he can be innocent.

Vices arise, for the most part, from the civilized state doing violence to nature, and yet it is our own vocation as human beings to emerge from our crude state of nature as animals. Perfect art becomes nature again.

Everything in education depends on establishing the right principles throughout and making them comprehensible and acceptable to children. Children must learn to substitute detesting things because they are disgusting and absurd for abhorrence out of hatred; they must learn to have inner aversion replace the external aversion to human beings or to divine punishment, to have self-estimation and inner worth replace the opinions of human beings, to have the inner value of actions and deeds replace words and emotions, understanding replace feeling, and joy and piety with good humor replace morose, timid, and gloomy devotion.

But above all things one must also guard children from ever overestimating *merita fortunae*.[8]

As concerns the education of children with a view to religion, the first question is whether it is feasible to teach religious concepts to children at an early age. There has been a great deal of controversy over this point in pedagogy. Religious concepts always presuppose some theology. Now could the young, who do not know the world, do not know themselves, be taught some theology? Could the young, who do not yet know duty, be in a position to comprehend an immediate duty to God? This much is certain, that if it were feasible that children should witness no acts of veneration towards the highest being, never even hear the name of God, it might be the proper order of things to guide them first to the ends and to that which benefits the human being, to sharpen their power of judgment, to instruct them in the order and beauty of the works of nature, then to add a wider knowledge of the structure of the universe, and only then to reveal to them the concept of a highest being, a lawgiver. But this is not possible in our present situation, and if one wanted to teach them something about God only at a late stage, and they nevertheless heard and witnessed so-called services to Him, then this would produce either indifference or perverted concepts in them for example, a fear of God's power. But since it is to be feared that these ideas might settle down in children's fantasy, one must in order to avoid this seek to teach them religious concepts at an early age. However, this must not be memory work, mere imitation and solely mimicry work rather the path which one chooses must always be in conformity with nature. Even without having abstract concepts of duty, of obligations, of good or bad conduct, children will understand that there is a law of duty that it is not ease, usefulness, and the like which should determine them but rather something universal which is not dependent on the whims of human beings. However, the teacher must also produce this concept for himself.

At first everything must be attributed to nature, but later nature itself must be attributed to God; how, for example, at first everything is oriented toward the preservation of the species and their balance, but at the same time from a wider perspective everything is also oriented towards the human being, so that he may make himself happy.

The concept of God might first best be made clear by analogy with that of the father under whose care we are. In the process one can then point out with great advantage the unity of humankind as that of a family.

But what then is religion? Religion is the law in us, in so far as it receives emphasis from a lawgiver and judge above us; it is morals applied to the knowledge of God. If religion is not combined with morality, then it becomes nothing more than currying favor. Singing praises, prayers, and going to church should only give the human being new strength, new courage for improvement, or they should be the expression of a heart inspired by the idea of duty. They are only preparations for good works, but not good works themselves, and one cannot please the highest being otherwise than by becoming a better human being.

With a child one must first begin with the law that it has in itself. The human being is contemptible to himself when he is vicious. This is grounded in the human being himself, and is not so merely because God has forbidden evil. For it is not necessary that the lawgiver also at the same time be the author of the law. Thus a prince can forbid stealing in his land, and yet he could not be declared the author of the prohibition of theft. From this the human being learns to understand that his good conduct alone makes him worthy of happiness. The divine law must appear at the same time as a law of nature, for it is not arbitrary. That is why to all morality there belongs religion.

But one must not begin with theology. A religion which is founded merely on theology can never contain anything moral. In such a religion one will have only fear on the one hand and intentions and dispositions geared towards reward on the other, resulting merely in a superstitious cult. Morality must therefore come first, theology then follows, and this is what is called religion.

The law within us is called conscience. Properly speaking, conscience is the application of our actions to this law. The reproaches of conscience will be without effect if one does not think of it as the representative of God, who has erected a sublime seat above us but also a judge's seat within us. If religion is not added to moral conscientiousness, the latter has no effect. Religion without moral conscientiousness is a superstitious worship. People want to serve God when they, for example, praise Him, and extol His power and wisdom, without thinking how they might fulfill the divine laws, yes, without even once knowing and inquiring into His power, wisdom, and so forth. These praises are an opiate for the conscience of such people and a cushion on which it is supposed to sleep peacefully.

Children cannot grasp all religious concepts, but nevertheless there are some that one must teach them; however, these must just be more negative than positive. To have children rattle off formulas is of no use and produces only a perverted concept of piety. True worship of God consists in acting according to God's will, and this one must teach to children. One must see to it that the name of God is not so often misused, by children as well as by oneself. If one uses it in congratulations, even with pious intent, this is just as much an abuse. The concept of God should fill man with reverence each time His name is pronounced, and he should therefore use it seldom and never frivolously. The child must learn to feel reverence before God, as the lord of life and of the whole world; further, as the provider for human beings, and thirdly and finally as their judge. It is said that *Newton* always stopped for a while and meditated when he uttered God's name.

By means of a unified elucidation of the concepts of God and of duty the child learns all the better to respect the divine provision for creatures, and will thus be protected from the propensity toward destruction and cruelty which expresses itself in so many ways in the torture of small animals. At the same time, one should also instruct the youth to discover the good in evil; for example, beasts of prey and insects are models of cleanliness and of industry.

Evil human beings awaken us to the law. Birds who hunt worms are protectors of the garden, and so forth.

One must therefore teach some concepts of the highest being to children, so that, when they see others praying and so forth, they may know to whom and why such is being done. But these concepts must be only few in number and, as said before, be merely negative. Moreover, one must begin to teach them to children already from early youth, but always see to it that they do not value human beings according to their religious observances, for in spite of the diversity of religions there is nevertheless unity of religion everywhere.

The development of these inclinations in the young man is mechanical and, as is the case with all instincts, they develop without even having an object. It is thus impossible to keep the young man in uncertainty here and in the innocence which is connected with it. But silence only makes things go from bad to worse. One sees this in the education of our ancestors. In the education of more recent times it is correctly assumed that one must speak openly, clearly, and decidedly with the young man about it. This is admittedly a delicate point, because one does not like to look at it as an object of public conversation. But everything turns out well if one speaks about it with dignified seriousness and by addressing the youth's inclinations.

The thirteenth or fourteenth year is usually the time when the inclination toward sex develops itself in the young man (if it occurs earlier, it would have to be because children have been seduced and spoiled through bad examples). At that point, their power of judgment is also already developed, and nature has prepared them at this time so that one can speak to them about these things.

Nothing weakens the mind as well as the body of the human being more than the kind of lust which is directed towards oneself, and it is entirely contrary to the nature of the human being. But this lust also must not be concealed from the young man. It must be placed before him in all its atrocity, he must be told that he thereby makes himself useless for the reproduction of the species, that through it the bodily powers are ruined the most, that it brings on premature old age and that his mind will suffer a great deal in the process, and so forth.

One can escape from the impulses to this lust through continuous occupation, by not devoting more time to bed and sleep than is necessary. By means of these constant occupations, one must put the thoughts about it out of one's mind. For even if the object only remains in the imagination, it still corrodes the vital power. If one directs one's inclination towards the other sex, one always still finds some resistance, but if one directs it towards oneself, then one can satisfy it at any time. The physical effect is extremely harmful, but the consequences as regards morality are far worse yet. Here one transgresses the boundaries of nature, and inclination rages without arrest because no real satisfaction takes place. Teachers of grown youths have raised the question whether it is allowable for a young man to get involved with the other sex. If one of the two must be chosen, then the latter is certainly better. In the former case he acts contrary to nature, but here he does not. Nature has called him to manhood as soon as he comes of age, and therefore also to reproduce his species; but the needs which the human being necessarily has in a civilized state are such that at this stage he cannot always already educate his children. He thus violates the civil order. Therefore it is best, indeed, it is a duty, that the young man wait until he is capable of regular marriage. He then acts not only as a good human being, but also as a good citizen.

The young man should learn early to foster a decent respect for the other sex, to earn its respect through activity which is free from vice, and thus to strive after the high prize of a happy marriage.

A second difference which the young man begins to make around the time he enters society consists in the knowledge of the differences of classes and the inequality of human beings. As a child he must not be allowed to notice these things. One must not even allow him to give orders to the servants. If he sees that the parents give orders to the servants, one can if need be say to him: "We give them bread, and in return for it they obey us; you do not do this, and therefore they need not obey you." Children know nothing of these differences if parents merely do not teach them this delusion. One must show the young man that the inequality of human beings is an institution which has arisen because one man has tried to obtain advantages over another. The awareness of the equality of human beings in the face of civic inequality can be imparted to him little by little.

One must see to it that the young man values himself absolutely and not according to others. The high esteem of others in matters which do not make up the worth of the human being at all is vanity. Further, one must also stress to him conscientiousness in all things, and here as everywhere not merely to appear so but to strive to be so. One must emphasize to him that he must absolutely not let a carefully considered resolution become an empty resolution; it is better to make no resolution and leave the matter in doubt.—He must also be taught contentedness with external circumstances and endurance in working: *sustine et abstine*; as well as moderation in pleasures. If one does not merely demand pleasures but also wants to work patiently one will become a useful member of the commonwealth and protect oneself from boredom.

Further, one must stress cheerfulness and good humor to the young man. Cheerfulness of heart arises from having nothing to reproach oneself for. One must also stress even-temperedness. Through practice one can bring oneself to always be able to be a cheerful member of society.—

One must also exhort him to look upon many a thing always as a duty. An action must be valued by me not because it agrees with my inclination but because I fulfill my duty through it.—

One must stress to him philanthropy towards others and then also cosmopolitan dispositions. In our soul there is something that makes us take an interest 1) in our own self, 2) in others with whom we have grown up, and then also 3) an interest in the best for the world must come to pass. One must make children familiar with this interest so that they may warm their souls with it. They must rejoice at the best for the world even if it is not to the advantage of their fatherland or to their own gain.—

Further one must emphasize to the young man that he should place little value on the enjoyment of the amusements of life. The childish fear of death will then cease. One must point out to the young man that the enjoyment does not deliver what the prospect promised.—

Finally, one must also stress to him the necessity of settling accounts with himself each day, so that at the end of his life he is able to estimate the value of his life.

## Notes

1. We know as much as we can remember.
2. Future oblivion.
3. The world in pictures. In 1658 Czech philosopher of education John Amos Comenius (1592–1670) published a textbook titled *Orbis Pictus*, often considered the first picture book intended for children.
4. Servile disposition.
5. Mercenary disposition.
6. Endure and sustain.
7. Hurry with leisure.
8. Good fortune.

# Afterword

## Robert B. Louden[*]

*Lectures on Pedagogy* is not a book that Kant himself published, but rather a poorly edited compendium of his views on education culled from lecture notes that he prepared and used for a course on practical pedagogy at the University of Königsberg. Toward the end of his life, when poor health prevented him from producing a good manuscript for publication, Kant offered his notes on pedagogy to his younger colleague Friedrich Theodor Rink, with instructions to select out from them the most useful ones for the public. However, the quality of Rink's work as an editor of Kant's writings has been uniformly criticized over the years. *Lectures on Pedagogy*, for instance, as editors of subsequent editions never tire of pointing out, is repetitive and not well organized. Did Rink publish all or only some of Kant's notes? Did he rearrange the order of those that he did publish, and were any deletions or additions made? Unfortunately, we do not have definitive answers to any of these questions, for the original notes that Kant handed over to Rink have not survived.

Nevertheless, despite its flaws, *Lectures on Pedagogy* remains Kant's central work on education. Although he gave considerable and repeated attention to educational questions in many of his own published writings, particularly the essays on the philosophy of history, the popular anthropology lectures, and the famous works on ethics, aesthetics, and philosophy of religion, his discussions of pedagogical issues in these latter works are often sporadic and subsidiary to his central concerns. On the other hand, in *Lectures on Pedagogy* educational concerns are always front and center, even when the authorial integrity of some of its specific claims have been challenged. Thus in order to arrive at a fully developed and authentically Kantian philosophy of education, one really needs to study Rink's short text in conjunction with Kant's voluminous and difficult published writings—a daunting task for even the most dedicated student. In what follows, I shall offer some signposts through this difficult territory.

## Stages of Education/Stages of History

In the opening paragraph of the *Lectures*, Kant announces that what he means by "educa-

---

[*] Robert B. Louden is Professor of Philosophy at the University of Southern Maine.

tion" is a three-stage process of care, discipline, and formation (9: 441).[1] Later he asks whether the education of individuals should "imitate the course followed by the development of humanity in general through its generations" (9: 446), and at this point it becomes clear that his position on the stages of education essentially mirrors his conception of the stages of world history. In other words, Kant's educational theory is strongly influenced by his philosophy of history.

The root idea behind Kant's schema of stages of both education and history is that of the gradual development of humanity out of natural predispositions. As he states in the *Lectures*: "Many germs lie within humanity, and now it is our business to develop the natural predispositions proportionally and to unfold humanity from its germs and to make it happen that the human being reaches his vocation [*Bestimmung*—this important term can also be rendered as 'destiny']" (9: 445). An explicit teleology is thus always present in Kant's discussions of education and history—both aim at the perfection of humanity. But 'humanity' is meant here primarily in a cultural and moral sense: how do individual members of the biological species *Homo sapiens* become fully human? At bottom, it is an extremely ambitious story of the growth of freedom out of nature through rational control of instinct and desire, culminating eventually in a single world community where all human beings are accorded a dignity that is beyond price. And on Kant's view education has a major role to play in achieving this goal: "the human being can only become human through education. He is nothing except what education makes of him" (9: 443).[2]

The first stage of education is *care*. Kant defines it at the beginning of the *Lectures* simply as "the precaution of the parents that children not make any harmful use of their powers" (9: 441), and the primary stress here is simply on protecting the young so that they do not injure themselves in the course of their natural development. But later, in discussing the distinction between physical and practical education, he also includes under "care" (which is part of physical education) numerous bits of advice about what foods, drinks, and activities are appropriate for young children. Much of his advice concerning care appears to be borrowed from Rousseau's *Emile*,[3] and is today perhaps of only antiquarian interest, in part because it is sometimes based on false empirical data. At the same time, it is possible that some of his remarks concerning the care of young children may stem from his own personal experience as a house tutor or private teacher (*Hofmeister*) in the homes of two or three families near Königsberg from 1748–54, after his student years. In later life Kant is said to have remarked that "in the whole world there was never a worse tutor" than he, but the testimony of the families who employed him suggests that he was in fact a much better tutor than he thought.

In terms of the history of humanity, this first stage of education corresponds to the very earliest period of human existence, when (Kant conjectures) our ancestors were still purely instinctual creatures who blindly and unreflectively obeyed the promptings of their natural inclinations and desires—a time before humans were conscious of "reason as a faculty that can extend itself beyond the limits within which all animals are held" (*Conjectural Beginning of Human History*, 8: 112). Once they became aware of their capacity to choose between alternative courses of action and ways of life, early humans were freed from the limitations of instinct that nature imposes on other animals. They stepped over an abyss from which there was no turning back.

The second stage of education is *discipline*. Discipline "changes animal nature into human nature" (9: 441). Changing animal nature into human by no means entails eradicating or demolishing instincts, desires, and inclinations—a radical change of this sort would result in beings who were no longer human. Rather, it refers to the ability (an ability which itself is one of humanity's germs or natural predispositions) to control them through the exercise of reason. As Kant remarks in a later work, *Religion within the Boundaries of Mere Reason* (1793):

> *Considered in themselves* natural inclinations are *good*, i. e. not reprehensible, and to want to extirpate them would not only be futile but harmful and blameworthy as well; we must rather only curb them, so that they will not wear each other out but will instead be harmonized into a whole called happiness.
>
> (6: 58)

Or, as he puts it in the *Lectures*: "to discipline means to seek to prevent animality from doing damage to humanity, both in the individual and in society. Discipline is therefore merely the taming of savagery" (9: 449).

But even Kant's counsel to curb rather than extirpate inclinations fails to capture fully the enormous task of discipline. As Aristotle emphasized, human beings need to train their inclinations and emotions so that the right feelings are expressed in the right way at the right time, about the right things, and toward the right people (see *Nicomachean Ethics* II.6 1106b21–24). Kant is often accused of ignoring the positive role of feeling in human development in both his ethical and educational theory, but this is a misreading. For instance, in *The Metaphysics of Morals* (1797) he stresses, "what is done not with pleasure but merely as compulsory service has no inner worth for him who so responds to his duty" (6: 484). Virtuous people take pleasure in doing what is morally required.

Discipline, like care, forms part of what Kant calls "negative" education. The main goal is not to interfere with nature except when absolutely necessary—e. g., in order to prevent children from injuring themselves. Here as well, Kant echoes Rousseau. In *Emile* we read:

> [T]he first education should be merely negative. It consists not in teaching virtue or truth, but in preserving the heart from vice and from the spirit from error. . . . Do the opposite of what is usually done and you will almost always do right. Exercise body, senses, powers, but keep the mind inactive as long as possible. Let childhood ripen in children.

However, despite Kant's Rousseauian emphasis on the negative character of discipline, there are also positive dispositions to be fostered during this second stage—e.g., obedience, truthfulness, sociability (9: 481–84), and, above all, self-control.

The corresponding second stage in the history of humanity is *civilization*. Human beings at this level of development have begun "the transition from the crudity of a merely animal nature into humanity, from the go-cart of instinct to the guidance of reason" (*Conjectural Beginning of Human History* 8: 115). They have begun to replace the rule of instinct with the rule of law, and they have developed an immense variety of cultural practices and institutions in their dispersion over all corners of the globe. But as for the grounding of moral character, the ultimate goal in Kant's philosophy of history, they still have a long way to go: "We are *cultivated* in a high degree by art and science. We are *civilized*, perhaps to the point of being overburdened, by all sorts of social decorum and propriety. But very much is lacking before we can be held to be already *moralized*" (*Idea for a Universal History with a Cosmopolitan Aim* 8: 26).

The third stage of education is formation (*Bildung*—also rendered as 'culture'). The important term '*Bildung*', which is often said to embody "the German theory of education," is used very broadly by Kant and later writers to refer not only to education and culture generally, but also to the entire process of self-realization. Kant also occasionally uses the more familiar term '*Kultur*' as a synonym for *Bildung*.

Discipline, as we saw earlier, involves the negative task of curbing the natural inclinations to make way for humanity; formation or culture is the positive stage of education, and involves fostering human beings' natural talents and abilities. At one point in the *Lectures on Pedagogy* Kant defines culture tersely by stating that "it is the procurement of skillfulness" (9: 449; cf. 466). Human beings are skillful when they can attain their chosen ends, whatever these ends may be. Culture imparts skill, and skill enables us to achieve our goals. Under the broad terms "*Bildung*" and "*Kultur*", Kant also includes more specific educational activities such as instruction (9: 441, 449, 452), teaching (9: 449), and guidance (9: 452).

In his philosophy of history writings Kant usually refers to the third stage of human history as "moralization" (*Moralisierung*); a future level of development where all members of the species will consistently act from moral motives. However, while he does include a fairly detailed discussion of moral education at the end of the *Lectures* (9: 486–99), and while he certainly holds that moral character is the ultimate goal of human development, *Bildung*, the third stage of education, does not actually correspond to moralization, the third stage of history. For moral character as Kant understands it is ultimately a free choice for which each moral agent is responsible—a choice that is not causally determined by nature or nurture. The development of moral character can be and is fostered by a variety of cultural factors, including not only good educational institutions but also the establishment of an effective international justice system that successfully restrains nation-states' "vain and violent aims of expansion," aims which themselves "ceaselessly constrain the slow endeavor of the inner *Bildung* of their citizens' way of thinking" (*Idea for a Universal History*, 8: 26). But these needed external institutions alone cannot guarantee moral character. Rather, what is called for is "the transformation of one's way of thinking and the founding of a character" through an act of freedom; "a *revolution* in the disposition of the human being" (*Religion within the Boundaries of Mere Reason* 6: 48, 47). Moral education and institutional reform can help prepare the way for the radical transformation that Kant calls moralization, but they alone cannot bring it about. Ultimately, it is a free choice on the part of each individual.

On Kant's view, civilization and culture are essentially coterminous stages of human historical development. Both have occurred together, ever since our ancestors first broke free from the dominion of instinct. And *Bildung*, the third stage of education, is still part of this second stage of history: "We live in a time of disciplinary training, culture, and civilization, but not by any means in a time of moralization" (*Lectures on Pedagogy* 9: 451).

In sum, Kant understands both education and history as a developmental process involving the gradual realization of inherent human powers and capacities; the growth of freedom through rational control of instinct and desire. The final goal is human perfection, where 'perfection' is understood not just as technical and cultural achievement, but, ultimately, moral transformation.

## Revolution/Experimentalism/Naturalism

Readers who know Kant only through his major philosophical works and the endless commentaries on them are in for some surprises when they turn to his writings on education. For in these latter texts he espouses several unexpected doctrines, each of which can be traced to his strong endorsement of Johann Bernard Basedow's experimental school, the Philanthropinum Institute, founded in Dessau in 1774. In 1776–77 Kant published two short *Essays Regarding the Philanthropinum* (2: 445–52), both of which are in large part fundraising appeals for the project, and in the *Friedländer* anthropology transcription (1775–76) he refers to Basedow's school as "the greatest phenomenon which has appeared in this century for the improvement of the perfection of humanity" (25: 722–23).

## Revolution

One of Kant's least popular doctrines in his political philosophy is his firm rejection of the right to revolution. For instance, in *The Metaphysics of Morals* he states plainly that "a people cannot offer any resistance to the legislative head of a state which would be consistent with right [*Recht*]" (6: 320; cf. 322). However, in his educational theory he advocates not gradual reform but revolution. In the second *Essay Regarding the Philanthropinum* he writes:

> It is futile to expect this salvation of the human species from a gradual improvement of the schools. They must be transformed if something good is to come out of them because they are defective in their original organization, and even the teachers must acquire a new *Bildung*. Not a slow *reform*, but a swift *revolution* can bring this about.
>
> (2: 449)

Baesdow's school, Kant noted, was organized "in a radically new way according to the genuine method" (2: 449). And this is precisely what was needed, for it is widely acknowledged that the existing schools were grossly deficient. According to one frequently-cited account,

> Youth was in those days, for most children, a sadly harassed period. Instruction was hard and heartlessly severe. Grammar was beaten into the memory, so were portions of Scripture and poetry. A common school punishment was to learn by heart Psalm 119. Schoolrooms were dismally dark. No one conceived it possible that youth could find pleasure in any kind of work, or that they had eyes for anything but reading and writing. The profligate age of Louis XIV inflicted on the poor children of the upper classes hair curled by the barber and smeared with powder and pomade, laced coats, knee-breeches, silk stockings, and a dagger at the side—for active, lively children the severest torture.[4]

Basedow and his followers were opposed to all of this. In their schools (the original Philanthropinum in Dessau was soon imitated by a number of other schools in Germany and

Switzerland), memorization was kept to a minimum, pupils were not forced to study, and teachers did not use corporal punishment. Learning through games was stressed, and physical education became an important part of the curriculum. Instruction was given in the pupils' native tongue, and Latin and French were taught by the conversational method. Last but definitely not least, the Philanthropinum schools were cosmopolitan rather than nationalist in orientation, free from religious indoctrination (even Jewish students were admitted), and open to students from all social classes.

Unfortunately, Basedow's school never attracted sufficient students or funding, despite Kant's strong efforts on both fronts. And part of the blame must be placed on Basedow's lack of administrative and people skills.

Although Kant remained firmly committed to the need for fundamental educational change throughout his career, his early revolutionary zeal softened somewhat in his later years. In addressing the question of how human progress is best achieved in *The Conflict of the Faculties* (1798), he notes that to believe it "will eventually happen by means of the *Bildung* of youth in domestic instruction, then in schools on both the lowest and highest level, in intellectual and moral culture fortified by religious doctrine, . . . is a plan which is scarcely likely to achieve the desired success" (7: 92–93). Rather, he continues, "progress is to be expected only on the condition of a wisdom from above (which bears the name of providence if it is invisible to us)" (7: 93). This starkly religious appeal would have surprised the radical Basedow, but Kant also adds a final cosmopolitan note on which the two would agree: human beings must also learn to "renounce wars of aggression altogether" (7: 93), so that governments will be able to invest more in education.

### Experimentalism

Like other philosophers in the German idealist tradition, Kant normally advocates an extremely top-heavy relationship between theory and practice, according to which reason and theory must always guide practice—never vice versa. For instance, in the *Critique of Pure Reason* he praises Galileo and other scientists for discerning that "reason has insight only into what it itself produces according to its own design; that it must take the lead with principles," and for compelling "nature to answer its questions, rather than letting nature guide its movements" (B xiii). And in his practical philosophy he also insists that "the worth of practice rests entirely on its conformity with the theory underlying it" (*On the Common Saying: That May be Correct in Theory, But it Is of No Use in Practice* 8: 277). Human beings must realize that they do not have "moles' eyes fixed on experience"; rather, their eyes "belong to a being made to stand erect and look at the heavens" (8: 277).

Another surprise in the *Lectures on Pedagogy*, however, is Kant's demand for experimentalism. Experiments are needed in education, and the kind of experiments called for should not simply be viewed as handmaidens of preordained theory. In defending Basedow's Philanthropinum against its conservative critics, Kant states:

> It is even commonly imagined that experiments in education are not necessary, and that one can already judge by reason alone whether something will be good or bad. But this is very mistaken, and experience teaches us that our experiments often show quite different effects from the ones expected. One sees therefore that since experiments

matter, no one generation can present a complete plan of education. The only experimental school which to an extent made a beginning in establishing a course was the Dessau Institute. We must let it keep this glory regardless of the many mistakes of which one could accuse it (mistakes found in all conclusions that come from experiments)—viz., that new experiments are always required.

(9: 451)

What is most surprising about this passage is its strong empirical tone—its denial that reason must always lead the way over experience, and its assertion that experiments are valuable precisely because they sometimes lead to results that reason did not forsee. In his more canonical writings, Kant defends an anti-empiricist model of scientific inquiry, one that "sees science as from the beginning a product of reason, guided by a priori principles both in setting its aims and in setting the guiding principles for making its observations and its systematic presentation of their results."[5] Although Kant, like many optimistic educational theorists before and since, does express the hope that the art of education will eventually be "transformed into science" (9: 447), the picture of science defended in the *Lectures on Pedagogy* is a refreshingly open-ended and empirical one.[6]

## Naturalism

Insofar as he maintains that moral principles cannot be derived from facts of nature, Kant is a stern anti-naturalist in his ethical theory. For instance, the concept of a 'moral ought', he asserts in the *Critique of Pure Reason*,

> expresses a species of necessity and a connection with grounds which does not occur anywhere else in the whole of nature. In nature the understanding can only cognize *what exists*, or has been, or will be. It is impossible that something in it *ought to be* other than what, in all these time-relations, it in fact is; indeed, the *ought*, if one has merely the course of nature before one's eyes, has no significance whatsoever.

(A 546/B 575)

And because he holds that moral principles cannot be derived from empirical facts, Kant is also adamantly opposed to any and all moral theories that are based merely on biological or cultural-historical facts about human beings. He insists on a "pure moral philosophy," one that is "completely cleansed of everything that may be only empirical and belongs to anthropology" (*Groundwork of the Metaphysics of Morals* 4: 389).

A third surprise in Kant's writings on education is his refreshing appeal to a kind of naturalism. ("A kind," because, as Hume famously remarked, "nature" is a word "than which there is none more ambiguous and equivocal."[7] There are many kinds of naturalism.) In his second *Essay Regarding the Philanthropinum*, he asserts that all schools save one "were spoiled at the outset, ... because everything in them works against nature" (2: 449). Basedow's Philanthropinum alone employs the correct educational method, one that "is wisely derived from nature itself and not slavishly copied from old habit and unexperienced ages" (2: 449).

The kind of naturalism invoked here is one that we encountered earlier, in our discussion of the 'negative' education advocated by Rousseau. At bottom, it hints of a proto-Romantic glorification of nature; a conviction that natural processes are good and departures from them bad. However, at least on Kant's understanding, it is not an outlook that seeks to derive the ethical from the natural. The concept 'good' is not derived from nature; rather nature is simply viewed as good. Ultimately, the naturalism of his educational writings is a species of *weak* naturalism: much that we find in nature is good, though natural facts in themselves do not establish or justify moral principles. And any moral theory that is to be applied successfully to human beings needs to be consistent with the facts of human nature. Accordingly, education, one of the primary external influences on human moral development, needs a method that is "wisely derived from nature itself."

## Morality and Education

Morality occupies the biggest space within Kant's theory of education, in large part because of the explicit teleology behind his concepts of education and history. As we have seen, education and history both aim at the realization of morality throughout the human species. As he declares at the end of the *Collins* lecture on ethics: "The final end of the human race is moral perfection. . . . How then are we to seek this perfection, and from where is it to be hoped for? From nowhere else but education" (27: 470–71). At the same time, as also noted earlier, education ultimately plays only a preparatory role in the grounding of moral character, because even the best educational institution cannot guarantee that its graduates will become morally good people. Moral character on Kant's view is not causally determined by nature or nurture, but is rather a free choice for which each individual bears responsibility. In the language of his mature philosophy, educational institutions affect human beings' empirical or phenomenal character, but not their non-empirical or noumenal character. Keeping these two background points in mind, let us now turn to Kant's perspective on the methods and goals of moral education.

## Methods of Moral Education

Kant's position on the methods of moral education is fairly straightforward, although—as is often the case in his educational theory—the full story does not emerge from the *Lectures on Pedagogy* alone. To a certain extent, his views on how to teach ethics are the same as his views on how to teach other subjects. The student's level of emotional and cognitive development should be the primary criterion in choosing a teaching method, not the subject matter or the instructor's personal preference. For instance, in his discussion of the "Doctrine of the Method of Ethics" at the end of the *Metaphysics of Morals* (one of his best texts on moral education), he advocates what he calls an 'erotematic' teaching method (from the Greek *eromai*, "to ask or inquire")—essentially, question-and-answer rather than lecture. For the primary goal of moral education is to show the student "that he himself can think" (6: 478) about morality rather than just listen to other people's (including teachers') opinions about it. Kant then subdivides the erotematic method into the dialogical approach, "where the teacher questions the pupils' *reason*"; and the catechistic, "where he merely questions their *memory*" (6: 478). He also discusses these two varieties of the erotematic teaching style (along with its counterpart, the lecture or 'acroamatic' approach—from the Greek *akroamai*, "to listen to") in many of his logic lectures (see, e.g., *Jäsche* 9: 149–50, *Pölitz* 24: 599, *Busolt* 24: 684, *Dohna-Wundlacken* 24: 780).

Accordingly, "the first and most essential" instrument for teaching ethics to young students is "a *moral* catechism" (*Metaphysics of Morals* 6: 478; cf. *Critique of Practical Reason* 5: 154) or "catechism of right" (*Lectures on Pedagogy* 9: 490). Catechisms—summaries of the main principles of a doctrine presented in the form of question-and-answer—were used for centuries by Christian educators to teach young people about the main tenets of faith, and Kant is borrowing from this earlier tradition of moral education. But his moral catechism differs from Christian catechisms in two basic ways. First, it is "purely moral" (*Critique of Practical Reason* 5: 154)—i. e., unmixed with religious or theological doctrines. On Kant's view, the validity of moral principles is not contingent on religion but rather a matter of rational argument and agreement: "on its own behalf morality in no way needs religion . . . but is rather self-sufficient by virtue of pure practical reason" (*Religion within the Boundaries of Mere Reason* 6: 3). Second, and related, the moral catechism must precede any religious education in the student's life. Again, moral principles are to be rationally justified independently of religious faith. And religion itself needs to be grounded in morality, for "if religion is not combined with morality, then it becomes nothing more than currying favor. . . . Morality must therefore come first" (*Lectures on Pedagogy* 9: 494–95).

In the *Lectures* Kant offers only a brief summary of what a moral catechism should look like: "it would have to contain cases which would be popular, which occur in ordinary life, and which would always naturally raise the question whether something is right or not" (9: 490). In *The Metaphysics of Morals* he presents a fragment of an actual catechism, one that stresses basic moral concepts such as the nature of happiness, inclination, autonomy, and duty (6: 480–82). A complete catechism, which he does not provide, would be extensive, "for it must be carried out through all the articles of virtue and vice" (6: 482).

Kant's employment of case studies in his moral catechism is based on the cognitive development and natural curiosity of children. Children are not yet able to reason autonomously about moral principles, and at the beginning their ability to think about moral issues is best fostered through contact with concrete examples. But even though the pupil is "not yet ready for speculation" about the rational foundations of ethics, he naturally takes an interest in specific moral questions, and in analyzing them with a teacher he will "feel the progress of his power of judgment" (*Critique of Practical Reason* 5: 154). However, while discussing case studies does help foster students' native interest in morality, Kant stresses that what is most important are the underlying principles by which the cases are properly appraised. Ultimately, it is not specific examples of virtuous human beings or morally right action but rather the moral law itself "that must serve as the constant standard of a teacher's instruction" (*The Metaphysics of Morals* 6: 480).

With the introduction of dialogue, the second stage of the erotematic teaching method, students adopt a more active role in their moral education, asking questions of teachers in addition to providing answers to their questions. In the *Critique of Practical Reason* Kant offers a brief hint of what he has in mind. Describing a discussion with a 10-year-old boy concerning "the mark by which pure virtue is tested," Kant advocates using real examples drawn from "the biographies of ancient and modern times" in a manner that encourages the student to reach his own conclusion "without being directed to it by a teacher" (5: 154–55).

Taken together, the moral catechism and dialogical method form half of what Kant calls "ethical didactics"—essentially, moral education strategies for teachers to use with students. The "practical counterpoint" to these two techniques is what Kant calls "ascetics," "in which is taught not only the concept of virtue but also how to put into practice and cultivate the *capacity for* as well as the will to virtue" (*The Metaphysics of Morals* 6: 411–12). Moral ascetics (from the Greek *askêtês*, one who practices an art) in Kant's etymological sense refers not to rigorous self-denial, renunciation of the flesh, etc., but merely to the practice rather than the theory of virtue. But it is largely a self-discipline that students must practice on themselves. The teacher's role here is limited to helping students grasp the correct principles for cultivating and practicing virtue. The main principle Kant stresses is the importance of taking pleasure and joy in doing one's duty (6: 484)—ironically, the exact opposite of what some critics claim to find in Kant's ethics.

Didactics and ascetics form the two divisions of Kant's "doctrine of method" for ethics, for they can both "be presented as a *science*" (6: 478)—in this context, a body of knowledge that can be set forth systematically and taught by means of rules. Casuistry, the art of resolving particular cases by applying general principles (from the Latin *cāsus*, case), forms the final component in Kant's methods of moral education. Casuistry is needed in moral education because rules are never self-deploying. There are no rules that can show us how to apply principles to specific cases; thus good judgment—which is always needed in ethics but rarely found—must remain an art to be cultivated through practice rather than a science to be learned through study.

### Goals of Moral Education

Kantian moral education of course aims to teach children "the duties that they have to fulfill" (*Lectures* 9: 488); but, more importantly, it also strives to foster a number of interconnected attitudes and dispositions that are preliminary to but essential for morality as Kant understands it. Perhaps the clearest example of the latter is the goal of instilling cosmopolitan dispositions in students. Students must learn to become citizens of the world, and to respect the inherent dignity and moral equality of all human beings: "they must rejoice at the best for the world even if it is not to the advantage of their fatherland or to their own gain" (9: 499). Education everywhere must aim not at national or parental goals (both of which are usually vocational in nature), but at human perfection. As Kant stresses earlier in the *Lectures*:

> Parents usually care only that their children get on well in the world, and . . . princes regard their subjects merely as instruments for their own designs. Parents care for the home, princes for the state. Neither have as their final end the best for the world and the perfection to which humanity is destined, and for which it also has the predisposition. However, the design for a plan of education must be made in a cosmopolitan manner.
>
> (9: 448)

This strong cosmopolitan orientation is also present in several other Enlightenment educational reform efforts; e. g., Basedow's Philanthropinum. But in Kant's case it connects directly to a core theme in his ethical theory. Educational plans that serve merely parental or national purposes are morally objectionable because they violate the categorical imperative to treat all human beings as ends in themselves: they treat students as tools (cf. *Groundwork for the Metaphysics of Morals* 4: 429).

The most important task of moral education is what Kant calls "the grounding of character," and this too is essentially shorthand for instilling a number of interrelated dispositions. At one point in the *Lectures* he states: "the first effort in moral character is the grounding of character. Character consists in the aptitude of acting from maxims" (9: 481). In the generic sense, a "maxim" is simply the underlying principle that guides one's action— thus, every action has a maxim. But Kant adds that the person who has character acts from a special type of maxim—one that originates "from the human being's own understanding" (9: 481). People who have character act autonomously from principles that can originate in their own reason rather than from rules that are externally imposed by others. As he remarks in *Anthropology from a Pragmatic Point of View*: "He who has character derives his conduct from a source that he has opened by himself" (7: 293). Later in the *Lectures* he states that the grounding of character "consists in the firm resolution of willing to do something, and then also in the actual performance of it" (9: 487). Now the stress is on strength of will and control of one's desires and passions; perseverance in the face of adversity.

Evil as well as good people, however, may possess independent judgment and strength of will. On Kant's view, the crucial distinguishing mark of morally good people is that they consistently act from maxims that can be "universalized"—that is, they act from principles that could be accepted and acted on by everyone. Those who are not morally good do not act from universalizable maxims. Human beings are moralized when they have acquired deep-seated dispositions to act on universalizable maxims, to treat all human beings as ends in themselves, and to regard all people as lawgiving members in a universal kingdom of ends. The moral educator's task is to instill these dispositions in individual students. Kant's philosophy of history points to a future condition where all members of the human race have acquired them.

Many Enlightenment intellectuals believed that human beings would be morally transformed through the growth of education, participation in democratic polities dedicated to the rule of law, free trade between nations, and the establishment of an effective international justice system that would stand up for human rights everywhere and eventually put an end to war.[8] Gradually, the right sort of external institutional development would lead to inner moral transformation. But while he is certainly sympathetic to this global reform movement, Kant's metaphysical commitment to free will prevents him from being a full-fledged member. External change does not guarantee internal change; good moral character is ultimately a free choice and not a causal outcome of social reform efforts.

John Dewey, in a famous passage in *Democracy and Education*, defines all of philosophy as philosophy of education.[9] Kant does not go quite this far, but in the preceding account I have tried to indicate some of the strong connections that exist between his philosophy of education, his philosophy of history, his ethical theory, and his anthropology. At bottom, education for Kant is about the effort to realize our humanity: "the human being can only become human through education" (9: 443).

## Notes

1. References to Kant's writings are cited by volume and page number in the standard "Academy" edition of his works, except for quotations from the *Critique of Pure Reason*, which are cited by the customary use of the pagination of its first ("A") and second ("B") editions.

2. John Locke expresses a similar conviction at the beginning of *Some Thoughts Concerning Education*: "I think I may say that of all the men we meet with, nine parts of ten are what they are, good or evil, useful or not, by their education. It is that which makes the great difference in mankind." Despite their strongly different philosophical orientations, Locke and Kant—indeed, Enlightenment intellectuals generally—stand united in their conviction that education is of supreme importance in human life.

3. Rousseau was a major influence on Kant's intellectual development. In a famous note that he wrote in the margins of his own copy of his 1764 book, *Observations on the Feeling of the Beautiful and the Sublime*, he states:

   > I am myself by inclination an investigator. I feel a complete thirst for knowledge and an eager unrest to go further in it as well as satisfaction at every acquisition. There was a time when I believed that this alone could constitute the honor of mankind, and I had contempt for the rabble who know nothing. *Rousseau* brought me around. This blinding superiority disappeared, I learned to honor human beings, and I would find myself far more useless than the common laborer if I did not believe that this consideration could impart to all others a value in establishing the rights of humanity (20: 44).

4. Karl von Raumer, *Geschichte der Pädagogik*, 4 vols. (Stuttgart: Samuel Gottlieb Liesching, 1843), 2: 278. This passage from Raumer is cited by Robert Herbert Quick, *Essays on Educational Reformers* (New York: D. Appleton and Company, 1896), pp. 274–75; and F. V. N. Painter, *A History of Education*, revised ed. (New York: D. Appleton and Company, 1906), p. 274.

5. Allen W. Wood, *Kant* (Malden, MA: Blackwell, 2005), p. 82.

6. As William K. Frankena notes, in his advocacy of experimentalism in education Kant represents "a strong anticipation of Dewey" [*Three Historical Philosophies of Education: Aristotle, Kant, Dewey* (Glenview, IL: Scott, Foresman and Company, 1965), p. 83; cf. 138–40].

7. David Hume, *A Treatise of Human Nature*, ed. L. A. Selby-Bigge and P. H. Nidditch, 2nd ed. (Oxford: Clarendon Press, 1978), III.I.ii.

8. For further discussion, see Robert B. Louden, *The World We Want: How and Why the Ideals of the Enlightenment Still Elude Us* (New York: Oxford University Press, 2007).

9. "If we are willing to conceive education as the process of forming fundamental dispositions, intellectual and emotional, toward nature and freedom, philosophy may even be defined *as the general theory of education.*" *The Middle Works of John Dewey*, 1899–1924, ed. Jo Ann Boydston (Carbondale: Southern Illinois University Press, 1980), 9: 328.

# 7

# Mary Wollstonecraft

**Mary Wollstonecraft** (1759–1797), born in England, had little formal education. During the French Revolution she lived in Paris, where she was close to many of its leading political figures. She worked as a writer, translator, and reviewer. Eventually she married the English political philosopher William Godwin and had a daughter, Mary, but died soon after from an infection contracted during childbirth. Her daughter wed the famed poet Percy Bysshe Shelley, and herself achieved literary fame as the author of *Frankenstein*. Mary Wollstonecraft's influential writings are widely regarded as critical to the development of feminism.

# *A Vindication of the Rights of Woman*

## Introduction

After considering the historic page, and viewing the living world with anxious solicitude, the most melancholy emotions of sorrowful indignation have depressed my spirits, and I have sighed when obliged to confess, that either nature has made a great difference between man and man, or that the civilization which has hitherto taken place in the world has been very partial. I have turned over various books written on the subject of education, and patiently observed the conduct of parents and the management of schools; but what has been the result?—a profound conviction that the neglected education of my fellow-creatures is the grand source of the misery I deplore; and that women, in particular, are rendered weak and wretched by a variety of concurring causes, originating from one hasty conclusion. The conduct and manners of women, in fact, evidently prove that their minds are not in a healthy state; for, like the flowers which are planted in too rich a soil, strength and usefulness are sacrificed to beauty; and the flaunting leaves, after having pleased a fastidious eye, fade, disregarded on the stalk, long before the season when they ought to have arrived at maturity.—One cause of this barren blooming I attribute to a false system of education, gathered from the books written on this subject by men who, considering females rather as women than human creatures, have been more anxious to make them alluring mistresses than affectionate wives and rational mothers; and the understanding of the sex has been so bubbled by this specious homage, that the civilized women of the present century, with a few exceptions, are only anxious to inspire love, when they ought to cherish a nobler ambition, and by their abilities and virtues exact respect.

In a treatise, therefore, on female rights and manners, the works which have been particularly written for their improvement must not be overlooked; especially when it is asserted, in direct terms, that the minds of women are enfeebled by false refinement; that the books of instruction, written by men of genius, have had the same tendency as more frivolous productions; and that, in the true style of Mahometanism, they are treated as a kind of subordinate beings, and not as a part of the human species, when improveable reason is allowed to be the dignified distinction which raises men above the brute creation, and puts a natural sceptre in a feeble hand.

Yet, because I am a woman, I would not lead my readers to suppose that I mean violently to agitate the contested question respecting the equality or inferiority of the sex; but as the subject lies in my way, and I cannot pass it over without subjecting the main tendency of my reasoning to misconstruction, I shall stop a moment to deliver, in a few words, my opinion.—In the government of the physical world it is observable that the female in point of strength is, in general, inferior to the male. This is the law of nature; and it does not appear to be suspended or abrogated in favour of woman. A degree of physical superiority cannot, therefore, be denied—and it is a noble prerogative! But not content with this natural pre-eminence, men endeavour to sink us still lower, merely to render us alluring objects for a moment; and women, intoxicated by the adoration which men, under the influence of their senses, pay them, do not seek to obtain a durable interest in their hearts, or to become the friends of the fellow creatures who find amusement in their society.

I am aware of an obvious inference:—from every quarter have I heard exclamations against masculine women; but where are they to be found? If by this appellation men mean to inveigh against their ardour in hunting, shooting, and gaming, I shall most cordially join in the cry; but if it be against the imitation of manly virtues, or, more properly speaking, the attainment of those talents and virtues, the exercise of which ennobles the human character, and which raise females in the scale of animal being, when they are comprehensively termed mankind;—all those who view them with a philosophic eye must, I should think, wish with me, that they may every day grow more and more masculine.

This discussion naturally divides the subject. I shall first consider women in the grand light of human creatures, who, in common with men, are placed on this earth to unfold their faculties; and afterwards I shall more particularly point out their peculiar designation. . . .

My own sex, I hope, will excuse me, if I treat them like rational creatures, instead of flattering their *fascinating* graces, and viewing them as if they were in a state of perpetual childhood, unable to stand alone. I earnestly wish to point out in what true dignity and human happiness consists—I wish to persuade women to endeavour to acquire strength, both of mind and body, and to convince them that the soft phrases, susceptibility of heart, delicacy of sentiment, and refinement of taste, are almost synonymous with epithets of weakness, and that those beings who are only the objects of pity and that kind of love, which has been termed its sister, will soon become objects of contempt.

Dismissing then those pretty feminine phrases, which the men condescendingly use to soften our slavish dependence, and despising that weak elegancy of mind, exquisite sensibility, and sweet docility of manners, supposed to be the sexual characteristics of the weaker vessel, I wish to show that elegance is inferior to virtue, that the first object of laudable ambition is to obtain a character as a human being, regardless of the distinction of sex; and that secondary views should be brought to this simple touchstone.

## Chapter II

### The Prevailing Opinion of a Sexual Character Discussed

. . . By individual education, I mean, for the sense of the word is not precisely defined, such an attention to a child as will slowly sharpen the senses, form the temper, regulate the passions as they begin to ferment, and set the understanding to work before the body arrives at maturity; so that the man may only have to proceed, not to begin, the important task of learning to think and reason.

To prevent any misconstruction, I must add, that I do not believe that a private education can work the wonders which some sanguine writers have attributed to it. Men and women must be educated, in a great degree, by the opinions and manners of the society they live in. In every age there has been a stream of popular opinion that has carried all before it, and given a family character, as it were, to the century. It may then fairly be inferred, that, till society be differently constituted, much cannot be expected from education. It is, however, sufficient for my present purpose to assert, that, whatever effect circumstances have on the abilities, every being may become virtuous by the exercise of its own reason; for if but one being was created with vicious inclinations, that is positively bad, what can save us from atheism? or if we worship a God, is not that God a devil?

Consequently, the most perfect education, in my opinion, is such an exercise of the understanding as is best calculated to strengthen the body and form the heart. Or, in other words, to enable the individual to attain such habits of virtue as will render it independent. In fact, it is a farce to call any being virtuous whose virtues do not result from the exercise of its own reason. This was Rousseau's opinion respecting men: I extend it to women, and confidently assert that they have been drawn out of their sphere by false refinement, and not by an endeavour to acquire masculine qualities. Still the regal homage which they receive is so intoxicating, that till the manners of the times are changed, and formed on more reasonable principles, it may be impossible to convince them that the illegitimate power, which they obtain, by degrading themselves, is a curse, and that they must return to nature and equality, if they wish to secure the placid satisfaction that unsophisticated affections impart. But for this epoch we must wait—wait, perhaps, till kings and nobles, enlightened by reason, and, preferring the real dignity of man to childish state, throw off their gaudy hereditary trappings: and if then women do not resign the arbitrary power of beauty—they will prove that they have *less* mind than man.

I may be accused of arrogance; still I must declare what I firmly believe, that all the writers who have written on the subject of female education and manners . . . have contributed to render women more artificial, weak characters, than they would otherwise have been; and, consequently, more useless members of society. . . .

I now principally allude to Rousseau, for his character of Sophia is, undoubtedly, a captivating one, though it appears to me grossly unnatural; however it is not the superstructure, but the foundation of her character, the principles on which her education was built, that I mean to attack; nay, warmly as I admire the genius of that able writer, whose opinions I shall often have occasion to cite, indignation always takes place of admiration, and the rigid frown of insulted virtue effaces the smile of complacency, which his eloquent periods are wont to raise, when I read his voluptuous reveries. Is this the man, who, in his ardour for virtue, would banish all the soft arts of peace, and almost carry us back to Spartan discipline? Is this the man who delights to paint the useful struggles of passion, the triumphs of good dispositions, and the heroic flights which carry the glowing soul out of itself?—How are these mighty sentiments lowered when he describes the pretty foot and enticing airs of his little favourite! But, for the present, I waive the subject, and, instead of severely reprehending the transient effusions of overweening sensibility, I shall only observe, that whoever has cast a benevolent eye on society, must often have been gratified by the sight of humble mutual love, not dignified by sentiment, or strengthened by a union in intellectual pursuits. The domestic trifles of the day have afforded matters for cheerful converse, and innocent caresses have softened toils which did not require great exercise of mind or stretch of thought: yet, has not the sight of this moderate felicity excited more tenderness than respect? An emotion similar to what we feel when children are playing, or animals sporting, whilst the contemplation of the noble struggles of suffering merit has raised admiration, and carried our thoughts to that world where sensation will give place to reason.

Women are, therefore, to be considered either as moral beings, or so weak that they must be entirely subjected to the superior faculties of men.

Let us examine this question. Rousseau declares that a woman should never, for a moment, feel herself independent, that she should be governed by fear to exercise her *natural* cunning, and made a coquetish slave in order to render her a more alluring object of desire, a *sweeter* companion to man, whenever he chooses to relax himself. He carries the arguments, which he pretends to draw from the indications of nature, still further, and insinuates that truth and fortitude, the corner stones of all human virtue, should be cultivated with certain restrictions, because, with respect to the female character, obedience is the grand lesson which ought to be impressed with unrelenting rigour.

What nonsense! when will a great man arise with sufficient strength of mind to puff away the fumes which pride and sensuality have thus spread over the subject! If women are by nature inferior to men, their virtues must be the same in quality, if not in degree, or virtue is a relative idea; consequently, their conduct should be founded on the same principles, and have the same aim.

Connected with man as daughters, wives, and mothers, their moral character may be estimated by their manner of fulfilling those simple duties; but the end, the grand end of their exertions should be to unfold their own faculties and acquire the dignity of conscious virtue. They may try to render their road pleasant; but ought never to forget, in common with man, that life yields not the felicity which can satisfy an immortal soul, I do not mean to insinuate, that either sex should be so lost in abstract reflections or distant views, as to forget the affections and duties that lie before them, and are, in truth, the means appointed to produce the fruit of life; on the contrary, I would warmly recommend them, even while I assert, that they afford most satisfaction when they are considered in their true, sober light.

Probably the prevailing opinion, that woman was created for man, may have taken its rise from Moses's poetical story; yet, as very few, it is presumed, who have bestowed any serious thought on the subject, ever supposed that Eve was, literally speaking, one of Adam's ribs, the deduction must be allowed to fall to the ground; or, only be so far admitted as it proves that man, from the remotest antiquity, found it convenient to exert his strength to subjugate his companion, and his invention to show that she ought to have her neck bent under the yoke, because the whole creation was only created for his convenience or pleasure. . . .

Let me reason with the supporters of this opinion who have any knowledge of human nature, do they imagine that marriage can eradicate the habitude of life? The woman who has only been taught to please will soon find that her charms are oblique sunbeams, and that they cannot have much effect on her husband's heart when they are seen every day, when the summer is passed and gone. Will she then have sufficient native energy to look into herself for comfort, and cultivate her dormant faculties? or, is it not more rational to expect that she will try to please other men; and, in the emotions raised by the expectation of new conquests, endeavour to forget the mortification her love or pride has received? When the husband ceases to be a lover—and the time will inevitably come, her desire of pleasing will then grow languid, or become a spring of bitterness; and love, perhaps, the most evanescent of all passions, gives place to jealousy or vanity.

I now speak of women who are restrained by principle or prejudice; such women, though they would shrink from an intrigue with real abhorrence, yet, nevertheless, wish to be convinced by the homage of gallantry that they are cruelly neglected by their husbands; or, days and weeks are spent in dreaming of the happiness enjoyed by congenial souls till their health is undermined and their spirits broken by discontent. How then can the great art of pleasing be such a necessary study? it is only useful to a mistress; the chaste wife, and serious mother, should only consider her power to please as the polish of her virtues, and the affection of her husband as one of the comforts that render her task less difficult and her life happier.—But, whether she be loved or neglected, her first wish should be to make herself respectable, and not to rely for all her happiness on a being subject to like infirmities with herself. . . .


**Chapter XII**


**On National Education**

The good effects resulting from attention to private education will ever be very confined, and the parent who really puts his own hand to the plow, will always, in some degree, be disappointed, till education becomes a grand national concern. A man cannot retire into a desert with his child, and if he did he could not bring himself back to childhood, and become the proper friend and play-fellow of an infant or youth. And when children are confined to the society of men and women, they very soon acquire that kind of premature manhood which stops the growth of every vigorous power of mind or body. In order to open their faculties they should be excited to think for themselves; and this can only be done by mixing a number of children together, and making them jointly pursue the same objects.

A child very soon contracts a benumbing indolence of mind, which he has seldom sufficient vigour afterwards to shake off, when he only asks a question instead of seeking for information, and then relies implicitly on the answer he receives. With his equals in age this could never be the case, and the subjects of inquiry, though they might be influenced, would not be entirely under the direction of men, who frequently damp, if not destroy, abilities, by bringing them forward too hastily: and too hastily they will infallibly be brought forward, if the child be confined to the society of a man, however sagacious that man may be.

Besides, in youth the seeds of every affection should be sown, and the respectful regard, which is felt for a parent, is very different from the social affections that are to constitute the happiness of life as it advances. Of these equality is the basis, and an intercourse of sentiments unclogged by that observant seriousness which prevents disputation, though it may not inforce submission. Let a child have ever such an affection for his parent, he will always languish to play and prattle with children; and the very respect he feels, for filial esteem always has a dash of fear mixed with it, will, if it do not teach him cunning, at least prevent him from pouring out the little secrets which first open the heart to friendship and confidence, gradually leading to more expansive benevolence. Added to this, he will never acquire that frank ingenuousness of behaviour, which young people can only attain by being frequently in society where they dare to speak what they think; neither afraid of being reproved for their presumption, nor laughed at for their folly.

Forcibly impressed by the reflections which the sight of schools, as they are at present conducted, naturally suggested, I have formerly delivered my opinion rather warmly in favour of a private education; but further experience has led me to view the subject in a different light. I still, however, think schools, as they are now regulated, the hot-beds of vice and folly, and the knowledge of human nature, supposed to be attained there, merely cunning selfishness.

At school boys become gluttons and slovens, and, instead of cultivating domestic affections, very early rush into the libertinism which destroys the constitution before it is formed; hardening the heart as it weakens the understanding.

I should, in fact, be averse to boarding-schools, if it were for no other reason than the unsettled state of mind which the expectation of the vacations produce. On these the children's thoughts are fixed with eager anticipating hopes, for, at least, to speak with moderation, half of the time, and when they arrive they are spent in total dissipation and beastly indulgence.

But, on the contrary, when they are brought up at home, though they may pursue a plan of study in a more orderly manner than can be adopted when near a fourth part of the year is actually spent in idleness, and as much more in regret and anticipation; yet they there acquire too high an opinion of their own importance, from being allowed to tyrannize over servants, and from the anxiety expressed by most mothers, on the score of manners, who, eager to teach the accomplishments of a gentleman, stifle, in their birth, the virtues of a man. Thus brought into company when they ought to be seriously employed, and treated like men when they are still boys, they become vain and effeminate.

The only way to avoid two extremes equally injurious to morality, would be to contrive some way of combining a public and private education. Thus to make men citizens two natural steps might be taken, which seem directly to lead to the desired point; for the domestic affections, that first open the heart to the various modifications of humanity, would be cultivated, whilst the children were nevertheless allowed to spend great part of their time, on terms of equality, with other children. . . .

Few, I believe, have had much affection for mankind, who did not first love their parents, their brothers, sisters, and even the domestic brutes, whom they first played with. The exercise of youthful sympathies forms the moral temperature; and it is the recollection of these first affections and pursuits that gives life to those that are afterwards more under the direction of reason. In youth, the fondest friendships are formed, the genial juices mounting at the same time, kindly mix; or, rather the heart, tempered for the reception of friendship, is accustomed to seek for pleasure in something more noble than the churlish gratification of appetite.

In order then to inspire a love of home and domestic pleasures, children ought to be educated at home, for riotous holidays only make them fond of home for their own sakes. Yet, the vacations, which do not foster domestic affections, continually disturb the course of study, and render any plan of improvement abortive which includes temperance; still, were they abolished, children would be entirely separated from their parents, and I question whether they would become better citizens by sacrificing the preparatory affections, by destroying the force of relationships that render the marriage state as necessary as respectable. But, if a private education produce self-importance, or insulate a man in his family, the evil is only shifted, not remedied.

This train of reasoning brings me back to a subject, on which I mean to dwell, the necessity of establishing proper day-schools.

But, these should be national establishments, for whilst school-masters are dependent on the caprice of parents, little exertion can be expected from them, more than is necessary to please ignorant people. Indeed, the necessity of a master's giving the parents some sample of the boy's abilities, which during the vacation is shewn to every visitor, is productive of more mischief than would at first be supposed. For it is seldom done entirely, to speak with moderation, by the child itself; thus the master countenances falsehood, or winds the poor machine up to some extraordinary exertion, that injures the wheels, and stops the progress of gradual improvement. The memory is loaded with unintelligible words, to make a show of, without the understanding's acquiring any distinct ideas: but only that education deserves emphatically to be termed cultivation of mind, which teaches young people how to begin to think. The imagination should not be allowed to debauch the understanding before it gained strength, or vanity will become the fore-runner of vice: for every way of exhibiting the acquirements of a child is injurious to its moral character.

How much time is lost in teaching them to recite what they do not understand? whilst, seated on benches, all in their best array, the mammas listen with astonishment to the parrot-like prattle, uttered in solemn cadences, with all the pomp of ignorance and folly. Such exhibitions only serve to strike the spreading fibres of vanity through the whole mind; for they neither teach children to speak fluently, nor behave gracefully. So far from it, that these frivolous pursuits might comprehensively be termed the study of affectation; for we now rarely see a simple, bashful boy, though few people of taste were ever disgusted by that awkward sheepishness so natural to the age, which schools and an early introduction into society, have changed into impudence and apish grimace. . . .

With what disgust have I heard sensible women, for girls are more restrained and cowed than boys, speak of the wearisome confinement, which they endured at school. Not allowed, perhaps, to step out of one broad walk in a superb garden, and obliged to pace with steady deportment stupidly backwards and forwards, holding up their heads and turning out their toes, with shoulders braced back, instead of bounding, as nature directs to complete her own design, in the various attitudes so conducive to health.[1] The pure animal spirits, which make both mind and body shoot out, and unfold the tender blossoms of hope, are turned sour, and vented in vain wishes or pert repinings, that contract the faculties and spoil the temper; else they mount to the brain, and sharpening the understanding before it gains proportionable strength, produce that pitiful cunning which disgracefully characterizes the female mind—and I fear will ever characterize it whilst women remain the slaves of power! . . .

I have already animadverted on the bad habits which females acquire when they are shut up together; and, I think, that the observation may fairly be extended to the other sex, till the natural inference is drawn which I have had in view throughout—that to improve both sexes they ought, not only in private families, but in public schools, to be educated together. If marriage be the cement of society, mankind should all be educated after the same model, or the intercourse of the sexes will never deserve the name of fellowship, nor will women ever fulfil the peculiar duties of their sex, till they become enlightened citizens, till they become free by being enabled to earn their own subsistence, independent of men; in the same manner, I mean, to prevent misconstruction, as one man is independent of another. Nay, marriage will never be held sacred till women, by being brought up with men, are prepared to be their companions rather than their mistresses; for the mean doublings of cunning will ever render them contemptible, whilst oppression renders them timid. So convinced am I of this truth, that I will venture to predict that virtue will never prevail in society till the virtues of both sexes are founded on reason; and, till the affections common to both are allowed to gain their due strength by the discharge of mutual duties.

Were boys and girls permitted to pursue the same studies together, those graceful decencies might early be inculcated which produce modesty without those sexual distinctions that taint the mind. Lessons of politeness, and that formulary of decorum, which treads on the heels of falsehood, would be rendered useless by habitual propriety of behaviour. Not, indeed, put on for visitors like the courtly robe of politeness, but the sober effect of cleanliness of mind. Would not this simple elegance of sincerity be a chaste homage paid to domestic affections, far surpassing the meretricious compliments that shine with false lustre in the heartless intercourse of fashionable life? But, till more understanding preponderates in society, there will ever be a want of heart and taste, and the harlot's *rouge* will supply the place of that celestial suffusion which only virtuous affections can give to the face. Gallantry, and what is called love, may subsist without simplicity of character; but the main pillars of friendship, are respect and confidence—esteem is never founded on it cannot tell what!

A taste for the fine arts requires great cultivation; but not more than a taste for the virtuous affections; and both suppose that enlargement of mind which opens so many sources of mental pleasure. Why do people hurry to noisy scenes, and crowded circles? I should answer, because they want activity of mind, because they have not cherished the virtues of the heart. They only, therefore, see and feel in the gross, and continually pine after variety, finding every thing that is simple insipid.

This argument may be carried further than philosophers are aware of, for if nature destined woman, in particular, for the discharge of domestic duties, she made her susceptible of the attached affections in a great degree. Now women are notoriously fond of pleasure; and, naturally must be so according to my definition, because they cannot enter into the minutiæ of domestic taste; lacking judgment, the foundation of all taste. For the understanding, in spite of sensual cavillers, reserves to itself the privilege of conveying pure joy to the heart.

With what a languid yawn have I seen an admirable poem thrown down, that a man of true taste returns to, again and again with rapture; and, whilst melody has almost suspended respiration, a lady has asked me where I bought my gown. I have seen also an eye glanced coldly over a most exquisite picture, rest, sparkling with pleasure, on a caricature rudely sketched; and whilst some terrific feature in nature has spread a sublime stillness through my soul, I have been desired to observe the pretty tricks of a lap-dog, that my perverse fate forced me to travel with. Is it surprising that such a tasteless being should rather caress this dog than her children? Or, that she should prefer the rant of flattery to the simple accents of sincerity?

To illustrate this remark I must be allowed to observe, that men of the first genius, and most cultivated minds, have appeared to have the highest relish for the simple beauties of nature; and they must have forcibly felt, what they have so well described, the charm which natural affections, and unsophisticated feelings spread round the human character. It is this power of looking into the heart, and responsively vibrating with each emotion, that enables the poet to personify each passion, and the painter to sketch with a pencil of fire.

True taste is ever the work of the understanding employed in observing natural effects; and till women have more understanding, it is vain to expect them to possess domestic taste. Their lively senses will ever be at work to harden their hearts, and the emotions struck out of them will continue to be vivid and transitory, unless a proper education store their mind with knowledge.

It is the want of domestic taste, and not the acquirement of knowledge, that takes women out of their families, and tears the smiling babe from the breast that ought to afford it nourishment. Women have been allowed to remain in ignorance, and slavish dependence, many, very many years, and still we hear of nothing but their fondness of pleasure and sway, their preference of rakes and soldiers, their childish attachment to toys, and the vanity that makes them value accomplishments more than virtues.

History brings forward a fearful catalogue of the crimes which their cunning has produced, when the weak slaves have had sufficient address to over-reach their masters. In France, and in how many other countries, have men been the luxurious despots, and women the crafty ministers?—Does this prove that ignorance and dependence domesticate them? Is not their folly the by-word of the libertines, who relax in their society; and do not men of sense continually lament that an immoderate fondness for dress and dissipation carries the mother of a family for ever from home? Their hearts have not been debauched by knowledge, or their minds led astray by scientific pursuits; yet, they do not fulfil the peculiar duties which as women they are called upon by nature to fulfil. On the contrary, the state of warfare which subsists between the sexes, makes them employ those wiles, that often frustrate the more open designs of force.

When, therefore, I call women slaves, I mean in a political and civil sense; for, indirectly they obtain too much power, and are debased by their exertions to obtain illicit sway.

Let an enlightened nation then try what effect reason would have to bring them back to nature, and their duty; and allowing them to share the advantages of education and government with man, see whether they will become better, as they grow wiser and become free. They cannot be injured by the experiment; for it is not in the power of man to render them more insignificant than they are at present.

To render this practicable, day schools, for particular ages, should be established by government, in which boys and girls might be educated together. The school for the younger children, from five to nine years of age, ought to be absolutely free and open to all classes. A sufficient number of masters should also be chosen by a select committee, in each parish, to whom any complaint of negligence, &c. might be made, if signed by six of the children's parents.

Ushers would then be unnecessary; for I believe experience will ever prove that this kind of subordinate authority is particularly injurious to the morals of youth. What, indeed, can tend to deprave the character more than outward submission and inward contempt? Yet how can boys be expected to treat an usher with respect, when the master seems to consider him in the light of a servant, and almost to countenance the ridicule which becomes the chief amusement of the boys during the play hours?

But nothing of this kind could occur in an elementary day-school, where boys and girls, the rich and poor, should meet together. And to prevent any of the distinctions of vanity, they should be dressed alike, and all obliged to submit to the same discipline, or leave the school. The school-room ought to be surrounded by a large piece of ground, in which the children might be usefully exercised, for at this age they should not be confined to any sedentary employment for more than an hour at a time. But these relaxations might all be rendered a part of elementary education, for many things improve and amuse the senses, when introduced as a kind of show, to the principles of which, dryly laid down, children would turn a deaf ear. For instance, botany, mechanics, and astronomy. Reading, writing, arithmetic, natural history, and some simple experiments in natural philosophy, might fill up the day; but these pursuits should never encroach on gymnastic plays in the open air. The elements of religion, history, the history of man, and politics, might also be taught by conversations, in the socratic form.

After the age of nine, girls and boys, intended for domestic employments, or mechanical trades, ought to be removed to other schools, and receive instruction, in some measure appropriated to the destination of each individual, the two sexes being still together in the morning; but in the afternoon, the girls should attend a school, where plain-work, mantua-making, millinery, &c. would be their employment.

The young people of superior abilities, or fortune, might now be taught, in another school, the dead and living languages, the elements of science, and continue the study of history and politics, on a more extensive scale, which would not exclude polite literature.

Girls and boys still together? I hear some readers ask: yes. And I should not fear any other consequence than that some early attachment might take place; which, whilst it had the best effect on the moral character of the young people, might not perfectly agree with the views of the parents, for it will be a long time, I fear, before the world will be so far enlightened that parents, only anxious to render their children virtuous, shall allow them to choose companions for life themselves.

Besides, this would be a sure way to promote early marriages, and from early marriages the most salutary physical and moral effects naturally flow. What a different character does a married citizen assume from the selfish coxcomb, who lives, but for himself, and who is often afraid to marry lest he should not be able to live in a certain style. Great emergencies excepted, which would rarely occur in a society of which equality was the basis, a man can only be prepared to discharge the duties of public life, by the habitual practice of those inferiour ones which form the man.

In this plan of education the constitution of boys would not be ruined by the early debaucheries, which now make men so selfish, or girls rendered weak and vain, by indolence, and frivolous pursuits. But, I presuppose, that such a degree of equality should be established between the sexes as would shut out gallantry and coquetry, yet allow friendship and love to temper the heart for the discharge of higher duties.

These would be schools of morality—and the happiness of man, allowed to flow from the pure springs of duty and affection, what advances might not the human mind make? Society can only be happy and free in proportion as it is virtuous; but the present distinctions, established in society, corrode all private, and blast all public virtue.

I have already inveighed against the custom of confining girls to their needle, and shutting them out from all political and civil employments; for by thus narrowing their minds they are rendered unfit to fulfil the peculiar duties which nature has assigned them.

Only employed about the little incidents of the day, they necessarily grow up cunning. My very soul has often sickened at observing the sly tricks practised by women to gain some foolish thing on which their silly hearts were set. Not allowed to dispose of money, or call any thing their own, they learn to turn the market penny; or, should a husband offend, by staying from home, or give rise to some emotions of jealousy—a new gown, or any pretty bawble, smooths Juno's angry brow.

But these *littlenesses* would not degrade their character, if women were led to respect themselves, if political and moral subjects were opened to them; and, I will venture to affirm, that this is the only way to make them properly attentive to their domestic duties.—An active mind embraces the whole circle of its duties, and finds time enough for all. It is not, I assert, a bold attempt to emulate masculine virtues; it is not the enchantment of literary pursuits, or the steady investigation of scientific subjects, that leads women astray from duty. No, it is indolence and vanity—the love of pleasure and the love of sway, that will reign paramount in an empty mind. I say empty emphatically, because the education which women now receive scarcely deserves the name. For the little knowledge that they are led to acquire, during the important years of youth, is merely relative to accomplishments; and accomplishments without a bottom, for unless the understanding be cultivated, superficial and monotonous is every grace. Like the charms of a made up face, they only strike the senses in a crowd; but at home, wanting mind, they want variety. The consequence is obvious; in gay scenes of dissipation we meet the artificial mind and face, for those who fly from solitude dread, next to solitude, the domestic circle; not having it in their power to amuse or interest, they feel their own insignificance, or find nothing to amuse or interest themselves.

Besides, what can be more indelicate than a girls's *coming out* in the fashionable world? Which, in other words, is to bring to market a marriageable miss, whose person is taken from one public place to another, richly caparisoned. Yet, mixing in the giddy circle under restraint, these butterflies long to flutter at large, for the first affection of their souls is their own persons, to which their attention has been called with the most sedulous care whilst they were preparing for the period that decides their fate for life. Instead of pursuing this idle routine, sighing for tasteless show, and heartless state, with what dignity would the youths of both sexes form attachments in the schools that I have cursorily pointed out; in which, as life advanced, dancing, music, and drawing, might be admitted as relaxations, for at these schools young people of fortune ought to remain, more or less, till they were of age. Those, who were designed for particular professions, might attend, three or four mornings in the week, the schools appropriated for their immediate instruction.

I only drop these observations at present, as hints; rather, indeed, as an outline of the plan I mean, than a digested one; but I must add, that I highly approve of . . . making the children and youths independent of the masters respecting punishments. They should be tried by their peers, which would be an admirable method of fixing sound principles of justice in the mind, and might have the happiest effect on the temper, which is very early soured or irritated by tyranny, till it becomes peevishly cunning, or ferociously overbearing.

My imagination darts forward with benevolent fervour to greet these amiable and respectable groups, in spite of the sneering of cold hearts, who are at liberty to utter, with frigid self-importance, the damning epithet—romantic; the force of which I shall endeavour to blunt by repeating the words of an eloquent moralist.—"I know not whether the allusions of a truly humane heart, whose zeal renders every thing easy, be not preferable to that rough and repulsing reason, which always finds an indifference for the public good, the first obstacle to whatever would promote it."

I know that libertines will also exclaim, that woman would be unsexed by acquiring strength of body and mind, and that beauty, soft bewitching beauty! would no longer adorn the daughters of men. I am of a very different opinion, for I think that, on the contrary, we should then see dignified beauty, and true grace; to produce which, many powerful physical and moral causes would concur.—Not relaxed beauty, it is true, or the graces of helplessness; but such as appears to make us respect the human body as a majestic pile fit to receive a noble inhabitant, in the relics of antiquity.

I do not forget the popular opinion that the Grecian statues were not modelled after nature. I mean, not according to the proportions of a particular man; but that beautiful limbs and features were selected from various bodies to form an harmonious whole. This might, in some degree, be true. The fine ideal picture of an exalted imagination might be superiour to the materials which the statuary found in nature, and thus it might with propriety be termed rather the model of mankind than of a man. It was not, however, the mechanical selection of limbs and features; but the ebullition of an heated fancy that burst forth, and the fine senses and enlarged understanding of the artist selected the solid matter, which he drew into this glowing focus.

I observed that it was not mechanical, because a whole was produced—a model of that grand simplicity, of those concurring energies, which arrest our attention and command our reverence. For only insipid lifeless beauty is produced by a servile copy of even beautiful nature. Yet, independent of these observations, I believe that the human form must have been far more beautiful than it is at present, because extreme indolence, barbarous ligatures, and many causes, which forcibly act on it, in our luxurious state of society, did not retard its expansion, or render it deformed. Exercise and cleanliness appear to be not only the surest means of preserving health, but of promoting beauty, the physical causes only considered; yet, this is not sufficient, moral ones must concur, or beauty will be merely of that rustic kind which blooms on the innocent, wholesome, countenances of some country people, whose minds have not been exercised. To render the person perfect, physical and moral beauty ought to be attained at the same time; each lending and receiving force by the combination. Judgment must reside on the brow, affection and fancy beam in the eye, and humanity curve the cheek, or vain is the sparkling of the finest eye or the elegantly turned finish of the fairest features: whilst in every motion that displays the active limbs and well-knit joints, grace and modesty should appear. But this fair assemblage is not to be brought together by chance; it is the reward of exertions calculated to support each other; for judgment can only be acquired by reflection, affection by the discharge of duties, and humanity by the exercise of compassion to every living creature.

Humanity to animals should be particularly inculcated as a part of national education, for it is not at present one of our national virtues. Tenderness for their humble dumb domestics, amongst the lower class, is oftener to be found in a savage than a civilized state. For civilization prevents that intercourse which creates affection in the rude hut, or mud hovel, and leads uncultivated minds who are only depraved by the refinements which prevail in the society, where they are trodden under foot by the rich, to domineer over them to revenge the insults that they are obliged to bear from their superiors.

This habitual cruelty is first caught at school, where it is one of the rare sports of the boys to torment the miserable brutes that fall in their way. The transition, as they grow up, from barbarity to brutes to domestic tyranny over wives, children, and servants, is very easy. Justice, or even benevolence, will not be a powerful spring of action unless it extend to the whole creation; nay, I believe that it may be delivered as an axiom, that those who can see pain, unmoved, will soon learn to inflict it.

The vulgar are swayed by present feelings, and the habits which they have accidentally acquired; but on partial feelings much dependence cannot be placed, though they be just; for, when they are not invigorated by reflection, custom weakens them, till they are scarcely perceptible. The sympathies of our nature are strengthened by pondering cogitations, and deadened by thoughtless use. Macbeth's heart smote him more for one murder, the first, than for a hundred subsequent ones, which were necessary to back it. But, when I used the epithet vulgar, I did not mean to confine my remark to the poor, for partial humanity, founded on present sensations, or whim, is quite as conspicuous, if not more so, amongst the rich.

The lady who sheds tears for the bird starved in a snare, and execrates the devils in the shape of men, who goad to madness the poor ox, or whip the patient ass, tottering under a burden above its strength, will, nevertheless, keep her coachman and horses whole hours waiting for her, when the sharp frost bites, or the rain beats against the well-closed windows which do not admit a breath of air to tell her how roughly the wind blows without. And she who takes her dogs to bed, and nurses them with a parade of sensibility, when sick, will suffer her babes to grow up crooked in a nursery. This illustration of my argument is drawn from a matter of fact. The woman whom I allude to was handsome, reckoned very handsome, by those who do not miss the mind when the face is plump and fair; but her understanding had not been led from female duties by literature, nor her innocence debauched by knowledge. No, she was quite feminine, according to the masculine acceptation of the word; and, so far from loving these spoiled brutes that filled the place which her children ought to have occupied, she only lisped out a pretty mixture of French and English nonsense, to please the men who flocked round her. The wife, mother, and human creature, were all swallowed up by the factitious character which an improper education and the selfish vanity of beauty had produced.

I do not like to make a distinction without a difference, and I own that I have been as much disgusted by the fine lady who took her lap-dog to her bosom instead of her child; as by the ferocity of a man, who, beating his horse, declared, that he knew as well when he did wrong, as a Christian.

This brood of folly shows how mistaken they are who, if they allow women to leave their harems, do not cultivate their understandings, in order to plant virtues in their hearts. For had they sense, they might acquire that domestic taste which would lead them to love with reasonable subordination their whole family, from their husband to the house-dog; nor would they ever insult humanity in the person of the most menial servant by paying more attention to the comfort of a brute, than to that of a fellow-creature.

My observations on national education are obviously hints; but I principally wish to enforce the necessity of educating the sexes together to perfect both, and of making children sleep at home that they may learn to love home; yet to make private support, instead of smothering, public affections, they should be sent to school to mix with a number of equals, for only by the jostlings of equality can we form a just opinion of ourselves.

To render mankind more virtuous, and happier of course, both sexes must act from the same principle; but how can that be expected when only one is allowed to see the reasonableness of it? To render also the social compact truly equitable, and in order to spread those enlightening principles, which alone can meliorate the fate of man, women must be allowed to found their virtue on knowledge, which is scarcely possible unless they be educated by the same pursuits as men.

## Note

1. I remember a circumstance that once came under my own observation, and raised my indignation. I went to visit a little boy at a school where young children were prepared for a larger one. The master took me into the school-room, but whilst I walked down a broad gravel walk, I could not help observing that the grass grew very luxuriantly on each side of me. I immediately

asked the child some questions, and found that the poor boys were not allowed to stir off the walk, and that the master sometimes permitted sheep to be turned in to crop the untrodden grass. The tyrant of this domain used to sit by a window that overlooked the prison yard, and one nook turning from it, where the unfortunate babes could sport freely, he enclosed, and planted it with potatoes. The wife likewise was equally anxious to keep the children in order, lest they should dirty or tear their clothes.

# Afterword

## Jane Roland Martin*

### Rational Women

. . . It cannot be denied that the conceptual framework of *A Vindication* is derivative. Wollstonecraft is a daughter of the Enlightenment, a true eighteenth-century rationalist whose world view is indebted to John Locke and his intellectual descendants. Reason serves as the starting point for Wollstonecraft's political philosophy, as for Locke's. She believes that there are rights that human beings inherit because they are rational creatures; that rationality forms the basis of these rights because reason, itself God-given, enables them to grasp truth and thus acquire knowledge of right and wrong; that the possession of reason raises humans above brute creation; and that through its exercise they become moral, and ultimately political, agents.

*A Vindication* belongs to the same powerful intellectual tradition as the American Declaration of Independence. In its emphasis on the rationality of man and on the connections between reason, on the one hand, and virtue, natural rights, and equality, on the other, Wollstonecraft's political philosophy is neither more nor less original than Thomas Jefferson's. Both thinkers share the Enlightenment belief in the efficacy of knowledge and the reign of reason in the state as in the individual; both understand that although man is born rational, his reason does not mature by itself but must be cultivated through education. Yet while Wollstonecraft embraces a world view shared by others, she is the one who argues systematically for bringing women into its domain. The originality and profundity of her ideas are not to be found in her eighteenth-century rationalism per se but in the way she extends the fundamental tenets of that philosophy to women. In *A Vindication* Wollstonecraft sets herself a threefold task: to rebut the presumption that women are not rational but are slaves to their passions; to show that if the rights of man are extended to females, women's domestic duties will not suffer; and to propose an education and upbringing for

* Jane Roland Martin is Professor Emerita of Philosophy at the University of Massachusetts, Boston.

females that will sufficiently develop their ability to reason independently so that they will clearly deserve the same political rights as men.

In carrying out her first task Wollstonecraft's strategy is brilliant; she puts her opponents in the awkward position of being committed to the thesis that women are not human beings. This is accomplished by her claim that there are only two possibilities: either women are human beings or they are brutes; there is no middle ground. Since her opponents presumably believe, as she does, that rationality is the defining characteristic of being human, the trap is set; those who would deny female reason automatically relegate their wives and daughters to the realm of brute creation.

Wollstonecraft knows better than to expect all her readers to shrink from classifying women as brutes. Given the choice of attributing reason to women or assigning them to a lower order of creation, some will undoubtedly prefer the latter option. Thus, she does not rest content to force her opponents to choose between two unpalatable alternatives; she also shifts the burden of proof onto those who would deny the rationality of women.

To this end Wollstonecraft distinguishes between female appearance and female nature. Readily granting that most women do not seem to be rational creatures, she acknowledges that Sophie is not merely a figment of Rousseau's imagination but is alive and well in the England of her day, as she was in the France of his. However, Wollstonecraft attributes the existence of Sophies in the world to their upbringing and environment rather than to their nature. Look at the way girls are raised! Look at their education! She argues that women are social constructions; therefore, whether by nature they are rational creatures or mere brutes one cannot say, for in the majority of cases their experiences, their training, and their instruction positively forbid their development of reason.

Wollstonecraft documents for her readers the details of what today we call female socialization. In so doing she reveals a sensitivity to the educative powers of the community perhaps matched only by Plato. As we have seen, Plato was well aware of the phenomenon of socialization; hence his program of censorship. But while Plato saw the dangers of exposing future guardians to stories in which gods and heroes were cowardly or quarrelsome, he failed to recognize the special ways in which a society can stunt the development of reason in females. Enlightenment thinkers acknowledged that reason's development could be stunted. Indeed, one of their central tenets was that the ills of society derived not from the exercise of reason but from its stultification by existing social institutions, that if reason were allowed to rule, progress would be assured. Part of Wollstonecraft's originality lies in her perception that it is both formal institutions such as the church and the informal education society transmits that prevent reason from developing.

Confident in her insights into female socialization, Wollstonecraft proposes an experiment in living. Since women have been denied the very sort of education necessary for the development of reason and instead have been brought up to be Sophies, it is impossible, she says, to know if they are rational by nature. Instead of continuing to give girls an education designed to produce more Sophies, provide them with one sufficient to cultivate their understanding, she suggests, and then see if women are not rational creatures. The burden of proof thus shifts: those who would deny women's rationality must first give females an education similar to that given males and must then evaluate its results.

Wollstonecraft even tells her readers how to interpret these results. Should you find—and you well may, she says—that the reason of males is more highly developed than that of females, do not conclude that females are not rational; any differences in rationality that emerge between the sexes will be ones of degree, not kind, for reason is everywhere the same. Thus, to succeed, the experiment to prove that women do not by nature possess reason must show that *no* understanding is cultivated in females by a rationalistic education.

Wollstonecraft's approach to her second task, to show that women's domestic duties do not suffer when the rights of man are extended to females, is as inspired as her approach to the first. One would expect her simply to assert that citizenship is compatible with the wife–mother role, but she goes well beyond this. By redefining the wife–mother role, she makes the performance of women's domestic duties and even domestic tranquility dependent on the extension of the rights of man to woman and also a natural consequence of it.

According to Wollstonecraft, to be a good mother a woman must be intelligent. How can a woman void of reflection be capable of educating her children? How can she discern what is proper for them? How can she incline them to those virtues she is unacquainted with or to that merit of which she has no idea? Thinking is not enough, however. Steadiness of purpose is also necessary to the maternal character, and this requires strength of mind, as opposed simply to an active mental life. Good mothers, Wollstonecraft insists, will often be obliged "to act contrary to the present impulse of tenderness or compassion," on the one hand, because they must exemplify order, "the soul of virtue," and, on the other, because to be useful they must have a plan of conduct and be resolute enough to persevere in carrying it out. In effect, to mother well a woman must be precisely what Rousseau's ideal citizen must be: her own legislator.

This redefinition of mothering has clear implications for marriage. The sense and the independence of mind required of the good mother are possessed by few women "who are taught to depend entirely on their husbands"; indeed, a woman with sufficient judgment to manage her children "will not submit, right or wrong, to her husband." Thus, Rousseau's conception of the wife who obeys even her husband's unjust commands is rejected once and for all. Wollstonecraft's daughters must be their own persons in their relations to their husbands as well as to their children. Whereas for Rousseau harmonious marriage is predicated on the subordination of women, Wollstonecraft makes the equality of husband and wife its central feature.

Upon the equality of the marriage relation rests the rational affection Wollstonecraft considers to be the only enduring attachment between a husband and a wife. Love, which she associates with instability, disappears quickly in marriage, Wollstonecraft repeatedly says. "To seek for a secret that would render it constant, would be as wild a search as for the philosopher's stone, or the grand panacea." The master and mistress of a family "ought not to continue to love each other with passion," for if love does not subside into friendship it will be succeeded by indifference. In the rational affection that for Wollstonecraft constitutes the only satisfactory marriage bond, the fondness of a lordly protector has no place. Instead, there must be mutual regard and respect. . . .

Wollstonecraft places women in the home, but she makes the home a brand-new place by changing both its emotional atmosphere and its social relationships. For Wollstonecraft, equality and rational affection are the essence of the harmonious union Rousseau sought in *Emile*, book 5.

Wollstonecraft accomplishes her second task by incorporating the characteristics the Enlightenment associated with the good citizen into her redefinition of the wife–mother role. Rationality and personal autonomy in the sense of self-government: these are the traits thought to be required for citizenship, and these are the traits she attributes to good mothers and successful wives. Place Sophie in the polity—teach her to be her own legislator, let her exercise her reason in the interests of society as a whole—and she may be unwilling or unable to subordinate her judgment at home continually to Emile's. But Wollstonecraft's daughters are supposed to be their own legislators at home. Hence the personal autonomy and the rationality they must exercise as citizens will not incapacitate them for their domestic duties; indeed, their domestic pursuits will be enhanced once women are granted the rights of men. "We shall not see women affectionate till more equality be established in society," Wollstonecraft says. And she appeals to "the history of all nations" in arguing that women will not fulfill their family duties if they are confined to domestic pursuits. "Unless their minds take a wider range," she warns, the wife–mother role itself will suffer.

Just as Rousseau envisions a society in which males are both citizens and husband–fathers, Wollstonecraft posits one in which females do double duty. Her daughters are to be wife–mothers *and* citizens, their place in the polity providing essential nourishment for the performance of their domestic duties. A breathtaking conception of women's role, Wollstonecraft's vision stands in sharp contrast to Plato's as well as Rousseau's, for while the female guardians of the Just State are placed in the polity, they are taken out of the home. No motherhood for them, just childbearing. No marriage, just mating. It remains to be seen if the female education Wollstonecraft outlines is adequate to the dual role she assigns women and if her redefinition of the wife–mother role is itself tenable. But when we remember that Rousseau confines women to the home and Plato places the home out of bounds to them, whatever limitations her theory may have, we cannot doubt its power and depth.

## The Education of Emily

It must be understood that in attributing rationality to female nature Wollstonecraft is assigning to it simply the *capacity* to be rational. Her daughters are no more born with reason full blown than are Plato's female guardians. Like the guardians, the women in the good society Wollstonecraft contemplates possess at birth a potential for rational thought that can be developed only through education. The knowledge, skills, and habits of mind that constitute the exercise of reason do not automatically emerge as a person matures but must be acquired, and their acquisition is not a wholly informal process but requires systematic teaching and learning.

According to Enlightenment thought, the rights Wollstonecraft wants to extend to women properly belong only to those who can, through their use of reason, grasp natural law and in so doing distinguish right from wrong. Thus her interest is in the actual exercise of female reason, not just in the female potential for rationality. Her daughters must display the highly developed powers of reasoning and possess the abstract ideas that are the prerequisites for the possession of rights; they must be self-legislating individuals whose thought and action are grounded in knowledge and governed by reason. No wonder the third task she sets herself is to provide an account of female education. The intellectual qualities women must possess to deserve the rights of men are the very ones the Sophies Wollstonecraft perceives in her world lack because of their misdirected training.

The account of female education developed in *A Vindication* constitutes a rejection of Sophie, but not of Rousseau. The most perfect education, Wollstonecraft says, "is such an exercise of the understanding as is best calculated to strengthen the body and form the heart. Or, in other words, to enable the individual to attain such habits of virtue as will render it independent. In fact, it is a farce to call any being virtuous whose virtues do not result from the exercise of reason. *This was Rousseau's opinion respecting men: I extend it to women*" (emphasis added). And indeed she does, for the qualities Wollstonecraft wants females to possess in the society she envisions are precisely the ones Rousseau wants Emile to acquire. Female Emiles, or Emilys, as I will henceforth call them—these are the women Wollstonecraft would have rise out of the ashes of the Sophies she abhors.

Given Wollstonecraft's object of extending the rights of men to women, it is hardly surprising that she claims for her daughters the educational ideal Rousseau sets for Emile. If Emily can become the rational autonomous agent Emile is supposed to be, she argues, there will be no grounds for barring her from full-fledged citizenship.

Curiously enough, although Wollstonecraft appropriates the guiding ideal of Emile's education for her daughters, the educational program she prescribes for Emily differs from Emile's in important aspects. In the first place, Emily is not to live apart from society, as Emile is. "A man cannot retire into a desert with his child, and if he did he could not bring himself back to childhood, and become the proper friend and playfellow of an infant or youth," Wollstonecraft says. She adds that children who are confined to the society of adults "very soon acquire that kind of premature manhood which stops the growth of every vigorous power of mind or body." If they are to think for themselves, children must mix with their fellows and jointly pursue the same objects. Otherwise, a child will rely on the answers elicited by his questions and will contract "a benumbing indolence of mind."

Wollstonecraft's wariness of what she calls "private education" also stems from her belief that in youth "the seeds of every affection should be sown, and the respectful regard which is felt for a parent, is very different from the social affections which are to constitute the happiness of life as it advances." Equality and "an intercourse of sentiments" unclogged by seriousness are the basis of the social affections, she suggests, and neither of these is to be found in the relation between parent—or, presumably, tutor—and child.

Wollstonecraft is as opposed to boarding schools as she is to a private education of the sort Rousseau prescribes for Emile. She finds these schools to be "hot-beds of vice and folly, and the knowledge of human nature supposed to be attained there merely cunning selfishness." Boys become gluttons and slovens in boarding schools; instead of cultivating domestic affections, they harden the heart. The way to avoid the equally injurious extremes of public (boarding school) education and private (home) education, in her view, is to send children to day schools, so that they can be educated both with the family and with other children.

The best education, she insists, is one in which both sexes in school, as in the family, are educated together. "Were boys and girls permitted to pursue the same studies together," she says, "those graceful decencies might early be inculcated which produce modesty without those sexual distinctions that taint the mind." Thus she rejects not only Rousseau's doctrine of a different education for males and females but his doctrine of a separate education for the two sexes. Like Plato, she advocates coeducation, where this is understood to entail both identical education and the mixing together of the sexes, although she does advocate separate instruction in the afternoons for those girls and boys who are "intended for domestic employments, or mechanical trades."

Wollstonecraft wants her daughters and sons to be educated "after the same model", but if the ideal she holds up for them is derived from Rousseau, the methods she proposes are not his. The early education Wollstonecraft would give Emily is a good deal more verbal and abstract than the one Rousseau would give Emile. The elementary education Wollstonecraft's children are to pursue up to age nine includes reading and writing as well as botany, mechanics, astronomy, arithmetic, natural history, simple experiments in natural philosophy, and the elements of religion, history, and politics. Moreover, she conceives of Emily's education in a way he does not conceive of Emile's—namely, as a list of subjects to be studied.

Wollstonecraft acknowledges that young children "should not be confined to any sedentary employment for more than an hour at a time" and that relaxation and exercise can themselves be considered a part of elementary education insofar as they "improve and amuse the senses." Her very defense of relaxation, however, and her insistence that the studies she lists should never encroach on gymnastic play in the open air reveal her commitment to a form of education Rousseau vehemently rejects for the young Emile. Emile's pursuits, too, are not sedentary. He walks with his tutor, watches the sun rise, observes the stars, plants a garden, attends a fair where he encounters a magician. But in the course of his activities, he becomes educated. Since he learns at his own pace while engaged in occupations that interest him, he needs no periods of recess and recreation in which to let off steam and regain his powers of concentration.

Plato takes education to be a pervasive feature of a society, and Rousseau takes it to be a pervasive feature of a child's life. Of course, it is the tutor's task to ensure that the education Emile receives from the activities in which he engages is the right sort. If Emile is to become an independent thinker, the tutor most pose questions that take genuine thought for him to answer; if he is to acquire firsthand experience of the world, he must be left on his own even to make mistakes; if he is to learn from nature and things rather than from books, his attention must be directed to particular phenomena such as night clouds passing between him and the moon or a stick dropped into the water.

Once the form Emile's education is to take becomes clear, it is easy to understand why manipulation is a part of it. Since Emile's learning is to be a by-product of his activities without his realizing it, his environment must be controlled so that he will undertake activities that will yield the desired learning, his attention must be directed to phenomena that will arouse his curiosity, and his thought processes must be engaged through conversation and dialogue. But it should not be supposed that Wollstonecraft's reason for rejecting the portion of Rousseau's philosophy that so delights progressive educators is that it is manipulative. Without reference to those books of *Emile* containing Rousseau's most creative educational ideas, she simply espouses a model of education for both sexes that in structure and content resembles the very education for boys that was anathema to Rousseau.

The education Wollstonecraft claims for Emily is relatively traditional in form and it is intellectualistic in content. In these important aspects it resembles that of Plato's guardians rather than of Emile. But while Plato initiates the guardians of his Just State into abstract studies at a relatively late age after a long regimen of music and gymnastics, Wollstonecraft does so from the beginning. She does stress Emily's physical education. The gymnastic play in the open air she prescribes is not meant simply to curb Emily's restlessness and boredom. The infancy of all children should be passed "in harmless gambols", and we would hear of no "infantine" airs, she says, "if girls were allowed to take sufficient exercise, and not confined in close rooms till their muscles are relaxed, and their powers of digestion destroyed." For Wollstonecraft, as for Plato, physical education is no frill. Yet if she makes it an integral component of female education, like Plato she ultimately justifies it by its contribution not simply to good health but to reason and virtue.

## A False Dilemma

. . . A political imagery underlies Wollstonecraft's theory of the human personality as it does Plato's. She considers the human soul or psyche to be made up of parts that necessarily stand to one another in the relation of governor and governed. Moreover, she assumes that some part or parts of the psyche must govern the others, and that the ruling element must be everywhere and eternally the same and must be the ultimate source of control. No give and take, no interaction, no sensitivity to context in this sovereignty model of personality. Either reason rules absolutely or passion does. The sovereignty model allows Wollstonecraft to construct an Emily who is a counter to Rousseau's Sophie: in Sophie the passions and senses will rule, in Emily reason will rule; in Sophie reason will forever be subordinate to feeling, in Emily feeling will always be suppressed by reason. The problem with this model, however, is that it forces one to choose between Sophie and Emile . . . for it does not accommodate personalities . . . in which there is no one fixed source of authority.

To do Wollstonecraft justice, it must be pointed out that she mentions feeling and passion with approval in many passages of *A Vindication*. She speaks, for example, of "those nobler passions that open and enlarge the soul," says that God willed "that the passions should unfold our reason," calls passions "spurs to action." She also wants women to feel affection for their husbands; indeed, the friendship upon which marriage ought to be founded is, she says, "the most sublime of all affections." And she advocates an education that will "form the heart" and insists that she wants the heart, as well as the understanding, to be "opened by cultivation."

Yet Wollstonecraft gives Emily feelings and emotions only to take them away. After saying that the passions are spurs to action and open the mind, she adds, "but they sink into mere appetites, become a personal and momentary gratification, when the object is gained." Hence reason must "teach passion to submit to necessity." After insisting that education forms the heart, she describes this task as the development of virtues resulting from the exercise of reason. In truth, the pages of *A Vindication* reveal Wollstonecraft's ambivalence about feeling and emotion. On the one hand, men have superior judgment and fortitude because "they give a freer scope to the grand passions." "It is not against strong, persevering passions; but romantic feelings that I wish to guard the female heart by exercising the understanding," she says. On the other hand, the passions are capricious "winds of life" and inherently dangerous.

Acknowledging that the most difficult task in the education of both sexes "is so to adjust instruction as not to narrow the understanding, whilst the heart is warmed by the generous juices of spring, just raised by the electric fermentation of the season; nor to dry up the feelings by employing the mind in investigations remote from life." Wollstonecraft is nonetheless required by her own ambivalence and by the sovereignty model of personality to educate Emily . . . [with] only two choices: the absolute subjection of feeling and emotion to reason or the absolute subjection of reason to feeling and emotion. Having rejected the latter option, only the former is open to her.

## Different Roles, Same Education

Wollstonecraft locates the precedent for Emily's education in rational self-control in Emile, but Rousseau would be the first to acknowledge that Emile himself is modeled after the guardians of the Just State, indeed, that Plato's *Republic* supplies a precedent for extending Emile's education to women. He and Plato would both remind Wollstonecraft, however, that Plato's educational program presupposes the abolition of institutions she wants to preserve—private home, family, marriage, and child rearing—and of the traditional female role itself. And he would question her assumption, as Plato no doubt would too, that it is coherent to embrace Plato's radicalism concerning women's education while adopting Rousseau's traditionalism concerning women's domestic functions.

Wollstonecraft might defend herself by claiming that in her philosophy education is not tied to social roles. A careful reading of *A Vindication* leaves no doubt, however, that Wollstonecraft embraces a version of Plato's production model of education. It is true that she says that education is viewed in a false light when it is not considered "as the first step to form a being advancing gradually towards perfection; but only as a preparation for life." The operative word in this passage is *only*. In her view, as in Plato's and Rousseau's, the function of education is to equip people to carry out the particular societal roles to which they are suited by nature. In other words, she accepts Plato's Functional Postulate and also his Postulate of Specialized Natures. Whereas Plato assumes that each person is born more apt for one task than another, Wollstonecraft assumes that women are born with an aptitude for two tasks corresponding to two societal roles, that of citizen and that of wife–mother. That she thinks education should not only prepare people for their pre-assigned roles in society does not, therefore, warrant detaching her account of female education from her theory of women's place.

Wollstonecraft might also defend herself by pointing out that she advocates citizenship for women and redefines both marriage and motherhood so as to make a place for reason in the wife–mother role. So she does. Yet in retaining the domestic sphere Plato abolishes, and in giving women responsibility for carrying on the activities and duties associated with it while advocating an education designed for those who have no such responsibility, Wollstonecraft leaves her theory of female education vulnerable to the criticism that Emily's education is not well suited to one of the societal roles for which it is supposed to prepare her. . . .

In particular, one must ask if a woman whose feelings are always subdued by reason will show her children enough affection, if she will possess the requisite nurturing capacities, if she will provide the warmth and the physical affection they need, if she will delight in their company.

It is scarcely an exaggeration to say that an ideal of the educated woman lies at the very center of *A Vindication*. Since Wollstonecraft's concern is women, we should not be surprised that historians of education have ignored this book. However, recent scholarship on *A Vindication* also tends to overlook the fact that Wollstonecraft presents us with an educational ideal. Concentrating on her defense of female rationality and her arguments for extending the rights of men to women, this body of work acknowledges Wollstonecraft's critique of Sophie's education and her insights into female socialization. Her positive philosophy of women's education is scarcely examined, however. This scholarship notes that she claims for her daughters the education of men as well as their rights. But it accepts without question the appropriateness for women of an education whose guiding ideal resembles the one constructed for Plato's guardians and for Emile.

As we know, the family that will be Emily's is not supposed to be patriarchal. Still, Emily is the one destined to bear primary responsibility for carrying on its domestic and nurturant tasks. In Wollstonecraft's social vision, Emily's husband is as dependent on Emily in domestic affairs as Emile is on Sophie. Her decision to give Emily Emile's education cannot therefore be viewed as unproblematic and leads to obvious questions about the adequacy of Emily's preparation for running a household. . . . Here let us confine ourselves to the issue of whether, in holding up for Emily an ideal of rational self-control, Wollstonecraft does not neglect her education in nurturing capacities and in the care, concern, and connection so essential for Emily's family functions in general and for her mothering responsibilities in particular.

Many people in Wollstonecraft's time would have argued that the attitudes, skills, behavior, and traits of character needed by mothers are inborn in women and emerge automatically as they mature and so would maintain that there is no reason to take these into account in a theory of female education. . . .

Despite her assertion that motherhood is woman's duty by nature, however, Wollstonecraft is no instinctualist: indeed, *A Vindication* can be read as an attack on instinctual theories of woman's nature. It is possible, nevertheless, that although she dismisses instinctualism, Wollstonecraft assumes that the feelings and emotions she herself believes are required for good maternal practice develop automatically in females. In the context of chastising mothers who do not suckle their young, she asserts that "a mutual care produces a new mutual sympathy" between mother and child and that affections "must grow out of the habitual exercise of a mutual sympathy." Perhaps, then, she believes that the deliberate cultivation of the feelings, emotions, and passions associated with good mothering is not necessary because these can be learned in the course of doing. . . .

When Wollstonecraft was writing, mother love as we tend to think of it was not a given, and neither was suckling one's young. She recognized that the two phenomena are related, but she oversimplified the connections between them. Nursing cannot be counted on to produce enduring maternal affection in those who do not want a child in the first place, in those who want children but do not want to be bothered with them, or in those who are experiencing great economic, social, or psychological stress. That it can be counted on in the case of women who are educated to be Emiles is also doubtful. But assuming for the sake of argument that it can be, we must remember that, given the structure of society Wollstonecraft posits, a good mother will tend to exhibit, besides affection, awareness of and sensitivity to her child's feelings and situation, protective love and a desire to foster her child's growth, and a sense of connection with her child. Surely the many cases we see today of child abuse, neglect, and abandonment; failure to protect children from incest; and inability to enter into one's children's plans and projects cannot all be attributed to a failure to nurse. . . .

Needless to say, education cannot by itself solve large-scale social problems. Neither child abuse nor incest will disappear just because an effort is made to help people become nurturant and caring. But that education is not a social panacea does not mean that it can do no good at all. In individual instances an education for nurturance and care may improve the quality of mothering; in some cases it may even prevent harm from being done to children. Moreover, the point to keep in mind here is that whatever efficacy education for mothering may have, the internal logic of Wollstonecraft's philosophy requires that Emily be provided such education. Given Wollstonecraft's acceptance of Plato's Functional Postulate that the task of education is to prepare people to fill necessary societal roles, given her rejection of the instinctualist position, and given her insistence that women have primary responsibility for child rearing, her theory of female education must include education for mothering.

We have already seen that Wollstonecraft embraces Plato's Functional Postulate as well as a version of his Postulate of Specialized Natures. In view of her coeducational scheme it should be clear that she also accepts the Identity Postulate of same role, same education. In contrast to Plato, however, Wollstonecraft believes that a person can be suited by nature for more than one societal role and that at least some roles can be shared by people whose natures are not identical. Thus her daughters are destined to be citizens and wife–mothers and her sons to be citizens and husband–fathers. In effect, then, she embraces a modified Postulate of Specialized Natures and also a modified Correspondence Postulate, which maintains that societal roles and human nature correspond to one another although not necessarily in one-to-one relation. Wollstonecraft denies the Difference Postulate altogether, however, for her daughters must perform two societal roles, one of which differs from that of her sons; yet the education the two sexes are to receive is to be identical.

Both of these deviations from Plato's production model of education can be traced back to Rousseau. Just as Wollstonecraft intends Emily to be a citizen and a wife–mother, Rousseau wants Emile to be a citizen and a husband–father; just as Emily is to receive an education designed specifically to fit her for the one role of citizen, so is Emile. Rousseau would, of course, defend his prescription of an identical education for Emile's two societal roles by pointing out their essential oneness: in the small fatherland that is the family, as in the large one, Emile is to be sovereign. Likewise, Wollstonecraft would remind us how similar the wife–mother and citizen roles are in her social vision. That there can be considerable overlap between social roles is undeniable. Still, if the overlapping characteristic of some roles gives the lie to the assumption that totally different educations are required to fit people for different roles, the assumption that different roles require no differences in training is questionable. Certainly, for Wollstonecraft's daughters there are significant differences between their two roles, which their education ignores at its peril.

As we know, Emile is not adequately educated to be a good husband and father. How unlikely, then, that his education will help Emily become a good wife–mother! In truth, in her understandable outrage at the education Rousseau proposes for Sophie, Wollstonecraft fails to notice that whatever plausibility his account of Emile's education may have is due to Sophie's existence. Rousseau knows this. He recognizes that the Platonic ideal of a self-governing individual in whom reason rules is incomplete and that a well-constructed philosophy of education must include both an account of education for citizenship and an account of education for carrying on the reproductive processes of society. Rousseau's mistake is to insist that these two kinds of education be assigned on the basis of sex. Furthermore, in constructing Emile's education he forgets that, according to his own social vision, Emile is to live his life in the family he and Sophie are to establish.

Rousseau's fundamental insight that Emile's education is partial is overlooked by Wollstonecraft, in part, perhaps, because, in her concern to reveal Rousseau's misogyny, she ignores Sophie's positive qualities. On balance, Sophie is definitely not a person to admire. Nevertheless, although she is passive and manipulative, she is also the one with the patience and gentleness, zeal and affection necessary for rearing children, the one with the tenderness and care "required to maintain the union of the whole family," and the one who is willing and able to make the lives of her loved ones "agreeable and sweet." Because Sophie acquires through her education the attributes so necessary for carrying on the reproductive processes of society, it makes a certain amount of sense that Emile does not. But not a great deal of sense, for as Sophie's husband, father of her children, and head of family, one would hope that he too would be tender and caring and disposed to make the lives of his loved ones agreeable and sweet. Be that as it may, it makes no sense at all to advocate Emile's and *only* Emile's education for both sexes—no sense, that is, if one cares about the quality of child rearing and family living.

Wollstonecraft does care about the quality of domestic life, indeed, she cares about it passionately, but her rationalistic philosophical framework does not permit her to claim for her daughters the education in Sophie's virtues that those with responsibility for carrying on the reproductive processes of society must have. Wollstonecraft's rationalism is thus the source of both her strength and her weakness. It allows her to extend the rights of men to women, thereby bringing women into the domain of citizenship. As we know, this in itself is no guarantee of political equality, but at least it puts women in a position from which to begin to pursue that elusive goal. At the same time, her rationalism allows Wollstonecraft to demonstrate the compatibility of the citizen and the wife–mother role, something neither Plato nor Rousseau attempts. Wollstonecraft accomplishes this by the revolutionary strategy of altering the patriarchal family structure. This is no guarantee of sex equality either, but if the total abolition of patriarchy requires women's economic independence, Wollstonecraft's conception of the relationship of husband and wife at least sets the stage for egalitarian marriage.

Wollstonecraft's rationalism serves also to illuminate aspects of mothering that even today are too often ignored. Intelligence and a certain stability of character are seldom considered maternal qualities, yet they are as important to child rearing as to other activities, and it is to Wollstonecraft's credit that she brings this out so clearly. In particular, she highlights the parts reason and self-control play in the educative aspects of mothering. Arguing that Sophie will not have "sufficient character to manage a family or educate children," she makes it very clear that the duty of forming her child's character cannot be successfully fulfilled by a mother who herself is ruled by whim and caprice.

Finally, Wollstonecraft's rationalism inspires her to claim for women the academic education historically reserved for men and, like Plato, to recommend a system of coeducation. Unfortunately, these proposals pose the same problems of male-based methods, male-biased disciplines, and genderized traits for her daughters as they do for Plato's guardians. Wollstonecraft is sensitive, as Plato is not, to the differential socialization of girls and boys. Yet she extends to her daughters the education of men without addressing the question of whether Emily will be at a serious disadvantage in an educational scheme that takes Emile as its norm. Wollstonecraft is sensitive also to the fact that a woman whose intelligence is cultivated is considered masculine, and yet she appropriates Emile's image for Emily without addressing the questions of what education can do to ensure that Emily will not be considered abnormal by others and ultimately by herself or of how she is to receive the respect and esteem Wollstonecraft considers to be prerequisites of equality.

Despite these problems, Emily's education is such an improvement on Sophie's that it seems almost churlish to criticize it. Yet . . . the academic education that is to make her own reason sovereign . . . must . . . be criticized not only for the harm its male-based methods, curriculum, and mold do to Emily but for the one-sidedness that is itself, of course, a function of its genderized origins. As the example of Emile makes clear, Emily's rationalistic education will not equip her for the citizenship Wollstonecraft would give her. Bonds of sympathy and an affection for the state are as important for Wollstonecraft as for Plato and Rousseau, but one can have little confidence that Emily's education will foster them. Like Rousseau, Wollstonecraft thinks that the seeds of civic sympathy and affection must be planted in the home: "If you wish to make good citizens, you must first exercise the affections of a son and a brother. This is the only way to expand the heart; for public affections, as well as public virtues, must ever grow out of the private character, or they are merely meteors that shoot athwart a dark sky, and disappear as they are gazed at and admired." Yet the reationalism of the domestic environment Emily will create makes one wonder if her family, any more than Sophie's, can succeed in performing its patriotic duty.

The one-sided female education Wollstonecraft proposes is in part a function of a definition of the wife–mother role that makes Sophie's virtues of nurturance and care all but invisible. We can appreciate the theoretical and practical considerations that lead Wollstonecraft to define marriage and mothering in strict rationalistic terms. Still, in making her case for the rights of women, this great feminist philosopher presents us with an ideal of female education that gives pride of place to traits traditionally associated with males at the expense of others traditionally associated with females.

Wollstonecraft denies not only Sophie's coquettishness but her concern for detail, not only her guile but her quickness of perception. She disparages women for thinking more about the incidental occurrences on a journey than the end in view, as men would. And she scorns women's sensibility. . . . [T]he only alternative Wollstonecraft posits to the life of abstract reason extolled by Plato is one of intellectual poverty. Yet Wollstonecraft gives us no good reason to believe that delicacy and quickness of perception are inferior qualities, that the ongoing details of a journey are necessarily of less importance than the end in view, that in all contexts it is better to suppress than to act upon one's immediate feelings. . . .

Wollstonecraft is not to be faulted for embracing a rationalism that enabled her to write a classic work on the rights of women. She is not to be faulted for claiming an intellectually demanding education for her daughters. But those of us today who want to claim an education for women should recognize the limitations of her philosophical framework. . . .

# 8
## John Stuart Mill

**John Stuart Mill** (1806–1873), was the leading British philosopher of the nineteenth century. Born in London, he received an intense early education from his father, James Mill, a philosophical and political writer. While pursuing a career in the East India Company, John Stuart Mill published widely in philosophy, political theory, and economics. He also served as a member of Parliament. A strong influence on his life and thought was Harriet Taylor, whom he met in 1831 and married two decades later.

## *Inaugural Address at St. Andrews*

In complying with the custom which prescribes that the person whom you have called by your suffrages to the honorary presidency of your University should embody in an Address a few thoughts on the subjects which most nearly concern a seat of liberal education, let me begin by saying, that this usage appears to me highly commendable. Education, in its larger sense, is one of the most inexhaustible of all topics. Though there is hardly any subject on which so much has been written, by so many of the wisest men, it is as fresh to those who come to it with a fresh mind, a mind not hopelessly filled full with other people's conclusions, as it was to the first explorers of it; and notwithstanding the great mass of excellent things which have been said respecting it, no thoughtful person finds any lack of things both great and small still waiting to be said, or waiting to be developed and followed out to their consequences. Education, moreover, is one of the subjects which most essentially require to be considered by various minds, and from a variety of points of view. For, of all many-sided subjects, it is the one which has the greatest number of sides. Not only does it include whatever we do for ourselves, and whatever is done for us by others, for the express purpose of bringing us somewhat nearer to the perfection of our nature; it does more: in its largest acceptation, it comprehends even the indirect effects produced on character and on the human faculties, by things of which the direct purposes are quite different; by laws, by forms of government, by the industrial arts, by modes of social life; nay, even by physical facts not dependent on human will; by climate, soil, and local position. Whatever helps to shape the human being—to make the individual what he is, or hinder him from being what he is not—is part of his education. And a very bad education it often is, requiring all that can be done by cultivated intelligence and will, to counteract its tendencies. To take an obvious instance: the niggardliness of Nature in some places, by engrossing the whole energies of the human being in the mere preservation of life, and her over-bounty in others, affording a sort of brutish subsistence on too easy terms, with hardly any exertion of the human faculties, are both hostile to the spontaneous growth and development of the mind; and it is at those two extremes of the scale that we find human societies in the state of most unmitigated savagery. I shall confine myself, however, to education in the narrower sense; the culture which each generation purposely gives to those who are to be its successors, in order to qualify them for at least keeping up, and if possible for raising, the level of improvement which has been attained. Nearly all here present are daily occupied either in receiving or in giving this sort of education; and the part of it which most concerns you at present is that in which you are yourselves engaged—the stage of education which is the appointed business of a national University.

The proper function of a University in national education is tolerably well understood. At least there is a tolerably general agreement about what a University is not. It is not a place of professional education. Universities are not intended to teach the knowledge required to fit men for some special mode of gaining their livelihood. Their object is not to make skilful lawyers, or physicians, or engineers, but capable and cultivated human beings. It is very right that there should be public facilities for the study of professions. It is well that there should be Schools of Law, and of Medicine, and it would be well if there were schools of engineering, and the industrial arts. The countries which have such institutions are greatly the better for them; and there is something to be said for having them in the same localities, and under the same general superintendence, as the establishments devoted to education properly so called. But these things are no part of what every generation owes to the next, as that on which its civilization and worth will principally depend. They are needed only by a comparatively few, who are under the strongest private inducements to acquire them by their own efforts; and even those few do not require them until after their education, in the ordinary sense, has been completed. Whether those whose speciality they are, will learn them as a branch of intelligence or as a mere trade, and whether, having learned them, they will make a wise and conscientious use of them or the reverse, depends less on the manner in which they are taught their profession, than upon what sort of minds they bring to it—what kind of intelligence, and of conscience, the general system of education has developed in them. Men are men before they are lawyers, or physicians, or merchants, or manufacturers; and if you make them capable and sensible men, they will make themselves capable and sensible lawyers or physicians. What professional men should carry away with them from a University, is not professional knowledge, but that which should direct the use of their professional knowledge, and bring the light of general culture to illuminate the technicalities of a special pursuit. Men may be competent lawyers without general education, but it depends on general education to make them philosophic lawyers—who demand, and are capable of apprehending, principles, instead of merely cramming their memory with details. And so of all other useful pursuits, mechanical included. Education makes a man a more intelligent shoe-maker, if that be his occupation, but not by teaching him how to make shoes; it does so by the mental exercise it gives, and the habits it impresses.

This, then, is what a mathematician would call the higher limit of University education: its province ends where education, ceasing to be general, branches off into departments adapted to the individual's destination in life. The lower limit is more difficult to define. A University is not concerned with elementary instruction: the pupil is supposed to have acquired that before coming here. But where does elementary instruction end, and the higher studies begin? Some have given a very wide extension to the idea of elementary instruction. According to them, it is not the office of a University to give instruction in single branches of knowledge from the commencement. What the pupil should be taught here (they think), is to methodize his knowledge: to look at every separate part of it in its relation to the other parts, and to the whole; combining the partial glimpses which he has obtained of the field of human knowledge at different points, into a general map, if I may so speak, of the entire region; observing how all knowledge is connected, how we ascend to one branch by means of another, how the higher modifies the lower, and the lower helps us to understand the higher; how every existing reality is a compound of many properties, of which each science or distinct mode of study reveals but a small part, but the whole of which must be included to enable us to know it truly as a fact in Nature, and not as a mere abstraction.

This last stage of general education, destined to give the pupil a comprehensive and connected view of the things which he has already learned separately, includes a philosophic study of the Methods of the sciences; the modes in which the human intellect proceeds from the known to the unknown. We must be taught to generalize our conception of the resources which the human mind possesses for the exploration of nature; to understand how man discovers the real facts of the world, and by what tests he can judge whether he has really found them. And doubtless this is the crown and consummation of a liberal education: but before we restrict a University to this highest department of instruction—before we confine it to teaching, not knowledge, but the philosophy of knowledge—we must be assured that the knowledge itself has been acquired elsewhere. Those who take this view of the function of a University are not wrong in thinking that the schools, as distinguished from the Universities, ought to be adequate to teaching every branch of general instruction required by youth, so far as it can be studied apart from the rest. But where are such schools to be found? Since science assumed its modern character, nowhere; and in these islands less even than elsewhere. This ancient kingdom, thanks to its great religious reformers, had the inestimable advantage, denied to its southern sister, of excellent parish schools, which gave, really and not in pretence, a considerable amount of valuable literary instruction to the bulk of the population, two centuries earlier than in any other country. But schools of a still higher description have been, even in Scotland, so few and inadequate, that the Universities have had to perform largely the functions which ought to be performed by schools; receiving students at an early age, and undertaking not only the work for which the schools should have prepared them, but much of the preparation itself. Every Scottish University is not a University only, but a High School, to supply the deficiency of other schools. And if the English Universities do not do the same, it is not because the same need does not exist, but because it is disregarded. Youths come to the Scottish Universities ignorant, and are there taught. The majority of those who come to the English Universities come still more ignorant, and ignorant they go away.

In point of fact, therefore, the office of a Scottish University comprises the whole of a liberal education, from the foundations upwards. And the scheme of your Universities has, almost from the beginning, really aimed at including the whole, both in depth and in breadth. You have not, as the English Universities so long did, confined all the stress of your teaching, all your real effort to teach, within the limits of two subjects, the classical languages and mathematics. You did not wait till the last few years to establish a Natural Science and a Moral Science Tripos. Instruction in both those departments was organized long ago; and your teachers of those subjects have not been nominal professors, who did not lecture: some of the greatest names in physical and in moral science have taught in your Universities, and by their teaching contributed to form some of the most distinguished intellects of the last and present centuries. To comment upon the course of education at the Scottish Universities is to pass in review every essential department of general culture. The best use, then, which I am able to make of the present occasion, is to offer a few remarks on each of those departments, considered in its relation to human cultivation at large; adverting to the nature of the claims which each has to a place in liberal education; in what special manner they each conduce to the improvement of the individual mind and the benefit of the race; and how they all conspire to the common end, the strengthening, exalting, purifying, and beautifying of our common nature, and the fitting out of mankind with the necessary mental implements for the work they have to perform through life.

Let me first say a few words on the great controversy of the present day with regard to the higher education, the difference which most broadly divides educational reformers and conservatives; the vexed question between the ancient languages, and the modern sciences and arts; whether general education should be classical—let me use a wider expression, and say literary—or scientific. A dispute as endlessly, and often as fruitlessly agitated as that old controversy which it resembles, made memorable by the names of Swift and Sir William Temple in England, and Fontenelle in France—the contest for superiority between the ancients and the moderns. This question, whether we should be taught the classics or the sciences, seems to me, I confess, very like a dispute whether painters should cultivate drawing or coloring, or, to use a more homely illustration, whether a tailor should make coats or trousers. I can only reply by the question, Why not both? Can anything deserve the name of a good education which does not include literature and science too? If there were no more to be said than that scientific education teaches us to think, and literary education to express our thoughts, do we not require both? and is not anyone a poor, maimed, lopsided fragment of humanity who is deficient in either? We are not obliged to ask ourselves whether it is more important to know the languages or the sciences. Short as life is, and shorter still as we make it by the time we waste on things which are neither business, nor meditation, nor pleasure, we are not so badly off that our scholars need be ignorant of the laws and properties of the world they live in, or our scientific men destitute of poetic feeling and artistic cultivation, I am amazed at the limited conception which many educational reformers have formed to themselves of a human being's power of acquisition. The study of science, they truly say, is indispensable: our present education neglects it: there is truth in this too, though it is not all truth: and they think it impossible to find room for the studies which they desire to encourage, but by turning out, at least from general education, those which are now chiefly cultivated. How absurd, they say, that the whole of boyhood should be taken up in acquiring an imperfect knowledge of two dead languages. Absurd indeed: but is the human mind's capacity to learn, measured by that of Eton and Westminster to teach? I should prefer to see these reformers pointing their attacks against the shameful inefficiency of the schools, public and private, which pretend to teach these two languages and do not. I should like to hear them denounce the wretched methods of teaching, and the criminal idleness and supineness, which waste the entire boyhood of the pupils without really giving to most of them more than a smattering, if even that, of the only kind of knowledge which is even pretended to be cared for. Let us try what conscientious and intelligent teaching can do, before we presume to decide what cannot be done.

Scotland has on the whole, in this respect, been considerably more fortunate than England. Scotch youths have never found it impossible to leave school or the University having learned somewhat of other things besides Greek and Latin; and why? Because Greek and Latin have been better taught. A beginning of classical instruction has all along been made in the common schools; and the common schools of Scotland, like her Universities, have never been the mere shams that the English Universities were during the last century, and the greater part of the English classical schools still are. The only tolerable Latin Grammars for school purposes that I know of, which had been produced in these islands until very lately, were written by Scotchmen. Reason, indeed, is beginning to find its way by gradual infiltration even into English schools, and to maintain a contest, though as yet a very unequal one, against routine. A few practical reformers of school tuition, of whom Arnold was the most eminent, have made a beginning of amendment in many things; but reforms, worthy of the name, are always slow, and reform even of governments and churches is not so slow as that of schools, for there is the great preliminary difficulty of fashioning the instruments; of teaching the teachers. If all the improvements in the mode of teaching languages which are already sanctioned by experience, were adopted into our classical schools, we should soon cease to hear of Latin and Greek as studies which must engross the school years, and render impossible any other acquirements. If a boy learned Greek and Latin on the same principle on which a mere child learns with such ease and rapidity any modern language, namely, by acquiring some familiarity with the vocabulary by practice and repetition, before being troubled with grammatical rules,—those rules being acquired with tenfold greater facility when the cases to which they apply are already familiar to the mind,—an average schoolboy, long before the age at which schooling terminates, would be able to read fluently and with intelligent interest any ordinary Latin or Greek author in prose or verse, would have a competent knowledge of the grammatical structure of both languages, and have had time besides for an ample amount of scientific instruction. I might go much farther; but I am as unwilling to speak out all that I think practicable in this matter, as George Stephenson was about railways, when he calculated the average speed of a train at ten miles an hour, because if he had estimated it higher, the practical men would have turned a deaf ear to him, as that most unsafe character in their estimation, an enthusiast and a visionary. The results have shown, in that case, who was the real practical man. What the results would show in the other case, I will not attempt to anticipate. But I will say confidently, that if the two classical languages were properly taught, there would be no need whatever for ejecting them from the school course, in order to have sufficient time for everything else that need be included therein.

Let me say a few words more on this strangely limited estimate of what it is possible for human beings to learn, resting on a tacit assumption that they are already as efficiently taught as they ever can be. So narrow a conception not only vitiates our idea of education, but actually, if we receive it, darkens our anticipations as to the future progress of mankind. For if the inexorable conditions of human life make it useless for one man to attempt to know more than one thing, what is to become of the human intellect as facts accumulate? In every generation, and now more rapidly than ever, the things which it is necessary that somebody should know are more and more multiplied. Every department of knowledge becomes so loaded with details, that one who endeavors to know it with minute accuracy, must confine himself to a smaller and smaller portion of the whole extent: every science and art must be cut up into subdivisions, until each man's portion, the district which he thoroughly knows, bears about the same ratio to the whole range of useful knowledge that the art of putting on a pin's head does to the field of human industry. Now, if, in order to know that little completely, it is necessary to remain wholly ignorant of all the rest, what will soon be the worth of a man, for any human purpose except his own infinitesimal fraction of human wants and requirements? His state will be even worse than that of simple ignorance. Experience proves that there is no one study or pursuit, which, practised to the exclusion of all others, does not narrow and pervert the mind; breeding in it a class of prejudices special to that pursuit, besides a general prejudice, common to all narrow specialities, against large views, from an incapacity to take in and appreciate the grounds of them. We should have to expect that human nature would be more and more dwarfed, and unfitted for great things, by its very proficiency in small ones. But matters are not so bad with us: there is no ground for so dreary an anticipation. It is not the utmost limit of human acquirement to know only one thing, but to combine a minute knowledge of one or a few things with a general knowledge of many things. By a general knowledge I do not mean a few vague impressions. An eminent man, one of whose writings is part of the course of this University, Archbishop Whately, has well discriminated between a general knowledge and a superficial knowledge. To have a general knowledge of a subject is to know only its leading truths, but to know these not superficially but thoroughly, so as to have a true conception of the subject in its great features; leaving the minor details to those who require them for the purposes of their special pursuit. There is no incompatibility between knowing a wide range of subjects up to this point, and some one subject with the completeness required by those who make it their principal occupation. It is this combination which gives an enlightened public: a body of cultivated intellects, each taught by its attainments in its own province what real knowledge is, and knowing enough of other subjects to be able to discern who are those that know them better. The amount of knowledge is not to be lightly estimated, which qualifies us for judging to whom we may have recourse for more. The elements of the more important studies being widely diffused, those who have reached the higher summits find a public capable of appreciating their superiority, and prepared to follow their lead. It is thus, too, that minds are formed capable of guiding and improving public opinion on the greater concerns of practical life. Government and civil society are the most complicated of all subjects accessible to the human mind; and he who would deal competently with them as a thinker, and not as a blind follower of a party, requires not only a general knowledge of the leading facts of life, both moral and material, but an understanding exercised and disciplined in the principles and rules of sound thinking, up to a point which neither the experience of life, nor any one science or branch of knowledge, affords. Let us understand, then, that it should be our aim in learning, not merely to know the one thing which is to be our principal occupation, as well as it can be known, but to do this and also to know something of all the great subjects of human interest; taking care to know that something accurately; marking well the dividing line between what we know accurately and what we do not; and remembering that our object should be to obtain a true view of nature and life in their broad outline, and that it is idle to throw away time upon the details of anything which is to form no part of the occupation of our practical energies.

It by no means follows, however, that every useful branch of general, as distinct from professional, knowledge, should be included in the curriculum of school or University studies. There are things which are better learned out of school, or when the school years, and even those usually passed in a Scottish University, are over. I do not agree with those reformers who would give a regular and prominent place in the school or University course to modern languages. This is not because I attach small importance to the knowledge of them. No one can in our age be esteemed a well-instructed person who is not familiar with at least the French language, so as to read French books with ease; and there is great use in cultivating a familiarity with German. But living languages are so much more easily acquired by intercourse with those who use them in daily life; a few months in the country itself, if properly employed, go so much farther than as many years of school lessons; that it is really waste of time for those to whom that easier mode is attainable, to labor at them with no help but that of books and masters: and it will in time be made attainable, through international schools and colleges, to many more than at present. Universities do enough to facilitate the study of modern languages, if they give a mastery over that ancient language which is the foundation of most of them, and the possession of which makes it easier to learn four or five of the continental languages than it is to learn one of them without it. Again, it has always seemed to me a great absurdity that history and geography should be taught in schools; except in elementary schools for the children of the laboring classes, whose subsequent access to books is limited. Who ever really learned history and geography except by private reading? and what an utter failure a system of education must be, if it has not given the pupil a sufficient taste for reading to seek for himself those most attractive and easily intelligible of all kinds of knowledge! Besides, such history and geography as can be taught in schools exercise none of the faculties of the intelligence except the memory. A University is indeed the place where the student should be introduced to the Philosophy of History; where professors who not merely know the facts, but have exercised their minds on them, should initiate him into the causes and explanations, so far as within our reach, of the past life of mankind in its principal features. Historical criticism also—the tests of historical truth—are a subject to which his attention may well be drawn in this stage of his education. But of the mere facts of history, as commonly accepted, what educated youth of any mental activity does not learn as much as is necessary, if he is simply turned loose into an historical library? What he needs on this, and on most other matters of common information, is, not that he should be taught it in boyhood, but that abundance of books should be accessible to him.

The only languages, then, and the only literature, to which I would allow a place in the ordinary curriculum, are those of the Greeks and Romans; and to these I would preserve the position in it which they at present occupy. That position is justified, by the great value, in education, of knowing well some other cultivated language and literature than one's own, and by the peculiar value of those particular languages and literatures.

There is one purely intellectual benefit from a knowledge of languages, which I am specially desirous to dwell on. Those who have seriously reflected on the causes of human error, have been deeply impressed with the tendency of mankind to mistake words for things. Without entering into the metaphysics of the subject, we know how common it is to use words glibly and with apparent propriety, and to accept them confidently when used by others, without ever having had any distinct conception of the things denoted by them. To quote again from Archbishop Whately, it is the habit of mankind to mistake familiarity for accurate knowledge. As we seldom think of asking the meaning of what we see every day, so when our ears are used to the sound of a word or a phrase, we do not suspect that it conveys no clear idea to our minds, and that we should have the utmost difficulty in defining it, or expressing, in any other words, what we think we understand by it. Now, it is obvious in what manner this bad habit tends to be corrected by the practice of translating with accuracy from one language to another, and hunting out the meanings expressed in a vocabulary with which we have not grown familiar by early and constant use. I hardly know any greater proof of the extraordinary genius of the Greeks, than that they were able to make such brilliant achievements in abstract thought, knowing, as they generally did, no language but their own. But the Greeks did not escape the effects of this deficiency. Their greatest intellects, those who laid the foundation of philosophy and of all our intellectual culture, Plato and Aristotle, are continually led away by words; mistaking the accidents of language for real relations in nature, and supposing that things which have the same name in the Greek tongue must be the same in their own essence. There is a well-known saying of Hobbes, the far-reaching significance of which you will more and more appreciate in proportion to the growth of your own intellect: "Words are the counters of wise men, but the money of fools." With the wise man a word stands for the fact which it represents; to the fool it is itself the fact. To carry on Hobbes's metaphor, the counter is far more likely to be taken for merely what it is, by those who are in the habit of using many different kinds of counters. But, besides the advantage of possessing another cultivated language, there is a further consideration equally important. Without knowing the language of a people, we never really know their thoughts, their feelings, and their type of character: and unless we do possess this knowledge, of some other people than ourselves, we remain, to the hour of our death, with our intellects only half expanded. Look at a youth who has never been out of his family circle: he never dreams of any other opinions or ways of thinking than those he has been bred up in; or, if he has heard of any such, attributes them to some moral defect, or inferiority of nature or education. If his family are Tory, he cannot conceive the possibility of being a Liberal; if Liberal, of being a Tory. What the notions and habits of a single family are to a boy who has had no intercourse beyond it, the notions and habits of his own country are to him who is ignorant of every other. Those notions and habits are to him human nature itself; whatever varies from them is an unaccountable aberration which he cannot mentally realize: the idea that any other ways can be right, or as near an approach to right as some of his own, is inconceivable to him. This does not merely close his eyes to the many things which every country still has to learn from others: it hinders every country from reaching the improvement which it could otherwise attain by itself. We are not likely to correct any of our opinions or mend any of our ways, unless we begin by conceiving that they are capable of amendment: but merely to know that foreigners think differently from ourselves, without understanding why they do so, or what they really do think, does but confirm us in our self-conceit, and connect our national vanity with the preservation of our own peculiarities. Improvement consists in bringing our opinions into nearer agreement with facts; and we shall not be likely to do this while we look at facts only through glasses colored by those very opinions. But since we cannot divest ourselves of preconceived notions, there is no known means of eliminating their influence but by frequently using the differently colored glasses of other people: and those of other nations, as the most different, are the best.

But if it is so useful, on this account, to know the language and literature of any other cultivated and civilized people, the most valuable of all to us in this respect are the languages and literature of the ancients. No nations of modern and civilized Europe are so unlike one another, as the Greeks and Romans are unlike all of us; yet without being, as some remote Orientals are, so totally dissimilar, that the labor of a life is required to enable us to understand them. Were this the only gain to be derived from a knowledge of the ancients, it would already place the study of them in a high rank among enlightening and liberalizing pursuits. It is of no use saying that we may know them through modern writings. We may know something of them in that way; which is much better than knowing nothing. But modern books do not teach us ancient thought; they teach us some modern writer's notion of ancient thought. Modern books do not show us the Greeks and Romans; they tell us some modern writer's opinions about the Greeks and Romans. Translations are scarcely better. When we want really to know what a person thinks or says, we seek it at first hand from himself. We do not trust to another person's impression of his meaning, given in another person's words; we refer to his own. Much more is it necessary to do so when his words are in one language, and those of his reporter in another. Modern phraseology never conveys the exact meaning of a Greek writer; it cannot do so, except by a diffuse explanatory circumlocution which no translator dares use. We must be able, in a certain degree, to think in Greek, if we would represent to ourselves how a Greek thought; and this not only in the abstruse region of metaphysics, but about the political, religious, and even domestic concerns of life. I will mention a further aspect of this question, which, though I have not the merit of originating it, I do not remember to have seen noticed in any book. There is no part of our knowledge which it is more useful to obtain at first hand—to go to the fountain head for— than our knowledge of history. Yet this, in most cases, we hardly ever do. Our conception of the past is not drawn from its own records, but from books written about it, containing not the facts, but a view of the facts which has shaped itself in the mind of somebody of our own or a very recent time. Such books are very instructive and valuable; they help us to understand history, to interpret history, to draw just conclusions from it; at the worst, they set us the example of trying to do all this; but they are not themselves history. The knowledge they give is upon trust, and even when they have done their best, it is not only incomplete, but partial, because confined to what a few modern writers have seen in the materials, and have thought worth picking out from among them. How little we learn of our own ancestors from Hume, or Hallam, or Macaulay, compared with what we know if we add to what these tell us, even a little reading of contemporary authors and documents! The most recent historians are so well aware of this, that they fill their pages with extracts from the original materials, feeling that these extracts are the real history, and their comments and thread of narrative are only helps towards understanding it. Now, it is part of the great worth to us of our Greek and Latin studies, that in them we do read history in the original sources. We are in actual contact with contemporary minds; we are not dependent on hearsay; we have something by which we can test and check the representations and theories of modern historians. It may be asked, Why then not study the original materials of modern history? I answer, It is highly desirable to do so; and let me remark by the way, that even this requires a dead language; nearly all the documents prior to the Reformation, and many subsequent to it, being written in Latin. But the exploration of these documents, though a most useful pursuit, cannot be a branch of education. Not to speak of their vast extent, and the fragmentary nature of each, the strongest reason is, that in learning the spirit of our own past ages, until a comparatively recent period, from contemporary writers, we learn hardly anything else. Those authors, with a few exceptions, are little worth reading on their own account. While, in studying the great writers of antiquity, we are not only learning to understand the ancient mind, but laying in a stock of wise thought and observation, still valuable to ourselves; and at the same time making ourselves familiar with a number of the most perfect and finished literary compositions which the human mind has produced—compositions which, from the altered conditions of human life, are likely to be seldom paralleled, in their sustained excellence, by the times to come.

Even as mere languages, no modern European language is so valuable a discipline to the intellect as those of Greece and Rome, on account of their regular and complicated structure. Consider for a moment what grammar is. It is the most elementary part of logic. It is the beginning of the analysis of the thinking process. The principles and rules of grammar are the means by which the forms of language are made to correspond with the universal forms of thought. The distinctions between the various parts of speech, between the cases of nouns, the moods and tenses of verbs, the functions of particles, are distinctions in thought, not merely in words. Single nouns and verbs express objects and events, many of which can be cognized by the senses: but the modes of putting nouns and verbs together, express the relations of objects and events, which can be cognized only by the intellect; and each different mode corresponds to a different relation. The structure of every sentence is a lesson in logic. The various rules of syntax oblige us to distinguish between the subject and predicate of a proposition, between the agent, the action, and the thing acted upon; to mark when an idea is intended to modify or qualify, or merely to unite with, some other idea; what assertions are categorical, what only conditional; whether the intention is to express similarity or contrast, to make a plurality of assertions conjunctively or disjunctively; what portions of a sentence, though grammatically complete within themselves, are mere members or subordinate parts of the assertion made by the entire sentence. Such things form the subject-matter of universal grammar; and the languages which teach it best are those which have the most definite rules, and which provide distinct forms for the greatest number of distinctions in thought, so that if we fail to attend precisely and accurately to any of these, we cannot avoid committing a solecism in language. In these qualities the classical languages have an incomparable superiority over every modern language, and over all languages, dead or living, which have a literature worth being generally studied.

But the superiority of the literature itself, for purposes of education, is still more marked and decisive. Even in the substantial value of the matter of which it is the vehicle, it is very far from having been superseded. The discoveries of the ancients in science have been greatly surpassed, and as much of them as is still valuable loses nothing by being incorporated in modern treatises: but what does not so well admit of being transferred bodily, and has been very imperfectly carried off even piecemeal, is the treasure which they accumulated of what may be called the wisdom of life; the rich store of experience of human nature and conduct, which the acute and observing minds of those ages, aided in their observations by the greater simplicity of manners and life, consigned to their writings, and most of which retains all its value. The speeches in Thucydides; the Rhetoric, Ethics, and Politics of Aristotle; the Dialogues of Plato; the Orations of Demosthenes; the Satires, and especially the Epistles of Horace; all the writings of Tacitus; the great work of Quintilian, a repertory of the best thoughts of the ancient world on all subjects connected with education; and, in a less formal manner, all that is left to us of the ancient historians, orators, philosophers, and even dramatists, are replete with remarks and maxims of singular good sense and penetration, applicable both to political and to private life: and the actual truths we find in them are even surpassed in value by the encouragement and help they give us in the pursuit of truth. Human invention has never produced anything so valuable, in the way both of stimulation and of discipline to the inquiring intellect, as the dialectics of the ancients, of which many of the works of Aristotle illustrate the theory, and those of Plato exhibit the practice. No modern writings come near to these, in teaching, both by precept and example, the way to investigate truth, on those subjects, so vastly important to us, which remain matters of controversy, from the difficulty or impossibility of bringing them to a directly experimental test. To question all things; never to turn away from any difficulty; to accept no doctrine either from ourselves or from other people without a rigid scrutiny by negative criticism, letting no fallacy, or incoherence, or confusion of thought, slip by unperceived; above all, to insist upon having the meaning of a word clearly understood before using it, and the meaning of a proposition before assenting to it; these are the lessons we learn from the ancient dialecticians. With all this vigorous management of the negative element, they inspire no scepticism about the reality of truth, or indifference to its pursuit. The noblest enthusiasm, both for the search after truth and for applying it to its highest uses, pervades these writers, Aristotle no less than Plato, though Plato has incomparably the greater power of imparting those feelings to others. In cultivating, therefore, the ancient languages as our best literary education, we are all the while laying an admirable foundation for ethical and philosophical culture. In purely literary excellence—in perfection of form—the pre-eminence of the ancients is not disputed. In every department which they attempted,—and they attempted almost all,—their composition, like their sculpture, has been to the greatest modern artists an example, to be looked up to with hopeless admiration, but of inappreciable value as a light on high, guiding their own endeavors. In prose and in poetry, in epic, lyric, or dramatic, as in historical, philosophical, and oratorical art, the pinnacle on which they stand is equally eminent. I am now speaking of the form, the artistic perfection of treatment; for, as regards substance, I consider modern poetry to be superior to ancient, in the same manner, though in a less degree, as modern science: it enters deeper into nature. The feelings of the modern mind are more various, more complex and manifold, that those of the ancients ever were. The modern mind is, what the ancient mind was not, brooding and self-conscious; and its meditative self-consciousness has discovered depths in the human soul which the Greeks and Romans did not dream of, and would not have understood. But what they had got to express, they expressed in a manner which few even of the greatest moderns have seriously attempted to rival. It must be remembered that they had more time, and that they wrote chiefly for a select class, possessed of leisure. To us who write in a hurry for people who read in a hurry, the attempt to give an equal degree of finish would be loss of time. But to be familiar with perfect models is not the less important to us because the element in which we work precludes even the effort to equal them. They show us at least what excellence is, and make us desire it, and strive to get as near to it as is within our reach. And this is the value to us of the ancient writers, all the more emphatically, because their excellence does not admit of being copied, or directly imitated. It does not consist in a trick which can be learned, but in the perfect adaptation of means to ends. The secret of the style of the great Greek and Roman authors is, that it is the perfection of good sense. In the first place, they never use a word without a meaning, or a word which adds nothing to the meaning. They always (to begin with) had a meaning; they knew what they wanted to say; and their whole purpose was to say it with the highest degree of exactness and completeness, and bring it home to the mind with the greatest possible clearness and vividness. It never entered into their thoughts to conceive of a piece of writing as beautiful in itself, abstractedly from what it had to express: its beauty must all be subservient to the most perfect expression of the sense. The *curiosa felicitas* which their critics ascribed in a pre-eminent degree to Horace, expresses the standard at which they all aimed. Their style is exactly described by Swift's definition, "the right words in the right places." Look at an oration of Demosthenes; there is nothing in it which calls attention to itself as style at all: it is only after a close examination we perceive that every word is what it should be, and where it should be, to lead the hearer smoothly and imperceptibly into the state of mind which the orator wishes to produce. The perfection of the workmanship is only visible in the total absence of any blemish or fault, and of anything which checks the flow of thought and feeling, anything which even momentarily distracts the mind from the main purpose. But then (as has been well said) it was not the object of Demosthenes to make the Athenians cry out, "What a splendid speaker!" but to make them say, "Let us march against Philip!" It was only in the decline of ancient literature that ornament began to be cultivated merely as ornament. In the time of its maturity, not the merest epithet was put in because it was thought beautiful in itself; nor even for a merely descriptive purpose, for epithets purely descriptive were one of the corruptions of style which abound in Lucan, for example: the word had no business there unless it brought out some feature which was wanted, and helped to place the object in the light which the purpose of the composition required. These conditions being complied with, then indeed the intrinsic beauty of the means used was a source of additional effect, of which it behooved them to avail themselves, like rhythm and melody of versification. But these great writers knew that ornament for the sake of ornament, ornament which attracts attention to itself, and shines by its own beauties, only does so by calling off the mind from the main object, and thus not only interferes with the higher purpose of human discourse, which ought, and generally professes, to have some matter to communicate, apart from the mere excitement of the moment, but also spoils the perfection of the composition as a piece of fine art, by destroying the unity of effect. This, then, is the first great lesson in composition to be learned from the classical authors. The second is, not to be prolix. In a single paragraph, Thucydides can give a clear and vivid representation of a battle, such as a reader who has once taken it into his mind can seldom forget. The most powerful and affecting piece of narrative perhaps in all historical literature, is the account of the Sicilian catastrophe in his seventh book; yet how few pages does it fill! The ancients were concise, because of the extreme pains they took with their compositions; almost all moderns are prolix, because they do not. The great ancients could express a thought so perfectly in a few words or sentences, that they did not need to add any more: the moderns, because they cannot bring it out clearly and completely at once, return again and again, heaping sentence upon sentence, each adding a little more elucidation, in hopes that, though no single sentence expresses the full meaning, the whole together may give a sufficient notion of it. In this respect I am afraid we are growing worse, instead of better, for want of time and patience, and from the necessity we are in of addressing almost all writings to a busy and imperfectly prepared public. The demands of modern life are such, the work to be done, the mass to be worked upon, are so vast, that those who have anything particular to say—who have, as the phrase goes, any message to deliver—cannot afford to devote their time to the production of masterpieces. But they would do far worse than they do, if there had never been masterpieces, or if they had never known them. Early familiarity with the perfect makes our most imperfect production far less bad than it otherwise would be. To have a high standard of excellence often makes the whole difference of rendering our work good when it would otherwise be mediocre.

For all these reasons I think it important to retain these two languages and literatures in the place they occupy, as a part of liberal education, that is, of the education of all who are not obliged by their circumstances to discontinue their scholastic studies at a very early age. But the same reasons which vindicate the place of classical studies in general education, show also the proper limitation of them. They should be carried as far as is sufficient to enable the pupil, in after life, to read the great works of ancient literature with ease. Those who have leisure and inclination to make scholarship, or ancient history, or general philology, their pursuit, of course require much more; but there is no room for more in general education. The laborious idleness in which the schooltime is wasted away in the English classical schools deserves the severest reprehension. To what purpose should the most precious years of early life be irreparably squandered in learning to write bad Latin and Greek verses? I do not see that we are much the better even for those who end by writing good ones. I am often tempted to ask the favorites of nature and fortune, whether all the serious and important work of the world is done, that their time and energy can be spared for these *nugae difficiles*. I am not blind to the utility of composing in a language, as a means of learning it accurately. I hardly know any other means equally effectual. But why should not prose composition suffice? What need is there of original composition at all? if that can be called original which unfortunate school-boys, without any thoughts to express, hammer out on compulsion from mere memory, acquiring the pernicious habit which a teacher should consider it one of his first duties to repress—that of merely stringing together borrowed phrases? The exercise in composition, most suitable to the requirements of learners, is that most valuable one, of retranslating from translated passages of a good author: and to this might be added, what still exists in many Continental places of education, occasional practice in talking Latin. There would be something to be said for the time spent in the manufacture of verses, if such practice were necessary for the enjoyment of ancient poetry; though it would be better to lose that enjoyment than to purchase it at so extravagant a price. But the beauties of a great poet would be a far poorer thing than they are, if they only impressed us through a knowledge of the technicalities of his art. The poet needed those technicalities: they are not necessary to us. They are essential for criticising a poem, but not for enjoying it. All that is wanted is sufficient familiarity with the language, for its meaning to reach us without any sense of effort, and clothed with the associations on which the poet counted for producing his effect. Whoever has this familiarity, and a practised ear, can have as keen a relish of the music of Virgil and Horace, as of Gray, or Burns, or Shelley, though he know not the metrical rules of a common Sapphic or Alcaic. I do not say that these rules ought not to be taught, but I would have a class apart for them, and would make the appropriate exercises an optional, not a compulsory part of the school teaching.

Much more might be said respecting classical instruction, and literary cultivation in general, as a part of liberal education. But it is time to speak of the uses of scientific instruction; or rather its indispensable necessity, for it is recommended by every consideration which pleads for any high order of intellectual education at all.

The most obvious part of the value of scientific instruction—the mere information that it gives—speaks for itself. We are born into a world which we have not made; a world whose phenomena take place according to fixed laws, of which we do not bring any knowledge into the world with us. In such a world we are appointed to live, and in it all our work is to be done. Our whole working power depends on knowing the laws of the world—in other words, the properties of the things which we have to work with, and to work among, and to work upon. We may and do rely, for the greater part of this knowledge, on the few who in each department make its acquisition their main business in life. But unless an elementary knowledge of scientific truths is diffused among the public, they never know what is certain and what is not, or who are entitled to speak with authority and who are not: and they either have no faith at all in the testimony of science, or are the ready dupes of charlatans and impostors. They alternate between ignorant distrust, and blind, often misplaced, confidence. Besides, who is there who would not wish to understand the meaning of the common physical facts that take place under his eye? Who would not wish to know why a pump raises water, why a lever moves heavy weights, why it is hot at the tropics and cold at the poles, why the moon is sometimes dark and sometimes bright, what is the cause of the tides? Do we not feel that he who is totally ignorant of these things, let him be ever so skilled in a special profession, is not an educated man, but an ignoramus? It is surely no small part of education to put us in intelligent possession of the most important and most universally interesting facts of the universe, so that the world which surrounds us may not be a sealed book to us, uninteresting because unintelligible. This, however, is but the simplest and most obvious part of the utility of science, and the part which, if neglected in youth, may be the most easily made up for afterwards. It is more important to understand the value of scientific instruction as a training and disciplining process, to fit the intellect for the proper work of a human being. Facts are the materials of our knowledge, but the mind itself is the instrument; and it is easier to acquire facts, than to judge what they prove, and how, through the facts which we know, to get to those which we want to know.

The most incessant occupation of the human intellect throughout life is the ascertainment of truth. We are always needing to know what is actually true about something or other. It is not given to us all to discover great general truths that are a light to all men and to future generations; though with a better general education the number of those who could do so would be far greater than it is. But we all require the ability to judge between the conflicting opinions which are offered to us as vital truths; to choose what doctrines we will receive in the matter of religion, for example; to judge whether we ought to be Tories, Whigs, or Radicals, or to what length it is our duty to go with each; to form a rational conviction on great questions of legislation and internal policy, and on the manner in which our country should behave to dependencies and to foreign nations. And the need we have of knowing how to discriminate truth, is not confined to the larger truths. All through life it is our most pressing interest to find out the truth about all the matters we are concerned with. If we are farmers we want to find what will truly improve our soil; if merchants, what will truly influence the markets of our commodities; if judges, or jurymen, or advocates, who it was that truly did an unlawful act, or to whom a disputed right truly belongs. Every time we have to make a new resolution or alter an old one, in any situation in life, we shall go wrong unless we know the truth about the facts on which our resolution depends. Now, however different these searchers for truth may look, and however unlike they really are in their subject-matter, the methods of getting at truth, and the tests of truth, are in all cases much the same. There are but two roads by which truth can be discovered—observation and reasoning; observation, of course, including experiment. We all observe, and we all reason, and therefore, more or less successfully, we all ascertain truths: but most of us do it very ill, and could not get on at all were we not able to fall back on others who do it better. If we could not do it in any degree, we should be mere instruments in the hands of those who could: they would be able to reduce us to slavery. Then how shall we best learn to do this? By being shown the way in which it has already been successfully done. The process by which truth is attained, reasoning and observation, have been carried to their greatest known perfection in the physical sciences. As classical literature furnishes the most perfect types of the art of expression, so do the physical sciences those of the art of thinking. Mathematics, and its application to astronomy and natural philosophy, are the most complete example of the discovery of truths by reasoning; experimental science, of their discovery by direct observation. In all these cases we know that we can trust the operation, because the conclusions to which it has led have been found true by subsequent trial. It is by the study of these, then, that we may hope to qualify ourselves for distinguishing truth, in cases where there do not exist the same ready means of verification.

In what consists the principal and most characteristic difference between one human intellect and another? In their ability to judge correctly of evidence. Our direct perceptions of truth are so limited,—we know so few things by immediate intuition, or, as it used to be called, by simple apprehension,—that we depend, for almost all our valuable knowledge, on evidence external to itself; and most of us are very unsafe hands at estimating evidence, where an appeal cannot be made to actual eyesight. The intellectual part of our education has nothing more important to do than to correct or mitigate this almost universal infirmity—this summary and substance of nearly all purely intellectual weakness. To do this with effect needs all the resources which the most perfect system of intellectual training can command. Those resources, as every teacher knows, are but of three kinds: first, models; secondly, rules; thirdly, appropriate practice. The models of the art of estimating evidence are furnished by science; the rules are suggested by science; and the study of science is the most fundamental portion of the practice.

Take, in the first instance, mathematics. It is chiefly from mathematics we realize the fact that there actually is a road to truth by means of reasoning; that anything real, and which will be found true when tried, can be arrived at by a mere operation of the mind. The flagrant abuse of mere reasoning in the days of the schoolmen, when men argued confidently to supposed facts of outward nature without properly establishing their premises, or checking the conclusions by observation, created a prejudice in the modern, and especially in the English mind, against deductive reasoning altogether, as a mode of investigation. The prejudice lasted long, and was upheld by the misunderstood authority of Lord Bacon; until the prodigious applications of mathematics to physical science—to the discovery of the laws of external nature—slowly and tardily restored the reasoning process to the place which belongs to it as a source of real knowledge. Mathematics, pure and applied, are still the great conclusive example of what can be done by reasoning. Mathematics also habituates us to several of the principal precautions for the safety of the process. Our first studies in geometry teach us two invaluable lessons. One is, to lay down at the beginning, in express and clear terms, all the premises from which we intend to reason. The other is, to keep every step in the reasoning distinct and separate from all the other steps, and to make each step safe before proceeding to another; expressly stating to ourselves, at every joint in the reasoning, what new premise we there introduce. It is not necessary that we should do this at all times, in all our reasonings. But we must be always able and ready to do it. If the validity of our argument is denied, or if we doubt it ourselves, that is the way to check it. In this way we are often enabled to detect at once the exact place where paralogism or confusion get in: and after sufficient practice we may be able to keep them out from the beginning. It is to mathematics, again, that we owe our first notion of a connected body of truth; truths which grow out of one another, and hang together so that each implies all the rest; that no one of them can be questioned without contradicting another or others, until in the end it appears that no part of the system can be false unless the whole is so. Pure mathematics first gave us this conception; applied mathematics extends it to the realm of physical nature. Applied mathematics shows us that not only the truths of abstract number and extension, but the external facts of the universe, which we apprehend by our senses, form, at least in a large part of all nature, a web similarly held together. We are able, by reasoning from a few fundamental truths, to explain and predict the phenomena of material objects: and what is still more remarkable, the fundamental truths were themselves found out by reasoning; for they are not such as are obvious to the senses, but had to be inferred by a mathematical process from a mass of minute details, which alone came within the direct reach of human observation. When

Newton, in this manner, discovered the laws of the solar system, he created, for all posterity, the true idea of science. He gave the most perfect example we are ever likely to have, of that union of reasoning and observation, which by means of facts that can be directly observed, ascends to laws which govern multitudes of other facts—laws which not only explain and account for what we see, but give us assurance beforehand of much that we do not see, much that we never could have found out by observation, though, having been found out, it is always verified by the result.

While mathematics, and the mathematical sciences, supply us with a typical example of the ascertainment of truth by reasoning,—those physical sciences which are not mathematical, such as chemistry, and purely experimental physics, show us in equal perfection the other mode of arriving at certain truth, by observation, in its most accurate form—that of experiment. The value of mathematics in a logical point of view is an old topic with mathematicians, and has even been insisted on so exclusively as to provoke a counter-exaggeration, of which a well-known essay by Sir William Hamilton is an example: but the logical value of experimental science is comparatively a new subject; yet there is no intellectual discipline more important than that which the experimental sciences afford. Their whole occupation consists in doing well, what all of us, during the whole of life, are engaged in doing, for the most part badly. All men do not affect to be reasoners, but all profess, and really attempt, to draw inferences from experience: yet hardly anyone, who has not been a student of the physical sciences, sets out with any just idea of what the process of interpreting experience really is. If a fact has occurred once or oftener, and another fact has followed it, people think they have got an experiment, and are well on the road towards showing that the one fact is the cause of the other. If they did but know the immense amount of precaution necessary to a scientific experiment; with what sedulous care the accompanying circumstances are contrived and varied, so as to exclude every agency but that which is the subject of the experiment—or, when disturbing agencies cannot be excluded, the minute accuracy with which their influence is calculated and allowed for, in order that the residue may contain nothing but what is due to the one agency under examination; if these things were attended to, people would be much less easily satisfied that their opinions have the evidence of experience; many popular notions and generalizations which are in all mouths, would be thought a great deal less certain than they are supposed to be; but we should begin to lay the foundation of really experimental knowledge on things which are now the subjects of mere vague discussion, where one side finds as much to say and says it as confidently as another, and each person's opinion is less determined by evidence than by his accidental interest or prepossession. In politics, for instance, it is evident to whoever comes to the study from that of the experimental sciences, that no political conclusions of any value for practice can be arrived at by direct experience. Such specific experience as we can have serves only to verify, and even that insufficiently, the conclusions of reasoning. Take any active force you please in politics; take the liberties of England, or free trade: how should we know that either of these things conduced to prosperity, if we could discern no tendency in the things themselves to produce it? If we had only the evidence of what is called our experience, such prosperity as we enjoy might be owing to a hundred other causes, and might have been obstructed, not promoted, by these. All true political science is, in one sense of the phrase, *à priori*, being deduced from the tendencies of things—tendencies known either through our general experience of human nature, or as the result of an analysis of the course of history, considered as a progressive evolution. It requires, therefore, the union of induction and deduction, and the mind that is equal to it must have been well disciplined in both. But familiarity with scientific experiment at least does the useful service of inspiring a wholesome scepticism about the conclusions which the mere surface of experience suggests.

The study, on the one hand, of mathematics and its applications, on the other, of experimental science, prepares us for the principal business of the intellect, by the practice of it in the most characteristic cases, and by familiarity with the most perfect and successful models of it. But in great things as in small, examples and models are not sufficient: we want rules as well. Familiarity with the correct use of a language in conversation and writing does not make rules of grammar unnecessary; nor does the amplest knowledge of sciences of reasoning and experiment dispense with rules of logic. We may have heard correct reasonings and seen skilful experiments all our lives—we shall not learn by mere imitation to do the like, unless we pay careful attention to how it is done. It is much easier in these abstract matters, than in purely mechanical ones, to mistake bad work for good. To mark out the difference between them is the province of logic. Logic lays down the general principles and laws of the search after truth; the conditions which, whether recognized or not, must actually have been observed if the mind has done its work rightly. Logic is the intellectual complement of mathematics and physics. Those sciences give the practice, of which Logic is the theory. It declares the principles, rules, and precepts, of which they exemplify the observance.

The science of Logic has two parts; ratiocinative and inductive logic. The one helps to keep us right in reasoning from premises, the other in concluding from observation. Ratiocinative logic is much older than inductive, because reasoning in the narrower sense of the word is an easier process than induction, and the science which works by mere reasoning, pure mathematics, had been carried to a considerable height while the sciences of observation were still in the purely empirical period. The principles of ratiocination, therefore, were the earliest understood and systematized, and the logic of ratiocination is even now suitable to an earlier stage in education than that of induction. The principles of induction cannot be properly understood without some previous study of the inductive sciences; but the logic of reasoning, which was already carried to a high degree of perfection by Aristotle, does not absolutely require even a knowledge of mathematics, but can be sufficiently exemplified and illustrated from the practice of daily life.

Of Logic I venture to say, even if limited to that of mere ratiocination, the theory of names, propositions, and the syllogism, that there is no part of intellectual education which is of greater value, or whose place can so ill be supplied by anything else. Its uses, it is true, are chiefly negative; its function is, not so much to teach us to go right, as to keep us from going wrong. But in the operations of the intellect it is so much easier to go wrong than right; it is so utterly impossible for even the most vigorous mind to keep itself in the path but by maintaining a vigilant watch against all deviations, and noting all the by-ways by which it is possible to go astray—that the chief difference between one reasoner and another consists in their less or greater liability to be misled. Logic points out all the possible ways in which, starting from true premises, we may draw false conclusions. By its analysis of the reasoning process, and the forms it supplies for stating and setting forth our reasonings, it enables us to guard the points at which a fallacy is in danger of slipping in, or to lay our fingers upon the place where it has slipped in. When I consider how very simple the theory of reasoning is, and how short a time is sufficient for acquiring a thorough knowledge of its principles and rules, and even considerable expertness in applying them, I can find no excuse for omission to study it on the part of anyone who aspires to succeed in any intellectual pursuit. Logic is the great disperser of hazy and confused thinking: it clears up the fogs which hide from us our own ignorance, and make us believe that we understand a subject when we do not. We must not be led away by talk about inarticulate giants who do great deeds without knowing how, and see into the most recondite truths without any of the ordinary helps, and without being able to explain to other people how they reach their conclusions, nor consequently to convince any other people of the truth of them. There may be such men, as there are deaf and dumb persons who do clever things; but for all that, speech and hearing are faculties by no means to be dispensed with. If you want to know whether you are thinking rightly, put your thoughts into words. In the very attempt to do this you will find yourselves, consciously or unconsciously, using logical forms. Logic compels us to throw our meaning into distinct propositions, and our reasonings into distinct steps. It makes us conscious of all the implied assumptions on which we are proceeding, and which, if not true, vitiate the entire process. It makes us aware what extent of doctrine we commit ourselves to by any course of reasoning, and obliges us to look the implied premises in the face, and make up our minds whether we can stand to them. It makes our opinions consistent with themselves and with one another, and forces us to think clearly, even when it cannot make us think correctly. It is true that error may be consistent and systematic as well as truth; but this is not the common case. It is no small advantage to see clearly the principles and consequences involved in our opinions, and which we must either accept, or else abandon those opinions. We are much nearer to finding truth when we search for it in broad daylight. Error, pursued rigorously to all that is implied in it, seldom fails to get detected by coming into collision with some known and admitted fact.

You will find abundance of people to tell you that logic is no help to thought, and that people cannot be taught to think by rules. Undoubtedly rules by themselves, without practice, go but a little way in teaching anything. But if the practice of thinking is not improved by rules, I venture to say it is the only difficult thing done by human beings that is not so. A man learns to saw wood principally by practice, but there are rules for doing it, grounded on the nature of the operation, and if he is not taught the rules, he will not saw well until he has discovered them for himself. Wherever there is a right way and a wrong, there must be a difference between them, and it must be possible to find out what the difference is; and when found out and expressed in words, it is a rule for the operation. If anyone is inclined to disparage rules, I say to him, try to learn anything which there are rules for, without knowing the rules, and see how you succeed. To those who think lightly of the school logic, I say, take the trouble to learn it. You will easily do so in a few weeks, and you will see whether it is of no use to you in making your mind clear, and keeping you from stumbling in the dark over the most outrageous fallacies. Nobody, I believe, who has really learned it, and who goes on using his mind, is insensible to its benefits, unless he started with a prejudice, or, like some eminent English and Scottish thinkers of the past century, is under the influence of a reaction against the exaggerated pretensions made by the schoolmen, not so much in behalf of logic as of the reasoning process itself. Still more highly must the use of logic be estimated, if we include in it, as we ought to do, the principles and rules of Induction as well as of Ratiocination. As the one logic guards us against bad deduction, so does the other against bad generalization, which is a still more universal error. If men easily err in arguing from one general proposition to another, still more easily do they go wrong in interpreting the observations made by themselves and others. There is nothing in which an untrained mind shows itself more hopelessly incapable, than in drawing the proper general conclusions from its own experience. And even trained minds, when all their training is on a special subject, and does not extend to the general principles of induction, are only kept right when there are ready opportunities of verifying their inferences by facts. Able scientific men, when they venture upon subjects in which they have no facts to check them, are often found drawing conclusions or making generalizations from their experimental knowledge, such as any sound theory of induction would show to be utterly unwarranted. So true is it that practice alone, even of a good kind, is not sufficient without principles and rules. Lord Bacon had the great merit of seeing that rules were necessary, and conceiving, to a very considerable extent, their true character. The defects of his conception were such as were inevitable while the inductive sciences were only in the earliest stage of their progress, and the highest efforts of the human mind in that direction had not yet been made. Inadequate as the Baconian view of induction was, and rapidly as the practice outgrew it, it is only within a generation or two that any considerable improvement has been made in the theory; very much through the impulse given by two of the many distinguished men who have adorned the Scottish Universities—Dugald Stewart and Brown.

I have given a very incomplete and summary view of the educational benefits derived from instruction in the more perfect sciences, and in the rules for the proper use of the intellectual faculties which the practice of those sciences has suggested. There are other sciences, which are in a more backward state, and tax the whole powers of the mind in its mature years, yet a beginning of which may be beneficially made in university studies, while a tincture of them is valuable even to those who are never likely to proceed farther. The first is physiology; the science of the laws of organic and animal life, and especially of the structure and functions of the human body. It would be absurd to pretend that a profound knowledge of this difficult subject can be acquired in youth, or as a part of general education. Yet an acquaintance with its leading truths is one of those acquirements which ought not to be the exclusive property of a particular profession. The value of such knowledge for daily uses has been made familiar to us all by the sanitary discussions of late years. There is hardly one among us who may not, in some position of authority, be required to form an opinion and take part in public action on sanitary subjects. And the importance of understanding the true conditions of health and disease—of knowing how to acquire and preserve that healthy habit of body which the most tedious and costly medical treatment so often fails to restore when once lost—should secure a place in general education for the principal maxims of hygiene, and some of those even of practical medicine. For those who aim at high intellectual cultivation, the study of physiology has still greater recommendations, and is, in the present state of advancement of the higher studies, a real necessity. The practice which it gives in the study of nature is such as no other physical science affords in the same kind, and is the best introduction to the difficult questions of politics and social life. Scientific education, apart from professional objects, is but a preparation for judging rightly of Man, and of his requirements and interests. But to this final pursuit, which has been called *par excellence* the proper study of mankind, physiology is the most serviceable of the sciences, because it is the nearest. Its subject is already Man: the same complex and manifold being, whose properties are not independent of circumstance, and immovable from age to age, like those of the ellipse and hyperbola, or of sulphur and phosphorus, but are infinitely various, indefinitely modifiable by art or accident, graduating by the nicest shades into one another, and reacting upon one another in a thousand ways, so that they are seldom capable of being isolated and observed separately. With the difficulties of the study of a being so constituted, the physiologist, and he alone among scientific inquirers, is already familiar. Take what view we will of man as a spiritual being, one part of his nature is far more like another than either of them is like anything else. In the organic world we study nature under disadvantages very similar to those which affect the study of moral and political phenomena: our means of making experiments are almost as limited, while the extreme complexity of the facts makes the conclusions of general reasoning unusually precarious, on account of the vast number of circumstances that conspire to determine every result. Yet, in spite of these obstacles, it is found possible in physiology to arrive at a considerable number of well-ascertained and important truths. This, therefore, is an excellent school in which to study the means of overcoming similar difficulties elsewhere. It is in physiology, too, that we are first introduced to some of the conceptions which play the greatest part in the moral and social sciences, but which do not occur at all in those of inorganic nature; as, for instance, the idea of predisposition, and of predisposing causes, as distinguished from exciting causes. The operation of all moral forces is immensely influenced by predisposition: without that element, it is impossible to explain the commonest facts of history and social life. Physiology is also the first science in which we recognize the influence of habit—the tendency of something to happen again merely because it has happened before. From physiology, too, we get our clearest notion of what is meant by development or evolution. The growth of a plant or animal from the first germ is the typical specimen of a phenomenon which rules through the whole course of the history of man and society—increase of function, through expansion and differentiation of structure by internal forces. I cannot enter into the subject at greater length; it is enough if I throw out hints which may be germs of further thought in yourselves. Those who aim at high intellectual achievements may be assured that no part of their time will be less wasted, than that which they employ in becoming familiar with the methods and with the main conceptions of the science of organization and life.

Physiology, at its upper extremity, touches on Psychology, or the Philosophy of Mind: and without raising any disputed questions about the limits between Matter and Spirit, the nerves and brain are admitted to have so intimate a connection with the mental operations, that the student of the last cannot dispense with a considerable knowledge of the first. The value of psychology itself need hardly be expatiated upon in a Scottish University; for it has always been there studied with brilliant success. Almost everything which has been contributed from these islands towards its advancement since Locke and Berkeley, has until very lately, and much of it even in the present generation, proceeded from Scottish authors and Scottish professors. Psychology, in truth, is simply the knowledge of the laws of human nature. If there is anything that deserves to be studied by man, it is his own nature and that of his fellow-men: and if it is worth studying at all, it is worth studying scientifically, so as to reach the fundamental laws which underlie and govern all the rest. With regard to the suitableness of this subject for general education, a distinction must be made. There are certain observed laws of our thoughts and of our feelings which rest upon experimental evidence, and, once seized, are a clew to the interpretation of much that we are conscious of in ourselves, and observe in one another. Such, for example, are the laws of association. Psychology, so far as it consists of such laws,—I speak of the laws themselves, not of their disputed applications,—is as positive and certain a science as chemistry, and fit to be taught as such. When, however, we pass beyond the bounds of these admitted truths, to questions which are still in controversy among the different philosophical schools—how far the higher operations of the mind can be explained by association, how far we must admit other primary principles—what faculties of the mind are simple, what complex, and what is the composition of the latter—above all, when we embark upon the sea of metaphysics properly so called, and inquire, for instance, whether time and space are real existences, as is our spontaneous impression, or forms of our sensitive faculty, as is maintained by Kant, or complex ideas generated by association; whether matter and spirit are conceptions merely relative to our faculties, or facts existing *per se*, and in the latter case, what is the nature and limit of our knowledge of them; whether the will of man is free or determined by causes, and what is the real difference between the two doctrines; matters on which the most thinking men, and those who have given most study to the subjects, are still divided; it is neither to be expected nor desired that those who do not specially devote themselves to the higher departments of speculation should employ much of their time in attempting to get to the bottom of these questions. But it is a part of liberal education to know that such controversies exist, and, in a general way, what has been said on both sides of them. It is instructive to know the failures of the human intellect as well as its successes, its imperfect as well as its perfect attainments; to be aware of the open questions, as well as of those which have been definitively resolved. A very summary view of these disputed matters may suffice for the many; but a system of education is not intended solely for the many; it has to kindle the aspirations and aid the efforts of those who are destined to stand forth as thinkers above the multitude: and for these there is hardly to be found any discipline comparable to that which these metaphysical controversies afford. For they are essentially questions about the estimation of evidence; about the ultimate grounds of belief; the conditions required to justify our most familiar and intimate convictions; and the real meaning and import of words and phrases which we have used from infancy as if we understood all about them, which are even at the foundation of human language, yet of which no one except a metaphysician has rendered to himself a complete account. Whatever philosophical opinions the study of these questions may lead us to adopt, no one ever came out of the discussion of them without increased vigor of understanding, an increased demand for precision of thought and language, and a more careful and exact appreciation of the nature of proof. There never was any sharpener of the intellectual faculties superior to the Berkeleian controversy. There is even now no reading more profitable to students—confining myself to writers in our own language, and notwithstanding that so many of their speculations are already obsolete—than Hobbes and Locke, Reid and Stewart, Hume, Hartley, and Brown; on condition that these great thinkers are not read passively, as masters to be followed, but actively, as supplying materials and incentives to thought. To come to our own contemporaries, he who has mastered Sir William Hamilton and your own lamented Ferrier as distinguished representatives of one of the two great schools of philosophy, and an eminent Professor in a neighboring University, Professor Bain, probably the greatest living authority in the other, has gained a practice in the most searching methods of philosophic investigation applied to the most arduous subjects, which is no inadequate preparation for any intellectual difficulties that he is ever likely to be called on to resolve.

In this brief outline of a complete scientific education, I have said nothing about direct instruction in that which it is the chief of all the ends of intellectual education to qualify us for—the exercise of thought on the great interests of mankind as moral and social beings—ethics and politics, in the largest sense. These things are not, in the existing state of human knowledge, the subject of a science, generally admitted and accepted. Politics cannot be learned once for all, from a text-book, or the instructions of a master. What we require to be taught on that subject, is to be our own teachers. It is a subject on which we have no masters to follow; each must explore for himself, and exercise an independent judgment. Scientific politics do not consist in having a set of conclusions ready made, to be applied everywhere indiscriminately, but in setting the mind to work in a scientific spirit to discover in each instance the truths applicable to the given case. And this, at present, scarcely any two persons do in the same way. Education is not entitled, on this subject, to recommend any set of opinions as resting on the authority of established science. But it can supply the student with materials for his own mind, and helps to use them. It can make him acquainted with the best speculations on the subject, taken from different points of view; none of which will be found complete, while each embodies some considerations really relevant, really requiring to be taken into the account. Education may also introduce us to the principal facts which have a direct bearing on the subject, namely, the different modes or stages of civilization that have been found among mankind, and the characteristic properties of each. This is the true purpose of historical studies, as prosecuted in a University. The leading facts of ancient and modern history should be known by the student from his private reading: if that knowledge be wanting, it cannot possibly be supplied here. What a Professor of History has to teach, is the meaning of those facts. His office is to help the student in collecting from history what are the main differences between human beings, and between the institutions of society, at one time or place and at another; in picturing to himself human life and the human conception of life, as they were at the different stages of human development; in distinguishing between what is the same in all ages and what is progressive, and forming some incipient conception of the causes and laws of progress. All these things are as yet very imperfectly understood even by the most philosophic inquirers, and are quite unfit to be taught dogmatically. The object is to lead the student to attend to them; to make him take interest in history not as a mere narrative, but as a chain of causes and effects still unwinding itself before his eyes, and full of momentous consequences to himself and his descendants; the unfolding of a great epic or dramatic action, to terminate in the happiness or misery, the elevation or degradation, of the human race; an unremitting conflict between good and evil powers, of which every act done by any of us, insignificant as we are, forms one of the incidents; a conflict in which even the smallest of us cannot escape from taking part, in which whoever does not help the right side is helping the wrong, and for our share in which, whether it be greater or smaller, and let its actual consequences be visible or in the main invisible, no one of us can escape the responsibility. Though education cannot arm and equip its pupils for this fight with any complete philosophy either of politics or of history, there is much positive instruction that it can give them, having a direct bearing on the duties of citizenship. They should be taught the outlines of the civil and political institutions of their own country, and in a more general way, of the more advanced of the other civilized nations. Those branches of politics, or of the laws of social life, in which there exists a collection of facts or thoughts sufficiently shifted and methodized to form the beginning of a science, should be taught *ex professo*. Among the chief of these is Political Economy; the sources and conditions of wealth and material prosperity for aggregate bodies of human beings. This study approaches nearer to the rank of a science, in the sense in which we apply that name to the physical sciences, than anything else connected with politics yet does. I need not enlarge on the important lessons which it affords for the guidance of life, and for the estimation of laws and institutions, or on the necessity of knowing all that it can teach in order to have true views of the course of human affairs, or form plans for their improvement which will stand actual trial. The same persons who cry down Logic will generally warn you against Political Economy. It is unfeeling, they will tell you. It recognizes unpleasant facts. For my part, the most unfeeling thing I know of is the law of gravitation: it breaks the neck of the best and most amiable person without scruple, if he forgets for a single moment to give heed to it. The winds and waves too are very unfeeling. Would you advise those who go to sea to deny the winds and waves—or to make use of them, and find the means of guarding against their dangers? My advice to you is to study the great writers on Political Economy, and hold firmly by whatever in them you find true; and depend upon it that if you are not selfish or hardhearted already, Political Economy will not make you so. Of no less importance than Political Economy is the study of what is called Jurisprudence; the general principles of law; the social necessities which laws are required to meet; the features common to all systems of law, and the differences between them; the requisites of good legislation, the proper mode of constructing a legal system, and the best constitution of courts of justice and modes of legal procedure. These things are not only the chief part of the business of government, but the vital concern of every citizen; and their improvement affords a wide scope for the energies of any duly prepared mind, ambitious of contributing towards the better condition of the human race. For this, too, admirable helps have been provided by writers of our own or of a very recent time. At the head of them stands Bentham, undoubtedly the greatest master who ever devoted the labor of a life to let in light on the subject of law, and who is the more intelligible to nonprofessional persons, because, as his way is, he builds up the subject from its foundation in the facts of human life, and shows, by careful consideration of ends and means, what law might and ought to be, in deplorable contrast with what it is. Other enlightened jurists have followed with contributions of two kinds, as the type of which I may take two works, equally admirable in their respective times. Mr. Austin, in his Lectures on Jurisprudence, takes for his basis the Roman law, the most elaborately consistent legal system which history has shown us in actual operation, and that which the greatest number of accomplished minds have employed themselves in harmonizing. From this he singles out the principles and distinctions which are of general applicability, and employs the powers and resources of a most precise and analytic mind to give to those principles and distinctions a philosophic basis, grounded in the universal reason of mankind, and not in mere technical convenience. Mr. Maine, in his treatise on Ancient Law in its relations to Modern Thought, shows from the history of law, and from what is known of the primitive institutions of mankind, the origin of much that has lasted till now, and has a firm footing both in the laws and in the ideas of modern times; showing that many of these things never originated in reason, but are relics of the institutions of barbarous society, modified more or less by civilization, but kept standing by the persistency of ideas which were the offspring of those barbarous institutions, and have survived their parent. The path opened by Mr. Maine has been followed up by others, with additional illustrations of the influence of obsolete ideas on modern institutions, and of obsolete institutions on modern ideas; an action and reaction which perpetuate, in many of the greatest concerns, a mitigated barbarism; things being continually accepted as dictates of nature and necessities of life, which, if we knew all, we should see to have originated in artificial arrangements of society, long since abandoned and condemned.

To these studies I would add International Law; which I decidedly think should be taught in all Universities, and should form part of all liberal education. The need of it is far from being limited to diplomatists and lawyers: it extends to every citizen. What is called the Law of Nations is not properly law, but a part of ethics; a set of moral rules, accepted as authoritative by civilized states. It is true that these rules neither are nor ought to be of eternal obligation, but do and must vary more or less from age to age, as the consciences of nations become more enlightened and the exigencies of political society undergo change. But the rules mostly were at their origin, and still are, an application of the maxims of honesty and humanity to the intercourse of states. They were introduced by the moral sentiments of mankind, or by their sense of the general interest, to mitigate the crimes and sufferings of a state of war, and to restrain governments and nations from unjust or dishonest conduct towards one another in time of peace. Since every country stands in numerous and various relations with the other countries of the world, and many, our own among the number, exercise actual authority over some of these, a knowledge of the established rules of international morality is essential to the duty of every nation, and therefore of every person in it who helps to make up the nation, and whose voice and feeling form a part of what is called public opinion. Let not any one pacify his conscience by the delusion that he can do no harm if he takes no part, and forms no opinion. Bad men need nothing more to compass their ends, than that good men should look on and do nothing. He is not a good man who, without a protest, allows wrong to be committed in his name, and with the means which he helps to supply, because he will not trouble himself to use his mind on the subject. It depends on the habit of attending to and looking into public transactions, and on the degree of information and solid judgment respecting them that exists in the community, whether the conduct of the nation as a nation, both within itself and towards others, shall be selfish, corrupt, and tyrannical, or rational and enlightened, just and noble.

Of these more advanced studies, only a small commencement can be made at schools and Universities; but even this is of the highest value, by awakening an interest in the subjects, by conquering the first difficulties, and injuring the mind to the kind of exertion which the studies require, by implanting a desire to make further progress, and directing the student to the best tracks and the best helps. So far as these branches of knowledge have been acquired, we have learned, or been put into the way of learning, our duty, and our work in life.

Knowing it, however, is but half the work of education; it still remains, that what we know, we shall be willing and determined to put in practice. Nevertheless, to know the truth is already a great way towards disposing us to act upon it. What we see clearly and apprehend keenly, we have a natural desire to act out. "To see the best, and yet the worst pursue," is a possible but not a common state of mind; those who follow the wrong have generally first taken care to be voluntarily ignorant of the right. They have silenced their conscience, but they are not knowingly disobeying it. If you take an average human mind while still young, before the objects it has chosen in life have given it a turn in any bad direction, you will generally find it desiring what is good, right, and for the benefit of all; and if that season is properly used to implant the knowledge and give the training which shall render rectitude of judgment more habitual than sophistry, a serious barrier will have been erected against the inroads of selfishness and falsehood. Still, it is a very imperfect education which trains the intelligence only, but not the will. No one can dispense with an education directed expressly to the moral as well as the intellectual part of his being. Such education, so far as it is direct, is either moral or religious; and these may either be treated as distinct, or as different aspects of the same thing. The subject we are now considering is not education as a whole, but scholastic education, and we must keep in view the inevitable limitations of what schools and Universities can do. It is beyond their power to educate morally or religiously. Moral and religious education consists in training the feelings and the daily habits; and these are, in the main, beyond the sphere and inaccessible to the control of public education. It is the home, the family, which gives us the moral or religious education we really receive: and this is completed, and modified, sometimes for the better, often for the worse, by society, and the opinions and feelings with which we are there surrounded. The moral or religious influence which a University can exercise, consists less in any express teaching, than in the pervading tone of the place. Whatever it teaches, it should teach as penetrated by a sense of duty; it should present all knowledge as chiefly a means to worthiness of life, given for the double purpose of making each of us practically useful to his fellow-creatures, and of elevating the character of the species itself; exalting and dignifying our nature. There is nothing which spreads more contagiously from teacher to pupil than elevation of sentiment: often and often have students caught from the living influence of a professor a contempt for mean and selfish objects, and a noble ambition to leave the world better than they found it, which they have carried with them throughout life. In these respects, teachers of every kind have natural and peculiar means of doing with effect what everyone who mixes with his fellow-beings, or addresses himself to them in any character, should feel bound to do to the extent of his capacity and opportunities. What is special to a University on these subjects belongs chiefly, like the rest of its work, to the intellectual department. A University exists for the purpose of laying open to each succeeding generation, as far as the conditions of the case admit, the accumulated treasure of the thoughts of mankind. As an indispensable part of this, it has to make known to them what mankind at large, their own country, and the best and wisest individual men, have thought on the great subjects of morals and religion. There should be, and there is in most Universities, professorial instruction in moral philosophy; but I could wish that this instruction were of a somewhat different type from what is ordinarily met with. I could wish that it were more expository, less polemical, and above all less dogmatic. The learner should be made acquainted with the principal systems of moral philosophy which have existed and been practically operative among mankind, and should hear what there is to be said for each: the Aristotelian, the Epicurean, the Stoic, the Judaic, the Christian in the various modes of its interpretation, which differ almost as much from one another as the teachings of those earlier schools. He should be made familiar with the different standards of right and wrong which have been taken as the basis of ethics; general utility, natural justice, natural rights, a moral sense, principles of practical reason, and the rest. Among all these, it is not so much the teacher's business to take a side, and fight stoutly for some one against the rest, as it is to direct them all towards the establishment and preservation of the rules of conduct most advantageous to mankind. There is not one of these systems which has not its good side; not one from which there is not something to be learned by the votaries of the others; not one which is not suggested by a keen, though it may not always be a clear, perception of some important truths, which are the prop of the system, and the neglect or undervaluing of which in other systems, is their characteristic infirmity. A system which may be as a whole erroneous, is still valuable, until it has forced upon mankind a sufficient attention to the portion of truth which suggested it. The ethical teacher does his part best, when he points out how each system may be strengthened even on its own basis, by taking into more complete account the truths which other systems have realized more fully and made more prominent. I do not mean that he should encourage an essentially sceptical eclecticism. While placing every system in the best aspect it admits of, and endeavoring to draw from all of them the most salutary consequences compatible with their nature, I would by no means debar him from enforcing by his best arguments his own preference for some one of the number. They cannot be all true; though those which are false as theories may contain particular truths, indispensable to the completeness of the true theory. But on this subject, even more than on any of those I have previously mentioned, it is not the teacher's business to impose his own judgment, but to inform and discipline that of his pupil.

And this same clew, if we keep hold of it, will guide us through the labyrinth of conflicting thought into which we enter when we touch the great question of the relation of education to religion. As I have already said, the only really effective religious education is the parental—that of home and childhood. All that social and public education has in its power to do, further than by a general pervading tone of reverence and duty, amounts to little more than the information which it can give; but this is extremely valuable. I shall not enter into the question which has been debated with so much vehemence in the last and present generation, whether religion ought to be taught at all in Universities and public schools, seeing that religion is the subject of all others on which men's opinions are most widely at variance. On neither side of this controversy do the disputants seem to me to have sufficiently freed their minds from the old notion of education, that it consists in the dogmatic inculcation from authority, of what the teacher deems true. Why should it be impossible, that information of the greatest value, on subjects connected with religion, should be brought before the student's mind; that he should be made acquainted with so important a part of the national thought, and of the intellectual labors of past generations, as those relating to religion, without being taught dogmatically the doctrines of any church or sect? Christianity being an historical religion, the sort of religious instruction which seems to me most appropriate to a University is the study of ecclesiastical history. If teaching, even on matters of scientific certainty, should aim quite as much at showing how the results are arrived at, as at teaching the results themselves, far more, then, should this be the case on subjects where there is the widest diversity of opinion among men of equal ability, and who have taken equal pains to arrive at the truth. This diversity should of itself be a warning to a conscientious teacher that he has no right to impose his opinion authoritatively upon a youthful mind. His teaching should not be in the spirit of dogmatism, but in that of inquiry. The pupil should not be addressed as if his religion has been chosen for him, but as one who will have to choose it for himself. The various Churches, established and unestablished, are quite competent to the task which is peculiarly theirs—that of teaching each its own doctrines, as far as necessary, to its own rising generation. The proper business of a University is different; not to tell us from authority what we ought to believe, and make us accept the belief as a duty, but to give us information and training, and help us to form our own belief in a manner worthy of intelligent beings, who seek for truth at all hazards, and demand to know all the difficulties, in order that they may be better qualified to find, or recognize, the most satisfactory mode of resolving them. The vast importance of these questions—the great results as regards the conduct of our lives, which depend upon our choosing one belief or another—are the strongest reasons why we should not trust our judgment when it has been formed in ignorance of the evidence, and why we should not consent to be restricted to a one-sided teaching, which informs us of what a particular teacher or association of teachers receive as true doctrine and sound argument, but of nothing more.

I do not affirm that a University, if it represses free thought and inquiry, must be altogether a failure, for the freest thinkers have often been trained in the most slavish seminaries of learning. The great Christian reformers were taught in Roman Catholic Universities; the sceptical philosophers of France were mostly educated by the Jesuits. The human mind is sometimes impelled all the more violently in one direction, by an over-zealous and demonstrative attempt to drag it in the opposite. But this is not what Universities are appointed for—to drive men from them, even into good, by excess of evil. A University ought to be a place of free speculation. The more diligently it does its duty in all other respects, the more certain it is to be that. The old English Universities, in the present generation, are doing better work than they have done within human memory in teaching the ordinary studies of their curriculum; and one of the consequences has been, that whereas they formerly seemed to exist mainly for the repression of independent thought, and the chaining up of the individual intellect and conscience, they are now the great foci of free and manly inquiry, to the higher and professional classes, south of the Tweed. The ruling minds of those ancient seminaries have at last remembered that to place themselves in hostility to the free use of the understanding, is to abdicate their own best privilege, that of guiding it. A modest deference, at least provisional, to the united authority of the specially instructed, is becoming in a youthful and imperfectly formed mind; but when there is no united authority—when the specially instructed are so divided and scattered that almost any opinion can boast of some high authority, and no opinion whatever can claim all; when, therefore, it can never be deemed extremely improbable that one who uses his mind freely may see reason to change his first opinion; then, whatever you do, keep, at all risks, your minds open: do not barter away your freedom of thought. Those of you who are destined for the clerical profession are, no doubt, so far held to a certain number of doctrines, that, if they ceased to believe them, they would not be justified in remaining in a position in which they would be required to teach insincerely. But use your influence to make those doctrines as few as possible. It is not right that men should be bribed to hold out against conviction—to shut their ears against objections, or, if the objections penetrate, to continue professing full and unfaltering belief when their confidence is already shaken. Neither is it right that, if men honestly profess to have changed some of their religious opinions, their honesty should as a matter of course exclude them from taking a part for which they may be admirably qualified, in the spiritual instruction of the nation. The tendency of the age, on both sides of the ancient Border, is towards the relaxation of formularies, and a less rigid constraction of articles. This very circumstance, by making the limits of orthodoxy less definite, and obliging everyone to draw the line for himself, is an embarrassment to consciences. But I hold entirely with those clergymen who elect to remain in the national church, so long as they are able to accept its articles and confessions in any sense or with any interpretation consistent with common honesty, whether it be the generally received interpretation or not. If all were to desert the church who put a large and liberal construction on its terms of communion, or who would wish to see those terms widened, the national provision for religious teaching and worship would be left utterly to those who take the narrowest, the most literal, and purely textual view of the formularies; who, though by no means necessarily bigots for their allies, and who, however great their merits may be,—and they are often very great,—yet, if the church is improvable, are not the most likely persons to improve it. Therefore, if it were not an impertinence in me to tender advice in such a matter, I should say, let all who conscientiously can, remain in the church. A church is far more easily improved from within than from without. Almost all the illustrious reformers of religion began by being clergymen; but they did not think that their profession as clergymen was inconsistent with being reformers. They mostly indeed ended their days outside the churches in which they were born; but it was because the churches, in an evil hour for themselves, cast them out. They did not think it any business of theirs to withdraw. They thought they had a better right to remain in the fold, than those had who expelled them.

I have now said what I had to say on the two kinds of education which the system of schools and Universities is intended to promote—intellectual education and moral education; knowledge and the training of the knowing faculty, conscience and that of the moral faculty. These are the two main ingredients of human culture; but they do not exhaust the whole of it. There is a third division, which, if subordinate, and owing allegiance to the two others, is barely inferior to them, and not less needful to the completeness of the human being; I mean the aesthetic branch; the culture which comes through poetry and art, and may be described as the education of the feelings, and the cultivation of the beautiful. This department of things deserves to be regarded in a far more serious light than is the custom of these countries. It is only of late, and chiefly by a superficial imitation of foreigners, that we have begun to use the word Art by itself, and to speak of Art as we speak of Science, or Government, or Religion: we used to talk of the Arts, and more specifically of the Fine Arts: and even by them were vulgarly meant only two forms of art, Painting and Sculpture, the two which as a people we cared least about—which were regarded even by the more cultivated among us as little more than branches of domestic ornamentation, a kind of elegant upholstery. The very words "Fine Arts" called up a notion of frivolity, of great pains expended on a rather trifling object—on something which differed from the cheaper and commoner arts of producing pretty things, mainly by being more difficult, and by giving fops an opportunity of pluming themselves on caring for it, and on being able to talk about it. This estimate extended in no small degree, though not altogether, even to poetry, the queen of arts, but, in Great Britain, hardly included under the name. It cannot exactly be said that poetry was little thought of; we were proud of our Shakespeare and Milton, and in one period at least of our history, that of Queen Anne, it was a high literary distinction to be a poet; but poetry was hardly looked upon in any serious light, or as having much value except as an amusement or excitement, the superiority of which over others principally consisted in being that of a more refined order of minds. Yet the celebrated saying of Fletcher of Saltoun, "Let who will make the laws of a people if I write their songs," might have taught us how great an instrument for acting on the human mind we were undervaluing. It would be difficult for anybody to imagine that "Rule Britannia," for example, or "Scots wha hae," had no permanent influence on the higher region of human character: some of Moore's songs have done more for Ireland than all Grattan's speeches: and songs are far from being the highest or most impressive form of poetry. On these subjects, the mode of thinking and feeling of other countries was not only not intelligible, but not credible, to an average Englishman.

To find Art ranking on a complete equality, in theory at least, with Philosophy, Learning, and Science—as holding an equally important place among the agents of civilization and among the elements of the worth of humanity; to find even painting and sculpture treated as great social powers, and the art of a country as a feature, in its character and condition, little inferior in importance to either its religion or its government; all this only did not amaze and puzzle Englishmen, because it was too strange for them to be able to realize it, or, in truth, to believe it possible: and the radical difference of feeling on this matter between the British people and those of France, Germany, and the Continent generally, is one among the causes of that extraordinary inability to understand one another, which exists between England and the rest of Europe, while it does not exist to anything like the same degree between one nation of Continental Europe and another. It may be traced to the two influences which have chiefly shaped the British character since the days of the Stuarts: commercial money-getting business, and religious Puritanism. Business, demanding the whole of the faculties, and whether pursued from duty or the love of gain, regarding as a loss of time whatever does not conduce directly to the end; Puritanism, which, looking upon every feeling of human nature, except fear and reverence for God, as a snare, if not as partaking of sin, looked coldly, if not disapprovingly, on the cultivation of the sentiments. Different causes have produced different effects in the Continental nations; among whom it is even now observable that virtue and goodness are generally for the most part an affair of the sentiments, while with us they are almost exclusively an affair of duty. Accordingly, the kind of advantage which we have had over many other countries in point of morals—I am not sure that we are not losing it—has consisted in greater tenderness of conscience. In this we have had on the whole a real superiority, though one principally negative; for conscience is with most men a power chiefly in the way of restraint—a power which acts rather in staying our hands from any great wickedness, than by the direction it gives to the general course of our desires and sentiments. One of the commonest types of character among us is that of a man all whose ambition is self-regarding; who has no higher purpose in life than to enrich or raise in the world himself and his family; who never dreams of making the good of his fellow-creatures or of his country an habitual object, further than giving away, annually or from time to time, certain sums in charity; but who has a conscience sincerely alive to whatever is generally considered wrong, and would scruple to use any very illegitimate means for attaining his self-interested objects. While it will often happen in other countries that men whose feelings and whose active energies point strongly in an unselfish direction, who have the love of their country, of human improvement, of human freedom, even of virtue, in great strength and of whose thoughts and activity a large share is devoted to disinterested objects, will yet, in the pursuit of these or of any other objects that they strongly desire, permit themselves to do wrong things which the other man, though intrinsically, and taking the whole of his character, farther removed from what a human being ought to be, could not bring himself to commit. It is of no use to debate which of these two states of mind is the best, or rather the least bad. It is quite possible to cultivate the conscience and the sentiments too. Nothing hinders us from so training a man that he will not, even for a disinterested purpose, violate the moral law, and also feeding and encouraging those high feelings, on which we mainly rely for lifting men above low and sordid objects, and giving them a higher conception of what constitutes success in life. If we wish men to practise virtue, it is worth while trying to make them love virtue, and feel it an object in itself, and not a tax paid for leave to pursue other objects. It is worth training them to feel, not only actual wrong or actual meanness, but the absence of noble aims and endeavors, as not merely blamable but also degrading; to have a feeling of the miserable smallness of mere self in the face of this great universe, of the collective mass of our fellow-creatures, in the face of past history and of the indefinite future—the poorness and insignificance of human life if it is to be all spent in making things comfortable for ourselves and our kin, and raising ourselves and them a step or two on the social ladder.

Thus feeling, we learn to respect ourselves only so far as we feel capable of nobler objects: and if unfortunately those by whom we are surrounded do not share our aspirations, perhaps disapprove the conduct to which we are prompted by them—to sustain ourselves by the ideal sympathy of the great characters in history, or even in fiction, and by the contemplation of an idealized posterity: shall I add, of ideal perfection embodied in a Divine Being? Now, of this elevated tone of mind the great source of inspiration is poetry, and all literature so far as it is poetical and artistic. We may imbibe exalted feelings from Plato, or Demosthenes, or Tacitus, but it is in so far as those great men are not solely philosophers, or orators, or historians, but poets and artists. Nor is it only loftiness, only the heroic feelings, that are bred by poetic cultivation. Its power is as great in calming the soul as in elevating it—in fostering the milder emotions, as the more exalted. It brings home to us all those aspects of life which take hold of our nature on its unselfish side, and lead us to identify our joy and grief with the good or ill of the system of which we form a part; and all those solemn or pensive feelings, which, without having any direct application to conduct, incline us to take life seriously, and predispose us to the reception of anything which comes before us in the shape of duty. Who does not feel a better man after a course of Dante, or of Wordsworth, or, I will add, of Lucretius or the Georgics, or after brooding over Gray's Elegy, or Shelley's Hymn to Intellectual Beauty? I have spoken of poetry, but all the other modes of art produce similar effects in their degree. The races and nations whose senses are naturally finer and their sensuous perceptions more exercised than ours, receive the same kind of impressions from painting and sculpture; and many of the more delicately organized among themselves do the same. All the arts of expression tend to keep alive and in activity the feelings they express. Do you think that the great Italian painters would have filled the place they did in the European mind, would have been universally ranked among the greatest men of their time, if their productions had done nothing for it but to serve as the decoration of a public hall or a private *salon?* Their Nativities and Crucifixions, their glorious Madonnas and Saints, were to their susceptible Southern countrymen the great school not only of devotional, but of all the elevated and all the imaginative feelings. We colder Northerns may approach to a conception of this function of art when we listen to an oratorio of Handel, or give ourselves up to the emotions excited by a Gothic cathedral. Even apart from any specific emotional expression, the mere contemplation of beauty of a high order produces in no small degree this elevating effect on the character. The power of natural scenery addresses itself to the same region of human nature which corresponds to Art. There are few capable of feeling the sublimer order of natural beauty, such as your own Highlands and other mountain regions afford, who are not, at least temporarily, raised by it above the littlenesses of humanity, and made to feel the puerility of the petty objects which set men's interests at variance, contrasted with the nobler pleasures which all might share. To whatever avocations we may be called in life, let us never quash these susceptibilities within us, but carefully seek the opportunities of maintaining them in exercise. The more prosaic our ordinary duties, the more necessary it is to keep up the tone of our minds by frequent visits to that higher region of thought and feeling, in which every work seems dignified in proportion to the ends for which, and the spirit in which, it is done; where we learn, while eagerly seizing every opportunity of exercising higher faculties and performing higher duties, to regard all useful and honest work as a public function, which may be ennobled by the mode of performing it—which has not properly any other nobility than what that gives—and which, if ever so humble, is never mean but when it is meanly done, and when the motives from which it is done are mean motives.

There is, besides, a natural affinity between goodness and the cultivation of the Beautiful, when it is real cultivation, and not a mere unguided instinct. He who has learned what beauty is, if he be of a virtuous character, will desire to realize it in his own life—will keep before himself a type of perfect beauty in human character, to light his attempts at self-culture. There is a true meaning in the saying of Goethe, though liable to be misunderstood and perverted, that the Beautiful is greater than the Good; for it includes the Good, and adds something to it: it is the Good made perfect, and fitted with all the collateral perfections which make it a finished and completed thing. Now, this sense of perfection, which would make us demand from every creation of man the very utmost that it ought to give, and render us intolerant of the smallest fault in ourselves or in anything we do, is one of the results of Art cultivation. No other human productions come so near to perfection as works of pure Art. In all other things, we are, and may reasonably be, satisfied if the degree of excellence is as great as the object immediately in view seems to us to be worth: but in Art, the perfection is itself the object. If I were to define Art, I should be inclined to call it, the endeavor after perfection in execution. If we meet with even a piece of mechanical work which bears the marks of being done in this spirit—which is done as if the workman loved it, and tried to make it as good as possible, though something less good would have answered the purpose for which it was ostensibly made—we say that he has worked like an artist. Art, when really cultivated, and not merely practised empirically, maintains, what it first gave the conception of, an ideal Beauty, to be eternally aimed at, though surpassing what can be actually attained; and by this idea it trains us never to be completely satisfied with imperfection in what we ourselves do and are: to idealize, as much as possible, every work we do, and most of all, our own characters and lives.

And now, having travelled with you over the whole range of the materials and training which a University supplies as a preparation for the higher uses of life, it is almost needless to add any exhortation to you to profit by the gift. Now is your opportunity for gaining a degree of insight into subjects larger and far more ennobling than the minutiae of a business or a profession, and for acquiring a facility of using your minds on all that concerns the higher interests of man, which you will carry with you into the occupations of active life, and which will prevent even the short intervals of time which that may leave you, from being altogether lost for noble purposes. Having once conquered the first difficulties, the only ones of which the irksomeness surpasses the interest; having turned the point beyond which what was once a task becomes a pleasure; in even the busiest after-life, the higher powers of your mind will make progress imperceptibly, by the spontaneous exercise of your thoughts, and by the lessons you will know how to learn from daily experience. So, at least, it will be if in your earlier studies you have fixed your eyes upon the ultimate end from which those studies take their chief value—that of making you more effective combatants in the great fight which never ceases to rage between Good and Evil, and more equal to coping with the ever new problems which the changing course of human nature and human society present to be resolved. Aims like these commonly retain the footing which they have once established in the mind; and their presence in our thoughts keeps our higher faculties in exercise, and makes us consider the acquirements and powers which we store up at any time of our lives, as a mental capital, to be freely expended in helping forward any mode which presents itself of making mankind in any respect wiser or better, or placing any portion of human affairs on a more sensible and rational footing than its existing one. There is not one of us who may not qualify himself so to improve the average amount of opportunities, as to leave his fellow-creatures some little the better for the use he has known how to make of his intellect. To make this little greater, let us strive to keep ourselves acquainted with the best thoughts that are brought forth by the original minds of the age; that we may know what movements stand most in need of our aid, and that, as far as depends on us, the good seed may not fall on a rock, and perish without reaching the soil in which it might have germinated and flourished. You are to be a part of the public who are to welcome, encourage, and help forward the future intellectual benefactors of humanity; and you are, if possible, to furnish your contingent to the number of those benefactors. Nor let anyone be discouraged by what may seem, in moments of despondency, the lack of time and of opportunity. Those who know how to employ opportunities will often find that they can create them: and what we achieve depends less on the amount of time we possess, than on the use we make of our time. You and your like are the hope and resource of your country in the coming generation. All great things which that generation is destined to do, have to be done by some like you; several will assuredly be done by persons for whom society has done much less, to whom it has given far less preparation, than those whom I am now addressing. I do not attempt to instigate you by the prospect of direct rewards, either earthly or heavenly; the less we think about being rewarded in either way, the better for us. But there is one reward which will not fail you, and which may be called disinterested, because it is not a consequence, but it is inherent in the very fact of deserving it; the deeper and more varied interest you will feel in life: which will give it tenfold its value, and a value which will last to the end. All merely personal objects grow less valuable as we advance in life: this not only endures, but increases.

# Afterword

## Elizabeth Anderson[*]

American universities usually introduce students to utilitarianism through the work of John Stuart Mill. This choice makes pedagogical sense: John Stuart Mill is a vastly more interesting, accessible, and readable author than Jeremy Bentham, the acknowledged founder of utilitarianism. Yet the choice is apt to lead to confusions, both about Mill, who departed in significant ways from orthodox utilitarianism, and about mainstream utilitarianism, which never accepted Mill's innovative departures. Mill thought that orthodox utilitarianism expressed important truths, but not the whole truth, about politics and morals.

The creative tensions in Mill's life work between enduring doctrines of utilitarianism and sophisticated emendations are particularly evident in Mill's philosophy of education. Utilitarians have always viewed education as a key tool for moral progress. To orthodox utilitarians, progress consisted in bringing happiness to the masses, not just to elites. A democratic temperament pervades utilitarian thought. From the conservative, elitist perspective of the day, this democratic temperament threatened the highest values of civilization. Mill's philosophy of education can be viewed as attempting to reconceive the conflict between democracy and elitism. There are significant elitist strands in Mill's thought. But this elitism reflects Mill's attempt to perfect and advance rather than restrain democracy, by paying attention to the intellectual and sentimental prerequisites of successful democratic practice.

Orthodox utilitarianism identified important relations between democracy and education. Utilitarianism was originally proposed as a theory of legislation. It directs legislators to pass laws that tend to produce the maximum happiness or pleasure of the members of society. To this end, we need legislators who are motivated to pursue the maximum happiness, and who have the knowledge of what means will produce this end. Periodic democratic elections provide the motive: if politicians don't give the people what will make them happy, the majority will elect someone else to exercise power. Scientific education provides the knowledge: legislators and civil servants must be trained in the principles of logic and empirical investigation through mathematics and the natural sciences, and study the modern social scientific disciplines of economics, psychology, sociology, and law. Science is the key to determining what policies would be effective in promoting happiness.

* Elizabeth Anderson is Professor of Philosophy and Women's Studies at the University of Michigan.

Utilitarianism is democratic not simply in advocating the political structures of democracy, such as the universal franchise, majority rule, and periodic elections. It is also, in an important sense, *culturally* democratic. The aim of government is to maximize pleasure, regardless of who enjoys it. One unit of pleasure counts the same, whether it is enjoyed by a noble aristocrat, a refined aesthete, or a lowly worker. Furthermore, orthodox utilitarianism treats all tastes as equal. One unit of pleasure counts the same, regardless of its source. Bentham insisted that so long as the quantities of pleasure were the same, "pushpin is as good as poetry." Since no pleasures are intrinsically superior to any others, there is no sense to be made of trying to improve or uplift people's aims. Orthodox utilitarianism therefore seeks only to satisfy people's given desires. It is anti-elitist, both in the sense of disparaging the usefulness of elites and in downgrading elite conceptions of value. Orthodox utilitarians regarded elites with distrust, as people who tried to maintain their privileges by keeping the masses ignorant and submissive.

These two democratic themes in utilitarianism—one about governance, the other about culture—inspired revolutionary changes in education. The vast expansion of mass education, and the dominance in modern universities of schools of applied sciences such as medicine, engineering, and business, owe much to the influence of utilitarian thinking. Utilitarianism also inspired the dramatic reversal, over the past century, in the relative standing of the liberal arts disciplines. Consider the prestige hierarchy of liberal arts disciplines currently entrenched in most modern universities. Mathematics and the natural sciences stand on top, holding the greatest authority in virtue of their unmatched rigor, empirical success, and technological applications. The social sciences stand in the middle, seeking greater prestige by trying to copy the methods and thus the empirical and practical successes of the natural sciences. The arts and humanities lie on the bottom, held in suspicion as useless luxuries, thought to be lacking either intellectual rigor or a coherent rationale for their pursuit, but hanging on out of a vague sense that something would be missing if their study were not continued. Theology has suffered even worse ignominy, having been expelled from most public universities and marginalized in divinity schools.

This hierarchy of liberal arts reflects utilitarian sensibilities. It is evident that the natural sciences, and hoped that the social sciences, can dramatically advance human happiness, by improving medicine, economic policy, and the like. Empirical knowledge of causal connections helps us achieve our aims more effectively, and thereby increases happiness. It is less clear how the arts and humanities increase human happiness. Notoriously, undergraduates tend to regard the humanities as impractical, a humanities degree as imparting no valuable skills. Of what use are the humanities? Once tastes are democratized, one can no longer say that they uplift us. Perhaps, then, they entertain and divert us. But if, as Bentham claimed, poetry is no better than pushpin, then why make poetry an object of serious study rather than discretionary indulgence? And how many people really do get much happiness out of studying medieval literature, say? An orthodox utilitarian justification of the arts and humanities is not easy to find. But perhaps it is not impossible. Theology, however, has virtually no chance of finding a utilitarian rationale. Most utilitarians regarded theology as nothing more than pernicious superstitions propagated by elites to keep the masses subdued.

This utilitarian hierarchy of liberal arts fundamentally challenged the conservative nineteenth century hierarchy in England. At that time the Church of England controlled most universities. Theology was the most prestigious discipline. Classical studies came next, with a peculiar emphasis on drilling students in composing Greek and Latin verse. Mathematics followed. Finally, England's top universities treated the study of the natural and social sciences with disdain. In contrast with the educational policies of France and Germany, which supported university-based science and engineering programs, England relied to a surprising degree on its tradition of independent invention, tinkering, and amateur science to promote industrial progress.

Like the utilitarians, English conservatives based their hierarchy of liberal arts on dual theories of governance and culture. But their theories were elitist ones, borrowed partly from classical sources, partly from Christian ones. Consider first governance. The ends of government were determined not by surveying the given wants of the masses, but by consulting the supposedly higher, eternal values supported by the Church and the classics. The tiny aristocratic elite comprised the only people fit to rule because only they could be trusted to uphold such noble values. Legislative skill depended on rhetoric, the art of persuasion, rather than social science. Theology and the humanities, especially Greek and Latin rhetoric and verse, were therefore most important for those destined to govern.

Consider next elite cultural values. The liberal arts were originally contrasted with the servile arts: they were the arts that fit a man for freedom rather than servitude. Freedom here referred to a particular class standing open only to propertied men. Free men were men whose independent wealth freed them from the burdens of toiling for a living so that they could pursue nobler ends at leisure. Where the servile arts taught workers how to supply the basic needs of life, the liberal arts taught free men the higher ends of life. The humanities enjoyed special prestige as the disciplines that taught men such uplifting values. This class-based ideology also ranked the theoretical or "pure" sciences over the practical or applied sciences. Workers pursued the applied sciences such as engineering for merely instrumental reasons connected to the necessities and conveniences of life. By contrast, men of leisure pursued the pure sciences for their own sakes.

In nineteenth-century England, this conservative model of education was fairly decrepit. It suffered from the obsolescence of the rationale for learning classical languages. Latin was once the common language of all educated Europeans, obviously indispensable to any person aspiring to higher learning. Now it was a dead language, of no use in communicating fresh ideas. Yet English universities stressed Latin and Greek composition, at the expense of reading great works of ancient literature and studying ancient history and philosophy. This distorted emphasis was due in part to the contradictions between classical and Christian values. The ancient Greek philosophers pursued reason freely where it led them, which was nowhere near Christianity. The Church suppressed free inquiry in the universities, and showed little interest in developing students' critical and analytical skills. Anglican doctrine was taught as dogma, insulated from critical scrutiny. Serious study of ancient Greek and Roman philosophers and statesmen would have raised questions that the Church would rather were not entertained. Students did learn some mathematics, although rarely at an advanced level. And math classes were valued more for the discipline and obedience they instilled through boring drill and rote exercises, than for their potential to sharpen students' analytical reasoning skills or to enable them to understand the basis of physical laws.

In this controversy between English educational traditions and orthodox utilitarian theory, where did John Stuart Mill stand? Consider his 1867 "Inaugural Address delivered to the University of St Andrews." Here Mill stood squarely with the utilitarians in stressing the centrality of the modern empirical sciences to higher education, the importance of advanced mathematics and logic, and the dangers of dogmatically enforcing theological and moral views at the expense of free inquiry. Today's reader might find Mill's lengthy defense of these ideas tedious, for they express what we take to be obvious truths today. What modern university could take itself seriously that did not devote considerable resources to teaching the natural and social sciences? But Mill was fighting an ossified system of education that hardly recognized the value of these disciplines.

A closer reading of the "Inaugural Address" answers a question many humanities students have asked themselves: granting that universities ought to offer courses in the natural and social sciences, why must every student be required to take them? What is the utility to an English major of taking physics? Mill offered two arguments. First, the physical sciences offer the most successful examples of the use of observation and reasoning to attain truth. They therefore stand as models for the other disciplines. This methodological argument has had lasting influence on the social sciences, with mixed results.

Mill's second argument is more interesting. The curricular battle between utilitarians and conservative elites was framed as a conflict between modern science and ancient arts, between technical education and the cultivated intellect. Democracy needs technically trained experts who know how to determine effective means to satisfy people's wants. Many utilitarians could see less need for a democracy to have a class of broadly educated intellects. Mill disagreed. The fundamental purpose of a university is not to train professionals or experts but to produce cultivated human beings. An enlightened public is necessary to democracy, to prevent an otherwise credulous population from being duped by charlatans posing as experts and promoting absurd or destructive policies. The class of broadly educated people needn't acquire expertise in all the sciences. But they should know enough of the leading principles of each to be able to tell the difference between a charlatan and a real expert, and thereby to know where to turn when expertise is needed. Mill thereby turns the elite ideal of the liberally educated, cultivated intellect to the service of democracy, rather than against it.

Thus Mill rejected the alternatives presented by both the reforming, utilitarian scientific moderns and the conservative, humanistic traditionalists. Universities did not have to choose between a scientific curriculum and one centered on classical studies. They could teach both. Mill was not merely proposing to meet each educational camp halfway. In important respects, he stepped outside their debates altogether. Although classical studies retained a prominent position in Mill's scheme, he mercilessly criticized the absurd waste of forcing students to compose poetry in Greek and Latin. He urged instead that it turn away from composition toward ancient history and literature. Why study the ancients? Not for the reason today's conservatives offer, that there lie the fundamental principles of "Western Civilization." On the contrary, Mill thought the ancients worth studying precisely for how alien they are. The classical curriculum was Mill's version of multicultural education: its point is to get students out of the habit of parochial thinking, to recognize that their own customs, thoughts, and culture are neither universal nor necessary. (Modern cultures, he thought, were best studied directly, through travel to foreign lands rather than university courses.)

Nor did Mill endorse the conservative view that the ancients are to be valued for teaching that there is an immutable hierarchy of human beings, and for exemplifying the highest spiritual levels of this hierarchy. On the contrary, although he praised the ancients for holding up an example of excellence that could inspire moderns, he judged them to be spiritually simple and superficial compared to complex, brooding, self-conscious, psychologically insightful moderns. In his comparisons of ancients and moderns, Mill rejected the view that the pursuit of excellence requires the anti-democratic belief in a rank order of human beings. Instead, the ancients and moderns exemplify diverse dimensions of excellence and deficiency. The ancients are better at literary form and dialectical reasoning, the moderns at natural science and literary substance—that is, at expressing nuanced, complex, and deep feelings. We can learn even from those who are inferior to us in some respects, for they may be superior to us in others. Furthermore, as multiculturalism teaches us, we can learn from sheer cultural difference, too. In these passages we can hear Mill again undermining the simplistic dichotomy between elitism and democracy, conservative and utilitarian education.

More daringly, Mill challenged both reformers and traditionalists in upholding the importance of the fine arts, a subject absent from the favored curricula of both sides. He rejected Bentham's democracy of tastes in favor of cultivating "those high feelings, on which we mainly rely for lifting men above low and sordid objects, and giving them a higher conception of what constitutes success in life." Mill saw the fine arts as inspiring the higher feelings and sentiments that motivate people to pursue noble aims.

Here, perhaps, the elitist strains in Mill are most clear. But are they as anti-democratic as they seem? A closer reading suggests not. For the nobler feelings include most prominently the "feeling of the miserable smallness of mere self in the face of . . . the collective mass of our fellow creatures—the poorness and insignificance of human life if it is to be all spent in making things comfortable for ourselves and our kin, and raising ourselves and them a step or two on the social ladder." This passage appears to rebuke both elites and masses. As a check against elitist attitudes of individual superiority to the masses, he recommends humility before "the collective mass of our fellow creatures." Yet such humility cannot be based on the thought that the masses have worthier aims than elites: Mill instead castigates the masses for their small-minded egoistic materialism, and counsels them to aspire to higher aims. In other works, Mill made it clear that one function of an elite, educated class is to defend a vision of life's ends that transcends the petty selfishness, acquisitiveness, and social climbing of the middle-class.

Mill's "Inaugural Address" thus navigates a difficult course through the conflict between elitism and democracy. Mill sought a democratic culture without a democracy of tastes: a democracy that could affirm the higher worth of some conceptions of life over others. And he identified a need for an educated elite to sustain democracy. Government must draw upon the expertise of an educated elite to frame and administer effective laws. An educated elite was needed to prevent democracy from degenerating into demagoguery. It was needed, also, to sustain a vision of higher ends against the homogenizing forces of democracy that pressure individuals into mass conformity, and against the narrowing forces of middle-class, crass commercialism that focus people's minds on the material interests of themselves and their small circle. Mill called upon higher education to cultivate such an elite. . . .

Yet his educational elitism was not anti-democratic. He argued that a liberally educated elite was needed to play several indispensable roles in democracy: to supply the expertise needed to frame and administer sound laws, prevent the degeneration of democracy into demagoguery, and counter the conformist, narrow-minded, egoistic character of the dominant middle class. Study of the arts and humanities advanced the last project of countering the excessive influence of middle-class commercialism: freedom of inquiry into the proper ends of life promoted autonomy against conformism, study of the classics promoted cosmopolitanism over narrow parochialism, the arts helped cultivate imagination, broader sympathies, and nobler goals than petty egoism.

Overcome the sentiments of arrogance and deference, contempt and humility that interfere with people's effective participation in discussion of public affairs. He argued that we cultivate sympathy for others by participating in egalitarian institutions whose functioning demands that we frame common aims cooperatively and justify them on grounds that others can accept. These institutions teach the privileged to overcome their contempt for those occupying lower stations, and the disadvantaged to cast aside their deference in favor of autonomy and dignity.

Despite these powerful egalitarian strands in Mill's thought, Mill's devotion to egalitarianism was conditional. Mill was an imperialist as well as a democrat. He reconciled these two ideas through his progressive vision of history. Mill accepted the logic of paternalism in cases where a more advanced civilization could promote progress in backward civilizations by imperialism. Educational policies must always be designed with the aim of inspiring progress. In some cases, this meant supporting a cultural elite even at the expense of democratization. But Mill was confident that the end of human progress was an egalitarian society.

# 9
## Alfred North Whitehead

**Alfred North Whitehead** (1861–1947) was an English mathematician and philosopher who graduated from the University of Cambridge and eventually became a professor at Harvard University. With Bertrand Russell he wrote the monumental logical treatise *Principia Mathematica*. Subsequently he developed an influential metaphysical system in which the fundamental concept was process or change.

## *The Aims of Education*

### Chapter I

### The Aims of Education

Culture is activity of thought, and receptiveness to beauty and humane feeling. Scraps of information have nothing to do with it. A merely well-informed man is the most useless bore on God's earth. What we should aim at producing is men who possess both culture and expert knowledge in some special direction. Their expert knowledge will give them the ground to start from, and their culture will lead them as deep as philosophy and as high as art. We have to remember that the valuable intellectual development is self-development, and that it mostly takes place between the ages of sixteen and thirty. As to training, the most important part is given by mothers before the age of twelve. A saying due to Archbishop Temple illustrates my meaning. Surprise was expressed at the success in after-life of a man, who as a boy at Rugby had been somewhat undistinguished. He answered, "It is not what they are at eighteen, it is what they become afterwards that matters."

In training a child to activity of thought, above all things we must beware of what I will call "inert ideas"—that is to say, ideas that are merely received into the mind without being utilised, or tested, or thrown into fresh combinations.

In the history of education, the most striking phenomenon is that schools of learning, which at one epoch are alive with a ferment of genius, in a succeeding generation exhibit merely pedantry and routine. The reason is, that they are overladen with inert ideas. Education with inert ideas is not only useless: it is, above all things, harmful—*Corruptio optimi, pessima*. Except at rare intervals of intellectual ferment, education in the past has been radically infected with inert ideas. That is the reason why uneducated clever women, who have seen much of the world, are in middle life so much the most cultured part of the community. They have been saved from this horrible burden of inert ideas. Every intellectual revolution which has ever stirred humanity into greatness has been a passionate protest against inert ideas. Then, alas, with pathetic ignorance of human psychology, it has proceeded by some educational scheme to bind humanity afresh with inert ideas of its own fashioning.

Let us now ask how in our system of education we are to guard against this mental dryrot. We enunciate two educational commandments, "Do not teach too many subjects," and again, "What you teach, teach thoroughly."

The result of teaching small parts of a large number of subjects is the passive reception of disconnected ideas, not illumined with any spark of vitality. Let the main ideas which are introduced into a child's education be few and important, and let them be thrown into every combination possible. The child should make them his own, and should understand their application here and now in the circumstances of his actual life. From the very beginning of his education, the child should experience the joy of discovery. The discovery which he has to make, is that general ideas give an understanding of that stream of events which pours through his life, which is his life. By understanding I mean more than a mere logical analysis, though that is included. I mean "understanding" in the sense in which it is used in the French proverb, "To understand all, is to forgive all." Pedants sneer at an education which is useful. But if education is not useful, what is it? Is it a talent, to be hidden away in a napkin? Of course, education should be useful, whatever your aim in life. It was useful to Saint Augustine and it was useful to Napoleon. It is useful, because understanding is useful.

I pass lightly over that understanding which should be given by the literary side of education. Nor do I wish to be supposed to pronounce on the relative merits of a classical or a modern curriculum. I would only remark that the understanding which we want is an understanding of an insistent present. The only use of a knowledge of the past is to equip us for the present. No more deadly harm can be done to young minds than by depreciation of the present. The present contains all that there is. It is holy ground; for it is the past, and it is the future. At the same time it must be observed that an age is no less past if it existed two hundred years ago than if it existed two thousand years ago. Do not be deceived by the pedantry of dates. The ages of Shakespeare and of Molière are no less past than are the ages of Sophocles and of Virgil. The communion of saints is a great and inspiring assemblage, but it has only one possible hall of meeting, and that is, the present; and the mere lapse of time through which any particular group of saints must travel to reach that meeting-place, makes very little difference.

Passing now to the scientific and logical side of education, we remember that here also ideas which are not utilised are positively harmful. By utilising an idea, I mean relating it to that stream, compounded of sense perceptions, feelings, hopes, desires, and of mental activities adjusting thought to thought, which forms our life. I can imagine a set of beings which might fortify their souls by passively reviewing disconnected ideas. Humanity is not built that way—except perhaps some editors of newspapers.

In scientific training, the first thing to do with an idea is to prove it. But allow me for one moment to extend the meaning of "prove"; I mean—to prove its worth. Now an idea is not worth much unless the propositions in which it is embodied are true. Accordingly an essential part of the proof of an idea is the proof, either by experiment or by logic, of the truth of the propositions. But it is not essential that this proof of the truth should constitute the first introduction to the idea. After all, its assertion by the authority of respectable teachers is sufficient evidence to begin with. In our first contact with a set of propositions, we commence by appreciating their importance. That is what we all do in after-life. We do not attempt, in the strict sense, to prove or to disprove anything, unless its importance makes it worthy of that honour. These two processes of proof, in the narrow sense, and of appreciation, do not require a rigid separation in time. Both can be proceeded with nearly concurrently. But in so far as either process must have the priority, it should be that of appreciation by use.

Furthermore, we should not endeavour to use propositions in isolation. Emphatically I do not mean, a neat little set of experiments to illustrate Proposition I and then the proof of Proposition I, a neat little set of experiments to illustrate Proposition II and then the proof of Proposition II, and so on to the end of the book. Nothing could be more boring. Interrelated truths are utilised *en bloc*, and the various propositions are employed in any order, and with any reiteration. Choose some important applications of your theoretical subject; and study them concurrently with the systematic theoretical exposition. Keep the theoretical exposition short and simple, but let it be strict and rigid so far as it goes. It should not be too long for it to be easily known with thoroughness and accuracy. The consequences of a plethora of half-digested theoretical knowledge are deplorable. Also the theory should not be muddled up with the practice. The child should have no doubt when it is proving and when it is utilising. My point is that what is proved should be utilised, and that what is utilised should—so far as is practicable—be proved. I am far from asserting that proof and utilisation are the same thing.

At this point of my discourse, I can most directly carry forward my argument in the outward form of a digression. We are only just realising that the art and science of education require a genius and a study of their own; and that this genius and this science are more than a bare knowledge of some branch of science or of literature. This truth was partially perceived in the past generation; and headmasters, somewhat crudely, were apt to supersede learning in their colleagues by requiring left-hand bowling and a taste for football. But culture is more than cricket, and more than football, and more than extent of knowledge.

Education is the acquisition of the art of the utilisation of knowledge. This is an art very difficult to impart. Whenever a textbook is written of real educational worth, you may be quite certain that some reviewer will say that it will be difficult to teach from it. Of course it will be difficult to teach from it. If it were easy, the book ought to be burned; for it cannot be educational. In education, as elsewhere, the broad primrose path leads to a nasty place. . . .

We now return to my previous point, that theoretical ideas should always find important applications within the pupil's curriculum. This is not an easy doctrine to apply, but a very hard one. It contains within itself the problem of keeping knowledge alive, of preventing it from becoming inert, which is the central problem of all education.

The best procedure will depend on several factors, none of which can be neglected, namely, the genius of the teacher, the intellectual type of the pupils, their prospects in life, the opportunities offered by the immediate surroundings of the school, and allied factors of this sort. It is for this reason that the uniform external examination is so deadly. We do not denounce it because we are cranks, and like denouncing established things. We are not so childish. Also, of course, such examinations have their use in testing slackness. Our reason of dislike is very definite and very practical. It kills the best part of culture. When you analyse in the light of experience the central task of education, you find that its successful accomplishment depends on a delicate adjustment of many variable factors. The reason is that we are dealing with human minds, and not with dead matter. The evocation of curiosity, of judgment, of the power of mastering a complicated tangle of circumstances, the use of theory in giving foresight in special cases—all these powers are not to be imparted by a set rule embodied in one schedule of examination subjects.

I appeal to you, as practical teachers. With good discipline, it is always possible to pump into the minds of a class a certain quantity of inert knowledge. You take a text-book and make them learn it. So far, so good. The child then knows how to solve a quadratic equation. But what is the point of teaching a child to solve a quadratic equation? There is a traditional answer to this question. It runs thus: The mind is an instrument, you first sharpen it, and then use it; the acquisition of the power of solving a quadratic equation is part of the process of sharpening the mind. Now there is just enough truth in this answer to have made it live through the ages. But for all its half-truth, it embodies a radical error which bids fair to stifle the genius of the modern world. I do not know who was first responsible for this analogy of the mind to a dead instrument. For aught I know, it may have been one of the seven wise men of Greece, or a committee of the whole lot of them. Whoever was the originator, there can be no doubt of the authority which it has acquired by the continuous approval bestowed upon it by eminent persons. But whatever its weight of authority, whatever the high approval which it can quote, I have no hesitation in denouncing it as one of the most fatal, erroneous, and dangerous conceptions ever introduced into the theory of education. The mind is never passive; it is a perpetual activity, delicate, receptive, responsive to stimulus. You cannot postpone its life until you have sharpened it. Whatever interest attaches to your subject-matter must be evoked here and now; whatever powers you are strengthening in the pupil, must be exercised here and now; whatever possibilities of mental life your teaching should impart, must be exhibited here and now. That is the golden rule of education, and a very difficult rule to follow.

The difficulty is just this: the apprehension of general ideas, intellectual habits of mind, and pleasurable interest in mental achievement can be evoked by no form of words, however accurately adjusted. All practical teachers know that education is a patient process of the mastery of details, minute by minute, hour by hour, day by day. There is no royal road to learning through an airy path of brilliant generalisations. There is a proverb about the difficulty of seeing the wood because of the trees. That difficulty is exactly the point which I am enforcing. The problem of education is to make the pupil see the wood by means of the trees.

The solution which I am urging, is to eradicate the fatal disconnection of subjects which kills the vitality of our modern curriculum. There is only one subject-matter for education, and that is Life in all its manifestations. Instead of this single unity, we offer children—Algebra, from which nothing follows; Geometry, from which nothing follows; Science, from which nothing follows; History, from which nothing follows; a Couple of Languages, never mastered; and lastly, most dreary of all, Literature, represented by plays of Shakespeare, with philological notes and short analyses of plot and character to be in substance committed to memory. Can such a list be said to represent Life, as it is known in the midst of the living of it? The best that can be said of it is, that it is a rapid table of contents which a deity might run over in his mind while he was thinking of creating a world, and has not yet determined how to put it together. . . .

Fortunately, the specialist side of education presents an easier problem than does the provision of a general culture. For this there are many reasons. One is that many of the principles of procedure to be observed are the same in both cases, and it is unnecessary to recapitulate. Another reason is that specialist training takes place—or should take place—at a more advanced stage of the pupil's course, and thus there is easier material to work upon. But undoubtedly the chief reason is that the specialist study is normally a study of peculiar interest to the student. He is studying it because, for some reason, he wants to know it. This makes all the difference. The general culture is designed to foster an activity of mind; the specialist course utilises this activity. But it does not do to lay too much stress on these neat antitheses. As we have already seen, in the general course foci of special interest will arise; and similarly in the special study, the external connections of the subject drag thought outwards.

Again, there is not one course of study which merely gives general culture, and another which gives special knowledge. The subjects pursued for the sake of a general education are special subjects specially studied; and, on the other hand, one of the ways of encouraging general mental activity is to foster a special devotion. You may not divide the seamless coat of learning. What education has to impart is an intimate sense for the power of ideas, for the beauty of ideas, and for the structure of ideas, together with a particular body of knowledge which has peculiar reference to the life of the being possessing it.

The appreciation of the structure of ideas is that side of a cultured mind which can only grow under the influence of a special study. I mean that eye for the whole chess-board, for the bearing of one set of ideas on another. Nothing but a special study can give any appreciation for the exact formulation of general ideas, for their relations when formulated, for their service in the comprehension of life. A mind so disciplined should be both more abstract and more concrete. It has been trained in the comprehension of abstract thought and in the analysis of facts.

Finally, there should grow the most austere of all mental qualities; I mean the sense for style. It is an æsthetic sense, based on admiration for the direct attainment of a foreseen end, simply and without waste. Style in art, style in literature, style in science, style in logic, style in practical execution have fundamentally the same aesthetic qualities, namely, attainment and restraint. The love of a subject in itself and for itself, where it is not the sleepy pleasure of pacing a mental quarter-deck, is the love of style as manifested in that study.

Here we are brought back to the position from which we started, the utility of education. Style, in its finest sense, is the last acquirement of the educated mind; it is also the most useful. It pervades the whole being. The administrator with a sense for style hates waste; the engineer with a sense for style economises his material; the artisan with a sense for style prefers good work. Style is the ultimate morality of mind.

But above style, and above knowledge, there is something, a vague shape like fate above the Greek gods. That something is Power. Style is the fashioning of power, the restraining of power. But, after all, the power of attainment of the desired end is fundamental. The first thing is to get there. Do not bother about your style, but solve your problem, justify the ways of God to man, administer your province, or do whatever else is set before you.

Where, then, does style help? In this, with style the end is attained without side issues, without raising undesirable inflammations. With style you attain your end and nothing but your end. With style the effect of your activity is calculable, and foresight is the last gift of gods to men. With style your power is increased, for your mind is not distracted with irrelevancies, and you are more likely to attain your object. Now style is the exclusive privilege of the expert. Whoever heard of the style of an amateur painter, of the style of an amateur poet? Style is always the product of specialist study, the peculiar contribution of specialism to culture.

English education in its present phase suffers from a lack of definite aim, and from an external machinery which kills its vitality. Hitherto in this address I have been considering the aims which should govern education. In this respect England halts between two opinions. It has not decided whether to produce amateurs or experts. The profound change in the world which the nineteenth century has produced is that the growth of knowledge has given foresight. The amateur is essentially a man with appreciation and with immense versatility in mastering a given routine. But he lacks the foresight which comes from special knowledge. The object of this address is to suggest how to produce the expert without loss of the essential virtues of the amateur. . . .

When one considers in its length and in its breadth the importance of this question of the education of a nation's young, the broken lives, the defeated hopes, the national failures, which result from the frivolous inertia with which it is treated, it is difficult to restrain within oneself a savage rage. In the conditions of modern life the rule is absolute, the race which does not value trained intelligence is doomed. Not all your heroism, not all your social charm, not all your wit, not all your victories on land or at sea, can move back the finger of fate. To-day we maintain ourselves. To-morrow science will have moved forward yet one more step, and there will be no appeal from the judgment which will then be pronounced on the uneducated.

We can be content with no less than the old summary of educational ideal which has been current at any time from the dawn of our civilisation. The essence of education is that it be religious.

Pray, what is religious education?

A religious education is an education which inculcates duty and reverence. Duty arises from our potential control over the course of events. Where attainable knowledge could have changed the issue, ignorance has the guilt of vice. And the foundation of reverence is this perception, that the present holds within itself the complete sum of existence, backwards and forwards, that whole amplitude of time, which is eternity.

## Chapter III

### The Rhythmic Claims of Freedom and Discipline

. . . The antithesis in education between freedom and discipline is not so sharp as a logical analysis of the meanings of the terms might lead us to imagine. The pupil's mind is a growing organism. On the one hand, it is not a box to be ruthlessly packed with alien ideas: and, on the other hand, the ordered acquirement of knowledge is the natural food for a developing intelligence. Accordingly, it should be the aim of an ideally constructed education that the discipline should be the voluntary issue of free choice, and that the freedom should gain an enrichment of possibility as the issue of discipline. The two principles, freedom and discipline, are not antagonists, but should be so adjusted in the child's life that they correspond to a natural sway, to and fro, of the developing personality. It is this adaptation of freedom and discipline to the natural sway of development that I have elsewhere called The Rhythm of Education. I am convinced that much disappointing failure in the past has been due to neglect of attention to the importance of this rhythm. My main position is that the dominant note of education at its beginning and at its end is freedom, but that there is an intermediate stage of discipline with freedom in subordination: Furthermore, that there is not one unique threefold cycle of freedom, discipline, and freedom; but that all mental development is composed of such cycles, and of cycles of such cycles. Such a cycle is a unit cell, or brick; and the complete stage of growth is an organic structure of such cells. In analysing any one such cell, I call the first period of freedom the "stage of Romance," the intermediate period of discipline I call the "stage of Precision," and the final period of freedom is the "stage of Generalisation."

Let me now explain myself in more detail. There can be no mental development without interest. Interest is the *sine qua non* for attention and apprehension. You may endeavour to excite interest by means of birch rods, or you may coax it by the incitement of pleasurable activity. But without interest there will be no progress. Now the natural mode by which living organisms are excited towards suitable self-development is enjoyment. The infant is lured to adapt itself to its environment by its love of its mother and its nurse; we eat because we like a good dinner: we subdue the forces of nature because we have been lured to discovery by an insatiable curiosity: we enjoy exercise: and we enjoy the unchristian passion of hating our dangerous enemies. Undoubtedly pain is one subordinate means of arousing an organism to action. But it only supervenes on the failure of pleasure. Joy is the normal healthy spur for the *élan vital*. I am not maintaining that we can safely abandon ourselves to the allurement of the greater immediate joys. What I do mean is that we should seek to arrange the development of character along a path of natural activity, in itself pleasurable. The subordinate stiffening of discipline must be directed to secure some long-time good; although an adequate object must not be too far below the horizon, if the necessary interest is to be retained.

The second preliminary point which I wish to make, is the unimportance—indeed the evil—of barren knowledge. The importance of knowledge lies in its use, in our active mastery of it—that is to say, it lies in wisdom. It is a convention to speak of mere knowledge, apart from wisdom, as of itself imparting a peculiar dignity to its possessor. I do not share in this reverence for knowledge as such. It all depends on who has the knowledge and what he does with it. That knowledge which adds greatness to character is knowledge so handled as to transform every phase of immediate experience. It is in respect to the activity of knowledge that an over-vigorous discipline in education is so harmful. The habit of active thought, with freshness, can only be generated by adequate freedom. Undiscriminating discipline defeats its own object by dulling the mind. If you have much to do with the young as they emerge from school and from the university, you soon note the dulled minds of those whose education has consisted in the acquirement of inert knowledge. Also the deplorable tone of English society in respect to learning is a tribute to our educational failure. Furthermore, this overhaste to impart mere knowledge defeats itself. The human mind rejects knowledge imparted in this way. The craving for expansion, for activity, inherent in youth is disgusted by a dry imposition of disciplined knowledge. The discipline, when it comes, should satisfy a natural craving for the wisdom which adds value to bare experience.

But let us now examine more closely the rhythm of these natural cravings of the human intelligence. The first procedure of the mind in a new environment is a somewhat discursive activity amid a welter of ideas and experience. It is a process of discovery, a process of becoming used to curious thoughts, of shaping questions, of seeking for answers, of devising new experiences, of noticing what happens as the result of new ventures. This general process is both natural and of absorbing interest. We must often have noticed children between the ages of eight and thirteen absorbed in its ferment. It is dominated by wonder, and cursed be the dullard who destroys wonder. Now undoubtedly this stage of development requires help, and even discipline. The environment within which the mind is working must be carefully selected. It must, of course, be chosen to suit the child's stage of growth, and must be adapted to individual needs. In a sense it is an imposition from without; but in a deeper sense it answers to the call of life within the child. In the teacher's consciousness the child has been sent to his telescope to look at the stars, in the child's consciousness he has been given free access to the glory of the heavens. Unless, working somewhere, however obscurely, even in the dullest child, there is this transfiguration of imposed routine, the child's nature will refuse to assimilate the alien material. It must never be forgotten that education is not a process of packing articles in a trunk. Such a smile is entirely inapplicable. It is, of course, a process completely of its own peculiar genus. Its nearest analogue is the assimilation of food by a living organism: and we all know how necessary to health is palatable food under suitable conditions. When you have put your boots in a trunk, they will stay there till you take them out again; but this is not at all the case if you feed a child with the wrong food.

This initial stage of romance requires guidance in another way. After all the child is the heir to long ages of civilisation, and it is absurd to let him wander in the intellectual maze of men in the Glacial Epoch. Accordingly, a certain pointing out of important facts, and of simplifying ideas, and of usual names, really strengthens the natural impetus of the pupil. In no part of education can you do without discipline or can you do without freedom; but in the stage of romance the emphasis must always be on freedom, to allow the child to see for itself and to act for itself. My point is that a block in the assimilation of ideas inevitably arises when a discipline of precision is imposed before a stage of romance has run its course in the growing mind. There is no comprehension apart from romance. It is my strong belief that the cause of so much failure in the past has been due to the lack of careful study of the due place of romance. Without the adventure of romance, at the best you get inert knowledge without initiative, and at the worst you get contempt of ideas—without knowledge.

But when this stage of romance has been properly guided another craving grows. The freshness of inexperience has worn off; there is general knowledge of the groundwork of fact and theory: and, above all, there has been plenty of independent browsing amid first-hand experiences, involving adventures of thought and of action. The enlightenment which comes from precise knowledge can now be understood. It corresponds to the obvious requirements of common sense, and deals with familiar material. Now is the time for pushing on, for knowing the subject exactly, and for retaining in the memory its salient features. This is the stage of precision. This stage is the sole stage of learning in the traditional scheme of education, either at school or university. You had to learn your subject, and there was nothing more to be said on the topic of education. The result of such an undue extension of a most necessary period of development was the production of a plentiful array of dunces, and of a few scholars whose natural interest had survived the car of Juggernaut. There is, indeed, always the temptation to teach pupils a little more of fact and of precise theory than at that stage they are fitted to assimilate. If only they could, it would be so useful. We—I am talking of schoolmasters and of university dons—are apt to forget that we are only subordinate elements in the education of a grown man; and that, in their own good time, in later life our pupils will learn for themselves. The phenomena of growth cannot be hurried beyond certain very narrow limits. But an unskilful practitioner can easily damage a sensitive organism. Yet, when all has been said in the way of caution, there is such a thing as pushing on, of getting to know the fundamental details and the main exact generalisations, and of acquiring an easy mastery of technique. There is no getting away from the fact that things have been found out, and that to be effective in the modern world you must have a store of definite acquirement of the best practice. To write poetry you must study metre; and to build bridges you must be learned in the strength of material. Even the Hebrew prophets had learned to write, probably in those days requiring no mean effort. The untutored art of genius is—in the words of the Prayer Book—a vain thing, fondly invented.

During the stage of precision, romance is the background. The stage is dominated by the inescapable fact that there are right ways and wrong ways, and definite truths to be known. But romance is not dead, and it is the art of teaching to foster it amidst definite application to appointed task. It must be fostered for one reason, because romance is after all a necessary ingredient of that balanced wisdom which is the goal to be attained. But there is another reason: The organism will not absorb the fruits of the task unless its powers of apprehension are kept fresh by romance. The real point is to discover in practice that exact balance between freedom and discipline which will give the greatest rate of progress over the things to be known. I do not believe that there is any abstract formula which will give information applicable to all subjects, to all types of pupils, or to each individual pupil; except indeed the formula of rhythmic sway which I have been insisting on, namely, that in the earlier stage the progress requires that the emphasis be laid on freedom, and that in the later middle stage the emphasis be laid on the definite acquirement of allotted tasks. I freely admit that if the stage of romance has been properly managed, the discipline of the second stage is much less apparent, that the children know how to go about their work, want to make a good job of it, and can be safely trusted with the details. Furthermore, I hold that the only discipline, important for its own sake, is self-discipline, and that this can only be acquired by a wide use of freedom. But yet—so many are the delicate points to be considered in education—it is necessary in life to have acquired the habit of cheerfully undertaking imposed tasks. The conditions can be satisfied if the tasks correspond to the natural cravings of the pupil at his stage of progress, if they keep his powers at full stretch, and if they attain an obviously sensible result, and if reasonable freedom is allowed in the mode of execution.

The difficulty of speaking about the way a skilful teacher will keep romance alive in his pupils arises from the fact that what takes a long time to describe, takes a short time to do. The beauty of a passage of Virgil may be rendered by insisting on beauty of verbal enunci- ation, taking no longer than prosy utterance. The emphasis on the beauty of a mathematical argument, in its marshalling of general considerations to unravel complex fact, is the speedi- est mode of procedure. The responsibility of the teacher at this stage is immense. To speak the truth, except in the rare case of genius in the teacher, I do not think that it is possible to take a whole class very far along the road of precision without some dulling of the interest. It is the unfortunate dilemma that initiative and training are both necessary, and that training is apt to kill initiative.

But this admission is not to condone a brutal ignorance of methods of mitigating this untoward fact. It is not a theoretical necessity, but arises because perfect tact is unattainable in the treatment of each individual case. In the past the methods employed assassinated interest; we are discussing how to reduce the evil to its smallest dimensions. I merely utter the warning that education is a difficult problem, to be solved by no one simple formula.

In this connection there is, however, one practical consideration which is largely neg- lected. The territory of romantic interest is large, ill-defined, and not to be controlled by any explicit boundary. It depends on the chance flashes of insight. But the area of precise know- ledge, as exacted in any general education system, can be, and should be, definitely deter- mined. If you make it too wide you will kill interest and defeat your own object: if you make it too narrow your pupils will lack effective grip. Surely, in every subject in each type of curriculum, the precise knowledge required should be determined after the most anxious inquiry. This does not now seem to be the case in any effective way. For example, in the classical studies of boys destined for a scientific career—a class of pupils in whom I am greatly interested—What is the Latin vocabulary which they ought definitely to know? Also what are the grammatical rules and constructions which they ought to have mastered? Why not determine these once and for all, and then bend every exercise to impress just these on the memory, and to understand their derivatives, both in Latin and also in French and English. Then, as to other constructions and words which occur in the reading of texts, supply full information in the easiest manner. A certain ruthless definiteness is essential in education. I am sure that one secret of a successful teacher is that he has formulated quite clearly in his mind what the pupil has got to know in precise fashion. He will then cease from half-hearted attempts to worry his pupils with memorising a lot of irrelevant stuff of inferior importance. The secret of success is pace, and the secret of pace is concentration. But, in respect to precise knowledge, the watchword is pace, pace, pace. Get your knowledge quickly, and then use it. If you can use it, you will retain it.

We have now come to the third stage of the rhythmic cycle, the stage of generalisation. There is here a reaction towards romance. Something definite is now known; aptitudes have been acquired; and general rules and laws are clearly apprehended both in their formulation and their detailed exemplification. The pupil now wants to use his new weapons. He is an effective individual, and it is effects that he wants to produce. He relapses into the discursive adventures of the romantic stage, with the advantage that his mind is now a disciplined regiment instead of a rabble. In this sense, education should begin in research and end in research. After all, the whole affair is merely a preparation for battling with the immediate experiences of life, a preparation by which to qualify each immediate moment with relevant ideas and appropriate actions. An education which does not begin by evoking initiative and end by encouraging it must be wrong. For its whole aim is the production of active wisdom.

In my own work at universities I have been much struck by the paralysis of thought induced in pupils by the aimless accumulation of precise knowledge, inert and unutilised. It should be the chief aim of a university professor to exhibit himself in his own true character—that is, as an ignorant man thinking, actively utilising his small share of knowledge. In a sense, knowledge shrinks as wisdom grows: for details are swallowed up in principles. The details of knowledge which are important will be picked up *ad hoc* in each avocation of life, but the habit of the active utilisation of well-understood principles is the final possession of wisdom. The stage of precision is the stage of growing into the apprehension of principles by the acquisition of a precise knowledge of details. The stage of generalisations is the stage of shedding details in favour of the active application of principles, the details retreating into subconscious habits. We don't go about explicitly retaining in our own minds that two and two make four, though once we had to learn it by heart. We trust to habit for our elementary arithmetic. But the essence of this stage is the emergence from the comparative passivity of being trained into the active freedom of application. Of course, during this stage, precise knowledge will grow, and more actively than ever before, because the mind has experienced the power of definiteness, and responds to the acquisition of general truth, and of richness of illustration. But the growth of knowledge becomes progressively unconscious, as being an incident derived from some active adventure of thought.

So much for the three stages of the rhythmic unit of development. In a general way the whole period of education is dominated by this threefold rhythm. Till the age of thirteen or fourteen there is the romantic stage, from fourteen to eighteen the stage of precision, and from eighteen to two and twenty the stage of generalisation. But these are only average characters, tinging the mode of development as a whole. I do not think that any pupil completes his stages simultaneously in all subjects. For example, I should plead that while language is initiating its stage of precision in the way of acquisition of vocabulary and of grammar, science should be in its full romantic stage. The romantic stage of language begins in infancy with the acquisition of speech, so that it passes early towards a stage of precision; while science is a late comer. Accordingly a precise inculcation of science at an early age wipes out initiative and interest, and destroys any chance of the topic having any richness of content in the child's apprehension. Thus, the romantic stage of science should persist for years after the precise study of language has commenced.

There are minor eddies, each in itself a threefold cycle, running its course in each day, in each week, and in each term. There is the general apprehension of some topic in its vague possibilities, the mastery of the relevant details, and finally the putting of the whole subject together in the light of the relevant knowledge. Unless the pupils are continually sustained by the evocation of interest, the acquirement of technique, and the excitement of success, they can never make progress, and will certainly lose heart. Speaking generally, during the last thirty years the schools of England have been sending up to the universities a disheartened crowd of young folk, inoculated against any outbreak of intellectual zeal. The universities have seconded the efforts of the schools and emphasised the failure. Accordingly, the cheerful gaiety of the young turns to other topics, and thus educated England is not hospitable to ideas. When we can point to some great achievement of our nation—let us hope that it may be something other than a war—which has been won in the class-room of our schools, and not in their playing-fields, then we may feel content with our modes of education. . . .

# Afterword

## Nathaniel M. Lawrence[*]

## I. The Rhythm of Education

There is a natural rhythm, says Whitehead, that flows through all educational development. It has three main phases. In the phase of enthusiastic encounter whatever is at hand is interesting, attractive for itself, though bad teaching may kill the interest before any progress is made in the subject. Arithmetic is a common example. Whitehead calls this first stage the *Romantic* stage. The second stage, in which order and system are introduced, is the period in which the chronology of history (rather than just its tales), the grammar of language, and so on, should appear. Whitehead calls this the stage of *Precision*. The final phase, which, properly handled, is the beginning of a new romantic phase, is the one in which precision has done its work. In this phase the student, with an understanding of both the surface aspects and the structure of his study, is prepared to extend knowledge in the direction of acquiring and putting into order more of the world. . . . This stage Whitehead calls the stage of *Generalization*. . . .

### 1. *Romance*

The stage of Romance is a familiar one. It is the stage of excitement, interest, espousal. On this stage much of progressive education rested its starry hopes. Having discovered that immature motivation was important in its own right, progressive education often jettisoned discipline to an appalling degree. A story is told of a British child, increasingly restive before her return to her progressive school. On the last day of vacation she burst into tears and cried, "Mommy, when I go back to school, will I have to do exactly what I want to do?" Isn't there always a passion for order too? Babies want a stable world with a regularity of its own upon which they can depend. Why should this appetite vanish when they are old enough to go to school? Moreover, growth requires not merely creative expression and assimilation. It

[*] Nathaniel M. Lawrence was Professor of Philosophy at Williams College.

must have an orderly continuity and structure which makes further orderly growth possible; otherwise it is merely cancerous.

Here is one point at which the skill and sensitivity of the teacher become most important. When does the high-school teacher, for example, lead students from surface appreciation of T. S. Eliot's poetry into the analysis of the strict technique of Eliot's writings? At what point does the teacher introduce students to the mathematical method in the analysis of biological studies? Certainly not before the results to be obtained can be vaguely discerned and desired, but also not *merely* with the students' recognition that something is wanting in their own understanding. The students must be acquainted with the nature of their ignorance before they can get rid of it. The stage of Precision opens gradually out of that of Romance, but the emergence of the second stage must have its reasonableness in the subject matter. Otherwise the discipline is arbitrary and ineffective.

## 2. *Precision*

The second phase in the rhythm of education is that of Precision. It corresponds exactly to the phase in the actual occasion in which the entity organizes, harmonizes, and orders the diverse data it has acquired from the antecedent world. This phase, of course, "is barren without a previous stage of romance. . . ." "New facts are added, but they are the facts which fit into the analysis." It is the period of grammar in language, principles and laws in science and mathematics, and memorizing in history.

The stage of Precision is thus what was commonly regarded before progressivism as the whole of education. Get things right, get them thoroughly, and get them in order. Adulthood will be with you soon. Prepare yourself for the mantle of maturity! Now Whitehead's point is that the demands of Precision are inescapable, but they have a restricted place in the rhythm of education. They come *after* the romantic encounter and are justified by that encounter. Why bother with grammar; why not let the forms of the language rub off on students through repeated exposure? Because they will have need of a strop on which to sharpen their own capacities for expression. The grammar of a language is its living logic. Students will want to know, and know instinctively, through habitual analysis of the structure of a sentence, whether what they hear and read is rhetorically persuasive alone or logically sound. There is an interesting correlation between the decline of the teaching of structural grammar and the collapse of letter writing, on the one hand, and, on the other, the rise in gullibility to the use of mass media for political and advertising purposes. Yet literacy is supposed to be increasing. What then is the test of literacy? The number of people going to school or the results of their going to school?

There is a final point to be made about the need for early doses of discipline. This is the phase in which the students' strong points will emerge, tested by exacting demands. At that point in their education when they are thinking of their future professions, they need to know more than what they are "interested" or even "talented" in. They need to know in what kind of work they are willing to do hard, exacting, and detailed study. Colleges are plagued with high-testing students who believe that professions are chosen on the basis of interest and expect the teachers to supply the interest. Only a self-disciplined mind can rise to a higher level of understanding, where a new Romantic cycle begins.

### 3. *Generalization*

Whitehead says of the third and final stage of the actual occasion that it is that of satisfaction. Of the final stage of the educational cycle he says it is "Hegel's synthesis. It is a return to romanticism with added advantage of classified ideas and relevant technique. It is the fruition which has been the goal of the precise training. It is the final success." This stage is clearly a "reaction toward romance." In this sense, "The stage of precision is the stage of growing into the apprehension of principles by the acquisition of a precise knowledge of details. The stage of generalisations is the stage of shedding details in favour of the active application of principles, the details retreating into subconscious habits." Thus with the appearance of Generalization the cycle starts over.

The romance inherent in Generalization is that of research and writing. All true research and much creativity must begin with Generalization. A *re*-search presupposes an initial search. Mushrooms develop suddenly, "overnight," as everyone knows. But who knows how or why? No one knew twenty years ago. Yet the experiments that showed why were within the technical grasp of biologists a hundred years ago. The Bible contradicts itself, yet it embodies truths which we can hardly wave away. What shall we do, jettison scripture and start over again or swallow it whole? If we discriminate, then on what basis and why? The barefoot geniuses in art or literature soon lose their force. If they have no acquaintance with the fields in which they create, they have but little critical acumen as to what they should modify, what adapt, and what leave behind as mined out. The capacity to generalize plus some luck and curiosity are the basis for genuine advance in human understanding. In it lies the possibility of progress. . . .

Romance must be followed by Precision. Precision sets the stage for the ascent to a higher level, that of Generalization. And from the higher ground new vistas appear. A new stage of Romance is begun.

In conclusion, the clear picture of these phases must be qualified in three ways. (1) There are no sharp lines of division between the phases. One grades into another, ideally without jars or breaks, the phases of the cycle being a matter of emphasis at any given time. (2) There are cycles overlapping cycles. Language may be in a precise stage when the romance of science has just begun; in fact, perhaps it should be, for the mere recording of interesting scientific facts relies upon the capacity to use language with precision. (3) There are cycles within cycles. Even the individual lesson "should form an eddy cycle issuing in its own subordinate process." From the overlap of cycles of education and the inclusion of smaller cycles in larger ones arises the rhythmic continuity of the educational process, through which an individual continuously exists, yet changes and grows.


## II. The Aim of Education

The aim of education is to help in the self-production of a person, to secure a "balanced growth of individuality." The self-production arises from an innate "passion" which must be fed and satisfied from the collective resources of the society. As the person develops, the processes which make up a life become more various and more intricate. At one stage the baby digests only milk. At one stage the young child's greatest verbal development lies in the use of simple nouns and adjectives. Development means the appearance of new capacities and new skills, somehow integrated with the old. Throughout there is a continuous identity. This process is something like converting a rowboat to an ocean liner while the boat is in continuous service. The sound keel of past experience must be capitalized upon and lengthened. This is the source of "precision." Present need and present enthusiasm supply the motivation for the increased accommodation of new understanding. This is the source of "romanticism." But without generalization there is no stable deck on which to build future accommodations. Creative self-development rests upon it. This is one reason for the breadth of education at the college level. In an age of specialization no one advances in a profitable way whose general perspective is confined to a specialty.

The "balanced growth" which education aims to secure is constantly threatened. Curiously, it is threatened by progress itself. Whitehead once remarked that virtually every scientific conception which he learned in his youth had been either swept away or sharply modified. The rate of progress, he says, "is such that an individual human being, of ordinary length of life, will be called upon to face novel situations which find no parallel in his past." The result is that the "fixed person for the fixed duties," formerly a godsend, in the future will be a "public danger." Yet knowledge that is effective is "professionalised knowledge, supported by a restricted acquaintance with useful subjects subservient to it."

The common way of attempting to avoid the dilemma is to aim at an education which provides both the special professional training and general knowledge. But Whitehead is dubious about balancing a deep study of a few abstractions with a shallow study of many abstractions. "The make-weight which balances the thoroughness of the specialist intellectual training should be of a radically different *kind* from purely intellectual analytical knowledge." If the ailment of education lies in its abstractness, the breadth of a group of abstractions only spuriously balances the depth of another group.

What is this different kind of experience which must be present in education?

> What I mean is art and aesthetic education. It is, however, art in such a general sense of the term that I hardly like to call it by that name. Art is a special example. What we want is to draw out habits of aesthetic apprehension. . . . Thus "art" in the general sense which I require is any selection by which the concrete facts are so arranged as to elicit attention to particular values which are realisable by them.

Art, so conceived, may refer equally to sunsets or factories. If we undertake merely to treat the sunset in terms of the atmosphere, rotation of the earth, and so on, or the factory as a device for making salable products, we are engaged in the kind of abstraction which robs the soul of its need for value. We slip into such abstractions all the more readily if the educational pattern is forever training us to deal with abstractions alone. "This fertilisation of the soul is the reason for the necessity of art. . . . The soul cries aloud for release into change. . . . [But] great art is more than a transient refreshment. It is something which adds to the permanent richness of the soul's self-attainment."

These reflections of Whitehead come in mid-passage in his philosophical career, years after the major part of his educational writings. They constitute an important reflection on those writings. He has before him the major features of his own educationl theory, but these features are now seen in a different perspective. The level of Generalization has a new significance. It is not merely a return to Romance in that it provides us new vistas with fresh encounters looming. It is also a return to Romance in that it must include concrete confrontation with value. Precision is content with assuming the values of the things which it orders. Having devoted myself to the value of designing commercial buildings, I may, in the phase of Precision, acquire all the engineering and technical knowledge of materials required to practice my profession. But these buildings are sociological and aesthetic structures as well. The danger of professional precision is that it will never rise to the level of generalization where it is related to the values it will effect. "The type of generality," says Whitehead, "which above all is wanted, is the appreciation of the variety of value. I mean an aesthetic growth." Professional training, which "can only touch one side of education," largely depending on printed books, must be balanced by concrete contact with things perceived as being values for one another.

This is Whitehead's final word on the aim of education. He presents us with the picture of an actually physical, potentially mental organism, whose orderly growth depends on the skill with which the various cycles are interknit and inclusive of one another. Ideally they achieve upward and outward spirals of progress. But not only must they never be divorced from their use; they must also strive toward a generalization which can only be acquired by an aesthetic return to the concrete particulars that make up the context of each life.

Contemporary education faces a unique problem: a violent expansion in factual knowledge, analogous to the population explosion. But facts in isolation are by definition valueless. It is in the relation of facts to one another and to men that their value lies. Our romantic encounter with facts soon requires a precise rendering of them in an orderly and disciplined way. Thus we are poised on the edge of generality. The power to generalize requires the ability to abstract. But a preoccupation with abstraction disconnects us from reality. True generalization needs constantly to be balanced by a continuous contact with those actual aspects of the world which one's own restricted pursuits influence and effect. The time for developing this habit of perspective is during formal education. Otherwise, education collapses at the point that adulthood appears. Generalization, Whitehead would say, is for the sake of education, not vice versa.

Beyond a presentation of the place of conventional studies in English schools, we get no precise curricular recommendation from Whitehead. Who can foretell for all time what demands will be made on education? But he does give us an invariant pattern of *method* in the three phases through which any educational unit, great or small, must pass, and a conception of the achievement of the method, which is a generality of *personal* outlook, rather than the intellectual control of abstract generalization.

# 10
## John Dewey

**John Dewey** (1859–1952), born and bred in Burlington, Vermont, was the foremost America philosopher of the first half of the twentieth century. After receiving his Ph.D. from John Hopkins University, he taught for several years at the Universities of Minnesota, Michigan, and Chicago, and then spent most of his academic career as Professor of Philosophy at Columbia University. He served as President of both the American Psychological Association and the American Philosophical Association. His influence on the development of educational practice both in the United States and abroad was enormous.

## *Democracy and Education*

### Preface

The following pages embody an endeavor to detect and state the ideas implied in a democratic society and to apply these ideas to the problems of the enterprise of education. The discussion includes an indication of the constructive aims and methods of public education as seen from this point of view, and a critical estimate of the theories of knowing and moral development which were formulated in earlier social conditions, but which still operate, in societies nominally democratic, to hamper the adequate realization of the democratic ideal. As will appear from the book itself, the philosophy stated in this book connects the growth of democracy with the development of the experimental method in the sciences, evolutionary ideas in the biological sciences, and the industrial reorganization, and is concerned to point out the changes in subject matter and method of education indicated by these developments. . . .

## 1. Education as a Necessity of Life

### 1. Renewal of Life by Transmission

The most notable distinction between living and inanimate beings is that the former maintain themselves by renewal. A stone when struck resists. If its resistance is greater than the force of the blow struck, it remains outwardly unchanged. Otherwise, it is shattered into smaller bits. Never does the stone attempt to react in such a way that it may maintain itself against the blow, much less so as to render the blow a contributing factor to its own continued action. While the living thing may easily be crushed by superior force, it none the less tries to turn the energies which act upon it into means of its own further existence. If it cannot do so, it does not just split into smaller pieces (at least in the higher forms of life), but loses its identity as a living thing.

As long as it endures, it struggles to use surrounding energies in its own behalf. It uses light, air, moisture, and the material of soil. To say that it uses them is to say that it turns them into means of its own conservation. As long as it is growing, the energy it expends in thus turning the environment to account is more than compensated for by the return it gets: it grows. Understanding the word "control" in this sense, it may be said that a living being is one that subjugates and controls for its own continued activity the energies that would otherwise use it up. Life is a self-renewing process through action upon the environment.

In all the higher forms this process cannot be kept up indefinitely. After a while they succumb; they die. The creature is not equal to the task of indefinite self-renewal. But continuity of the life process is not dependent upon the prolongation of the existence of any one individual. Reproduction of other forms of life goes on in continuous sequence. And though, as the geological record shows, not merely individuals but also species die out, the life process continues in increasingly complex forms. As some species die out, forms better adapted to utilize the obstacles against which they struggled in vain come into being. Continuity of life means continual readaptation of the environment to the needs of living organisms.

We have been speaking of life in its lowest terms—as a physical thing. But we use the word "life" to denote the whole range of experience, individual and racial. When we see a book called the *Life of Lincoln* we do not expect to find within its covers a treatise on physiology. We look for an account of social antecedents; a description of early surroundings, of the conditions and occupation of the family; of the chief episodes in the development of character; of signal struggles and achievements; of the individual's hopes, tastes, joys and sufferings. In precisely similar fashion we speak of the life of a savage tribe, of the Athenian people, of the American nation. "Life" covers customs, institutions, beliefs, victories and defeats, recreations and occupations.

We employ the word "experience" in the same pregnant sense. And to it, as well as to life in the bare physiological sense, the principle of continuity through renewal applies. With the renewal of physical existence goes, in the case of human beings, the re-creation of beliefs, ideals, hopes, happiness, misery, and practices. The continuity of any experience, through renewing of the social group, is a literal fact. Education, in its broadest sense, is the means of this social continuity of life. Every one of the constituent elements of a social group, in a modern city as in a savage tribe, is born immature, helpless, without language, beliefs, ideas, or social standards. Each individual, each unit who is the carrier of the life-experience of his group, in time passes away. Yet the life of the group goes on.

The primary ineluctable facts of the birth and death of each one of the constituent members in a social group determine the necessity of education. On one hand, there is the contrast between the immaturity of the new-born members of the group—its future sole representatives—and the maturity of the adult members who possess the knowledge and customs of the group. On the other hand, there is the necessity that these immature members be not merely physically preserved in adequate numbers, but that they be initiated into the interests, purposes, information, skill, and practices of the mature members: otherwise the group will cease its characteristic life. Even in a savage tribe, the achievements of adults are far beyond what the immature members would be capable of if left to themselves. With the growth of civilization, the gap between the original capacities of the immature and the standards and customs of the elders increases. Mere physical growing up, mere mastery of the bare necessities of subsistence will not suffice to reproduce the life of the group. Deliberate effort and the taking of thoughtful pains are required. Beings who are born not only unaware of, but quite indifferent to, the aims and habits of the social group have to be rendered cognizant of them and actively interested. Education, and education alone, spans the gap.

Society exists through a process of transmission quite as much as biological life. This transmission occurs by means of communication of habits of doing, thinking, and feeling from the older to the younger. Without this communication of ideals, hopes, expectations, standards, opinions, from those members of society who are passing out of the group life to those who are coming into it, social life could not survive. If the members who compose a society lived on continuously, they might educate the new-born members, but it would be a task directed by personal interest rather than social need. Now it is a work of necessity.

If a plague carried off the members of a society all at once, it is obvious that the group would be permanently done for. Yet the death of each of its constituent members is as certain as if an epidemic took them all at once. But the graded difference in age, the fact that some are born as some die, makes possible through transmission of ideas and practices the constant reweaving of the social fabric. Yet this renewal is not automatic. Unless pains are taken to see that genuine and thorough transmission takes place, the most civilized group will relapse into barbarism and then into savagery. In fact, the human young are so immature that if they were left to themselves without the guidance and succor of others, they could not even acquire the rudimentary abilities necessary for physical existence. The young of human beings compare so poorly in original efficiency with the young of many of the lower animals, that even the powers needed for physical sustentation have to be acquired under tuition. How much more, then, is this the case with respect to all the technological, artistic, scientific, and moral achievements of humanity!

## 2. Education and Communication

So obvious, indeed, is the necessity of teaching and learning for the continued existence of a society that we may seem to be dwelling unduly on a truism. But justification is found in the fact that such emphasis is a means of getting us away from an unduly scholastic and formal notion of education. Schools are, indeed, one important method of the transmission which forms the dispositions of the immature; but it is only one means, and, compared with other agencies, a relatively superficial means. Only as we have grasped the necessity of more fundamental and persistent modes of tuition can we make sure of placing the scholastic methods in their true context.

Society not only continues to exist *by* transmission, *by* communication, but it may fairly be said to exist *in* transmission, *in* communication. There is more than a verbal tie between the words common, community, and communication. Men live in a community in virtue of the things which they have in common; and communication is the way in which they come to possess things in common. What they must have in common in order to form a community or society are aims, beliefs, aspirations, knowledge—a common understanding—like-mindedness as the sociologists say. Such things cannot be passed physically from one to another, like bricks; they cannot be shared as persons would share a pie by dividing it into physical pieces. The communication which insures participation in a common understanding is one which secures similar emotional and intellectual dispositions—like ways of responding to expectations and requirements.

Persons do not become a society by living in physical proximity, any more than a man ceases to be socially influenced by being so many feet or miles removed from others. A book or a letter may institute a more intimate association between human beings separated thousands of miles from each other than exists between dwellers under the same roof. Individuals do not even compose a social group because they all work for a common end. The parts of a machine work with a maximum of cooperativeness for a common result, but they do not form a community. If, however, they were all cognizant of the common end and all interested in it so that they regulated their specific activity in view of it, then they would form a community. But this would involve communication. Each would have to know what the other was about and would have to have some way of keeping the other informed as to his own purpose and progress. Consensus demands communication.

We are thus compelled to recognize that within even the most social group there are many relations which are not as yet social. A large number of human relationships in any social group are still upon the machine-like plane. Individuals use one another so as to get desired results, without reference to the emotional and intellectual disposition and consent of those used. Such uses express physical superiority, or superiority of position, skill, technical ability, and command of tools, mechanical or fiscal. So far as the relations of parent and child, teacher and pupil, employer and employee, governor and governed, remain upon this level, they form no true social group, no matter how closely their respective activities touch one another. Giving and taking of orders modifies action and results, but does not of itself effect a sharing of purposes, a communication of interests.

Not only is social life identical with communication, but all communication (and hence all genuine social life) is educative. To be a recipient of a communication is to have an enlarged and changed experience. One shares in what another has thought and felt and in so far, meagerly or amply, has his own attitude modified. Nor is the one who communicates left unaffected. Try the experiment of communicating, with fullness and accuracy, some experience to another, especially if it be somewhat complicated, and you will find your own attitude toward your experience changing; otherwise you resort to expletives and ejaculations. The experience has to be formulated in order to be communicated. To formulate requires getting outside of it, seeing it as another would see it, considering what points of contact it has with the life of another so that it may be got into such form that he can appreciate its meaning. Except in dealing with commonplaces and catch phrases one has to assimilate, imaginatively, something of another's experience in order to tell him intelligently of one's own experience. All communication is like art. It may fairly be said, therefore, that any social arrangement that remains vitally social, or vitally shared, is educative to those who participate in it. Only when it becomes cast in a mold and runs in a routine way does it lose its educative power.

In final account, then, not only does social life demand teaching and learning for its own permanence, but the very process of living together educates. It enlarges and enlightens experience; it stimulates and enriches imagination; it creates responsibility for accuracy and vividness of statement and thought. A man really living alone (alone mentally as well as physically) would have little or no occasion to reflect upon his past experience to extract its net meaning. The inequality of achievement between the mature and the immature not only necessitates teaching the young, but the necessity of this teaching gives an immense stimulus to reducing experience to that order and form which will render it most easily communicable and hence most usable.

## 3. The Place of Formal Education

There is, accordingly, a marked difference between the education which every one gets from living with others, as long as he really lives instead of just continuing to subsist, and the deliberate educating of the young. In the former case the education is incidental; it is natural and important, but it is not the express reason of the association. While it may be said, without exaggeration, that the measure of the worth of any social institution, economic, domestic, political, legal, religious, is its effect in enlarging and improving experience; yet this effect is not a part of its original motive, which is limited and more immediately practical. Religious associations began, for example, in the desire to secure the favor of overruling powers and to ward off evil influences; family life in the desire to gratify appetites and secure family perpetuity; systematic labor, for the most part, because of enslavement to others, etc. Only gradually was the by-product of the institution, its effect upon the quality and extent of conscious life, noted, and only more gradually still was this effect considered as a directive factor in the conduct of the institution. Even to-day, in our industrial life, apart from certain values of industriousness and thrift, the intellectual and emotional reaction of the forms of human association under which the world's work is carried on receives little attention as compared with physical output.

But in dealing with the young, the fact of association itself as an immediate human fact, gains in importance. While it is easy to ignore in our contact with them the effect of our acts upon their disposition, or to subordinate that educative effect to some external and tangible result, it is not so easy as in dealing with adults. The need of training is too evident; the pressure to accomplish a change in their attitude and habits is too urgent to leave these consequences wholly out of account. Since our chief business with them is to enable them to share in a common life we cannot help considering whether or no we are forming the powers which will secure this ability. If humanity has made some headway in realizing that the ultimate value of every institution is its distinctively human effect—its effect upon conscious experience—we may well believe that this lesson has been learned largely through dealings with the young.

We are thus led to distinguish, within the broad educational process which we have been so far considering, a more formal kind of education—that of direct tuition or schooling. In undeveloped social groups, we find very little formal teaching and training. Savage groups mainly rely for instilling needed dispositions into the young upon the same sort of association which keeps adults loyal to their group. They have no special devices, material, or institutions for teaching save in connection with initiation ceremonies by which the youth are inducted into full social membership. For the most part, they depend upon children learning the customs of the adults, acquiring their emotional set and stock of ideas, by sharing in what the elders are doing. In part, this sharing is direct, taking part in the occupations of adults and thus serving an apprenticeship; in part, it is indirect, through the dramatic plays in which children reproduce the actions of grown-ups and thus learn to know what they are like. To savages it would seem preposterous to seek out a place where nothing but learning was going on in order that one might learn.

But as civilization advances, the gap between the capacities of the young and the concerns of adults widens. Learning by direct sharing in the pursuits of grown-ups becomes increasingly difficult except in the case of the less advanced occupations. Much of what adults do is so remote in space and in meaning that playful imitation is less and less adequate to reproduce its spirit. Ability to share effectively in adult activities thus depends upon a prior training given with this end in view. Intentional agencies—schools—and explicit material—studies—are devised. The task of teaching certain things is delegated to a special group of persons.

Without such formal education, it is not possible to transmit all the resources and achievements of a complex society. It also opens a way to a kind of experience which would not be accessible to the young, if they were left to pick up their training in informal association with others, since books and the symbols of knowledge are mastered.

But there are conspicuous dangers attendant upon the transition from indirect to formal education. Sharing in actual pursuit, whether directly or vicariously in play, is at least personal and vital. These qualities compensate, in some measure, for the narrowness of available opportunities. Formal instruction, on the contrary, easily becomes remote and dead—abstract and bookish, to use the ordinary words of depreciation. What accumulated knowledge exists in low grade societies is at least put into practice; it is transmuted into character; it exists with the depth of meaning that attaches to its coming within urgent daily interests.

But in an advanced culture much which has to be learned is stored in symbols. It is far from translation into familiar acts and objects. Such material is relatively technical and superficial. Taking the ordinary standard of reality as a measure, it is artificial. For this measure is connection with practical concerns. Such material exists in a world by itself, unassimilated to ordinary customs of thought and expression. There is the standing danger that the material of formal instruction will be merely the subject matter of the schools, isolated from the subject matter of life-experience. The permanent social interests are likely to be lost from view. Those which have not been carried over into the structure of social life, but which remain largely matters of technical information expressed in symbols, are made conspicuous in schools. Thus we reach the ordinary notion of education: the notion which ignores its social necessity and its identity with all human association that affects conscious life, and which identifies it with imparting information about remote matters and the conveying of learning through verbal signs: the acquisition of literacy.

Hence one of the weightiest problems with which the philosophy of education has to cope is the method of keeping a proper balance between the informal and the formal, the incidental and the intentional, modes of education. When the acquiring of information and of technical intellectual skill do not influence the formation of a social disposition, ordinary vital experience fails to gain in meaning, while schooling, in so far, creates only "sharps" in learning—that is, egoistic specialists. To avoid a split between what men consciously know because they are aware of having learned it by a specific job of learning, and what they unconsciously know because they have absorbed it in the formation of their characters by intercourse with others, becomes an increasingly delicate task with every development of special schooling.

## Summary

It is the very nature of life to strive to continue in being. Since this continuance can be secured only by constant renewals, life is a self-renewing process. What nutrition and reproduction are to physiological life, education is to social life. This education consists primarily in transmission through communication. Communication is a process of sharing experience till it becomes a common possession. It modifies the disposition of both the parties who partake in it. That the ulterior significance of every mode of human association lies in the contribution which it makes to the improvement of the quality of experience is a fact most easily recognized in dealing with the immature. That is to say, while every social arrangement is educative in effect, the educative effect first becomes an important part of the purpose of the association in connection with the association of the older with the younger. As societies become more complex in structure and resources, the need of formal or intentional teaching and learning increases. As formal teaching and training grow in extent, there is the danger of creating an undesirable split between the experience gained in more direct associations and what is acquired in school. This danger was never greater than at the present time, on account of the rapid growth in the last few centuries of knowledge and technical modes of skill.

## 2. Education as a Social Function

### 1. The Nature and Meaning of Environment

We have seen that a community or social group sustains itself through continuous self-renewal, and that this renewal takes place by means of the educational growth of the immature members of the group. By various agencies, unintentional and designed, a society transforms uninitiated and seemingly alien beings into robust trustees of its own resources and ideals. Education is thus a fostering, a nurturing, a cultivating, process. All of these words mean that it implies attention to the conditions of growth. We also speak of rearing, raising, bringing up—words which express the difference of level which education aims to cover. Etymologically, the word education means just a process of leading or bringing up. When we have the outcome of the process in mind, we speak of education as shaping, forming, molding activity—that is, a shaping into the standard form of social activity. In this chapter we are concerned with the general features of the *way* in which a social group brings up its immature members into its own social form.

Since what is required is a transformation of the quality of experience till it partakes in the interests, purposes, and ideas current in the social group, the problem is evidently not one of mere physical forming. Things can be physically transported in space; they may be bodily conveyed. Beliefs and aspirations cannot be physically extracted and inserted. How then are they communicated? Given the impossibility of direct contagion or literal inculcation, our problem is to discover the method by which the young assimilate the point of view of the old, or the older bring the young into likemindedness with themselves.

The answer, in general formulation, is: By means of the action of the environment in calling out certain responses. The required beliefs cannot be hammered in; the needed attitudes cannot be plastered on. But the particular medium in which an individual exists leads him to see and feel one thing rather than another; it leads him to have certain plans in order that he may act successfully with others; it strengthens some beliefs and weakens others as a condition of winning the approval of others. Thus it gradually produces in him a certain system of behavior, a certain disposition of action. The words "environment," "medium" denote something more than surroundings which encompass an individual. They denote the specific *continuity* of the surroundings with his own active tendencies. An inanimate being is, of course, continuous with its surroundings; but the environing circumstances do not, save metaphorically, constitute an environment. For the inorganic being is not *concerned* in the influences which affect it. On the other hand, some things which are remote in space and time from a living creature, especially a human creature, may form his environment even more truly than some of the things close to him. The things with which a man *varies* are his genuine environment. Thus the activities of the astronomer vary with the stars at which he gazes or about which he calculates. Of his immediate surroundings, his telescope is most intimately his environment. The environment of an antiquarian, as an antiquarian, consists of the remote epoch of human life with which he is concerned, and the relics, inscriptions, etc., by which he establishes connections with that period.

In brief, the environment consists of those conditions that promote or hinder, stimulate or inhibit, the *characteristic* activities of a living being. Water is the environment of a fish because it is necessary to the fish's activities—to its life. The north pole is a significant element in the environment of an arctic explorer, whether he succeeds in reaching it or not, because it defines his activities, makes them what they distinctively are. Just because life signifies not bare passive existence (supposing there is such a thing), but a way of acting, environment or medium signifies what enters into this activity as a sustaining or frustrating condition.

## 2. The Social Environment

A being whose activities are associated with others has a social environment. What he does and what he can do depend upon the expectations, demands, approvals, and condemnations of others. A being connected with other beings cannot perform his own activities without taking the activities of others into account. For they are the indispensable conditions of the realization of his tendencies. When he moves he stirs them and reciprocally. We might as well try to imagine a business man doing business, buying and selling, all by himself, as to conceive it possible to define the activities of an individual in terms of his isolated actions. The manufacturer moreover is as truly socially guided in his activities when he is laying plans in the privacy of his own countinghouse as when he is buying his raw material or selling his finished goods. Thinking and feeling that have to do with action in association with others is as much a social mode of behavior as is the most overt cooperative or hostile act.

What we have more especially to indicate is how the social medium nurtures its immature members. There is no great difficulty in seeing how it shapes the external habits of action. Even dogs and horses have their actions modified by association with human beings; they form different habits because human beings are concerned with what they do. Human beings control animals by controlling the natural stimuli which influence them; by creating a certain environment in other words. Food, bits and bridles, noises, vehicles, are used to direct the ways in which the natural or instinctive responses of horses occur. By operating steadily to call out certain acts, habits are formed which function with the same uniformity as the original stimuli. If a rat is put in a maze and finds food only by making a given number of turns in a given sequence, his activity is gradually modified till he habitually takes that course rather than another when he is hungry.

Human actions are modified in a like fashion. A burnt child dreads the fire; if a parent arranged conditions so that every time a child touched a certain toy he got burned, the child would learn to avoid that toy as automatically as he avoids touching fire. So far, however, we are dealing with what may be called *training* in distinction from educative teaching. The changes considered are in outer action rather than in mental and emotional dispositions of behavior. The distinction is not, however, a sharp one. The child might conceivably generate in time a violent antipathy, not only to that particular toy, but to the class of toys resembling it. The aversion might even persist after he had forgotten about the original burns; later on he might even invent some reason to account for his seemingly irrational antipathy. In some cases, altering the external habit of action by changing the environment to affect the stimuli to action will also alter the mental disposition concerned in the action. Yet this does not always happen; a person trained to dodge a threatening blow, dodges automatically with no corresponding thought or emotion. We have to find, then, some differentia of training from education.

A clue may be found in the fact that the horse does not really share in the social use to which his action is put. Some one else uses the horse to secure a result which is advantageous by making it advantageous to the horse to perform the act—he gets food, etc. But the horse, presumably, does not get any new interest. He remains interested in food, not in the service he is rendering. He is not a partner in a shared activity. Were he to become a copartner, he would, in engaging in the conjoint activity, have the same interest in its accomplishment which others have. He would share their ideas and emotions.

Now in many cases—too many cases—the activity of the immature human being is simply played upon to secure habits which are useful. He is trained like an animal rather than educated like a human being. His instincts remain attached to their original objects of pain or pleasure. But to get happiness or to avoid the pain of failure he has to act in a way agreeable to others. In other cases, he really shares or participates in the common activity. In this case, his original impulse is modified. He not merely acts in a way agreeing with the actions of others, but, in so acting, the same ideas and emotions are aroused in him that animate the others. A tribe, let us say, is warlike. The successes for which it strives, the achievements upon which it sets store, are connected with fighting and victory. The presence of this medium incites bellicose exhibitions in a boy, first in games, then in fact when he is strong enough. As he fights he wins approval and advancement; as he refrains, he is disliked, ridiculed, shut out from favorable recognition. It is not surprising that his original belliger-ent tendencies and emotions are strengthened at the expense of others, and that his ideas turn to things connected with war. Only in this way can he become fully a recognized member of his group. Thus his mental habitudes are gradually assimilated to those of his group.

If we formulate the principle involved in this illustration, we shall perceive that the social medium neither implants certain desires and ideas directly, nor yet merely establishes certain purely muscular habits of action, like "instinctively" winking or dodging a blow. Setting up conditions which stimulate certain visible and tangible ways of acting is the first step. Making the individual a sharer or partner in the associated activity so that he feels its success as his success, its failure as his failure, is the completing step. As soon as he is possessed by the emotional attitude of the group, he will be alert to recognize the special ends at which it aims and the means employed to secure success. His beliefs and ideas, in other words, will take a form similar to those of others in the group. He will also achieve pretty much the same stock of knowledge since that knowledge is an ingredient of his habitual pursuits.

The importance of language in gaining knowledge is doubtless the chief cause of the common notion that knowledge may be passed directly from one to another. It almost seems as if all we have to do to convey an idea into the mind of another is to convey a sound into his ear. Thus imparting knowledge gets assimilated to a purely physical process. But learning from language will be found, when analyzed, to confirm the principle just laid down. It would probably be admitted with little hesitation that a child gets the idea of, say, a hat by using it as other persons do; by covering the head with it, giving it to others to wear, having it put on by others when going out, etc. But it may be asked how this principle of shared activity applies to getting through speech or reading the idea of, say, a Greek helmet, where no direct use of any kind enters in. What shared activity is there in learning from books about the discovery of America?

Since language tends to become the chief instrument of learning about many things, let us see how it works. The baby begins of course with mere sounds, noises, and tones having no meaning, expressing, that is, no idea. Sounds are just one kind of stimulus to direct response, some having a soothing effect, others tending to make one jump, and so on. The sound h-a-t would remain as meaningless as a sound in Choctaw, a seemingly inarticulate grunt, if it were not uttered in connection with an action which is participated in by a number of people. When the mother is taking the infant out of doors, she says "hat" as she puts something on the baby's head. Being taken out becomes an interest to the child; mother and child not only go out with each other physically, but both are *concerned* in the going out; they enjoy it in common. By conjunction with the other factors in activity the sound "hat" soon gets the same meaning for the child that it has for the parent; it becomes a sign of the activity into which it enters. The bare fact that language consists of sounds which are *mutually intelligible* is enough of itself to show that its meaning depends upon connection with a shared experience.

In short, the sound h-a-t gains meaning in precisely the same way that the thing "hat" gains it, by being used in a given way. And they acquire the same meaning with the child which they have with the adult because they are used in a common experience by both. The guarantee for the same manner of use is found in the fact that the thing and the sound are first employed in a *joint* activity, as a means of setting up an active connection between the child and a grown-up. Similar ideas or meanings spring up because both persons are engaged as partners in an action where what each does depends upon and influences what the other does. If two savages were engaged in a joint hunt for game, and a certain signal meant "move to the right" to the one who uttered it, and "move to the left" to the one who heard it, they obviously could not successfully carry on their hunt together. Understanding one another means that objects, including sounds, have the same value for both with respect to carrying on a common pursuit.

After sounds have got meaning through connection with other things employed in a joint undertaking, they can be used in connection with other like sounds to develop new meanings, precisely as the things for which they stand are combined. Thus the words in which a child learns about, say, the Greek helmet originally got a meaning (or were understood) by use in an action having a common interest and end. They now arouse a new meaning by inciting the one who hears or reads to rehearse imaginatively the activities in which the helmet has its use. For the time being, the one who understands the words "Greek helmet" becomes mentally a partner with those who used the helmet. He engages, through his imagination, in a shared activity. It is not easy to get the *full* meaning of words. Most persons probably stop with the idea that "helmet" denotes a queer kind of headgear a people called the Greeks once wore. We conclude, accordingly, that the use of language to convey and acquire ideas is an extension and refinement of the principle that things gain meaning by being used in a shared experience or joint action; in no sense does it contravene that principle. When words do not enter as factors into a shared situation, either overtly or imaginatively, they operate as pure physical stimuli, not as having a meaning or intellectual value. They set activity running in a given groove, but there is no accompanying conscious purpose or meaning. Thus, for example, the plus sign may be a stimulus to perform the act of writing one number under another and adding the numbers, but the person forming the act will operate much as an automaton would unless he realizes the meaning of what he does.

## 3. The Social Medium as Educative

Our net result thus far is that social environment forms the mental and emotional disposition of behavior in individuals by engaging them in activities that arouse and strengthen certain impulses, that have certain purposes and entail certain consequences. A child growing up in a family of musicians will inevitably have whatever capacities he has in music stimulated, and, relatively, stimulated more than other impulses which might have been awakened in another environment. Save as he takes an interest in music and gains a certain competency in it, he is "out of it"; he is unable to share in the life of the group to which he belongs. Some kinds of participation in the life of those with whom the individual is connected are inevitable; with respect to them, the social environment exercises an educative or formative influence unconsciously and apart from any set purpose.

In savage and barbarian communities, such direct participation (constituting the indirect or incidental education of which we have spoken) furnishes almost the sole influence for rearing the young into the practices and beliefs of the group. Even in present-day societies, it furnishes the basic nurture of even the most insistently schooled youth. In accord with the interests and occupations of the group, certain things become objects of high esteem; others of aversion. Association does not create impulses of affection and dislike, but it furnishes the objects to which they attach themselves. The way our group or class does things tends to determine the proper objects of attention, and thus to prescribe the directions and limits of observation and memory. What is strange or foreign (that is to say outside the activities of the groups) tends to be morally forbidden and intellectually suspect. It seems almost incredible to us, for example, that things which we know very well could have escaped recognition in past ages. We incline to account for it by attributing congenital stupidity to our forerunners and by assuming superior native intelligence on our own part. But the explanation is that their modes of life did not call for attention to such facts, but held their minds riveted to other things. Just as the senses require sensible objects to stimulate them, so our powers of observation, recollection, and imagination do not work spontaneously, but are set in motion by the demands set up by current social occupations. The main texture of disposition is formed, independently of schooling, by such influences. What conscious, deliberate teaching can do is at most to free the capacities thus formed for fuller exercise, to purge them of some of their grossness, and to furnish objects which make their activity more productive of meaning.

While this "unconscious influence of the environment" is so subtle and pervasive that it affects every fibre of character and mind, it may be worth while to specify a few directions in which its effect is most marked. First, the habits of language. Fundamental modes of speech, the bulk of the vocabulary, are formed in the ordinary intercourse of life, carried on not as a set means of instruction but as a social necessity. The babe acquires, as we well say, the *mother* tongue. While speech habits thus contracted may be corrected or even displaced by conscious teaching, yet, in times of excitement, intentionally acquired modes of speech often fall away, and individuals relapse into their really native tongue. Secondly, manners. Example is notoriously more potent than precept. Good manners come, as we say, from good breeding or rather are good breeding; and breeding is acquired by habitual action, in response to habitual stimuli, not by conveying information. Despite the never ending play of conscious correction and instruction, the surrounding atmosphere and spirit is in the end the chief agent in forming manners. And manners are but minor morals. Moreover in major morals, conscious instruction is likely to be efficacious only in the degree in which it falls in with the general "walk and conversation" of those who constitute the child's social environment. Thirdly, good taste and aesthetic appreciation. If the eye is constantly greeted by harmonious objects, having elegance of form and color, a standard of taste naturally grows up. The effect of a tawdry, unarranged, and over-decorated environment works for the deterioration of taste, just as meagre and barren surroundings starve out the desire for beauty. Against such odds, conscious teaching can hardly do more than convey second-hand information as to what others think. Such taste never becomes spontaneous and personally engrained, but remains a labored reminder of what those think to whom one has been taught to look up. To say that the deeper standards of judgments of value are framed by the situations into which a person habitually enters is not so much to mention a fourth point, as it is to point out a fusion of those already mentioned. We rarely recognize the extent in which our conscious estimates of what is worth while and what is not, are due to standards of which we are not conscious at all. But in general it may be said that the things which we take for granted without inquiry or reflection are just the things which determine our conscious thinking and decide our conclusions. And these habitudes which lie below the level of reflection are just those which have been formed in the constant give and take of relationship with others.

## 4. The School as a Special Environment

The chief importance of this foregoing statement of the educative process which goes on willynilly is to lead us to note that the only way in which adults consciously control the kind of education which the immature get is by controlling the environment in which they act, and hence think and feel. We never educate directly, but indirectly by means of the environment. Whether we permit chance environments to do the work, or whether we design environments for the purpose makes a great difference. And any environment is a chance environment so far as its educative influence is concerned unless it has been deliberately regulated with reference to its educative effect. An intelligent home differs from an unintelligent one chiefly in that the habits of life and intercourse which prevail are chosen, or at least colored, by the thought of their bearing upon the development of children. But schools remain, of course, the typical instance of environments framed with express reference to influencing the mental and moral disposition of their members.

Roughly speaking, they come into existence when social traditions are so complex that a considerable part of the social store is committed to writing and transmitted through written symbols. Written symbols are even more artificial or conventional than spoken; they cannot be picked up in accidental intercourse with others. In addition, the written form tends to select and record matters which are comparatively foreign to everyday life. The achievements accumulated from generation to generation are deposited in it even though some of them have fallen temporarily out of use. Consequently as soon as a community depends to any

considerable extent upon what lies beyond its own territory and its own immediate generation, it must rely upon the set agency of schools to insure adequate transmission of all its
resources. To take an obvious illustration: The life of the ancient Greeks and Romans has
profoundly influenced our own, and yet the ways in which they affect us do not present
themselves on the surface of our ordinary experiences. In similar fashion, peoples still existing, but remote in space, British, Germans, Italians, directly concern our own social affairs,
but the nature of the interaction cannot be understood without explicit statement and
attention. In precisely similar fashion, our daily associations cannot be trusted to make clear
to the young the part played in our activities by remote physical energies, and by invisible
structures. Hence a special mode of social intercourse is instituted, the school, to care for
such matters.

This mode of association has three functions sufficiently specific, as compared with
ordinary associations of life, to be noted. First, a complex civilization is too complex to be
assimilated *in toto*. It has to be broken up into portions, as it were, and assimilated piecemeal,
in a gradual and graded way. The relationships of our present social life are so numerous and
so interwoven that a child placed in the most favorable position could not readily share in
many of the most important of them. Not sharing in them, their meaning would not be
communicated to him, would not become a part of his own mental disposition. There would
be no seeing the trees because of the forest. Business, politics, art, science, religion, would
make all at once a clamor for attention; confusion would be the outcome. The first office of
the social organ we call the school is to provide a *simplified* environment. It selects the
features which are fairly fundamental and capable of being responded to by the young. Then
it establishes a progressive order, using the factors first acquired as means of gaining insight
into what is more complicated.

In the second place, it is the business of the school environment to eliminate, so far as
possible, the unworthy features of the existing environment from influence upon mental
habitudes. It establishes a purified medium of action. Selection aims not only at simplifying
but at weeding out what is undesirable. Every society gets encumbered with what is trivial,
with dead wood from the past, and with what is positively perverse. The school has the duty
of omitting such things from the environment which it supplies, and thereby doing what it
can to counteract their influence in the ordinary social environment. By selecting the best for
its exclusive use, it strives to reenforce the power of this best. As a society becomes more
enlightened, it realizes that it is responsible *not* to transmit and conserve the whole of its
existing achievements, but only such as make for a better future society. The school is its
chief agency for the accomplishment of this end.

In the third place, it is the office of the school environment to balance the various
elements in the social environment, and to see to it that each individual gets an opportunity
to escape from the limitations of the social group in which he was born, and to come into
living contact with a broader environment. Such words as "society" and "community" are
likely to be misleading, for they have a tendency to make us think there is single thing
corresponding to the single word. As a matter of fact, a modern society is many societies
more or less loosely connected. Each household with its immediate extension of friends
makes a society; the village or street group of playmates is a community; each business
group, each club, is another. Passing beyond these more intimate groups, there is in a country

like our own a variety of races, religious affiliations, economic divisions. Inside the modern city, in spite of its nominal political unity, there are probably more communities, more differing customs, traditions, aspirations, and forms of government or control, than existed in an entire continent at an earlier epoch.

Each such group exercises a formative influence on the active dispositions of its members. A clique, a club, a gang, a Fagin's household of thieves, the prisoners in a jail, provide educative environments for those who enter into their collective or conjoint activities, as truly as a church, a labor union, a business partnership, or a political party. Each of them is a mode of associated or community life, quite as much as is a family, a town, or a state. There are also communities whose members have little or no direct contact with one another, like the guild of artists, the republic of letters, the members of the professional learned class scattered over the face of the earth. For they have aims in common, and the activity of each member is directly modified by knowledge of what others are doing.

In the olden times, the diversity of groups was largely a geographical matter. There were many societies, but each, within its own territory, was comparatively homogeneous. But with the development of commerce, transportation, intercommunication, and emigration, countries like the United States are composed of a combination of different groups with different traditional customs. It is this situation which has, perhaps more than any other one cause, forced the demand for an educational institution which shall provide something like a homogeneous and balanced environment for the young. Only in this way can the centrifugal forces set up by juxtaposition of different groups within one and the same political unit be counteracted. The intermingling in the school of youth of different races, differing religions, and unlike customs creates for all a new and broader environment. Common subject matter accustoms all to a unity of outlook upon a broader horizon than is visible to the members of any group while it is isolated. The assimilative force of the American public school is eloquent testimony to the efficacy of the common and balanced appeal.

The school has the function also of coordinating within the disposition of each individual the diverse influences of the various social environments into which he enters. One code prevails in the family; another, on the street; a third, in the workshop or store; a fourth, in the religious association. As a person passes from one of the environments to another, he is subjected to antagonistic pulls, and is in danger of being split into a being having different standards of judgment and emotion for different occasions. This danger imposes upon the school a steadying and integrating office.

### Summary

The development within the young of the attitudes and dispositions necessary to the continuous and progressive life of a society cannot take place by direct conveyance of beliefs, emotions, and knowledge. It takes place through the intermediary of the environment. The environment consists of the sum total of conditions which are concerned in the execution of the activity characteristic of a living being. The social environment consists of all the activities of fellow beings that are bound up in the carrying on of the activities of any one of its members. It is truly educative in its effect in the degree in which an individual shares or participates in some conjoint activity. By doing his share in the associated activity, the individual appropriates the purpose which actuates it, becomes familiar with its methods and subject matters, acquires needed skill, and is saturated with its emotional spirit.

The deeper and more intimate educative formation of disposition comes, without conscious intent, as the young gradually partake of the activities of the various groups to which they may belong. As a society becomes more complex, however, it is found necessary to provide a special social environment which shall especially look after nurturing the capacities of the immature. Three of the more important functions of this special environment are: simplifying and ordering the factors of the disposition it is wished to develop; purifying and idealizing the existing social customs; creating a wider and better balanced environment than that by which the young would be likely, if left to themselves, to be influenced.

## 3. Education as Direction

### 1. The Environment as Directive

We now pass to one of the special forms which the general function of education assumes: namely, that of direction, control, or guidance. Of these three words, direction, control, and guidance, the last best conveys the idea of assisting through cooperation the natural capacities of the individuals guided; control conveys rather the notion of an energy brought to bear from without and meeting some resistance from the one controlled; direction is a more neutral term and suggests the fact that the active tendencies of those directed are led in a certain continuous course, instead of dispersing aimlessly. Direction expresses the basic function, which tends at one extreme to become a guiding assistance and at another, a regulation or ruling. But in any case, we must carefully avoid a meaning sometimes read into the term "control." It is sometimes assumed, explicitly or unconsciously, that an individual's tendencies are naturally purely individualistic or egoistic, and thus antisocial. Control then denotes the process by which he is brought to subordinate his natural impulses to public or common ends. Since, by conception, his own nature is quite alien to this process and opposes it rather than helps it, control has in this view a flavor of coercion or compulsion about it. Systems of government and theories of the state have been built upon this notion, and it has seriously affected educational ideas and practices. But there is no ground for any such view. Individuals are certainly interested, at times, in having their own way, and their own way may go contrary to the ways of others. But they are also interested, and chiefly interested upon the whole, in entering into the activities of others and taking part in conjoint and cooperative doings. Otherwise, no such thing as a community would be possible. And there would not even be any one interested in furnishing the policeman to keep a semblance of harmony unless he thought that thereby he could gain some personal advantage. Control, in truth, means only an emphatic form of direction of powers, and covers the regulation gained by an individual through his own efforts quite as much as that brought about when others take the lead.

In general, every stimulus directs activity. It does not simply excite it or stir it up, but directs it toward an object. Put the other way around, a response is not just a re-action, a protest, as it were, against being disturbed; it is, as the word indicates, an answer. It meets the stimulus, and corresponds with it. There is an adaptation of the stimulus and response to each other. A light is the stimulus to the eye to see something, and the business of the eye is to see. If the eyes are open and there is light, seeing occurs; the stimulus is but a condition of the fulfillment of the proper function of the organ, not an outside interruption. To some extent, then, all direction or control is a guiding of activity to its own end; it is an assistance in doing fully what some organ is already tending to do.

This general statement needs, however, to be qualified in two respects. In the first place, except in the case of a small number of instincts, the stimuli to which an immature human being is subject are not sufficiently definite to call out, in the beginning, specific responses. There is always a great deal of superfluous energy aroused. This energy may be wasted, going aside from the point; it may also go against the successful performance of an act. It does harm by getting in the way. Compare the behavior of a beginner in riding a bicycle with that of the expert. There is little axis of direction in the energies put forth; they are largely dispersive and centrifugal. Direction involves a focusing and fixating of action in order that it may be truly a response, and this requires an elimination of unnecessary and confusing movements. In the second place, although no activity can be produced in which the person does not cooperate to some extent, yet a response may be of a kind which does not fit into the sequence and continuity of action. A person boxing may dodge a particular blow success-fully, but in such a way as to expose himself the next instant to a still harder blow. Adequate control means that the successive acts are brought into a continuous order; each act not only meets its immediate stimulus but helps the acts which follow.

In short, direction is both simultaneous and successive. At a given time, it requires that, from all the tendencies that are partially called out, those be selected which centre energy upon the point of need. Successively, it requires that each act be balanced with those which precede and come after, so that *order* of activity is achieved. *Focusing and ordering are thus the two aspects of direction, one spatial, the other temporal.* The first insures hitting the mark; the second keeps the balance required for further action. Obviously, it is not possible to separate them in practice as we have distinguished them in idea. Activity must be centered at a given time *in such a way* as to prepare for what comes next. The problem of the immediate response is complicated by one's having to be on the lookout for future occurrences.

Two conclusions emerge from these general statements. On the one hand, purely external direction is impossible. The environment can at most only supply stimuli to call out responses. These responses proceed from tendencies already possessed by the individual. Even when a person is frightened by threats into doing something, the threats work only because the person has an instinct of fear. If he has not, or if, though having it, it is under his own control, the threat has no more influence upon him than light has in causing a person to see who has no eyes. While the customs and rules of adults furnish stimuli which direct as well as evoke the activities of the young, the young, after all, participate in the direction which their actions finally take. In the strict sense, nothing can be forced upon them or into them. To overlook this fact means to distort and pervert human nature. To take into account the contribution made by the existing instincts and habits of those directed is to direct them economically and wisely. Speaking accurately, all direction is but *re*-direction; it shifts the activities already going on into another channel. Unless one is cognizant of the energies which are already in operation, one's attempts at direction will almost surely go amiss.

On the other hand, the control afforded by the customs and regulations of others may be short-sighted. It may accomplish its immediate effect, but at the expense of throwing the subsequent action of the person out of balance. A threat may, for example, prevent a person from doing something to which he is naturally inclined by arousing fear of disagreeable consequences if he persists. But he may be left in the position which exposes him later on to influences which will lead him to do even worse things. His instincts of cunning and slyness may be aroused, so that things henceforth appeal to him on the side of evasion and trickery more than would otherwise have been the case. Those engaged in directing the actions of others are always in danger of overlooking the importance of the sequential development of those they direct.

## 2. Modes of Social Direction

Adults are naturally most conscious of directing the conduct of others when they are immediately aiming so to do. As a rule, they have such an aim consciously when they find themselves resisted; when others are doing things they do not wish them to do. But the more permanent and influential modes of control are those which operate from moment to moment continuously without such deliberate intention on our part.

1. When others are not doing what we would like them to or are threatening disobedience, we are most conscious of the need of controlling them and of the influences by which they are controlled. In such cases, our control becomes most direct, and at this point we are most likely to make the mistakes just spoken of. We are even likely to take the influence of superior force for control, forgetting that while we may lead a horse to water we cannot make him drink; and that while we can shut a man up in a penitentiary we cannot make him penitent. In all such cases of immediate action upon others, we need to discriminate between physical results and moral results. A person may be in such a condition that forcible feeding or enforced confinement is necessary for his own good. A child may have to be snatched with roughness away from a fire so that he shall not be burnt. But no improvement of disposition, no educative effect, need follow. A harsh and commanding tone may be effectual in keeping a child away from the fire, and the same desirable physical effect will follow as if he had been snatched away. But there may be no more obedience of a moral sort in one case than in the other. A man can be prevented from breaking into other persons' houses by shutting him up, but shutting him up may not alter his disposition to commit burglary. When we confuse a physical with an educative result, we always lose the chance of enlisting the person's own participating disposition in getting the result desired, and thereby of developing within him an intrinsic and persisting direction in the right way.

In general, the occasion for the more conscious acts of control should be limited to acts which are so instinctive or impulsive that the one performing them has no means of foreseeing their outcome. If a person cannot foresee the consequences of his act, and is not capable of understanding what he is told about its outcome by those with more experience, it is impossible for him to guide his act intelligently. In such a state, every act is alike to him. Whatever moves him does move him, and that is all there is to it. In some cases, it is well to permit him to experiment, and to discover the consequences for himself in order that he may act intelligently next time under similar circumstances. But some courses of action are too discommoding and obnoxious to others to allow of this course being pursued. Direct disapproval is now resorted to. Shaming, ridicule, disfavor, rebuke, and punishment are used. Or contrary tendencies in the child are appealed to to divert him from his troublesome line of behavior. His sensitiveness to approbation, his hope of winning favor by an agreeable act, are made use of to induce action in another direction.

2. These methods of control are so obvious (because so intentionally employed) that it would hardly be worth while to mention them if it were not that notice may now be taken, by way of contrast, of the other more important and permanent mode of control. This other method resides in the ways in which persons, with whom the immature being is associated, *use things*; the instrumentalities with which they accomplish their own ends. The very existence of the social medium in which an individual lives, moves, and has his being is the standing effective agency of directing his activity.

This fact makes it necessary for us to examine in greater detail what is meant by the social environment. We are given to separating from each other the physical and social environments in which we live. The separation is responsible on one hand for an exaggeration of the moral importance of the more direct or personal modes of control of which we have been speaking; and on the other hand for an exaggeration, in current psychology and philosophy, of the *intellectual* possibilities of contact with a purely physical environment. There is not, in fact, any such thing as the direct influence of one human being on another apart from use of the physical environment as an intermediary. A smile, a frown, a rebuke, a word of warning or encouragement, all involve some physical change. Otherwise, the attitude of one would not get over to alter the attitude of another. Comparatively speaking, such modes of influence may be regarded as personal. The physical medium is reduced to a mere means of personal contact. In contrast with such direct modes of mutual influence, stand associations in common pursuits involving the use of things as means and as measures of results. Even if the mother never told her daughter to help her, or never rebuked her for not helping, the child would be subjected to direction in her activities by the mere fact that she was engaged, along with the parent, in the household life. Imitation, emulation, the need of working together, enforce control.

If the mother hands the child something needed, the latter must reach the thing in order to get it. Where there is giving there must be taking. The way the child handles the thing after it is got, the use to which it is put, is surely influenced by the fact that the child has watched the mother. When the child sees the parent looking for something, it is as natural for it also to look for the object and to give it over when it finds it, as it was, under other circumstances, to receive it. Multiply such an instance by the thousand details of daily intercourse, and one has a picture of the most permanent and enduring method of giving direction to the activities of the young.

In saying this, we are only repeating what was said previously about participating in a joint activity as the chief way of forming disposition. We have explicitly added, however, the recognition of the part played in the joint activity by the *use of things*. The philosophy of learning has been unduly dominated by a false psychology. It is frequently stated that a person learns by merely having the qualities of things impressed upon his mind through the gateway of the senses. Having received a store of sensory impressions, association or some power of mental synthesis is supposed to combine them into ideas—into things with a *meaning*. An object, stone, orange, tree, chair, is supposed to convey different impressions of color, shape, size, hardness, smell, taste, etc., which aggregated together constitute the characteristic meaning of each thing. But as matter of fact, it is the characteristic use to which the thing is put, because of its specific qualities, which supplies the meaning with which it is identified. A chair is a thing which is put to one use; a table, a thing which is employed for another purpose; an orange is a thing which costs so much, which is grown in warm climes, which is eaten, and when eaten has an agreeable odor and refreshing taste, etc.

The difference between an adjustment to a physical stimulus and a *mental* act is that the latter involves response to a thing in its *meaning*; the former does not. A noise may make me jump without my mind being implicated. When I hear a noise and run and get water and put out a blaze, I respond intelligently; the sound meant fire, and fire meant need of being extinguished. I bump into a stone, and kick it one side purely physically. I put it to one side for fear some one will stumble upon it, intelligently; I respond to a meaning which the thing has. I am startled by a thunderclap whether I recognize it or not—more likely, if I do not recognize it. But if I say, either out loud or to myself, that is thunder, I respond to the disturbance as a meaning. My behavior has a mental quality. When things have a meaning for us, we *mean* (intend, propose) what we do: when they do not, we act blindly, unconsciously, unintelligently.

In both kinds of responsive adjustment, our activities are directed or controlled. But in the merely blind response, direction is also blind. There may be training, but there is no education. Repeated responses to recurrent stimuli may fix a habit of acting in a certain way. All of us have many habits of whose import we are quite unaware, since they were formed without our knowing what we were about. Consequently they possess us, rather than we them. They move us; they control us. Unless we become aware of what they accomplish, and pass judgment upon the worth of the result, we do not control them. A child might be made to bow every time he met a certain person by pressure on his neck muscles, and bowing would finally become automatic. It would not, however, be an act of recognition or deference on his part, till he did it with a certain end in view—as having a certain meaning. And not till he knew what he was about and performed the act for the sake of its meaning could he be said to be "brought up" or educated to act in a certain way. To have an *idea* of a thing is thus not just to get certain sensations from it. It is to be able to respond to the thing in view of its place in an inclusive scheme of action; it is to foresee the drift and probable consequence of the action of the thing upon us and of our action upon it.

To have the same ideas about things which others have, to be like-minded with them, and thus to be really members of a social group, is therefore to attach the same meanings to things and to acts which others attach. Otherwise, there is no common understanding, and no community life. But in a shared activity, each person refers what he is doing to what the other is doing and *vice-versa*. That is, the activity of each is placed in the same inclusive situation. To pull at a rope at which others happen to be pulling is not a shared or conjoint activity, unless the pulling is done with knowledge that others are pulling and for the sake of either helping or hindering what they are doing. A pin may pass in the course of its manufacture through the hands of many persons. But each may do his part without knowledge of what others do or without any reference to what they do; each may operate simply for the sake of a separate result—his own pay. There is, in this case, no common consequence to which the several acts are referred, and hence no genuine intercourse or association, in spite of juxtaposition, and in spite of the fact that their respective doings contribute to a single outcome. But if each views the consequences of his own acts as having a bearing upon what others are doing and takes into account the consequences of their behavior upon himself, then there is a common mind; a common intent in behavior. There is an understanding set up between the different contributors; and this common understanding controls the action of each.

Suppose that conditions were so arranged that one person automatically caught a ball and then threw it to another person who caught and automatically returned it; and that each so acted without knowing where the ball came from or went to. Clearly, such action would be without point or meaning. It might be physically controlled, but it would not be socially directed. But suppose that each becomes aware of what the other is doing, and becomes interested in the other's action and thereby interested in what he is doing himself as connected with the action of the other. The behavior of each would then be intelligent; and socially intelligent and guided. Take one more example of a less imaginary kind. An infant is hungry, and cries while food is prepared in his presence. If he does not connect his own state with what others are doing, nor what they are doing with his own satisfaction, he simply reacts with increasing impatience to his own increasing discomfort. He is physically controlled by his own organic state. But when he makes a back and forth reference, his whole attitude changes. He takes an interest, as we say; he takes note and watches what others are doing. He no longer reacts just to his own hunger, but behaves in the light of what others are doing for its prospective satisfaction. In that way, he also no longer just gives way to hunger without knowing it, but he notes, or recognizes, or identifies his own state. It becomes an object for him. His attitude toward it becomes in some degree intelligent. And in such noting of the meaning of the actions of others and of his own state, he is socially directed.

It will be recalled that our main proposition had two sides. One of them has now been dealt with: namely, that physical things do not influence mind (or form ideas and beliefs) except as they are implicated in action for prospective consequences. The other point is persons modify *one another's dispositions* only through the special use they make of physical conditions. Consider first the case of so-called expressive movements to which others are sensitive; blushing, smiling, frowning, clinching of fists, natural gestures of all kinds. In themselves, these are not expressive. They are organic parts of a person's attitude. One does not blush to show modesty or embarrassment to others, but because the capillary circulation alters in response to stimuli. But others *use* the blush, or a slightly perceptible tightening of the muscles of a person with whom they are associated, as a sign of the state in which that person finds himself, and as an indication of what course to pursue. The frown signifies an imminent rebuke for which one must prepare, or an uncertainty and hesitation which one must, if possible, remove by saying or doing something to restore confidence.

A man at some distance is waving his arms wildly. One has only to preserve an attitude of detached indifference, and the motions of the other person will be on the level of any remote physical change which we happen to note. If we have no concern or interest, the waving of the arms is as meaningless to us as the gyrations of the arms of a windmill. But if interest is aroused, we begin to participate. We refer his action to something we are doing ourselves or that we should do. We have to judge the meaning of his act in order to decide what to do. Is he beckoning for help? Is he warning us of an explosion to be set off, against which we should guard ourselves? In one case, his action means to run toward him; in the other case, to run away. In any case, it is the change he effects in the physical environment which is a sign to us of how we should conduct ourselves. Our action is *socially* controlled because we endeavor to refer what we are to do to the same situation in which he is acting.

Language is, as we have already seen (p. 389), a case of this joint reference of our own action and that of another to a common situation. Hence its unrivaled significance as a means of social direction. But language would not be this efficacious instrument were it not that it takes place upon a background of coarser and more tangible use of physical means to accomplish results. A child sees persons with whom he lives using chairs, hats, tables, spades, saws, plows, horses, money, in certain ways. If he has any share at all in what they are doing, he is led thereby to use things in the same way, or to use other things in a way which will fit in. If a chair is drawn up to a table, it is a sign that he is to sit in it; if a person extends his right hand, he is to extend his; and so on in a never ending stream of detail. The prevailing habits of using the products of human art and the raw materials of nature constitute by all odds the deepest and the most pervasive mode of social control. When children go to school, they already have "minds"—they have knowledge and dispositions of judgment which may be appealed to through the use of language. But these "minds" are the organized habits of intelligent response which they have previously acquired by putting things to use in connection with the way other persons use things. The control is inescapable; it saturates disposition.

The net outcome of the discussion is that the fundamental means of control is not personal but intellectual. It is not "moral" in the sense that a person is moved by direct personal appeal from others, important as is this method at critical junctures. It consists in the habits of *understanding*, which are set up in using objects in correspondence with others, whether by way of cooperation and assistance or rivalry and competition. *Mind* as a concrete thing is precisely the power to understand things in terms of the use made of them; a socialized mind is the power to understand them in terms of the use to which they are turned in joint or shared situations. *And mind in this sense is the method of social control.*

### 3. Imitation and Social Psychology

We have already noted the defects of a psychology of learning which places the individual mind naked, as it were, in contact with physical objects, and which believes that knowledge, ideas, and beliefs accrue from their interaction. Only comparatively recently has the predominating influence of association with fellow beings in the formation of mental and moral disposition been perceived. Even now it is usually treated as a kind of adjunct to an alleged method of learning by direct contact with things, and as merely supplementing knowledge of the physical world with knowledge of persons. The purport of our discussion is that such a view makes an absurd and impossible separation between persons and things. Interaction with things may form habits of external adjustment. But it leads to activity having a meaning and conscious intent only when things are used to produce a result. And the only way one person can modify the mind of another is by using physical conditions, crude or artificial, so as to evoke some answering activity from him. Such are our two main conclusions. It is desirable to amplify and enforce them by placing them in contrast with the theory which uses a psychology of supposed *direct* relationships of human beings to one another as an adjunct to the psychology of the supposed direct relation of an individual to physical objects. In substance, this so-called social psychology has been built upon the notion of imitation. Consequently, we shall discuss the nature and role of imitation in the formation of mental disposition.

According to this theory, social control of individuals rests upon the instinctive tendency of individuals to imitate or copy the actions of others. The latter serve as models. The imitative instinct is so strong that the young devote themselves to conforming to the patterns set by others and reproducing them in their own scheme of behavior. According to our theory, what is here called imitation is a misleading name for partaking with others in a use of things which leads to consequences of common interest.

The basic error in the current notion of imitation is that it puts the cart before the horse. It takes an effect for the cause of the effect. There can be no doubt that individuals in forming a social group are like-minded; they understand one another. They tend to act with the same controlling ideas, beliefs, and intentions, given similar circumstances. Looked at from without, they might be said to be engaged in "imitating" one another. In the sense that they are doing much the same sort of thing in much the same sort of way, this would be true enough. But "imitation" throws no light upon *why* they so act; it repeats the fact as an explanation of itself. It is an explanation of the same order as the famous saying that opium puts men to sleep because of its dormitive power.

Objective likeness of acts and the mental satisfaction found in being in conformity with others are baptized by the name imitation. This social fact is then taken for a psychological force, which produced the likeness. A considerable portion of what is called imitation is simply the fact that persons being alike in structure respond in the same way to like stimuli. Quite independently of imitation, men on being insulted get angry and attack the insulter. This statement may be met by citing the undoubted fact that response to an insult takes place in different ways in groups having different customs. In one group, it may be met by recourse to fisticuffs, in another by a challenge to a duel, in a third by an exhibition of contemptuous disregard. This happens, so it is said, because the model set for imitation is different. But there is no need to appeal to imitation. The mere fact that customs are different means that the actual stimuli to behavior are different. Conscious instruction plays a part; prior approvals and disapprovals have a large influence. Still more effective is the fact that unless an individual acts in the way current in his group, he is literally out of it. He can associate with others on intimate and equal terms only by behaving in the way in which they behave. The pressure that comes from the fact that one is let into the group action by acting in one way and shut out by acting in another way is unremitting. What is called the effect of imitation is mainly the product of conscious instruction and of the selective influence exercised by the unconscious confirmations and ratifications of those with whom one associates.

Suppose that some one rolls a ball to a child; he catches it and rolls it back, and the game goes on. Here the stimulus is not just the sight of the ball, or the sight of the other rolling it. It is the *situation*—the game which is playing. The response is not merely rolling the ball back; it is rolling it back so that the other one may catch and return it,—that the game may continue. The "pattern" or model is not the action of the other person. The whole situation requires that each should adapt his action in view of what the other person has done and is to do. Imitation may come in but its role is subordinate. The child has an interest on his own account; he wants to keep it going. He may then note how the other person catches and holds the ball in order to improve his own acts. He imitates the means of doing, not the end or thing to be done. And he imitates the means because he wishes, on his own behalf, as part of his own initiative, to take an effective part in the game. One has only to consider how completely the child is dependent from his earliest days for successful execution of his purposes upon fitting his acts into those of others to see what a premium is put upon behaving as others behave, and of developing an understanding of them in order that he may so behave. The pressure for likemindedness in action from this source is so great that it is quite superfluous to appeal to imitation.

As matter of fact, imitation of ends, as distinct from imitation of means which help to reach ends, is a superficial and transitory affair which leaves little effect upon disposition. Idiots are especially apt at this kind of imitation; it affects outward acts but not the meaning of their performance. When we find children engaging in this sort of mimicry, instead of encouraging them (as we would do if it were an important means of social control) we are more likely to rebuke them as apes, monkeys, parrots, or copy cats. Imitation of means of accomplishment is, on the other hand, an intelligent act. It involves close observation, and judicious selection of what will enable one to do better something which he already is trying to do. Used for a purpose, the imitative instinct may, like any other instinct, become a factor in the development of effective action.

This excursus should, accordingly, have the effect of reenforcing the conclusion that genuine social control means the formation of a certain mental disposition; a way of *understanding* objects, events, and acts which enables one to participate effectively in associated activities. Only the friction engendered by meeting resistance from others leads to the view that it takes place by forcing a line of action contrary to natural inclinations. Only failure to take account of the situations in which persons are mutually concerned (or interested in acting responsively to one another) leads to treating imitation as the chief agent in promoting social control.

## 4. Some Applications to Education

Why does a savage group perpetuate savagery, and a civilized group civilization? Doubtless the first answer to occur to mind is because savages are savages; beings of low-grade intelligence and perhaps defective moral sense. But careful study has made it doubtful whether their native capacities are appreciably inferior to those of civilized man. It has made it certain that native differences are not sufficient to account for the difference in culture. In a sense the mind of savage peoples is an effect, rather than a cause, of their backward institutions. Their social activities are such as to restrict their objects of attention and interest, and hence to limit the stimuli to mental development. Even as regards the objects that come within the scope of attention, primitive social customs tend to arrest observation and imagination upon qualities which do not fructify in the mind. Lack of control of natural forces means that a scant number of natural objects enter into associated behavior. Only a small number of natural resources are utilized and they are not worked for what they are worth. The advance of civilization means that a larger number of natural forces and objects have been transformed into instrumentalities of action, into means for securing ends. We start not so much with superior capacities as with superior stimuli for evocation and direction of our capacities. The savage deals largely with crude stimuli; we have *weighted* stimuli.

Prior human efforts have made over natural conditions. As they originally existed they were indifferent to human endeavors. Every domesticated plant and animal, every tool, every utensil, every appliance, every manufactured article, every aesthetic decoration, every work of art means a transformation of conditions once hostile or indifferent to characteristic human activities into friendly and favoring conditions. Because the activities of children today are controlled by these selected and charged stimuli, children are able to traverse in a short lifetime what the race has needed slow, tortured ages to attain. The dice have been loaded by all the successes which have preceded.

Stimuli conductive to economical and effective response, such as our system of roads and means of transportation, our ready command of heat, light, and electricity, our ready-made machines and apparatus for every purpose, do not, by themselves or in their aggregate, constitute a civilization. But the uses to which they are put are civilization, and without the things the uses would be impossible. Time otherwise necessarily devoted to wresting a livelihood from a grudging environment and securing a precarious protection against its inclemencies is freed. A body of knowledge is transmitted, the legitimacy of which is guaranteed by the fact that the physical equipment in which it is incarnated leads to results that square with the other facts of nature. Thus these appliances of art supply a protection, perhaps our chief protection, against a recrudescence of these superstitious beliefs, those fanciful myths and infertile imaginings about nature in which so much of the best intellectual power of the past has been spent. If we add one other factor, namely, that such appliances be not only used, but *used in the interests of a truly shared or associated life*, then the appliances become the *positive* resources of civilization. If Greece, with a scant tithe of our material resources, achieved a worthy and noble intellectual and artistic career, it is because Greece operated for social ends such resources as it had.

But whatever the situation, whether one of barbarism or civilization, whether one of stinted control of physical forces, or of partial enslavement to a mechanism not yet made tributary to a shared experience, things as they enter into action furnish the educative conditions of daily life and direct the formation of mental and moral disposition.

Intentional education signifies, as we have already seen, a specially selected environment, the selection being made on the basis of materials and method specifically promoting growth in the desired direction. Since language represents the physical conditions that have been subjected to the maximum transformation in the interests of social life—physical things which have lost their original quality in becoming social tools—it is appropriate that language should play a large part compared with other appliances. By it we are led to share vicariously in past human experience, thus widening and enriching the experience of the present. We are enabled, symbolically and imaginatively, to anticipate situations. In countless ways, language condenses meanings that record social outcomes and presage social outlooks. So significant is it of a liberal share in what is worth while in life that unlettered and uneducated have become almost synonymous.

The emphasis in school upon this particular tool has, however, its dangers:—dangers which are not theoretical but exhibited in practice. Why is it, in spite of the fact that teaching by pouring in, learning by a passive absorption, are universally condemned, that they are still so entrenched in practice? That education is not an affair of "telling" and being told, but an active and constructive process, is a principle almost as generally violated in practice as conceded in theory. Is not this deplorable situation due to the fact that the doctrine is itself merely told? It is preached; it is lectured; it is written about. But its enactment into practice requires that the school environment be equipped with agencies for doing, with tools and physical materials, to an extent rarely attained. It requires that methods of instruction and administration be modified to allow and to secure direct and continuous occupations with things. Not that the use of language as an educational resource should lessen; but that its use should be more vital and fruitful by having its normal connection with shared activities. "These things ought ye to have done, and not to have left the others undone." And for the school "these things" mean equipment with the instrumentalities of cooperative or joint activity.

For when the schools depart from the educational conditions effective in the out-of-school environment, they necessarily substitute a bookish, a pseudo-intellectual spirit for a social spirit. Children doubtless go to school to learn, but it has yet to be proved that learning occurs most adequately when it is made a separate conscious business. When treating it as a business of this sort tends to preclude the social sense which comes from sharing in an activity of common concern and value, the effort at isolated intellectual learning contradicts its own aim. We may secure motor activity and sensory excitation by keeping an individual by himself, but we cannot thereby get him to understand the meaning which things have in the life of which he is a part. We may secure technical specialized ability in algebra, Latin or botany, but not the kind of intelligence which directs ability to useful ends. Only by engaging in a joint activity, where one person's use of material and tools is consciously referred to the use other persons are making of their capacities and appliances, is a social direction of disposition attained.

## Summary

The natural or native impulses of the young do not agree with the life-customs of the group into which they are born. Consequently they have to be directed or guided. This control is not the same thing as physical compulsion; it consists in centering the impulses acting at any one time upon some specific end and in introducing an order of continuity into the sequence of acts. The action of others is always influenced by deciding what stimuli shall call out their actions. But in some cases as in commands, prohibitions, approvals, and disapprovals, the stimuli proceed from persons with a direct view to influencing action. Since in such cases we are most conscious of controlling the action of others, we are likely to exaggerate the importance of this sort of control at the expense of a more permanent and effective method. The basic control resides in the nature of the situations in which the young take part. In social situations the young have to refer their way of acting to what others are doing and make it fit in. This directs their action to a common result, and gives an understanding common to the participants. For all *mean* the same thing, even when performing different acts. This common understanding of the means and ends of action is the essence of social control. It is indirect, or emotional and intellectual, not direct or personal. Moreover it is intrinsic to the disposition of the person, not external and coercive. To achieve this internal control through identity of interest and understanding is the business of education. While books and conversation can do much, these agencies are usually relied upon too exclusively. Schools require for their full efficiency more opportunity for conjoint activities in which those instructed take part, so that they may acquire a *social* sense of their own powers and of the materials and appliances used.

## 4. Education as Growth

### 1. The Conditions of Growth

In directing the activities of the young, society determines its own future in determining that of the young. Since the young at a given time will at some later date compose the society of that period, the latter's nature will largely turn upon the direction children's activities were given at an earlier period. This cumulative movement of action toward a later result is what is meant by growth.

The primary condition of growth is immaturity. This may seem to be a mere truism— saying that a being can develop only in some point in which he is undeveloped. But the prefix "im" of the word immaturity means something positive, not a mere void or lack. It is noteworthy that the terms "capacity" and "potentiality" have a double meaning, one sense being negative, the other positive. Capacity may denote mere receptivity, like the capacity of a quart measure. We may mean by potentiality a merely dormant or quiescent state—a capacity to become something different under external influences. But we also mean by capacity an ability, a power; and by potentiality potency, force. Now when we say that immaturity means the possibility of growth, we are not referring to absence of powers which may exist at a later time; we express a force positively present—the *ability* to develop.

Our tendency to take immaturity as mere lack, and growth as something which fills up the gap between the immature and the mature is due to regarding childhood *comparatively*, instead of intrinsically. We treat it simply as a privation because we are measuring it by adulthood as a fixed standard. This fixes attention upon what the child has not, and will not have till he becomes a man. This comparative standpoint is legitimate enough for some purposes, but if we make it final, the question arises whether we are not guilty of an overweening presumption. Children, if they could express themselves articulately and sincerely, would tell a different tale; and there is excellent adult authority for the conviction that for certain moral and intellectual purposes adults must become as little children.

The seriousness of the assumption of the negative quality of the possibilities of immaturity is apparent when we reflect that it sets up as an ideal and standard a static end. The fulfillment of growing is taken to mean an *accomplished* growth: that is to say, an Ungrowth, something which is no longer growing. The futility of the assumption is seen in the fact that every adult resents the imputation of having no further possibilities of growth; and so far as he finds that they are closed to him mourns the fact as evidence of loss, instead of falling back on the achieved as adequate manifestation of power. Why an unequal measure for child and man?

Taken absolutely, instead of comparatively, immaturity designates a positive force or ability,—the *power* to grow. We do not have to draw out or educe positive activities from a child, as some educational doctrines would have it. Where there is life, there are already eager and impassioned activities. Growth is not something done to them; it is something they do. The positive and constructive aspect of possibility gives the key to understanding the two chief traits of immaturity, dependence and plasticity. (1) It sounds absurd to hear dependence spoken of as something positive, still more absurd as a power. Yet if helplessness were all there were in dependence, no development could ever take place. A merely impotent being has to be carried, forever, by others. The fact that dependence is accompanied by growth in ability, not by an ever increasing lapse into parasitism, suggests that it is already something constructive. Being merely sheltered by others would not promote growth. For (2) it would only build a wall around impotence. With reference to the physical world, the child is helpless. He lacks at birth and for a long time thereafter power to make his way physically, to make his own living. If he had to do that by himself, he would hardly survive an hour. On this side his helplessness is almost complete. The young of the brutes are immeasurably his superiors. He is physically weak and not able to turn the strength which he possesses to coping with the physical environment.

1. The thoroughgoing character of this helplessness suggests, however, some compensating power. The relative ability of the young of brute animals to adapt themselves fairly well to physical conditions from an early period suggests the fact that their life is not intimately bound up with the life of those about them. They are compelled, so to speak, to have physical gifts because they are lacking in social gifts. Human infants, on the other hand, can get along with physical incapacity just because of their social capacity. We sometimes talk and think as if they simply happened to be *physically* in a social environment; as if social forces exclusively existed in the adults who take care of them, they being passive recipients. If it were said that children are themselves marvelously endowed with *power* to enlist the cooperative attention of others, this would be thought to be a backhanded way of saying that others are marvelously attentive to the needs of children. But observation shows that children are gifted with an equipment of the first order for social intercourse. Few grownup persons retain all of the flexible and sensitive ability of children to vibrate sympathetically with the attitudes and doings of those about them. Inattention to physical things (going with incapacity to control them) is accompanied by a corresponding intensification of interest and attention as to the doings of people. The native mechanism of the child and his impulses all tend to facile social responsiveness. The statement that children, before adolescence, are egotistically self-centered, even if it were true, would not contradict the truth of this statement. It would simply indicate that their social responsiveness is employed on their own behalf, not that it does not exist. But the statement is not true as matter of fact. The facts which are cited in support of the alleged pure egoism of children really show the intensity and directness with which they go to their mark. If the ends which form the mark seem narrow and selfish to adults, it is only because adults (by means of a similar engrossment in their day) have mastered these ends, which have consequently ceased to interest them. Most of the remainder of children's alleged native egoism is simply an egoism which runs counter to an adult's egoism. To a grown-up person who is too absorbed in his own affairs to take an interest

in children's affairs, children doubtless seem unreasonably engrossed in *their* own affairs.

From a social standpoint, dependence denotes a power rather than a weakness; it involves interdependence. There is always a danger that increased personal independence will decrease the social capacity of an individual. In making him more self-reliant, it may make him more self-sufficient; it may lead to aloofness and indifference. It often makes an individual so insensitive in his relations to others as to develop an illusion of being really able to stand and act alone—an unnamed form of insanity which is responsible for a large part of the remediable suffering of the world.

2. The specific adaptability of an immature creature for growth constitutes his *plasticity*. This is something quite different from the plasticity of putty or wax. It is not a capacity to take on change of form in accord with external pressure. It lies near the pliable elasticity by which some persons take on the color of their surroundings while retaining their own bent. But it is something deeper than this. It is essentially the ability to learn from experience; the power to retain from one experience something which is of avail in coping with the difficulties of a later situation. This means power to modify actions on the basis of the results of prior experiences, the power to *develop dispositions*. Without it, the acquisition of habits is impossible.

It is a familiar fact that the young of the higher animals, and especially the human young, have to *learn* to utilize their instinctive reactions. The human being is born with a greater number of instinctive tendencies than other animals. But the instincts of the lower animals perfect themselves for appropriate action at an early period after birth, while most of those of the human infant are of little account just as they stand. An original specialized power of adjustment secures immediate efficiency, but, like a railway ticket, it is good for one route only. A being who, in order to use his eyes, ears, hands, and legs, has to experiment in making varied combinations of their reactions, achieves a control that is flexible and varied. A chick, for example, pecks accurately at a bit of food in a few hours after hatching. This means that definite coordinations of activities of the eyes in seeing and of the body and head in striking are perfected in a few trials. An infant requires about six months to be able to gauge with approximate accuracy the action in reaching which will coordinate with his visual activities; to be able, that is, to tell whether he can reach a seen object and just how to execute the reaching. As a result, the chick is limited by the relative perfection of its original endowment. The infant has the advantage of the *multitude* of instinctive tentative reactions and of the experiences that accompany them, even though he is at a temporary disadvantage because they cross one another. In learning an action, instead of having it given ready-made, one of necessity learns to vary its factors, to make varied combinations of them, according to change of circumstances. A possibility of continuing progress is opened up by the fact that in learning one act, methods are developed good for use in other situations. Still more important is the fact that the human being acquires a habit of learning. He learns to learn.

The importance for human life of the two facts of dependence and variable control has been summed up in the doctrine of the significance of prolonged infancy. This prolongation is significant from the standpoint of the adult members of the group as well as from that of the young. The presence of dependent and learning beings is a stimulus to nurture and affection. The need for constant continued care was probably a chief means in transforming

temporary cohabitations into permanent unions. It certainly was a chief influence in forming habits of affectionate and sympathetic watchfulness; that constructive interest in the
well-being of others which is essential to associated life. Intellectually, this moral development meant the introduction of many new objects of attention; it stimulated foresight and
planning for the future. Thus there is a reciprocal influence. Increasing complexity of social
life requires a longer period of infancy in which to acquire the needed powers; this prolongation of dependence means prolongation of plasticity, or power of acquiring variable and
novel modes of control. Hence it provides a further push to social progress.

## 2. Habits as Expressions of Growth

We have already noted that plasticity is the capacity to retain and carry over from prior
experience factors which modify subsequent activities. This signifies the capacity to acquire
habits, or develop definite dispositions. We have now to consider the salient features of
habits. In the first place, a habit is a form of executive skill, of efficiency in doing. A habit
means an ability to use natural conditions as means to ends. It is an active control of the
environment through control of the organs of action. We are perhaps apt to emphasize the
control of the body at the expense of control of the environment. We think of walking,
talking, playing the piano, the specialized skills characteristic of the etcher, the surgeon, the
bridge-builder, as if they were simply ease, deftness, and accuracy on the part of the organism. They are that, of course; but the measure of the value of these qualities lies in the
economical and effective control of the environment which they secure. To be able to walk is
to have certain properties of nature at our disposal—and so with all other habits.

Education is not infrequently defined as consisting in the acquisition of those habits that
effect an adjustment of an individual and his environment. The definition expresses an
essential phase of growth. But it is essential that adjustment be understood in its active sense
of *control* of means for achieving ends. If we think of a habit simply as a change wrought in
the organism, ignoring the fact that this change consists in ability to effect subsequent
changes in the environment, we shall be led to think of "adjustment" as a conformity to
environment as wax conforms to the seal which impresses it. The environment is thought of
as something fixed, providing in its fixity the end and standard of changes taking place in the
organism; adjustment is just fitting ourselves to this fixity of external conditions. Habit as
*habituation* is indeed something *relatively* passive; we get used to our surroundings—to our
clothing, our shoes, and gloves; to the atmosphere as long as it is fairly equable; to our daily
associates, etc. Conformity to the environment, a change wrought in the organism without
reference to ability to modify surroundings, is a marked trait of such habituations. Aside
from the fact that we are not entitled to carry over the traits of such adjustments (which
might well be called *accommodations,* to mark them off from active adjustments) into habits
of active use of our surroundings, two features of habituations are worth notice. In the first
place, we get used to things by *first* using them.

Consider getting used to a strange city. At first, there is excessive stimulation and excessive and ill-adapted response. Gradually certain stimuli are selected because of their rele-
vancy, and others are degraded. We can say either that we do not respond to them any longer,
or more truly that we have effected a persistent response to them—an equilibrium of

adjustment. This means, in the second place, that this enduring adjustment supplies the background upon which are made specific adjustments, as occasion arises. We are never interested in changing the *whole* environment; there is much that we take for granted and accept just as it already is. Upon this background our activities focus at certain points in an endeavor to introduce needed changes. Habituation is thus our adjustment to an environment which at the time we are not concerned with modifying, and which supplies a leverage to our active habits.

Adaptation, in fine, is quite as much adaptation *of* the environment to our own activities as of our activities *to* the environment. A savage tribe manages to live on a desert plain. It adapts itself. But its adaptation involves a maximum of accepting, tolerating, putting up with things as they are, a maximum of passive acquiescence, and a minimum of active control, of subjection to use. A civilized people enters upon the scene. It also adapts itself. It introduces irrigation; it searches the world for plants and animals that will flourish under such conditions; it improves, by careful selection, those which are growing there. As a consequence, the wilderness blossoms as a rose. The savage is merely habituated; the civilized man has habits which transform the environment.

The significance of habit is not exhausted, however, in its executive and motor phase. It means formation of intellectual and emotional disposition as well as an increase in ease, economy, and efficiency of action. Any habit marks an *inclination*—an active preference and choice for the conditions involved in its exercise. A habit does not wait, Micawberlike, for a stimulus to turn up so that it may get busy; it actively seeks for occasions to pass into full operation. If its expression is unduly blocked, inclination shows itself in uneasiness and intense craving. A habit also marks an intellectual disposition. Where there is a habit, there is acquaintance with the materials and equipment to which action is applied. There is a definite way of understanding the situations in which the habit operates. Modes of thought, of observation and reflection, enter as forms of skill and of desire into the habits that make a man an engineer, an architect, a physician, or a merchant. In unskilled forms of labor, the intellectual factors are at minimum precisely because the habits involved are not of a high grade. But there are habits of judging and reasoning as truly as of handling a tool, painting a picture, or conducting an experiment.

Such statements are, however, understatements. The habits of mind involved in habits of the eye and hand supply the latter with their significance. Above all, the intellectual element in a habit fixes the relation of the habit to varied and elastic use, and hence to continued growth. We speak of *fixed* habits. Well, the phrase may mean powers so well established that their possessor always has them as resources when needed. But the phrase is also used to mean ruts, routine ways, with loss of freshness, open-mindedness, and originality. Fixity of habit may mean that something has a fixed hold upon us, instead of our having a free hold upon things. This fact explains two points in a common notion about habits: their identification with mechanical and external modes of action to the neglect of mental and moral attitudes, and the tendency to give them a bad meaning, an identification with "bad habits." Many a person would feel surprised to have his aptitude in his chosen profession called a habit, and would naturally think of his use of tobacco, liquor, or profane language as typical of the meaning of habit. A habit is to him something which has a hold on him, something not easily thrown off even though judgment condemn it.

Habits reduce themselves to routine ways of acting, or degenerate into ways of action to which we are enslaved just in the degree in which intelligence is disconnected from them. Routine habits are unthinking habits; "bad" habits are habits so severed from reason that they are opposed to the conclusions of conscious deliberation and decision. As we have seen, the acquiring of habits is due to an original plasticity of our natures: to our ability to vary responses till we find an appropriate and efficient way of acting. Routine habits, and habits that possess us instead of our possessing them, are habits which put an end to plasticity. They mark the close of power to vary. There can be no doubt of the tendency of organic plasticity, of the physiological basis, to lessen with growing years. The instinctively mobile and eagerly varying action of childhood, the love of new stimuli and new developments, too easily passes into a "settling down," which means aversion to change and a resting on past achievements. Only an environment which secures the full use of intelligence in the process of forming habits can counteract this tendency. Of course, the same hardening of the organic conditions affects the physiological structures which are involved in thinking. But this fact only indicates the need of persistent care to see to it that the function of intelligence is invoked to its maximum possibility. The short-sighted method which falls back on mechanical routine and repetition to secure external efficiency of habit, motor skill without accompanying thought, marks a deliberate closing in of surroundings upon growth.

## 3. The Educational Bearings of the Conception of Development

We have had so far but little to say in this chapter about education. We have been occupied with the conditions and implications of growth. If our conclusions are justified, they carry with them, however, definite educational consequences. When it is said that education is development, everything depends upon *how* development is conceived. Our net conclusion is that life is development, and that developing, growing, is life. Translated into its educational equivalents, this means (*i*) that the educational process has no end beyond itself; it is its own end; and that (*ii*) the educational process is one of continual reorganizing, reconstructing, transforming.

1. Development when it is interpreted in *comparative* terms, that is, with respect to the special traits of child and adult life, means the direction of power into special channels: the formation of habits involving executive skill, definiteness of interest, and specific objects of observation and thought. But the comparative view is not final. The child has specific powers; to ignore that fact is to stunt or distort the organs upon which his growth depends. The adult uses his powers to transform his environment, thereby occasioning new stimuli which redirect his powers and keep them developing. Ignoring this fact means arrested development, a passive accommodation. Normal child and normal adult alike, in other words, are engaged in growing. The difference between them is not the difference between growth and no growth, but between the modes of growth appropriate to different conditions. With respect to the development of powers devoted to coping with specific scientific and economic problems we may say the child should be growing in manhood. With respect to sympathetic curiosity, unbiased responsiveness, and openness of mind, we may say that the adult should be growing in childlikeness. One statement is as true as the other.

Three ideas which have been criticized, namely, the merely privative nature of immaturity, static adjustment to a fixed environment, and rigidity of habit, are all connected with a false idea of growth or development,—that it is a movement toward a fixed goal. Growth is regarded as *having* an end, instead of *being* an end. The educational counterparts of the three fallacious ideas are first, failure to take account of the instinctive or native powers of the young; secondly, failure to develop initiative in coping with novel situations; thirdly, an undue emphasis upon drill and other devices which secure automatic skill at the expense of personal perception. In all cases, the adult environment is accepted as a standard for the child. He is to be brought up *to* it.

Natural instincts are either disregarded or treated as nuisances—as obnoxious traits to be suppressed, or at all events to be brought into conformity with external standards. Since conformity is the aim, what is distinctively individual in a young person is brushed aside, or regarded as a source of mischief or anarchy. Conformity is made equivalent to uniformity. Consequently, there are induced lack of interest in the novel, aversion to progress, and dread of the uncertain and the unknown. Since the end of growth is outside of and beyond the process of growing, external agents have to be resorted to to induce movement towards it. Whenever a method of education is stigmatized as mechanical, we may be sure that external pressure is brought to bear to reach an external end.

2. Since in reality there is nothing to which growth is relative save more growth, there is nothing to which education is subordinate save more education. It is a commonplace to say that education should not cease when one leaves school. The point of this commonplace is that the purpose of school education is to insure the continuance of education by organizing the powers that insure growth. The inclination to learn from life itself and to make the conditions of life such that all will learn in the process of living is the finest product of schooling.

When we abandon the attempt to define immaturity by means of fixed comparison with adult accomplishments, we are compelled to give up thinking of it as denoting lack of desired traits. Abandoning this notion, we are also forced to surrender our habit of thinking of instruction as a method of supplying this lack by pouring knowledge into a mental and moral hole which awaits filling. Since life means growth, a living creature lives as truly and positively at one stage as at another, with the same intrinsic fullness and the same absolute claims. Hence education means the enterprise of supplying the conditions which insure growth, or adequacy of life, irrespective of age. We first look with impatience upon immaturity, regarding it as something to be got over as rapidly as possible. Then the adult formed by such educative methods looks back with impatient regret upon childhood and youth as a scene of lost opportunities and wasted powers. This ironical situation will endure till it is recognized that living has its own intrinsic quality and that the business of education is with that quality.

Realization that life is growth protects us from that so-called idealizing of childhood which in effect is nothing but lazy indulgence. Life is not to be identified with every superficial act and interest. Even though it is not always easy to tell whether what appears to be mere surface fooling is a sign of some nascent as yet untrained power, we must remember that manifestations are not to be accepted as ends in themselves. They are signs of possible growth. They are to be turned into means of development, of carrying power forward, not indulged or cultivated for their own sake. Excessive attention to surface phenomena (even in the way of rebuke as well as of encouragement) may lead to their fixation and thus to arrested development. What impulses are moving toward, not what they have been, is the important thing for parent and teacher. The true principle of respect for immaturity cannot be better put than in the words of Emerson: "Respect the child. Be not too much his parent. Trespass not on his solitude. But I hear the outcry which replies to this suggestion: Would you verily throw up the reins of public and private discipline; would you leave the young child to the mad career of his own passions and whimsies, and call this anarchy a respect for the child's nature? I answer,—Respect the child, respect him to the end, but also respect yourself. . . . The two points in a boy's training are, to keep his *naturel* and train off all but that; to keep his *naturel,* but stop off his uproar, fooling, and horse-play; keep his nature *and arm it with knowledge in the very direction in which it points.*" And as Emerson goes on to show this reverence for childhood and youth instead of opening up an easy and easy-going path to the instructors, "involves at once immense claims on the time, the thought, on the life of the teacher. It requires time, use, insight, event, all the great lessons and assistances of God; and only to think of using it implies character and profoundness."

## Summary

Power to grow depends upon need for others and plasticity. Both of these conditions are at their height in childhood and youth. Plasticity or the power to learn from experience means the formation of habits. Habits give control over the environment, power to utilize it for human purposes. Habits take the form both of habituation, or a general and persistent balance of organic activities with the surroundings, and of active capacities to readjust activity to meet new conditions. The former furnishes the background of growth; the latter constitute growing. Active habits involve thought, invention, and initiative in applying capacities to new aims. They are opposed to routine which marks an arrest of growth. Since growth is the characteristic of life, education is all one with growing; it has no end beyond itself. The criterion of the value of school education is the extent in which it creates a desire for continued growth and supplies means for making the desire effective in fact. . . .

## 6. Education as Conservative and Progressive

### 3. Education as Reconstruction

In its contrast with the ideas both of unfolding of latent powers from within, and of formation from without, whether by physical nature or by the cultural products of the past, the ideal of growth results in the conception that education is a constant reorganizing or reconstructing of experience. It has all the time an immediate end, and so far as activity is educative, it reaches that end—the direct transformation of the quality of experience. Infancy, youth, adult life,—all stand on the same educative level in the sense that what is really *learned* at any and every stage of experience constitutes the value of that experience, and in the sense that it is the chief business of life at every point to make living thus contribute to an enrichment of its own perceptible meaning.

We thus reach a technical definition of education: It is that reconstruction or reorganization of experience which adds to the meaning of experience, and which increases ability to direct the course of subsequent experience. (1) The increment of meaning corresponds to the increased perception of the connections and continuities of the activities in which we are engaged. The activity begins in an impulsive form; that is, it is blind. It does not know what it is about; that is to say, what are its interactions with other activities. An activity which brings education or instruction with it makes one aware of some of the connections which had been imperceptible. To recur to our simple example, a child who reaches for a bright light gets burned. Henceforth he *knows* that a certain act of touching in connection with a certain act of vision (and *vice-versa*) means heat and pain; or, a certain light means a source of heat. The acts by which a scientific man in his laboratory learns more about flame differ no whit in principle. By doing certain things, he makes perceptible certain connections of heat with other things, which had been previously ignored. Thus his acts in relation to these things get more meaning; he knows better what he is doing or "is about" when he has to do with them; he can *intend* consequences instead of just letting them happen—all synonymous ways of saying the same thing. At the same stroke, the flame has gained in meaning; all that is known about combustion, oxidation, about light and temperature, may become an intrinsic part of its intellectual content.

(2) The other side of an educative experience is an added power of subsequent direction or control. To say that one knows what he is about, or can intend certain consequences, is to say, of course, that he can better anticipate what is going to happen; that he can, therefore, get ready or prepare in advance so as to secure beneficial consequences and avert undesirable ones. A genuinely educative experience, then, one in which instruction is conveyed and ability increased, is contradistinguished from a routine activity on one hand, and a capricious activity on the other. *(a)* In the latter one "does not care what happens"; one just lets himself go and avoids connecting the consequences of one's act (the evidences of its connections with other things) with the act. It is customary to frown upon such aimless random activity, treating it as willful mischief or carelessness or lawlessness. But there is a tendency to seek the cause of such aimless activities in the youth's own disposition, isolated from everything else. But in fact such activity is explosive, and due to maladjustment with surroundings. Individuals act capriciously whenever they act under external dictation, or from being told, without having a purpose of their own or perceiving the bearing of the deed upon other acts. One may learn by doing something which he does not understand; even in the most intelligent action, we do much which we do not mean, because the largest portion of the connections of the act we consciously intend are not perceived or anticipated. But we learn only because after the act is performed we note results which we had not noted before. But much work in school consists in setting up rules by which pupils are to act of such a sort that even after pupils have acted, they are not led to see the connection between the result—say the answer—and the method pursued. So far as they are concerned, the whole thing is a trick and a kind of miracle. Such action is essentially capricious, and leads to capricious habits. *(b)* Routine action, action which is automatic, may increase skill to do a *particular* thing. In so far, it might be said to have an educative effect. But it does not lead to new perceptions of bearings and connections; it limits rather than widens the meaning-horizon. And since the environment changes and our way of acting has to be modified in order successfully

to keep a balanced connection with things, an isolated uniform way of acting becomes disastrous at some critical moment. The vaunted "skill" turns out gross ineptitude.

The essential contrast of the idea of education as continuous reconstruction with the other one-sided conceptions which have been criticized in this and the previous chapter is that it identifies the end (the result) and the process. This is verbally self-contradictory, but only verbally. It means that experience as an active process occupies time and that its later period completes its earlier portion; it brings to light connections involved, but hitherto unperceived. The later outcome thus reveals the meaning of the earlier, while the experience as a whole establishes a bent or disposition toward the things possessing this meaning. Every such continuous experience or activity is educative, and all education resides in having such experiences.

It remains only to point out (what will receive more ample attention later) that the reconstruction of experience may be social as well as personal. For purposes of simplification we have spoken in the earlier chapters somewhat as if the education of the immature which fills them with the spirit of the social group to which they belong, were a sort of catching up of the child with the aptitudes and resources of the adult group. In static societies, societies which make the maintenance of established custom their measure of value, this conception applies in the main. But not in progressive communities. They endeavor to shape the experiences of the young so that instead of reproducing current habits, better habits shall be formed, and thus the future adult society be an improvement on their own. Men have long had some intimation of the extent to which education may be consciously used to eliminate obvious social evils through starting the young on paths which shall not produce these ills, and some idea of the extent in which education may be made an instrument of realizing the better hopes of men. But we are doubtless far from realizing the potential efficacy of education as a constructive agency of improving society, from realizing that it represents not only a development of children and youth but also of the future society of which they will be the constituents.

## Summary

Education may be conceived either retrospectively or prospectively. That is to say, it may be treated as process of accommodating the future to the past, or as an utilization of the past for a resource in a developing future. The former finds its standards and patterns in what has gone before. The mind may be regarded as a group of contents resulting from having certain things presented. In this case, the earlier presentations constitute the material to which the later are to be assimilated. Emphasis upon the value of the early experiences of immature beings is most important, especially because of the tendency to regard them as of little account. But these experiences do not consist of externally presented material, but of interaction of native activities with the environment which progressively modifies both the activities and the environment. . . .

The same principle of criticism applies to theories which find the primary subject matter of study in the cultural products—especially the literary products—of man's history. Isolated from their connection with the present environment in which individuals have to act, they become a kind of rival and distracting environment. Their value lies in their use to increase the meaning of the things with which we have actively to do at the present time. The idea of education advanced in these chapters is formally summed up in the idea of continuous reconstruction of experience, an idea which is marked off from education as preparation for a remote future, as unfolding, as external formation, and as recapitulation of the past.

## 7. The Democratic Conception in Education

For the most part, save incidentally, we have hitherto been concerned with education as it may exist in any social group. We have now to make explicit the differences in the spirit, material, and method of education as it operates in different types of community life. To say that education is a social function, securing direction and development in the immature through their participation in the life of the group to which they belong, is to say in effect that education will vary with the quality of life which prevails in a group. Particularly is it true that a society which not only changes but which has the ideal of such change as will improve it, will have different standards and methods of education from one which aims simply at the perpetuation of its own customs. To make the general ideas set forth applicable to our own educational practice, it is, therefore, necessary to come to closer quarters with the nature of present social life.

## 1. The Implications of Human Association

Society is one word, but many things. Men associate together in all kinds of ways and for all kinds of purposes. One man is concerned in a multitude of diverse groups, in which his associates may be quite different. It often seems as if they had nothing in common except that they are modes of associated life. Within every larger social organization there are numerous minor groups: not only political subdivisions, but industrial, scientific, religious, associations. There are political parties with differing aims, social sets, cliques, gangs, corporations, partnerships, groups bound closely together by ties of blood, and so in endless variety. In many modern states, and in some ancient, there is great diversity of populations, of varying languages, religions, moral codes, and traditions. From this standpoint, many a minor political unit, one of our large cities, for example, is a congeries of loosely associated societies, rather than an inclusive and permeating community of action and thought.[1]

The terms society, community, are thus ambiguous. They have both a eulogistic or normative sense, and a descriptive sense; a meaning *de jure* and a meaning *de facto*. In social philosophy, the former connotation is almost always uppermost. Society is conceived as one by its very nature. The qualities which accompany this unity, praiseworthy community of purpose and welfare, loyalty to public ends, mutuality of sympathy, are emphasized. But when we look at the facts which the term *denotes* instead of confining our attention to its intrinsic *connotation*, we find not unity, but a plurality of societies, good and bad. Men banded together in a criminal conspiracy, business aggregations that prey upon the public while serving it, political machines held together by the interest of plunder, are included. If it is said that such organizations are not societies because they do not meet the ideal requirements of the notion of society, the answer, in part, is that the conception of society is then made so "ideal" as to be of no use, having no reference to facts; and in part, that each of these organizations, no matter how opposed to the interests of other groups, has something of the praiseworthy qualities of "Society" which hold it together. There is honor among thieves, and a band of robbers has a common interest as respects its members. Gangs are marked by fraternal feeling, and narrow cliques by intense loyalty to their own codes. Family life may be marked by exclusiveness, suspicion, and jealousy as to those without, and yet be a model of amity and mutual aid within. Any education given by a group tends to socialize its members, but the quality and value of the socialization depends upon the habits and aims of the group.

Hence, once more, the need of a measure for the worth of any given mode of social life. In seeking this measure, we have to avoid two extremes. We cannot set up, out of our heads, something we regard as an ideal society. We must base our conception upon societies which actually exist, in order to have any assurance that our ideal is a practicable one. But, as we have just seen, the ideal cannot simply repeat the traits which are actually found. The problem is to extract the desirable traits of forms of community life which actually exist, and employ them to criticize undesirable features and suggest improvement. Now in any social group whatever, even in a gang of thieves, we find some interest held in common, and we find a certain amount of interaction and cooperative intercourse with other groups. From these two traits we derive our standard. How numerous and varied are the interests which are consciously shared? How full and free is the interplay with other forms of association? If we apply these considerations to, say, a criminal band, we find that the ties which consciously hold the members together are few in number, reducible almost to a common interest in plunder; and that they are of such a nature as to isolate the group from other groups with respect to give and take of the values of life. Hence, the education such a society gives is partial and distorted. If we take, on the other hand, the kind of family life which illustrates the standard, we find that there are material, intellectual, aesthetic interests in which all participate and that the progress of one member has worth for the experience of other members—it is readily communicable—and that the family is not an isolated whole, but enters intimately into relationships with business groups, with schools, with all the agencies of culture, as well as with other similar groups, and that it plays a due part in the political organization and in return receives support from it. In short, there are many interests consciously communicated and shared; and there are varied and free points of contact with other modes of association.

I. Let us apply the first element in this criterion to a despotically governed state. It is not true there is no common interest in such an organization between governed and governors. The authorities in command must make some appeal to the native activities of the subjects, must call some of their powers into play. Talleyrand said that a government could do everything with bayonets except sit on them. This cynical declaration is at least a recognition that the bond of union is not merely one of coercive force. It may be said, however, that the activities appealed to are themselves unworthy and degrading—that such a government calls into functioning activity simply capacity for fear. In a way, this statement is true. But it overlooks the fact that fear need not be an undesirable factor in experience. Caution, circumspection, prudence, desire to foresee future events so as to avert what is harmful, these desirable traits are as much a product of calling the impulse of fear into play as is cowardice and abject submission. The real difficulty is that the appeal to fear is *isolated*. In evoking dread and hope of specific tangible reward—say comfort and ease—many other capacities are left untouched. Or rather, they are affected, but in such a way as to pervert them. Instead of operating on their own account they are reduced to mere servants of attaining pleasure and avoiding pain.

This is equivalent to saying that there is no extensive number of common interests; there is no free play back and forth among the members of the social group. Stimulation and response are exceedingly one-sided. In order to have a large number of values in common, all the members of the group must have an equable opportunity to receive and to take from others. There must be a large variety of shared undertakings and experiences. Otherwise, the influences which educate some into masters, educate others into slaves. And the experience of each party loses in meaning, when the free interchange of varying modes of life-experience is arrested. A separation into a privileged and a subject-class prevents social endosmosis. The evils thereby affecting the superior class are less material and less perceptible, but equally real. Their culture tends to be sterile, to be turned back to feed on itself; their art becomes a showy display and artificial; their wealth luxurious; their knowledge over-specialized; their manners fastidious rather than humane.

Lack of the free and equitable intercourse which springs from a variety of shared interests makes intellectual stimulation unbalanced. Diversity of stimulation means novelty, and novelty means challenge to thought. The more activity is restricted to a few definite lines—as it is when there are rigid class lines preventing adequate interplay of experiences—the more action tends to become routine on the part of the class at a disadvantage, and capricious, aimless, and explosive on the part of the class having the materially fortunate position. Plato defined a slave as one who accepts from another the purposes which control his conduct. This condition obtains even where there is no slavery in the legal sense. It is found wherever men are engaged in activity which is socially serviceable, but whose service they do not understand and have no personal interest in. Much is said about scientific management of work. It is a narrow view which restricts the science which secures efficiency of operation to movements of the muscles. The chief opportunity for science is the discovery of the relations of a man to his work—including his relations to others who take part—which will enlist his intelligent interest in what he is doing. Efficiency in production often demands division of labor. But it is reduced to a mechanical routine unless workers see the technical, intellectual, and social relationships involved in what they do, and engage in their work because of the motivation furnished by such perceptions. The tendency to reduce such things as efficiency of activity and scientific management to purely technical externals is evidence of the one-sided stimulation of thought given to those in control of industry—those who supply its aims. Because of their lack of all-round and well-balanced social interest, there is not sufficient stimulus for attention to the human factors and relationships in industry. Intelligence is narrowed to the factors concerned with technical production and marketing of goods. No doubt, a very acute and intense intelligence in these narrow lines can be developed, but the failure to take into account the significant social factors means none the less an absence of mind, and a corresponding distortion of emotional life.

II. This illustration (whose point is to be extended to all associations lacking reciprocity of interest) brings us to our second point. The isolation and exclusiveness of a gang or clique brings its antisocial spirit into relief. But this same spirit is found wherever one group has interests "of its own" which shut it out from full interaction with other groups, so that its prevailing purpose is the protection of what it has got, instead of reorganization and progress through wider relationships. It marks nations in their isolation from one another; families which seclude their domestic concerns as if they had no connection with a larger life; schools when separated from the interest of home and community; the divisions of rich and poor; learned and unlearned. The essential point is that isolation makes for rigidity and formal institutionalizing of life, for static and selfish ideals within the group. That savage tribes regard aliens and enemies as synonymous is not accidental. It springs from the fact that they have identified their experience with rigid adherence to their past customs. On such a basis it is wholly logical to fear intercourse with others, for such contact might dissolve custom. It would certainly occasion reconstruction. It is a commonplace that an alert and expanding mental life depends upon an enlarging range of contact with the physical environment. But the principle applies even more significantly to the field where we are apt to ignore it—the sphere of social contacts.

Every expansive era in the history of mankind has coincided with the operation of factors which have tended to eliminate distance between peoples and classes previously hemmed off from one another. Even the alleged benefits of war, so far as more than alleged, spring from the fact that conflict of peoples at least enforces intercourse between them and thus accidentally enables them to learn from one another, and thereby to expand their horizons. Travel, economic and commercial tendencies, have at present gone far to break down external barriers; to bring peoples and classes into closer and more perceptible connection with one another. It remains for the most part to secure the intellectual and emotional significance of this physical annihilation of space.

## 2. The Democratic Ideal

The two elements in our criterion both point to democracy. The first signifies not only more numerous and more varied points of shared common interest, but greater reliance upon the recognition of mutual interests as a factor in social control. The second means not only freer interaction between social groups (once isolated so far as intention could keep up a separation) but change in social habit—its continuous readjustment through meeting the new situations produced by varied intercourse. And these two traits are precisely what characterize the democratically constituted society.

Upon the educational side, we note first that the realization of a form of social life in which interests are mutually interpenetrating, and where progress, or readjustment, is an important consideration, makes a democratic community more interested than other communities have cause to be in deliberate and systematic education. The devotion of democracy to education is a familiar fact. The superficial explanation is that a government resting upon popular suffrage cannot be successful unless those who elect and who obey their governors are educated. Since a democratic society repudiates the principle of external authority, it must find a substitute in voluntary disposition and interest; these can be created only by education. But there is a deeper explanation. A democracy is more than a form of government; it is primarily a mode of associated living, of conjoint communicated experience. The extension in space of the number of individuals who participate in an interest so that each has to refer his own action to that of others, and to consider the action of others to give point and direction to his own, is equivalent to the breaking down of those barriers of class, race, and national territory which kept men from perceiving the full import of their activity. These more numerous and more varied points of contact denote a greater diversity of stimuli to which an individual has to respond; they consequently put a premium on variation in his action. They secure a liberation of powers which remain suppressed as long as the incitations to action are partial, as they must be in a group which in its exclusiveness shuts out many interests.

The widening of the area of shared concerns, and the liberation of a greater diversity of personal capacities which characterize a democracy, are not of course the product of deliberation and conscious effort. On the contrary, they were caused by the development of modes of manufacture and commerce, travel, migration, and intercommunication which flowed from the command of science over natural energy. But after greater individualization on one hand, and a broader community of interest on the other have come into existence, it is a matter of deliberate effort to sustain and extend them. Obviously a society to which stratification into separate classes would be fatal, must see to it that intellectual opportunities are accessible to all on equable and easy terms. A society marked off into classes need be specially attentive only to the education of its ruling elements. A society which is mobile, which is full of channels for the distribution of a change occurring anywhere, must see to it that its members are educated to personal initiative and adaptability. Otherwise, they will be overwhelmed by the changes in which they are caught and whose significance or connections they do not perceive. The result will be a confusion in which a few will appropriate to themselves the results of the blind and externally directed activities of others.

## 3. The Platonic Educational Philosophy

Subsequent chapters will be devoted to making explicit the implications of the democratic ideas in education. In the remaining portions of this chapter, we shall consider the educational theories which have been evolved in three epochs when the social import of education was especially conspicuous. The first one to be considered is that of Plato. No one could better express than did he the fact that a society is stably organized when each individual is doing that for which he has aptitude by nature in such a way as to be useful to others (or to contribute to the whole to which he belongs); and that it is the business of education to discover these aptitudes and progressively to train them for social use. Much which has been said so far is borrowed from what Plato first consciously taught the world. But conditions which he could not intellectually control led him to restrict these ideas in their application. He never got any conception of the indefinite plurality of activities which may characterize an individual and a social group, and consequently limited his view to a limited number of *classes* of capacities and of social arrangements.

Plato's starting point is that the organization of society depends ultimately upon knowledge of the end of existence. If we do not know its end, we shall be at the mercy of accident and caprice. Unless we know the end, the good, we shall have no criterion for rationally deciding what the possibilities are which should be promoted, nor how social arrangements are to be ordered. We shall have no conception of the proper limits and distribution of activities—what he called justice—as a trait of both individual and social organization. But how is the knowledge of the final and permanent good to be achieved? In dealing with this question we come upon the seemingly insuperable obstacle that such knowledge is not possible save in a just and harmonious social order. Everywhere else the mind is distracted and misled by false valuations and false perspectives. A disorganized and factional society sets up a number of different models and standards. Under such conditions it is impossible for the individual to attain consistency of mind. Only a complete whole is fully self-consistent. A society which rests upon the supremacy of some factor over another irrespective of its rational or proportionate claims, inevitably leads thought astray. It puts a premium on certain things and slurs over others, and creates a mind whose seeming unity is forced and distorted. Education proceeds ultimately from the patterns furnished by institutions, customs, and laws. Only in a just state will these be such as to give the right education; and only those who have rightly trained minds will be able to recognize the end, and ordering principle of things. We seem to be caught in a hopeless circle. However, Plato suggested a way out. A few men, philosophers or lovers of wisdom—or truth—may by study learn at least in outline the proper patterns of true existence. If a powerful ruler should form a state after these patterns, then its regulations could be preserved. An education could be given which would sift individuals, discovering what they were good for, and supplying a method of assigning each to the work in life for which his nature fits him. Each doing his own part, and never transgressing, the order and unity of the whole would be maintained.

It would be impossible to find in any scheme of philosophic thought a more adequate recognition on one hand of the educational significance of social arrangements and, on the other, of the dependence of those arrangements upon the means used to educate the young. It would be impossible to find a deeper sense of the function of education in discovering and developing personal capacities, and training them so that they would connect with the activities of others. Yet the society in which the theory was propounded was so undemocratic that Plato could not work out a solution for the problem whose terms he clearly saw.

While he affirmed with emphasis that the place of the individual in society should not be determined by birth or wealth or any conventional status, but by his own nature as discovered in the process of education, he had no perception of the uniqueness of individuals. For him they fall by nature into classes, and into a very small number of classes at that. Consequently the testing and sifting function of education only shows to which one of three classes an individual belongs. There being no recognition that each individual constitutes his own class, there could be no recognition of the infinite diversity of active tendencies and combinations of tendencies of which an individual is capable. There were only three types of faculties or powers in the individual's constitution. Hence education would soon reach a static limit in each class, for only diversity makes change and progress.

In some individuals, appetites naturally dominate; they are assigned to the laboring and trading class, which expresses and supplies human wants. Others reveal, upon education, that over and above appetites, they have a generous, outgoing, assertively courageous disposition. They become the citizen-subjects of the state; its defenders in war; its internal guardians in peace. But their limit is fixed by their lack of reason, which is a capacity to grasp the universal. Those who possess this are capable of the highest kind of education, and become in time the legislators of the state—for laws are the universals which control the particulars of experience. Thus it is not true that in intent, Plato subordinated the individual to the social whole. But it is true that lacking the perception of the uniqueness of every individual, his incommensurability with others, and consequently not recognizing that a society might change and yet be stable, his doctrine of limited powers and classes came in net effect to the idea of the subordination of individuality.

We cannot better Plato's conviction that an individual is happy and society well organized when each individual engages in those activities for which he has a natural equipment, nor his conviction that it is the primary office of education to discover this equipment to its possessor and train him for its effective use. But progress in knowledge has made us aware of the superficiality of Plato's lumping of individuals and their original powers into a few sharply marked-off classes; it has taught us that original capacities are indefinitely numerous and variable. It is but the other side of this fact to say that in the degree in which society has become democratic, social organization means utilization of the specific and variable qualities of individuals, not stratification by classes. Although his educational philosophy was revolutionary, it was none the less in bondage to static ideals. He thought that change or alteration was evidence of lawless flux; that true reality was unchangeable. Hence while he would radically change the existing state of society, his aim was to construct a state in which change would subsequently have no place. The final end of life is fixed; given a state framed with this end in view, not even minor details are to be altered. Though they might not be inherently important, yet if permitted they would inure the minds of men to the idea of change, and hence be dissolving and anarchic. The breakdown of his philosophy is made apparent in the fact that he could not trust to gradual improvements in education to bring about a better society which should then improve education, and so on indefinitely. Correct education could not come into existence until an ideal state existed, and after that education would be devoted simply to its conservation. For the existence of this state he was obliged to trust to some happy accident by which philosophic wisdom should happen to coincide with possession of ruling power in the state.

## 4. The "Individualistic" Ideal of the Eighteenth Century

In the eighteenth-century philosophy we find ourselves in a very different circle of ideas. "Nature" still means something antithetical to existing social organization; Plato exercised a great influence upon Rousseau. But the voice of nature now speaks for the diversity of individual talent and for the need of free development of individuality in all its variety. Education in accord with nature furnishes the goal and the method of instruction and discipline. Moreover, the native or original endowment was conceived, in extreme cases, as nonsocial or even as antisocial. Social arrangements were thought of as mere external expedients by which these nonsocial individuals might secure a greater amount of private happiness for themselves.

Nevertheless, these statements convey only an inadequate idea of the true significance of the movement. In reality its chief interest was in progress and in social progress. The seeming antisocial philosophy was a somewhat transparent mask for an impetus toward a wider and freer society—towards cosmopolitanism. The positive ideal was humanity. In membership in humanity, as distinct from a state, man's capacities would be liberated; while in existing political organizations his powers were hampered and distorted to meet the requirements and selfish interests of the rulers of the state. The doctrine of extreme individualism was but the counterpart, the obverse, of ideals of the indefinite perfectibility of man and of a social organization having a scope as wide as humanity. The emancipated individual was to become the organ and agent of a comprehensive and progressive society.

The heralds of this gospel were acutely conscious of the evils of the social estate in which they found themselves. They attributed these evils to the limitations imposed upon the free powers of man. Such limitation was both distorting and corrupting. Their impassioned devotion to emancipation of life from external restrictions which operated to the exclusive advantage of the class to whom a past feudal system consigned power, found intellectual formulation in a worship of nature. To give "nature" full swing was to replace an artificial, corrupt, and inequitable social order by a new and better kingdom of humanity. Unrestrained faith in Nature as both a model and a working power was strengthened by the advances of natural science. Inquiry freed from prejudice and artificial restraints of church and state had revealed that the world is a scene of law. The Newtonian solar system, which expressed the reign of natural law, was a scene of wonderful harmony, where every force balanced with every other. Natural law would accomplish the same result in human relations, if men would only get rid of the artificial man-imposed coercive restrictions.

Education in accord with nature was thought to be the first step in insuring this more social society. It was plainly seen that economic and political limitations were ultimately dependent upon limitations of thought and feeling. The first step in freeing men from external chains was to emancipate them from the internal chains of false beliefs and ideals. What was called social life, existing institutions, were too false and corrupt to be entrusted with this work. How could it be expected to undertake it when the undertaking meant its own destruction? "Nature" must then be the power to which the enterprise was to be left. Even the extreme sensationalistic theory of knowledge which was current derived itself from this conception. To insist that mind is originally passive and empty was one way of glorifying the possibilities of education. If the mind was a wax tablet to be written upon by objects, there were no limits to the possibility of education by means of the natural environment. And since the natural world of objects is a scene of harmonious "truth," this education would infallibly produce minds filled with the truth.

## 5. Education as National and as Social

As soon as the first enthusiasm for freedom waned, the weakness of the theory upon the constructive side became obvious. Merely to leave everything to nature was, after all, but to negate the very idea of education; it was to trust to the accidents of circumstance. Not only was some method required but also some positive organ, some administrative agency for carrying on the process of instruction. The "complete and harmonious development of all powers," having as its social counterpart an enlightened and progressive humanity, required definite organization for its realization. Private individuals here and there could proclaim the gospel; they could not execute the work. A Pestalozzi could try experiments and exhort philanthropically inclined persons having wealth and power to follow his example. But even Pestalozzi saw that any effective pursuit of the new educational ideal required the support of the state. The realization of the new education destined to produce a new society was, after all, dependent upon the activities of existing states. The movement for the democratic idea inevitably became a movement for publicly conducted and administered schools.

So far as Europe was concerned, the historic situation identified the movement for a state-supported education with the nationalistic movement in political life—a fact of incalculable significance for subsequent movements. Under the influence of German thought in particular, education became a civic function and the civic function was identified with the realization of the ideal of the national state. The "state" was substituted for humanity; cosmopolitanism gave way to nationalism. To form the citizen, not the "man," became the aim of education.[2] The historic situation to which reference is made is the after-effects of the Napoleonic conquests, especially in Germany. The German states felt (and subsequent events demonstrate the correctness of the belief) that systematic attention to education was the best means of recovering and maintaining their political integrity and power. Externally they were weak and divided. Under the leadership of Prussian statesmen they made this condition a stimulus to the development of an extensive and thoroughly grounded system of public education.

This change in practice necessarily brought about a change in theory. The individualistic theory receded into the background. The state furnished not only the instrumentalities of public education but also its goal. When the actual practice was such that the school system, from the elementary grades through the university faculties, supplied the patriotic citizen and soldier and the future state official and administrator and furnished the means for military, industrial, and political defense and expansion, it was impossible for theory not to emphasize the aim of social efficiency. And with the immense importance attached to the nationalistic state, surrounded by other competing and more or less hostile states, it was equally impossible to interpret social efficiency in terms of a vague cosmopolitan humanitarianism. Since the maintenance of a particular national sovereignty required subordination of individuals to the superior interests of the state both in military defense and in struggles for international supremacy in commerce, social efficiency was understood to imply a like subordination. The educational process was taken to be one of disciplinary training rather than of personal development. Since, however, the ideal of culture as complete development of personality persisted, educational philosophy attempted a reconciliation of the two ideas. The reconciliation took the form of the conception of the "organic" character of the state. The individual in his isolation is nothing; only in and through an absorption of the aims and meaning of organized institutions does he attain true personality. What appears to be his subordination to political authority and the demand for sacrifice of himself to the commands of his superiors is in reality but making his own the objective reason manifested in the state—the only way in which he can become truly rational. The notion of development which we have seen to be characteristic of institutional idealism (as in the Hegelian philosophy) was just such a deliberate effort to combine the two ideas of complete realization of personality and thoroughgoing "disciplinary" subordination to existing institutions.

The extent of the transformation of educational philosophy which occurred in Germany in the generation occupied by the struggle against Napoleon for national independence, may be gathered from Kant, who well expresses the earlier individual-cosmopolitan ideal. In his treatise on Pedagogics, consisting of lectures given in the later years of the eighteenth century, he defines education as the process by which man becomes man. Mankind begins its history submerged in nature—not as Man who is a creature of reason, while nature furnishes only instinct and appetite. Nature offers simply the germs which education is to develop and perfect. The peculiarity of truly human life is that man has to create himself by his own voluntary efforts; he has to make himself a truly moral, rational, and free being. This creative effort is carried on by the educational activities of slow generations. Its acceleration depends upon men consciously striving to educate their successors not for the existing state of affairs but so as to make possible a future better humanity. But there is the great difficulty. Each generation is inclined to educate its young so as to get along in the present world instead of with a view to the proper end of education: the promotion of the best possible realization of humanity as humanity. Parents educate their children so that they may get on; princes educate their subjects as instruments of their own purposes.

Who, then, shall conduct education so that humanity may improve? We must depend upon the efforts of enlightened men in their private capacity. "All culture begins with private men and spreads outward from them. Simply through the efforts of persons of enlarged inclinations, who are capable of grasping the ideal of a future better condition, is the gradual approximation of human nature to its end possible. . . . Rulers are simply interested in such training as will make their subjects better tools for their own intentions." Even the subsidy by rulers of privately conducted schools must be carefully safeguarded. For the rulers' interest in the welfare of their own nation instead of in what is best for humanity, will make them, if they give money for the schools, wish to draw their plans. We have in this view an express statement of the points characteristic of the eighteenth-century individualistic cosmo-politanism. The full development of private personality is identified with the aims of humanity as a whole and with the idea of progress. In addition we have an explicit fear of the hampering influence of a state-conducted and state-regulated education upon the attainment of these ideas. But in less than two decades after this time, Kant's philosophic successors, Fichte and Hegel, elaborated the idea that the chief function of the state is educational; that in particular the regeneration of Germany is to be accomplished by an education carried on in the interests of the state, and that the private individual is of necessity an egoistic, irrational being, enslaved to his appetites and to circumstances unless he submits voluntarily to the educative discipline of state institutions and laws. In this spirit, Germany was the first country to undertake a public, universal, and compulsory system of education extending from the primary school through the university, and to submit to jealous state regulation and supervision all private educational enterprises.

Two results should stand out from this brief historical survey. The first is that such terms as the individual and the social conceptions of education are quite meaningless taken at large, or apart from their context. Plato had the ideal of an education which should equate individual realization and social coherency and stability. His situation forced his ideal into the notion of a society organized in stratified classes, losing the individual in the class. The eighteenth-century educational philosophy was highly individualistic in form, but this form was inspired by a noble and generous social ideal: that of a society organized to include humanity, and providing for the indefinite perfectibility of mankind. The idealistic philosophy of Germany in the early nineteenth century endeavored again to equate the ideals of a free and complete development of cultured personality with social discipline and political subordination. It made the national state an intermediary between the realization of private personality on one side and of humanity on the other. Consequently, it is equally possible to state its animating principle with equal truth either in the classic terms of "harmonious development of all the powers of personality" or in the more recent terminology of "social efficiency." All this reenforces the statement which opens this chapter: The conception of education as a social process and function has no definite meaning until we define the kind of society we have in mind.

These considerations pave the way for our second conclusion. One of the fundamental problems of education in and for a democratic society is set by the conflict of a nationalistic and a wider social aim. The earlier cosmopolitan and "humanitarian" conception suffered both from vagueness and from lack of definite organs of execution and agencies of administration. In Europe, in the Continental states particularly, the new idea of the importance of education for human welfare and progress was captured by national interests and harnessed to do a work whose social aim was definitely narrow and exclusive. The social aim of education and its national aim were identified, and the result was a marked obscuring of the meaning of a social aim.

This confusion corresponds to the existing situation of human intercourse. On the one hand, science, commerce, and art transcend national boundaries. They are largely international in quality and method. They involve interdependencies and cooperation among the peoples inhabiting different countries. At the same time, the idea of national sovereignty has never been as accentuated in politics as it is at the present time. Each nation lives in a state of suppressed hostility and incipient war with its neighbors. Each is supposed to be the supreme judge of its own interests, and it is assumed as matter of course that each has interests which are exclusively its own. To question this is to question the very idea of national sovereignty which is assumed to be basic to political practice and political science. This contradiction (for it is nothing less) between the wider sphere of associated and mutually helpful social life and the narrower sphere of exclusive and hence potentially hostile pursuits and purposes, exacts of educational theory a clearer conception of the meaning of "social" as a function and test of education than has yet been attained.

Is it possible for an educational system to be conducted by a national state and yet the full social ends of the educative process not be restricted, constrained, and corrupted? Internally, the question has to face the tendencies, due to present economic conditions, which split society into classes some of which are made merely tools for the higher culture of others. Externally, the question is concerned with the reconciliation of national loyalty, of patriotism, with superior devotion to the things which unite men in common ends, irrespective of national political boundaries. Neither phase of the problem can be worked out by merely negative means. It is not enough to see to it that education is not actively used as an instrument to make easier the exploitation of one class by another. School facilities must be secured of such amplitude and efficiency as will in fact and not simply in name discount the effects of economic inequalities, and secure to all the wards of the nation equality of equipment for their future careers. Accomplishment of this end demands not only adequate administrative provision of school facilities, and such supplementation of family resources as will enable youth to take advantage of them, but also such modification of traditional ideals of culture, traditional subjects of study and traditional methods of teaching and discipline as will retain all the youth under educational influences until they are equipped to be masters of their own economic and social careers. The ideal may seem remote of execution, but the democratic ideal of education is a farcical yet tragic delusion except as the ideal more and more dominates our public system of education.

The same principle has application on the side of the considerations which concern the relations of one nation to another. It is not enough to teach the horrors of war and to avoid everything which would stimulate international jealousy and animosity. The emphasis must be put upon whatever binds people together in cooperative human pursuits and results, apart from geographical limitations. The secondary and provisional character of national sovereignty in respect to the fuller, freer, and more fruitful association and intercourse of all human beings with one another must be instilled as a working disposition of mind. If these applications seem to be remote from a consideration of the philosophy of education, the impression shows that the meaning of the idea of education previously developed has not been adequately grasped. This conclusion is bound up with the very idea of education as a freeing of individual capacity in a progressive growth directed to social aims. Otherwise a democratic criterion of education can only be inconsistently applied.

## Summary

Since education is a social process, and there are many kinds of societies, a criterion for educational criticism and construction implies a *particular* social ideal. The two points selected by which to measure the worth of a form of social life are the extent in which the interests of a group are shared by all its members, and the fullness and freedom with which it interacts with other groups. An undesirable society, in other words, is one which internally and externally sets up barriers to free intercourse and communication of experience. A society which makes provision for participation in its good of all its members on equal terms and which secures flexible readjustment of its institutions through interaction of the different forms of associated life is in so far democratic. Such a society must have a type of education which gives individuals a personal interest in social relationships and control, and the habits of mind which secure social changes without introducing disorder.

Three typical historic philosophies of education were considered from this point of view. The Platonic was found to have an ideal formally quite similar to that stated, but which was compromised in its working out by making a class rather than an individual the social unit. The so-called individualism of the eighteenth-century enlightenment was found to involve the notion of a society as broad as humanity, of whose progress the individual was to be the organ. But it lacked any agency for securing the development of its ideal as was evidenced in its falling back upon Nature. The institutional idealistic philosophies of the nineteenth century supplied this lack by making the national state the agency, but in so doing narrowed the conception of the social aim to those who were members of the same political unit, and reintroduced the idea of the subordination of the individual to the institution.

## 8. Aims in Education

### 1. The Nature of an Aim

The account of education given in our earlier chapters virtually anticipated the results reached in a discussion of the purport of education in a democratic community. For it assumed that the aim of education is to enable individuals to continue their education—or that the object and reward of learning is continued capacity for growth. Now this idea cannot be applied to *all* the members of a society except where intercourse of man with man is mutual, and except where there is adequate provision for the reconstruction of social habits and institutions by means of wide stimulation arising from equitably distributed interests. And this means a democratic society. In our search for aims in education, we are not concerned, therefore, with finding an end outside of the educative process to which education is subordinate. Our whole conception forbids. We are rather concerned with the contrast which exists when aims belong within the process in which they operate and when they are set up from without. And the latter state of affairs must obtain when social relationships are not equitably balanced. For in that case, some portions of the whole social group will find their aims determined by an external dictation; their aims will not arise from the free growth of their own experience, and their nominal aims will be means to more ulterior ends of others rather than truly their own.

Our first question is to define the nature of an aim so far as it falls within an activity, instead of being furnished from without. We approach the definition by a contrast of mere *results* with *ends*. Any exhibition of energy has results. The wind blows about the sands of the desert; the position of the grains is changed. Here is a result, an effect, but not an *end*. For there is nothing in the outcome which completes or fulfills what went before it. There is mere spatial redistribution. One state of affairs is just as good as any other. Consequently there is no basis upon which to select an earlier state of affairs as a beginning, a later as an end, and to consider what intervenes as a process of transformation and realization.

Consider for example the activities of bees in contrast with the changes in the sands when the wind blows them about. The results of the bees' actions may be called ends not because they are designed or consciously intended, but because they are true terminations or completions of what has preceded. When the bees gather pollen and make wax and build cells, each step prepares the way for the next. When cells are built, the queen lays eggs in them; when eggs are laid, they are sealed and bees brood them and keep them at a temperature required to hatch them. When they are hatched, bees feed the young till they can take care of themselves. Now we are so familiar with such facts, that we are apt to dismiss them on the ground that life and instinct are a kind of miraculous thing anyway. Thus we fail to note what the essential characteristic of the event is; namely, the significance of the temporal place and order of each element; the way each prior event leads into its successor while the successor takes up what is furnished and utilizes it for some other stage, until we arrive at the end, which, as it were, summarizes and finishes off the process.

Since aims relate always to results, the first thing to look to when it is a question of aims, is whether the work assigned possesses intrinsic continuity. Or is it a mere serial aggregate of acts, first doing one thing and then another? To talk about an educational aim when approximately each act of a pupil is dictated by the teacher, when the only order in the sequence of his acts is that which comes from the assignment of lessons and the giving of directions by another, is to talk nonsense. It is equally fatal to an aim to permit capricious or discontinuous action in the name of spontaneous self-expression. An aim implies an orderly and ordered activity, one in which the order consists in the progressive completing of a process. Given an activity having a time span and cumulative growth within the time succession, and aim means foresight in advance of the end or possible termination. If bees anticipated the consequences of their activity, if they perceived their end in imaginative foresight, they would have the primary element in an aim. Hence it is nonsense to talk about the aim of education—or any other undertaking—where conditions do not permit of foresight of results, and do not stimulate a person to look ahead to see what the outcome of a given activity is to be.

In the next place the aim as a foreseen end gives direction to the activity; it is not an idle view of a mere spectator, but influences the steps taken to reach the end. The foresight functions in three ways. In the first place, it involves careful observation of the given conditions to see what are the means available for reaching the end, and to discover the hindrances in the way. In the second place, it suggests the proper order or sequence in the use of means. It facilitates an economical selection and arrangement. In the third place, it makes choice of alternatives possible. If we can predict the outcome of acting this way or that, we can then compare the value of the two courses of action; we can pass judgment upon their relative desirability. If we know that stagnant water breeds mosquitoes and that they are likely to carry disease, we can, disliking that anticipated result, take steps to avert it. Since we do not anticipate results as mere intellectual onlookers, but as persons concerned in the outcome, we are partakers in the process which produces the result. We intervene to bring about this result or that.

Of course these three points are closely connected with one another. We can definitely foresee results only as we make careful scrutiny of present conditions, and the importance of the outcome supplies the motive for observations. The more adequate our observations, the more varied is the scene of conditions and obstructions that presents itself, and the more numerous are the alternatives between which choice may be made. In turn, the more numerous the recognized possibilities of the situation, or alternatives of action, the more meaning does the chosen activity possess, and the more flexibly controllable is it. Where only a single outcome has been thought of, the mind has nothing else to think of; the meaning attaching to the act is limited. One only steams ahead toward the mark. Sometimes such a narrow course may be effective. But if unexpected difficulties offer themselves, one has not as many resources at command as if he had chosen the same line of action after a broader survey of the possibilities of the field. He cannot make needed readjustments readily.

The net conclusion is that acting with an aim is all one with acting intelligently. To foresee a terminus of an act is to have a basis upon which to observe, to select, and to order objects and our own capacities. To do these things means to have a mind—for mind is precisely intentional purposeful activity controlled by perception of facts and their relationships to one another. To have a mind to do a thing is to foresee a future possibility; it is to have a plan for its accomplishment; it is to note the means which make the plan capable of execution and the obstructions in the way,—or, if it is really a *mind* to do the thing and not a vague aspiration—it is to have a plan which takes account of resources and difficulties. Mind is capacity to refer present conditions to future results, and future consequences to present conditions. And these traits are just what is meant by having an aim or a purpose. A man is stupid or blind or unintelligent—lacking in mind—just in the degree in which in any activity he does not know what he is about, namely, the probable consequences of his acts. A man is imperfectly intelligent when he contents himself with looser guesses about the outcome than is needful, just taking a chance with his luck, or when he forms plans apart from study of the actual conditions, including his own capacities. Such relative absence of mind means to make our feelings the measure of what is to happen. To be intelligent we must "stop, look, listen" in making the plan of an activity.

To identify acting with an aim and intelligent activity is enough to show its value—its function in experience. We are only too given to making an entity out of the abstract noun "consciousness." We forget that it comes from the adjective "conscious." To be conscious is to be aware of what we are about; conscious signifies the deliberate, observant, planning traits of activity. Consciousness is nothing which we have which gazes idly on the scene around one or which has impressions made upon it by physical things; it is a name for the purposeful quality of an activity, for the fact that it is directed by an aim. Put the other way about, to have an aim is to act with meaning, not like an automatic machine; it is to *mean* to do something and to perceive the meaning of things in the light of that intent.

## 2. The Criteria of Good Aims

We may apply the results of our discussion to a consideration of the criteria involved in a correct establishing of aims. (1) The aim set up must be an outgrowth of existing conditions. It must be based upon a consideration of what is already going on; upon the resources and difficulties of the situation. Theories about the proper end of our activities—educational and moral theories—often violate this principle. They assume ends lying *outside* our activities; ends foreign to the concrete make-up of the situation; ends which issue from some outside source. Then the problem is to bring our activities to bear upon the realization of these externally supplied ends. They are something for which we *ought* to act. In any case such "aims" limit intelligence; they are not the expression of mind in foresight, observation, and choice of the better among alternative possibilities. They limit intelligence because, given readymade, they must be imposed by some authority external to intelligence, leaving to the latter nothing but a mechanical choice of means.

(2) We have spoken as if aims could be completely formed prior to the attempt to realize them. This impression must now be qualified. The aim as it first emerges is a mere tentative sketch. The act of striving to realize it tests its worth. If it suffices to direct activity success-fully, nothing more is required, since its whole function is to set a mark in advance; and at times a mere hint may suffice. But usually—at least in complicated situations—acting upon it brings to light conditions which had been overlooked. This calls for revision of the original aim; it has to be added to and subtracted from. An aim must, then, be *flexible*; it must be capable of alteration to meet circumstances. An end established externally to the process of action is always rigid. Being inserted or imposed from without, it is not supposed to have a working relationship to the concrete conditions of the situation. What happens in the course

of action neither confirms, refutes, nor alters it. Such an end can only be insisted upon. The failure that results from its lack of adaptation is attributed simply to the perverseness of conditions, not to the fact that the end is not reasonable under the circumstances. The value of a legitimate aim, on the contrary, lies in the fact that we can use it to change conditions. It is a method for dealing with conditions so as to effect desirable alterations in them. A farmer who should passively accept things just as he finds them would make as great a mistake as he who framed his plans in complete disregard of what soil, climate, etc., permit. One of the evils of an abstract or remote external aim in education is that its very inapplicability in practice is likely to react into a haphazard snatching at immediate conditions. A good aim surveys the present state of experience of pupils, and forming a tentative plan of treatment, keeps the plan constantly in view and yet modifies it as conditions develop. The aim, in short, is experimental, and hence constantly growing as it is tested in action.

(3) The aim must always represent a freeing of activities. The term *end in view* is suggestive, for it puts before the mind the termination or conclusion of some process. The only way in which we can define an activity is by putting before ourselves the objects in which it terminates—as one's aim in shooting is the target. But we must remember that the *object* is only a mark or sign by which the mind specifies the *activity* one desires to carry out. Strictly speaking, not the target but *hitting* the target is the end in view; one *takes* aim by means of the target, but also by the sight on the gun. The different objects which are thought of are means of *directing* the activity. Thus one aims at, say, a rabbit; what he wants is to shoot straight: a certain kind of activity. Or, if it is the rabbit he wants, it is not rabbit apart from his activity, but as a factor in activity; he wants to eat the rabbit, or to show it as evidence of his marksmanship—he wants to do something with it. The doing with the thing, not the thing in isolation, is his end. The object is but a phase of the active end,—continuing the activity successfully. This is what is meant by the phrase, used above, "freeing activity."

In contrast with fulfilling some process in order that activity may go on, stands the static character of an end which is imposed from without the activity. It is always conceived of as fixed; it is *something* to be attained and possessed. When one has such a notion, activity is a mere unavoidable means to something else; it is not significant or important on its own account. As compared with the end it is but a necessary evil; something which must be gone through before one can reach the object which is alone worth while. In other words, the external idea of the aim leads to a separation of means from end, while an end which grows up within an activity as plan for its direction is always both ends and means, the distinction being only one of convenience. Every means is a temporary end until we have attained it. Every end becomes a means of carrying activity further as soon as it is achieved. We call it end when it marks off the future direction of the activity in which we are engaged; means when it marks off the present direction. Every divorce of end from means diminishes by that much the significance of the activity and tends to reduce it to a drudgery from which one would escape if he could. A farmer has to use plants and animals to carry on his farming activities. It certainly makes a great difference to his life whether he is fond of them, or whether he regards them merely as means which he has to employ to get something else in which alone he is interested. In the former case, his entire course of activity is significant; each phase of it has its own value. He has the experience of realizing his end at every stage; the postponed aim, or end in view, being merely a sight ahead by which to keep his activity going fully and freely. For if he does not look ahead, he is more likely to find himself blocked. The aim is as definitely a *means* of action as is any other portion of an activity.

## 3. Applications in Education

There is nothing peculiar about educational aims. They are just like aims in any directed occupation. The educator, like the farmer, has certain things to do, certain resources with which to do, and certain obstacles with which to contend. The conditions with which the farmer deals, whether as obstacles or resources, have their own structure and operation independently of any purpose of his. Seeds sprout, rain falls, the sun shines, insects devour, blight comes, the seasons change. His aim is simply to utilize these various conditions; to make his activities and their energies work together, instead of against one another. It would be absurd if the farmer set up a purpose of farming, without any reference to these conditions of soil, climate, characteristics of plant growth, etc. His purpose is simply a foresight of the consequences of his energies connected with those of the things about him, a foresight used to direct his movements from day to day. Foresight of possible consequences leads to more careful and extensive observation of the nature and performances of the things he had to do with, and to laying out a plan—that is, of a certain order in the acts to be performed.

It is the same with the educator, whether parent or teacher. It is as absurd for the latter to set up their "own" aims as the proper objects of the growth of the children as it would be for the farmer to set up an ideal of farming irrespective of conditions. Aims mean acceptance of responsibility for the observations, anticipations, and arrangements required in carrying on a function—whether farming or educating. Any aim is of value so far as it assists observation, choice, and planning in carrying on activity from moment to moment and hour to hour; if it gets in the way of the individual's own common sense (as it will surely do if imposed from without or accepted on authority) it does harm.

And it is well to remind ourselves that education as such has no aims. Only persons, parents, and teachers, etc., have aims, not an abstract idea like education. And consequently their purposes are indefinitely varied, differing with different children, changing as children grow and with the growth of experience on the part of the one who teaches. Even the most valid aims which can be put in words will, as words, do more harm than good unless one recognizes that they are not aims, but rather suggestions to educators as to how to observe, how to look ahead, and how to choose in liberating and directing the energies of the concrete situations in which they find themselves. As a recent writer has said: "To lead this boy to read Scott's novels instead of old Sleuth's stories; to teach this girl to sew; to root out the habit of bullying from John's make up; to prepare this class to study medicine,—these are samples of the millions of aims we have actually before us in the concrete work of education."

Bearing these qualifications in mind, we shall proceed to state some of the characteristics found in all good educational aims. (I) An educational aim must be founded upon the intrinsic activities and needs (including original instincts and acquired habits) of the given individual to be educated. The tendency of such an aim as preparation is, as we have seen, to omit existing powers, and find the aim in some remote accomplishment or responsibility. In general, there is a disposition to take considerations which are dear to the hearts of adults and set them up as ends irrespective of the capacities of those educated. There is also an inclination to propound aims which are so uniform as to neglect the specific powers and requirements of an individual, forgetting that all learning is something which happens to an individual at a given time and place. The larger range of perception of the adult is of great value in observing the abilities and weaknesses of the young, in deciding what they may amount to. Thus the artistic capacities of the adult exhibit what certain tendencies of the child are capable of; if we did not have the adult achievements we should be without assurance as to the significance of the drawing, reproducing, modeling, coloring activities of childhood. So if it were not for adult language, we should not be able to see the import of the babbling impulses of infancy. But it is one thing to use adult accomplishments as a context in which to place and survey the doings of childhood and youth; it is quite another to set them up as a fixed aim without regard to the concrete activities of those educated.

(2) An aim must be capable of translation into a method of cooperating with the activities of those undergoing instruction. It must suggest the kind of environment needed to liberate and to organize *their* capacities. Unless it lends itself to the construction of specific procedures, and unless these procedures test, correct, and amplify the aims, the latter is worthless. Instead of helping the specific task of teaching, it prevents the use of ordinary judgment in observing and sizing up the situation. It operates to exclude recognition of everything except what squares up with the fixed end in view. Every rigid aim just because it is rigidly given seems to render it unnecessary to give careful attention to concrete conditions. Since it *must* apply anyhow, what is the use of noting details which do not count?

The vice of externally imposed ends has deep roots. Teachers receive them from superior authorities; these authorities accept them from what is current in the community. The teachers impose them upon children. As a first consequence, the intelligence of the teacher is not free, it is confined to receiving the aims laid down from above. Too rarely is the individual teacher so free from the dictation of authoritative supervisor, textbook on methods, prescribed course of study, etc., that he can let his mind come to close quarters with the pupil's mind and the subject matter. This distrust of the teacher's experience is then reflected in lack of confidence in the responses of pupils. The latter receive their aims through a double or treble external imposition, and are constantly confused by the conflict between the aims which are natural to their own experience at the time and those in which they are taught to acquiesce. Until the democratic criterion of the intrinsic significance of every growing experience is recognized, we shall be intellectually confused by the demand for adaptation to external aims.

(3) Educators have to be on their guard against ends that are alleged to be general and ultimate. Every activity, however specific, is, of course, general in its ramified connections, for it leads out indefinitely into other things. So far as a general idea makes us more alive to these connections, it cannot be too general. But "general" also means "abstract," or detached from all specific context. And such abstractness means remoteness, and throws us back, once more, upon teaching and learning as mere means of getting ready for an end disconnected from the means. That education is literally and all the time its own reward means that no alleged study or discipline is educative unless it is worth while in its own immediate having. A truly general aim broadens the outlook; it stimulates one to take more consequences (connections) into account. This means a wider and more flexible observation of means. The more interacting forces, for example, the farmer takes into account, the more varied will be

his immediate resources. He will see a greater number of possible starting places, and a greater number of ways of getting at what he wants to do. The fuller one's conception of possible future achievements, the less his present activity is tied down to a small number of alternatives. If one knew enough, one could start almost anywhere and sustain his activities continuously and fruitfully.

Understanding then the term general or comprehensive aim simply in the sense of a broad survey of the field of present activities, we shall take up some of the larger ends which have currency in the educational theories of the day, and consider what light they throw upon the immediate concrete and diversified aims which are always the educator's real concern. We premise (as indeed immediately follows from what has been said) that there is no need of making a choice among them or regarding them as competitors. When we come to act in a tangible way we have to select or choose a particular act at a particular time, but any number of comprehensive ends may exist without competition, since they mean simply different ways of looking at the same scene. One cannot climb a number of different mountains simultaneously, but the views had when different mountains are ascended supplement one another: they do not set up incompatible, competing worlds. Or, putting the matter in a slightly different way, one statement of an end may suggest certain questions and observations, and another statement another set of questions, calling for other observations. Then the more general ends we have, the better. One statement will emphasize what another slurs over. What a plurality of hypotheses does for the scientific investigator, a plurality of stated aims may do for the instructor.

## Summary

An aim denotes the result of any natural process brought to consciousness and made a factor in determining present observation and choice of ways of acting. It signifies that an activity has become intelligent. Specifically it means foresight of the alternative consequences attendant upon acting in a given situation in different ways, and the use of what is anticipated to direct observation and experiment. A true aim is thus opposed at every point to an aim which is imposed upon a process of action from without. The latter is fixed and rigid; it is not a stimulus to intelligence in the given situation, but is an externally dictated order to do such and such things. Instead of connecting directly with present activities, it is remote, divorced from the means by which it is to be reached. Instead of suggesting a freer and better balanced activity, it is a limit set to activity. In education, the currency of these externally imposed aims is responsible for the emphasis put upon the notion of preparation for a remote future and for rendering the work of both teacher and pupil mechanical and slavish. . . .

## 10. Interest and Discipline

### 1. The Meaning of the Terms

We have already noticed the difference in the attitude of a spectator and of an agent or participant. The former is indifferent to what is going on; one result is just as good as another, since each is just something to look at. The latter is bound up with what is going on; its outcome makes a difference to him. His fortunes are more or less at stake in the issue of events. Consequently he does whatever he can to influence the direction present occurrences take. One is like a man in a prison cell watching the rain out of the window; it is all the same to him. The other is like a man who has planned an outing for the next day which continuing rain will frustrate. He cannot, to be sure, by his present reactions affect to-morrow's weather, but he may take some steps which will influence future happenings, if only to postpone the proposed picnic. If a man sees a carriage coming which may run over him, if he cannot stop its movement, he can at least get out of the way if he foresees the consequence in time. In many instances, he can intervene even more directly. The attitude of a participant in the course of affairs is thus a double one: there is solicitude, anxiety concerning future consequences, and a tendency to act to assure better, and avert worse, consequences.

There are words which denote this attitude: concern, interest. These words suggest that a person is bound up with the possibilities inhering in objects; that he is accordingly on the lookout for what they are likely to do to him; and that, on the basis of his expectation or foresight, he is eager to act so as to give things one turn rather than another. Interest and aims, concern and purpose, are necessarily connected. Such words as aim, intent, end, emphasize the *results* which are wanted and striven for; they take for granted the personal attitude of solicitude and attentive eagerness. Such words as interest, affection, concern, motivation, emphasize the bearing of what is foreseen upon the individual's fortunes, and his active desire to act to secure a possible result. They take for granted the objective changes. But the difference is but one of emphasis; the meaning that is shaded in one set of words is illuminated in the other. *What* is anticipated is objective and impersonal; to-morrow's rain; the possibility of being run over. But for an active being, a being who partakes of the consequences instead of standing aloof from them, there is at the same time a personal response. The difference imaginatively foreseen makes a present difference, which finds expression in solicitude and effort. While such words as affection, concern, and motive indicate an attitude of personal preference, they are always attitudes toward *objects*—toward what is foreseen. We may call the phase of objective foresight intellectual, and the phase of personal concern emotional and volitional, but there is no separation in the facts of the situation.

Such a separation could exist only if the personal attitudes ran their course in a world by themselves. But they are always responses to what is going on in the situation of which they are a part, and their successful or unsuccessful expression depends upon their interaction with other changes. Life activities flourish and fail only in connection with changes of the environment. They are literally bound up with these changes; our desires, emotions, and affections are but various ways in which our doings are tied up with the doings of things and persons about us. Instead of marking a purely personal or subjective realm, separated from the objective and impersonal, they indicate the non-existence of such a separate world. They afford convincing evidence that changes in things are not alien to the activities of a self, and that the career and welfare of the self are bound up with the movement of persons and things. Interest, concern, mean that self and world are engaged with each other in a developing situation.

The word interest, in its ordinary usage, expresses *(i)* the whole state of active development, *(ii)* the objective results that are foreseen and wanted, and *(iii)* the personal emotional inclination. *(i)* An occupation, employment, pursuit, business is often referred to as an interest. Thus we say that a man's interest is politics, or journalism, or philanthropy, or archaeology, or collecting Japanese prints, or banking. *(ii)* By an interest we also mean the point at which an object touches or engages a man; the point where it influences him. In some legal transactions a man has to prove "interest" in order to have a standing at court. He has to show that some proposed step concerns his affairs. A silent partner has an interest in a business, although he takes no active part in its conduct because its prosperity or decline affects his profits and liabilities. *(iii)* When we speak of a man as interested in this or that the emphasis falls directly upon his personal attitude. To be interested is to be absorbed in, wrapped up in, carried away by, some object. To take an interest is to be on the alert, to care about, to be attentive. We say of an interested person both that he has lost himself in some affair and that he has found himself in it. Both terms express the engrossment of the self in an object.

When the place of interest in education is spoken of in a depreciatory way, it will be found that the second of the meanings mentioned is first exaggerated and then isolated. Interest is taken to mean merely the effect of an object upon personal advantage or disadvantage, success or failure. Separated from any objective development of affairs, these are reduced to mere personal states of pleasure or pain. Educationally, it then follows that to attach importance to interest means to attach some feature of seductiveness to material otherwise indifferent; to secure attention and effort by offering a bribe of pleasure. This procedure is properly stigmatized as "soft" pedagogy; as a "soup-kitchen" theory of education.

But the objection is based upon the fact—or assumption—that the forms of skill to be acquired and the subject matter to be appropriated have no interest on their own account: in other words, they are supposed to be irrelevant to the normal activities of the pupils. The remedy is not in finding fault with the doctrine of interest, any more than it is to search for some pleasant bait that may be hitched to the alien material. It is to discover objects and modes of action, which are connected with present powers. The function of this material in engaging activity and carrying it on consistently and continuously *is* its interest. If the material operates in this way, there is no call either to hunt for devices which will make it interesting or to appeal to arbitrary, semi-coerced effort.

The word interest suggests, etymologically, what is *between,*—that which connects two things otherwise distant. In education, the distance covered may be looked at as temporal. The fact that a process takes time to mature is so obvious a fact that we rarely make it explicit. We overlook the fact that in growth there is ground to be covered between an initial stage of process and the completing period; that there is something intervening. In learning, the present powers of the pupil are the initial stage; the aim of the teacher represents the remote limit. Between the two lie *means*—that is middle conditions:—acts to be performed; difficulties to be overcome; appliances to be used. Only *through* them, in the literal time sense, will the initial activities reach a satisfactory consummation.

These intermediate conditions are of interest precisely because the development of existing activities into the foreseen and desired end depends upon them. To be means for the achieving of present tendencies, to be "between" the agent and his end, to be of interest, are different names for the same thing. When material has to be made interesting, it signifies that as presented, it lacks connection with purposes and present power: or that if the connection be there, it is not perceived. To make it interesting by leading one to realize the connection that exists is simply good sense; to make it interesting by extraneous and artificial inducements deserves all the bad names which have been applied to the doctrine of interest in education.

So much for the meaning of the term interest. Now for that of discipline. Where an activity takes time, where many means and obstacles lie between its initiation and completion, deliberation and persistence are required. It is obvious that a very large part of the everyday meaning of will is precisely the deliberate or conscious disposition to persist and endure in a planned course of action in spite of difficulties and contrary solicitations. A man of strong will, in the popular usage of the words, is a man who is neither fickle nor half-hearted in achieving chosen ends. His ability is executive; that is, he persistently and energetically strives to execute or carry out his aims. A weak will is unstable as water.

Clearly there are two factors in will. One has to do with the foresight of results, the other with the depth of hold the foreseen outcome has upon the person. (i) Obstinacy is persistence but it is not strength of volition. Obstinacy may be mere animal inertia and insensitiveness. A man keeps on doing a thing just because he has got started, not because of any clearly thought-out purpose. In fact, the obstinate man generally declines (although he may not be quite aware of his refusal) to make clear to himself what his proposed end is; he has a feeling that if he allowed himself to get a clear and full idea of it, it might not be worth while. Stubbornness shows itself even more in reluctance to criticize ends which present themselves than it does in persistence and energy in use of means to achieve the end. The really executive man is a man who ponders his ends, who makes his ideas of the results of his actions as clear and full as possible. The people we called weak-willed or self-indulgent always deceive themselves as to the consequences of their acts. They pick out some feature which is agreeable and neglect all attendant circumstances. When they begin to act, the disagreeable results they ignored begin to show themselves. They are discouraged, or complain of being thwarted in their good purpose by a hard fate, and shift to some other line of action. That the primary difference between strong and feeble volition is intellectual, consisting in the degree of persistent firmness and fullness with which consequences are thought out, cannot be over-emphasized.

(ii) There is, of course, such a thing as a speculative tracing out of results. Ends are then foreseen, but they do not lay deep hold of a person. They are something to look at and for curiosity to play with rather than something to achieve. There is no such thing as over-intellectuality, but there is such a thing as a one-sided intellectuality. A person "takes it out" as we say in considering the consequences of proposed lines of action. A certain flabbiness of fibre prevents the contemplated object from gripping him and engaging him in action. And most persons are naturally diverted from a proposed course of action by unusual, unforeseen obstacles, or by presentation of inducements to an action that is directly more agreeable.

A person who is trained to consider his actions, to undertake them deliberately, is in so far forth disciplined. Add to this ability a power to endure in an intelligently chosen course in face of distraction, confusion, and difficulty, and you have the essence of discipline. Discipline means power at command; mastery of the resources available for carrying through the action undertaken. To know what one is to do and to move to do it promptly and by use of the requisite means is to be disciplined, whether we are thinking of an army or a mind. Discipline is positive. To cow the spirit, to subdue inclination, to compel obedience, to mortify the flesh, to make a subordinate perform an uncongenial task—these things are or are not disciplinary according as they do or do not tend to the development of power to recognize what one is about and to persistence in accomplishment.

It is hardly necessary to press the point that interest and discipline are connected, not opposed. (i) Even the more purely intellectual phase of trained power—apprehension of what one is doing as exhibited in consequences—is not possible without interest. Deliberation will be perfunctory and superficial where there is no interest. Parents and teachers often complain—and correctly—that children "do not want to hear, or want to understand." Their minds are not upon the subject precisely because it does not touch them; it does not enter into their concerns. This is a state of things that needs to be remedied, but the remedy is not in the use of methods which increase indifference and aversion. Even punishing a child for inattention is one way of trying to make him realize that the matter is *not* a thing of complete unconcern; it is one way of arousing "interest," or bringing about a sense of connection. In the long run, its value is measured by whether it supplies a mere physical excitation to act in the way desired by the adult or whether it leads the child "to think"—that is, to reflect upon his acts and impregnate them with aims. (ii) That interest is requisite for executive persistence is even more obvious. Employers do not advertise for workmen who are not interested in what they are doing. If one were engaging a lawyer or a doctor, it would never occur to one to reason that the person engaged would stick to his work more conscientiously if it was so uncongenial to him that he did it merely from a sense of obligation. Interest measures—or rather is—the depth of the grip which the foreseen end has upon one in moving one to act for its realization.

## 2. The Importance of the Idea of Interest in Education

Interest represents the moving force of objects—whether perceived or presented in imagination—in any experience having a purpose. In the concrete, the value of recognizing the dynamic place of interest in an educative development is that it leads to considering individual children in their specific capabilities, needs, and preferences. One who recognizes the importance of interest will not assume that all minds work in the same way because they happen to have the same teacher and textbook. Attitudes and methods of approach and response vary with the specific appeal the same material makes, this appeal itself varying with difference of natural aptitude, of past experience, of plan of life, and so on. But the facts of interest also supply considerations of general value to the philosophy of education. Rightly understood, they put us on our guard against certain conceptions of mind and of subject matter which have had great vogue in philosophic thought in the past, and which exercise a serious hampering influence upon the conduct of instruction and discipline. Too frequently mind is set over the world of things and facts to be known; it is regarded as something existing in isolation, with mental states and operations that exist independently. Knowledge is then regarded as an external application of purely mental existences to the things to be known, or else as a result of the impressions which this outside subject matter makes on mind, or as a combination of the two. Subject matter is then regarded as something complete in itself; it is just something to be learned or known, either by the voluntary application of mind to it or through the impressions it makes on mind.

The facts of interest show that these conceptions are mythical. Mind appears in experience, as ability to respond to present stimuli on the basis of anticipation of future possible consequences, and with a view to controlling the kind of consequences that are to take place. The things, the subject matter known, consist of whatever is recognized as having a bearing upon the anticipated course of events, whether assisting or retarding it. These statements are too formal to be very intelligible. An illustration may clear up their significance.

You are engaged in a certain occupation, say writing with a typewriter. If you are an expert, your formed habits take care of the physical movements and leave your thoughts free to consider your topic. Suppose, however, you are not skilled, or that, even if you are, the machine does not work well. You then have to use intelligence. You do not wish to strike the keys at random and let the consequences be what they may; you wish to record certain words in a given order so as to make sense. You attend to the keys, to what you have written, to your movements, to the ribbon or the mechanism of the machine. Your attention is not distributed indifferently and miscellaneously to any and every detail. It is centered upon whatever has a bearing upon the effective pursuit of your occupation. Your look is ahead, and you are concerned to note the existing facts because and in so far as they are factors in the achievement of the result intended. You have to find out what your resources are, what conditions are at command, and what the difficulties and obstacles are. This foresight and this survey with reference to what is foreseen constitute mind. Action that does not involve such a forecast of results and such an examination of means and hindrances is either a matter of habit or else it is blind. In neither case is it intelligent. To be vague and uncertain as to what is intended and careless in observation of conditions of its realization is to be, in that degree, stupid or partially intelligent.

If we recur to the case where mind is not concerned with the physical manipulation of the instruments but with what one intends to write, the case is the same. There is an activity in process; one is taken up with the development of a theme. Unless one writes as a phonograph talks, this means intelligence; namely, alertness in foreseeing the various conclusions to which present data and considerations are tending, together with continually renewed observation and recollection to get hold of the subject matter which bears upon the conclusions to be reached. The whole attitude is one of concern with what is to be, and with what is so far as the latter enters into the movement towards the end. Leave out the direction which depends upon foresight of possible future results, and there is no intelligence in present behavior. Let there be imaginative forecast but no attention to the conditions upon which its attainment depends, and there is self-deception or idle dreaming—abortive intelligence.

If this illustration is typical, mind is not a name for something complete by itself; it is a name for a course of action in so far as that is intelligently directed; in so far, that is to say, as aims, ends, enter into it, with selection of means to further the attainment of aims. Intelligence is not a peculiar possession which a person owns; but a person is intelligent in so far as the activities in which he plays a part have the qualities mentioned. Nor are the activities in which a person engages, whether intelligently or not, exclusive properties of himself; they are something in which he *engages and partakes*. Other things, the independent changes of other things and persons, cooperate and hinder. The individual's act may be initial in a course of events, but the outcome depends upon the interaction of his response with energies supplied by other agencies. Conceive mind as anything but one factor partaking along with others in the production of consequences, and it becomes meaningless.

The problem of instruction is thus that of finding material which will engage a person in specific activities having an aim or purpose of moment or interest to him, and dealing with things not as gymnastic appliances but as conditions for the attainment of ends. The remedy for the evils attending the doctrine of formal discipline previously spoken of, is not to be found by substituting a doctrine of specialized disciplines, but by reforming the notion of mind and its training. Discovery of typical modes of activity, whether play or useful occupations, in which individuals are concerned, in whose outcome they recognize they have something at stake, and which cannot be carried through without reflection and use of judgment to select material of observation and recollection, is the remedy. In short, the root of the error long prevalent in the conception of training of mind consists in leaving out of account movements of things to future results in which an individual shares, and in the direction of which observation, imagination, and memory are enlisted. It consists in regarding mind as complete in itself, ready to be directly applied to a present material.

In historic practice the error has cut two ways. On one hand, it has screened and protected traditional studies and methods of teaching from intelligent criticism and needed revisions. To say that they are "disciplinary" has safeguarded them from all inquiry. It has not been enough to show that they were of no use in life or that they did not really contribute to the cultivation of the self. That they were "disciplinary" stifled every question, subdued every doubt, and removed the subject from the realm of rational discussion. By its nature, the allegation could not be checked up. Even when discipline did not accrue as matter of fact, when the pupil even grew in laxity of application and lost power of intelligent self-direction, the fault lay with him, not with the study or the methods of teaching. His failure was but proof that he needed more discipline, and thus afforded a reason for retaining the old methods. The responsibility was transferred from the educator to the pupil because the material did not have to meet specific tests; it did not have to be shown that it fulfilled any particular need or served any specific end. It was designed to discipline in general, and if it failed, it was because the individual was unwilling to be disciplined.

In the other direction, the tendency was towards a negative conception of discipline, instead of an identification of it with growth in constructive power of achievement. As we have already seen, will means an attitude towards the future, towards the production of possible consequences, an attitude involving effort to foresee clearly and comprehensively the probable results of ways of acting, and an active identification with some anticipated consequences. Identification of will, or effort, with mere strain, results when a mind is set up, endowed with powers that are only to be applied to existing material. A person just either will or will not apply himself to the matter in hand. The more indifferent the subject matter, the less concern it has for the habits and preferences of the individual, the more demand there is for an effort to bring the mind to bear upon it—and hence the more discipline of will. To attend to material because there is something to be done in which the person is concerned is *not* disciplinary in this view; not even if it results in a desirable increase of constructive power. Application just for the sake of application, for the sake of training, is alone disciplinary. This is more likely to occur if the subject matter presented is uncongenial, for then there is no motive (so it is supposed) except the acknowledgment of duty or the value of discipline. The logical result is expressed with literal truth in the words of an American humorist: "It makes no difference what you teach a boy so long as he doesn't like it."

The counterpart of the isolation of mind from activities dealing with objects to accomplish ends is isolation of the subject matter to be learned. In the traditional schemes of education, subject matter means so much material to be studied. Various branches of study represent so many independent branches, each having its principles of arrangement complete within itself. History is one such group of facts; algebra another; geography another, and so on till we have run through the entire curriculum. Having a ready-made existence on their own account, their relation to mind is exhausted in what they furnish it to acquire. This idea corresponds to the conventional practice in which the program of school work, for the day, month, and successive years, consists of "studies" all marked off from one another, and each supposed to be complete by itself—for educational purposes at least.

Later on a chapter is devoted to the special consideration of the meaning of the subject matter of instruction. At this point, we need only to say that, in contrast with the traditional theory, anything which intelligence studies represents things in the part which they play in the carrying forward of active lines of interest. Just as one "studies" his typewriter as part of the operation of putting it to use to effect results, so with any fact or truth. It becomes an object of study—that is, of inquiry and reflection—when it figures as a factor to be reckoned with in the completion of a course of events in which one is engaged and by whose outcome one is affected. Numbers are not objects of study just because they are numbers already constituting a branch of learning called mathematics, but because they represent qualities and relations of the world in which our action goes on, because they are factors upon which the accomplishment of our purposes depends. Stated thus broadly, the formula may appear abstract. Translated into details, it means that the act of learning or studying is artificial and ineffective in the degree in which pupils are merely presented with a lesson to be learned. Study is effectual in the degree in which the pupil realizes the place of the numerical truth he is dealing with in carrying to fruition activities in which he is concerned. This connection of an object and a topic with the promotion of an activity having a purpose is the first and the last word of a genuine theory of interest in education.

### 3. Some Social Aspects of the Question

While the theoretical errors of which we have been speaking have their expressions in the conduct of schools, they are themselves the outcome of conditions of social life. A change confined to the theoretical conviction of educators will not remove the difficulties, though it should render more effective efforts to modify social conditions. Men's fundamental attitudes toward the world are fixed by the scope and qualities of the activities in which they partake. The ideal of interest is exemplified in the artistic attitude. Art is neither merely internal nor merely external; merely mental nor merely physical. Like every mode of action, it brings about changes in the world. The changes made by some actions (those which by contrast may be called mechanical) are external; they are just shifting things about. No ideal reward, no enrichment of emotion and intellect, accompanies them. Others contribute to the maintenance of life, and to its external adornment and display. Many of our existing social activities, industrial and political, fall in these two classes. Neither the people who engage in them, nor those who are directly affected by them, are capable of full and free interest in their work. Because of the lack of any purpose in the work for the one doing it, or because of the restricted character of its aim, intelligence is not adequately engaged. The same conditions force many people back upon themselves. They take refuge in an inner play of sentiment and fancies. They are aesthetic but not artistic, since their feelings and ideas are turned upon themselves, instead of being methods in acts which modify conditions. Their mental life is sentimental; an enjoyment of an inner landscape. Even the pursuit of science may become an asylum of refuge from the hard conditions of life—not a temporary retreat for the sake of recuperation and clarification in future dealings with the world. The very word art may become associated not with specific transformation of things, making them more significant for mind, but with stimulations of eccentric fancy and with emotional indulgences. The separation and mutual contempt of the "practical" man and the man of theory or culture, the divorce of fine and industrial arts, are indications of this situation. Thus interest and mind are either narrowed, or else made perverse. Compare what was said in an earlier chapter about the one-sided meanings which have come to attach to the ideas of efficiency and of culture.

This state of affairs must exist so far as society is organized on a basis of division between laboring classes and leisure classes. The intelligence of those who do things becomes hard in the unremitting struggle with things; that of those freed from the discipline of occupation becomes luxurious and effeminate. Moreover, the majority of human beings still lack economic freedom. Their pursuits are fixed by accident and necessity of circumstance; they are not the normal expression of their own powers interacting with the needs and resources of the environment. Our economic conditions still relegate many men to a servile status. As a consequence, the intelligence of those in control of the practical situation is not liberal. Instead of playing freely upon the subjugation of the world for human ends, it is devoted to the manipulation of other men for ends that are non-human in so far as they are exclusive.

This state of affairs explains many things in our historic educational traditions. It throws light upon the clash of aims manifested in different portions of the school system; the narrowly utilitarian character of most elementary education, and the narrowly disciplinary or cultural character of most higher education. It accounts for the tendency to isolate intellectual matters till knowledge is scholastic, academic, and professionally technical, and for the widespread conviction that liberal education is opposed to the requirements of an education which shall count in the vocations of life.

But it also helps define the peculiar problem of present education. The school cannot immediately escape from the ideals set by prior social conditions. But it should contribute through the type of intellectual and emotional disposition which it forms to the improvement of those conditions. And just here the true conceptions of interest and discipline are full of significance. Persons whose interests have been enlarged and intelligence trained by dealing with things and facts in active occupations having a purpose (whether in play or work) will be those most likely to escape the alternatives of an academic and aloof knowledge and a hard, narrow, and merely "practical" practice. To organize education so that natural active tendencies shall be fully enlisted in doing something, while seeing to it that the doing requires observation, the acquisition of information, and the use of a constructive imagination, is what most needs to be done to improve social conditions. To oscillate between drill exercises that strive to attain efficiency in outward doing without the use of intelligence, and an accumulation of knowledge that is supposed to be an ultimate end in itself, means that education accepts the present social conditions as final, and thereby takes upon itself the responsibility for perpetuating them. A reorganization of education so that learning takes place in connection with the intelligent carrying forward of purposeful activities is a slow work. It can only be accomplished piecemeal, a step at a time. But this is not a reason for nominally accepting one educational philosophy and accommodating ourselves in practice to another. It is a challenge to undertake the task of reorganization courageously and to keep at it persistently.

## Summary

Interest and discipline are correlative aspects of activity having an aim. Interest means that one is identified with the objects which define the activity and which furnish the means and obstacles to its realization. Any activity with an aim implies a distinction between an earlier incomplete phase and later completing phase; it implies also intermediate steps. To have an interest is to take things as entering into such a continuously developing situation, instead of taking them in isolation. The time difference between the given incomplete state of affairs and the desired fulfillment exacts effort in transformation; it demands continuity of attention and endurance. This attitude is what is practically meant by will. Discipline or development of power of continuous attention is its fruit.

The significance of this doctrine for the theory of education is twofold. On the one hand it protects us from the notion that mind and mental states are something complete in themselves, which then happen to be applied to some ready-made objects and topics so that knowledge results. It shows that mind and intelligent or purposeful engagement in a course of action into which things enter are identical. Hence to develop and train mind is to provide an environment which induces such activity. On the other side, it protects us from the notion that subject matter on its side is something isolated and independent. It shows that subject matter of learning is identical with all the objects, ideas, and principles which enter as resources or obstacles into the continuous intentional pursuit of a course of action. The developing course of action, whose end and conditions are perceived, is the unity which holds together what are often divided into an independent mind on one side and an independent world of objects and facts on the other. . . .

## 12. Thinking in Education

### 1. The Essentials of Method

No one doubts, theoretically, the importance of fostering in school good habits of thinking. But apart from the fact that the acknowledgment is not so great in practice as in theory, there is not adequate theoretical recognition that all which the school can or need do for pupils, so far as their *minds* are concerned (that is, leaving out certain specialized muscular abilities), is to develop their ability to think. The parceling out of instruction among various ends such as acquisition of skill (in reading, spelling, writing, drawing, reciting); acquiring information (in history and geography), *and* training of thinking is a measure of the ineffective way in which we accomplish all three. Thinking which is not connected with increase of efficiency in action, and with learning more about ourselves and the world in which we live, has something the matter with it just as thought. And skill obtained apart from thinking is not connected with any sense of the purposes for which it is to be used. It consequently leaves a man at the mercy of his routine habits and of the authoritative control of others, who know what they are about and who are not especially scrupulous as to their means of achievement. And information severed from thoughtful action is dead, a mind-crushing load. Since it simulates knowledge and thereby develops the poison of conceit, it is a most powerful obstacle to further growth in the grace of intelligence. The sole direct path to enduring improvement in the methods of instruction and learning consists in centering upon the conditions which exact, promote, and test thinking. Thinking *is* the method of intelligent learning, of learning that employs and rewards mind. We speak, legitimately enough, about the method of thinking, but the important thing to bear in mind about method is that thinking is method, the method of intelligent experience in the course which it takes.

I. The initial stage of that developing experience which is called thinking is *experience.* This remark may sound like a silly truism. It ought to be one; but unfortunately it is not. On the contrary, thinking is often regarded both in philosophic theory and in educational practice as something cut off from experience, and capable of being cultivated in isolation. In fact, the inherent limitations of experience are often urged as the sufficient ground for attention to thinking. Experience is then thought to be confined to the senses and appetites; to a mere material world, while thinking proceeds from a higher faculty (of reason), and is occupied with spiritual or at least literary things. So, oftentimes, a sharp distinction is made between pure mathematics as a peculiarly fit subject matter of thought (since it has nothing to do with physical existences) and applied mathematics, which has utilitarian but not mental value.

Speaking generally, the fundamental fallacy in methods of instruction lies in supposing that experience on the part of pupils may be assumed. What is here insisted upon is the necessity of an actual empirical situation as the initiating phase of thought. Experience is here taken as previously defined: trying to do something and having the thing perceptibly do something to one in return. The fallacy consists in supposing that we can begin with ready-made subject matter of arithmetic, or geography, or whatever, irrespective of some direct personal experience of a situation. Even the kindergarten and Montessori techniques are so anxious to get at intellectual distinctions, without "waste of time," that they tend to ignore—or reduce—the immediate crude handling of the familiar material of experience, and to introduce pupils at once to material which expresses the intellectual distinctions which adults have made. But the first stage of contact with any new material, at whatever age of maturity, must inevitably be of the trial and error sort. An individual must actually try, in play or work, to do something with material in carrying out his own impulsive activity, and then note the interaction of his energy and that of the material employed. This is what happens when a child at first begins to build with blocks, and it is equally what happens when a scientific man in his laboratory begins to experiment with unfamiliar objects.

Hence the first approach to any subject in school, if thought is to be aroused and not words acquired, should be as unscholastic as possible. To realize what an experience, or empirical situation, means, we have to call to mind the sort of situation that presents itself outside of school; the sort of occupations that interest and engage activity in ordinary life. And careful inspection of methods which are permanently successful in formal education, whether in arithmetic or learning to read, or studying geography, or learning physics or a foreign language, will reveal that they depend for their efficiency upon the fact that they go back to the type of the situation which causes reflection out of school in ordinary life. They give the pupils something to do, not something to learn; and the doing is of such a nature as to demand thinking, or the intentional noting of connections; learning naturally results.

That the situation should be of such a nature as to arouse thinking means of course that it should suggest something to do which is not either routine or capricious—something, in other words, presenting what is new (and hence uncertain or problematic) and yet sufficiently connected with existing habits to call out an effective response. An effective response means one which accomplishes a perceptible result, in distinction from a purely haphazard activity, where the consequences cannot be mentally connected with what is done. The most significant question which can be asked, accordingly, about any situation or experience proposed to induce learning is what quality of problem it involves.

At first thought, it might seem as if usual school methods measured well up to the standard here set. The giving of problems, the putting of questions, the assigning of tasks, the magnifying of difficulties, is a large part of school work. But it is indispensable to discriminate between genuine and simulated or mock problems. The following questions may aid in making such discrimination. *(a)* Is there anything *but* a problem? Does the question naturally suggest itself within some situation of personal experience? Or is it an aloof thing, a problem only for the purposes of conveying instruction in some school topic? Is it the sort of trying that would arouse observation and engage experimentation outside of school? *(b)* Is it the pupil's own problem, or is it the teacher's or textbook's problem, made a problem for the pupil only because he cannot get the required mark or be promoted or win the teacher's approval, unless he deals with it? Obviously, these two questions overlap. They are two ways of getting at the same point: Is the experience a personal thing of such a nature as inherently to stimulate and direct observation of the connections involved, and to lead to inference and its testing? Or is it imposed from without, and is the pupil's problem simply to meet the external requirement?

Such questions may give us pause in deciding upon the extent to which current practices are adapted to develop reflective habits. The physical equipment and arrangements of the average schoolroom are hostile to the existence of real situations of experience. What is there similar to the conditions of everyday life which will generate difficulties? Almost everything testifies to the great premium put upon listening, reading, and the reproduction of what is told and read. It is hardly possible to overstate the contrast between such conditions and the situations of active contact with things and persons in the home, on the playground, in fulfilling of ordinary responsibilities of life. Much of it is not even comparable with the questions which may arise in the mind of a boy or girl in conversing with others or in reading books outside of the school. No one has ever explained why children are so full of questions outside of the school (so that they pester grown-up persons if they get any encouragement), and the conspicuous absence of display of curiosity about the subject matter of school lessons. Reflection on this striking contrast will throw light upon the question of how far customary school conditions supply a context of experience in which problems naturally suggest themselves. No amount of improvement in the personal technique of the instructor will wholly remedy this state of things. There must be more actual material, more *stuff*, more appliances, and more opportunities for doing things, before the gap can be overcome. And where children are engaged in doing things and in discussing what arises in the course of their doing, it is found, even with comparatively indifferent modes of instruction, that children's inquiries are spontaneous and numerous, and the proposals of solution advanced, varied, and ingenious.

As a consequence of the absence of the materials and occupations which generate real problems, the pupil's problems are not his; or, rather, they are his *only as* a pupil, not as a human being. Hence the lamentable waste in carrying over such expertness as is achieved in dealing with them to the affairs of life beyond the schoolroom. A pupil has a problem, but it is the problem of meeting the peculiar requirements set by the teacher. His problem becomes that of finding out what the teacher wants, what will satisfy the teacher in recitation and examination and outward deportment. Relationship to subject matter is no longer direct. The occasions and material of thought are not found in the arithmetic or the history or geography itself, but in skillfully adapting that material to the teacher's requirements. The pupil studies, but unconsciously to himself the objects of his study are the conventions and standards of the school system and school authority, not the nominal "studies." The thinking thus evoked is artifically one-sided at the best. At its worst, the problem of the pupil is not how to meet the requirements of school life, but how to *seem* to meet them—or, how to come near enough to meeting them to slide along without an undue amount of friction. The type of judgment formed by these devices is not a desirable addition to character. If these statements give too highly colored a picture of usual school methods, the exaggeration may at least serve to illustrate the point: the need of active pursuits, involving the use of material to accomplish purposes, if there are to be situations which normally generate problems occasioning thoughtful inquiry.

II. There must be *data* at command to supply the considerations required in dealing with the specific difficulty which has presented itself. Teachers following a "developing" method sometimes tell children to think things out for themselves as if they could spin them out of their own heads. The material of thinking is not thoughts, but actions, facts, events, and the relations of things. In other words, to think effectively one must have had, or now have, experiences which will furnish him resources for coping with the difficulty at hand. A difficulty is an indispensable stimulus to thinking, but not all difficulties call out thinking. Sometimes they overwhelm and submerge and discourage. The perplexing situation must be sufficiently like situations which have already been dealt with so that pupils will have some control of the means of handling it. A large part of the art of instruction lies in making the difficulty of new problems large enough to challenge thought, and small enough so that, in addition to the confusion naturally attending the novel elements, there shall be luminous familiar spots from which helpful suggestions may spring.

In one sense, it is a matter of indifference by what psychological means the subject matter for reflection is provided. Memory, observation, reading, communication, are all avenues for supplying data. The relative proportion to be obtained from each is a matter of the specific features of the particular problem in hand. It is foolish to insist upon observation of objects presented to the senses if the student is so familiar with the objects that he could just as well recall the facts independently. It is possible to induce undue and crippling dependence upon sense-presentations. No one can carry around with him a museum of all the things whose properties will assist the conduct of thought. A well-trained mind is one that has a maximum of resources behind it, so to speak, and that is accustomed to go over its past experiences to see what they yield. On the other hand, a quality or relation of even a familiar object may previously have been passed over, and be just the fact that is helpful in dealing with the question. In this case direct observation is called for. The same principle applies to the use to be made of observation on one hand and of reading and "telling" on the other. Direct observation is naturally more vivid and vital. But it has its limitations; and in any case it is a necessary part of education that one should acquire the ability to supplement the narrowness of his immediately personal experiences by utilizing the experiences of others. Excessive reliance upon others for data (whether got from reading or listening) is to be depreciated. Most objectionable of all is the probability that others, the book or the teacher, will supply solutions ready-made, instead of giving material that the student has to adapt and apply to the question in hand for himself.

There is no inconsistency in saying that in schools there is usually both too much and too little information supplied by others. The accumulation and acquisition of information for purposes of reproduction in recitation and examination is made too much of. "Knowledge," in the sense of information, means the working capital, the indispensable resources, of further inquiry; of finding out, or learning, more things. Frequently it is treated as an end itself, and then the goal becomes to heap it up and display it when called for. This static, cold-storage ideal of knowledge is inimical to educative development. It not only lets occasions for thinking go unused, but it swamps thinking. No one could construct a house on ground cluttered with miscellaneous junk. Pupils who have stored their "minds" with all kinds of material which they have never put to intellectual uses are sure to be hampered when they try to think. They have no practice in selecting what is appropriate, and no criterion to go by; everything is on the same dead static level. On the other hand, it is quite open to question whether, if information actually functioned in experience through use in application to the student's own purposes, there would not be need of more varied resources in books, pictures, and talks than are usually at command.

III. The correlate in thinking of facts, data, knowledge already acquired, is suggestions, inferences, conjectured meanings, suppositions, tentative explanations:—*ideas*, in short. Careful observation and recollection determine what is given, what is already there, and hence assured. They cannot furnish what is lacking. They define, clarify, and locate the question; they cannot supply its answer. Projection, invention, ingenuity, devising come in for that purpose. The data *arouse* suggestions, and only by reference to the specific data can we pass upon the appropriateness of the suggestions. But the suggestions run beyond what is, as yet, actually *given* in experience. They forecast possible results, things *to* do, not facts (things already done). Inference is always an invasion of the unknown, a leap from the known.

In this sense, a thought (what a thing suggests but is not as it is presented) is creative,—an incursion into the novel. It involves some inventiveness. What is suggested must, indeed, be familiar in *some* context; the novelty, the inventive devising, clings to the new light in which it is seen, the different use to which it is put. When Newton thought of his theory of gravitation, the creative aspect of his thought was not found in its materials. They were familiar; many of them commonplaces—sun, moon, planets, weight, distance, mass, square of numbers. These were not original ideas; they were established facts. His originality lay in the *use* to which these familiar acquaintances were put by introduction into an unfamiliar context. The same is true of every striking scientific discovery, every great invention, every admirable artistic production. Only silly folk identify creative originality with the extraordinary and fanciful; others recognize that its measure lies in putting everyday things to uses which had not occurred to others. The operation is novel, not the materials out of which it is constructed.

The educational conclusion which follows is that *all* thinking is original in a projection of considerations which have not been previously apprehended. The child of three who discovers what can be done with blocks, or of six who finds out what he can make by putting five cents and five cents together, is really a discoverer, even though everybody else in the world knows it. There is a genuine increment of experience; not another item mechanically added on, but enrichment by a new quality. The charm which the spontaneity of little children has for sympathetic observers is due to perception of this intellectual originality. The joy which children themselves experience is the joy of intellectual constructiveness—of creativeness, if the word may be used without misunderstanding.

The educational moral I am chiefly concerned to draw is not, however, that teachers would find their own work less of a grind and strain if school conditions favored learning in the sense of discovery and not in that of storing away what others pour into them; nor that it would be possible to give even children and youth the delights of personal intellectual productiveness—true and important as are these things. It is that no thought, no idea, can possibly be conveyed as an idea from one person to another. When it is told, it is, to the one to whom it is told, another given fact, not an idea. The communication may stimulate the other person to realize the question for himself and to think out a like idea, or it may smother his intellectual interest and suppress his dawning effort at thought. But what he *directly* gets cannot be an idea. Only by wrestling with the conditions of the problem at first hand, seeking and finding his own way out, does he think. When the parent or teacher has provided the conditions which stimulate thinking and has taken a sympathetic attitude toward the activities of the learner by entering into a common or conjoint experience, all has been done which a second party can do to instigate learning. The rest lies with the one directly concerned. If he cannot devise his own solution (not of course in isolation, but in correspondence with the teacher and other pupils) and find his own way out he will not learn, not even if he can recite some correct answer with one hundred per cent accuracy. We can and do supply ready-made "ideas" by the thousand; we do not usually take much pains to see that the one learning engages in significant situations where his own activities generate, support, and clinch ideas—that is, perceived meanings or connections. This does not mean that the teacher is to stand off and look on; the alternative to furnishing ready-made subject matter and listening to the accuracy with which it is reproduced is not quiescence, but participation, sharing, in an activity. In such shared activity, the teacher is a learner, and the learner is, without knowing it, a teacher—and upon the whole, the less consciousness there is, on either side, of either giving or receiving instruction, the better.

IV. Ideas, as we have seen, whether they be humble guesses or dignified theories, are anticipations of possible solutions. They are anticipations of some continuity or connection of an activity and a consequence which has not as yet shown itself. They are therefore tested by the operation of acting upon them. They are to guide and organize further observations, recollections, and experiments. They are intermediate in learning, not final. All educational reformers, as we have had occasion to remark, are given to attacking the passivity of traditional education. They have opposed pouring in from without, and absorbing like a sponge; they have attacked drilling in material as into hard and resisting rock. But it is not easy to secure conditions which will make the getting of an idea identical with having an experience which widens and makes more precise our contact with the environment. Activity, even self-activity, is too easily thought of as something merely mental, cooped up within the head, or finding expression only through the vocal organs.

While the need of application of ideas gained in study is acknowledged by all the more successful methods of instruction, the exercises in application are sometimes treated as devices for *fixing* what has already been learned and for getting greater practical skill in its manipulation. These results are genuine and not to be despised. But practice in applying what has been gained in study ought primarily to have an intellectual quality. As we have already seen, thoughts just as thoughts are incomplete. At best they are tentative; they are suggestions, indications. They are standpoints and methods for dealing with situations of experience. Till they are applied in these situations they lack full point and reality. Only application tests them, and only testing confers full meaning and a sense of their reality. Short of use made of them, they tend to segregate into a peculiar world of their own. It may be seriously questioned whether the philosophies (to which reference has been made in section 2 of chapter 10) which isolate mind and set it over against the world did not have their origin in the fact that the reflective or theoretical class of men elaborated a large stock of ideas which social conditions did not allow them to act upon and test. Consequently men were thrown back into their own thoughts as ends in themselves.

However this may be, there can be no doubt that a peculiar artificiality attaches to much of what is learned in schools. It can hardly be said that many students consciously think of the subject matter as unreal; but it assuredly does not possess for them the kind of reality which the subject matter of their vital experiences possesses. They learn not to expect that sort of reality of it; they become habituated to treating it as having reality for the purposes of recitations, lessons, and examinations. That it should remain inert for the experiences of daily life is more or less a matter of course. The bad effects are twofold. Ordinary experience does not receive the enrichment which it should; it is not fertilized by school learning. And the attitudes which spring from getting used to and accepting half-understood and ill-digested material weaken vigor and efficiency of thought.

If we have dwelt especially on the negative side, it is for the sake of suggesting positive measures adapted to the effectual development of thought. Where schools are equipped with laboratories, shops, and gardens, where dramatizations, plays, and games are freely used, opportunities exist for reproducing situations of life, and for acquiring and applying information and ideas in the carrying forward of progressive experiences. Ideas are not segregated, they do not form an isolated island. They animate and enrich the ordinary course of life. Information is vitalized by its function; by the place it occupies in direction of action.

The phrase "opportunities exist" is used purposely. They may not be taken advantage of; it is possible to employ manual and constructive activities in a physical way, as means of getting just bodily skill; or they may be used almost exclusively for "utilitarian," *i.e.*, pecuniary, ends. But the disposition on the part of upholders of "cultural" education to assume that such activities are merely physical or professional in quality, is itself a product of the philosophies which isolate mind from direction of the course of experience and hence from action upon and with things. When the "mental" is regarded as a self-contained separate realm, a counterpart fate befalls bodily activity and movements. They are regarded as at the best mere external annexes to mind. They may be necessary for the satisfaction of bodily needs and the attainment of external decency and comfort, but they do not occupy a necessary place in mind nor enact an indispensable role in the completion of thought. Hence they have no place in a liberal education—*i.e.*, one which is concerned with the interests of intelligence. If they come in at all, it is as a concession to the material needs of the masses. That they should be allowed to invade the education of the élite is unspeakable. This conclusion follows irresistibly from the isolated conception of mind, but by the same logic it disappears when we perceive what mind really is—namely, the purposive and directive factor in the development of experience.

While it is desirable that all educational institutions should be equipped so as to give students an opportunity for acquiring and testing ideas and information in active pursuits typifying important social situations, it will, doubtless, be a long time before all of them are thus furnished. But this state of affairs does not afford instructors an excuse for folding their hands and persisting in methods which segregate school knowledge. Every recitation in every subject gives an opportunity for establishing cross connections between the subject matter of the lesson and the wider and more direct experiences of everyday life. Classroom instruction falls into three kinds. The least desirable treats each lesson as an independent whole. It does not put upon the student the responsibility of finding points of contact between it and other lessons in the same subject, or other subjects of study. Wiser teachers see to it that the student is systematically led to utilize his earlier lessons to help understand the present one, and also to use the present to throw additional light upon what has already been acquired. Results are better, but school subject matter is still isolated. Save by accident, out-of-school experience is left in its crude and comparatively irreflective state. It is not subject to the refining and expanding influences of the more accurate and comprehensive material of direct instruction. The latter is not motivated and impregnated with a sense of reality by being intermingled with the realities of everyday life. The best type of teaching bears in mind the desirability of affecting this interconnection. It puts the student in the habitual attitude of finding points of contact and mutual bearings.

## Summary

Processes of instruction are unified in the degree in which they centre in the production of good habits of thinking. While we may speak, without error, of the method of thought, the important thing is that thinking is the method of an educative experience. The essentials of method are therefore identical with the essentials of reflection. They are first that the pupil have a genuine situation of experience—that there be a continuous activity in which he is interested for its own sake; secondly, that a genuine problem develop within this situation as a stimulus to thought; third, that he possess the information and make the observations needed to deal with it; fourth, that suggested solutions occur to him which he shall be responsible for developing in an orderly way; fifth, that he have opportunity and occasion to test his ideas by application, to make their meaning clear and to discover for himself their validity.

## 13. The Nature of Method

### 1. The Unity of Subject Matter and Method

The trinity of school topics is subject matter, methods, and administration or government. We have been concerned with the two former in recent chapters. It remains to disentangle them from the context in which they have been referred to, and discuss explicitly their nature. We shall begin with the topic of method, since that lies closest to the considerations of the last chapter. Before taking it up, it may be well, however, to call express attention to one implication of our theory; the connection of subject matter and method with each other. The idea that mind and the world of things and persons are two separate and independent realms—a theory which philosophically is known as dualism—carries with it the conclusion that method and subject matter of instruction are separate affairs. Subject matter then becomes a ready-made systematized classification of the facts and principles of the world of nature and man. Method then has for its province a consideration of the ways in which this antecedent subject matter may be best presented to and impressed upon the mind; or, a consideration of the ways in which the mind may be externally brought to bear upon the matter so as to facilitate its acquisition and possession. In theory, at least, one might deduce from a science of the mind as something existing by itself a complete theory of methods of learning, with no knowledge of the subjects to which the methods are to be applied. Since many who are actually most proficient in various branches of subject matter are wholly innocent of these methods, this state of affairs gives opportunity for the retort that pedagogy, as an alleged science of methods of the mind in learning, is futile;—a mere screen for concealing the necessity a teacher is under of profound and accurate acquaintance with the subject in hand.

But since thinking is a directed movement of subject matter to a completing issue, and since mind is the deliberate and intentional phase of the process, the notion of any such split is radically false. The fact that the material of a science is organized is evidence that it has already been subjected to intelligence; it has been methodized, so to say. Zoology as a systematic branch of knowledge represents crude, scattered facts of our ordinary acquaintance with animals after they have been subjected to careful examination, to deliberate supplementation, and to arrangement to bring out connections which assist observation, memory, and further inquiry. Instead of furnishing a starting point for learning, they mark out a consummation. Method means that arrangement *of* subject matter which makes it most effective in use. Never is method something outside of the material.

How about method from the standpoint of an individual who is dealing with subject matter? Again, it is not something external. It is simply an effective treatment *of* material—efficiency meaning such treatment as utilizes the material (puts it to a purpose) with a minimum of waste of time and energy. We can distinguish a *way* of acting, and discuss it by itself; but the way *exists* only as a way-of-dealing-with-material. Method is not antithetical to subject matter; it is the effective direction of subject matter to desired results. It is antithetical to random and ill-considered action,—ill-considered signifying ill-adapted.

The statement that method means directed movement of subject matter towards ends is formal. An illustration may give it content. Every artist must have a method, a technique, in doing his work. Piano playing is not hitting the keys at random. It is an orderly way of using them, and the order is not something which exists ready-made in the musician's hands or brain prior to an activity dealing with the piano. Order is found in the disposition of acts which use the piano and the hands and brain so as to achieve the result intended. It is the action of the piano directed to accomplish the purpose of the piano as a musical instrument. It is the same with "pedagogical" method. The only difference is that the piano is a mechanism constructed in advance for a single end; while the material of study is capable of indefinite uses. But even in this regard the illustration may apply if we consider the infinite variety of kinds of music which a piano may produce, and the variations in technique required in the different musical results secured. Method in any case is but an effective way of employing some material for some end.

These considerations may be generalized by going back to the conception of experience. Experience as the perception of the connection between something tried and something undergone in consequence is a process. Apart from effort to control the course which the process takes, there is no distinction of subject matter and method. There is simply an activity which includes both what an individual does and what the environment does. A piano player who had perfect mastery of his instrument would have no occasion to distinguish between his contribution and that of the piano. In well-formed, smooth-running functions of any sort,—skating, conversing, hearing music, enjoying a landscape,—there is no consciousness of separation of the method of the person and of the subject matter. In whole-hearted play and work there is the same phenomenon.

When we reflect upon an experience instead of just having it, we inevitably distinguish between our own attitude and the objects toward which we sustain the attitude. When a man is eating, he is eating *food*. He does not divide his act into eating *and* food. But if he makes a scientific investigation of the act, such a discrimination is the first thing he would effect. He would examine on the one hand the properties of the nutritive material, and on the other hand the acts of the organism in appropriating and digesting. Such reflection upon experience gives rise to a distinction of *what* we experience (the experienc*ed*) and the experienc*ing*—the *how*. When we give names to this distinction we have subject matter and method as our terms. There is the thing seen, heard, loved, hated, imagined, and there is the act of seeing, hearing, loving, hating, imagining, etc.

This distinction is so natural and so important for certain purposes, that we are only too apt to regard it as a separation in existence and not as a distinction in thought. Then we make a division between a self and the environment or world. This separation is the root of the dualism of method and subject matter. That is, we assume that knowing, feeling, willing, etc., are things which belong to the self or mind in its isolation, and which then may be brought to bear upon an independent subject matter. We assume that the things which belong in isolation to the self or mind have their own laws of operation irrespective of the modes of active energy of the object. These laws are supposed to furnish method. It would be no less absurd to suppose that men can eat without eating something, or that the structure and movements of the jaws, throat muscles, the digestive activities of stomach, etc., are not what they are *because* of the material with which their activity is engaged. Just as the organs of the organism are a continuous part of the very world in which food materials exist, so the capacities of seeing, hearing, loving, imagining are intrinsically connected with the subject matter of the world. They are more truly ways in which the environment enters into experience and functions there than they are independent acts brought to bear upon things. Experience, in short, is not a combination of mind and world, subject and object, method and subject matter, but is a single continuous interaction of a great diversity (literally countless in number) of energies.

For the purpose of *controlling* the course of direction which the moving unity of experience takes we draw a mental distinction between the how and the what. While there is no *way* of walking or of eating or of learning over and above the actual walking, eating, and studying, there are certain elements in the act which give the key to its more effective control. Special attention to these elements makes them more obvious to perception (letting other factors recede for the time being from conspicuous recognition). Getting an idea of *how* the experience proceeds indicates to us what factors must be secured or modified in order that it may go on more successfully. This is only a somewhat elaborate way of saying that if a man watches carefully the growth of several plants, some of which do well and some of which amount to little or nothing, he may be able to detect the special conditions upon which the prosperous development of a plant depends. These conditions, stated in an orderly sequence, would constitute the method or way or manner of its growth. There is no difference between the growth of a plant and the prosperous development of an experience. It is not easy, in either case, to seize upon just the factors which make for its best movement. But study of cases of success and failure and minute and extensive comparison, helps to seize upon causes. When we have arranged these causes in order, we have a method of procedure or a technique.

A consideration of some evils in education that flow from the isolation of method from subject matter will make the point more definite. *(i)* In the first place, there is the neglect (of which we have spoken) of concrete situations of experience. There can be no discovery of a method without cases to be studied. The method is derived from observation of what actually happens, with a view to seeing that it happen better next time. But in instruction and discipline, there is rarely sufficient opportunity for children and youth to have the direct normal experiences from which educators might derive an idea of method or order of best development. Experiences are had under conditions of such constraint that they throw little or no light upon the normal course of an experience to its fruition. "Methods" have then to be authoritatively recommended to teachers, instead of being an expression of their own intelligent observations. Under such circumstances, they have a mechanical uniformity, assumed to be alike for all minds. Where flexible personal experiences are promoted by providing an environment which calls out directed occupations in work and play, the methods ascertained will vary with individuals—for it is certain that each individual has something characteristic in his way of going at things.

*(ii)* In the second place, the notion of methods isolated from subject matter is responsible for the false conceptions of discipline and interest already noted. When the effective way of managing material is treated as something readymade apart from material, there are just three possible ways in which to establish a relationship lacking by assumption. One is to utilize excitement, shock of pleasure, tickling the palate. Another is to make the consequences of not attending painful; we may use the menace of harm to motivate concern with the alien subject matter. Or a direct appeal may be made to the person to put forth effort without any reason. We may rely upon immediate strain of "will." In practice, however, the latter method is effectual only when instigated by fear of unpleasant results.

*(iii)* In the third place, the act of learning is made a direct and conscious end in itself. Under normal conditions, learning is a product and reward of occupation with subject matter. Children do not set out, consciously, to learn walking or talking. One sets out to give his impulses for communication and for fuller intercourse with others a show. He learns in consequence of his direct activities. The better methods of teaching a child, say, to read, follow the same road. They do not fix his attention upon the fact that he has to learn something and so make his attitude self-conscious and constrained. They engage his activities, and in the process of engagement he learns: the same is true of the more successful methods in dealing with number or whatever. But when the subject matter is not used in carrying forward impulses and habits to significant results, it is just something to be learned. The pupil's attitude to it is just that of having to learn it. Conditions more unfavorable to an alert and concentrated response would be hard to devise. Frontal attacks are even more wasteful in learning than in war. This does not mean, however, that students are to be seduced unaware into preoccupation with lessons. It means that they shall be occupied with them for real reasons or ends, and not just as something to be learned. This is accomplished whenever the pupil perceives the place occupied by the subject matter in the fulfilling of some experience.

*(iv)* In the fourth place, under the influence of the conception of the separation of mind and material, method tends to be reduced to a cut and dried routine, to following mechanically prescribed steps. No one can tell in how many school-rooms children reciting in arithmetic or grammar are compelled to go through, under the alleged sanction of method, certain preordained verbal formulae. Instead of being encouraged to attack their topics directly, experimenting with methods that seem promising and learning to discriminate by the consequences that accrue, it is assumed that there is one fixed method to be followed. It is also naïvely assumed that if the pupils make their statements and explanations in a certain form of "analysis," their mental habits will in time conform. Nothing has brought pedagogical theory into greater disrepute than the belief that it is identified with handing out to teachers recipes and models to be followed in teaching. Flexibility and initiative in dealing with problems are characteristic of any conception to which method is a way of managing material to develop a conclusion. Mechanical rigid woodenness is an inevitable corollary of any theory which separates mind from activity motivated by a purpose.

## 2. Method as General and as Individual

In brief, the method of teaching is the method of an art, of action intelligently directed by ends. But the practice of a fine art is far from being a matter of extemporized inspirations. Study of the operations and results of those in the past who have greatly succeeded is essential. There is always a tradition, or schools of art, definite enough to impress beginners, and often to take them captive. Methods of artists in every branch depend upon thorough acquaintance with materials and tools; the painter must know canvas, pigments, brushes, and the technique of manipulation of all his appliances. Attainment of this knowledge requires persistent and concentrated attention to objective materials. The artist studies the progress of his own attempts to see what succeeds and what fails. The assumption that there are no alternatives between following ready-made rules and trusting to native gifts, the inspiration of the moment and undirected "hard work," is contradicted by the procedures of every art.

Such matters as knowledge of the past, of current technique, of materials, of the ways in which one's own best results are assured, supply the material for what may be called *general* method. There exists a cumulative body of fairly stable methods for reaching results, a body authorized by past experience and by intellectual analysis, which an individual ignores at his peril. As was pointed out in the discussion of habit-forming (p. 410), there is always a danger that these methods will become mechanized and rigid, mastering an agent instead of being powers at command for his own ends. But it is also true that the innovator who achieves anything enduring, whose work is more than a passing sensation, utilizes classic methods more than may appear to himself or to his critics. He devotes them to new uses, and in so far transforms them.

Education also has its general methods. And if the application of this remark is more obvious in the case of the teacher than of the pupil, it is equally real in the case of the latter. Part of his learning, a very important part, consists in *becoming* master of the methods which the experience of others has shown to be most efficient in like cases of getting knowledge. These general methods are in no way opposed to individual initiative and originality—to personal ways of doing things. On the contrary they are reenforcements of them. For there is radical difference between even the most general method and a prescribed rule. The latter is a *direct* guide to action; the former operates indirectly through the enlightenment it supplies as to ends and means. It operates, that is to say, through intelligence, and not through conformity to orders externally imposed. Ability to use even in a masterly way an established technique gives no warranty of artistic work, for the latter also depends upon an animating idea.

If knowledge of methods used by others does not directly tell us what to do, or furnish ready-made models, how does it operate? What is meant by calling a method intellectual? Take the case of a physician. No mode of behavior more imperiously demands knowledge of established modes of diagnosis and treatment than does his. But after all cases are *like*, not identical. To be used intelligently, existing practices, however authorized they may be, have to be adapted to the exigencies of particular cases. Accordingly, recognized procedures indicate to the physician what inquiries to set on foot for himself, what measures to *try*. They are standpoints from which to carry on investigations; they economize a survey of the features of the particular case by suggesting the things to be especially looked into. The physician's own personal attitudes, his own ways (individual methods) of dealing with the situation in which he is concerned, are not subordinated to the general principles of procedure, but are facilitated and directed by the latter. The instance may serve to point out the value to the teacher of a knowledge of the psychological methods and the empirical devices found useful in the past. When they get in the way of his own common sense, when they come between him and the situation in which he has to act, they are worse than useless. But if he has acquired them as intellectual aids in sizing up the needs, resources, and difficulties of the unique experiences in which he engages, they are of constructive value. In the last resort, just because *everything* depends upon his own methods of response, *much* depends upon how far he can utilize, in making his own response, the knowledge which has accrued in the experience of others.

As already intimated, every word of this account is directly applicable also to the method of the pupil, the way of learning. To suppose that students, whether in the primary school or in the university, can be supplied with models of method to be followed in acquiring and expounding a subject is to fall into a self-deception that has lamentable consequences. (See p. 454.) One must make his own reaction in any case. Indications of the standardized or general methods used in like cases by others—particularly by those who are already experts—are of worth or of harm according as they make his personal reaction more intelligent or as they induce a person to dispense with exercise of his own judgment.

If what was said earlier (see p. 447) about originality of thought seemed overstrained, demanding more of education than the capacities of average human nature permit, the difficulty is that we lie under the incubus of a superstition. We have set up the notion of mind at large, of intellectual method that is the same for all. Then we regard individuals as differing in the *quantity* of mind with which they are charged. Ordinary persons are then expected to be ordinary. Only the exceptional are allowed to have originality. The measure of difference between the average student and the genius is a measure of the absence of originality in the former. But this notion of mind in general is a fiction. How one person's abilities compare in quantity with those of another is none of the teacher's business. It is irrelevant to his work. What is required is that every individual shall have opportunities to employ his own powers in activities that have meaning. Mind, individual method, originality (these are convertible terms) signify the *quality* of purposive or directed action. If we act upon this conviction, we shall secure more originality even by the conventional standard than now develops. Imposing an alleged uniform general method upon everybody breeds mediocrity in all but the very exceptional. And measuring originality by deviation from the mass breeds eccentricity in them. Thus we stifle the distinctive quality of the many, and save in rare instances (like, say, that of Darwin) infect the rare geniuses with an unwholesome quality.

## 3. The Traits of Individual Method

The most general features of the method of knowing have been given in our chapter on thinking. They are the features of the reflective situation: Problem, collection and analysis *of data*, projection and elaboration of suggestions or ideas, experimental application and testing; the resulting conclusion or judgment. The specific elements of an individual's method or way of attack upon a problem are found ultimately in his native tendencies and his acquired habits and interests. The method of one will vary from that of another (and *properly* vary) as his original instinctive capacities vary, as his past experiences and his preferences vary. Those who have already studied these matters are in possession of information which will help teachers in understanding the responses different pupils make, and help them in guiding these responses to greater efficiency. Child-study, psychology, and a knowledge of social environment supplement the personal acquaintance gained by the teacher. But methods remain the personal concern, approach, and attack of an individual, and no catalogue can ever exhaust their diversity of form and tint.

Some attitudes may be named, however, which are central in effective intellectual ways of dealing with subject matter. Among the most important are directness, open-mindedness, single-mindedness (or whole-heartedness), and responsibility.

1. It is easier to indicate what is meant by directness through negative terms than in positive ones. Self-consciousness, embarrassment, and constraint are its menacing foes. They indicate that a person is not immediately concerned with subject matter. Something has come between which deflects concern to side issues. A self-conscious person is partly thinking about his problem and partly about what others think of his performances. Diverted energy means loss of power and confusion of ideas. Taking an attitude is by no means identical with being conscious of one's attitude. The former is spontaneous, naïve, and simple. It is a sign of whole-souled relationship between a person and what he is dealing with. The latter is not of necessity abnormal. It is sometimes the easiest way of correcting a false method of approach, and of improving the effectiveness of the means one is employing,—as golf players, piano players, public speakers, etc., have occasionally to give especial attention to their position and movements. But this need *is* occasional and temporary. When it is effectual a person thinks of himself in terms of what is to be done, as one means among others of the realization of and end—as in the case of a tennis player practicing to get the "feel" of a stroke. In abnormal cases, one thinks of himself not as part of the agencies of execution, but as a separate object—as when the player strikes an attitude thinking of the impression it will make upon spectators, or is worried because of the impression he fears his movements give rise to.

Confidence is a good name for what is intended by the term directness. It should not be confused, however, with *self*-confidence which may be a form of self-consciousness—or of "cheek." Confidence is not a name for what one thinks or feels about his attitude; it is not reflex. It denotes the straight-forwardness with which one goes at what he has to do. It denotes not *conscious* trust in the efficacy of one's powers but unconscious faith in the possibilities of the situation. It signifies rising to the needs of the situation.

We have already pointed out (see p. 454) the objections to making students emphatically aware of the fact that they are studying or learning. Just in the degree in which they are induced by the conditions to be so aware, they are *not* studying and learning. They are in a divided and complicated attitude. Whatever methods of a teacher call a pupil's attention off from what he has to do and transfer it to his own attitude towards what he is doing impair directness of concern and action. Persisted in, the pupil acquires a permanent tendency to fumble, to gaze about aimlessly, to look for some clue of action beside that which the subject matter supplies. Dependence upon extraneous suggestions and directions, a state of foggy confusion, take the place of that sureness with which children (and grown-up people who have not been sophisticated by "education") confront the situations of life.

2. Open-mindedness. Partiality is, as we have seen, an accompaniment of the existence of interest, since this means sharing, partaking, taking sides in some movement. All the more reason, therefore, for an attitude of mind which actively welcomes suggestions and relevant information from all sides. In the chapter on Aims it was shown that foreseen ends are factors in the development of a changing situation. They are the means by which the direction of action is controlled. They are subordinate to the situation, therefore, not the situation to them. They are not ends in the sense of finalities to which everything must be bent and sacrificed. They are, as foreseen, *means* of guiding the development of a situation. A target is not the future goal of shooting; it is the centering factor in a present shooting. Openness of mind means accessibility of mind to any and every consideration that will throw light upon the situation that needs to be cleared up, and that will help determine the consequences of acting this way or that. Efficiency in accomplishing ends which have been settled upon as unalterable can coexist with a narrowly opened mind. But intellectual growth means constant expansion of horizons and consequent formation of new purposes and new responses. These are impossible without an active disposition to welcome points of view hitherto alien; an active desire to entertain considerations which modify existing purposes. Retention considerations which modify existing purposes. Retention of capacity to grow is the reward of such intellectual hospitality. The worst thing about stubbornness of mind, about prejudices, is that they arrest development; they shut the mind off from new stimuli. Open-mindedness means retention of the childlike attitude; closed-mindedness means premature intellectual old age.

Exorbitant desire for uniformity of procedure and for prompt external results are the chief foes which the open-minded attitude meets in school. The teacher who does not permit and encourage diversity of operation in dealing with questions is imposing intellectual blinders upon pupils—restricting their vision to the one path the teacher's mind happens to approve. Probably the chief cause of devotion to rigidity of method is, however, that it seems to promise speedy, accurately measurable, correct results. The zeal for "answers" is the explanation of much of the zeal for rigid and mechanical methods. Forcing and overpressure have the same origin, and the same result upon alert and varied intellectual interest.

Open-mindedness is not the same as empty-mindedness. To hang out a sign saying "Come right in; there is no one at home" is not the equivalent of hospitality. But there is a kind of passivity, willingness to let experiences accumulate and sink in and ripen, which is an essential of development. Results (external answers or solutions) may be hurried; processes may not be forced. They take their own time to mature. Were all instructors to realize that the quality of mental process, not the production of correct answers, is the measure of educative growth something hardly less than a revolution in teaching would be worked.

3. Single-mindedness. So far as the word is concerned, much that was said under the head of "directness" is applicable. But what the word is here intended to convey is *completeness* of interest, unity of purpose; the absence of suppressed but effectual ulterior aims for which the professed aim is but a mask. It is equivalent to mental integrity. Absorption, engrossment, full concern with subject matter for its own sake, nurture it. Divided interest and evasion destroy it.

Intellectual integrity, honesty, and sincerity are at bottom not matters of conscious purpose but of quality of active response. Their acquisition is fostered of course by conscious intent, but self-deception is very easy. Desires are urgent. When the demands and wishes of others forbid their direct expression they are easily driven into subterranean and deep channels. Entire surrender, and whole-hearted adoption of the course of action demanded by others are almost impossible. Deliberate revolt or deliberate attempts to deceive others may result. But the more frequent outcome is a confused and divided state of interest in which one is fooled as to one's own real intent. One tries to serve two masters at once. Social instincts, the strong desire to please others and get their approval, social training, the general sense of duty and of authority, apprehension of penalty, all lead to a half-hearted effort to conform, to "pay attention to the lesson," or whatever the requirement is. Amiable individuals want to do what they are expected to do. Consciously the pupil thinks he is doing this. But his own desires are not abolished. Only their evident exhibition is suppressed. Strain of attention to what is hostile to desire is irksome; in spite of one's *conscious* wish, the underlying desires determine the main course of thought, the deeper emotional responses. The mind wanders from the nominal subject and devotes itself to what is intrinsically more desirable. A systematized divided attention expressing the duplicity of the state of desire is the result.

One has only to recall his own experiences in school or at the present time when outwardly employed in actions which do not engage one's desires and purposes, to realize how prevalent is this attitude of divided attention—double-mindedness. We are so used to it that we take it for granted that a considerable amount of it is necessary. It may be; if so, it is the more important to face its bad intellectual effects. Obvious is the loss of energy of thought immediately available when one is consciously trying (or trying to seem to try) to attend to one matter, while unconsciously one's imagination is spontaneously going out to more congenial affairs. More subtle and more permanently crippling to efficiency of intellectual activity is a fostering of habitual self-deception, with the confused sense of reality which accompanies it. A double standard of reality, one for our own private and more or less concealed interests, and another for public and acknowledged concerns, hampers, in most of us, integrity and completeness of mental action. Equally serious is the fact that a split is set up between conscious thought and attention and impulsive blind affection and desire. Reflective dealings with the material of instruction is constrained and half-hearted; attention wanders. The topics to which it wanders are unavowed and hence intellectually illicit; transactions with them are furtive. The discipline that comes from regulating response by deliberate inquiry having a purpose fails; worse than that, the deepest concern and most congenial enterprises of the imagination (since they centre about the things dearest to desire) are casual, concealed. They enter into action in ways which are unacknowledged. Not subject to rectification by consideration of consequences, they are demoralizing.

School conditions favorable to this division of mind between avowed, public, and socially responsible undertakings, and private, ill-regulated, and suppressed indulgences of thought are not hard to find. What is sometimes called "stern discipline," *i.e.*, external coercive pressure, has this tendency. Motivation through rewards extraneous to the thing to be done has a like effect. Everything that makes schooling merely preparatory works in this direction. Ends being beyond the pupil's present grasp, other agencies have to be found to procure immediate attention to assigned tasks. Some responses are secured, but desires and affections not enlisted must find other outlets. Not less serious is exaggerated emphasis upon drill exercises designed to produce skill in action, independent of any engagement of thought—exercises having no purpose but the production of automatic skill. Nature abhors a mental vacuum. What do teachers imagine is happening to thought and emotion when the latter get no outlet in the things of immediate activity? Were they merely kept in temporary abeyance, or even only calloused, it would not be a matter of so much moment. But they are not abolished; they are not suspended; they are not suppressed—save with reference to the task in question. They follow their own chaotic and undisciplined course. What is native, spontaneous, and vital in mental reaction goes unused and untested, and the habits formed are such that these qualities become less and less available for public and avowed ends.

4. Responsibility. By responsibility as an element in intellectual attitude is meant the disposition to consider in advance the probable consequences of any projected step and deliberately to accept them: to accept them in the sense of taking them into account, acknowledging them in action, not yielding a mere verbal assent. Ideas, as we have seen, are intrinsically standpoints and methods for bringing about a solution of a perplexing situation; forecasts calculated to influence responses. It is only too easy to think that one accepts a statement or believes a suggested truth when one has not considered its implications; when one has made but a cursory and superficial survey of what further things one is committed to by acceptance. Observation and recognition, belief and assent, then become names for lazy acquiescence in what is externally presented.

It would be much better to have fewer facts and truths in instruction—that is, fewer things supposedly accepted,—if a smaller number of situations could be intellectually worked out to the point where conviction meant something real—some identification of the self with the type of conduct demanded by facts and foresight of results. The most permanent bad results of undue complication of school subjects and congestion of school studies and lessons are not the worry, nervous strain, and superficial acquaintance that follow (serious as these are), but the failure to make clear what is involved in really knowing and believing a thing. Intellectual responsibility means severe standards in this regard. These standards can be built up only through practice in following up and acting upon the meaning of what is acquired.

Intellectual *thoroughness* is thus another name for the attitude we are considering. There is a kind of thoroughness which is almost purely physical: the kind that signifies mechanical and exhausting drill upon all the details of a subject. Intellectual thoroughness is *seeing a thing through*. It depends upon a unity of purpose to which details are subordinated, not upon presenting a multitude of disconnected details. It is manifested in the firmness with which the full meaning of the purpose is developed, not in attention, however "conscientious" it may be, to the steps of action externally imposed and directed.

## Summary

Method is a statement of the way the subject matter of an experience develops most effectively and fruitfully. It is derived, accordingly, from observation of the course of experiences where there is no conscious distinction of personal attitude and manner from material dealt with. The assumption that method is something separate is connected with the notion of the isolation of mind and self from the world of things. It makes instruction and learning formal, mechanical, constrained. While methods are individualized, certain features of the normal course of an experience to its fruition may be discriminated, because of the fund of wisdom derived from prior experiences and because of general similarities in the materials dealt with from time to time. Expressed in terms of the attitude of the individual the traits of good method are straightforwardness, flexible intellectual interest or open-minded will to learn, integrity of purpose, and acceptance of responsibility for the consequences of one's activity including thought.

## 14. The Nature of Subject Matter

### 1. Subject Matter of Educator and of Learner

So far as the nature of subject matter in principle is concerned, there is nothing to add to what has been said (see p. 440). It consists of the facts observed, recalled, read, and talked about, and the ideas suggested, in course of a development of a situation having a purpose. This statement needs to be rendered more specific by connecting it with the materials of school instruction, the studies which make up the curriculum. What is the significance of our definition in application to reading, writing, mathematics, history, nature study, drawing, singing, physics, chemistry, modern and foreign languages, and so on?

Let us recur to two of the points made earlier in our discussion. The educator's part in the enterprise of education is to furnish the environment which stimulates responses and directs the learner's course. In last analysis, *all* that the educator can do is modify stimuli so that response will as surely as is possible result in the formation of desirable intellectual and emotional dispositions. Obviously studies or the subject matter of the curriculum have intimately to do with this business of supplying an environment. The other point is the necessity of a social environment to give meaning to habits formed. In what we have termed informal education, subject matter is carried directly in the matrix of social intercourse. It is what the persons with whom an individual associates do and say. This fact gives a clue to the understanding of the subject matter of formal or deliberate instruction. A connecting link is found in the stories, traditions, songs, and liturgies which accompany the doings and rites of a primitive social group. They represent the stock of meanings which have been precipitated out of previous experience, which are so prized by the group as to be identified with their conception of their own collective life. Not being obviously a part of the skill exhibited in the daily occupations of eating, hunting, making war and peace, constructing rugs, pottery, and baskets, etc., they are consciously impressed upon the young; often, as in the initiation ceremonies, with intense emotional fervor. Even more pains are consciously taken to perpetuate the myths, legends, and sacred verbal formulae of the group than to transmit the directly useful customs of the group just because they cannot be picked up, as the latter can be in the ordinary processes of association.

As the social group grows more complex, involving a greater number of acquired skills which are dependent, either in fact or in the belief of the group, upon standard ideas deposited from past experience, the content of social life gets more definitely formulated for purposes of instruction. As we have previously noted, probably the chief motive for consciously dwelling upon the group life, extracting the meanings which are regarded as most important and systematizing them in a coherent arrangement, is just the need of instructing the young so as to perpetuate group life. Once started on this road of selection, formulation, and organization, no definite limit exists. The invention of writing and of printing gives the operation an immense impetus. Finally, the bonds which connect the subject matter of school study with the habits and ideals of the social group are disguised and covered up. The ties are so loosened that it often appears as if there were none; as if subject matter existed simply as knowledge on its own independent behoof, and as if study were the mere act of mastering it for its own sake, irrespective of any social values. Since it is highly important for practical reasons to counteract this tendency, the chief purposes of our theoretical discussion are to make clear the connection which is so readily lost from sight, and to show in some detail the social content and function of the chief constituents of the course of study.

The points need to be considered from the standpoint of instructor and of student. To the former, the significance of a knowledge of subject matter, going far beyond the present knowledge of pupils, is to supply definite standards and to reveal to him the possibilities of the crude activities of the immature. (*i*) The material of school studies translates into concrete and detailed terms the meanings of current social life which it is desirable to transmit. It puts clearly before the instructor the essential ingredients of the culture to be perpetuated, in such an organized form as to protect him from the haphazard efforts he would be likely to indulge in if the meanings had not been standardized. (*ii*) A knowledge of the ideas which have been achieved in the past as the outcome of activity places the educator in a position to perceive the meaning of the seeming impulsive and aimless reactions of the young, and to provide the stimuli needed to direct them so that they will amount to something. The more the educator knows of music the more he can perceive the possibilities of the inchoate musical impulses of a child. Organized subject matter represents the ripe fruitage of experiences like theirs, experiences involving the same world, and powers and needs similar to theirs. It does not represent perfection or infallible wisdom; but it is the best at command to further new experiences which may, in some respects at least, surpass the achievements embodied in existing knowledge and works of art.

From the standpoint of the educator, in other words, the various studies represent working resources, available capital. Their remoteness from the experience of the young is not, however, seeming; it is real. The subject matter of the learner is not, therefore, it cannot be, identical with the formulated, the crystallized, and systematized subject matter of the adult; the material as found in books and in works of art, etc. The latter represents the *possibilities* of the former; not its existing state. It enters directly into the activities of the expert and the educator, not into that of the beginner, the learner. Failure to bear in mind the difference in subject matter from the respective standpoints of teacher and student is responsible for most of the mistakes made in the use of texts and other expressions of preexistent knowledge.

The need for a knowledge of the constitution and functions, in the concrete, of human nature is great just because the teacher's attitude to subject matter is so different from that of the pupil. The teacher presents in actuality what the pupil represents only in *posse*. That is, the teacher already knows the things which the student is only learning. Hence the problem of the two is radically unlike. When engaged in the direct act of teaching, the instructor needs to have subject matter at his fingers' ends; his attention should be upon the attitude and response of the pupil. To understand the later in its interplay with subject matter is his task, while the pupil's mind, naturally, should be not on itself but on the topic in hand. Or to state the same point in a somewhat different manner: the teacher should be occupied not with subject matter in itself but in its interaction with the pupil's present needs and capacities. Hence simple scholarship is not enough. In fact, there are certain features of scholarship or mastered subject matter—taken by itself—which get in the way of effective teaching *unless* the instructor's habitual attitude is one of concern with its interplay in the pupil's own experience. In the first place, his knowledge extends indefinitely beyond the range of the pupil's acquaintance. It involves principles which are beyond the immature pupil's understanding and interest. In and of itself, it may no more represent the living world of the pupil's experience than the astronomer's knowledge of Mars represents a baby's acquaintance with the room in which he stays. In the second place, the method of organization of the material of achieved scholarship differs from that of the beginner. It is not true that the experience of the young is unorganized—that it consists of isolated scraps. But it is organized in connection with direct practical centres of interest. The child's home is, for example, the organizing centre of his geographical knowledge. His own movements about the locality, his journeys abroad, the tales of his friends, give the ties which hold his items of information together. But the geography of the geographer, of the one who has already developed the implications of these smaller experiences, is organized on the basis of the relationship which the various facts bear to one another—not the relations which they bear to his house, bodily movements, and friends. To the one who is learned, subject matter is extensive, accurately defined, and logically interrelated. To the one who is learning, it is fluid, partial, and connected through his personal occupations.[3] The problem of teaching is to keep the experience of the student moving in the direction of what the expert already knows. Hence the need that the teacher know both subject matter and the characteristic needs and capacities of the student.

## 2. The Development of Subject Matter in the Learner

It is possible, without doing violence to the facts, to mark off three fairly typical stages in the growth of subject matter in the experience of the learner. In its first estate, knowledge exists as the content of intelligent ability—power to do. This kind of subject matter, or known material, is expressed in familiarity or acquaintance with things. Then this material gradually is surcharged and deepened through communicated knowledge or information. Finally, it is enlarged and worked over into rationally or logically organized material—that of the one who, relatively speaking, is expert in the subject.

1. The knowledge which comes first to persons, and that remains most deeply engrained, is knowledge of *how to do*; how to walk, talk, read, write, skate, ride a bicycle, manage a machine, calculate, drive a horse, sell goods, manage people, and so on indefinitely. The popular tendency to regard instinctive acts which are adapted to an end as a sort of miraculous knowledge, while unjustifiable, is evidence of the strong tendency to identify intelligent control of the means of action with knowledge. When education, under the influence of a scholastic conception of knowledge which ignores everything but scientifically formulated facts and truths, fails to recognize that primary or initial subject matter always exists as matter of an active doing, involving the use of the body and the handling of material, the subject matter of instruction is isolated from the needs and purposes of the learner, and so becomes just a something to be memorized and reproduced upon demand. Recognition of

the natural course of development, on the contrary, always sets out with situations which involve learning by doing. Arts and occupations form the initial stage of the curriculum, corresponding as they do to knowing how to go about the accomplishment of ends.

Popular terms denoting knowledge have always retained the connection with ability in action lost by academic philosophies. Ken and can are allied words. Attention means caring for a thing, in the sense of both affection and of looking out for its welfare. Mind means carrying out instructions in action—as a child minds his mother—and taking care of something—as a nurse minds the baby. To be thoughtful, considerate, means to heed the claims of others. Apprehension means dread of undesirable consequences, as well as intellectual grasp. To have good sense or judgement is to know the conduct a situation calls for; discernment is not making distinctions for the sake of making them, an exercise reprobated as hair splitting, but is insight into an affair with reference to acting. Wisdom has never lost its association with the proper direction of life. Only in education, never in the life of farmer, sailor, merchant, physician, or laboratory experimenter, does knowledge mean primarily a store of information aloof from doing.

Having to do with things in an intelligent way issues in acquaintance or familiarity. The things we are best acquainted with are the things we put to frequent use—such things as chairs, tables, pen, paper, clothes, food, knives and forks on the commonplace level, differentiating into more special objects according to a person's occupations in life. Knowledge of things in that intimate and emotional sense suggested by the word acquaintance is a precipitate from our employing them with a purpose. We have acted with or upon the thing so frequently that we can anticipate how it will act and react—such is the meaning of familiar acquaintance. We are ready for a familiar thing; it does not catch us napping, or play unexpected tricks with us. This attitude carries with it a sense of congeniality or friendliness, of ease and illumination; while the things with which we are not accustomed to deal are strange, foreign, cold, remote, "abstract."

II. But it is likely that elaborate statements regarding this primary stage of knowledge will darken understanding. It includes practically all of our knowledge which is not the result of deliberate technical study. Modes of purposeful doing includes dealings with persons as well as things. Impulses of communication and habits of intercourse have to be adapted to maintaining successful connections with others; a large fund of social knowledge accrues. As a part of this intercommunication one learns much from others. They tell of their experiences and of the experiences which, in turn, have been told them. In so far as one is interested or concerned in these communications, their matter becomes a part of one's own experience. Active connections with others are such an intimate and vital part of our own concerns that it is impossible to draw sharp lines, such as would enable us to say, "Here my experience ends; there yours begins." In so far as we are partners in common undertakings, the things which others communicate to us as the consequences of their particular share in the enterprise blend at once into the experience resulting from our own special doings. The ear is as much an organ of experience as the eye or hand; the eye is available for reading reports of what happens beyond its horizon. Things remote in space and time affect the issue of our actions quite as much as things which we can smell and handle. They really concern us, and, consequently, any account of them which assists us in dealing with things at hand falls within personal experience.

Information is the name usually given to this kind of subject matter. The place of communication in personal doing supplies us with a criterion for estimating the value of informational material in school. Does it grow naturally out of some question with which the student is concerned? Does it fit into his more direct acquaintance so as to increase its efficacy and deepen its meaning? If it meets these two requirements, it is educative. The amount heard or read is of no importance—the more the better, *provided* the student has a need for it and can apply it in some situation of his own.

But it is not so easy to fulfill these requirements in actual practice as it is to lay them down in theory. The extension in modern times of the area of intercommunication; the invention of appliances for securing acquaintance with remote parts of the heavens and bygone events of history; the cheapening of devices, like printing, for recording and distributing information—genuine and alleged—have created an immense bulk of communicated subject matter. It is much easier to swamp a pupil with this than to work it into his direct experiences. All too frequently it forms another strange world which just overlies the world of personal acquaintance. The sole problem of the student is to learn, for school purposes, for purposes of recitations and promotions, the constituent parts of this strange world. Probably the most conspicuous connotation of the word knowledge for most persons to-day is just the body of facts and truths ascertained by others; the material found in the rows and rows of atlases, cyclopedias, histories, biographies, books of travel, scientific treatises, on the shelves of libraries.

The imposing stupendous bulk of this material has unconsciously influenced men's notions of the nature of knowledge itself. The statements, the propositions, in which knowledge, the issue of active concern with problems, is deposited, are taken to be themselves knowledge. The record of knowledge, independent of its place as an outcome of inquiry and a resource in further inquiry, is taken to *be* knowledge. The mind of man is taken captive by the spoils of its prior victories; the spoils, not the weapons and the acts of waging the battle against the unknown, are used to fix the meaning of knowledge, of fact, and truth.

If this identification of knowledge with propositions stating information has fastened itself upon logicians and philosophers, it is not surprising that the same ideal has almost dominated instruction. The "course of study" consists largely of information distributed into various branches of study, each study being subdivided into lessons presenting in serial cut-off portions of the total store. In the seventeenth century, the store was still small enough so that men set up the ideal of a complete encyclopedic mastery of it. It is now so bulky that the impossibility of any one man's coming into possession of it all is obvious. But the educational ideal has not been much affected. Acquisition of a modicum of information in each branch of learning, or at least in a selected group, remains the principle by which the curriculum, from elementary school through college, is formed; the easier portions being assigned to the earlier years, the more difficult to the later.

The complaints of educators that learning does not enter into character and affect conduct; the protests against memoriter work, against cramming, against gradgrind preoccupation with "facts," against devotion to wire-drawn distinctions and ill-understood rules and principles, all follow from this state of affairs. Knowledge which is mainly second-hand, other men's knowledge, tends to become merely verbal. It is no objection to information that it is clothed in words; communication necessarily takes place through words. But in the degree in which what is communicated cannot be organized into the existing experience of the learner, it becomes *mere* words: that is, pure sense-stimuli, lacking in meaning. Then it operates to call out mechanical reactions, ability to use the vocal organs to repeat statements, or the hand to write or to do "sums."

To be informed is to be posted; it is to have at command the subject matter needed for an effective dealing with a problem, and for giving added significance to the search for solution and to the solution itself. Informational knowledge is the material which can be fallen back upon as given, settled, established, assured in a doubtful situation. It is a kind of bridge for mind in its passage from doubt to discovery. It has the office of an intellectual middleman. It condenses and records in available form the net results of the prior experiences of mankind, as an agency of enhancing the meaning of new experiences. When one is told that Brutus assassinated Caesar, or that the length of the year is three hundred sixty-five and one fourth days, or that the ratio of the diameter of the circle to its circumference is 3.1415 . . . one receives what is indeed knowledge for others, but for him it is a stimulus to knowing. His acquisition of *knowledge* depends upon his response to what is communicated.

### 3. Science or Rationalized Knowledge

Science is a name for knowledge in its most characteristic form. It represents in its degree, the perfected outcome of learning,—its consummation. What is known, in a given case, is what is sure, certain, settled, disposed of; that which we think *with* rather than that which we think about. In its honorable sense, knowledge is distinguished from opinion, guesswork, specula-tion, and mere tradition. In knowledge, things are *ascertained*; they are *so* and not dubiously otherwise. But experience makes us aware that there is difference between intellectual cer-tainty of *subject matter* and *our* certainty. We are made, so to speak, for belief; credulity is natural. The undisciplined mind is averse to suspense and intellectual hesitation; it is prone to assertion. It likes things undisturbed, settled, and treats them as such without due warrant. Familiarity, common repute, and congeniality to desire are readily made measuring rods of truth. Ignorance gives way to opinionated and current error,—a greater foe to learning than ignorance itself. A Socrates is thus led to declare that consciousness of ignorance is the beginning of effective love of wisdom, and a Descartes to say that science is born of doubting.

We have already dwelt upon the fact that subject matter, or data, and ideas have to have their worth tested experimentally: that in themselves they are tentative and provisional. Our predilection for premature acceptance and assertion, our aversion to suspended judgment, are signs that we tend naturally to cut short the process of testing. We are satisfied with superficial and immediate short-visioned applications. If these work out with moderate satisfactoriness, we are content to suppose that our assumptions have been confirmed. Even in the case of failure, we are inclined to put the blame not on the inadequacy and incorrect-ness of our data and thoughts, but upon our hard luck and the hostility of circumstance. We charge the evil consequence not to the error of our schemes and our incomplete inquiry into conditions (thereby getting material for revising the former and stimulus for extending the latter) but to untoward fate. We even plume ourselves upon our firmness in clinging to our conceptions in spite of the way in which they work out.

Science represents the safeguard of the race against these natural propensities and the evils which flow from them. It consists of the special appliances and methods which the race has slowly worked out in order to conduct reflection under conditions whereby its procedures and results are tested. It is artificial (an acquired art), not spontaneous; learned, not native. To this fact is due the unique, the invaluable place of science in education, and also the dangers which threaten its right use. Without initiation into the scientific spirit one is not in possession of the best tools which humanity has so far devised for effectively directed reflection. One in that case not merely conducts inquiry and learning without the use of the best instruments, but fails to understand the full meaning of knowledge. For he does not become acquainted with the traits that mark off opinion and assent from authorized conviction. On the other hand, the fact that science marks the perfecting of knowing in highly specialized conditions of technique renders its results, taken by themselves, remote from ordinary experience—a quality of aloofness that is popularly designated by the term abstract. When this isolation appears in instruction, scientific information is even more exposed to the dangers attendant upon presenting ready-made subject matter than are other forms of information.

Science has been defined in terms of method of inquiry and testing. At first sight, this definition may seem opposed to the current conception that science is organized or systematized knowledge. The opposition, however, is only seeming, and disappears when the ordinary definition is completed. Not organization but the *kind* of organization effected by adequate methods of tested discovery marks off science. The knowledge of a farmer is systematized in the degree in which he is competent. It is organized on the basis of relation of means to ends—practically organized. Its organization *as* knowledge (that is, in the eulogistic sense of adequately tested and confirmed) is incidental to its organization with reference to securing crops, live-stock, etc. But scientific subject matter is organized with specific reference to the successful conduct of the enterprise of discovery, to knowing as a specialized undertaking.

Reference to the kind of assurance attending science will shed light upon this statement. It is *rational* assurance,—logical warranty. The ideal of scientific organization is, therefore, that every conception and statement shall be of such a kind as to follow from others and to lead to others. Concepts and propositions mutually imply and support one another. This double relation of "leading to and confirming" is what is meant by the terms logical and rational. The everyday conception of water is more available for ordinary uses of drinking, washing, irrigation, etc., than the chemist's notion of it. The latter's description of it as $H_2O$ is superior from the standpoint of place and use in inquiry. It states the nature of water in a way which connects it with knowledge of other things, indicating to one who understands it how the knowledge is arrived at and its bearings upon other portions of knowledge of the structure of things. Strictly speaking, it does not indicate the objective relations of water any more than does a statement that water is transparent, fluid, without taste or odor, satisfying to thirst, etc. It is just as true that water has these relations as that it is constituted by two molecules of hydrogen in combination with one of oxygen. But for the *particular purpose* of conducting discovery with a view to ascertainment of fact, the latter relations are fundamental. The more one emphasizes organization as a mark of science, then, the more he is committed to a recognition of the primacy of method in the definition of science. For method defines the kind of organization in virtue of which science is science.

## 4. Subject Matter as Social

Our next chapters will take up various school activities and studies and discuss them as successive stages in that evolution of knowledge which we have just been discussing. It remains to say a few words upon subject matter as social, since our prior remarks have been mainly concerned with its intellectual aspect. A difference in breadth and depth exists even in vital knowledge; even in the data and ideas which are relevant to real problems and which are motivated by purposes. For there is a difference in the social scope of purposes and the social importance of problems. With the wide range of possible material to select from, it is important that education (especially in all its phases short of the most specialized) should use a criterion of social worth.

All information and systematized scientific subject matter have been worked out under the conditions of social life and have been transmitted by social means. But this does not prove that all is of equal value for the purposes of forming the disposition and supplying the equipment of members of present society. The scheme of a curriculum must take account of the adaptation of studies to the needs of the existing community life; it must select with the intention of improving the life we live in common so that the future shall be better than the past. Moreover, the curriculum must be planned with reference to placing essentials first, and refinements second. The things which are socially most fundamental, that is, which have to do with the experiences in which the widest groups share, are the essentials. The things which represent the needs of specialized groups and technical pursuits are secondary. There is truth in the saying that education must first be human and only after that professional. But those who utter the saying frequently have in mind in the term human only a highly specialized class: the class of learned men who preserve the classic traditions of the past. They forget that material is humanized in the degree in which it connects with the common interests of men as men.

Democratic society is peculiarly dependent for its maintenance upon the use in forming a course of study of criteria which are broadly human. Democracy cannot flourish where the chief influences in selecting subject matter of instruction are utilitarian ends narrowly conceived for the masses, and, for the higher education of the few, the traditions of a specialized cultivated class. The notion that the "essentials" of elementary education are the three R's mechanically treated, is based upon ignorance of the essentials needed for realization of democratic ideals. Unconsciously it assumes that these ideals are unrealizable; it assumes that in the future, as in the past, getting a livelihood, "making a living," must signify for most men and women doing things which are not significant, freely chosen, and ennobling to those who do them; doing things which serve ends unrecognized by those engaged in them, carried on under the direction of others for the sake of pecuniary reward. For preparation of large numbers for a life of this sort, and only for this purpose, are mechanical efficiency in reading, writing, spelling and figuring, together with attainment of a certain amount of muscular dexterity, "essentials." Such conditions also infect the education called liberal, with illiberality. They imply a somewhat parasitic cultivation bought at the expense of not having the enlightenment and discipline which come from concern with the deepest problems of common humanity. A curriculum which acknowledges the social responsibilities of education must present situations where problems are relevant to the problems of living together, and where observation and information are calculated to develop social insight and interest.

## Summary

The subject matter of education consists primarily of the meanings which supply content to existing social life. The continuity of social life means that many of these meanings are contributed to present activity by past collective experience. As social life grows more complex these factors increase in number and import. There is need of special selection, formulation, and organization in order that they may be adequately transmitted to the new generation. But this very process tends to set up subject matter as something of value just by itself, apart from its function in promoting the realization of the meanings implied in the present experience of the immature. Especially is the educator exposed to the temptation to conceive his task in terms of the pupil's ability to appropriate and reproduce the subject matter in set statements, irrespective of its organization into his activities as a developing social member. The positive principle is maintained when the young begin with active occupations having a social origin and use, and proceed to a scientific insight in the materials and laws involved, through assimilating into their more direct experience the ideas and facts communicated by others who have had a larger experience. . . .

## 18. Educational Values

The considerations involved in a discussion of educational values have already been brought out in the discussion of aims and interests. The specific values usually discussed in educational theories coincide with aims which are usually urged. They are such things as utility, culture, information, preparation for social efficiency, mental discipline or power, and so on. The aspect of these aims in virtue of which they are valuable has been treated in our analysis of the nature of interest, and there is no difference between speaking of art as an interest or concern and referring to it as a value. It happens, however, that discussion of values has usually been centered about a consideration of the various ends subserved by specific subjects of the curriculum. It has been a part of the attempt to justify those subjects by pointing out the significant contributions to life accruing from their study. An explicit discussion of educational values thus affords an opportunity for reviewing the prior discussion of aims and interests on one hand and of the curriculum on the other, by bringing them into connection with one another.

## 1. The Nature of Realization or Appreciation

Much of our experience is indirect; it is dependent upon signs which intervene between the things and ourselves, signs which stand for or represent the former. It is one thing to have been engaged in war, to have shared its dangers and hardships; it is another thing to hear or read about it. All language, all symbols, are implements of an indirect experience; in technical language the experience which is procured by their means is "mediated." It stands in contrast with an immediate, direct experience, something in which we take part vitally and at first hand, instead of through the intervention of representative media. As we have seen, the scope of personal, vitally direct experience is very limited. If it were not for the intervention of agencies for representing absent and distant affairs, our experience would remain almost on the level of that of the brutes. Every step from savagery to civilization is dependent upon the invention of media which enlarge the range of purely immediate experience and give it deepened as well as wider meaning by connecting it with things which can only be signified or symbolized. It is doubtless this fact which is the cause of the disposition to identify an uncultivated person with an illiterate person—so dependent are we on letters for effective representative or indirect experience.

At the same time (as we have also had repeated occasion to see) there is always a danger that symbols will not be truly representative; danger that instead of really calling up the absent and remote in a way to make it enter a present experience, the linguistic media of representation will become an end in themselves. Formal education is peculiarly exposed to this danger, with the result that when literacy supervenes, mere bookishness, what is popularly termed the academic, too often comes with it. In colloquial speech, the phrase a "realizing sense" is used to express the urgency, warmth, and intimacy of a direct experience in contrast with the remote, pallid, and coldly detached quality of a representative experience. The terms "mental realization" and "appreciation" (or *genuine* appreciation) are more elaborate names for the realizing sense of a thing. It is not possible to define these ideas except by synonyms, like "coming home to one," "really taking it in," etc., for the only way to appreciate what is meant by a direct experience of a thing is by having it. But it is the difference between reading a technical description of a picture, and seeing it; or between just seeing it and being moved by it; between learning mathematical equations about light and being carried away by some peculiarly glorious illumination of a misty landscape.

We are thus met by the danger of the tendency of technique and other purely representative forms to encroach upon the sphere of direct appreciations; in other words, the tendency to assume that pupils have a foundation of direct realization of situations sufficient for the superstructure of representative experience erected by formulated school studies. This is not simply a matter of quantity or bulk. Sufficient direct experience is even more a matter of quality; it must be of a sort to connect readily and fruitfully with the symbolic material of instruction. Before teaching can safely enter upon conveying facts and ideas through the media of signs, schooling must provide genuine situations in which personal participation brings home the import of the material and the problems which it conveys. From the standpoint of the pupil, the resulting experiences are worth while on their own account; from the standpoint of the teacher, they are also means of supplying subject matter required for understanding instruction involving signs, and of evoking attitudes of open-mindedness and concern as to the material symbolically conveyed.

In the outline given of the theory of educative subject matter, the demand for this background of realization or appreciation is met by the provision made for play and active occupations embodying typical situations. Nothing need be added to what has already been said except to point out that while the discussion dealt explicitly with the subject matter of primary education, where the demand for the available background of direct experience is most obvious, the principle applies to the primary or elementary phase of every subject. The first and basic function of laboratory work, for example, in a high school or college in a new field, is to familiarize the student at first hand with a certain range of facts and problems—to give him a "feeling" for them. Getting command of technique and of methods of reaching and testing generalizations is at first secondary to getting appreciation. As regards the primary-school activities, it is to be borne in mind that the fundamental intent is not to amuse nor to convey information with a minimum of vexation nor yet to acquire skill,—though these results may accrue as by-products,—but to enlarge and enrich the scope of experience, and to keep alert and effective the interest in intellectual progress.

The rubric of appreciation supplies an appropriate head for bringing out three further principles: the nature of effective or real (as distinct from nominal) standards of value; the place of the imagination in appreciative realizations; and the place of the fine arts in the course of study.

1. The nature of standards of valuation. Every adult has acquired, in the course of his prior experience and education, certain measures of the worth of various sorts of experience. He has learned to look upon qualities like honesty, amiability, perseverance, loyalty, as moral goods; upon certain classics of literature, painting, music, as aesthetic values, and so on. Not only this, but he has learned certain rules for these values—the golden rule in morals; harmony, balance, etc., proportionate distribution in aesthetic goods; definition, clarity, system in intellectual accomplishments. These principles are so important as standards of judging the worth of new experiences that parents and instructors are always tending to teach them directly to the young. They overlook the danger that standards so taught will be *merely* symbolic; that is, largely conventional and verbal. In reality, working as distinct from professed standards depend upon what an individual has himself specifically appreciated to be deeply significant in concrete situations. An individual may have learned that certain characteristics are conventionally esteemed in music; he may be able to converse with some correctness about classic music; he may even honestly believe that these traits constitute his own musical standards. But if in his own past experience, what he has been most accustomed to and has most enjoyed is ragtime, his active or working measures of valuation are fixed on the ragtime level. The appeal actually made to him in his own personal realization fixes his attitude much more deeply than what he has been taught as the proper thing to say; his habitual disposition thus fixed forms his real "norm" of valuation in subsequent musical experiences.

Probably few would deny this statement as to musical taste. But it applies equally well in judgments of moral and intellectual worth. A youth who has had repeated experience of the full meaning of the value of kindliness toward others built into his disposition has a measure of the worth of generous treatment of others. Without this vital appreciation, the duty and virtue of unselfishness impressed upon him by others as a standard remains purely a matter of symbols which he cannot adequately translate into realities. His "knowledge" is second-handed; it is only a knowledge that others prize unselfishness as an excellence, and esteem him in the degree in which he exhibits it. Thus there grows up a split between a person's professed standards and his actual ones. A person may be aware of the *results* of this struggle between his inclinations and his theoretical opinions; he suffers from the conflict between doing what is really dear to him and what he has learned will win the approval of others. But of the split itself he is unaware; the result is a kind of unconscious hypocrisy, an instability of disposition. In similar fashion, a pupil who has worked through some confused intellectual situation and fought his way to clearing up obscurities in a definite outcome, appreciates the value of clarity and definition. He has a standard which can be depended upon. He may be trained externally to go through certain motions of analysis and division of subject matter and may acquire information about the value of these processes as standard logical functions, but unless it somehow comes home to him at some point as an appreciation of his own, the significance of the logical norms—so-called—remains as much an external piece of information as, say, the names of rivers in China. He may be able to recite, but the recital is a mechanical rehearsal.

It is, then, a serious mistake to regard appreciation as if it were confined to such things as literature and pictures and music. Its scope is as comprehensive as the work of education itself. The formation of habits is a purely mechanical thing unless habits are also *tastes*—habitual modes of preference and esteem, an effective sense of excellence. There are adequate grounds for asserting that the premium so often put in schools upon external "discipline," and upon marks and rewards, upon promotion and keeping back, are the obverse of the lack of attention given to life situations in which the meaning of facts, ideas, principles, and problems is vitally brought home.

2. Appreciative realizations are to be distinguished from symbolic or representative experiences. They are not to be distinguished from the work of the intellect or understanding. Only a personal response involving imagination can possibly procure realization even of pure "facts." The imagination is the medium of appreciation in every field. The engagement of the imagination is the only thing that makes any activity more than mechanical. Unfortunately, it is too customary to identify the imaginative with the imaginary, rather than with a warm and intimate taking in of the full scope of a situation. This leads to an exaggerated estimate of fairy tales, myths, fanciful symbols, verse, and something labeled "Fine Art," as agencies for developing imagination and appreciation; and, by neglecting imaginative vision in other matters, leads to methods which reduce much instruction to an unimaginative acquiring of specialized skill and amassing of load of information. Theory, and—to some extent—practice, have advanced far enough to recognize that play-activity is an imaginative enterprise. But it is still usual to regard this activity as a specially marked-off stage of childish growth, and to overlook the fact that the difference between play and what is regarded as serious employment should be not a difference between the presence and absence of imagination, but a difference in the materials with which imagination is occupied. The result is an unwholesome exaggeration of the fantastic and "unreal" phases of childish play and a deadly reduction of serious occupation to a routine efficiency prized simply for its external tangible results. Achievement comes to denote the sort of thing that a well-planned machine can do better than a human being can, and the main effect of education, the achieving of a life of rich significance, drops by the wayside, Meantime mind-wandering and wayward fancy are nothing but the unsuppressible imagination cut loose from concern with what is done.

An adequate recognition of the play of imagination as the medium of realization of every kind of thing which lies beyond the scope of direct physical response is the sole way of escape from mechanical methods in teaching. The emphasis put in this book, in accord with many tendencies in contemporary education, upon activity, will be misleading if it is not recognized that the imagination is as much a normal and integral part of human activity as is muscular movement. The educative value of manual activities and of laboratory exercises, as well as of play, depends upon the extent in which they aid in bringing about a sensing of the *meaning* of what is going on. In effect, if not in name, they are dramatizations. Their utilitarian value in forming habits of skill to be used for tangible results is important, but not when isolated from the appreciative side. Were it not for the accompanying play of imagination, there would be no road from a direct activity to representative knowledge; for it is by imagination that symbols are translated over into a direct meaning and integrated with a narrower activity so as to expand and enrich it. When the representative creative imagination is made merely literary and mythological, symbols are rendered mere means of directing physical reactions of the organs of speech.

3. In the account previously given nothing was explicitly said about the place of literature and the fine arts in the course of study. The omission at that point was intentional. At the outset, there is no sharp demarcation of useful, or industrial, arts and fine arts. The activities . . . contain within themselves the factors later discriminated into fine and useful arts. As engaging the emotions and the imagination, they have the qualities which give the fine arts their quality. As demanding method or skill, the adaptation of tools to materials with constantly increasing perfection, they involve the element of technique indispensable to artistic production. From the standpoint of product, or the *work* of art, they are naturally defective, though even in this respect when they comprise genuine appreciation they often have a rudimentary charm. As experiences they have both an artistic and an aesthetic quality. When they emerge into activities which are tested by their product and when the socially serviceable value of the product is emphasized, they pass into useful or industrial arts. When they develop in the direction of an enhanced appreciation of the immediate qualities which appeal to taste, they grow into fine arts.

In one of its meanings, appreciation is opposed to depreciation. It denotes an enlarged, an *intensified* prizing, not merely a prizing, much less—like depreciation—a lowered and degraded prizing. This enhancement of the qualities which make any ordinary experience appealing, appropriable—capable of full assimilation—and enjoyable, constitutes the prime function of literature, music, drawing, painting, etc., in education. They are not the exclusive agencies of appreciation in the most general sense of that word; but they are the chief agencies of an intensified, enhanced appreciation. As such, they are not only intrinsically and directly enjoyable, but they serve a purpose beyond themselves. They have the office, in increased degree, of all appreciation in fixing taste, in forming standards for the worth of later experiences. They arouse discontent with conditions which fall below their measure; they create a demand for surroundings coming up to their own level. They reveal a depth and range of meaning in experiences which otherwise might be mediocre and trivial. They supply, that is, organs of vision. Moreover, in their fullness they represent the concentration and consummation of elements of good which are otherwise scattered and incomplete. They select and focus the elements of enjoyable worth which make any experience directly enjoyable. They are not luxuries of education, but emphatic expressions of that which makes any education worth while.

## 2. The Valuation of Studies

The theory of educational values involves not only an account of the nature of appreciation as fixing the measure of subsequent valuations, but an account of the specific directions in which these valuations occur. To value means primarily to prize, to esteem; but secondarily it means to apprize, to estimate. It means, that is, the act of cherishing something, holding it dear, and also the act of passing judgment upon the nature and amount of its value as compared with something else. To value in the latter sense is to valuate or evaluate. The distinction coincides with that sometimes made between intrinsic and instrumental values. Intrinsic values are not objects of judgment, they cannot (as intrinsic) be compared, or regarded as greater and less, better or worse. They are invaluable; and if a thing is invaluable, it is neither more nor less so than any other invaluable. But occasions present themselves when it is necessary to choose, when we must let one thing go in order to take another. This establishes an order of preference, a greater and less, better and worse. Things judged or passed upon have to be estimated in relation to some third thing, some further end. With respect to that, they are means, or instrumental values.

We may imagine a man who at one time thoroughly enjoys converse with his friends, at another the hearing of a symphony; at another the eating of his meals; at another the reading of a book; at another the earning of money, and so on. As an appreciative realization, each of these is an intrinsic value. It occupies a particular place in life; it serves its own end, which cannot be supplied by a substitute. There is no question of comparative value, and hence none of valuation. Each is the specific good which it is, and that is all that can be said. In its own place, none is a means to anything beyond itself. But there may arise a situation in which they compete or conflict, in which a choice has to be made. Now comparison comes in. Since a choice has to be made, we want to know the respective claims of each competitor. What is to be said for it? What does it offer in comparison with, as balanced over against, some other possibility? Raising these questions means that a particular good is no longer an end in itself, an intrinsic good. For if it were, its claims would be incomparable, imperative. The question is now as to its status as a means of realizing something else, which is then the invaluable of *that* situation. If a man has just eaten, or if he is well fed generally and the opportunity to hear music is a rarity, he will probably prefer the music to eating. In the given situation that will render the greater contribution. If he is starving, or if he is satiated with music for the time being, he will naturally judge food to have the greater worth. In the abstract or at large, apart from the needs of a particular situation in which choice has to be made, there is no such thing as degrees or order of value.

Certain conclusions follow with respect to educational values. We cannot establish a hierarchy of values among studies. It is futile to attempt to arrange them in an order, beginning with one having least worth and going on to that of maximum value. In so far as any study has a unique or irreplaceable function in experience, in so far as it marks a characteristic enrichment of life, its worth is intrinsic or incomparable. Since education is not a means to living, but is identical with the operation of living a life which is fruitful and inherently significant, the only ultimate value which can be set up is just the process of living itself. And this is not an end to which studies and activities are subordinate means; it is the whole of which they are ingredients. And what has been said about appreciation means that every study in one of its aspects ought to have just such ultimate significance. It is as true of arithmetic as it is of poetry that in some place and at some time it ought to be a good to be appreciated on its own account—just as an enjoyable experience, in short. If it is not, then when the time and place come for it to be used as a means or instrumentality, it will be in just that much handicapped. Never having been realized or appreciated for itself, one will miss something of its capacity as a resource for other ends.

It equally follows that when we compare studies as to their values, that is, treat them as means to something beyond themselves, that which controls their proper valuation is found in the specific situation in which they are to be used. The way to enable a student to apprehend the instrumental value of arithmetic is not to lecture him upon the benefit it will be to him in some remote and uncertain future, but to let him discover that success in something he is interested in doing depends upon ability to use number.

It also follows that the attempt to distribute distinct sorts of value among different studies is a misguided one, in spite of the amount of time recently devoted to the undertaking. Science for example may have *any* kind of value, depending upon the situation into which it enters as a means. To some the value of science may be military; it may be an instrument in strengthening means of offense or defense; it may be technological, a tool for engineering; or it may be commercial—an aid in the successful conduct of business; under other conditions, its worth may be philanthropic—the service it renders in relieving human suffering; or again it may be quite conventional—of value in establishing one's social status as an "educated" person. As matter of fact, science serves all these purposes, and it would be an arbitrary task to try to fix upon one of them as its "real" end. All that we can be sure of educationally is that science should be taught so as to be an end in itself in the lives of students—something worth while on account of its own unique intrinsic contribution to the experience of life. Primarily it must have "appreciation value." If we take something which seems to be at the opposite pole, like poetry, the same sort of statement applies. It may be that, at the present time, its chief value is the contribution it makes to the enjoyment of leisure. But that may represent a degenerate condition rather than anything necessary. Poetry has historically been allied with religion and morals; it has served the purpose of penetrating the mysterious depths of things. It has had an enormous patriotic value. Homer to the Greeks was a Bible, a textbook of morals, a history, and a national inspiration. In any case, it may be said that an education which does not succeed in making poetry a resource in the business of life as well as in its leisure, has something the matter with it—or else the poetry is artificial poetry.

The same considerations apply to the value of a study or a topic of a study with reference to its motivating force. Those responsible for planning and teaching the course of study should have grounds for thinking that the studies and topics included furnish both direct increments to the enriching of lives of the pupils and also materials which they can put to use in other concerns of direct interest. Since the curriculum is always getting loaded down with purely inherited traditional matter and with subjects which represent mainly the energy of some influential person or group of persons in behalf of something dear to them, it requires constant inspection, criticism, and revision to make sure it is accomplishing its purpose. Then there is always the probability that it represents the values of adults rather than those of children and youth, or those of pupils a generation ago rather than those of the present day. Hence a further need for a critical outlook and survey. But these considerations do not mean that for a subject to have motivating value to a pupil (whether intrinsic or instrumental) is the same thing as for him to be aware of the value, or to be able to tell what the study is good for.

In the first place, as long as any topic makes an immediate appeal, it is not necessary to ask what it is good for. This is a question which can be asked only about instrumental values. Some goods are not good *for* anything; they are just goods. Any other notion leads to an absurdity. For we cannot stop asking the question about an instrumental good, one whose value lies in its being good *for* something, unless there is at some point something intrinsically good, good for itself. To a hungry, healthy child, food is a good of the situation; we do not have to bring him to consciousness of the ends subserved by food in order to supply a motive to eat. The food in connection with his appetite *is* a motive. The same thing holds of mentally eager pupils with respect to many topics. Neither they nor the teacher could possibly foretell with any exactness the purposes learning is to accomplish in the future; nor as long as the eagerness continues is it advisable to try to specify particular goods which are to come of it. The proof of a good is found in the fact that the pupil responds; his response *is* use. His response to the material shows that the subject functions in his life. It is unsound to urge that, say, Latin has a value *per se* in the abstract, just as a study, as a sufficient justification for teaching it. But it is equally absurd to argue that unless teacher or pupil can point out some definite assignable future use to which it is to be put, it lacks justifying value. When pupils are genuinely concerned in learning Latin, that is of itself proof that it possesses value. The most which one is entitled to ask in such cases is whether in view of the shortness of time, there are not other things of intrinsic value which in addition have greater instrumental value.

This brings us to the matter of instrumental values—topics studied because of some end beyond themselves. If a child is ill and his appetite does not lead him to eat when food is presented, or if his appetite is perverted so that he prefers candy to meat and vegetables, conscious reference to results is indicated. He needs to be made conscious of consequences as a justification of the positive or negative value of certain objects. Or the state of things may be normal enough, and yet an individual not be moved by some matter because he does not grasp how his attainment of some intrinsic good depends upon active concern with what is presented. In such cases, it is obviously the part of wisdom to establish consciousness of connection. In general what is desirable is that a topic be presented in such a way that it either have an immediate value, and require no justification, or else be perceived to be a means of achieving something of intrinsic value. An instrumental value then has the intrinsic value of being a means to an end.

It may be questioned whether some of the present pedagogical interest in the matter of values of studies is not either excessive or else too narrow. Sometimes it appears to be a labored effort to furnish an apologetic for topics which no longer operate to any purpose, direct or indirect, in the lives of pupils. At other times, the reaction against useless lumber seems to have gone to the extent of supposing that no subject or topic should be taught unless some quite definite future utility can be pointed out by those making the course of study or by the pupil himself, unmindful of the fact that life is its own excuse for being; and that definite utilities which can be pointed out are themselves justified only because they increase the experienced content of life itself.

### 3. The Segregation and Organization of Values

It is of course possible to classify in a general way the various valuable phases of life. In order to get a survey of aims sufficiently wide (see p. 432) to give breadth and flexibility to the enterprise of education, there is some advantage in such a classification. But it is a great mistake to regard these values as ultimate ends to which the concrete satisfactions of experience are subordinate. They are nothing but generalizations, more or less adequate, of concrete goods. Health, wealth, efficiency, sociability, utility, culture, happiness itself are only abstract terms which sum up a multitude of particulars. To regard such things as standards for the valuation of concrete topics and process of education is to subordinate to an abstraction the concrete facts from which the abstraction is derived. They are not in any true sense standards of valuation; these are found, as we have previously seen, in the *specific realizations* which form tastes and habits of preference. They are, however, of significance as points of view elevated above the details of life whence to survey the field and see how its constituent details are distributed, and whether they are well proportioned.

No classification can have other than a provisional validity. The following may prove of some help. We may say that the kind of experience to which the work of the schools should contribute is one marked by executive competency in the management of resources and obstacles encountered (efficiency); by sociability, or interest in the direct companionship of others; by aesthetic taste or capacity to appreciate artistic excellence in at least some of its classic forms; by trained intellectual method, or interest in some mode of scientific achievement; and by sensitiveness to the rights and claims of others—conscientiousness. And while these considerations are not standards of value, they are useful criteria for survey, criticism, and better organization of existing methods and subject matter of instruction.

The need of such general points of view is the greater because of a tendency to segregate educational values due to the isolation from one another of the various pursuits of life. The idea is prevalent that different studies represent separate kinds of values, and that the curriculum should, therefore, be constituted by gathering together various studies till a sufficient variety of independent values have been cared for. The following quotation does not use the word value, but it contains the notion of a curriculum constructed on the idea that there are a number of separate ends to be reached, and that various studies may be evaluated by referring each study to its respective end. "Memory is trained by most studies, but best by languages and history; taste is trained by the more advanced study of languages, and still better by English literature; imagination by all higher language teaching, but chiefly by Greek and Latin poetry; observation by science work in the laboratory, though some training is to be got from the earlier stages of Latin and Greek; for expression, Greek and Latin composition come first and English composition next; for abstract reasoning, mathematics stands almost alone; for concrete reasoning, science comes first, then geometry; for social reasoning, the Greek and Roman historians and orators come first, and general history next. Hence the narrowest education which can claim to be at all complete includes Latin, one modern language, some history, some English literature, and one science."

There is much in the wording of this passage which is irrelevant to our point and which must be discounted to make it clear. The phraseology betrays the particular provincial tradition within which the author is writing. There is the unquestioned assumption of "faculties" to be trained, and a dominant interest in the ancient languages; there is comparative disregard of the earth on which men happen to live and the bodies they happen to carry around with them. But with allowances made for these matters (even with their complete abandonment) we find much in contemporary educational philosophy which parallels the fundamental notion of parceling out special values to segregated studies. Even when some one end is set up as a standard of value, like social efficiency or culture, it will often be found to be but a verbal heading under which a variety of disconnected factors are comprised. And although the general tendency is to allow a greater variety of values to a given study than does the passage quoted, yet the attempt to inventory a number of values attaching to each study and to state the amount of each value which the given study possesses emphasizes an implied educational disintegration.

As matter of fact, such schemes of values of studies are largely but unconscious justifications of the curriculum with which one is familiar. One accepts, for the most part, the studies of the existing course and then assigns values to them as a sufficient reason for their being taught. Mathematics is said to have, for example, disciplinary value in habituating the pupil to accuracy of statement and closeness of reasoning; it has utilitarian value in giving command of the arts of calculation involved in trade and the arts; culture value in its enlargement of the imagination in dealing with the most general relations of things; even religious value in its concept of the infinite and allied ideas. But clearly mathematics does not accomplish such results because it is endowed with miraculous potencies called values; it has these values if and when it accomplishes these results, and not otherwise. The statements may help a teacher to a larger vision of the possible results to be effected by instruction in mathematical topics. But unfortunately, the tendency is to treat the statement as indicating powers inherently residing in the subject, whether they operate or not, and thus to give it a rigid justification. If they do not operate, the blame is put not on the subject as taught, but on the indifference and recalcitrancy of pupils.

This attitude toward subjects is the obverse side of the conception of experience or life as a patchwork of independent interests which exist side by side and limit one another. Students of politics are familiar with a check and balance theory of the powers of government. There are supposed to be independent separate functions, like the legislative, executive, judicial, administrative, and all goes well if each of these checks all the others and thus creates an ideal balance. There is a philosophy which might well be called the check and balance theory of experience. Life presents a diversity of interests. Left to themselves, they tend to encroach on one another. The ideal is to prescribe a special territory for each till the whole ground of experience is covered, and then see to it each remains within its own boundaries. Politics, business, recreation, art, science, the learned professions, polite intercourse, leisure, represent such interests. Each of these ramifies into many branches: business into manual occupations, executive positions, bookkeeping, railroading, banking, agriculture, trade and commerce, etc., and so with each of the others. An ideal education would then supply the means of meeting these separate and pigeon-holed interests. And when we look at the schools, it is easy to get the impression that they accept this view of the nature of adult life, and set for themselves the task of meeting its demands. Each interest is acknowledged as a kind of fixed institution to which something in the course of study must correspond. The course of study must then have some civics and history politically and patriotically viewed; some utilitarian studies; some science; some art (mainly literature of course); some provision for recreation; some moral education; and so on. And it will be found that a large part of current agitation about schools is concerned with clamor and controversy about the due meed of recognition to be given to each of these interests, and with struggles to secure for each its due share in the course of study; or, if this does not seem feasible in the existing school system, then to secure a new and separate kind of schooling to meet the need. In the multitude of educations education is forgotten.

The obvious outcome is congestion of the course of study, over-pressure and distraction of pupils, and a narrow specialization fatal to the very idea of education. But these bad results usually lead to more of the same sort of thing as a remedy. When it is perceived that after all the requirements of a full life experience are not met, the deficiency is not laid to the isolation and narrowness of the teaching of the existing subjects, and this recognition made the basis of reorganization of the system. No, the lack is something to be made up for by the introduction of still another study, or, if necessary, another kind of school. And as a rule those who object to the resulting overcrowding and consequent superficiality and distraction, usually also have recourse to a merely quantitative criterion: the remedy is to cut off a great many studies as fads and frills, and return to the good old curriculum of the three R's in elementary education and the equally good and equally old-fashioned curriculum of the classics and mathematics in higher education.

The situation has, of course, its historic explanation. Various epochs of the past have had their own characteristic struggles and interests. Each of these great epochs has left behind itself a kind of cultural deposit, like a geologic stratum. These deposits have found their way into educational institutions in the form of studies, distinct courses of study, distinct types of schools. With the rapid change of political, scientific, and economic interests in the last century, provision had to be made for new values. Though the older courses resisted, they have had at least in this country to retire their pretensions to a monopoly. They have not, however, been reorganized in content and aim; they have only been reduced in amount. The new studies, representing the new interests, have not been used to transform the method and aim of all instruction; they have been injected and added on. The result is a conglomerate, the cement of which consists in the mechanics of the school program or time table. Thence arises the scheme of values and standards of value which we have mentioned.

This situation in education represents the divisions and separations which obtain in social life. The variety of interests which should mark any rich and balanced experience have been torn asunder and deposited in separate institutions with diverse and independent purposes and methods. Business is business, science is science, art is art, politics is politics, social intercourse is social intercourse, morals is morals, recreation is recreation, and so on. Each possesses a separate and independent province with its own peculiar aims and ways of proceeding. Each contributes to the others only externally and accidentally. All of them together make up the whole of life by just apposition and addition. What does one expect from business save that it should furnish money, to be used in turn for making more money and for support of self and family, for buying books and pictures, tickets to concerts which may afford culture, and for paying taxes, charitable gifts and other things of social and ethical value? How unreasonable to expect that the pursuit of business should be itself a culture of the imagination, in breadth and refinement; that it should directly, and not through the money which it supplies, have social service for its animating principle and be conducted as an enterprise in behalf of social organization! The same thing is to be said, *mutatis mutandis*, of the pursuit of art or science or politics or religion. Each has become specialized not merely in its appliances and its demands upon time, but in its aim and animating spirit. Unconsciously, our course of studies and our theories of the educational values of studies reflect this division of interests.

The point at issue in a theory of educational value is then the unity or integrity of experience. How shall it be full and varied without losing unity of spirit? How shall it be one and yet not narrow and monotonous in its unity? Ultimately, the question of values and a standard of values is the moral question of the organization of the interests of life. Educationally, the question concerns that organization of schools, materials, and methods which will operate to achieve breadth and richness of experience. How shall we secure breadth of outlook without sacrificing efficiency of execution? How shall we secure the diversity of interests, without paying the price of isolation? How shall the individual be rendered executive *in* his intelligence instead of at the cost of his intelligence? How shall art, science, and politics reenforce one another in an enriched temper of mind instead of constituting ends pursued at one another's expense? How can the interests of life and the studies which enforce them enrich the common experience of men instead of dividing men from one another? With the questions of reorganization thus suggested, we shall be concerned in the concluding chapters.

## Summary

Fundamentally, the elements involved in a discussion of value have been covered in the prior discussion of aims and interests. But since educational values are generally discussed in connection with the claims of the various studies of the curriculum, the consideration of aim and interest is here resumed from the point of view of special studies. The term "value" has two quite different meanings. On the one hand, it denotes the attitude of prizing a thing, finding it worth while, for its own sake, or intrinsically. This is a name for a full or complete experience. To value in this sense is to appreciate. But to value also means a distinctively intellectual act—an operation of comparing and judging—to valuate. This occurs when direct full experience is lacking, and the question arises which of the various possibilities of a situation is to be preferred in order to reach a full realization, or vital experience.

We must not, however, divide the studies of the curriculum into the appreciative, those concerned with intrinsic value, and the instrumental, concerned with those which are of value or ends beyond themselves. The formation of proper standards in any subject depends upon a realization of the contribution which it makes to the immediate significance of experience, upon a direct appreciation. Literature and the fine arts are of peculiar value because they represent appreciation at its best—a heightened realization of meaning through selection and concentration. But every subject at some phase of its development should possess, what is for the individual concerned with it, an aesthetic quality.

Contribution to immediate intrinsic values in all their variety in experience is the only criterion for determining the worth of instrumental and derived values in studies. The tendency to assign separate values to each study and to regard the curriculum in its entirety as a kind of composite made by the aggregation of segregated values is a result of the isolation of social groups and classes. Hence it is the business of education in a democratic social group to struggle against this isolation in order that the various interests may reenforce and play into one another. . . .

## 26. Theories of Morals

### 1. The Inner and the Outer

Since morality is concerned with conduct, any dualisms which are set up between mind and activity must reflect themselves in the theory of morals. Since the formulations of the separation in the philosophic theory of morals are used to justify and idealize the practices employed in moral training, a brief critical discussion is in place. It is a commonplace of educational theory that the establishing of character is a comprehensive aim of school instruction and discipline. Hence it is important that we should be on our guard against a conception of the relations of intelligence to character which hampers the realization of the aim, and on the look-out for the conditions which have to be provided in order that the aim may be successfully acted upon.

The first obstruction which meets us is the currency of moral ideas which split the course of activity into two opposed factors, often named respectively the inner and outer, or the spiritual and the physical. This division is a culmination of the dualism of mind and the world, soul and body, end and means, which we have so frequently noted. In morals it takes the form of a sharp demarcation of the motive of action from its consequences, and of character from conduct. Motive and character are regarded as something purely "inner," existing exclusively in consciousness, while consequences and conduct are regarded as out-side of mind, conduct having to do simply with the movements which carry out motives; consequences with what happens as a result. Different schools identify morality with either the inner state of mind or the outer act and results, each in separation from the other.

Action with a purpose is deliberate; it involves a consciously foreseen end and a mental weighing of considerations pro and con. It also involves a conscious state of longing or desire for the end. The deliberate choice of an aim and of a settled disposition of desire takes time. During this time complete overt action is suspended. A person who does not have his mind made up, does not know what to do. Consequently he postpones definite action so far as possible. His position may be compared to that of a man considering jumping across a ditch. If he were sure he could or could not make it, definite activity in some direction would occur. But if he considers, he is in doubt; he hesitates. During the time in which a single overt line of action is in suspense, his activities are confined to such redistributions of energy within the organism as will prepare a determinate course of action. He measures the ditch with his eyes; he brings himself taut to get a feel of the energy at his disposal; he looks about for other ways across, he reflects upon the importance of getting across. All this means an accentuation of consciousness; it means a turning in upon the individual's own attitudes, powers, wishes, etc.

Obviously, however, this surging up of personal factors into conscious recognition is a part of the whole activity in its temporal development. There is not first a purely psychical process, followed abruptly by a radically different physical one. There is one continuous behavior, proceeding from a more uncertain, divided, hesitating state to a more overt, determinate, or complete state. The activity at first consists mainly of certain tensions and adjustments within the organism; as these are coordinated into a unified attitude, the organism as a whole acts—some definite act is undertaken. We may distinguish, of course, the more explicitly conscious phase of the continuous activity as mental or psychical. But that only identifies the mental or psychical to mean the indeterminate, formative state of an activity which in its fullness involves putting forth of overt energy to modify the environment.

Our conscious thoughts, observations, wishes, aversions are important, because they represent inchoate, nascent activities. They fulfill their destiny in issuing, later on, into specific and perceptible acts. And these inchoate, budding organic readjustments are important because they are our sole escape from the dominion of routine habits and blind impulse. They are activities having a *new* meaning in process of development. Hence, normally, there is an accentuation of personal consciousness whenever our instincts and ready formed habits find themselves blocked by novel conditions. Then we are thrown back upon ourselves to reorganize our own attitude before proceeding to a definite and irretrievable course of action. Unless we try to drive our way through by sheer brute force, we must modify our organic resources to adapt them to the specific features of the situation in which we find ourselves. The conscious deliberating and desiring which precede overt action are, then, the methodic personal readjustment implied in activity in uncertain situations.

This role of mind in continuous activity is not always maintained, however. Desires for something different, aversion to the given state of things caused by the blocking of successful activity, stimulates the imagination. The picture of a different state of things does not always function to aid ingenious observation and recollection to find a way out and on. Except where there is a disciplined disposition, the tendency is for the imagination to run loose. Instead of its objects being checked up by conditions with reference to their practicability in execution, they are allowed to develop because of the immediate emotional satisfaction which they yield. When we find the successful display of our energies checked by uncongenial surroundings, natural and social, the easiest way out is to build castles in the air and let them be a substitute for an actual achievement which involves the pains of thought. So in overt action we acquiesce, and build up an imaginary world in mind. This break between thought and conduct is reflected in those theories which make a sharp separation between mind as inner and conduct and consequences as merely outer.

For the split may be more than an incident of a particular individual's experience. The social situation may be such as to throw the class given to articulate reflection back into their own thoughts and desires without providing the means by which these ideas and aspirations can be used to reorganize the environment. Under such conditions, men take revenge, as it were, upon the alien and hostile environment by cultivating contempt for it, by giving it a bad name. They seek refuge and consolation within their own states of mind, their own imaginings and wishes, which they compliment by calling both more real and more ideal than the despised outer world. Such periods have recurred in history. In the early centuries of the Christian era, the influential moral systems of Stoicism, of monastic and popular Christianity and other religious movements of the day, took shape under the influence of such conditions. The more action which might express prevailing ideals was checked, the more the inner possession and cultivation of ideals was regarded as self-sufficient—as the essence of morality. The external world in which activity belongs was thought of as morally indifferent. Everything lay in having the right motive, even though that motive was not a moving force in the world. Much the same sort of situation recurred in Germany in the later eighteenth and early nineteenth centuries; it led to the Kantian insistence upon the good will as the sole moral good, the will being regarded as something complete in itself, apart from action and from the changes or consequences effected in the world. Later it led to an idealization of existing institutions as themselves the embodiment of reason.

The purely internal morality of "meaning well," of having a good disposition regardless of what comes of it, naturally led to a reaction. This is generally known as either hedonism or utilitarianism. It was said in effect that the important thing morally is not what a man is inside of his own consciousness, but what he *does*—the consequences which issue, the changes he actually effects. Inner morality was attacked as sentimental, arbitrary, dogmatic, subjective—as giving men leave to dignify and shield any dogma congenial to their self-interest or any caprice occurring to imagination by calling it an intuition or an ideal of conscience. Results, conduct, are what counts; they afford the sole measure of morality.

Ordinary morality, and hence that of the schoolroom, is likely to be an inconsistent compromise of both views. On one hand, certain states of feeling are made much of; the individual must "mean well," and if his intentions are good, if he had the right sort of emotional consciousness, he may be relieved of responsibility for full results in conduct. But since, on the other hand, certain things have to be done to meet the convenience and the requirements of others, and of social order in general, there is great insistence upon the doing of certain things, irrespective of whether the individual has any concern or intelligence in their doing. He must toe the mark; he must have his nose held to the grindstone; he must obey; he must form useful habits; he must learn self-control,—all of these precepts being understood in a way which emphasizes simply the immediate thing tangibly done, irrespective of the spirit of thought and desire in which it is done, and irrespective therefore of its effect upon other less obvious doings.

It is hoped that the prior discussion has sufficiently elaborated the method by which both of these evils are avoided. One or both of these evils must result wherever individuals, whether young or old, cannot engage in a progressively cumulative undertaking under conditions which engage their interest and require their reflection. For only in such cases is it possible that the disposition of desire and thinking should be an organic factor *in* overt and obvious conduct. Given a consecutive activity embodying the student's own interest, where a definite result is to be obtained, and where neither routine habit nor the following of dictated directions nor capricious improvising will suffice, and there the rise of conscious purpose, conscious desire, and deliberate reflection are inevitable. They are inevitable as the spirit and quality of an activity having specific consequences, not as forming an isolated realm of inner consciousness.

## 2. The Opposition of Duty and Interest

Probably there is no antithesis more often set up in moral discussion than that between acting from "principle" and from "interest." To act on principle is to act disinterestedly, according to a general law, which is above all personal considerations. To act according to interest is, so the allegation runs, to act selfishly, with one's own personal profit in view. It substitutes the changing expediency of the moment for devotion to unswerving moral law. The false idea of interest underlying this opposition has already been criticized (see Chapter 10), but some moral aspects of the question will now be considered.

A clue to the matter may be found in the fact that the supporters of the "interest" side of the controversy habitually use the term "self-interest." Starting from the premises that unless there is interest in an object or idea, there is no motive force, they end with the conclusion that even when a person claims to be acting from principle or from a sense of duty, he really acts as he does because there "is something in it" for himself. The premiss is sound; the conclusion false. In reply the other school argues that since man is capable of generous self-forgetting and even self-sacrificing action, he is capable of acting without interest. Again the premiss is sound, and the conclusion false. The error on both sides lies in a false notion of the relation of interest and the self.

Both sides assume that the self is a fixed and hence isolated quantity. As a consequence, there is a rigid dilemma between acting for an interest of the self and without interest. If the self is something fixed antecedent to action, then acting from interest means trying to get more in the way of possessions for the self—whether in the way of fame, approval of others, power over others, pecuniary profit, or pleasure. Then the reaction from this view as a cynical depreciation of human nature leads to the view that men who act nobly act with no interest at all. Yet to an unbiased judgment it would appear plain that a man must be interested in what he is doing or he would not do it. A physician who continues to serve the sick in a plague at almost certain danger to his own life must be interested in the efficient performance of his profession—more interested in that than in the safety of his own bodily life. But it is distorting facts to say that this interest is merely a mask for an interest in something else which he gets by continuing his customary services—such as money or good repute or virtue; that it is only a means to an ulterior selfish end. The moment we recognize that the self is not something ready-made, but something in continuous formation through choice of action, the whole situation clears up. A man's interest in keeping at his work in spite of danger to life means that his self is found *in* that work; if he finally gave up, and preferred his personal safety or comfort, it would mean that he preferred to be *that* kind of a self. The mistake lies in making a separation between interest and self, and supposing that the latter is the end to which interest in objects and acts and others is a mere means. In fact, self and interest are two names for the same fact; the kind and amount of interest actively taken in a thing reveals and measures the quality of selfhood which exists. Bear in mind that interest means the active or moving *identity* of the self with a certain object, and the whole alleged dilemma falls to the ground.

Unselfishness, for example, signifies neither lack of interest in what is done (that would mean only machine-like indifference) nor selflessness—which would mean absence of virility and character. As employed everywhere outside of this particular theoretical controversy, the term "unselfishness" refers to the kind of aims and objects which habitually interest a man. And if we make a mental survey of the kind of interests which evoke the use of this epithet, we shall see that they have two intimately associated features. (*i*) The generous self consciously identifies itself with the *full* range of relationships implied in its activity, instead of drawing a sharp line between itself and considerations which are excluded as alien or indifferent; *(ii)* it readjusts and expands its *past* ideas of itself to take in new consequences as they become perceptible. When the physician began his career he may not have thought of a pestilence; he may not have consciously identified himself with service under such conditions. But, if he has a normally growing or active self, when he finds that his vocation involves such risks, he willingly adopts them as integral portions of his activity. The wider or larger self which means inclusion instead of denial of relationships is identical with a self which enlarges in order to assume previously unforeseen ties.

In such crises of readjustment—and the crisis may be slight as well as great—there may be a transitional conflict of "principle" with "interest." It is the nature of a habit to involve ease in the accustomed line of activity. It is the nature of a readjusting of habit to involve an effort which is disagreeable—something to which a man has deliberately to hold himself. In other words, there is a tendency to identify the self—or take interest—in what one has got used to, and to turn away the mind with aversion or irritation when an unexpected thing which involves an unpleasant modification of habit comes up. Since in the past one has done one's duty without having to face such a disagreeable circumstances, why not go on as one has been? To yield to this temptation means to narrow and isolate the thought of the self—to treat it as complete. Any habit, no matter how efficient in the past, which has become set, may at any time bring this temptation with it. To act from principle in such an emergency is not to act on some abstract principle, or duty at large; it is to act upon the *principle of a course of action*, instead of upon the *circumstances* which have attended it. The principle of a physician's conduct is its animating aim and spirit—the care for the diseased. The principle is not what justifies an activity, for the principle is but another name for the continuity of the activity. If the activity as manifested in its consequences is undesirable, to act upon principle is to accentuate its evil. And a man who prides himself upon acting upon principle is likely to be a man who insists upon having his own way without learning from experience what is the better way. He fancies that some abstract principle justifies his course of action without recognizing that his principle needs justification.

Assuming, however, that school conditions are such as to provide desirable occupations, it is interest in the occupation as a whole—that is, in its continuous development—which keeps a pupil at his work in spite of temporary diversions and unpleasant obstacles. Where there is no activity having a growing significance, appeal to principle is either purely verbal, or a form of obstinate pride or an appeal to extraneous considerations clothed with a dignified title. Undoubtedly there are junctures where momentary interest ceases and attention flags, and where reenforcement is needed. But what carries a person over these hard stretches is not loyalty to duty in the abstract, but interest in his occupation. Duties are "offices"—they are the specific acts needed for the fulfilling of a function—or, in homely language, doing one's job. And the man who is genuinely interested in his job is the man who is able to stand temporary discouragement, to persist in the face of obstacles, to take the lean with the fat: he makes an interest out of meeting and overcoming difficulties and distractions.

## 3. Intelligence and Character

A noteworthy paradox often accompanies discussions of morals. On the one hand, there is an identification of the moral with the rational. Reason is set up as a faculty from which proceed ultimate moral intuitions, and sometimes, as in the Kantian theory, it is said to supply the only proper moral motive. On the other hand, the value of concrete, everyday intelligence is constantly underestimated, and even deliberately depreciated. Morals is often thought to be an affair with which ordinary knowledge has nothing to do. Moral knowledge is thought to be a thing apart, and conscience is thought of as something radically different from consciousness. This separation, if valid, is of especial significance for education. Moral education in school is practically hopeless when we set up the development of character as a supreme end, and at the same time treat the acquiring of knowledge and the development of understanding, which of necessity occupy the chief part of school time, as having nothing to do with character. On such a basis, moral education is inevitably reduced to some kind of catechetical instruction, or lessons about morals. Lessons "about morals" signify as matter of course lessons in what other people think about virtues and duties. It amounts to something only in the degree in which pupils happen to be already animated by a sympathetic and dignified regard for the sentiments of others. Without such a regard, it has no more influence on character than information about the mountains of Asia; with a servile regard, it increases dependence upon others, and throws upon those in authority the responsibility for conduct. As a matter of fact, direct instruction in morals has been effective only in social groups where it was a part of the authoritative control of the many by the few. Not the teaching as such but the reenforcement of it by the whole régime of which it was an incident made it effective. To attempt to get similar results from lessons about morals in a democratic society is to rely upon sentimental magic.

At the other end of the scale stands the Socratic-Platonic teaching which identifies knowledge and virtue—which holds that no man does evil knowingly but only because of ignorance of the good. This doctrine is commonly attacked on the ground that nothing is more common than for a man to know the good and yet do the bad: not knowledge, but habituation or practice, and motive are what is required. Aristotle, in fact, at once attacked the Platonic teaching on the ground that moral virtue is like an art, such as medicine; the experienced practitioner is better than a man who has theoretical knowledge but no practical experience of disease and remedies. The issue turns, however, upon what is meant by knowledge. Aristotle's objection ignored the gist of Plato's teaching to the effect that man could not attain a theoretical insight into the good except as he had passed through years of practical habituation and strenuous discipline. Knowledge of the good was not a thing to be got either from books or from others, but was achieved through a prolonged education. It was the final and culminating grace of a mature experience of life. Irrespective of Plato's position, it is easy to perceive that the term knowledge is used to denote things as far apart as intimate and vital personal realization,—a conviction gained and tested in experience,—and a second-handed, largely symbolic, recognition that persons in general believe so and so—a devitalized remote information. That the latter does not guarantee conduct, that it does not profoundly affect character, goes without saying. But if knowledge means something of the same sort as our conviction gained by trying and testing that sugar is sweet and quinine bitter, the case stands otherwise. Every time a man sits on a chair rather than on a stove, carries an umbrella when it rains, consults a doctor when ill—or in short performs any of the thousand acts which make up his daily life, he proves that knowledge of a certain kind finds direct issue in conduct. There is every reason to suppose that the same sort of knowledge of good has a like expression; in fact "good" is an empty term unless it includes the satisfactions experienced in such situations as those mentioned. Knowledge that other persons are supposed to know something might lead one to act so as to win the approbation others attach to certain actions, or at least so as to give others the impression that one agrees with them; there is no reason why it should lead to personal initiative and loyalty in behalf of the beliefs attributed to them.

It is not necessary, accordingly, to dispute about the proper meaning of the term knowledge. It is enough for educational purposes to note the different qualities covered by the one name, to realize that it is knowledge gained at first hand through the exigencies of experience which affects conduct in significant ways. If a pupil learns things from books simply in connection with school lessons and for the sake of reciting what he has learned when called upon, then knowledge will have effect upon *some* conduct—namely upon that of reproducing statements at the demand of others. There is nothing surprising that such "knowledge" should not have much influence in the life out of school. But this is not a reason for making a divorce between knowledge and conduct, but for holding in low esteem this kind of knowledge. The same thing may be said of knowledge which relates merely to an isolated and technical speciality; it modifies action but only in its own narrow line. In truth, the problem of moral education in the schools is one with the problem of securing knowledge—the knowledge connected with the system of impulses and habits. For the use to which any known fact is put depends upon its connections. The knowledge of dynamite of a safecracker may be identical in verbal form with that of a chemist; in fact, it is different, for it is knit into connection with different aims and habits, and thus has a different import.

Our prior discussion of subject matter as proceeding from direct activity having an immediate aim, to the enlargement of meaning found in geography and history, and then to scientifically organized knowledge, was based upon the idea of maintaining a vital connection between knowledge and activity. What is learned and employed in an occupation having an aim and involving cooperation with others is moral knowledge, whether consciously so regarded or not. For it builds up a social interest and confers the intelligence needed to make that interest effective in practice. Just because the studies of the curriculum represent standard factors in social life, they are organs of initiation into social values. As mere school studies, their acquisition has only a technical worth. Acquired under conditions where their social significance is realized, they feed moral interest and develop moral insight. Moreover, the qualities of mind discussed under the topic of method of learning are all of them intrinsically moral qualities. Open-mindedness, single-mindedness, sincerity, breadth of outlook, thoroughness, assumption of responsibility for developing the consequences of ideas which are accepted, are moral traits. The habit of identifying moral characteristics with external conformity to authoritative prescriptions may lead us to ignore the ethical value of these intellectual attitudes, but the same habit tends to reduce morals to a dead and machine-like routine. Consequently while such an attitude has moral results, the results are morally undesirable—above all in a democratic society where so much depends upon personal disposition.

## 4. The Social and the Moral

All of the separations which we have been criticizing—and which the idea of education set forth in the previous chapters is designed to avoid—spring from taking morals too narrowly,—giving them, on one side, a sentimental goody-goody turn without reference to effective ability to do what is socially needed, and, on the other side, overemphasizing convention and tradition so as to limit morals to a list of definitely stated acts. As a matter of fact, morals are as broad as acts which concern our relationships with others. And potentially this includes all our acts, even though their social bearing may not be thought of at the time of performance. For every act, by the principle of habit, modifies disposition—it sets up a certain kind of inclination and desire. And it is impossible to tell when the habit thus strengthened may have a direct and perceptible influence on our association with others. Certain traits of character have such an obvious connection with our social relationships that we call them "moral" in an emphatic sense—truthfulness, honesty, chastity, amiability, etc. But this only means that they are, as compared with some other attitudes, central:—that they carry other attitudes with them. They are moral in an emphatic sense not because they are isolated and exclusive, but because they are so intimately connected with thousands of other attitudes which we do not explicitly recognize—which perhaps we have not even names for. To call them virtues in their isolation is like taking the skeleton for the living body. The bones are certainly important, but their importance lies in the fact that they support other organs of the body in such a way as to make them capable of integrated effective activity. And the same is true of the qualities of character which we specifically designate virtues. Morals concern nothing less than the whole character, and the whole character is identical with the man in all his concrete make-up and manifestations. To possess virtue does not signify to have cultivated a few nameable and exclusive traits; it means to be fully and adequately what one is capable of becoming through association with others in all the offices of life.

The moral and the social quality of conduct are, in the last analysis, identical with each other. It is then but to restate explicitly the import of our earlier chapters regarding the social function of education to say that the measure of the worth of the administration, curriculum, and methods of instruction of the school is the extent to which they are animated by a social spirit. And the great danger which threatens school work is the absence of conditions which make possible a permeating social spirit; this is the great enemy of effective moral training. For this spirit can be actively present only when certain conditions are met.

(i) In the first place, the school must itself be a community life in all which that implies. Social perceptions and interests can be developed only in a genuinely social medium—one where there is give and take in the building up of a common experience. Informational statements about things can be acquired in relative isolation by any one who previously has had enough intercourse with others to have learned language. But realization of the *meaning* of the linguistic signs is quite another matter. That involves a context of work and play in association with others. The plea which has been made for education through continued constructive activities in this book rests upon the fact they afford an opportunity for a social atmosphere. In place of a school set apart from life as a place for learning lessons, we have a miniature social group in which study and growth are incidents of present shared experience. Playgrounds, shops, workrooms, laboratories not only direct the natural active tendencies of youth, but they involve intercourse, communication, and cooperation,—all extending the perception of connections.

*(ii)* The learning in school should be continuous with that out of school. There should be a free interplay between the two. This is possible only when there are numerous points of contact between the social interests of the one and of the other. A school is conceivable in which there should be a spirit of companionship and shared activity, but where its social life would no more represent or typify that of the world beyond the school walls than that of a monastery. Social concern and understanding would be developed, but they would not be available outside; they would not carry over. The proverbial separation of town and gown, the cultivation of academic seclusion, operate in this direction. So does such adherence to the culture of the past as generates a reminiscent social spirit, for this makes an individual feel more at home in the life of other days than in his own. A professedly cultural education is peculiarly exposed to this danger. An idealized past becomes the refuge and solace of the spirit; present-day concerns are found sordid, and unworthy of attention. But as a rule, the absence of a social environment in connection with which learning is a need and a reward is the chief reason for the isolation of the school; and this isolation renders school knowledge inapplicable to life and so infertile in character.

A narrow and moralistic view of morals is responsible for the failure to recognize that all the aims and values which are desirable in education are themselves moral. Discipline, natural development, culture, social efficiency, are moral traits—marks of a person who is a worthy member of that society which it is the business of education to further. There is an old saying to the effect that it is not enough for a man to be good; he must be good for something. The something for which a man must be good is capacity to live as a social member so that what he gets from living with others balances with what he contributes. What he gets and gives as a human being, a being with desires, emotions, and ideas, is not external possessions, but a widening and deepening of conscious life—a more intense, disciplined, and expanding realization of meanings. What he *materially* receives and gives is at most opportunities and means for the evolution of conscious life. Otherwise, it is neither giving nor taking, but a shifting about of the position of things in space, like the stirring of water and sand with a stick. Discipline, culture, social efficiency, personal refinement, improvement of character are but phases of the growth of capacity nobly to share in such a balanced experience. And education is not a mere means to such a life. Education is such a life. To maintain capacity for such education is the essence of morals. For conscious life is a continual beginning afresh.

## Summary

The most important problem of moral education in the school concerns the relationship of knowledge and conduct. For unless the learning which accrues in the regular course of study affects character, it is futile to conceive the moral end as the unifying and culminating end of education. When there is no intimate organic connection between the methods and materials of knowledge and moral growth, particular lessons and modes of discipline have to be resorted to: knowledge is not integrated into the usual springs of action and the outlook on life, while morals become moralistic—a scheme of separate virtues.

The two theories chiefly associated with the separation of learning from activity, and hence from morals, are those which cut off inner disposition and motive—the conscious personal factor—from deeds as purely physical and outer; and which set action from interest in opposition to that from principle. Both of these separations are overcome in an educational scheme where learning is the accompaniment of continuous activities or occupations which have a social aim and utilize the materials of typical social situations. For under such conditions, the school becomes itself a form of social life, a miniature community and one in close interaction with other modes of associated experience beyond school walls. All education which develops power to share effectively in social life is moral. It forms a character which not only does the particular deed socially necessary but one which is interested in that continuous readjustment which is essential to growth. Interest in learning from all the contacts of life is the essential moral interest.

## Notes

1. See p. 393.
2. There is a much neglected strain in Rousseau tending intellectually in this direction. He opposed the existing state of affairs on the ground that it formed *neither* the citizen nor the man. Under existing conditions, he preferred to try for the latter rather than for the former. But there are many sayings of his which point to the formation of the citizen as ideally the higher, and which indicate that his own endeavor, as embodied in the *Emile*, was simply the best makeshift the corruption of the times permitted him to sketch.
3. Since the learned man should also still be a learner, it will be understood that these contrasts are relative, not absolute. But in the earlier stages of learning at least they are practically all-important.

# Afterword

## Sidney Hook*

John Dewey's *Democracy and Education* continues to be a classic in the philosophy of education. . . . It illuminates directly or indirectly all the basic issues that are central today to the concerns of intelligent educators or lay people interested in education. . . .

I shall present briefly three leading ideas which seem to me central to Dewey's philosophy of education. They are his theory of experience, his conception of democracy, and his emphasis on scientific method in education. . . .

## I

Let us sort out the meanings of these terms in Dewey's discussion. For him experience is not everything or anything that happens to a person, although there is a sense in ordinary discourse in which any happening is an experience, like birth or death, an accidental fall, or an unexpected blow. As Dewey uses the term, it refers to a pattern of events in which the organism is deliberately or with some awareness attending or acting upon something and undergoing or suffering the consequences of the action. Education is the process by which on the basis of present experiences we make future experiences more accessible, meaningful, or controllable. That is why for Dewey experience and education are not synonymous. Those who talk of life as a school and any or every experience as its curriculum, so to speak, miss this crucial distinction and overlook the fact that some experiences may be uneducational, crippling the powers to meet, understand, and possibly control the inescapable flow of future experiences. They also overlook the fact that one learns not only from one's own experience but from the experiences of others too, something ignored or denied by some fashionable movements in education. Education goes on in all types of society, democratic or undemocratic. Consequently it cannot be identified with democratic processes.

The most striking and insightful contributions of *Democracy and Education* fall within the field of the psychology of education or learning. In inquiring into the conditions, factors, and activities that make for effective education, especially teaching and learning in schools and classrooms, what Dewey has to say about interest and discipline, motivation and effort,

---

* Sidney Hook was Professor of Philosophy at New York University.

method and subject matter, and a number of allied themes has stood the test of further inquiry since his day. In exploring these topics Dewey uncovers the profound influence of certain philosophical and psychological assumptions of the past on some deplorable present-day educational practices. Most of these practices are derived from a dualistic theory of mind and body which, according to Dewey's analysis, converts functional distinctions in the "moving unities of experience" into separations of existence. Thus mind is considered separate from the body, whose activity is viewed as an alien influence on how the mind learns; the self is divided from its environing physical and social world; the objects of experience are regarded as completely external to the modes of experiencing them; and, therefore, the methods of learning are isolated from the subject matters learned. Among the evils of education, or rather schooling, that Dewey sees as consequences of isolating the way we learn from what we learn are the failure to make use of "the concrete situations of experience," reliance upon the twin inducements of fear and bribes to motivate learning, and mindless use of rote methods and mechanical routines.

So far, regardless of the social philosophy one holds, it would be possible to accept and implement what Dewey says about how to improve the quality of education for any particular person or group. Dewey's insights into the psychology of education could be used in educating an absolute monarch or the guardians and rulers of a Platonic republic. But when we ask ourselves what should education be for society as a whole, we cannot give an intelligible answer unless we have a definable notion of a desirable society. The criteria of a desirable society are derived by Dewey from the features that are found wherever any social group exists and prospers. These criteria are twofold—the degree of shared interests within the society and the freedom to develop new interests, both common and personal. "How numerous and varied are the interests which are commonly shared? How full and free is the interplay with other forms of association?" Using these as moral criteria, the superiority of the democratic community to all other forms of communal association is easy to establish.

Actually this derivation of the validity of democratic society is circular, and some may even claim it is question-begging because the very choice of criteria presupposes an ideal family. But the point that is central here is not the justification of democracy but its conception—how it is to be understood—and the educational corollaries of that conception. . . .

## II

Democracy in most contexts refers to a form of government or a political process by which those who rule are elected by the freely given consent of a majority of the adults governed. Although Dewey was a democrat in this sense, he did not regard democracy or any other political process or institution as an end in itself. He realized that a democracy could function poorly and that it was capable of acting abominably, *e.g.*, in its treatment of minorities in the South or elsewhere. All his life he criticized the functioning of American democracy in the light of a more basic conception of democracy which he called "moral and ideal."

The essence of Dewey's view was that democracy was committed to an equality of concern for each individual in the community to develop as a person. Education was the chief means by which those personal capacities were to be discovered and liberated. Education would enable human beings to achieve their maximum *distinctive* growth in harmony with their fellows. . . .

For Dewey growth is an inclusive and not a single exclusive end. It embraces *all* the positive intellectual, emotional, and moral ends that appear in everybody's easy schedule of the good life and the good education—growth in skills and powers, knowledge and appreciation, value and thought. For Dewey, however, it is not enough to list these ends; they must be brought into living and relevant relation to the developing powers and habits and imagination of the individual person. We grow not by worshiping values, but by realizing them in our daily behavior. The pattern of realization is an individual thing even when the values are common. There are different rates of growth, different styles of growth; but when they maximize our powers to grow they are all ways by which we grow in maturity. We are mature to the extent that we form habits of reasonable expectation on the basis of what we know about the world, our fellows, and ourselves—to the extent that we can cope with an ever-changing environment, make sense of new experience, and escape both the petrifactions of routine and the blind outburst of impulse. The growth, consequently, which Dewey identifies with genuine and desirable education is a shorthand expression for the direction of change in a great variety of growths—intellectual, emotional, and moral. It excludes, therefore, the kinds of growth which interfere with or reverse the direction of change in this variety of growths—it excludes growths in prejudice, arbitrariness, hate, invidious prestige, power and status, and even that miscellany of knowledge which burdens a mind not in training for a quiz show. More important still, it becomes clear why in the interests of growth Dewey became a critic of specialized and narrow vocationalism, of merely professionalized education, and why he became the protagonist of a liberal and general education . . . imbued with . . . equality of concern for all persons. . . .

## III

Equality of concern is not the same thing as equal treatment. It is compatible with unequal treatment, provided this treatment is required by the necessities of intellectual and emotional growth in each case. "Moral equality," he says, "means incommensurability, the inapplicability of common and quantitative standards. It means intrinsic qualities which require *unique* opportunities and *differential* manifestation. . . ." The principle of moral equality or ideal democracy is the most revolutionary principle in the world because its scope embraces all social institutions.

Any honest reading of Dewey indicates that individuals come first in the order of concern, and that to be an individual is to be different in some distinctive and important way even though many things are shared in common with others. Conceptually, it is very difficult to express this union of equality of concern and difference of treatment in a formal rule. But we may illustrate it by reference to another institution: In a healthy and happy family where children vary in age, strength and intellectual gifts, it would be absurd for parents to treat them equally—absurd precisely because they are considered equal, valued equally. . . .

The paradigm of an ideal family in which the parents are wise and benevolent cannot, of course, be used with respect to democratic society as a whole. For such a society is self-governing and must strictly abide by majority rule after respecting the rights of other individuals. Dewey, it should be noted, even in politics was never an absolute majoritarian or believer in unlimited government; the validity of majority rule presupposes respect for the equal political and civil rights of minorities. The family model is more appropriate to the school, especially on the elementary level, for it recognizes the indispensable and active role of the teacher and the legitimate restraints that may be put on students when their experimental activities may result in harm to themselves or others. Until students are mature enough to take over the direction of their own education, of necessity there must be an asymmetry in the role and intellectual authority of the teacher with respect to them. The excesses of progressive education, which made it a byword among those who took the curriculum of studies seriously, flowed from a failure to realize this.

## IV

With this conception of democracy in education, we can see how Dewey uses it in masterly fashion to criticize the traditional methods of education and its curricular content, down to the specific details of the three R's, history, geography, and other academic disciplines. In every case he traces the effect of inherited class interests and prejudices in narrowing and mechanizing what was considered "essential," in separating the purely intellectual studies from purely practical ones, in identifying the former with liberal education, and by separating such education from concern with the great social problems and responsibilities of the age infecting it with illiberality. At the same time he evaluates the institutions of existing society in the light of what would be required to make democratic education pervasive. While this might seem to involve an adjustment of the schools to the existing economic, political, and nationalist order, he argues convincingly that, rather, it entails a continuous and profound transformation of social life which will bring all citizens into a greater participation in determining the ends and goals of their activity. In the processes of production, distribution, communication, and exchange, individuals should more and more enter actively in the planning of goals, the sharing of roles and responsibilities instead of being, like machines and raw material, at the beck of decisions that they cannot influence or even indirectly control. From the vantage point of his educational ideal,

> An undesirable society, in other words, is one which internally and externally sets up barriers to free intercourse and communication of experience. A society which makes provision for participation in its good of all its members on equal terms and which secures flexible readjustment of its institutions through interaction of the different forms of associated life is in so far democratic. Such a society must have a type of education which gives individuals a personal interest in social relationships and control, and the habits of mind which secure social changes without introducing disorder.

Once these social changes are introduced, and they must be introduced democratically, not from above by a beloved leader or a vanguard political party, and without violence which usually serves the purpose of reaction, then the division or separation between the concepts of culture and utility, and their attendant curricular practices, can be banished from formal schooling.

The centrality of multiple forms of active participation in Dewey's conception of democracy distinguishes it from conventional views of formal political democracy in which citizens merely choose at stated intervals between alternatives set by others. . . . At the same time we can see why Dewey rejects any view, whether Platonic or technocratic, which makes one small group by virtue of its theoretical concern with the ends of life the best qualified to rule over the masses who have been educated only in the use of means and instruments in behalf of goals beyond their ken or competence. For him, when education has not been narrowly circumscribed by the needs of a class society, there are no experts in wisdom. And as for the rule of experts in any field, without disputing their expertise, Dewey holds that one does not need to be an expert in order to evaluate the recommendations of experts. Otherwise democratic government would be impossible. . . .

## V

The trouble with much of our education, John Dewey complained long before his critics, is that most children do not learn as much and as well as they can learn. Modern education, by enlisting scientific psychology, attempts to get them to learn as much and as well as they can. Its *program* is to hold the stick up to the very top level of each individual's capacity, and by engaging interest, elicit the effort and drive that will take him or her as close to the top as possible. If it fails in this program, it is not because it is too scientific, but because it is not scientific enough. Of course, there are normative tasks which the school must face, and no one has stressed the importance of the moral aspects of education more than Dewey. But when it is relevant to ask the questions—What ought our behavior be? What is worth pursuing and possessing? What is the best thing to say or do in this situation?—can we improve on Dewey's reply that such questions are to be answered not by habit, not by drift, not by intuition, not by revelation, but by critical intelligence informed by all the relevant facts in the situation? And by intelligence he means the use of the *pattern* of scientific inquiry, as distinct from the specific techniques of specific subject matters. For Dewey, the ultimate authority in liberal civilization is the authority of scientific method, broadly interpreted as the method of intelligence. . . .

Dewey's concept of intelligence involves the education of emotion, volition and perception, and not merely formal reasoning power or the exercise of what is sometimes called the *mind* or *intellect* considered in isolation from observation, experiment, and practice. "There is no such thing as over-intellectuality," he wrote in *Democracy and Education*, "but there is such a thing as one-sided intellectuality."

If we reject scientific method, the method of free intelligence, as the supreme authority in judgment of both fact and value, what can we substitute in its stead? Every alternative involves at some point an institutional authority which, historical evidence shows, lends itself to abuse, which proclaims itself to be above all interests and becomes the expression of a particular interest invested with the symbols of public authority.

Dewey's educational philosophy must still hurdle some great obstacles before it can be made socially effective. In a sense, this philosophy promises too much. As it conceives education, teaching becomes much more complex, much more of an art than conventional modes. It requires that teachers be much abler than most of them are at present likely to be. . . .

## VI

What makes a good teacher, like what makes a good education, must be considered in relation to certain values. What we are seeking are the criteria of a good teacher in a democratic society whose educational system has embraced the fundamental aims we have previously outlined.

(a) The first criterion is intellectual competence. By this I mean not only the truism that teachers should have a mastery of the subject matter and should keep abreast of important developments but that they should have some capacity for analysis. Without this capacity, they cannot develop it in their students. . . .

Related to intellectual competence is the willingness to countenance, if not to encourage, rational opposition and spirited critical dissent by students. The inquiring mind even among youth sometimes probes deeply. Only teachers unsure of themselves will resent embarrassing questions to which the only honest reply must be a confession of ignorance. Intellectual independence is such a rare virtue that the good teacher positively welcomes it, despite the occasional excesses of youthful dogmatism and exuberance. . . .

(b) Intellectual competence is necessary but not sufficient for good teaching. It must be accompanied by a quality of patience towards beginners which accepts as natural the first groping steps towards understanding by the uninitiated. The "simple" and the "obvious" are relative to antecedent skills and knowledge. Failure to see and act on this is responsible for intellectual brow-beating by otherwise competent teachers and for the air, deliberately only half-concealed, of suffering the hopeless stupidity of those who are stumbling their way forward. The intellectually quick, and all teachers should be quick, have a tendency towards intellectual impatience. The impatience but not the quickness must be curbed. Patience is something that can be learned, except by certain temperaments who should never be entrusted with a class. Good teaching is not found where a star teacher holds forth for the benefit only of star pupils, but where some participating response is evoked from every normal member of the class. Nothing is easier than to yield to the pleasures of colloquy with the exceptional students of a class—and nothing is more unfair to the rest, in whom this builds up intense resentment, oddly enough not against the teacher but against their exceptional classmates. Special provision should be made for the instruction of superior students, but a good teacher does not let their special needs dominate the class to the exclusion of the legitimate educational needs of the others.

(c) The third characteristic of good teaching is ability to plan a lesson, without mechanically imposing it on the class, in those subjects where basic materials have to be acquired, and to guide the development of discussion to a cumulative result in subjects in which the seminar method is used. The bane of much . . . teaching is improvisation. Improvisation is not only legitimate but unavoidable in motivating interest and finding points of departure or illustration for principles. But it cannot replace the planful survey of subject matter and problems, nor provide direction to discussion. . . .

What the teacher must aim at is to make each class hour an integrated experience with an aesthetic, if possible a dramatic, unity of its own. Without a spontaneity that can point up the give and take of discussion, and a skill in weaving together what the students themselves contribute, preparation will not save the hour from dullness. The pall of dullness which hangs over the memories of school days in the minds of many unfortunately envelops the whole question of education.

(d) Another important quality the good teacher possesses is knowledge of human beings. . . . The more one studies students, the more differences they reveal. These differences need not be relevant to what they are trying to learn; but sometimes they are. A teacher devoid of this knowledge cannot solve the problem of motivation or evoke full participation from his or her class. . . .

The secret of intellectual vitality in the classroom, when a theorem is being derived for the twentieth time or when an elementary point in the grammar of a foreign language is being explained or when the nerve of an old philosophic argument is being laid bare, lies in experiencing the situation as a fresh problem in communication rather than one in personal discovery. Or, putting it a little differently, it consists in getting the students to reach the familiar conclusion with a sense of having made their own discovery. The task is to make as many as possible see as much as possible of what they have not seen before. It is this perennial challenge, which cannot be adequately met without a knowledge of people, that keeps the good teacher alive. . . .

(e) [G]ood teaching requires sympathy . . ., a positive attitude of imaginative concern with the personal needs of others. . . . Those who teach large numbers and never get to know their students have a tendency to regard all but a brilliant few as a dull, cloddish mass. Reduce the number in each class, shorten the perspective, and no one worthy of being a teacher will fail to see the interesting variety of potentiality in every group. . . . In each person there is some unique quality of charm, intelligence, or character, some promise and mystery that invites attention and nurture. The teacher who seeks it will find it.

Students respond to sympathy for their special intellectual needs like plants to sunshine and rain. They undertake more and achieve more. . . .

(f) The good teacher, to close our inventory of traits, possesses vision. It is the source of both intellectual enthusiasm and detachment in the face of inevitable failures and disappointments. Without vision he or she . . . cannot inspire a passion for excellence. The vision . . . must not obtrude itself into the details of instruction. Its presence should be inferrable from the spirit with which the instruction is carried on. It should operate in such a way as to lift up the students' hearts and minds beyond matters of immediate concern and enable them to see the importance of a point of view. Wherever an intellectually stimulating teacher is found, there will also be found some large perspective of interest that lights up the corners of his or her subject matter. If students catch fire from it, it should not be in order to believe some dogma but to strengthen them in the search for truth and to become more sensitive to visions that express other centers of experience. . . .

## VII

As committed as he was to democracy in education and education for democracy—where democracy is understood in an ethical not narrowly political sense—Dewey was unalterably opposed to indoctrination. He was . . . aware of the great social reforms and reconstructions that were necessary in order for the schools to realize . . . the moral ideals of the democratic society. And as a *citizen* he was always in the forefront of the battle for reform. But all the schools could legitimately do was "to form attitudes which will express themselves in intelligent social action." This, he says, "is something very different from indoctrination," because intelligence, alone of all virtues, is self-critical. Only those indoctrinate who are unable or unwilling to establish their conclusions by intelligent inquiry. Whatever his own views were, Dewey was confident that if they had merit they would be recognized as valid by those whom the schools in the exercise of their educational function had taught to study and deal with the social world and its problems responsibly, i.e., intelligently, scientifically conscientiously. . . .

## VIII

John Dewey's philosophy has still a great deal to teach us. But it is not the first nor the last word on our problems. . . .

[W]e must remember that we cannot succeed in education without succeeding in fields other than education—in community relations, in industry, in politics. Rates of progress are different in different fields and uncertain in all: but unless we can improve the quality of our local democratic communities, unless we can realize greater democracy in our personal lives and in our face-to-face relations with our neighbors, Dewey's educational philosophy will have only limited effectiveness.

In this sense, the battleground of education is coterminous with the whole of society. . . . Intelligence in the service of freedom and free men and women must reconstruct social institutions so that they provide equal opportunity and equal concern for all. Only thus can we provide an educational philosophy not only for present-day America, but also for the future—a future in which, as Dewey envisaged it, "freedom and fullness of human companionship is the aim, and intelligent cooperative experimentation the method."

# Permissions

## *Meno*

From *The Dialogues of Plato*, Volume I, translated by R. E. Allen. Copyright © 1984 by Yale University Press. Reprinted by permission of the publisher. The notes are those of Andrea Tschemplik and are copyright © 2005 by her and reprinted with her permission. Some of the translator's own notes that are included have been abbreviated.

## *The Republic*

From Plato, *The Republic*, edited by Andrea Tschemplik with a complete revision of the translation by John Llewelyn Davies and David James Vaughan, originally published in 1852 by Macmillan & Co. Copyright © 2005 by Rowman & Littlefield Publishers, Inc. Reprinted by permission of the publisher.

## Afterword

### Robert S. Brumbaugh

From Robert S. Brumbaugh and Nathaniel M. Lawrence, *Philosophers on Education: Six Essays on the Foundations of Western Thought*, Houghton Mifflin Company. Copyright © 1963 by the authors and reprinted by permission of their estates. The editor made minor changes to avoid what some readers might suppose to be sex-specific language.

## *Nicomachean Ethics*

From Aristotle, *Nicomachean Ethics*, translated by Martin Ostwald. Copyright © 1999 by Prentice Hall, Inc. Reprinted by permission of the publisher. The notes are written by the translator.

## *Politics*

From Aristotle, *Politics*, translated by Ernest Barker and revised by R. F. Stalley. Copyright © 1995 by Oxford University Press. Reprinted by permission of the publisher.

## Afterword

### Randall Curren

Published here for the first time. Copyright © 2008 by the author.

## *On the Teacher*

From Augustine, *The Teacher*, translated by Peter King. Copyright © 1995 by Hackett Publishing Company, Inc. Reprinted by permission of the publisher.

## Afterword

### Philip L. Quinn

From Philip L. Quinn, "Augustinian Learning," in *Philosophers on Education: New Historical Perspectives*, ed. Amelie Oksenberg Rorty. Copyright © 1998 by Routledge. Reprinted by permission of the publisher.

## *Some Thoughts Concerning Education*

From *Some Thoughts Concerning Education* (1693).

## Afterword

### Peter Gay

From Peter Gay, "Introduction," in *John Locke on Education*, ed. Peter Gay. Copyright © 1964 by the author. Reprinted by permission of the author.

## *Emile*

From *The Emile of Jean Jacques Rousseau*, translated by William Boyd. Originally published in 1956 by William Heinemann Ltd. Reprinted by permission of Teachers College Press.

## Afterword

### William Boyd

## *Lectures on Pedagogy*

## Afterword

### Robert B. Louden

## *A Vindication of the Rights of Woman*

## Afterword

### Jane Roland Martin

## *Inaugural Address at St. Andrews*

## Afterword

### Elizabeth Anderson

## The Aims of Education

From Alfred North Whitehead, *The Aims of Education and Other Essays*. Copyright © 1929 by The Macmillan Company. Reprinted by permission of The Free Press.

## Afterword

### Nathaniel M. Lawrence

From Robert S. Brumbaugh and Nathaniel M. Lawrence, *Philosophers on Education: Six Essays on the Foundations of Western Thought*. Houghton Mifflin Company. Copyright © 1963 by the authors and reprinted by permission of their estates. The editor made minor changes to avoid what some readers might suppose to be sex-specific language.

## Democracy and Education

From John Dewey, *The Middle Works*, 1899–1924, vol. 9 (1916), ed. Jo Ann Boydston. Copyright © 1980 by the Southern Illinois University Press. Reprinted by permission of the publisher. Page references in the text are altered from the original to reflect the pagination in this volume.

## Afterword

### Sidney Hook

This essay is drawn from various sources: Sidney Hook, "Introduction," John Dewey, *The Middle Works*, 1899–1924, vol. 9 (1916), ed. Jo Ann Boydston, copyright © 1980 by Southern Illinois University Press, reprinted by permission of the publisher; Sidney Hook, *Education & The Taming of Power*, La Salle Illinois, Open Court Publishing Company, 1973, reprinted by permission of the estate of Sidney Hook; *Education for Modern Man: A New Perspective*, New York, Alfred A. Knopf, 1963, reprinted by permission of the estate of Sidney Hook. The editor made minor changes to avoid what some readers might suppose to be sex-specific language.